KU-082-653

THE OXFORD UNIVERSITY PRESS AND THE SPREAD OF LEARNING

AN ILLUSTRATED HISTORY

1478–1978

The Oxford University Press and the Spread of Learning 1478–1978

AN ILLUSTRATED HISTORY
BY NICOLAS BARKER

WITH A PREFACE BY CHARLES RYSKAMP

OXFORD · AT THE CLARENDON PRESS

Oxford University Press, Walton Street, Oxford OX2 6DP

OXFORD LONDON GLASGOW
NEW YORK TORONTO MELBOURNE WELLINGTON
KUALA LUMPUR SINGAPORE JAKARTA HONG KONG TOKYO
DELHI BOMBAY CALCUTTA MADRAS KARACHI
NAIROBI DAR ES SALAAM CAPE TOWN

First published 1978
Reprinted 1978, 1979

British Library Cataloguing in Publication Data

Barker, Nicolas
The Oxford University Press and the spread of learning.
1. Oxford University Press – History
I. Title
338.7'61'07050942574 Z232.098 77–30541
ISBN 0–19–951086–5

Printed in Great Britain
at the University Press, Oxford
by Eric Buckley
Printer to the University

PREFACE

FOR five hundred years there has been a press at Oxford associated with the University to advance learning in the quadrangles of the colleges, the city and the country, and for the world. Oxford University Press has a unique tradition in the history of printing: no press is so old, no other press has come close to it in establishing such a large number of bases for publication throughout the world, none has published distinguished work over as many centuries in as many fields—in religion, the classics, mathematics, physics and astronomy, law and literature. It has accomplished more than rulers and diplomats, wars and treaties, to establish English as the common language of the world today, and to make English law known and respected generally; it has made the Bible available to millions in every part of the globe.

The story of the Press is as remarkable as the fact of its existence for five hundred years. This book is concerned with the internal struggles and conflicts that have always been characteristic of university politics, but here there are further complications because of feuds with other printers and booksellers about the most lucrative aspects of printing. The narrative therefore in part relates to colleges, universities, and committees, printers and patrons, editors and production managers. But it is chiefly the record of a few towering personalities and their legacy to all peoples. And it is about great books made easily available everywhere.

What we shall read and what we shall see in the dozens of pictures are at the heart of publishing; this is an illustrated chronicle of man's determination to advance learning. From the copying of manuscripts in Hellenistic times, to the Sosii in ancient Rome, to monastic *scriptoria* and the wandering scholars, to the Estiennes and the Elsevirs, to the steam-powered press of *The Times* in London in 1814, there is no story quite like this.

Americans frequently like to think of a college in terms of a teacher and a student on a bench, of Mark Hopkins on one end of a log and James Garfield on the other. Nicolas Barker, in the text which follows, repeats the words of an Oxford polymath who said that a university consists of a library and a press.

That idea and a few men are central to this history of a university and its press. In the beginning there was Theodoric Rood ('The Red'). A century later it was Robert Dudley, Earl of Leicester, Chancellor of the University of Oxford, who gave the University its licence to print in 1584. Then there were the four great 'architects' who built the learned press: William Laud (1573–1645), Archbishop of Canterbury, Chancellor of the University, who had the vision; John Fell (1625–86), Dean of Christ

Church, who was able to realize the vision and to achieve a distinction in printing not unlike that of Richelieu's Imprimerie Royale; Sir William Blackstone (1723–80), Solicitor-General to the Queen and the first Vinerian Professor of English Law, who reformed a decaying and mismanaged press and brought peace and prosperity to it with the publication of his four-volume, supremely masterful *Commentaries on the Laws of England*, 'the next thing to a constitution of England'; and Bartholomew Price (1818–98), Sedleian Professor of Natural Philosophy, the brilliant writer on calculus, who led the press into educational publishing and created a sound business enterprise. To their names we should add those of Charles Cannan (1858–1919), Dean of Trinity College, who established the now world-famous Oxford series (Classical Texts, English Texts, books of verse, etc.) and the modern press as we know it. And it was Sir Humphrey Milford (1877–1952), Publisher to the University, whose vigorous enterprise in establishing offices overseas forged a universal network of learning, the Oxford University Press.

This history is, of course, much more than the visions and intrigues, policies and publications, of these eight men. It is also the record of many other authors and printers, of book manufacture, paper-making, and type design. It actually begins with the wandering scholars of the twelfth century, then quickly moves on to 1478 and the first itinerant printer in Oxford, Theodoric Rood of Cologne, from whose press only seventeen books survive, and for some of these, no more than a few pages. Rood failed within ten years, when all of England's printers except Caxton went out of business. A second press lasted only three years, from 1517 to 1520. The permanent establishment of a press was not until 1584. Hitherto neglected manuscripts in Oxford were brought to the Printer to the University, and the various faculties collaborated with the Library and the Printer to form a true university press. In the first decades of the seventeenth century it turned from provincial printing to spreading higher learning throughout the world.

The books also became of international and lasting fame: the first description of the English colony at Virginia (John Smith's *Map of Virginia*, 1612); Robert Burton's *Anatomy of Melancholy* (1621); William Chillingworth's powerful defence of free inquiry (*The Religion of Protestants*, 1638); Francis Bacon's *Of the Advancement and Proficience of Learning* (1640); and the classic Arabic and Hebrew studies of Pococke and those in mathematics by Wallis. In the centuries which followed there were hundreds of books which became pre-eminent in every field of learning. They were books which were identified with the well-formulated programme of the Oxford University Press. Above all, there was the publication of the Bible, from the early printings of the Authorized or King James Version, and the beautiful folio Bibles in Fell types, to those for the British and Foreign Bible Society, then the Revised Version (1881–94), and the Scofield Reference Bible (1909). The success of the Oxford University Press through the ages is inseparably tied to the printing of the Bible and the *Book of Common Prayer*.

But in later years the history of the Press was as closely associated with all of the dictionaries, histories, 'companions', texts, and books of verse which bear the name of Oxford. There were the studies in language which culminated in the monumental *New* (or *Oxford*) *English Dictionary* (1884–1928), histories from Clarendon's to Morison's and Commager's, criticism of literature and art, and the publication of music. Oxford's name is as synonymous with these as it is with 'English' itself: Oxford English is still *the* English for hundreds of millions; Oxford's style—or Fowler's *Usage*—is still the best style.

Along the way one will also encounter many names and many remarkable books which are just as much part of the world of Oxford University Press as those mentioned above, but they may not so immediately call to mind the name of the Press. Halley's astronomy, Jowett's Plato, Clerk-Maxwell's physics, Anson's law and Bradley's philosophy, the poems of Gerard Manley Hopkins and Robert Bridges, or the history of Arnold Toynbee—they are all included in this story. There is even Lewis Carroll's *Alice in Wonderland.*

The five-hundredth anniversary of Oxford University Press is first being celebrated in New York, where its first overseas branch was located. That was a decade or two after the earliest American university presses were founded. Oxford Bibles had come to America with its original English settlers. By 1867 the Oxford Press was printing a *Book of Common Prayer* for the Protestant Episcopal Church in the United States. Since 1896 the American business has had its own, and outstanding, tradition of publications in many fields. The American offices are now located on Madison Avenue in New York, across the corner from The Pierpont Morgan Library, which has the finest collection of early English printing, including that of the first Oxford Press, outside of two or three in England. In recent years the Library has collaborated in the publication of some of its most important books with the Press. It is a very great honour for us in New York and at the Morgan Library to pay this tribute to the astonishing achievement of the Oxford University Press. I should like to give sincere thanks to the many members of the Press in Oxford, London, New York, and throughout the world who have made all this possible, in 1978, and during the preceding five hundred years.

CHARLES RYSKAMP
Director, The Pierpont Morgan Library

CONTENTS

PREFACE v

INTRODUCTION xi

The Early University and its Books 1

The First Press at Oxford 2

The Second Press 4

The Press Established at Oxford 6

The Successors of Joseph Barnes 8

The Acquisition of Printing Types 10

Laud's Vision of a University Press 11

The Survival of Laud's Vision 13

John Fell: the Vision Realized 14

The Fell Types 15

The Press at Work 18

The First Books 20

Illustrated Books 21

Printing the Bible: Pitt, Parker, and Guy 23

The End of the Partnership 25

The Roots of the English Language 26

Fell's Successors: Aldrich, Charlett, and the Clarendon Building 27

Thomas Hearne 30

The Bible Patent: John Baskett 31

Publishing after Hearne 32

William Blackstone 33

The Reformed Press 34

Resumption of the Bible Press 36

Technical Change 37

The Restoration of Classical Scholarship	38
Other Books, 1800–1850	40
Results of the Partnership: the New Building	41
The Growth of Evangelicalism and the Text of the Bible	42
Oriental Scholarship	43
Thomas Combe: Mechanization of the Press	43
The Royal Commission and its Effect on the Press	45
The Clarendon Press Series	46
Bartholomew Price: the Great Expansion	47
Horace Hart: The Rediscovery of the Fell Types	50
The London Business and the Revised Version	51
The New English Dictionary	51
The 'Oxford' Style	52
Charles Cannan: the Making of the Modern Press	53
The Expansion of the London Business: Sir Humphrey Milford	54
Recent Fine Printing	55
The American Branch	56
Other Branches Overseas	57
Publishing in Modern Times	58
Ephemera	60
Epilogue	60
APPENDIX. The Oxford Almanacks	61
INDEX	65
PLATES	*at end*

INTRODUCTION

EIGHT centuries have passed since the group of wandering scholars who had settled at Oxford began to organize teaching and learning on a regular basis, in a form which we now recognize as the beginning of the University. For almost as long, the possession, circulation, and manufacture of books have been part of the University's functions. It was not, however, until 1478 that the first printed book issued from an Oxford press, and inaugurated the connection between the University and the distribution of books in quantity from which the present Oxford University Press has grown.

In 1978, therefore, we celebrate the quincentenary of the introduction of printing at Oxford with a pictorial history of its subsequent progress, illustrated by the books, documents, and pictures which are its tangible record. The story, although it properly begins with the arrival of Theodoric Rood and the first learned and educational books that he printed, stretches back to the early thirteenth century when scribes, illuminators, and binders of books are already found in Oxford. Rood did not stay in Oxford, but a respectable number of books had appeared at a series of presses there by the seventeenth century, when, at the initiative of two great men, Archbishop Laud and Bishop Fell, the University Press in its present form was established.

Laud, as Chancellor of the University, provided for a press attached to the University in his revision of its statutes, confirmed by the Royal Charter which he obtained for it in 1636. But it was Fell who carried out what Laud had intended, and added his own distinctive component, the possession of special types for learned works. So it is the dark, dominant figure of John Fell, Dean of Christ Church and then Bishop of Oxford, who emerges as the real founder of the University Press. The Fell types (used and illustrated in this book) are among its most treasured possessions. It was Fell, again, who determined the type of books which still preoccupy the Press: learned and educational books, and the Bible. He also added a fourth strand in the Oxford Almanack, the annual illustrated calendar of the University, which vividly depicts and reflects the changing shape of the buildings and landscape of Oxford, and also the changing ideas and ideals that engaged it.

Fell was not without distinguished successors, but the difficulty of establishing a market for learned books led to a decline in the eighteenth century. From this, the Press was rescued by William Blackstone, the great academic lawyer. Blackstone reorganized the Press on terms which set it on a sound commercial footing, in time to meet the great new demand for the Bible which dominated the first half of the nineteenth century. At the same time, Thomas Gaisford, another Dean of Christ Church, revived the tradition of scholarly publishing.

The Press as it is today is the creation of Bartholomew Price, Professor of Natural Philosophy and the first permanent 'Secretary to the Delegates' or, in effect, manager of the whole business of the Press, whose connection with it, lasting nearly forty years, ended only with his death in 1898. Price saw the great potential demand for knowledge in Victorian England, and created and regulated the flow of books—learned works, educational books, and works of reference—with which the Oxford University Press met it. He saw the great *New English Dictionary* started, and the first branch overseas, in New York, opened. His successors have built on this foundation to make the Press the foremost academic publishing and printing business in the world.

This is the story set out and illustrated in the handsome pages of this quincentenary history. The five centuries and more of change and growth in the formation of this still unique enterprise are depicted here in a series of 375 items, landmarks only in a far larger and wider progress. Besides the books themselves, the original documents, portraits of the chief participants, and the Oxford background of the Almanacks are described and reproduced; there are 266 illustrations altogether, including four in full colour. Designed to form the basis of the quincentenary exhibitions at The Pierpont Morgan Library in New York, the University of Western Ontario, the Victoria and Albert Museum, and the Stadt- und Universitätsbibliothek, Frankfurt am Main, it will remain a permanent record of the pioneering role of the University of Oxford in disseminating learning.

The illustrations and descriptive text in this book are intended to be at once a catalogue of the exhibits shown at each of these places, and an extension of the picture of the Press's activity presented within the confines of each site. At the same time, the book may serve as a permanent memorial of the collection of diverse objects brought together on this occasion, as well as a picture of the events it describes.

The history of the Press as a whole has been better told, and at greater length, elsewhere. But pictures can provide a graphic illustration of certain themes which persist in the history of printing at Oxford, whose persistence seems less a deliberate than a natural product of the progress of the University itself. The text of the Bible itself, of classical writers (notably Aristotle) and the fathers of the Church; the history of England, and more especially the English language, from its earliest roots; the codification of human knowledge, in great systematic works of reference, and in particular again the establishment of the structure and use of the English language; theology, geography and maps, archaeology, law, natural history, and the sciences: all these can be found, occupying Oxford scholars and the Oxford press for the last five hundred years.

Both the Oxford University Press and the author have large debts of gratitude to record. Many people smoothed the path, never an easy one, of the exhibition. Our first debt is to the staff of The Pierpont Morgan Library, notably Mr. Charles Ryskamp, its director, Mr. Paul Needham, and Mr. Thomas Lange; Dr. Robert Lee, Director of Libraries, D. B. Weldon Library, University of Western Ontario, Mr. Anthony Burton, Assistant Keeper of the Library, Victoria and Albert Museum, and Professor Dr. D. Köttelwesen, Director of the Stadt- und Universitätsbibliothek, Frankfurt am Main, also provided invaluable help in the subsequent journey of the exhibition. Those who lent material for the exhibition equally deserve our thanks: All Souls College, the Ashmolean Museum, Balliol College, Brasenose College, the British and Foreign Bible Society, Christ Church, Corpus Christi College, the Fitzwilliam Museum, Jesus College, the National Portrait Gallery, Queen's College, The Pierpont Morgan Library, St. John's College, the Taylor Institution Library, Trinity College, and Worcester College. The University Archivist, Mr. Trevor Aston, was conspicuously kind in lending invaluable material, and the Bodleian Library not only provided the major share of items which the Press itself does not possess, but also considerable help in the compilation of the text, thanks to the kindness of Mr. Paul Morgan and Mr. Timothy Rogers. Miss Priscilla Barker and Olivia and Christian Barker provided material assistance to the author. Finally, Mr. J. W. Thomas has earned our special thanks for the accomplished skill, speed, and efficiency of his photography, of which the illustrations (a few excepted, which came from other sources) are the best testimony.

The author must distinguish his own personal gratitude to the staff of the Press, who have greatly eased his task: to Miss Elizabeth Knight, who co-ordinated and organized the work involved both in the exhibition and the book; Mr. Peter Sutcliffe, whose forthcoming history of the Press in modern times he was allowed to read in manuscript; Miss Linda Scovill, who bore the brunt of the burden laid on OUP New York; and to the University Printer and the many members of his staff who have taken part in the making of the book. But the largest of all these debts is due to Mr. Harry Carter, archivist and historian of the Press. His *History of the Oxford University Press: Volume I, to 1780* provided a structure, as well as most of the material, of the main part of the book; his unrivalled knowledge of the material, archival and physical, in the Press made its accumulation easy (for the author, at least); above all, his encyclopaedic knowledge, not just of the Press itself, but of the history of printing, of the University, and the course of scholarship generally have rescued me from many blunders; those that remain are my own.

I should like, finally, to record my thanks to the Secretary and Delegates of the Oxford University Press for honouring me with the commission to write this account of a tradition which it is their task to extend to future ages.

N. J. B.

THE EARLY UNIVERSITY AND ITS BOOKS

There was a town at the ford over the Thames long before a university was established. If Alfred did not, as the Elizabethan antiquaries fondly asserted, found the university, coins with his name were minted at Oxford. Domesday Book records over a thousand dwellings there, more than half ruinous or uninhabited—witness both of the town's size and of the thoroughness with which it was sacked by the Northmen in 1065. It prospered under the Norman sheriff Robert d'Oili, who restored, among much else, the church of St. Mary the Virgin. At some point in the second half of the twelfth century, a swarm of the wandering scholars found all over western Europe settled at Oxford. When Giraldus Cambrensis visited it in 1184–5, he found Masters and Faculties well established. At the beginning of the thirteenth century, the first Chancellor of the University was appointed by the Bishop of Lincoln, in whose see Oxford then was. The first evidence of the existence of the book trade is contemporary with this event.

1. Grant of Land in Cat Street by Elias Bradfot to William, son of Robert of Northampton, *c.* 1215 (University Archives, W.P.β F 46).

The parish of St. Mary the Virgin, and in particular Cat Street, which runs north from the High Street past the east end of the church, was the centre of the book trade from these early times. Cat Street itself was a mass of little tenements, many of them with stalls opening on to the street at ground-floor level. The land which Elias Bradfot dimitted to William lay between those of Laurence the Binder and Emma Rideratrix. The deed is witnessed by, among others, three illuminators, a scribe, and two parchminers (dealers in vellum for the writing or binding of books); all these were no doubt neighbours in Cat Street.

By the mid thirteenth century, these craftsmen were joined by stationers, owners of a stand or stall. They were originally valuers of all kinds of goods, and only came to deal mainly in books because they were the commonest pledge, or *cautio*, for a loan from the University Chest. Unredeemed pledged books were sold by the stationers. Anxious to control a trade directly concerned with the finances of the University, the Chancellor demanded and, between 1290 and 1355, got jurisdiction over it. Then the makers and sellers of books became servants of the University, and thus (as they were later called) 'privileged persons'.

2. University Statutes: 'Contra vendentes libros contra voluntatem stationarii', 27 January 1374; and 'De onere custodum', before 1380 (University Archives, Registrum A).

The writing of the earliest parts of Registrum A, which includes the Chancellor's record of the Statutes passed by Congregation, dates to the first years of the fourteenth century. The first of the two statutes relating to the book trade shows that seventy years later the stationers expected a regular trade in books beyond the occasional sale of unredeemed pledges. This trade was sufficiently steady to attract the unwelcome attention of unlicensed outside competitors. They bought ('plerique codices magni valoris ad partes exteras deferuntur'), and also sold ('veri domini librorum eorundem exquisitis coloribus seducuntur'), thus diminishing the profit of the university stationers. It is the familiar cry of the dealer in learned books, threatened by competition from the general trade.

The statute of 1380 is interesting, since it shows the special business of the university stationer. It was his duty, under penalty of confiscation or worse, to rent out exemplars, which were whole, complete, correct, and faithful copies of the original text. This requirement was partly due to the academic need for a 'set text'; it was equally necessary for the mechanical business of copying manuscripts by hand.

3. The Pecia system: St. Thomas Aquinas. Summa theologica, pars secunda (Worcester Cathedral MS. F 103).

From the middle of the thirteenth to the middle of the fourteenth century, the stationers were often also described as *exemplatores librorum*. It was their task to maintain and supply copies of required texts, and in a number of universities, beginning with Bologna *c.* 1200, they hired out their exemplars in quires or *peciae*. There were several advantages in this system: it accelerated copying (a copyist could return a quire when finished, which could then be leased to another), and it diminished the risk of loss. At Bologna students were expected to return each *pecia* within a week, with a fine if they were late and a larger fine if they lost it. Manuscripts copied in this manner have the end of each *pecia* marked in the margin with its number.

The Worcester manuscript of Aquinas is (so far as is known) a unique example of the survival of a stationer's *exemplar*. The most striking thing about it is that it contains a duplicate of the second quire, written in the same hand and repeating the same text (though not line for line) as the first. Stationers were obliged by university statute to keep their exemplars complete, and clearly protected themselves by making more than one copy. The expertise with which a professional scribe (as opposed to the students who rented the *peciae* to copy for their own purposes) could repeat his work is strikingly demonstrated here: it is, in effect, a form of duplication which anticipates printing in its mechanical precision.

The University of Oxford had its own *cista exemplarium*, a chest in which the University's *exemplaria* were kept and rented out on similar terms to *exemplatores*. Manuscript notes like 'peciam sequentem habet Cancellar. Oxon.' are found in some manuscripts. In the latter part of the fourteenth century, the system died out, for no obvious reason. It may have been due to the impact of outside competition, which evoked the University Statutes of 1374 and 1380. Evidently by then there was a sufficiency or more of *exemplaria*, which may have made *pecia*-copying unnecessary.

4. Letter of thanks to Humfrey, Duke of Gloucester, for the gift of 129 books to the University, 5 November 1439 (University Archives, Registrum F).

An Oxford polymath once said that a university consists of a library and a press. The University had books before Duke Humfrey's gift, but its size and the number of classical and humanistic books, representing the 'new learning' from Italy, provided a new foundation for the library. With the letter, the University sent its indenture or receipt for the books, recording the title of each and listing its *secundo folio*, the opening words of the second leaf, the identifying mark universally used in the Middle Ages. This gift was followed by others in 1441, totalling another 16, and in February 1444 the Duke added a final 134 more. A bequest of more books may have been diverted by Henry VI to his new foundation, King's College, at Cambridge.

Among the books given by Duke Humfrey was a translation by Leonardo Bruni of Aristotle's *Ethics*, a seminal work (as to both text and manner of translation) for the new humanism. It was one of the earliest books to be printed by the first Oxford printer.

THE FIRST PRESS AT OXFORD

If Duke Humfrey's gifts were generous, there was no shortage of books in fifteenth-century Oxford, to go by the number of scribes, illuminators, booksellers, and bookbinders recorded at work there. As earlier, they tended to live in the streets round the church of St. Mary the

Virgin, especially Cat Street. Several of them doubled the book trade with service to the University or colleges, like Christopher Coke, bookbinder and manciple of Neville's Hall. A surprising number of Oxford manuscripts are written by Dutch or German scribes: Frederic Naghel of Utrecht wrote out a Latin version of Plato's *Meno* in Oxford in 1423, and John Reynbold of Erfurt produced a massive set of Duns Scotus in 1460–5 for Bishop William Gray to give to Balliol. Wanderers like these from the Rhine valley were among those who spread the new art of printing throughout western Europe. Hence came the first Oxford printer.

His name was Theodoric, surnamed Rood ('the red' in Low German), from Cologne. So much can be learned from his books, of which seventeen altogether are now known. All our knowledge of his press depends on these books; there is no mention of it in contemporary records. Theodoric's presence is, however, attested in other directions: as 'Dyryke Dowcheman' he lived (and probably worked) in a house in the parish of St. Peter-in-the-East; 'Dydycke' was paid 23*s.* 4*d.* for mending and regilding a bedel's staff in 1481–2; by 1482–3 'Dedyck Teutonicus' had moved out of a tenement in the High Street. Evidently, English tongues found his name hard. Theodoric was at work in Oxford until 1485 and probably after; the date of his arrival is clouded by the best-known misprint in the history of Oxford printing. What, by all the typographical evidence, must be his first (or earliest surviving) book is dated '1468'; as its two successors in the same type are dated 1479, it is generally assumed that an 'x' slipped out of the date of the *Expositio in symbolum apostolorum.*

It is not clear whether Theodoric's press was a speculative venture or whether he was summoned by members of the University for a specific purpose, as the first printers at Paris were by the Rector of the Sorbonne. On balance, the former seems more likely. None of the surviving books bear any acknowledgement of local patronage, a matter in which the early printers were normally punctilious. There were in Cologne substantial capitalists who invested in printing, for whom printers worked on a contract basis. Caxton, visiting Cologne in 1470–1, had employed Johann Veldener, who subsequently became his supplier of type, in this way. It may be that Caxton's success suggested Theodoric's mission. Whether independent of or sponsored by local support, the books he printed were well chosen: they included texts established in the earlier Middle Ages, as well as those called for by the new humanism (among these were the first English printing of any classical Latin text, Cicero's *Pro Milone*, and Leonardo Bruni's translation of Aristotle's *Ethics*); Mirk's *Festial* (1486/7) was reprinted seventeen times up to 1532, and Lyndewood's *Constitutiones* (*c.* 1483) twelve times by 1557. Like Caxton, Rood may also have printed other religious and liturgical books (a class severely reduced during the Reformation); Henry Bradshaw suggested that the odd assortment of woodcut illustrations in the *Festial* were originally intended for a *Golden Legend* and a *Horae* of which no trace survives.

5. [Rufinus of Aquileia.] *Expositio Sancti Hieronymi in symbolum apostolorum.* Impressa Oxonie Et finita Anno Domini '1468' [1478].

Tyrannius Rufinus (*c.* 340–410) was for long the friend and supporter of Jerome, who eventually quarrelled with him for his support of the works of Origen. This comparison of the creed of Aquileia (where Rufinus was born) with that of Rome is still valuable evidence of church practice in the fourth century.

In the fifteenth century the creed was still firmly

attributed to St. Jerome, whose minor works were regularly found in collections in English medieval libraries. There is no telling what dictated its choice to Theodoric. With two other books, dated 1479 and 1480, it is set in a distinctive gothic type, broad, heavily ligatured, and with some letters with cursive characteristics, which is found in several contemporary versions in Cologne. It is closest to that used by the press which worked for Gerard ten Raem, but it shares some letters with founts used by Ulrich Zel, the first printer at Cologne, and Richard Pafraet, who migrated from Cologne to Deventer. None of the three Oxford books in this type bears the printer's name, but in view of the Cologne connection there is no reason to doubt that Theodoric printed them; there is as little reason to doubt the misdating of the first of them, although there are no signs of haste about it, nor is the date corrected in any surviving copy.

6. John Anwykyll (?). *Compendium totius grammaticae*, *c.* 1483.

One of the causes that may have brought Theodoric to Oxford was a revolution in the teaching of Latin grammar, which can be connected with the foundation of Magdalen College School in 1478. Dissatisfaction with the old mechanical system reflected in the Donatus *Ars minor* and the *Doctrinale* of Alexander Gallus had been felt in Oxford for some time. One of the objects of the new Magdalen College School was to teach Latin as a living language: the vivid examples rendered in English and Latin give a fair idea of the new method; to the modern reader they give an equally vivid picture of unaffected colloquial English at the time.

The first such book, the *Long parvula* attributed to John Stanbridge, usher at the school, was printed by Theodoric about 1481; only two leaves of it survive, and its identification depends on a later edition of 1509. Even the more substantial *Compendium* does not survive complete: forty-four leaves of one issue and six of another attest its success. Its title is only known from a later edition, printed at Deventer in 1489 by Theodoric's fellow Cologner Richard Pafraet, no doubt for the English market: *Compendium totius grammaticae ex variis autoribus, Laurentio, Servio, Perotto, diligenter collectum et versibus cum eorum interpretatione conscriptum, totius barbariei destructorium, et latine lingue ornamentum non minus preceptoribus quam pueris necessarium.* The destruction of barbarous diction, its necessity for masters as well as pupils, above all the citation of the great humanist grammarians Lorenzo Valla and Niccolò Perotti, make its revolutionary purpose clear; 'bad Latin was ceasing to be a second language, and good Latin was becoming a school subject.'[1] With the *Compendium* went the *Vulgaria Terentii*, a set of colloquial sentences from Terence's plays with translations, even clearer evidence of the desire to re-embed the roots of Latin, as spoken in schools and after, in good classical usage.

John Anwykyll was the first master of Magdalen College School; that he was author of the book is assumed from some verses attached to it praising William Waynflete (?1395–1486) by one John, who wrote the book at his instance. Whoever wrote it, it became the basis of Latin grammar as taught for the next 400 years. Stanbridge's *Accidence*, a development of it, was printed some fifty times, and ended its useful life in Scotland in the seventeenth century. The grammars of Whittington and Lily were even more successful. The *Vulgaria Terentii* was immediately reprinted by William de Machlinia, and by Gerard Leeu in Antwerp in 1486. It was the basis, in its turn, of the *Flowers for Latin speaking . . . out of Terence* of Nicholas Udall, the great sixteenth-century schoolmaster.

THE SECOND PRESS

The sudden end of the first Oxford Press cannot be explained by misjudgement of the market, but it cannot be a coincidence that all the other printers in England, in London and St. Albans, with the exception of Caxton, went out of business at about the same time. In 1484 Richard III's parliament passed an Act relaxing the restrictions on alien traders, and it is prob-

[1] Carter p. 8.

able that an influx of cheaper books printed abroad made it difficult for the local printers to continue unless, like Caxton, their books had no foreign competition. The Act continued in force until 1523, when foreign apprentices were banned, but by 1534, when protectionism for the local trade and the needs of government to control unauthorized printing combined in the Act forbidding the sale of bound books from abroad or any retail sale of books by aliens, printing in England was already expanding rapidly.

The same needs concentrated the trade in London, and there is no evidence to explain the brief appearance of the second Oxford Press in 1517–20, of which eight works are known. To judge by its types, the Press had some connection with Wynkyn de Worde's flourishing London business (as, perhaps, the St. Albans printer had with Caxton earlier). John Scolar, at work between December 1517 and June 1518, and Charles Kyrfoth, whose name appears on one book dated February 1519/20, are unknown elsewhere. Its output was decidedly more conservative than that of the first Press; it included two works by Walter Burley, one of the internationally famous Oxford scholars of the early fourteenth century, and a *Computus*, a simple method of calculating dates using Roman numerals. The emphasis is on the old scholastic educational tradition; there is none of the humanistic Latin and Greek found in the equally short-lived (1521–2) first Cambridge press at the same time.

7. Joannes Dedicus. *Quaestiones moralissime super libros Ethicorum*. In celeberima universitate Oxoniensi per me Iohannem Scolar . . . Anno domini M.CCCCC. decimo octavo. Mensis vero Maii die decimo quinto.

The author of this commentary on Aristotle's *Ethics* is unknown, but it belongs to a tradition of Aristotelian scholarship long predating Leonardo Bruni's translation. It is the longest (152 pages) and only substantial work printed at the second Press. Its principal interest lies in the elaborate privilege which John Scolar was careful to print with his work:

> It is forbidden by an edict under the seal of the chancery for anyone during seven years to print this excellent work, or sell it in a form paid for by another in the University of Oxford or within its precinct, on pain of losing all the books and five pounds sterling for every copy sold, wherever the books were printed, in addition to the other penalty provided by the edict. Don't think you can blind the crows.

Aldus had found it necessary to obtain a similar privilege for his edition of Theodore Gaza's Grammar in 1495 and subsequently, and the King of France and the Emperor first issued privileges in 1507 and 1512. This, however, was the first privilege issued in England (the first royal privilege comes six months later). Both Scolar and Kyrfoth put a device of the University's coat of arms in their books to emphasize their academic authority. Here, as elsewhere, the usefulness of their books to Oxford students is stressed in the introductory matter.

8. Robert Whittington. *De heteroclitis nominibus*. Oxonii impressa per me Ioannem Scolar . . . Anno domini M.CCCCC. decimo octavo Mensis vero Iunij die vicesimo septimo.

This is the only one of the pieces printed at the second Press which looks forward, rather than to the past medieval syllabus of the University. Robert Whittington was an old pupil of Stanbridge's from Magdalen College School, whose great moment came on 4 July 1513 when, on supplication to the Regents for the doctorate in grammar and rhetoric, 'he was crowned with laurel and allowed the exclusive use of a hood lined with silk'.[1] It was his subsequent assumption of the title *protovates Angliae*, rather than any defects in his work, that annoyed his fellow grammarians William Horman and William Lily. The pamphlet war which followed did nothing to halt the sales of Whittington's enormously successful grammar. In

[1] M. R. James, introduction to William Horman, *Vulgaria*, Oxford (for the Roxburghe Club), 1926, pp. xv–xvi.

various parts (of which this is only one and not the first edition of that) and forms, it went through at least 150 separate editions in the sixteenth century. But in the end William Lily had the last word, his grammar outlasting Whittington's by many years. Every other edition was printed in London, a fair indication of the ephemerality of the Press at Oxford.

THE PRESS ESTABLISHED AT OXFORD

In 1534, the same year as the Act against foreign books and booksellers, the University of Cambridge, alarmed by the risk of heresy, sought and got a royal charter which allowed three stationers and printers to practise there. Oxford, further from Europe so less prone to heretical influence, did not pursue the precedent. Nor did Cambridge exercise its privilege for nearly fifty years. In the interval, the charter of Philip and Mary to the Stationers' Company in 1557 had fastened the bond between government censorship and the London printers' determination to suppress competition. Despite the charter, Cambridge failed in its first attempt to set up a press in 1576, even though a Stationer was appointed as first printer, and when in 1583 Thomas Thomas, no Stationer, did set up, the Company sent a party down to break up his press.

Oxford was not to be outdone. Although unprotected by charter, the University took the risk; in August 1584 Convocation voted to lend £100 to Joseph Barnes, a bookseller licensed by the Vice-Chancellor since 1573, 'that he might have a press in the University for printing books the more easily'.[1] Barnes's venture was further supported by a committee of doctors appointed to decide on printing. The University did not, however, neglect its legal, or at least political, position.

9. Supplicatio ad illustrissimum comitem Leicestriae summum Oxoniensis academiae cancellarium pro Typographia Oxoniae erigenda (Bibliothèque Nationale MS. Clairambault 327, fols. 122–3).

This document is, in effect, a brief for the Chancellor of the University, Robert Dudley, Earl of Leicester, to plead with the Queen the University's case for printing at Oxford. It is anonymous, and may be the work of more than one hand. Its content is largely a conventional plea for the promulgation of learning, cast in terms to which no exception could be taken. The desire to keep up with Cambridge, which must have provoked it, is prudently omitted. The patriotic need to keep up with foreign universities, the too little known scholarship of Oxford, is commonplace. The reference to the earlier precedent of 'a man living in Oxford fifty years ago, more or less, who used to print books' shows how little was remembered of the earlier presses. Another reference to the probable good effect of the Press on 'the western parts of England, Wales, and the hitherto barbarous realm of Ireland' was politic, in view of the permanent anxiety of the government about the western marches and Ireland; it is further reflected in the intermittent but long-lived tradition of printing in Welsh at the Press.

But the crux of the document lies in two points: the presence in Oxford of important but neglected manuscripts, and above all of 'a substantial bookseller', Joseph Barnes, 'who would willingly print books if he were given privileges for four or five of his choice not now covered by privileges'. There is no documentary evidence of the result of this plea, but it was clearly successful, although Barnes did not get his privileges. The Star Chamber decree of 23 June 1586, regulating printing, expressly allowed one printer and one apprentice each to both Oxford and Cambridge.

[1] Registrum L 10, f. 281.

10. Portrait of Robert Dudley, Earl of Leicester (?1532–88), Chancellor of the University of Oxford (National Portrait Gallery).

When Leicester received the University's petition, his star was waning. He had been well on the way to fame and the favour of the Queen when he became Chancellor in 1564. He was now about to embark on his campaign in the Low Countries; it was the first time that the Queen had allowed him an independent command. But first, in January 1585, he paid a state visit to his University, staying with the Rector of Lincoln College, its Vice-Chancellor. This was the splendid martial figure whom the University had to thank for its licence to print.

11. *In adventum illustrissimi Lecestrensis comitis ad collegium Lincolniense carmen gratulatorium.* Oxoniae, ex aedibus Josephi Barnes, 1585.

No doubt Leicester's arrival at the gate of Lincoln College was the occasion of a formal reception, of which the recital of these verses may have been part. Perhaps this broadside, dated 11 January 1585, was presented to the Earl, at once a thank-offering for his intervention and solid evidence of its fruit. It was the forerunner of many longer sets of verses, including some in exotic languages, produced by the University to commemorate great occasions. (Two such sets, devoted to the memory of Leicester's nephew, Sir Philip Sidney, were printed by Barnes in 1587.) The play on the words 'comis' and 'Comes', the neat and tactful reference to Leicester as the Atlas of his University, Nestor of his country, and Achates of his Queen, are characteristic of the amiable rhetoric appropriate to them.

The large and handsome cut of the University Arms, and the variety of the types employed, show that Barnes had already invested some of his £100 well. They were to adorn his work for many years to come.

12. John Case. *Speculum moralium quaestionum in universam ethicen Aristotelis.* Oxoniae, ex officina typographica, Josephi Barnesii celeberrimae Academiae Oxoniensis typographi, 1585.

This was the first book from Barnes's press, which he prefaced with a long dedicatory epistle to Leicester. For the third time Aristotle's *Ethics*, this time in the form of *quaestio*, *oppositio*, and *responsio* appropriate to the disputations then held in the University schools, marks a turning-point in the history of the Press at Oxford. John Case was a prolific author; in 1568 he had been elected fellow of St. John's College, but 'being Popishly affected he left his fellowship and married and . . . read logic and philosophy to young men (mostly of the R.C. religion) in a private house in St Mary Magd. parish'.[1]

Barnes's epistle dwells at length on the history of printing and on the benefits that Leicester's benefaction has brought to the University.

13. St. John Chrysostom. *Homiliae sex, ex manuscriptis Codicibus Novi Collegii.* Oxoniae, ex officina typographica Josephi Barnesii, 1586.

This was the first book printed in Greek at the University. The sermons of St. John Chrysostom (*c.* 345–407) were popular in the sixteenth century; the first Greek book printed in England, by Reginald Wolfe in 1543, contained two of them. These were edited by John Harmar (?1555–1613), the Regius Professor of Greek. Harmar owed his chair, and his previous education at Winchester and New College, to the Earl of Leicester's patronage. His edition of Chrysostom, based on the manuscripts at New College (of which he was now a fellow), was a thank-offering. In 1588 Harmar was made headmaster of Winchester, and in 1595 Warden; he was also a prebendary of the cathedral. If his preferment was due to his patron, he was not unworthy of it. The Chrysostom was the first scholarly Greek text printed in England, and Harmar went on to take a leading part in the translation of the New Testament for the Authorized Version (King James Bible), finally printed in 1611.

14. Richard de Bury. *Philobiblon . . . sive de amore librorum, et institutione bibliothecae, tractatus pulcherrimus . . . cui Accessit appendix de manuscriptis Oxoniensibus.* Oxonii, excudebat Iosephus Barnesius, 1599.

The early printers were not slow to realize the virtues of this famous tract on bibliophily, written

[1] Anthony Wood, *Athenae Oxonienses*, ed. P. Bliss (1813–20), i. 685.

by the Bishop of Durham (1281–1345). The first edition was printed at Cologne, perhaps for the English market, in 1473. The first Oxford edition marked the most important event in the history of books in the University, the foundation of the library which still bears his name by Sir Thomas Bodley (1545–1613). The *Philobiblon* was dedicated to him and edited by Thomas James, fellow of New College, who became Bodley's first librarian in 1602, when the library was formally opened. The promised appendix only lists the authors whose works are to be found at Oxford. James's *Ecloga Oxonio-Cantabrigiensis*, the first printed catalogue of books at either university, appeared in London in 1600.

James remained Bodley's Librarian until 1620, when he resigned owing to ill health (the cold in the Bodleian took its toll of scholars), and became Dean of Wells. In 1605 and 1620, the full catalogues of the library which he compiled were printed, first by Barnes, the next by his successor, John Lichfield. The 1605 catalogue was dedicated to Henry, Prince of Wales, the white hope of English learning and letters cut off in his prime. The second and enlarged catalogue (it was dedicated to the King and Prince Charles) cost £112. 10*s*., a substantial sum.

15. Charles Butler. *The feminine monarchie Or a treatise concerning bees, and the due ordering of them.* At Oxford, printed by Joseph Barnes, 1609.

This was the first original (as the author is at pains to point out) work on bees to be published in England. Charles Butler (*d*. 1647), fellow of Magdalen College, was always original, a man slightly out of step with his time. His treatises on rhetoric and oratory, and above all his *English Grammar* (1633) with its peculiar system of phonetic spelling, show this and also his strong practical turn of mind. His *English Grammar* presses the advantages of English from its wide geographical use, which demands a common usage—a striking prophecy of English in the twentieth century. Equally, his work on bees contains some sharp reflections on the masculine basis of society.

Music was another subject on which Butler wrote a novel treatise, and in *The feminine monarchie* he attempted to reproduce the humming of a swarm of bees in musical notation. This occasioned the first use of music type at Oxford; Butler's interest in the mechanics of printing can also be seen elsewhere (21).

16. John Smith. *A map of Virginia with a description of the countrey, the Commodities, People, Government and Religion.* At Oxford, printed by Joseph Barnes, 1612.

It is still not clear why this first description of the English colony at Virginia came to be printed at Oxford. John Smith (1580–1631) sent back a report and map to the Council in England when he became head of the colony in 1608, and on his return to England set about the engraving of his map and the publication of his report, supplemented with the accounts of eight other colonists. The map was engraved by William Hole, who was already famous for his work on the title-pages and maps of the 1607 edition of Camden's *Britannia* (he also engraved the first music in England and the first English copper-plate writing manual). It is altogether a most unexpected publication from the provincial press, and the most probable explanation is that Smith entrusted the text to William Simmonds, fellow of Magdalen College, who had been out in Virginia.

Although Smith, having survived the romantic but difficult start of Virginia, transferred his energies to New England, he continued, in his *General Historie* (1624) and elsewhere, to promote the cause of colonization in America, of which his Oxford book was the first tract.

THE SUCCESSORS OF JOSEPH BARNES

Barnes retired in 1617 and died a year later, leaving goods worth £1,128. He was succeeded by John Lichfield, the first of a family long connected with Oxford printing. He had several partners. As long as they shared the Press, they were within the decree of the Court of Star Chamber of June 1586, which limited printing to London, 'excepte one presse in the universitye of Cambridge, and another presse in the universitie of Oxforde, and no moe'. But in 1627 Lichfield and his then partner William Turner quarrelled; they printed separately thereafter, each calling himself 'Printer to the University'. This was a matter of some scandal and unease to the University. In 1635 John Lichfield was succeeded by his son Leonard; William Turner continued until 1643. Successive generations of the Lichfield family went on printing at Oxford until well into the eighteenth century.

17. Peter Heylyn. *Microcosmos, or a little description of the great world.* At Oxford, printed by John Lichfield and James Short, printers to the famous University, 1621.

In 1621 two remarkable best-sellers made their first appearance, both printed at Oxford: Burton's *Anatomy of Melancholy*, and the first modern geography to be printed in English, Peter Heylin's *Microcosmos*. The latter is now forgotten, but in its time it was even more successful; eight Oxford editions in quarto up to 1639 were followed before the end of the century by another eight in folio, printed at London under the title of *Cosmographie*. It was a 'Treatise Historicall, Geographicall, Politicall, Theologicall' which for three generations was the source of information about the rest of the world (particularly Europe) most commonly used in England.

Peter Heylyn (1600–62) was a choleric controversialist, a 'bluster-master' in his enemy John Hacket's phrase, from his early days as a fellow of Magdalen College. He annoyed James I by saying in *Microcosmos* that 'France is the greater and more famous Kingdom than England'; 'is' was a misprint for 'was', he replied, and the passage referred to the time of Edward III, but he wisely suppressed it in later editions. His loyalty to Laud and his memory is a nicer side of his character; he lived to be restored to his canonry of Westminster at the Restoration.

18. Robert Burton. *The Anatomy of Melancholy. What it is, with all the kinds, causes, symptomes, prognostickes, & severall cures of it.* The fift edition. Oxford, printed for Henry Cripps [by L. Lichfield], 1638.

18A. *The Anatomy of Melancholy*. The fourth edition, 1632 (proof sheet).

Robert Burton (1577–1640) went as a commoner to Brasenose College in 1593, whence he was elected a student of Christ Church in 1599. There, 'in the most flourishing colledge of Europe', he led a quiet life, without event: 'I have lived a silent, sedentary, solitary, private life, *mihi et musis*, in the university, as long almost as *Xenocrates* in *Athens*, *ad senectam fere*, to learn wisdom as he did, penned up most part in my study.' The *Anatomy* is the one monument of his life, apart from those of his books (some rare) which he left to the Bodleian.

He was an inveterate amender of his work, which constantly grew. It first appeared in quarto, then in 1624 became a folio. In 1628 the famous engraved frontispiece by C. le Blond was added. Of the 1632 edition a number of proof-sheets have recently been discovered, used as endpapers in contemporary Oxford bindings. The 1638 edition had a curious history; it began life as an Edinburgh piracy, which was detected midway through and the sheets impounded and sent to Oxford, where the printing was completed. Burton presented copies of it to three Oxford colleges, Corpus Christi, the Brasenose of his youth, and Christ Church, whose copy, testimony of a long and happy association, is illustrated here.

19. *Catalogus universalis pro nundinis Francofurtensibus autumnalibus de anno* 1621. Francofurti, Typis ac sumptibus Sigismundi Latomi, 1621.

The Frankfurt book-fair was established before the end of the fifteenth century, and by the middle of the sixteenth its position at the centre of civilized Europe, its extensive trade connections with the other main printing towns of Europe, and habit now established for scholars and authors, as well as printers and booksellers, made its twice-yearly sessions an essential part of the book trade and literary life. In 1564 the first catalogue of all the fairs appeared at Augsburg, and from 1598 the Ratskanzlei at Frankfurt banned all private catalogues in favour of its own official version. This continued until 1749.

In the first century after the introduction of printing to England, the trade in books was essentially an import and local business. But at the end of the sixteenth century, authors and booksellers began to look for a market abroad for books printed in England. The early Frankfurt Fair catalogues were reprinted (technically, by piracy) in London, and London printed books appeared in the Fair catalogues. For the first time in 1621 Oxford printed books are found there too, the Bodleian catalogue of 1620, Robert Sanderson's *Logicae artis compendium* (1619), and an alchemical work by John Thornborough, Bishop of Worcester, Λιθοθεωρικός (1621). For the first time the Oxford Press was making a name outside the University and the indigenous book trade.

20. Mateo Aleman. *The Rogue: or, the life of Guzman de Alfarache*. Oxford, printed by William Turner, for Robert Allot, and are to be sold in Paul's Churchyard, 1630.

This is a literal reprint, errors and all, of the first London edition of 1622. It was no doubt printed for the London trade; Allot produced a third, corrected, edition there in 1634. It would be unremarkable if it were not the first novel to be printed at Oxford, and one of the liveliest of early English translations, fully worthy of its picaresque original. James Mabbe, the translator, spent most of his life at Oxford, as demy, fellow, and bursar of Magdalen College, apart from two years spent as secretary to Sir John Digby, ambassador at Madrid. There he acquired his taste for Guzman de Alfarache, and Cervantes and other Spanish authors, whom he also translated.

THE ACQUISITION OF PRINTING TYPES

21. Charles Butler. *Oratoriae libri duo*. Oxoniae, excudebat Guilielmus Turner, impensis authoris, 1629.

There had been little advance in the typographic equipment of the Oxford printers since Barnes's time. An interesting specimen of it comes in Butler's tract on oratory. Making the classic point that all sentences depend on variety, he analyses the *distinctiones*, which can be a difference of punctuation or letters; the latter differ in kind (Roman or Italic) or shape (capitals or lower-case letters), and in size. He illustrates the point with a range of type sizes, and a specimen of Roman, Italic, and 'English' or Black-letter. It shows the normal types available in Oxford at the time.

22. Portrait of Sir Henry Savile (1549–1622), attributed to Marcus Gheeraerts (Bodleian Library).

23. Matrices of the Greek type given to the University by Savile.

24. *Ultima linea Savilii sive in obitum clarissimi Domini Henrici Savilii*. Oxoniae, excudebant Johannes Lichfield et Jacobus Short, 1622.

25. *Camdeni insignia*. Oxoniae, excudebant Johannes Lichfield et Jacobus Short, Academiae typographi, 1624.

Sir Henry Savile, Warden of Merton College and later Provost of Eton, was a great benefactor of learning. His most notable achievement was the edition of the works of St. John Chrysostom in eight volumes, printed at the press that he established at Eton in 1610–13. In 1619 he gave his Greek type to the University, and the gift is recorded in *Ultima linea Savilii*, a record of his benefactions with verses to his memory.

The sources of his type, a large Great Primer Greek fitter for texts than Barnes's smaller type, are not clear. Savile had wanted a set of the celebrated *grecs du roi*, cut for François I by Claude Garamont. The type he got was a copy, probably bought at the Frankfurt book fair in 1608 and perhaps originally cut by Pierre Haultin *c.* 1580. The equipment given by Savile was first used in the University's tribute to William Camden (1551–1623), another great benefactor (founder of the chair of history) and scholar. It differs slightly from the type used by Savile at Eton (some sets of punches, matrices, and type do not always match), and has been augmented and adapted since. The bulk of it remains, a relic of the oldest gift of type to the University.

26. Broadside of types from the Leyden purchase in 1637.

27. Specimen of the Brevier Hebrew (Univ. Arch. S.E.P. P 17^b (4)).

28. Gerard Langbaine's Inventory of the matrices (Univ. Arch. S.E.P. P 17^b (3), fol. 47).

In 1637 the University, by now in possession of an income to devote to printing, decided to augment its equipment. Samuel Brown, a London bookseller and brother of one of the University proctors that year, went to Leyden and negotiated a purchase of types, matrices, and punches from the stock of the recently deceased typefounder Arend Cornelisz. van Hoogenacker. Altogether materials for eleven different types were acquired, the majority Hebrew. Although well thought of at the time, it was a bad bargain. Few of the founts were complete, and Gerard Langbaine, when he became Keeper of the Archives in 1644 and custodian of the types, was put to great pains to make up a reasonable set of Hebrew types and an Arabic. The result of his work can be seen below.

LAUD'S VISION OF A UNIVERSITY PRESS

29. Portrait of William Laud, Archbishop of Canterbury, Chancellor of the University (1573–1645). By Sir Anthony Van Dyck, 1636 (St. John's College).

30. Great Charter of Charles I to the University, 3 March 1636 (University Archives).

31. 'An Historical Account relating to the University of Oxford' in *The Second Volume of the Remains of . . . William Laud, . . . written by Himself*, ed. Henry Wharton (London, 1700).

When Laud became Chancellor in 1629 he set himself a number of tasks, among them the codifying of the University statutes and their consolidation in 'a large Charter' providing privileges equal to those of Cambridge, and the setting up of 'a Greek Press in London and Oxford, for Printing of the Library Manuscripts'.[1] The manuscripts were the Barocci Greek MSS. given to the Bodleian at Laud's instance by his predecessor, the Earl of Pembroke. The small, dignified, if impetuous, presence of Van Dyck's portrait was not to be crossed or thwarted. He acted quickly. The Press was provided for by Letters Patent of 12 November 1632, and confirmed by the Great Charter of 1636. It allowed the University three *typographi* (thus clearing the illegal position of Lichfield and Turner, of whom, however, Laud had a low opinion), and the right to print Bibles, already granted to Cambridge but otherwise reserved to the King's Printer. Elated, the University set up a Delegacy for Printing, and determined upon an edition of the chronicle of John Malalas, using Savile's types.

The practical implementation of these plans was constantly in Laud's mind. The new statutes which he drew up in 1633–4 provide, under *De typographis Universitatis*, for a learned 'Architypographus', whose task should be the superintendence of paper, presses, and type, down to the width of margins and the correction of correctors' errors. All this was settled in Laud's mind, formal rather than practical, but he saw the need to 'let your Privilege settle a while'. One thing needed for the Press was money, and the University killed two birds with one stone in 1637 by compounding with the Company of Stationers not to print books for which they had patents for £200 p.a. This provided the funds for the Leyden purchase, and in May that year Laud saw his vision on the brink of realization.

But the clouds were gathering, and Laud's attention was distracted to the political affairs which brought his downfall. Still, the foresight, industry, and force of character which he brought to bear on the University in the decade before the Civil War left an indelible mark on the Oxford Press.

[1] 'The Diary of the Life of Arch-Bishop Laud', in *The History of the Troubles and Tryal of . . . William Laud*, ed. H. Wharton (1695), pp. 68–9.

32. Pope Clement I. *Ad Corinthios epistola prior. Ex laceris reliquiis vetustissimi exemplaris Bibliothecae Regiae eruit, lacunas explevit, latinê vertit, & notis brevioribus illustravit, Patricius Iunius.* Excudebat Johannes Lichfield Academiae Typographus An. Dom. 1633.

Although Laud was obliged to leave 'the setting up of a learned Press' undone, his influence can be seen in one of the first works of modern textual scholarship to issue from an Oxford press, St. Clement's first letter to the Corinthians. The text had been found on some tattered leaves at the end of the Codex Alexandrinus, the great fifth-century Greek Bible manuscript given to Charles I in 1628 by the Patriarch of Constantinople, Cyril Lucaris. Patrick Young, the King's librarian, transcribed it and supplied a Latin translation and notes. Words and letters missing in the original that he was able to supply were printed in red, an original and useful editorial device.

Lichfield had already obliged Laud in 1631 by printing William Page's *Treatise of bowing at the name of Jesus*, a practice strongly approved by Laud. It may have been he who directed Young's work to Lichfield and persuaded the University to lend him Sir Henry Savile's Greek types, here used to good effect. It is likely that the University also supplied the corrector, although they did not pay for the printing: Young expresses his gratitude for royal generosity in the preface. Otherwise, all the constituents of a learned press are here: 'a scholar-editor with uncommercial motives, a printer equipped with uncommon type, a competent corrector, and someone willing to pay the cost with little prospect of recovering it' (Carter, p. 36).

33. William Chillingworth. *The religion of protestants a safe way of salvation.* Oxford, printed by Leonard Lichfield, printer to the University, 1638.

William Chillingworth (1602–44) was one of the most remarkable products of Laudian Oxford. Son of the mayor of Oxford and Laud's godson, he was educated at Oxford, and became a scholar and fellow of Trinity College, a friend of another coming man, Gilbert Sheldon, Archbishop of Canterbury to be. His great capacity soon brought him to the front of the controversy with Rome, but his own investigations into ecclesiastical authority forced him into acceptance of an infallible church. He was converted in 1629, and next year the Jesuits at Douai unwisely (given his endless self-questioning) set him to work on an account of his motives to conversion. His impartiality, relieved of the burden of controversy, reawoke; a series of patient letters from Laud redirected him, and he left Douai in 1631 for Oxford, where in 1634 he resumed his Protestant faith, although it was not until 1638 that he came, reluctantly, to subscribe to the articles of the Church of England.

He was doubly attacked now, both by Catholics as an apostate, and by puritans as one tainted by Rome. The heat of a dispute on the nature of charity led him to the library and congenial moderation of Sir Lucius Cary, Viscount Falkland, at Great Tew, where he wrote his *Religion of Protestants*, the classic defence of free inquiry and the necessity of personal conviction, detached from all systems. Its immediate success brought him modest preferment, and redoubled abuse from the extremists. With the war he, like Falkland, saw the best hope of peace in the royalist cause, but was taken prisoner, harassed, and soon after died. It was after the Restoration that his ideas came into their own; his work was reprinted nine times in various forms between 1664 and 1742. In literary style, as well as theology, it was a landmark in the history of the English Church.

34. Francis Bacon. *Of the advancement and proficience of learning or the partitions of sciences . . . Interpreted by Gilbert Wats.* Oxford, printed by Leon: Lichfield, printer to the University, for Rob: Young & Ed. Forrest, 1640.

The publication of the most substantial part of Bacon's *Instauratio magna* (first published in the author's Latin in 1623) was an end and a beginning. It was the last substantial work of scholarship to issue from the Oxford Press before the outbreak of war. It was also the form in which the lessons of Bacon's philosophical and scientific writing were communicated to the two groups, in London (Boyle's 'Invisible College') and in Oxford (the 'Philosophical Society of Oxford' that met in John Wilkins's rooms in Wadham), who remained 'inquisitive into natural philosophy and other parts of human learning' throughout the war. The 'New Philosophy' came into formal existence on 28 November 1660 when the group that met at

Gresham College resolved on the 'founding a Colledge for the promoting of Physico-Mathematicall Experimentall Learning', the future Royal Society.

Gilbert Watts died in 1657 before he could see the vindication of his long work of translation, but its importance in the transference of learned discourse from Latin to the vernacular can be seen in the fact that, from the first, the new Society's proceedings, the *Philosophical Transactions*, were in English.

THE SURVIVAL OF LAUD'S VISION

The war brought great change to the Oxford presses. The removal of King and court to Oxford doubled and redoubled the amount of work that came to them, for a pamphlet printed in the Royalist interest in Oxford would appear twice, once with an Oxford imprint and again with a false London imprint to show the King still had friends there; Parliament, not to be outdone, would alter the text in its own interest and issue it again with two imprints; each might in turn produce a formal rejoinder from the other side. Altogether, over 1,000 pieces came from the Oxford Press between 1641 and 1650, but—*silent enim inter arma leges*—few of them were works of scholarship in the sense that Laud intended.

35. Edward Pococke. *Specimen historiae Arabum, sive Gregorii Abul Farajii Malatiensis, de origine & moribus Arabum.* Oxoniae, Excudebat H. Hall, Impensis Humph: Robinson, in Caemeterio Paulino, ad insigne Trium Columbarum, 1650.

Laud's benefactions to the University included the splendid gift of manuscripts to the Bodleian, among them some in Middle Eastern languages then unequalled in England, and the endowment of a chair of Arabic. Edward Pococke (1604–91) learned his oriental languages as chaplain to the Turkey Merchants in Aleppo; in 1636 Laud appointed him to the new professorship, and sent him to the East again to collect manuscripts. Although oppressed for his Laudian connections during the war, he persevered with his work, and the *Specimen*, an elaborate set of essays attached to a thirteenth-century description of the Arabs, was the first product of it. The extensive use of Arabic and some Hebrew probably drew on the type purchased at Leyden.

Pococke followed this up with the *Porta Mosis* by the great thirteenth-century Talmudic scholar Moses Maimonides, with the Arabic text in Hebrew letters as originally written, and had an important part in establishing the oriental texts of Walton's Polyglot Bible, the great monument of English Scholarship under the Commonwealth. After the Restoration, he was able to continue his work uninterrupted, and established a European reputation in his field.

36. John Wallis. *Operum mathematicorum pars altera [prima].* Oxonii, excudebat L. Lichfield per T. Robinson, 1656[7].

John Wallis (1616–1703) was the most distinguished mathematician in England between William Oughtred and Isaac Newton. He was also a theologian and controversialist, and a respectable astronomer; in 1658 he succeeded Gerard Langbaine as Keeper of the University Archives, of which he was an enthusiastic custodian and protector. In 1649 he became Savilian Professor of Geometry, a chair he held for fifty-four years.

His *Opera Mathematica* was the foundation of Oxford's primacy in mathematics for over a century. Here Wallis prefigured the differential calculus, and invented the symbol ∞ for infinity. The work was a long time in the press, and in the event the second part appeared in the year before the first. The diagrams presented problems, but in general Lichfield surmounted the problem of mathematical setting very well.

37. Portrait of Gerard Langbaine (1609–58), Provost of Queen's College and Keeper of the Archives (Queen's College).

38. Langbaine's notes on the typefounding of Nicholas Nicholls (Univ. Arch. S.E.P. P 17[b] (3), fol. 43).

39. Langbaine's letter to Samuel Clarke, 7 December 1657 (B.L. Add. MS. 22905, fol. 9).

40. Portrait of Samuel Clarke (1625–69), Architypographus (Bodleian Library).

The maintenance of Laud's vision during the dark days of the war and after was largely due to Gerard Langbaine, a solid and resourceful defender of the University against enemy interference. He provided help for those like Pococke who were damaged by Laud's fall, and it was due to him that the learned press was not wholly neglected in hard times. He undertook the painful task (clearly neglected till now) of counting and identifying the typefounding material from Leyden (see 26–8), and got the London typefounder Nicholas Nicholls to cast type from the matrices and supplement the deficiencies in the fount, which (with a good deal of grumbling) he did in 1652. Nicholls also supplied a fount of Anglo-Saxon in 1656 for William Somner's new *Dictionarium Saxonico-Latino-Anglicum* (1659), the first work in any of the northern languages printed at Oxford, which awoke a new interest in them there (see 103–8). Only a month before he died, Langbaine wrote to Samuel Clarke, then at work on Walton's Polyglot, to tell him that the Vice-Chancellor was to call a meeting to discuss setting up a learned press.

Clarke's own appointment in May 1658 as Architypographus and Law Bedel (provided for by the Laudian statutes) seems to have been the only outcome of an initiative that otherwise died with Langbaine. Clarke was hampered by the fact that he was obliged to find his own security for the small sums of money advanced by the University or private individuals. Thus Pococke's Arabic translation of Grotius's *De veritate religionis Christianae*, 1660, intended for evangelism in the Levant, was paid for by Robert Boyle, although Clarke advanced the printer's costs. Clarke's only independent source of money (largely invested in the edition of Malalas planned by Laud in 1633) was the erratic payments for the non-exercise of the University's privilege paid by the Stationers and Bible-printers.

The Restoration did not, at first, alter Clarke's position; but in the year before he died (like Langbaine, he died young, of the cold in the Bodleian library, it was thought) a very considerable change took place. Clarke's delicate punctilious character, equally exact in matters of Hebrew scholarship and the names of the tulips which he planted in the garden of the house in Holywell which he pledged as security for the University's debt, emerges from his notebooks. Had he lived, he might have achieved much.

JOHN FELL: THE VISION REALIZED

41. Portrait of John Fell, with John Dolben and Richard Allestree. By Sir Godfrey Kneller (Christ Church).

42. Portrait of Gilbert Sheldon, Archbishop of Canterbury (All Souls College).

43. The Sheldonian Theatre as it is today, with Burghers's engraving of 1709.

44. Portrait of Thomas Yate, Principal of Brasenose College (Brasenose College).

45. Portrait of Sir Joseph Williamson (National Portrait Gallery).

46. Portrait of Sir Leoline Jenkins (Jesus College).

47. The first Delegates' Minute Book.

John Fell (1625–86) was the son of Samuel Fell, Dean of Christ Church in Laud's time and a loyal supporter of his plans for the University. Like Laud, he was not a popular man; like Laud again ('Great praise give we to God, and little laud to the devil'), he is apt to be remembered by a disparaging rhyme ('I do not love you, Dr. Fell . . .'). In 1660 he too became Dean of Christ Church, where he found much to do: the College was partly ruinous, and all else neglected. With his new canons, who included John Dolben (1625–86), the future Archbishop of York, and Richard Allestree (1619–81), he set to work. In 1666–9 he was Vice-Chancellor, and now found time for the setting up of an academic printing-house. He turned to Archbishop Sheldon, Chancellor of the University, to which he had given the 'Theatre' which bears his name as a place of solemn occasions. Fell persuaded Sheldon that, when not in use, the building might be used for printing. Composing frames and presses (no less than five, a large number then), all built locally, were moved in before the builders were out, late in 1668 or early in 1669.

In 1669 Fell was the most powerful man in the University, fortified by influential friends in London, but not so strong as to prevent Convocation voting down his nominee for the post of Architypographus, vacant at Clarke's death. This was a set-back, though not so great a one as the death of Clarke. But Fell would not be deterred. The imminent expiry of the Stationers' lease or covenant of forbearance at Lady Day 1672 suggested another scheme. Fell decided, with three partners, to take up the lease at a cost of £200 p.a., and 'undertake the whole affair of printing here'.

Of his three partners the most active was Thomas Yate, Principal of Brasenose. He was a man of some means: with Fell he had been on the Delegacy for printing re-established in 1662; he now became Fell's right hand in dealing with the business side of the partnership. Sir Leoline Jenkins was Principal of Jesus; he was also a judge of the Court of Admiralty and Prerogative Court of Canterbury. His legal opinion was essential to the partnership, as were his London chambers for browbeating the London trade. Sir Joseph Williamson, the future benefactor of Queen's College, was the friend at Court: secretary to Lord Arlington, he was soon to become Secretary of State and, as President of the Royal Society, a friend to learning. But first and last, it was Yate who counted most; he was, in modern terms, 'the Director, the Publicity Agent, the financier who supplied what capital Fell was not able to raise, and the Business Manager of the Theatre Press; as Works Manager he was assisted by the mechanical printer John Hall. He kept its accounts in his own hand, a hand as scholarly as it was minute, and corresponded with all and sundry, the estranged Stationers in London equally with the London paper factors expectant of his orders.'[1]

These were the men to whom on 22 August 1671 the Delegates recommended that a lease should be granted of the University's privilege of printing for three years from Lady Day 1672, for £200 p.a. From the start, Fell had a clear idea of what he would do himself and what Yate would attend to: 'The manage of the mony Affair is Mr. Principal's province, I concerne my selfe only in Letters.'[2]

THE FELL TYPES

48. Portrait of Thomas Marshall (Lincoln College).

49. Letter from Marshall to Fell, 2/12 April 1670 (Bodley MS. Rawl. D 398, fol. 122).

50. Fell's list of matrices and types bought in Holland (MS. Rawl. D 397, fol. 132).

51. Broadside showing the Dutch purchase.

By 'Letters' Fell meant type. For this he had an agent, Thomas Marshall (1621–85), a Laudian exile who had left Oxford in 1647 for Holland, where he remained as chaplain to the English Merchant Adventurers at Dordrecht. There he met Francis Junius, whose pupil he became; they worked together on the early Saxon and Gothic texts published by Junius. Samuel Clarke, making determined efforts to buy type for the new press in 1668, could find none in London, and turned to Marshall to find him the Dutch types admired throughout western Europe. After Clarke's death Fell took up the quest. In 1668 Marshall had become fellow of Lincoln College, and after his first successful purchase of types, returned to Oxford with hopes of becoming Rector of his college. After a second expedition to Holland to get more Roman, Italic, and Greek types, and 'a founder, an able workman, and if such a one may be had, one who

[1] John Johnson & Strickland Gibson, *Print and Privilege at Oxford to the year 1700* (1946), p. 60.

[2] Letter to Jenkins, 7 Jan. 1672. S.P. (Dom.) Car. II 362, no. 28.

THE FELL TYPES

A Selection

Double Pica

But all of these Injunctions were the genuine Acts of the *Convocation. The setting forth therefore was not by virtue of*

Great Primer

The Souldiers were in tumult, and seditiously prayed that they *may bee cassiered: not that they soe meant, but by espostulation*

English

And I have therefore spoken so much concerning the Citie in generall, as well to shew you, that the stakes betweene us and them, whose Citie is not *such, are not equall; as also to make knowne by effects, the worth of these men I am to*

Pica

Not that they have the most reason to bee prodigall of their lives, but rather such men, as if they live, may expect a change of fortune, *and whose losses are greatest, if they miscarry in*

Long Primer

Of all the sumptuous edifices which of late years have shot up in Oxford, and adorn'd the habitation of the muses, the new printing-house, commonly call'd Clarendon's Printing-house, strikes me with *particular pleasure and veneration: it is, I do assure your*

Small Pica

Sir. You are now upon a very good Way towards the setting up of a learned Press; & I like your Proposal well to keep your Matrices, *& your Letters You have gotten, safe; & in the*

Brevier

I was loth to write, because I know not how to comfort you, and God knows, I never knew what sorrow ment till now. All that I can say to you is, that you must obey the will and providence of God, and remember, that the Queens *Majesty bare the loss of Prince Henry with a magnanimous heart, and*

Double Pica Greek

ΟΙ μὲν πολλοὶ τῶν ἐνθάδε ἤδη εἰρηκότων ἐπαινοῦσι τὸν προσθέντα τῷ νόμῳ

English Greek

Θρᾳκης πολεσι, κατεπλευσε μὲν εἰς Ἀμφιπολιν, ἀλλ᾽ ὅμως μαχης γενομενης Βρασίδας

Long Primer Greek

Περὶ τῶν πέντε ἀστέρων τῶν καλουμένων πλανητῶν, διὰ τὸ κινησιν εχειν ιδιαν αὐτοῖς, λέγονται δὲ θεῶν ειναι πέντε· πρῶτον μὲν Διὸς φαίνοντα μέγαν, ὁ δεύτερος ἐκλήθη μὲν

Pica Black Letter

Notwithstanding what hath been said, let none that are godly take occasion hereby to entertaine too high conceipts of themselves

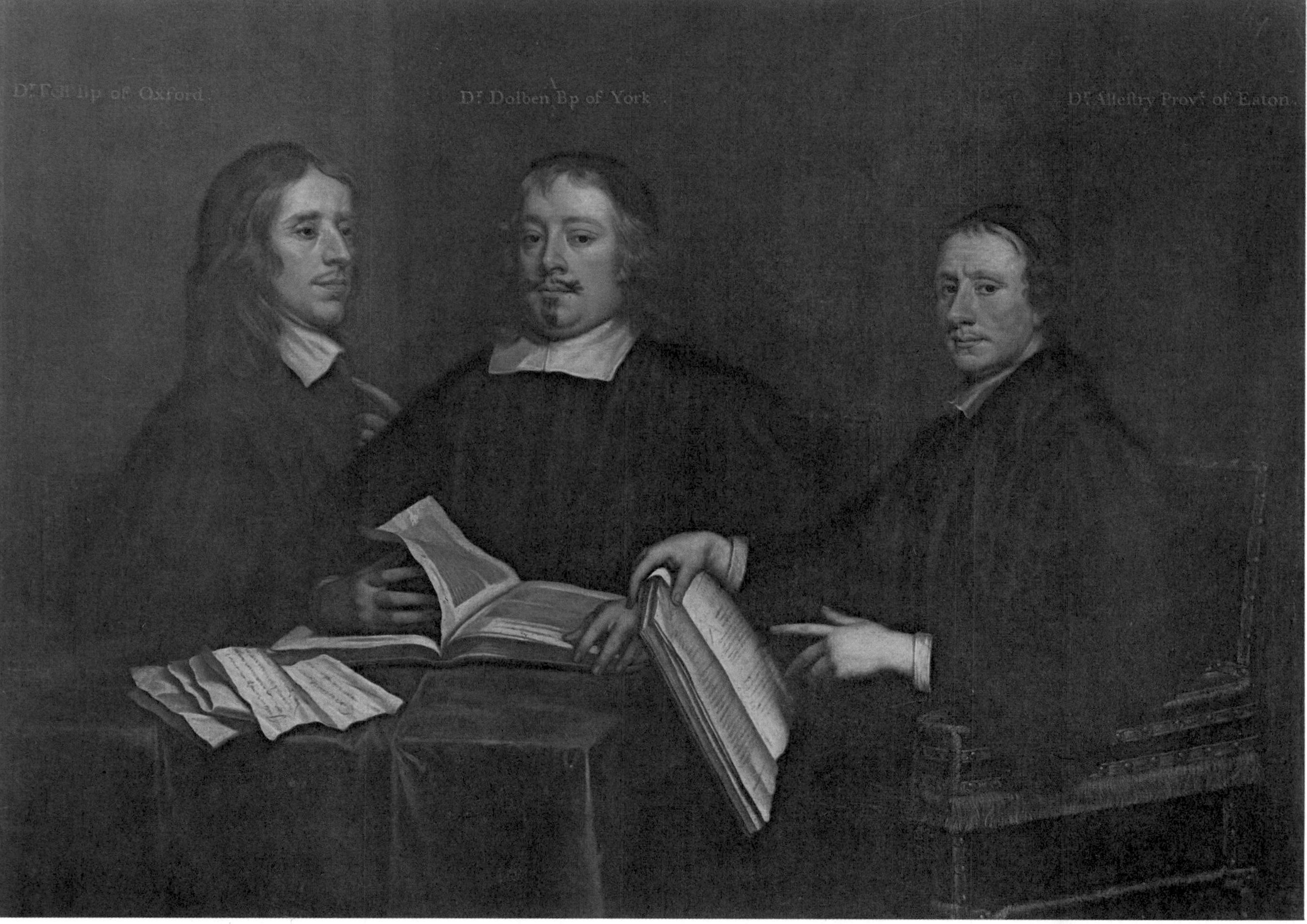
Dr Fell Bp of Oxford
Dr Dolben Bp of York
Dr Allestry Provt of Eaton

can also cut letters',[1] he succeeded as Rector of Lincoln, later becoming Dean of Gloucester.

The types that Marshall got, first from Abraham van Dijck and then Jacques Vallet, were mainly not of the newest cut by the celebrated Christoffel van Dijck, Abraham's father, who had died in the winter of 1669–70, but older. Some of them dated back to the sixteenth century, and were cut by some of the greatest of all punch-cutters, Claude Garamont (*d.* 1561), Pierre Haultin (*d.* 1588), and Robert Granjon (1513–89).

51A. The Paragon or Double Pica Greek of Robert Granjon: a punch, matrices, and type.

51B. Box, labelled 'garmoendt grix'.

When Fell persuaded 'poor Dr. Marshall to make a winter journey into Holland'[2] for a second time in 1671–2, one of his objectives was to buy matrices for 'Waesberg's Greeks'. Jan van Waesberge was a publisher, not a printer, but his name was probably on the books in the types Fell wanted. The Dutch printers were not willing to part with such material, but Marshall was lucky enough to find a merchant with Greek matrices taken as security for an unpaid debt. When he saw them, Fell was delighted: 'Such Greeks as I despaird of', he triumphantly called them.[3] He might well be elated. Three of the four types that Marshall got still survive at Oxford; all of them are of sixteenth-century Parisian workmanship of the first rank. The Paragon (or Double Pica, as it was known in England) was a particularly fine one, and can be identified with the 'large Greek on the model of the French King's on Paragon body' ordered by Plantin from the great punch-cutter Robert Granjon in 1565. The 'grecs du roi' ordered by François I from Granjon's predecessor Claude Garamont and based on the hand of his Cretan scribe Angelos Vergetios were widely imitated, but never, perhaps, to more brilliant effect than here. Seven punches and 234 matrices of the original cut survive, and almost as many characters were added after the type reached Oxford by Peter de Walpergen. The type continued in use for the grandest work as late as the Grenville Homer (see 169) in 1800–1.

The box probably brought the smaller, Long Primer, Greek that Marshall bought in 1670. The label is a corruption of 'Garamont', whose name was attached to the type by 1592; it indicated the size, not the author of the type, for it was cut by Robert Granjon.

52. The Nonpareil Roman and Italic: two boxes of matrices with type.

53. The Pica Italic: a box of matrices and punches for bigger capitals.

54. Specimen, showing the Pica Roman, annotated by Guillaume Le Bé II.

Marshall's second stay in Holland was cut short by the outbreak of war. He was forced to leave behind the precious matrices, but Captain Thomas Langley, in charge of the Harwich packet which continued to ply, was an enterprising man: 'Sir,' he wrote to Sir Joseph Williamson, 'I remember Dockter mashall tould me that thir is some thing He Left behind Him that he would Have adresed to you. I praye Iff they shall Come Lett thos comoditis Be put into small parsels: not exceding the Bulke of mony Bages, for by that menis I with Eas Conveyed the Last.'[4] So the matrices were smuggled out, disguised in money bags. The Nonpareil Roman and Italic are both the work of Pierre Haultin, a Huguenot who lived and worked at La Rochelle, a centre of French Calvinist printing. These types were used for the pocket vernacular Bibles that came from the presses there. In earlier days Haultin had worked in Paris. There Granjon was born and worked, although from time to time his skill in cutting Italics and ornaments (printers' flowers) took him to Lyons, where it was much appreciated. From 1564 to 1570 he worked for the great Antwerp printer Christophe Plantin, through whom his types were popularized in the Low Countries. The Pica Italic dates from this period, although Granjon probably cut it on his own account, not for Plantin. He ended his career at Rome, summoned by Pope Gregory XIII, cutting exotic types (among them a fine Arabic) for the missionary press set up by Cardinal Ferdinand de' Medici. The punches for large capitals do not properly belong to this type, and are of later date.

The Pica Roman, apart from eight substitute letters, is a type first cut by Garamont *c.* 1533–4

[1] Fell to Marshall (MS. Rawl. D 317, fol. 263).

[2] Fell to Jenkins, 29 Nov. 1671. S.P. (Dom.) Car. II, 244, no. 49.

[3] S.P. (Dom.) Car. II, 303, no. 18.

[4] Letter, 30 Mar. 1672 (S.P. Dom., Car. II, 304, no. 153).

and adapted by him later. Guillaume Le Bé I, the first of a distinguished family of punch-cutters, bought many of Garamont's matrices after his death. After Le Bé's death in 1598 his son, Guillaume II, sent a specimen of his stock to Plantin, with his own notes. The 'Cicero, de Garamond' corresponds with the Fell Pica Roman; 'Cicero' was the common name for the size called Pica in England (it probably derives from the great edition of Cicero by Peter Victorius, printed at Paris in 1538, in which Garamont's type was used).

55. A Specimen of the Types attributable to Peter de Walpergen, Oxford, 1957.

Walpergen's punches, matrixes, and types:

56. Canon Roman and Italic.

57. English Syriac.

58, 59. Double Pica Music, with a specimen of the manuscript copy and the Cathedral Service (Christ Church, Music MSS. nos. 33, 128).

Marshall found Fell his 'able workman', a young man called Harman Harmanszoon then working in the Van Dijck foundry, who arrived in Oxford by August 1672. His skill, however, was limited to casting type, whereas Fell wanted 'one who can cut letters'. It was probably Sir Leoline Jenkins, in Holland to negotiate the Peace of Nijmegen, who discovered Peter de Walpergen. Walpergen was a rolling stone: he may have been born in Frankfurt, and had already been to the East Indies when Jenkins found him. His stay in Oxford, where he died in 1703, was punctuated by troubles, financial and other; his taste for 'low company' embarrassed Fell. But he was a good engraver. His big Roman and Italic types (sizes missing from Marshall's purchases) have an individual, almost cranky, quality that typifies the Fell types for most people, chiefly because these are the sizes most often seen now. When he had a good model, his work was excellent. His Syriac, cut in 1681 and the first instance of punch-cutting and matrix-making at Oxford, is actually better than the letter of Walton's Polyglot on which it was based. His fine large Music was copied from the beautiful music script of a scribe employed by Henry Aldrich, who followed Fell as Dean of Christ Church in 1689. It seems to have been intended for a choral service-book for use in the cathedral, of which only part was ever printed.

60. *A specimen of the several sorts of letter given to the University by Dr. John Fell.* Oxford, Printed at the Theater, 1695.

In 1693 and again in 1695 the University (to whom Fell's executors made over all the equipment for printing that he bought) honoured his memory by printing a specimen of the types, adding those acquired later, and an inventory of the complete stock and furniture of the printing-house. The title-page shows a fine range of Walpergen's Roman types from Great Primer up to Canon. The large engraving of the University Arms was first used in 1695 for the University's mourning for Queen Mary, *Pietas Oxoniensis in obitum augustissimae & desideratissimae Reginae Mariae.*

THE PRESS AT WORK

61. Thomas Yate's memoranda (Univ. Arch. S.E.P. P 17[b] (1)[m]).

62. David Loggan's map of Oxford (1675), enlarged detail showing 'Tom Pun's House' and 'the new Print House'.

63. A type mould.

64. A composing frame, with cases of type, composing stick, galley and slice, and a compositor's candle.

65. Proofs of pages from *Epicteti enchiridion, Cebetis tabula: et Theophrasti characteres ethici*, Oxford, 1670, proof of sheet G.

66. Model of a common press, with brayer and ink-ball.

67. Ream label for paper supplied by Carbonel; a peel.

68. *A specimen of the several sorts of letter* (1693), inventory.

69. Warehouse-Keeper's accounts (Bodley MS. Rawl. D 397, fols. 404–26).

70. *Articles agreed upon by the Workmen of the University Printing-House, Oxford*, 1712.

In 1671, as he wrestled with the multifarious problems of setting up the Press, Yate set them down in some notes. Many of the issues are as live now as then. The duties of the works manager and corrector, the relative lengths of books (indicated by the last quire letter and the number of sheets in each), the choice of illustrations or the right page-size for school-books, length of run, prices, paper, ink—all needed an answer. Foremost was the question of premises: 'whether to build any roome under the wall of the Theater for composeing and Presse J. Hall thinks it absolutely necessary.' The Theatre, ill lit and to be vacated if needed for other purposes, was inconvenient. In February 1671, the Delegates approved a new building to be erected 'at the charge of the University', and the Vice-Chancellor's accounts for 1671–2 record the payment of £104 'for the new Print House under the East Wall of the Theater'. An existing house next to it called Tom Pun's House was acquired, which became 'the little Print House'; it had hearths, which the New Print House did not, and provided living-quarters for the warehouse-keeper. These places can be seen on Loggan's map, the New Print House leaning against the Theatre wall and the Little Print House adjoining.

Walpergen had his 'workhouse' in the Dean's Lodgings at Christ Church. He would need a fire to heat metal, and also type-moulds. This instrument, the crucial part of the invention of printing, held the matrix; the founder held it in his hand, and poured the molten type-metal into it with a ladle to cast a letter; the wooden sides acted as insulation and improved his grip.

In the Print House the compositors worked at their frames, on which the type-cases were laid, as at a standing desk. The frames, with handsome turned legs and panelled backs, were made by an Oxford joiner, John Rainsford, in 1668–9. Each compositor had his own stick, into which he set the type line by line; when it was full, he transferred it to the galley, in which it was held in position by the slice until the page was complete. Even outside the dark Theatre, a candle was necessary to see what he was doing. Three of the compositors were French (another was Dutch), which explains the instructions in French in a proof sheet, preserved in a contemporary binding, of Fell's New Year Book for 1670 (see 71).

The pressmen worked at a press, also made of wood; one man spread the ink with a brayer and conveyed it to the type with a pair of ink-balls, made of hide, the other laid on the paper, and pulled the arm of the press. Both compositors and pressmen worked long hours, although, since they were paid on a piece-work basis, they were free when the press was idle. Later, the workmen in the Bible Press formed a friendly society, whose principal purpose was to provide for widows and orphans; the difference in subscription rates for those 'smouting' (casual employees) and those who 'have a Place' shows that the work force still fluctuated with the volume of work available.

Paper made at Wolvercote, three miles from Oxford, was early used, but the Press was also approached by several paper merchants in London. After an unfortunate experience with the first, the 'undertakers' dealt with William Carbonel, the most substantial, who imported paper from France and Italy. It was packed in reams (the French *rames*) of 480 sheets, each ream marked with a label with the consignee's name. The Warehouse-Keeper, John Hall (son and grandson of Oxford printers), supervised deliveries and storage of paper, and its issue to the presses; it had to be damped for printing. The sheets were hung on lines afterwards to dry, and lifted on and off with a peel.

John Hall was also, Yate suggested, to purchase ink, and, as his accounts show, he was gradually trusted with the day-to-day business of the Press. His functions were sharply divided from those of the corrector, who in turn was told 'not to intermeddle in anything, but to mynd his bussinesse'.[1] The undertakers were determined to keep a close control of their business.

[1] Yate's memorandum, S.E.P., P 17^{b} $(1)^{m}$.

THE FIRST BOOKS

71. St. Clement. *d A Corinthios epistola.* Oxoniae, excudebant A. & L. Lichfield, 1669.

72. *Epicedia universitatis Oxoniensis, in obitum augustissimae principis Henriettae Mariae, Reginae matris.* Oxoniae, e typographia Sheldoniana, 1669.

73. *Συνοδικόν sive pandectae canonum SS. Apostolorum, et conciliorum ab Ecclesia Graeca receptorum . . . Gulielmus Beveregius . . . recensuit . . .* Oxonii, e Theatro Sheldoniano. Sumptibus Gulielmi Wells et Roberti Scott, bibliop. Lond., 1672.

The Press was not ready on New Year's Day 1669 when Fell, as was his custom, had a plain text, classical or patristic, printed to give as a return for the good wishes of the undergraduates of Christ Church. This purpose is set out in the preface to his text of Clement's Corinthians (a choice sanctioned by Laud's example). In August, however, when the Queen Mother died, the Press was ready, and the customary verses were issued 'from the Sheldonian Theatre' in October.

These pieces were trifles compared with the great enterprise with which Fell determined to start, the printing of the canons of the Eastern Church. He chose the editor, William Beveridge, and determined to dedicate his work to Archbishop Sheldon. The earliest minute of the meeting of the Delegates for Printing records their decision to entrust the work to Robert Scott, a leading London bookseller with connections all over Europe. All the University's resources were made available to him, but he had to buy in type, bring compositors expert in Greek from France and other men from London, in order to complete the two folio volumes of 1588 pages. It nearly broke Scott, but it was a triumph for Fell. To him, a pillar of the High Church, the tracing a strand of church history, beyond and apart from the papacy, to apostolic sanction, had a peculiar importance.

But there is no sign of an answering enthusiasm in the University. Convocation rejected Thomas Bennett, Fell's choice as successor to Samuel Clarke, and failed to proceed with the old edition of Malalas or the new Bodleian catalogue. In July 1671 Fell wrote to Jenkins: 'It is certain in that while the Charge of the Presse lyes at large in the hands of the University, it can never be lookt after, or managed to advantage.' He gave it one more chance: he promoted the worthless Architypographus, and offered Bennett again; again Convocation rejected him, preferring 'a Cambridge-man, and who I hear is crazed in his head, & void of all manage'.[1] After this, Fell determined to go his own way. Laud's vision should be realized, if not in the way that he had planned.

74. The first prospectus (All Souls College MS. 239, fol. 641).

75. Anthony Wood. *Historia et antiquitates universitatis Oxoniensis.* Oxonii, e Theatro Sheldoniano, 1674.

76. Thomas Hyde. *Catalogus impressorum librorum bibliothecae Bodlejanae in academia Oxoniensi.* Oxonii, e Theatro Sheldoniano, 1674.

77. [Richard Allestree.] *The ladies calling.* Oxford, Printed at the Theater, 1673.

78. (William Lily.) *A short introduction of grammar.* Oxford, Printed at the Theater, 1673.

79. Aesop. *Fabulae.* Engraved copperplate of the title-page of the lost edition.

By the Delegates' grant of the University's privileges to the partnership, Fell's ambitions for his Press were unleashed. He drew up a prospectus early in January 1672, which seems never to have got beyond this draft. After listing the 'Books begun' (the last of which appeared in 1732), he passes on to a magnificent range, from 'the greek Bible in a royal folio', and 'the history of Tamerlain in Arab. & Persian', to 'A history of Insects, more perfect than any yet extant'. Few of these dreams were realized as he had planned: in sum, they still represent the matter which engages all academic presses. The trumpet-call of great names from the past and the present Imprimerie Royale, the

[1] Fell to Jenkins, 12 Oct. 1671 (S.P. Dom., Car. II, 293, no. 116).

mingled plea to patriotism and commercial gain, echo Fell's high expectations and optimism.

Of the 'Books begun', the *Synodicon* was soon to be out. Anthony Wood (1632–95) had been at work on his history of Oxfordshire since 1660. He left his own account of his dealings with Fell, who wanted the history of the University only, and in Latin. He smoothed Wood's path to important documents in London, but annoyed him by censoring the text, which he got translated. Fell paid for this and the costs of printing (with £50 from Jenkins). The University paid Wood £100 for the copy and £50 for his extra trouble. It was a handsome book, dedicated by the undertakers (*procuratores rei Typographicae*) to the King. The engraved title significantly shows the King handing a charter to the kneeling person of the University, who offers him the book in return; in the background the Theatre can be seen.

The Catalogue of Printed Books in the Bodleian had been set in hand by the Delegates in July 1672 at the meeting before they approved Fell's assumption of the Press, at which they offered Hyde £100 for the copy. It ran to 706 pages: Hyde, dedicating it to Sheldon, makes much of his nine years of labour in the cold library; Hearne believed that Emmanuel Pritchard, the under-librarian, did most of the work. From the first, Yate saw the use to which it would be put: 'If wee print the Catalogue to do it in a Larg Letter, Larg Paper, a Larg Margent, and on Paper will beare Inke.'[1] It was widely bought interleaved for use as a catalogue of other libraries: a copy thus treated was the only catalogue of the Bibliothèque Mazarine until 1760, and John Locke used it to list his own books. The Vice-Chancellor paid the partners £725 for printing 1,000 copies, which had all sold by 1696.

The least successful of Fell's ventures was the school-book printing. Here, as with Bibles and almanacs, he was making war on entrenched enemies, who had long paid the University not to compete with them. It was the Stationers who came in October 1672 to offer Fell £120 p.a. to forbear printing their privileged books. By then, the partners had discovered that they could not compete with the cheap printers used by the Stationers. They had printed Aesop, Ovid's *Tristia*, and Cato's *Disticha* at costs of *2s. 7d.*, *1s. 2d.*, and $9\frac{1}{2}$*d.*: the Stationers' prices were *6d.*, *9d.*, and $2\frac{1}{2}$*d.* It was the same with the other two little books they had printed. In the end, the Stationers took all the stock at cost, and the partners settled for £100 p.a. The Stationers must have pulped the stock, for all that now survives is the handsome copperplate title-page for the Aesop. Lily's *Grammar* was the one exception: here the partners had signed a separate agreement with the patentee, Roger Norton, and continued to print it, in a text revised for Fell by Thomas Bennett, until 1733.

The Ladies Calling, by contrast, was the most successful of Fell's books. It was the sequel to the even more successful *Whole Duty of Man* (1658), and was one of seven books by the same author, whose identity was a closely guarded secret. There is little doubt that it was Fell's friend Richard Allestree, Regius Professor of Divinity, 1663–79, who let Fell print all the books that he wrote after the Press started. The earlier books were printed by the London trade, who found the later as attractive, and pirated them, to Fell's annoyance. 'Duty of Man's Works' were a staple of the Press up to 1720; their popularity continued until the nineteenth century.

ILLUSTRATED BOOKS

80. [Aratus.] 'Αράτου Σολέως Φαινόμενα καὶ Διοσημεῖα. Oxonii, e Theatro Sheldoniano, 1672.

81. David Loggan. *Oxonia illustrata.* Oxoniae, e Theatro Sheldoniano, 1675.

82. *The Oxford Almanack*, 1674.

83. Robert Morison. *Plantarum historia universalis Oxoniensis.* Oxonii, e Theatro Sheldoniano, 1672–99.

84. Accounts for Morison's work (Univ. Arch. S.E.P. 2. 28 (4)).

[1] Yate's memorandum, S.E.P. P 17^b (1)^m.

85. Humphrey Prideaux. *Marmora Oxoniensia.* Oxonii, e Theatro Sheldoniano, 1676.

86. Robert Plot. *The natural history of Oxfordshire.* Printed at the Theater in Oxford, for that Press, and Simon Miller, London, 1677.

87. Walter Charleton. *Exercitationes de differentiis et nominibus animalium.* Oxoniae, e Theatro Sheldoniano, 1677.

87A. *Rana piscatrix*: engraved copperplate.

88. Johann Scheffer. *The history of Lapland.* At the Theater in Oxford, 1674.

89. Woodblocks for initials, cut by George Edwards.

In many respects, Fell's model was Richelieu's Imprimerie Royale: the series of Byzantine historical texts, classics, Bibles, Richelieu's *Instruction du Chrestien*—all these are echoed in his list. In one respect, however, Fell's work was original: his taste for illustration. The Imprimerie Royale books often had engraved titles and frontispieces (Poussin was their artist, as Rubens earlier to the Plantin Press), but apart from the wood-blocks in *Histoire des connestables, chanceliers et gardes des sceaux* (1658), the illustrated books printed there are too close in time to those printed at Oxford for their influence to have been felt. Fell's models were the great Dutch illustrated books: the application to scholarly books was his own.

The first such book was the Aratus, his New Year Book for 1672. It had a fine engraved title by David Loggan, appointed *Publicus Academiae Sculptor* to the University in 1669, two double-page engraved celestial hemispheres, and other diagrams. Loggan's masterpiece was the great series of perspective views of the University, published in 1675 (some are found in copies of Wood's *Historia* the year before). These are a triumph of the rolling-press, which Loggan kept not in the Sheldonian but at Leonard Lichfield's house in Holywell.

Among Yate's memoranda is 'A Designe & cut for a Leafe Almanack on a Brasse plate'. The first of these, a magnificent 'vision of History' by Robert Streeter who had designed the ceiling of the Sheldonian Theatre, was printed on four sheets in 1674. It was perhaps over-large; there was no *Almanack* in 1675, but from 1676 onwards it was printed on a single royal sheet (the series is still unbroken).

In 1676 and until 1724, also without break, the *Almanack* was engraved (and sometimes also designed) by Michael Burghers, who worked for the University for some fifty-five years, beginning as a journeyman under Loggan. Loggan began Morison's *Plantarum historia*, but the bulk of the work was done by Burghers, although many engravers worked on it. Robert Morison (1620–83) was the King's Botanist. It was his intention, when he came to Oxford as Professor of Botany in 1669, to provide a more systematic classification of trees and plants than any yet. The plates were also more accurate, as well as beautiful. In other respects, it was not a good investment: the costs were large and never recovered, not least because the work was never completed. The University's loans to Morison and other expenses were a matter of anxiety, depicted in the many accounts drawn up for the book.

It may have been experience with Morison that prompted Fell to be brisk with another project, the publication of the inscriptions among the 'Arundel Marbles', the collection of Graeco-Roman sculpture and stones made by the 2nd Earl of Arundel and given to the University in 1667. Fell's chosen editor, Humphrey Prideaux, the future Dean of Norwich (1648–1724), was a favourite pupil. He could put off Fell urging him to finish the long-delayed Malalas ('We are continually pestered with letters from forrain parts to set it forth, out of a conceit that rare things ly hid therein, wereas more than halfe the book is stuffed with ridiculous and incredible lys'), but not Fell in need of copy. Prideaux protests that the defects in his edition, manifest enough, were due to the haste with which his notes were taken from him and set up piecemeal. Burghers provided engravings of all the reliefs, with a plate for the title-page, the first of many.

Plot's *Oxfordshire* was part of a large scheme for 'a journey through England and Wales, for the Promotion of Learning and Trade'; this was a specimen. Robert Plot, first 'custos' of the Ashmolean Museum at Oxford (1640–96), was Baconian in his interest in all things human and divine and in his reliance on direct observation. Although versed in modern science, he records popular legends, credible or otherwise. His topography is good, and Burghers's plates, of gentlemen's seats, fossils, plants, remarkable views, and curiosities natural and man-made, add to his lively and readable text. No more was published, apart from *Staffordshire*

(1686). Burghers also provided the new plates for the second edition of Charleton's *Exercitationes*, a work of varied interest, including unusual animals like the guinea-pig, a mixed collection of *fossilia*, and some unusual depictions of animal anatomy. The plate of the *rana piscatrix* is the only one now left.

The other artist on whom Fell depended in the early days was George Edwards, who cut the lively illustrations for Scheffer's *History of Lapland* on wood. The work itself is remarkably comprehensive, for it covers history, government, religion, costume, and customs; it was the first anthropological work from the Press. It also contained a grammar and specimens of the Lapp language, one of which suggested Longfellow's 'A boy's will is the wind's will'. The translation had an odd history: it 'was made by Mr. Acton Cremer (who was then Bach. of Arts at Xt Church), being an imposition set him by Bp. Fell for courting a Mistress at y^{t} Age, which the Bp. dislik'd, yet for all that he married'. [1]

Edwards also cut at least one small set of fantastic capitals for Fell, and probably another larger set, of the same kind. The blocks for both survive: the larger were used in Wood's *Historia*, and the smaller in *The Government of the Tongue* (2nd edn., 1674) and many times afterwards.

It is interesting to compare this wide range of illustrative material against the contemporary books of the Imprimerie Royale. It is hardly fair to set Wood and Loggan against the magnificent series of descriptions and plates of the royal fêtes and palaces. On the other hand the plates for Morison and Charleton make up in accuracy what they lack in grace compared with the *Mémoires pour servir à l'histoire naturelle* of Perrault and the *Plantes* of Dodart. Although Fell tried hard to persuade Edward Bernard to publish his Euclid, for which Edwards engraved 315 illustrations (never used), there is nothing to set beside the *Recueil de plusieurs traités de mathématiques* (1671–7). On the other hand, there is no French equivalent in archaeology or topography. Generous though Fell was, his plates could not compete with the splendid French engravers. Still, they were better than most work produced in England; more important, they bridged the gap between scholarship and what was still thought of as a purely decorative art. Fell's is the earliest co-ordinated attempt to provide practical illustrations.

PRINTING THE BIBLE: PITT, PARKER, AND GUY

90. Letter from Dr. John Fell to Sir Leoline Jenkins, 11 April 1672 (P.R.O., S.P. Dom., Car. II 305, No. 117).

91. Fell's draft prospectus for the annotated Bible (Bodley MS. Rawl. D 398, fol. 127).

92. Specimen of the annotated Bible, with Fell's directions to the annotators (Bodley MS. Smith 22, fol. 81).

93. *The Holy Bible, Containing the Old Testament And the New*. Oxford, at the Theater, 1675.

94. Τῆς Καινῆς Διαθήκης ἅπαντα (New Testament in Greek). E Theatro Sheldoniano, 1675.

95, 95A. *The Book of Common Prayer, and Administration of the Sacraments*. Oxford, At the Theater, 1675 (engraved title and plate).

96. Agreement between the partners and the Stationers' Company, 9 March 1675 (Stationers' Company Records).

97. Moses Pitt. *The English Atlas*. Oxford, at the Theater, for Moses Pitt, London, 1680.

98. *The Holy Bible*. Oxford: Printed at the Theater, 1685; bound for use in the Chapel Royal by Robert Steel.

The Bible had a large part in Fell's plans for the Press. Dominant in them was a great annotated Bible, too large a project to be realized. He wrote

[1] Thomas Hearne's diary, in *Remarks and Collections of Thomas Hearne* (O.H.S., 1885–1918), iii. 318.

hopefully to Jenkins, who had let him know that Sheldon ('my Lord') approved of it. Later he drew up a prospectus, a characteristic example of his high principles, high hopes, and high finance. He even had a specimen set up, on which he wrote his equally characteristic instructions for his protégé Thomas Smith. Some traces of this plan can be seen in the *Paraphrase of the Epistles of St Paul* (1675–8) by Fell's friend Obadiah Walker, Master of University College, which had a considerable success.

The plain text of the Bible, the Authorized or King James Version, was a different matter. The University's right to print it was specially mentioned in the Laudian charters; it was a right that could not be disputed by the King's Printer, the patentee, but one most dangerous to the established London trade. Opposition strengthened Fell's resolve: beaten on the school books, he determined to produce a Bible which would compete though not clash with the Stationers'. The result, a quarto (a format not used in London), is not pleasant to look at, although the *Book of Common Prayer* that went with it was redeemed by a fine engraved title, of which the plate still survives. However, it frightened the Stationers: in the new lease agreement with the partners in 1675 they conceded the right (properly theirs) 'to print singing psalmes with such Bibles as they [the partners] shall see cause to be printed'.[1]

It was a hollow triumph. The London trade had enough on its hands with Dutch piracies; they would stand no more competition. They undercut the Oxford prices, and the partners printed no more. Fell had, rather unexpectedly, altered the text of the Bible in one or two places, and imposed his own logical but unusual orthography on it. Prideaux, sharp again, observed: 'I must confesse, since Mr. Dean hath taken the liberty of inventeing a new way of spelleing and useing it therein, which I thinke will confound and alter the analogy of the English tongue, that I doe not at all approve thereof.'[2] Despite Prideaux's own spelling, there was a good deal of uniformity then, at least in print, and Fell's new style may have been a bar. Fell himself retreated to produce a text of the Greek New Testament, with variant readings. It was highly regarded, and made the basis of two subsequent editions.

In 1678, when the second lease ran out, Fell tried again: he offered the Stationers his unsold stock for £3,800 as a premium for its renewal. They refused, and Fell put the same terms to Moses Pitt. Pitt was a Cornishman, a man of large vision, after Fell's own heart. His great *Atlas*, projected in eleven volumes to rival the great Dutch Blaeu atlas, was to be printed at the Theatre (Fell and Yate were among the subscribers) in Elephant folio. Pitt accepted Fell's proposal, in partnership with two other Stationers, Peter Parker and Thomas Guy (founder of Guy's Hospital); all three were involved in the trade in Dutch pirated Bibles and at odds with the Stationers.

The new sublessees carried the war vigorously into the Stationers' own territory. They installed several presses in the Theatre (they were allowed four, but clearly exceeded), and set to work with such success that the King's Printers petitioned Council against them. They were referred to the courts, but did not bring up their case for five years, doing their best to break the sublessees by undercutting. They, however, were up to every trick of their opponents and more (Fell was embarrassed by some of their practices). Their success, 'whereby the Price of Bibles, for the Advantage of the Publick was brought down to less than Half of what they were before sold at; and many hundreds of thousands of Bibles, printed and sold, more than otherwise would have been; and our people at home, and abroad in our Plantations, furnished from hence, which before were wont to be furnished in vast Numbers from Holland',[3] must have pleased Fell immensely. When Henry Hills, Upper Warden of the Stationers' Company and chief of the King's Printers, came to Oxford to negotiate a settlement in 1685, Fell refused any compromise on Bible-printing, and, by suggesting that the Stationers should treat with the University rather than the partners, did his best to perpetuate the arrangement.

It was the making of the Oxford Bible business, which has grown by many times since then. The fine folio Bibles found their way to the Chapel Royal (the copy illustrated was bound by Robert Steel in black morocco with the cipher of William and Mary), and the pocket Bibles went with emigrants to 'the Plantations' in America, where the printing and sale of Bibles has grown beyond anything that Fell could have dreamed.

[1] *Print and Privilege*, pp. 165–7.

[2] *Letters of Humphrey Prideaux*, ed. E. M. Thompson (1875), p. 38.

[3] Letter from John Wallis to Edward Bernard, printed in *Philosophical Experiments of Robert Hooke* (1726), p. 221.

THE END OF THE PARTNERSHIP

99. Statement and accounts, 1672 (All Souls College MS. 239, fols. 666, 667).

100. File of titles registered for the Vice-Chancellor's *imprimatur* (Univ. Arch. S.E.P. P 17ᵇ (4)).

101. *An Account of the State of the Press*, 9 January 1679 [1680].

Before 1672 was out, Fell and Yate reviewed the progress they had made (the accounts are in Yate's hand, the statement in Fell's). They had done much, and the future seemed golden. If the event had been less fruitful than they had hoped, they still had much to be proud of. The file of their titles licensed by the Vice-Chancellor, first submitted in manuscript and then by a proof of the title-page, still exists with its original tawed leather thong. It is a long list, but not complete: the partners were not obliged to obtain a licence and sometimes did not.

The *Account of the State of the Press* is not one of Fell's proposals, but a justification of the partners' work and achievements, issued when the King's Printers were petitioning Council and legal action was threatened. It lists a total of seventy-seven works already published, and others ready for the press. Among the latter are Fell's great edition of Cyprian, which had long occupied him.

101A. St. Cyprian. *Opera recognita & illustrata per Joannem Oxoniensem Episcopum.* Oxonii, e Theatro Sheldoniano, Anno 1682.

In the programme that Fell drew up in 1672 'Cyprian according to the very many excellent uncollated Copies we have by us' had ranked high among 'the Greek & Latin fathers in their order', and by 1676 'the Undertakers . . . would begin with St. *Cyprian*'. This preference is hardly surprising, and it is supported by the new life of the saint added to the text, 'Annales Cyprianici' by John Pearson, Bishop of Chester. Cyprian, third-century bishop and martyr, held the modern belief that bishops are answerable directly to God, and that orthodoxy resides in their consensus. He had opposed the Novatian and Donatist heresies, and also the papacy over baptism; finally, he was martyred. The parallel with Laud was clear; Cyprian's model was dear to high Anglicans, threatened alike by Dissenters and Roman Catholics.

Fell's text, which runs to 856 pages, forcibly points the parallel. He is at pains to argue the falsity of dubious passages favouring the papacy. In echoing Cyprian's condemnation of those who made pagan sacrifice or alleged that they had, he drew vividly on his own memories of the Civil War. But these issues apart, Fell performed his task as an editor conscientiously and thoroughly, and Cyprian's last editor, Wilhelm Hartel in 1868–71, found little to change in his text. Perhaps the highest compliment paid to his scholarship was one he would have relished least. His work was pirated three times soon after his death, lastly by J.-L. de Lorme, an *émigré* printer in Amsterdam, employed by the Abbé Jean-Paul Bignon, whose scholarly ambitions for France closely followed Fell's: it is no coincidence that there are three copies of his edition in the Bibliothèque Nationale.

The copy illustrated is one presented by Fell to Richard King, who had taken his M.A. at Christ Church the previous year, and later became rector of Marston Bigott in Somerset.

102. Fell's Last Will and Testament, 11 June 1686 (Univ. Arch. Wills F).

Fell originally made his will in April 1685. Yate and Jenkins were both dead, and he evidently felt free to dispose of the lease and stock held by the partners, which he left in trust to the University. The trustees included Timothy Halton, Provost of Queen's College (perhaps representing Sir Joseph Williamson's interest), and Obadiah Walker. Fell was much hurt by Walker's defection to Rome early in 1686, and removed him from his last will, made shortly before his death on 10 July 1686. In this he directed his executors to 'carry on the Work of the press takeing to them the Advise and Direction' of Halton, Henry Aldrich, and John Mill, Principal of St. Edmund Hall and successor to Fell's interest in the Greek text of the New Testament.

He further added that 'all founts of letter bought with my money' should remain at the use of the Press, and that 'my founding Materialls of puncheons Matrices Moulds got together by me and others at great expence be carefully kept together by my Executors for the space of fower yeares next ensewing my decease'. This was the heart of the matter to Fell; without the means to produce type for learned books, an academic press could not flourish. So, if the executors then found 'the interests of learning and printing encouraged' in the University, they were to 'make over to the Chancellor Masters and Scholars as aforesaid the intire right and interest' in this material, or dispose of them as they thought fit. By this provision Fell was to restore to the University the means, which he had taken into his own hands, of realizing the vision that he and Laud had formed.

THE ROOTS OF THE ENGLISH LANGUAGE

103. Francis Junius, ed. *Caedmonis monachi paraphrasis poetica Genesios*. Amstelodami, apud Christophorum Cunradi, Typis & sumptibus Editoris, 1655.

104. Francis Junius & Thomas Marshall, edd. *Quatuor D. N. Jesu Christi Evangeliarum versiones perantiquae duo, Gothica scilicet et Anglo-Saxonica*. Dordrechti, Typis et sumptibus Junianis Excudebant Henricus & Joannes Essaei, 1665.

105. Junius's types.

106. George Hickes. *Institutiones grammaticae Anglo-Saxonicae, et Moeso-Gothicae*. Oxoniae, e Theatro Sheldoniano, 1689. Typis Junianis.

107. George Hickes. *Linguarum veterum septentrionalium Thesaurus grammatico-criticus & archaeologicus*. Oxoniae, e Theatro Sheldoniano, 170[3–]5.

108. Edward Lye, ed. *Francisci Junii Francisci filii Etymologicum Anglicanum*. Oxonii, e Theatro Sheldoniano, 1743.

Francis Junius (1589–1677) came to England in 1621 as librarian and tutor in the house of the Earl of Arundel. He stayed for thirty years and laid the foundation of modern scholarship in the northern languages, the roots of English. On his return to Holland, he published his first work on it, a text of the verse paraphrase of Genesis by Caedmon (*fl.* 670). Thomas Marshall visited him as a refugee and together they produced the diglot Gospels in Anglo-Saxon and Gothic, the latter the first printing of the translation of Ulfilas, the earliest Gothic text. In 1674 Junius returned to England, and spent his last years first with Marshall at Oxford, and then at Windsor, where his nephew Isaac Vossius was a canon; there he died in 1677. While at Oxford he bestowed his manuscripts and type on the University. The manuscripts went to the Bodleian Library; the punches and matrices for Anglo-Saxon, Gothic, and also Runic, together with several founts of type, came to Oxford by barge from Eton after his death. The type was put to use, but not the matrices and punches: they were lost in the Bodleian till 1697, when Humfrey Wanley and Edward Thwaites recovered them.

> Dr Hyde knew nothing of them, but at last told them he thought he had some old Punchions about his study, but he did not know how they come there, and presently produces a small box full, and taking out one, he pores upon it and at last wisely tells them that these could not be what they look'd after, for they are Æthiopic: but Mr Thwaites desiring a sight of them found that which he look'd upon to be Gothic, and in the box were almost all Junius's Saxon, Gothic and Runic Punchions, which they took away with them and a whole Oyster barrel full of old Greek Letter, which was discovered in another hole.[1]

In those twenty years, one major work appeared in Junius's types, the grammar of George Hickes (1642–1715). Hickes wrote this in the midst of other business during his brief period as Dean of Worcester. Deprived for refusing to take the Oath of Allegiance in August 1689, he led a wandering and difficult life as a leader of the non-jurors; in the midst of all this he somehow found time to complete his *Thesaurus*, a large expansion of his grammar, with a long historical account of the languages. Further, it included Humfrey Wanley's

[1] Letter from Thomas Tanner, 10 Aug. 1697, Bodl. MS. Ballard iv, fol. 30.

first essay in Anglo-Saxon palaeography. It was the culmination of the movement that began in 1659 with Somner's dictionary, and if the host of Saxon scholars called up by Hickes's work has found much to criticize in it, that does not belittle his achievement.

Among the manuscripts that Junius bequeathed to Oxford were two volumes of 'Etymologicon linguae Anglicanae'. For a long time an editor was sought in vain, until Edward Lye (1694–1767), vicar of Houghton Parva in Northamptonshire, undertook it. He taught himself Anglo-Saxon and Gothic, and corresponded with Eric Benzelius, Archbishop of Uppsala, with whom he later re-edited the Gothic Gospels. In 1743 the book came out, Lye modestly putting his name below Junius's. It was the first systematic etymology of the English Language, and had an immediate and lasting effect on its study. Dr. Samuel Johnson used it extensively in the compilation of his own dictionary, and from it stems the modern historical approach to lexicography.

FELL'S SUCCESSORS: ALDRICH, CHARLETT, AND THE CLARENDON BUILDING

109. Portrait of Henry Aldrich. By Sir Godfrey Kneller (Christ Church). Aldrich's drawing for *The Oxford Almanack*, 1676.

110. Printer's copy for Clarendon's *History of the Rebellion* (Bodley MS. Clar. 114 ff.).

111. Album of decorative designs by Aldrich, with Burghers's plates engraved after them.

112. Edward Hyde, Earl of Clarendon. *The history of the Rebellion and Civil Wars in England.* Oxford, printed at the Theater, An. Dom. 1702[–4]. With *The life of Edward Earl of Clarendon.* Written by himself. Oxford, at the Clarendon Printing-House, 1759.

113. Nicholas Hawksmoor's design for the Clarendon Building: south elevation (Worcester College).

114. Advertisement for the Press, 12 June 1705.

In 1690, the four years' interval prescribed in Fell's will elapsed, and the executors duly made over his printing equipment to the University. The direction of the Press continued without a break, for the three advisers appointed by Fell were among the Delegates of the Press who took on its management in 1691. The leading part was taken by Henry Aldrich (1647–1710), Dean of Christ Church from 1689. Although Fell's successor in both respects, and generally admired for scholarship and natural authority, he was very different from Fell. Although both, in an age of wigs, wore their own hair, Fell retained the appearance, as well as the outlook, of the pre-war era in which he grew up. Aldrich, however, was born ahead of his time: his interests, in the arts, music, and architecture, were unusual, although he turned his hand as easily to theological controversy, a tract on geometry, and another, influential in and after its time, on logic. His hand can be seen in much of the emblematical and decorative work engraved for the Press. The allegorical figures of the Seasons, Time, Juno, and so on which adorn the 1676 *Almanack* were drawn by him, and prints from his collection can frequently be identified as the iconographic source of later designs. His taste for allegory was not shared by Whig detractors of the University, who were apt to detect treason in what they could not understand.

The great landmark in Aldrich's management of the Press was the publication of Clarendon's *History of the Rebellion.* Edward Hyde (1609–74), Earl of Clarendon, had been Chancellor of the University from 1660 to his fall in 1667. This may have induced his sons to give the 'copy' in the book to Oxford. Extraordinary pains were taken with it: the text was specially transcribed from a copy made for Clarendon which was revised by the Bishop of Rochester, Thomas Sprat, and Aldrich, with the aim of simplifying and standardizing Clarendon's style. Aldrich, writing to Sprat on 28 August 1700, reveals a most modern preoccupation with these problems, foretelling the 'Oxford Style'. The corrector, Thomas Terry, said that it was 'most exactly printed from the written copie'; but the process of regularization caused further differences between copy and print.

Aldrich had a further share in Clarendon: he drew the designs for headpieces and initials which made the folio edition one of the handsomest books hitherto produced in England. An album containing his designs, in brown ink with brown and grey wash, shows how much of the originals the engravings, excellent though they are, have lost. The plates are still preserved. The album is now in the library of the Printer to the University; it once belonged to Horace Walpole.

Clarendon's *History* was a success, in terms of prestige and profit to the University. The folio edition was several times reprinted, and the first octavo (1705–6) was bought *en bloc* by a London stationer, Thomas Bennett, with whom the Delegates concerted the distribution of the folio. As with Loggan's *Oxonia illustrata*, copies were often finely bound in turkey leather. There were several Oxford binders capable of fine work: more than one worked on the set exhibited; volume 2 only was bound by Richard Sedgley, one of the finest of contemporary Oxford craftsmen.

The profits, however, did not (as is popularly supposed) pay for the new building, named after Clarendon, into which the Press moved in October 1713. Although a splendid example of Hawksmoor's work, it was not thought as convenient as the old Printing House, and for long people preferred 'At the Theater' to the new 'At the Clarendon Press'. The University raised the money (£6,185) itself; a large part came from the £2,000 premium exacted from the new lessee of the Bible Press, John Baskett.

The sale of academic books continued a problem. Neither Fell nor Yate, despite their ingenious financial expedients, solved it. 'The vending of books we never could compasse',[1] wrote Arthur Charlett (1655–1722), Master of University College, who had succeeded to Yate's old place in the Press. He did his best; his encouragement of authors, a wide correspondence soliciting subscriptions, buying and giving away books to likely patrons—all this he did. He also printed regular advertisements of books in print and forthcoming: that for 1705 includes Clarendon and Hickes among those 'recently published'; the astronomer Halley's edition of Apollonius Pergaeus is among those 'in the press'.

115. Thomas Gale. *Historiae Britannicae, Saxonicae, Anglo-Danicae, scriptores xv*. Oxoniae, e Theatro Sheldoniano, 1691.

116. Heinrich Wilhelm Ludolf. *Grammatica Russica*. Oxonii, e Theatro Sheldoniano, 1696.

117. [Edward Bernard.] *Catalogi librorum manuscriptorum Angliae et Hiberniae in unum collecti*. Oxoniae, e Theatro Sheldoniano, 1697 [1698].

118. Henry Maundrell. *A journey from Aleppo to Jerusalem at Easter* A.D. 1697. Oxford, printed at the Theater, 1703.

119. White Kennett. *Parochial Antiquities attempted in the history of Ambrosden, Burcester, and other adjacent parts in the counties of Oxford and Bucks*. Oxford, printed at the Theater, 1695.

120. Edward Wells. *A treatise of antient and present geography together with a sett of maps, design'd for the use of young students in the universities*. Oxford, printed at the Theater, 1701.

121. John Wallis. *Opera mathematica*. Oxoniae, e Theatro Sheldoniano, 1693–9.

122. Edmund Halley, ed. *Apollonii Pergaei Conicorum libri octo*. Oxoniae, e Theatro Sheldoniano, 1710.

123. David Wilkins, ed. *Novum Testamentum Ægyptium vulgo Copticum*. Oxonii, e Theatro Sheldoniano, 1716.

124. John Mill, ed. *Novum Testamentum cum lectionibus variantibus*. Oxonii, e Theatro Sheldoniano, 1707.

Thomas Gale (?1635–1702), the future Dean of York, was a scholar of wide range, taking in classics, geography, but above all the early chronicles of English history. The series *Historiae Britannicae et Anglicanae scriptores* was inaugurated under Fell (by William Fulman). The 1691 volume, the last to appear, included the spurious Annals of Croyland, as well as the Chronicle of Melrose (a valuable early Scotch source) and the Annals of Burton. Gale's texts, copied by himself, or else at his

[1] Historic Manuscripts Commission, *2nd Report*, p. 245[b].

expense, were not free from error, but he put into print a large number of early British historical documents, which remained staple texts until superseded by the Rolls Series in the nineteenth century.

Ludolf's Russian grammar was the first of its kind. It was due to the initiative of Edward Bernard, a Delegate from 1691. The University had the Cyrillic type cut at Amsterdam; it represents the Church-Slavonic script which was used for written and printed Russian until Peter the Great introduced the modernized forms of letters. Ludolf came to Oxford to oversee the printing: 300 copies were struck off, and all but fourteen sold by 1699. For modern scholars, Ludolf's work is invaluable as a description of the Russian language and how it was spoken in the seventeenth century.[1]

Edward Bernard (1638–96) was something of a disappointment to the Press. Although he was Savilian Professor of Astronomy, his interests lay more in ancient mathematical and linguistic texts. His long-promised editions of Euclid and Josephus never appeared, and his main work was published elsewhere. In 1691 he was able to retire from his chair and took charge of the long-projected union catalogue of the manuscript resources of British libraries. In its published form, it was less complete than had been hoped. Lambeth and most of the Cambridge libraries dropped out, and the catalogue of the Cottonian library by Thomas Smith was printed separately, though at Oxford. Bernard died before it was complete, and Charlett organized the last stages, in which Edmund Gibson and Humfrey Wanley were the most active of many collaborators. It was pioneering work, used as a guide to the manuscript resources of Britain, literary and historical, for many years.

Maundrell's *Journey* was one of the few best-sellers produced by the Press; its lively, readable style and the plates by Burghers made it different from the bulk of the learned work. It was reprinted seven times up to 1749, but as with Clarendon and its other valuable copies, the University farmed out its rights to the trade, only retaining the printing.

White Kennett's parochial history was, as its title suggests, intended as an exemplary work. Although Thomas Hearne (who disliked him) accused Kennett of 'putting in all the papers he met with',[2] the value of the documents he printed in full ranges far outside the limited demands of a history of Ambrosden and Bicester. It is, in fact, 'a microcosm of feudal history'. As a piece of publishing, it was a success: all but six of 312 copies printed sold within a year. Undoubtedly the handsome plates were an added attraction: they too were intended as an example for similar studies. Such works as Francis Peck's *Academia tertia Anglicana* (1728) show that the model was not lost on Kennett's successors.

Edward Wells (1667–1727), scholar of Christ Church and subsequently a country clergyman, was a prolific writer. He has several popular school-books on geography and mathematics to his name, an edition of the *Periegesis* of Dionysus that went through several editions, as well as homiletic, theological, and controversial writings. His *Treatise* was the first educational atlas to be printed at Oxford, and the maps, if smaller in scale than those of Pitt's great work, are fine examples of engraving. The work was a deserved success, and had reached a fifth edition by 1738.

John Wallis (1616–1703), already publishing at Oxford before Fell's time, became one of his most loyal and energetic supporters during the long dispute with the Stationers, carrying on the battle after Fell's death with a single-minded determination worthy of Fell. The collection of his complete works, grown since 1657, contained his famous *Algebra*, including methods devised with Leibniz and Newton, whose letters he also published, a series of texts on harmonics, ancient music, and other topics, and his grammar of English, first published in 1652 and several times reprinted. His scientific analysis of vocal sounds was the result of teaching 'dumb' children.

After his book was printed, one of the blocks was mislaid; it was found not long ago under the floorboards of the Sheldonian Theatre. Wallis lived to see his book in print, but his death deprived the Press of one of its loyalest defenders. As a mathematician and controversialist, he had a high reputation; in his linguistic work he was the forerunner of modern scientific methods.

Edmund Halley (1656–1742) succeeded Wallis, before becoming Astronomer Royal in 1721. Aldrich put him on to ancient Greek geometry, and in particular Apollonius, of whom Edward Bernard had transcribed several books known only from Arabic translations. Halley started with *De sectione* which Bernard had begun to translate, and 'deciphered' the rest, using the partial translation

[1] A full and fascinating account of this episode will be found in J. S. G. Simmons, 'H. W. Ludolf and the printing of his *Grammatica Russica* at Oxford in 1696', *Oxford Slavonic Papers*, i (1950), pp. 104–29.

[2] *Remarks and Collections of Thomas Hearne* (O.H.S.), i (1885), p. 244.

as a key. He continued with the work on conics, reconstructing the eighth book, entirely lost, from notes and quotations in later writers. His work was an astonishing combination of mathematical and linguistic genius which modern scholarship cannot fault.

The printing of the Coptic Gospels appeared in Fell's first draft proposals for the Press. Marshall, who undertook it, died with the work unfinished, and it was not taken up again till 1715 when David Wilkins, a German scholar, learning that Oxford had both the best manuscript and the type, came and edited the text. His work was defective in some ways, but his book remained unique for many years. First published in 1716, the last copy sold in 1907, a notable tribute to the Delegates' determination to keep an important book in print.

After Fell's death, John Mill devoted himself single-mindedly to the great Greek New Testament with all the variant readings, on which Fell had set his heart. Fell had found him, he recollected later, accumulating notes and 'vehemently insisted on my putting them in order and setting about an edition as soon as might be'. Mill lamented his death, and, taking his example, insisted on publishing the book himself. He completed it, a fortnight before he died. The 'exemplar Millianum' was a landmark in biblical scholarship: no one had attempted before the reconstruction of the stemma of the New Testament, and although Mill's work could not hope to be complete or accurate, it has provided the framework of all scholarly work in the field since.

THOMAS HEARNE

125. John Leland. *De rebus Britannicis Collectanea.* Oxonii, e Theatro Sheldoniano, 1715. Sumptibus Editoris.

126. William Roper. *Vita D. Thomae Mori equitis aurati, lingua Anglicana contexta.* Veneunt apud editorem, 1716.

127. William Camden. *Annales rerum Anglicarum et Hibernicarum regnante Elizabetha.* 1717.

Thomas Hearne (1678–1735) was, by fate and temperament, at odds with his time and the Oxford of which he was too fond to leave. Educated under White Kennett at St. Edmund Hall, he became Janitor at the Bodleian in 1701 and soon embarked on the series of publications which lasted the rest of his life. They and he were an embarrassment to the University: his non-juring principles were too apt to appear in his editorial matter, and it was felt that his 'private way of Publishing perverts the Press', as Archbishop Wake put it. His success made matters worse. Unlike the University, Hearne could compass 'vending'. The Delegates seldom printed less than 500 copies: Hearne would print 200–240, with 60–70 on large paper, and price them high; his subscribers were loyal, and he often sold out and found his books selling at a premium in the trade.

In 1713 a rash remark in his edition of Dodwell's *De parma equestri* induced the Heads of Houses to demand that the offending passage be removed before the book was published. This, however, did not impede his election as Architypographus in January 1715, the first man with practical experience since Clarke to hold the post. No doubt, too, his principles, if extreme, were sympathetic to many in the University. The Delegates, not unreasonably, were alarmed, and appointed a Warehouse-Keeper, rather as Fell had done with Hall, and the Vice-Chancellor told the new Architypographus: 'Mr Hearne, you are certainly the fittest person that is in Oxford for this place. But your principles are not suitable.' Piqued, Hearne resigned.

He was, however, unrepentant: the six volumes of Leland's invaluable collections, the foundation of English antiquarian studies, contained criticism of the removal of the Arundel marbles from the Theatre yard and of the Archbishop of Dublin for treason to James II; sheet Zzz of the first volume was the first (he was proud to boast) to be printed at the new Clarendon Printing House. He was forbidden to use 'Oxford' or 'the Theatre' in his imprints, and in his edition of Roper's Life of More substituted a Burghers plate showing a distant Oxford, with oxen heading towards the ford, labelled 'Vad. Boum Vet.' (the old oxen ford). But in Camden's *Annals* he defamed Henry VIII,

Queen Elizabeth, and the University. He was sued in the Chancellor's Court, which threatened expulsion (a severer punishment for him than most), but the case was allowed to drop, and Hearne continued, if more cautiously; he was allowed to use the imprint again.

Hearne was too individual, too prone to take offence, to have taken an active part in the running of the Press, but his long dealings with it, recorded in detail in his *Diary*, are a better guide to it than any other in the period. Like Mill's New Testament, Hearne's private printing made the University Press better known than its own publications.

THE BIBLE PATENT: JOHN BASKETT

128. *The Holy Bible.* Printed by John Baskett, Printer to the King's most Excellent Majesty, for Great Britain; and to the University, 1717.

129. John Baskett's accounts (Univ. Arch. S.E.P. Z 28 (5)).

130. The renewal of the lease of the Bible Press.

131. *The Holy Bible.* Printed for T. Wright and W. Gill, Printers to the University: and sold by R. Baldwin and S. Crowder, in Paternoster Row, London; and by W. Jackson, in Oxford, 1769.

Parker and Guy were undone by their own success. Their management of the Bible Press enabled them to contribute generously to the University's legal expenses in the action brought by the Stationers' Company, in course of which it was stated that they had no fewer than eleven presses and forty-eight apprentices and workmen. The case was finally settled out of court in March 1689, more or less on the terms suggested by Fell in 1685, the Stationers reserving only the right to a renewal of the covenant not to print their books. This generosity may have been deliberate. In 1691 Parker and Guy's lease ran out, and the Stationers put in a bid. This involved combining the business of the King's Printers with the Oxford Bible Press, in return for which they would pay an annual rent of £200, buy the surplus stock of the learned Press at 20 per cent profit to the University, 'Collect and send to Oxford-library, what Books are, or shall be, due to them' under the Licensing Act (1662), continue to print Bibles at prices to be fixed by the University, and settle any debts arising from the law-suit.

It was a generous offer. Although Parker and Guy made a counter-bid, loyally supported by John Wallis, the new Delegates, feeling perhaps that they had made more out of the Bible Press than was fair, accepted the Stationers' terms. John Baskett was early active in their plans. He supplied paper from 1695, personally financed the printing of Clarendon's *History* from 1707, and took a large number of the *Oxford Almanack* each year. In addition, he gradually bought up the shares in the King's Printers' business, and in 1711 negotiated a new lease of the Oxford Bible Press to run for twenty-one years from 1713 for himself (he settled separately with the Stationers' Company).

The first fruit of this was to be the printing of 'the Bible in a large Folio Volume, on fine Paper, & with a large, noble Letter, at the new Printing House in Oxford'. The determination, shared by Baskett and Charlett, that the Bible would be typographically distinguished, seems to have overridden care for the text, and the Bible became known as a 'Basket-ful of errors' or the Vinegar Bible (a headline in St. Luke's Gospel read 'the Parable of the Vinegar' for 'Vineyard'). It was none the less unequalled in English Bible-printing so far, and only Baskerville's (Cambridge, 1763) and Bruce Rogers's (Oxford, 1935) have been as distinguished in appearance. The Vinegar Bible was further decorated with copperplate headpieces and initials by Thornhill, Chéron, and Laguerre, the leading decorative artists of their day.

John Baskett died in 1742, and next year his sons overreached themselves. In 1743 a Bible was printed at Cambridge (the first since 1682) and also an extract of the Statutes. Against the latter the Basketts sued for infringement of their patent as King's Printers. Judgement was finally given in 1758, after a protracted case in which all the evidence, going back to 1534, was rehearsed, and the outcome was an assertion of the two Universities' rights. Soon after, Charles Eyre had bought the new lease of the King's Printers' business. He and Mark Baskett became competitors for the Oxford Bible Press, and, as in 1691, after an unseemly wrangle, the new lease was finally granted to a third party, Wright & Gill, prosperous London stationers. The terms of their new lease show that the Delegates had learned from previous experience: Clause 4 specifically provides for the printing of new and accurate texts of the Bible and Book of Common Prayer.

It was beginning to be realized that the right to print Bibles was not just a chattel, to be hawked to the highest bidder, but carried with it duties. Privilege had to be earned, the more so since a further judgement, in *The Stationers' Company* v. *Carnan* (1775), had abolished all other monopolies of print other than those governed by copyright law. The Delegates decided to have the text prepared by Dr. Paris for the Cambridge Bible collated with the 1611 and 1701 (Bishop Lloyd's) versions. Benjamin Blayney (1728–1801), fellow of Hertford College and later Regius Professor of Hebrew, was entrusted with this task. On the whole, he altered too much; in the manner of his time, he set too much store by consistency of usage and fact, and he did not understand Jacobean syntax. On the other hand, his knowledge of Hebrew improved the spelling of Hebrew names and words (for both rhythm and meaning), and diminished the over-use of italic to indicate words supplied and not in the Hebrew. Best of all, in an age given to over-capitalization, he left well alone. It is arguable that the Authorized Version saved English from the German practice of capitalizing all nouns. Blayney's work was not without critics, but it was an important beginning to the new task of never-ending vigilance over the sacred text.

PUBLISHING AFTER HEARNE

132. [Richard Allestree.] *The whole duty of man.* Oxford, printed for John Eyre, and sold by Thomas Page and W. Mount, and the booksellers of London and Westminster, 1730.

133. J. J. Dillenius. *Historia muscorum.* Oxonii, e Theatro Sheldoniano, 1741.

134. Richard Russell. *A dissertation concerning the use of sea water in diseases of the glands.* Oxford, printed at the Theatre, and sold by James Fletcher in the Turl, and J. and J. Rivington in St Paul's Church-Yard, London, 1753.

135. [Thomas Hanmer, ed.] *The works of Shakespear. In six volumes. Carefully revised and corrected by former editions, and adorned with sculptures designed and executed by the best hands.* Oxford, printed at the Theatre, 1743–4.

136. Engraved copperplate for one of the tailpieces for Hanmer's Shakespeare.

137. Robert Lowth. *De sacra poesi Hebraeorum.* Oxonii, e Typographeo Clarendoniano, 1753.

With the death of Charlett, the University lost any inclination to meddle directly with the intricacies of publishing: the Delegates managed the Press (through the Warehouse-Keeper) and farmed the privilege. The Heads of Houses monopolized the Delegacy, and apart from Thomas Delaune, President of St. John's College and chairman of the Delegates, who made off with most of the profits from Clarendon's *History*, they did very little. Even *The Whole Duty of Man* and its sequels, published successfully by the University in the past and still in strong demand, were neglected: the one Oxford edition of the eighteenth century was merely printed at the University Press for a London bookseller.

Johann Dill (Dillenius) was the first Sherardian Professor of Botany at Oxford, and his great natural history of mosses, with copper-engravings of some 600 species, was a substantial task. Unlike Morison earlier, however, Dillenius was obliged to finance his own publication, in which Sir Hans Sloane and other patrons assisted him.

Dr. Richard Russell was a pioneer of the use

Laws of England
Member for Hindon
Wilts

of sea water for glandular and skin diseases. He practised during the summer months at Brighton, which he set on the path to fame. Soon his prescription was popularized by royal example, and the custom of going to the seaside for summer holidays grew up, and has lasted ever since. The elegant cut on the title-page of his work shows the Theatre in an elaborate marine frame, flanked on either side with the figures of Neptune and Hygieia.

Sir Thomas Hanmer (1677–1746) retired from politics in 1727, and devoted his leisure to the preparation of a new and splendid text of Shakespeare. He first planned to publish it through the London trade by subscription, and came to Oxford by chance when he learned that no bookseller would take it on. The Delegates saw in it a chance for Oxford to honour Shakespeare (commended by Pope's example) and to restore credit to the Press. Hanmer paid for the plates after Francis Hayman, elegant but stylized exercises in the mode (popular all over Europe) of Watteau, but the Delegates paid for everything else, including new type by the great typefounder William Caslon and engraved ornaments by Gravelot, and gave two guineas 'for the pressmen to drink Sir Tho. Hanmer's health'. Hanmer was an erratic editor, but his design of getting back to the sources away from recent accretions, however ill executed, was the foundation of Shakespearian scholarship. His edition was a success: the edition of 600 was almost sold out on subscription, and if, in Johnson's phrase, 'its Pomp recommends it more than its Accuracy', it was promptly pirated and remained popular for the rest of the century.

In 1774 the House of Lords rejected a bill to establish perpetual copyright, and contributed indirectly to the decline of the Stationers' Company monopolies. Oxford acted promptly to safeguard its privilege, and with the help of its Chancellor, Lord North, secured an Act (1775) granting it copyright in such of its publications as were formally registered under the Act. Predictably, Clarendon's *History* and *Life* were chosen, and also Louth's lectures on Hebrew poetry. Robert Lowth (1710–87), Professor of Poetry 1741–50 and later Bishop of London, must have seemed a good investment for the future. His lectures on Hebrew poetry were printed three times, and his *English Grammar* was even more popular. But neither lasted, nor did the Delegates claim perpetual copyright again until 1870, when Ruskin's *Lectures on Art* were registered.

WILLIAM BLACKSTONE

138. Portrait of Sir William Blackstone, by Tilly Kettle (Bodleian Library).

139. 'Some thoughts on the Oxford Press.'

140. William Blackstone. *To the Reverend Doctor Randolph*. Oxford, printed [by Richard Walker & William Jackson] in the year 1757.

141. 'Orders of the Delegates of the Press, Mdcclviii.'

142. William Blackstone. *Commentaries on the laws of England*. Oxford, printed at the Clarendon Press, 1765–9.

William Blackstone (1723–80) was made a Delegate of the Press on 2 July 1755. It was a controversial appointment. Blackstone was then a fellow of All Souls College, a busy lawyer who had just begun to lecture on English law in the University. He was one of the new men who were determined to rid the University of the sleepy pluralistic rule of the Heads of Houses. The Press was one of their chosen battlefields, and Blackstone's contested nomination the first engagement of the campaign. His onslaught, short, fierce, but completely successful, ended in March 1758. Later that year he became the first Vinerian Professor of English Law and in 1763 Solicitor-General to the Queen. Confident success is depicted in the handsome gowned figure of Kettle's portrait.

Blackstone's first action was to investigate current practice elsewhere in the printing trade, taking advice from Samuel Richardson, novelist and master printer, among others. He discovered that the Press was badly organized and over-charged for its work. In 'Some Thoughts on the Oxford Press' he reported his findings to the Delegates, and offered a solution, the adoption of piece-work rates as used by London printers. His report was not discussed. Blackstone forced the pace. His supporters had sent the Vice-Chancellor, George Huddesford, a report on his nomination, to which Huddesford replied with a pamphlet, *Observations relating to the Delegates of the Press* (1756). Blackstone waited until Huddesford was succeeded by Thomas Randolph. Then he published his famous open letter on 21 May 1757, in which he exposed the sad state of the Press, the misapplication of funds intended for publication, and his own proposed cures.

Randolph paid no attention, but Blackstone kept up his pressure until January 1758. Then he reiterated his proposals, with a final threat 'to bring our Proceedings with relation to the Press . . . before another less indulgent Tribunal'; this brought opposition to a sudden end. On 1 February the Delegates resolved to keep a book (as he had suggested) with minutes of their meetings at one end and accounts at the other (these 'Orders of the Delegates' have been maintained continuously since); on 9 February his proposals to the Vice-Chancellor were accepted *in toto*; on 16 February the office of Warehouse-Keeper, occupied from his appointment after the Hearne fiasco to his death in 1756 by the incompetent and corrupt Stephen Richardson, was bestowed on Blackstone's candidate, Daniel Prince; finally, on 18 March, his carefully calculated piece-work wage and charge rates were put into force: two days earlier, the Vice-Chancellor Dr. Randolph himself proposed a vote of thanks to him for his hard work.

It would be hard to find in English history another such victory of reform with no significant compromise. It may have saved the Press from extinction, it almost certainly saved learned publishing by corporately owned university presses; it also shook Oxford profoundly, for what could be done in the Press could be done in other departments of the University. (Carter, pp. 330–1.)

The reverberations of Blackstone's campaign continued to be felt for another century, until the Royal Commission on the Universities (1852). Meanwhile, peace was sealed with the printing at the Press and publication in four quarto volumes (resting under Blackstone's hand in his portrait) of the work for which he is famous throughout the English-speaking world, his *Commentaries on the Laws of England*. These were the product of his earlier lectures: as a digest of historical growth and a co-ordination of the cumulative precedents of case-law, it is a miracle of organization, judgement, and common sense; it is the nearest thing to a constitution of England. Its wider importance was immediately recognized: Grenville quoted it against Blackstone to assert Wilkes's right to take his seat in the Commons in 1769. Translated into French, German, Italian, and Russian, it became the textbook of liberty and justice all over the world.

THE REFORMED PRESS

143. Samuel Johnson's letter to the Vice-Chancellor, 12 March 1776.

144. *Orders . . . for regulating the Prices of Printing at the University Press*, 1758.

145. Ἡ Καινὴ Διαθήκη. *Novum Testamentum iuxta exemplar Millianum.* Oxonii, e Typographeo Clarendoniano, 1763. Sumptibus Academiae.

146. *Specimen of the several sorts of printing-types belonging to the University of Oxford at the Clarendon Printing-House*, 1768.

147. Daniel Prince's letter to John Nichols.

On 9 July 1758 the Delegates appointed 'Mr Payne of Castle Street, London' as 'Warehouse-Keeper or Publisher' in London. It was the beginning of a new approach to selling academic books. 'Honest Tom Payne' was the most distinguished bookseller in London; he acted not only for the Clarendon Press, but also for Wright & Gill, the lessees of the Bible Press. The relationship with the Payne family, with Peter Elmsley and William Dawson, and later with the Parkers and the Gardners, was a close one, closer and more involved with the direction of the Press than their distant role as distributors would suggest; it lasted for over a century.

At first, however, there were difficulties. The Delegates, among them Blackstone, were opposed to any increase in discount to the trade, as the burden 'will in the end fall heaviest upon the Scholar or Consumer'.[1] The booksellers (Payne resigned in 1773, and was succeeded by Thomas Cadell and Peter Elmsley) protested that, without a discount which would leave an intermediate wholesaler with a margin, they could not get the books off their hands. They enlisted a distinguished advocate in Johnson, whose famous letter seems to have persuaded the Delegates. A discount of 25 per cent on Clarendon was sanctioned at once, and in 1779 Elmsley, and Prince at Oxford, were allowed 20 per cent on all books.

Daniel Prince had been brought up in the heart of the Oxford book trade. In 1756 he succeeded his uncle Richard Clements (to whom he had probably been apprenticed), as bookseller on the corner of Cat Street and New College Lane. He gave Blackstone much useful advice, and as the 'Warehouse Man and Overseer of the Press' (a deliberate extension of the Warehouse-Keeper's role) Prince served the Delegates well for twenty-six years. The first task set him was to catalogue the Press's books, types, and other furniture. His list of books and a specimen of the types were printed.

Reform of the typographical material was part of Blackstone's scheme and (no doubt advised by Prince) he negotiated with John Baskerville for a Greek type. Baskerville, whose new types had just taken literary Europe by storm, was engaged to print the Bible and Book of Common Prayer at Cambridge, and his punch-cutter, John Handy, may have been idle. It was not a great success: it was an uneasy compromise between the older models which Baskerville was shown in profusion and his own natural style. It did, however, serve as the model for one of the finest of English Greek types, cut by William Martin (brother of Robert, Baskerville's apprentice and successor) for William Bulmer.

Prince continued to add to the Press's equipment: more of Caslon's Roman and Italic types are to be seen taking the place of Fell types in the 1768 *Specimen of printing-types*; a new press was bought; and from 1778 paper was held in stock instead of being ordered for each book printed. Prince's accounts were a great improvement on his predecessor's, and both the quantity and quality of the Press's work increased during his time as overseer. Writing to his younger contemporary, John Nichols, a printer like himself as well as a historical writer, he could afford to be modest about his own achievements.

148. Richard Chandler. *Marmora Oxoniensia.* Oxonii, e Typographeo Clarendoniano Impensis Academiae, 1763.

149. Martin Lister. *Historia sive synopsis methodica conchyliorum.* Oxonii, e Typographeo Clarendoniano, 1770.

150. Thomas Warton. *The history of English Poetry.* London, printed for, and sold by J. Dodsley . . . and Messrs Fletcher at Oxford, 1774–81.

151, 151A. Thomas Hawkins. *The origin of the English drama.* Oxford, printed at the Clarendon-Press, for S. Leacroft, Charing Cross, London. And sold by D. Prince at Oxford, and J. Woodyear at Cambridge, 1773. With one of the original blocks.

153. Benjamin Kennicott, ed. *Vetus Testamentum Hebraicum, cum variis lectionibus.* Oxonii, e Typographeo Clarendoniano, 1776–80.

Humphrey Prideaux had been the first to admit that his *Marmora Oxoniensia* (1676) had suffered from haste, at Fell's rather than his own wish. In 1755 a new occasion for approaching the problem came with the gift to the University of another part of Lord Arundel's collection by the Dowager Countess of Pomfret. Richard Chandler (1738–1810), then a demy of Magdalen College, proposed a new catalogue in Imperial folio with seventy-six whole-page engraved plates. His text was painstaking but dull, except for the inscriptions, of which (including the Parian Chronicle which had defeated Prideaux) he produced acceptable texts. It was a splendid book, printed on fine paper made by James Whatman (the later inventor of wove paper), and the Delegates gave it to kings and other notables. It made Chandler's name. He was immediately employed by the Society of Dilettanti to travel in Asia Minor and Greece with Nicholas Revett (architect) and William Pars (artist), recording ancient remains. More magnificent folios appeared, and in 1775 Chandler published at the Press his own entertaining account of his travels. An equally splendid book was Lister's *Historia*, printed

[1] Draft memorandum (1759), in the 'Delegates' Book'.

from the old plates designed by the author's talented daughters, a revival of the Press's interest in natural history.

The simultaneous publication of Warton's *History of English Poetry* down to the Elizabethan age and Hawkins's *Origin of the English Drama*, a reprint of fourteen plays published 1515–1606, was a turning-point in the study of English literature. Neither was published by the Delegates, but by London booksellers; Warton's book, indeed, bears no sign of being printed at Oxford, although a letter from Prince to Nichols records its printing there. Thomas Warton (1728–90), Professor first of Poetry and then of Ancient History and Poet Laureate 1785–90, was an indifferent poet but the first scholar to explore early English on the same lines as those used for classical or Anglo-Saxon texts. Thomas Hawkins, chaplain of Magdalen College, who died young while his book was in the press, had supervised the second, and corrected, edition of Hanmer's Shakespeare (1771). This led him to read the earlier drama in order to emend Shakespeare, and gave him the idea of producing texts of them, adorned, in two cases, with skilful recutting of the original woodcuts; two of the blocks still survive.

Benjamin Kennicott (1718–83), fellow of Exeter College, was a member of the one Whig college in a University still mainly Tory. In 1753 he published a dissertation on the printed text of the Hebrew Bible, attributing certain obscurities to earlier scribal errors. This made him further unpopular with literalists, but he was encouraged by Robert Lowth and Thomas Secker, soon to be Archbishop of Canterbury. In 1760 the Delegates and Secker agreed to support his project of collating as many early manuscripts as he could find, and for the next twenty years Kennicott laboured on, supported mainly by subscriptions to the work, which came in from the King and all over the world. To his second volume Kennicott added a dissertation making clear that none of the variants he had found implied either doctrinal or historical change. But neither he nor his contemporaries saw his work as wasted labour: Dr. Johnson said 'that though the text should not be much mended thereby, yet it was no small advantage to know, that we had as good a text as the most consummate industry and diligence could procure'.[1]

152. Henry James Pye. *Faringdon Hill.* A poem in two books. Oxford: printed for Daniel Prince, & sold by J. Wilkie at No. 71 St. Paul's Church-Yard, London. 1774.

Contemporary poetry rarely engaged the Press in the eighteenth century, and the author of this conventional essay in the popular mode of topographic verse probably brought his work to Prince because he was the nearest printer. Henry James Pye (1745–1813) was born at Faringdon in Berkshire and went to Magdalen College. He contributed a poem to the University's verses on the birth of the Prince of Wales in 1762, and tried persistently to make his name as a poet without ever rising, in Sidney Lee's words, above 'a uniform dead level of dulness'. A prolific author and a busy local magistrate, he was rewarded by Pitt for six years' loyal service in parliament with the succession, in 1790, to Thomas Warton (see 150) as Poet Laureate: 'No selection could have more effectually deprived the post of reputable literary associations.' It also sealed Pye's fate. He is now irrevocably linked with his fellow poetasters, John Wolcot, Charles Small Pybus, and the author of *The birth and triumph of love*, in an epigram attributed to Porson:

> Poetis nos laetamur tribus
> Pye, Petro Pindar, Parvo Pybus.
> Si ulterius ire pergis
> Adde his Sir James Bland Burges.

RESUMPTION OF THE BIBLE PRESS

154. Agreement with William Jackson and Archibald Hamilton for the partnership in the Bible Press, 12 February 1780.

155. Catalogues of Bibles printed at Oxford, 1783–1812.

156. *The Holy Bible.* 1808.

157. *The Book of Common Prayer.* Oxford, printed at the Clarendon Press, by Dawson, Bensley, and Cooke, printers to the University, 1799.

[1] *Boswell's Life of Johnson*, ed. G. Birkbeck Hill, rev. L. F. Powell (1934–64), ii. 128.

158. *Novum Testamentum Vulgatae editionis. Sumptibus Academiae Oxoniensis in usum cleri Gallicani in Anglia exulantis.* Oxonii, e Typographeo Clarendoniano, 1796.

159. 'General Statement of the Partnership Account.'

The implications of *The Stationers' Company* v. *Carnan* were quickly felt at Oxford. The Stationers gave up their annual payment, now £550, to the lessees of the Oxford privilege for forbearing to print books in which the Stationers claimed an exclusive right. Wright & Gill, as their lease came up in 1779, reminded the Delegates of this fact, and of the damage done to a promising market by the War of Independence (perhaps aware that the ex-colonists had already begun to print the New Testament themselves). The University made one attempt to regain its other privileges but its Chancellor, Lord North, although Prime Minister, failed to persuade the Commons to restore their old rights to the three patentees. However, to compensate Oxford, he doubled the Stamp Duty on almanacs and gave £500 p.a. out of the proceeds to the University. Although the duty on almanacs was abolished in 1834, the annual subvention continues.

The result of this was to determine the University to take a more active part in the Bible Press. Wright & Gill's lease was not renewed, and a new agreement was concluded for a partnership in which the Delegates shared their right with an experienced London printer, Archibald Hamilton, and William Jackson, the owner of the 'New Printing Office' near Carfax where Blackstone printed his letter *To Doctor Randolph*. Jackson supervised the Oxford Bible Press to good effect; Hamilton saw to distribution in London.

Beginning in 1783, a broadside sheet catalogue of Bibles printed at Oxford was issued, with prices given. The range gradually expanded. The partners changed: Hamilton died in 1793 and was replaced by William Dawson; Jackson died in 1795 and was replaced by Joshua Cooke, who had succeeded to Daniel Prince's bookselling business, and Thomas Bensley, a distinguished London printer, became the third partner in the Oxford Press.

Thomas Bensley (*d.* 1833) was an enterprising if erratic printer, distinguished both for technical innovation and for typographic style. He was the principal patron of Vincent Figgins, a punch-cutter and typefounder of genius, whose types bridged the gap between the 'old face' of Caslon and the 'modern' types popularized by Bodoni and the Didot brothers with rare distinction. Bensley's sure typographic taste added new distinction to the more than respectable style of Jackson, and can be seen equally in the folio lectern Bible and Book of Common Prayer and in the cheap duodecimo editions.

One of the more unexpected products of the Press in this period was the Latin Vulgate New Testament, edited from the most recent French text by some of the *émigré* clergy at Winchester, of which 2,000 copies were printed in 1796. The costs of the edition were met by the University; all 2,000 copies were distributed free to French refugee priests, and another 2,000 were printed at the expense of the Duke of Buckingham.

With the new partnership, a new system of accounts was required. Hitherto it had been the business of the Warehouse-Keeper or Overseer of the Press to keep and present accounts. Now new and more elaborate figures for costs and revenue were required, and an annual balance was struck; the profits then recorded were distributed among the partners in proportion to their shareholding.

TECHNICAL CHANGE

160. Delegates' Order Book, 25 October 1796; 30 April & 1 May 1805; 17 October 1805; 21 October 1806.

161. An iron printing-press of the design produced by Earl Stanhope in 1805, with improvements by him and others.

162. *The Book of Common Prayer*, 1806.

163. *An account of the visit of His Royal Highness the Prince Regent and their Imperial and Royal Majesties the Emperor of Russia and the King of Prussia to the University of Oxford in June* 1814, 1815.

Charles, 3rd Earl Stanhope (1753–1816), was a polymathic genius to whom printing owes much. His first invention was the first commercially successful printing press made of iron. Developed soon after 1800, it was first marketed early in 1805. Bensley and Cooke had already in 1796 installed three presses, 'two of them on an improv'd construction', but these were evidently wooden or 'common' presses. Bensley was clearly interested in the Stanhope Press from an early stage, and when he and Cooke reported the installation of two of them in October 1805, he was able to produce a model of the press as a present from Lord Stanhope to the Delegates. Subsequently, Bensley with his London neighbour Richard Taylor acquired the rights in Koenig's first cylinder press, but it was some time before machine-powered presses were installed at Oxford.

A Stanhope press still survives at the Press. The brass plate on the staple is inscribed: 'No. 11. Peter Keir, Engineer Camden Town St. Pancras London'. After the original purchase, the Press added others from Keir in 1811. This one, which prints a large Royal sheet, is the only hand press left at the Press, where at one time as many as 65 were in use.

On 17 March 1805, the Delegates had received a letter from Andrew Wilson, who had been charged by Lord Stanhope with the exploitation of his other invention, stereotype, offering the process to them. Wilson had already concluded an agreement with Cambridge, and this clearly spurred the Delegates to come to terms with him: in June 1805 they signed an agreement whereby Wilson was bound to instruct Bensley and the Oxford manager of the printing business, Samuel Collingwood, in return for the large sum of £4,000.

It was not an easy process to master. The type pages were moulded in gypsum plaster, which had to dry quickly if it was to take the impression of the type cleanly; a clear dry atmosphere was needed, and good fires. Still, a year later, 2,000 copies of a 'Brevier Prayer Book' were printed from stereotype plates, and 'exhibited, finish'd, and ready for sale' to the Delegates. Despite continuing difficulties with smaller sizes of type, the partners persevered, and from 1810 on stereotype was a regular feature of the Bible Press.

In 1814, the war against France over and Napoleon in exile on Elba, the crowned heads of Europe paid a state visit to Oxford. The University Press put its best work into a short commemorative book, which is in effect a specimen of the Press's types and resources at the time. It is an elegant piece of work, definitely nineteenth-century in appearance: the break with the past signified by the new technical developments can be seen in the new typographic style of the Press. It was also one of Bensley's last achievements. In 1816, his accounts were called in question by the other partners; he was unable to answer a charge of misappropriation (which he had, however, himself reported), and he was excluded from the new partnership agreement in 1817.

THE RESTORATION OF CLASSICAL SCHOLARSHIP

164. Joannes Malalas. *Historia chronica*. Oxonii, e Theatro Sheldoniano, 1691.

165. Samuel Musgrave, ed. Εὐριπίδου τὰ σωζόμενα. *Euripidis quae extant omnia*. Oxonii, e Typographeo Clarendoniano, 1778.

166. Jonathan Toup, ed. *Dionysii Longini quae supersunt Graece et Latine*. Oxonii, e Typographeo Clarendoniano, 1778.

167. Thomas Tyrwhitt, ed. *Aristotelis de poetica liber*. Oxonii, e Typographeo Clarendoniano, 1794.

168. Daniel Wyttenbach, ed. *Plutarchi moralia, id est opera, exceptis vitis, reliqua*. Oxonii: e Typographeo Clarendoniano, 1795–1830.

169. [Richard Porson, ed.] Ὁμήρου Ἰλιὰς καὶ Ὀδύσσεια. Ἐξ ἐργαστηριου τυπογραφικοῦ Ἀκαδημιας τῆς ἐν Ὀξονίᾳ, 1801.

170. Martin Routh, ed. *Reliquiae sacrae*, 1814–18, 1848.

171. Thomas Gaisford. Portrait by H. W. Pickersgill (Christ Church).

172. Thomas Gaisford, ed. *Poetae Graeci minores*, 1814–20.

173. Thomas Gaisford, ed. *Suidae lexicon post Ludolphum Kusterum ad codices manuscriptos recensuit Thomas Gaisford*, 1834.

174. Karl Wilhelm Dindorf, ed. *Demosthenis Orationes*, 1846–51.

175. Immanuel Bekker, ed. *Oratores Attici*, 1822–8.

The edition of Malalas that Laud dreamed of and Prideaux scouted finally appeared in 1691. The text was seen through the press by John Mill, but it was not a credit to the Press. In 1690 Richard Bentley was staying in Oxford; Mill lent him proofs, and the resultant 'Epistola ad Millium', printed with the Malalas, was his first published work. He was only 28, but the range of his learning and acuteness of criticism in it made his reputation.

The rest of Bentley's career was devoted to the University of Cambridge and its Press. At Oxford, classical scholarship slept. A new generation of scholars, mostly German, ridiculed such efforts as were made. But, unknown to them, change was on its way. Samuel Musgrave (1732–80), a Plymouth doctor, achieved a self-taught dominance over the text of Euripides, and the Delegates gladly undertook his complete edition. He had already edited the *Hippolytus* in 1756, and the same generous style was adopted for the complete works; the text was set in the great Fell Paragon Greek, without accents (Musgrave himself suggested the despised Baskerville Greek, which was smaller).

Musgrave had been assisted by another good English scholar, Jeremiah Markland. A third, Jonathan Toup (1713–85), produced an equally distinguished and durable edition of Longinus, marked by the vigour and certainty of its emendations. Aristotle's *Poetics* had not ceased to occupy classical scholars at Oxford but without distinction until Tyrwhitt's posthumous edition appeared in 1794. Tyrwhitt (1730–86) was a scholar of wide range, including Shakespeare and Chaucer, and proof of the forgeries of Thomas Chatterton. His *Poetics* was the first modern edition of the text.

By now scholars from abroad had learned to think more respectfully of the Oxford Press, and Daniel Wyttenbach (1746–1820), Professor of Greek at Amsterdam and then Ruhnken's successor at Leyden, brought his edition of Plutarch to it. The Grenville Homer, edited by Porson, gave the Press a European reputation. Martin Routh, the centenarian President of Magdalen College (1755–1854), who edited two of Plato's dialogues in 1784, extended the range of textual scholarship to include the earliest Christian texts, a task which occupied many years of patient and laborious work.

The great and dominant figure in the new revival was Thomas Gaisford (1779–1855), Regius Professor of Greek (1812) and Dean of Christ Church from 1831. As a Delegate of the Press for nearly fifty years, he had a direct influence on its choice of books; as a Curator of the Bodleian he was instrumental in enriching it with many books, especially classical manuscripts. Above all he edited a large number of texts himself; his emendations were level-headed, but his work is chiefly remembered for the thoroughness with which he collated and reprinted earlier notes, especially early scholia. His edition of the lesser Greek poets, including Hesiod and Theocritus, was a model piece of work; his great Suidas formed the basis for later editions.

Gaisford was responsible for inviting major foreign scholars to edit texts for the Press, and among those who responded were Immanuel Bekker (1785–1871) and Karl Wilhelm Dindorf (1802–83). Bekker's edition of the Greek orators was the first comprehensive text ever to appear. Dindorf's Demosthenes was the last of a series, including Aeschylus, Sophocles, and others, which he produced for the Press. It was not, however, Gaisford, but an Oxford bookseller, Joseph Parker, who brought to the Press an edition, though not a critical one, of Thucydides (1830–5), by a more famous man, Thomas Arnold (1795–1842), the great headmaster of Rugby.

Gaisford's influence was not limited to the classics; he was a useful and practical Delegate, whose continuous presence rescued the Press from the uncertainty that followed the changes of 1780, and provided a successful staple for the first half of the nineteenth century.

OTHER BOOKS, 1800–1850

176. J. Torelli, ed. *Archimedis opera*, 1792.

177. James Bradley. *Observations*, 1798–1805.

178. Edward Pococke. *Specimen historiae Arabum*, ed. Joseph White, 1806.

179. Gilbert Burnet. *History of his own time*, ed. Martin Routh, 1823.

180. Joseph Addison. *Evidences of Christianity*, 1801.

181. John Keble. *The Christian year*, 1840.

182. Richard Hooker. *Works*, ed. John Keble, 1836.

183. James Ingram. *Inaugural lecture on Anglo-Saxon literature*, 1807.

184. James Ingram. *Memorials of Oxford*, 1832–7.

185. John le Neve. *Fasti ecclesiae Anglicanae*, ed. Sir Thomas Duffus Hardy, 1854.

186. Robert Montgomery. *Oxford, a poem*, 1831.

187. *Wyckliffe's Wycket*, 1828.

The great folio edition of the Greek text of Archimedes was one of the few Oxford contributions to scientific literature in this period. For the first time printed with the commentary of Eustocius, it remained the authoritative text for nearly a century. It was one of the last Oxford learned works in the grand manner: folios were to become rare.

The astronomical *Observations* of James Bradley (1693–1762) were an obligation which the Press was slow to fulfil. Bradley's work—as Savilian Professor of Astronomy and later Astronomer Royal, he had discovered the nutation of the earth's axis—was of some originality and deserved publication. Eventually, Abraham Robertson, also Savilian Professor, edited Bradley's papers and they were published in two volumes.

The Press had a tendency to reprint its old successes (Kennett's *Parochial Antiquities* and Wells's *Geography* were among them). Pococke's even earlier work on Arabic history was edited by Joseph White, and given an extremely elegant 'period' typographic form in which Bensley's hand can be seen.

Among Gaisford's achievements was a series of major English historic texts. These included a new edition of Clarendon (1819), and Martin Routh's edition of Burnet's *History of his own Time*, the other great account of England in the seventeenth century by one of the major participants in its history.

A bare quarter of a century separates the reprint (1801) of the century-old *Evidences of Christianity* by Joseph Addison (1672–1719) and the publication in 1827 of Keble's *Christian Year*, the greatest devotional classic of Victorian England. With Pusey, Keble (1792–1866) founded the 'Oxford Movement', the new High Church style for which Oxford stood in most Victorian eyes. It was offered to the Delegates first and declined by them on the ground that they did not publish devotional works. Joseph Parker, the Oxford bookseller (and also a partner in the Press), published it instead, and in 1840 the Press printed an edition, the 'nineteenth', for him.

Keble's edition of Richard Hooker (?1554–1606) was by far the most important of a series of reprints of the major English theologians. He took immense pains over it, as befitted the work of the greatest Anglican theologian, and printed some new material from Hooker's manuscript.

James Ingram (1774–1850) was Professor of Anglo-Saxon and President of Trinity. His inaugural lecture began a revival in Anglo-Saxon studies, to which he contributed an edition of the Saxon Chronicle (1823). He later turned to the history of Oxford, and his *Memorials*, issued in parts from 1832 and in three volumes in 1837, was distinguished by its elegant plates, and even more by the engravings in the text by Orlando Jewitt, a local engraver on wood, whose masterpiece it was.

Le Neve's *Fasti*, first printed in folio in 1716, became three fat octavo volumes in the new nineteenth-century style. Sir Thomas Duffus Hardy (1804–78), one of the first and greatest of British archivists, increased the volume of Le Neve's original records of all ecclesiastical dignitaries of the Church of England by nearly three times. Although it is in process of being re-edited now, it remains the one comprehensive source for its subject, and is still much used by historians.

Little original poetry came from the Press at this

period. Robert Montgomery (1807–55), whose religious verse had appeared before he was twenty-one and been much praised, matriculated at Oxford in February 1830. In April, Macaulay's famous review, a classic of literary castigation, appeared in the *Edinburgh Review*. But neither this, nor the local ridicule evoked by *Oxford*, had the slightest effect on the popularity of his work, which continued for the rest of his life and after.

With the departure of Bensley, the Press lost its distinction of typographic style. It was not used by William Pickering, the genius of English typography from 1820 to 1850. *Wyckliffe's Wycket*, however, might well have been published as one of his reprints of early English texts. Its editor, Samuel Pantin, dedicated it to William Van Mildert, the last Prince-Bishop of Durham.

RESULTS OF THE PARTNERSHIP: THE NEW BUILDING

188. Books printed at the Oxford University Press and sold by Joshua Cooke, Peter Elmsley, and David Bremner, 1798.

189. Delegates' Order Book, 29 April and 2 November 1825.

190. *The Microcosm of Oxford*, *c*. 1835.

191. Early nineteenth-century wood-blocks of the Clarendon Building and the Theatre.

192. *Novum Testamentum Graecum*, 1830.

In addition to the Bible Press partnership, the Delegates maintained the London distribution of their books through Peter Elmsley, and on his retirement about 1800 through his successors David Bremner and John Thomas Payne, son of 'Honest Tom'. They now put out special catalogues of Oxford books, to assist their sale. Elmsley's heir was his nephew, also called Peter Elmsley, (1773–1825), perhaps the greatest Greek scholar ever produced by Oxford; he became Principal of St. Alban Hall and Professor of Ancient History in 1823, and contributed to Gaisford's programme of classical texts, although his main work was published elsewhere.

Besides the London distributors, the Press still needed an Oxford bookseller, and the successor to Prince and Jackson was Joseph Parker, one of Prince's apprentices. He served the Press well, and when in 1810 there was a change in the Bible partnership, Parker became a partner, with Samuel Collingwood, superintendent of the 'Learned Side' (the two printing establishments were still separate), and Edward Gardner, who succeeded Payne (now a successful and eminent second-hand bookseller). Gardner was a bookbinder, who took charge of the London warehouse until 1851, when he was succeeded by his son. Joseph Parker, too, was succeeded by his nephew, John Henry Parker, in 1832. The younger Parker was publisher to the Oxford Movement, and his theological list ran parallel with the Press's without apparent conflict. He became more and more interested in archaeology, and in 1867, by now a rich man, he endowed the Keepership of the Ashmolean Museum and became the first Keeper himself.

All this activity meant a substantial growth in the Press's business, and with it the need for larger premises. In 1825, the Delegates decided to purchase a site in Walton Street, and a handsome new building was erected there between 1826 and 1830, to designs by Daniel Robertson and Edward Blore. It was still new when *The Microcosm of Oxford*, a delightful set of views, was printed by N. Whittock, the first lithographic printer in Oxford. Its novelty justified its appearance as a large folding frontispiece to Whittock's work.

The first book to be printed off in the new building was a Greek New Testament, edited by Charles Lloyd (1784–1829), Bishop of Oxford, patron and teacher of the men who made the Oxford Movement. Lloyd's Greek Testament was first published in 1827, and became one of the Press's steadiest sellers. It was still in print in 1863.

THE GROWTH OF EVANGELICALISM AND THE TEXT OF THE BIBLE

193. *The Holy Bible. Printed for the British and Foreign Bible Society*, 1812.

194. Letter from Samuel Collingwood to Joseph Tarn, 13 October 1812.

195. *The Holy Bible*, 1824.

196. *The Holy Bible, an exact reprint page for page of the Authorized Version published in the year 1611*, 1833.

197. *The Holy Bible, in the earliest English versions made by John Wycliffe and his followers. Edited by Josiah Forshall and Sir Frederic Madden*, 1850.

In 1804 the British and Foreign Bible Society was founded, its sole object 'to encourage a wider circulation of the Holy Scriptures, without note or comment'. It was, from the first, non-sectarian, its committee composed of 15 members of the Established Church, 15 dissenters, and 6 'resident foreigners'. It was the cornerstone of the new Evangelicalism which swept Britain, America, and by degrees the world. In 1804 the Society decided to commission the printing of Bibles on their own account, and the first stereotype New Testament was printed at the Cambridge University Press in 1805. Early in 1810, the Reverend Joseph Tarn wrote to William Dawson, the Oxford warehouseman in London, and began a correspondence which has continued ever since. The first Bible was printed for the Society at Oxford in 1812.

From 1812 the bulk of the correspondence was conducted by Samuel Collingwood, and his early remarks on the increased demand for Bibles, the need for better quality and lower prices, reflect the growing size and importance of the business. Collingwood himself became an enthusiastic supporter of the Society, helped to found the local branch, and punctually collected and transmitted subscriptions.

In 1824 the need to standardize the marginal notes, a task begun by Blayney, produced the Pica Reference Bible, in which the references to parallel passages were carefully collated and corrected. This text became the standard for the Oxford Reference Bibles, and was largely adopted outside the Press.

This progress was not unattended with controversy. The British and Foreign Bible Society was constantly under attack for its 'latitudinarian' views, and its refusal to alter its constitution to exclude non-Trinitarians led to the foundation of the Trinitarian Bible Society in 1831, which then and since has also printed many editions of the Bible at Oxford. The Press was directly attacked by the Reverend Thomas Curtis in an open letter, *The Existing Monopoly*, addressed to the Bishop of London in 1833, in which he condemned the participation of profit-making booksellers like Parker in privileges 'reposed for public benefit'. He had already addressed other strictures, complaining of the many inaccuracies carried over from Blayney's Bible, direct to Parker. This in turn suggested the literal reprint of the Authorized Version as visible testimony of Oxford's interest in the correctness of the scriptures that they printed. Copies were presented by the Delegates to the British and Foreign Bible Society and other interested parties.

In 1833 Parker told the Society that the 'profits of the Press never exceed 12½ per cent'; in 1802 Dawson, in discussion with one of the Cambridge Syndics, Isaac Milner, had told him that it 'ought to *net* ¼ or 25 per cent'. It is an interesting reflection on the expansion in a single generation. In the 1820s the British and Foreign Bible Society's orders for the Brevier Bible averaged 5,000, in the 1830s 10,000, and in the 1840s 30,000. The price was 6*s*. 8*d*. in 1832, and 4*s*. in 1850. The progress was sharpened by competition, owing to Adam Thomson, who like Curtis began with denunciation in *The Bible Monopoly inconsistent with Bible Circulation* (1840), and then set up his own press at Coldstream.

The Press's last contribution to Bible scholarship in this period was the 'English polyglot', the parallel edition of the several Wycliffite texts of the earliest English translation, which finally appeared in 1850. Josiah Forshall worked on it for twenty-five years, assisted by his successor as Keeper of Manuscripts at the British Museum, Sir Frederic Madden.

ORIENTAL SCHOLARSHIP

198. Joannes Uri. *Bibliothecae Bodleianae codicum manuscriptorum orientalium catalogus*, 1787.

199. H. H. Wilson ed. *Sankhya Karika or memorial verses on the Sankhya philosophy by Iswara Krisna*, 1837.

200. Edward Pusey. *Bibliothecae Bodleianae codicum manuscriptorum orientalium catalogus*, 1835.

201. Monier Williams. *A Sanskrit grammar*, 1847.

202. Friedrich Max Müller. *Rigveda*, 1849–73.

During the eighteenth century the primacy in oriental scholarship, in Persian and Indian languages, passed from the universities to the East India Company. Joannes Uri (1726–96), a Hungarian who studied at Leyden before coming to Oxford in 1766, was an isolated figure. He was invited to Oxford to undertake a catalogue of the oriental manuscripts, but his first volume, produced after twenty years' work, was not a success, its errata forming a conspicuous part of the second volume.

Oxford owes its entry into Sanskrit studies to a legacy for the foundation of a chair in the subject from Joseph Boden. The first professor, Horace Wilson (1786–1860), took up his appointment in 1832. There was only one kind of Sanskrit type available in England, an English Sanskrit cut by the Caslon foundry for Sir Charles Wilkins in 1808. This was acquired by the Press, and it was first used in Wilson's edition of Sankhya Karika, the first Sanskrit book to be printed at the Press, who printed it for the Oriental Translation Fund. It was published in London by A. J. Valpy.

Despite his other avocations, Pusey (1800–82) found time to honour a promise to complete Uri's catalogue. It took him six years, and is a monument of patient scholarship. As Regius Professor of Hebrew, he was also master of Samaritan and Aramaic, and his work on Sahidic texts was original: his Bodleian catalogue showed an equal knowledge of Arabic. It was an achievement the more remarkable since he lectured nine times a week and also contributed actively to 'Tracts for the Times'.

Monier Williams, later Sir Monier Monier-Williams (1819–99), succeeded Wilson as Boden Professor in 1860. The success of his *Sanskrit Grammar* was largely due to the energy and determination with which he promoted Indian studies. After a long campaign he achieved the foundation of the Indian Institute at Oxford, which has remained the centre for the study of Far Eastern languages in Oxford.

Max Müller (1823–1900) failed to get the Boden chair in 1860. It was almost the only disappointment in an energetic and successful career. His masterpiece in Sanskrit studies was his edition of the Rigveda with commentary. He also devoted a good deal of time to comparative philology, a discipline largely invented by himself, and his work is typified by the decent plain texts on every subject put out by the Press under his guidance, as well as his more massive works.

THOMAS COMBE: MECHANIZATION OF THE PRESS

203. Thomas Combe. Portrait by John Everett Millais (Ashmolean Museum).

204. The introduction of steam power.

205. *The Holy Bible*. Trial sheets from the Diamond 24mo edition, 1875.

206, 206A. Wolvercote Mill. Water-colour by J. Buckler, 1826; photograph by J. H. Stacy.

207. Combe, Bartholomew Price, and others at the Mill House (photograph by J. H. Stacy).

Thomas Combe was born at Leicester in 1797, the son of a printer and bookseller. He came to work for Joseph Parker, then went to London. In 1838 the post of Superintendent of the Clarendon Press (the 'Learned Side') fell vacant, and Combe was given the job. In 1841 he acquired two and a half shares in the Bible Press, of which he also became Superintendent. In 1853 when the two senior partners died he increased his holding in the Bible Press to eight shares. His plural capacity was acknowledged with the title Printer to the University.

Combe came to the Press at a fortunate time. Between 1808 and 1815 460,500 Bibles were printed there; in 1837–47 the number rose to 2,600,000. Combe soon became wealthy. The first steam presses had been installed just before he became Superintendent, and the change to steam power vastly accelerated the Press's output. The picture long post-dates its introduction, but the machine-room would not have looked very different in 1834, when the first steam-driven machines were put in.

As a young man Combe had become an active supporter of Newman and Pusey. With his wealth, he built churches and schools; he also started a regular Sunday school for boys at the Press. In 1848 Millais was introduced to Mr. and Mrs. Combe, and painted Combe's portrait the following year. Through Millais, the Combes met the other Pre-Raphaelites, to whom, with his long white beard, he was known as 'the Patriarch' (his wife became 'Mrs. Pat'). Soon he had become a discriminating and understanding patron, in particular of Holman Hunt, to whom he acted as financial adviser in all his complicated dealings with the London art trade.

Combe had long been interested in a thin, light, but opaque, paper for Bible and Prayer Books. According to legend (but no copy survives), he printed an edition of twenty-four copies of a small 24mo Bible on paper brought from the Far East, as early as 1842. In fact the paper was probably one made at Hanley for the pottery trade, and in 1875, when the idea was revived, Thomas Brittain and Sons of Hanley, as well as Wolvercote, were asked to supply what was now called 'Oxford India Paper'. It was a great success, and an increasing number of Oxford books, especially Bibles and Prayer Books, were printed on thinner paper.

In 1855 Combe had bought the freehold of the old Wolvercote paper-mill. The mill itself was of medieval origin, but paper was made there at least by 1674, when Plot records its existence. It was, apparently, George Edwards, the engraver, who had something to do with improvements in the mill, and in 1694 paper from it was first supplied for printing at the Press, and often thereafter. According to Holman Hunt, Combe decided to buy the mill because he was afraid that the Press might be deprived of the Bible privilege, and that the small saving of owning a paper-mill might count for much in a more sharply competitive market.

It may, on the other hand, have been because he liked it that Combe really decided to buy the mill and its surroundings. Holman Hunt and he would go for long walks in the neighbourhood. Whatever the reason, Combe managed it with his customary skill, and shortly before his death in 1872 sold it to the University. It may have been on this occasion that he was photographed with Bartholomew Price, Secretary to the Delegates, by J. H. Stacy, the Mill Manager.

208. Edward Hyde, Lord Clarendon. *Clarendon's History and his life, written by himself.* New edition from the original MSS. Oxford, At the Clarendon Press, 1843.

209. H. G. Liddell and R. Scott. *A Greek and English Lexicon, based on the work of Franz Passow*, 1843.

210. Charles Wordsworth. *Graecae Grammaticae rudimenta*, 1843.

211. Phineas Pett, ed. Virgil: *Opera.* Oxonii, e Typographeo Clarendoniano, 1795.

212. *Graecae grammaticae compendium*, 1819.

213. *Schemata geometrica*, 1806.

The success of the Press encouraged expansion in other directions. Clarendon's works had a special importance, since they were (now) the only works in which the University had perpetual copyright. The one-volume 'super royal 8vo' edition published in 1843 was one of the most attractive of mid nineteenth-century books printed at the Press; it remained in print until the 1950s.

Liddell and Scott, whose names are a byword for Greek lexicography in England, based their work on Passow's *Handwörterbuch der griechischen Sprache*, first published in 1830–1. As they worked, however, it became more and more their own. It was and has remained one of the pillars of Oxford's status in classical publishing.

It was Scott who saw to the correction and return of the specimen page, which still survives. The Delegates' order book records its progress: 3,000 copies were printed of the first edition, 6,000 of the second (1845) and third (1848); the fourth edition went up to 8,000 in 1854. An abridged version was equally successful.

Besides the upper end of the scholarly market, the Delegates began very slowly to tackle the market for school editions. Charles Wordsworth, Bishop of Brechin, produced his Greek grammar in 1844, and it too had a steady annual sale, rising from 5,000 in 1844 to 6,000 in 1853, reprinting pretty nearly every year. Earlier, the Press undertook the printing of a school Virgil, edited by Phineas Pett, who had produced a straight text of Caesar for the Delegates in 1780. For Westminster School, the Press printed a new edition of their standard Greek Grammar, the basically sixteenth-century *Graecae grammaticae compendium* (1819). Besides these Gaisford produced editions of several single plays by Euripides for Westminster, who also required the standard texts of Ovid and Aesop.

These were fairly conventional books. But in 1806 a rather less commonplace educational book was printed at the Press. *Schemata geometrica* has no text: it consists solely of figures from Euclid and others, which would have been demonstrated by the teacher. The publication of these books, like manuals of handwriting, was normally the business of specialists in copper-plate engraving, and it does not look as if this experiment at Oxford were a success.

THE ROYAL COMMISSION AND ITS EFFECT ON THE PRESS

The national movement for reform in the first half of the nineteenth century had a special focus at Oxford in the Tractarian movement. The religious questions asked by Keble and Newman were, however, echoed by other voices questioning the function of the University itself. In 1837 the Hebdomadal Board, perhaps provoked by a series of articles by Sir William Hamilton in the *Edinburgh Review* demanding state intervention, embarked on a revision of Laud's statutes. This did not prevent the appointment in 1850 of a Royal Commission to inquire into the state, discipline, studies, and revenues of the University. The Commissioners reported in 1852, and an Act of Parliament embodying their final recommendations was passed in 1854. The governing body of the University was reconstructed, non-collegiate students were admitted, fellowships and scholarships were thrown open, and the latter increased in value and number, new professorships were created, and the building of a science museum authorized.

The impact of this on the whole education system was considerable. In 1857 admission examinations in various centres were inaugurated, and with this went a demand for educational texts which had been vigorously advocated by Baden Powell (1796–1860), Savilian Professor of Geometry, one of the Commissioners appointed in 1850, and a strong supporter of 'the grand principle of comprehensive state education'.

Gradually these forces made themselves felt at the Press. They coincided with a reduction in the annual growth of Bible printing. The shrewd buying of the Bible societies prevented the privileged presses from combining to protect their prices; low prices put Bibles and Testaments within the reach of the poorest. Dry stereotyping and electrotyping were introduced in 1860 and 1863, but the technical expertise of Combe and his junior partner in the

Bible Press, Hall, could not compensate for this. Dividends to the Delegates and the other partners fell by a half. The only way out for the Delegates was to venture into the business of publishing themselves. The long association with the Parker family came to an end, and in May 1863 Alexander Macmillan (1818–92), a new and vigorous force in the London trade, was appointed publisher to the University: 'I hope it will turn out a good thing for them and for me', he wrote to his friend James Maclehose. 'They have great funds, and seem willing to employ them in useful and lucrative ways. They have a good many schemes for educational and other works, and want the guidance, as to business arrangements, of a publisher of experience. I hope I will not disappoint them.' [1]

THE CLARENDON PRESS SERIES

214. Richard Morris. Chaucer: *Prologue to the Canterbury Tales*, 1866.

215. G. W. Kitchin. Spenser: *The Faerie Queene*, Book 1, 1867.

216. Gustave Masson. *French Classics*, 1867.

217. W. Thomson & P. G. Tait. *A Treatise on Natural Philosophy*, 1868.

218. Mark Pattison. *Pope's Essay on Man*, 1870.

219. W. Stubbs. *Select Charters*, 1871.

220. W. W. Merry & Robinson Ellis. Homer: *Odyssey*, 1871.

221. Lewis Campbell & Evelyn Abbott. *Sophocles*, 1874.

It was on 12 June 1863 that the Delegates accepted a report from a committee which they had appointed to examine 'a proposal to publish educational works', and directed the same committee to put them into execution. The outcome was prompt. G. W. Kitchin, secretary to the committee and from 1866 the first full-time Secretary to the Delegates, produced his Spenser; other active editors in the English series were Richard Morris, one of the founders of the Early English Text Society, whose Chaucer was the first book in the series, and Mark Pattison, whose Pope was to omit 'all words, phrases, or passages unfit to be seen by ladies'. Abbott took charge of the Classical series, aided by the distinguished group of scholars from Benjamin Jowett's Balliol. Masson, modern languages master at Harrow, edited the French series single-handed. William Stubbs (1825–1901), Bishop of Oxford, set the medieval historian on a course charted by original documents followed at Oxford for two generations. An attempt to persuade Bryce, whose *Holy Roman Empire* achieved a European reputation in 1864, to write a textbook of German history failed. Finally, William Thomson, later Lord Kelvin, started the Natural Science series with a treatise on physics. Although the text was largely drafted by his coadjutor Peter Tait, the concept was Thomson's; the book was quickly translated into German by Thomson's friend Helmholtz.

Alexander Macmillan proved a generous supporter and vigorous publisher of the series, although it threatened to compete with his own books. In 1866 the whole series so far published was exhibited at the Great Exhibition in Paris; over the next thirty years, it expanded to cover the whole field of secondary education, and set a pattern which was imitated all over the world.

[1] C. L. Graves, *The Life and Letters of Alexander Macmillan* (1910), p. 205.

BARTHOLOMEW PRICE: THE GREAT EXPANSION

222. Bartholomew Price: a photograph by C. L. Dodgson (Lewis Carroll).

223. The Secretary's room, about 1886.

224. Bartholomew Price. *A treatise on infinitesimal calculus*, 1852–60.

225. Delegates' Order Book, 27 February 1868, 27 February 1873, and 20 June 1884.

After Laud, Fell, and Blackstone, Bartholomew Price (1818–98) was the fourth great man who may be claimed as architect of the Oxford University Press. A scholar of Pembroke College, he took a first-class degree in mathematics in 1840, becoming a fellow of his college in 1845. In the same year he became tutor and lecturer in mathematics. His first contact with the Press came with the publication of his *Treatise on infinitesimal calculus.* This magisterial work dealt with every branch of differential and integral calculus, and its application to algebra, geometry, and mechanics. It made Price's scholarly name; in 1852 he became a Fellow of the Royal Society, and next year Sedleian Professor of Natural Philosophy.

In 1861 Price, with his friend Henry Liddell (1811–98), Dean of Christ Church, and H. O. Coxe, Bodley's Librarian, became a Delegate of the Press. The new regime had its effect. First came the appointment of Macmillan, then the advance into educational publishing presaged by his appointment. The growth of the Delegates' business was immediate, and the need for a full-time executive staff soon made itself felt. In 1868 Price became Secretary to the Delegates, with far wider powers than Kitchin, and his great work began. He stimulated and curbed Macmillan's enthusiasm. The threat of competition with Macmillan's own thriving business was gradually removed as the Press's publishing assumed its own definite character.

In 1872 Combe died, and Price was sufficiently optimistic to persuade the Delegates to buy his eight shares (they had already bought the paper-mill at Wolvercote, and invested in a binding factory in London in 1870), and when in 1873 E. B. Gardner, the last independent keeper of the London warehouse, retired the Delegates bought his five shares as well. This substantial increase in his responsibilities no doubt suggested to Price the redrafting of his terms of employment. His business acumen and reputation grew together: he was on every major committee in the University, and a few words from him would settle the most complicated issues.

Price's task was strenuous, the more so when Benjamin Jowett, Master of Balliol, became Vice-Chancellor and with it chairman of the Delegates. In 1884 he asked to be allowed to resign, and the Delegates' minute records their uncertainty on how to replace so large a figure in their business (a photograph of the room in which he worked shows the simple style in which he conducted it). Jowett's appointee, Philip Lyttelton Gell, had his task delimited as 'to assist' Price, who as perpetual Delegate continued to have the largest say in the conduct of the Press's affairs. Price became Master of Pembroke College in 1891, and his activity in university affairs continued undiminished until his death on 29 December 1898. In the forty years of his association with the Press it had grown from a somnolent, self-contained attachment of a large printing-house to become the greatest academic publishing business in the world.

226. Lewis Carroll (C. L. Dodgson). *Alice's adventures in wonderland*, 1865.

One of Liddell's protégés at Christ Church was a young mathematician called Charles Dodgson (1832–98), who diverted his studies of plane geometry and formal logic with nonsense tales told to Liddell's daughter Alice. Written down and illustrated by Sir John Tenniel, then at the height of his career, *Alice in Wonderland* was printed at the Press in 1865, under the pseudonym Lewis Carroll. Not for the last time, the author was dissatisfied with the printing, and the printing was withdrawn: twenty copies at most survive. It must have been an embarrassment to Price; he was a friend of Dodgson's, who immortalized him in it (he was known as 'Bat' Price to his intimate friends):

> Twinkle, twinkle, little bat,
> How I wonder what you're at . . .

227. E. A. Freeman. *The history of the Norman conquest of England*, 1869–79.

Edward Augustus Freeman (1823–92) was already famous for his prodigious industry and outspoken comment on public affairs when the Press published his first great work on English history. It was the first major book to be published under the new regime, and it was followed by a series of massive works which drew heavily on the Press's resources, strained by the demands of buying up the Bible Press partners' shares. Together with Stubbs, whom he succeeded as Regius Professor of History in 1884, Freeman founded the modern history school at Oxford; his works set a standard for its academic study.

228. Benjamin Jowett. *The dialogues of Plato, translated into English, with analyses and introductions*, 1871.

An open scholar of Balliol College, Benjamin Jowett (1817–93) was so brilliant that he was elected a fellow while still an undergraduate. An enthusiastic teacher, he gave evidence to the Royal Commission supporting the poor scholar. Theology occupied much of his study, and his critical work on St. Paul led to suspicion of heresy, and his essay on the interpretation of scripture in *Essays and Reviews* (1860) made him one of the 'Septem contra Christum' as the authors were stigmatized. This famous episode in the liberalization of the Church of England did not prevent his election as Master of Balliol in 1870, where he was able to turn his passion for promoting the interests of young scholars to such effect that he made the college the great forcing-ground of intellectual ability. In the University, the civil service, and government, Balliol scholars came to have a dominant role.

The publication of his translation of Plato was instantly recognized as a major scholarly achievement, and (like Clarendon's *History*) perpetual copyright was claimed for it in the name of Balliol College. It was to dominate the teaching of Plato for a century after. In 1882, as Vice-Chancellor, he instituted an inquiry into the Press's unprofitable scholarly publishing and set on foot the publishing of plain texts for undergraduate (as opposed to school) use. By the time of his death he had become an institution:

> First come I. My name is Jowett.
> If it's knowledge, then I know it.
> If I don't, it isn't knowledge.
> I'm the Master of this College.

229. Sir James Clerk Maxwell. *A treatise on electricity and magnetism*, 1873.

Sir James Clerk Maxwell (1831–79) was educated at Edinburgh Academy and Cambridge, where he became first Professor of Experimental Physics in 1871. Building on Faraday's theory of 'fields of force' in electricity, he constructed a mathematical demonstration of electromagnetism which he published in the *Transactions of the Royal Society* in 1865. One of the consequences of this was the demonstration that electric waves travel at the speed of light, and that therefore light itself is an electromagnetic phenomenon. The full demonstration of this theory was given in the *Treatise on Electricity*, the Press's first (and perhaps most important) publication in modern science. In 1892 Heinrich Hertz, encouraged by Helmholtz, provided experimental proof of Maxwell's theory, and with it the solution of the problem of wireless telegraphy; a generation later, Maxwell's work formed the foundation of Einstein's theory of relativity. He was indeed 'the greatest theoretical physicist of the nineteenth century'.[1]

230. Sir William Anson: *The principles of the English law of contract*, 1879.

For thirty-three years Sir William Anson (1843–1914) was Warden of All Souls College. A Balliol scholar, he was elected to an All Souls fellowship in 1867, and was the first layman to become Warden. In 1898 he was briefly Vice-Chancellor of the University, but was then elected member of parliament for the University, and played an active part in the Education Act of 1902. But he is chiefly remembered for the work that grew from his Vinerian Readership in English Law, which Blackstone held before him. In spite of Blackstone's example, most books on English law before Anson were practical manuals. In studying the English law of contract, he set out for the first time its general principles, in a style of admirable lucidity, and in so doing broke down the old barriers between the practice and the academic study of law. It was an epoch-making work, which has passed through many editions, and has profoundly influenced both the teaching and practice of law in England and America.

231. F. J. Bell (trs.) and A. H. Garland (ed.). *Müller's certain variations in the vocal organs of the Passeres that have hitherto escaped notice*, 1878.

It was no less a figure than Charles Darwin who

[1] *Printing and the mind of man*, ed. John Carter and P. H. Muir (1967), p. 215.

recommended the Delegates to publish a translation of Müller's work on the vocal organs of the *Passeres*. An edition of 784 copies was duly printed, and published at 7*s*. 6*d*. As it was only eighty-two pages long, Price's intention had been to make it 5*s*., but he was dissuaded by Alexander Macmillan. Always optimistic ('If there are musicians who add physiological considerations to their studies they will certainly value such a book, or on the other hand physiologists who care about the musical result of voice organs'), even he urged the increase in price, asking 'How many people in each quarter are likely to buy such a book? Are they poor men to whom the difference of 5/- or 7/6 would be of importance?'

He was right to be sceptical. In the first year seven copies were sold, another in 1880, two more in 1881; after twenty-five years, the sales were twenty-one. It was a classic example of falling between two stools.

232. Frederick York Powell and Gudbrandt Vigfusson. *Corpus poeticum boreale*, 1881.

Frederick York Powell (1850–1904), Regius Professor of Modern History, was a polymath who published works of distinction in many fields but not that of modern history. His first work, a history of England to the Conquest (1876), was much praised; he was widely read in all the western languages from Icelandic to Portuguese, translated Omar Khayyám from the Persian, knew Maori and Romany; he invited Verlaine and Mallarmé to lecture at Oxford, and was reputed to know the boxing reports in the *Licensed Victuallers' Gazette* as well as the Kalevala or Beowulf. He was an active Delegate of the Press, an enthusiastic supporter of Price, and an ally of Ingram Bywater in the creation of the Oxford Classical Texts. (He insisted on the publication of Thomson's *Human Anatomy for Art Students* in 1897, delighted that 'the Delegates have published an improper book'.) It was he who said that a University consisted of a library and a press.

He is now chiefly remembered for his work with the Icelandic scholar Vigfusson in resurrecting and establishing the earliest Norse poetic texts. The *Corpus* was, however, more than this: Powell's essays made it effectively a history of the Icelandic and Norse people and their literature. His lively style of writing drew those who had been captivated by Dasent's translations to the academic study of the sources, which became, in the work of W. P. Ker, an inspiration to the founders of the school of English studies.

233. George Birkbeck Hill (ed.). *Boswell's Life of Johnson*, 1887.

The publication in six octavo volumes of a fully annotated text of Boswell's Life of Johnson was a new departure for the Press. George Birkbeck Hill (1835–1904) was for most of his life an invalid, who spent his leisure in exhaustive reading in eighteenth-century English literature. His proposal for an *editio maior* of Boswell was accepted in 1881 by the Delegates, through the influence of Jowett to whom, 'Johnsonianissimus', the work was eventually dedicated. Hill's long footnotes set a new standard for the scholarly edition of a modern English text, and his exhaustive knowledge of the whole world in which Johnson lived added a new dimension to Boswell's portrait. He continued his work with editions of Johnson's letters, the *Lives of the English Poets*, and the other contemporary lives of Johnson. Although his textual scholarship was inevitably less advanced, he laid the foundation for the standard edition of English authors, now embodied in the 'Oxford English Texts' series.

234. W. W. Skeat (ed.). *The complete works of Geoffrey Chaucer*, 1894–7.

Walter William Skeat (1835–1912) acquired his first knowledge of Anglo-Saxon at school, but read theology and mathematics at Cambridge, to which he returned in 1864 as a mathematical lecturer. He was, however, early involved in the Early English Text Society, for whom he edited his first text in 1865; in 1878 he became the first professor of Anglo-Saxon at Cambridge. He edited Piers Plowman, Chatterton, Ælfric's Lives of the Saints, and the Anglo-Saxon Gospels. His work for the *New English Dictionary* (see 246–8) produced his own *Etymological Dictionary*, published by the Press in 1879–82 and still in print; he also founded the English Dialect Society.

But perhaps the greatest of all his many contributions to the study of early English literature was his seven-volume annotated text of Chaucer. At last the greatest of pre-Shakespearian poets was given a proper critical text, with the apocrypha finally distinguished, and full explanatory notes; it provided a foundation not only for the study of Chaucer, but for the literature of his age. Many subsequent editors have built on his work, which is now supplanted by the edition of F. N. Robinson (1957). But his one-volume plain text of 1895 is still in print.

235. *The Holy Bible*, 1877.

The great Caxton exhibition of 1877, organized to commemorate the quatercentenary of the introduction of printing into England, was the occasion of one of the Press's most notable technical triumphs. A historical display of Bibles was one of the chief exhibits, and at the suggestion of Henry Stevens of Vermont, the famous bookseller, a Bible was printed and bound within twelve hours on the actual day on which the exhibition opened. Printing began at 2 a.m., and 100 sets of sheets were dispatched on the 9 a.m. train to London. They were bound in morocco, lettered and armed with the arms of the University in gold, at the Press Bindery, and a parcel of ten copies delivered to the exhibition at the South Kensington Museum before 2 p.m. when Mr. Gladstone, the Prime Minister, formally opened it. In his speech, he specially mentioned this fact as 'the climax and consummation of printing'.

It was also the swan song of the Old Bible Press. In 1884 E. Pickard Hall was superannuated, and the last shares were acquired by the Delegates. Led by Jowett, they felt that the new demands of the Press demanded changes which could only be achieved if they had absolute control of the means of production.

HORACE HART: THE REDISCOVERY OF THE FELL TYPES

236. Horace Hart: a photograph.

237. R. Ellis (ed.). *Catulli opera*, 1867.

238. C. H. O. Daniel. *A garland for Rachel*, 1881.

239. Robert Bridges (ed.). *The Yattendon Hymnal*, 1899.

240. Horace Hart. *Notes on a century of typography at the University Press, Oxford 1693–1794*, 1900.

241. The Press at the end of the nineteenth century: photographs.

In 1882 Horace Hart (1840–1916), then manager of the London printing-works of William Clowes & Sons, was appointed to the new position of Controller of the Press. He had to amalgamate the Learned and Bible Presses, still run as two separate businesses, employing type of different heights, and now antiquated presses. He standardized the type height, built a new extension to the machine-room, bought new presses and new matrices for learned works (mainly from Germany, since British typefounders refused to risk their sales of type), and installed machinery for the new processes of photo-lithography and collotype.

It was in 1893 that, probably prompted by York Powell, Hart first recast the Fell types. They had not been entirely disused. In 1867 Robinson Ellis, the foremost Oxford Latin scholar, drew attention to them (probably without knowing what they were) in his Clarendon Press series Catullus. Charles Daniel (1836–1919), fellow and later Provost of Worcester College, who printed antiquarian tracts at his private press, had a better idea, and obtained a fount of the Small Pica Roman and Italic in 1876, to reprint, appropriately, a Royalist Oxford tract.

In 1881 Daniel used the same type to print *A Garland for Rachel*, a set of seventeen poems addressed by various friends, among them C. L. Dodgson, to his daughter on her birthday. Another contributor was Robert Bridges (1844–1930), the future Poet Laureate, who had just retired to live not far from Oxford, at Yattendon in Berkshire. Bridges had already taken an interest in the typography of his published verse. He now seized on the recast Fell types, and used them to splendid effect in *The Yattendon Hymns*, a collection of hymns (some by Bridges), with the tunes in Walpergen's music type.

This example stimulated the revival of the use

of the Fell types by the Press itself. It also led Horace Hart to attempt a historical survey of the material which he now had laboriously looked out and put in good order. *Notes on a Century of Typography* was the result of seven years' work: it was itself a notable example of the use of the Fell types, and it set the seal on the restoration of Fell's legacy.

The earliest surviving photographs of the Press show what it was like in Hart's time: The quadrangle round which it was built was a garden (of which only one magnificent beech tree survives); inside, the new machinery can be seen in the various departments of the Press.

THE LONDON BUSINESS AND THE REVISED VERSION

242. Henry Frowde: a photograph.

243. *The Holy Bible, being the version set forth* A.D. 1611 *compared with the most ancient authorities and revised*, 1881, New Testament.

244. W. J. Craig (ed.). *The complete works of Shakespeare*, 1894.

245. *The Holy Bible*, 1894.

When Gardner retired, Henry Frowde (1841–1927), then 23, was appointed manager of the London warehouse. Business quickly grew. Frowde moved and enlarged the bindery, and expanded the premises at 7 Paternoster Row: 'Amen Corner' became more and more widely known. In 1881 Alexander Macmillan, no longer needed, retired and was rewarded with an honorary degree.

In 1870 the Convocation of Canterbury had entrusted the revision of the Authorized Version, the King James Bible, to a committee led by F. J. A. Hort, B. F. Westcott, and J. B. Lightfoot, all at one time professors of divinity at Cambridge. In 1873 the Universities of Oxford and Cambridge agreed to publish the text, contributing £20,000 to the expenses in exchange for exclusive copyright. Work proceeded fast: soon the new text was in proof, which was read and corrected with the most minute care. The interest generated by this 'culminating phase in the Victorian cult of the Bible' (R. C. K. Ensor) was immense: on the day that the New Testament was published, 17 May 1881, one million copies were sold. People were seen reading it in the street, and the New York publishers Appleton sent representatives on the steamer carrying stock for New York, who set up and stereotyped the entire text, so that two days after it arrived American printed and bound copies were on sale. The 22 May *Chicago Times* printed the entire text of the Gospels, Acts, and Epistle to the Romans, cabled from New York at a cost of $10,000.

Hundreds of thousands of copies were printed and reprinted in many formats; in the end, demand diminished (and left the Press with over-stocks), but not before it had built up the London business to new heights. Frowde capitalized ably on this in the harder days of the 1890s. He set on foot the 'Oxford Classics' series, for which the one-volume edition of Shakespeare with glossary of W. J. Craig (1843–1906) was the model. Another landmark came in 1894 with the publication of the 'Long primer 8vo Bible', the first to be published with comparative references in a narrow central column between the text columns. Bibles with 'centre refs.' became a new staple of the business.

THE NEW ENGLISH DICTIONARY

246. Sir James Murray and his staff: a photograph.

247. Sir James Murray, Henry Bradley, William Craigie, and C. T. Onions: *The New English Dictionary*. 1884–1928; a corrected proof.

248. *The Oxford English Dictionary*, Compact Edition, 1971.

249. *The Concise Oxford Dictionary*. 6th edition, by John Sykes, 1976.

The origins of the *New English Dictionary* can be traced back to 1857 when it was first proposed to members of the Philological Society by Richard Chenevix Trench, Dean of Westminster. The leading figure in the early discussions of its future was Frederick Furnivall, founder of the Early English Text Society. It was he who recruited James Murray (1837–1915), a Scottish bank clerk become master at Mill Hill School. In 1877 Furnivall finally approached the Press, and after some discussion—Max Müller gave his opinion on etymologies, and Murray's initial reluctance had to be overcome—an agreement was signed on 1 March 1879. The target was 7,000 pages in ten years. But allowances of length and time grew together. In January 1884 the first fascicle appeared, 352 pages long and covering A–Ant. That summer Murray moved to Oxford, and established the 'Scriptorium' in the Banbury Road, where he (and it) remained for the rest of his life.

In 1886 Henry Bradley was appointed by Gell to assist Murray, who was at first suspicious but gradually accepted him as an ally in his fluctuating relations with the Press. By 1896 Bywater discovered that A–F, now completed, presaged a total length of 12,800 pages: expenditure was £50,000 and revenue only £15,000 so far. There was a crisis: Murray and Bradley were rationed to a 6 : 1 ratio against Webster's Dictionary, and given another assistant, William Craigie. Slowly the work crept on: F–K complete in two volumes came out in 1901; Craigie finished R in 1910. Murray was knighted in 1908, but his hopes of seeing the great work finished on his eightieth birthday were not fulfilled: he died with letter T just complete. C. T. Onions joined the staff, who saw the last letters of the alphabet finished. On 5 January 1928 the last volume appeared: the definition and history of the English language was complete in 414,825 head-words.

No other single factor has assured the position of English as the twentieth-century lingua franca. Already by 1900 a Chinaman in Singapore advertised that he could teach English 'up to the letter G'. Long before it was complete, it was used as a quarry by the Fowler brothers to produce the *Concise* (1911) and *Pocket* (1925) *Oxford Dictionaries*. The new edition of the *Concise Oxford Dictionary*, published in 1976, is the latest in the battery of Oxford dictionaries at all lengths and levels which have grown from the great *N.E.D.*

THE 'OXFORD' STYLE

250. [Horace Hart.] *Rules for compositors and readers*, 1893.

251. H. W. Fowler. *Modern English usage*, 1927.

A preoccupation with standardized orthography can be traced in Oxford printing to Fell's eccentric but uniform spellings in his Bible (see 93), which provoked an interesting attack, *Friendly advice to the correctour of the English press at Oxford* (1682). Aldrich's letter to Sprat in 1700 (see 112) reflects the positively modern interest which he and Wallis took in the subject. It was part of Hart's reorganization of the Press to draw up rules for compositors and the Press's readers, some of whom, like J. C. Pembrey, a reader for 70 years, who corrected Max Müller's Sanskrit even though he knew no word of the language, had already a formidable reputation in the learned world. Hart's *Rules*, originally a pocket pamphlet of twenty-four pages, is now in its 38th edition; its bulk increased by ten times, it is, with Collins's *Authors and Printers Dictionary* (also published by the Press), the accepted authority on punctuation, italicization, word-division, capitalization, and difficult or controversial spellings or usage.

H. W. and F. G. Fowler first appeared on the Press's list as translators of Lucian in 1905. Their next project was for 'a sort of English composition manual, from the negative point of view, for journalists and amateur writers'. This grew into *The King's English* (1907), whose success showed the Fowlers' gift for apt and concise definition and (more than that) uncanny sense for the ambiguities and obscurities that vexed the majority of contemporary writers and speakers. The Fowlers moved on to the dictionaries, without deserting their first interest, and *Modern English Usage* (1927) canonized an authority as individual as firmly expressed.

CHARLES CANNAN: THE MAKING OF THE MODERN PRESS

252. Charles Cannan: a photograph.

253. Oxford Classical Texts: *Aristotelis Ethica Nicomachea. Recognovit brevique adnotatione critica instruxit I. Bywater*, 1894.

254. Oxford English Texts: *The poetical works of John Milton. Edited after the original texts by H. C. Beeching*, 1900.

255. *The Oxford Book of English Verse*, A.D. 1250–1900, *chosen and edited by Sir Arthur Quiller-Couch*, 1900.

256. C. R. L. Fletcher and Rudyard Kipling. *A school history of England*, 1911.

257. F. H. Bradley. *Essays on truth and reality*, 1914.

Charles Cannan (1858–1919) was a scholar of Corpus Christi College, and became fellow and dean of Trinity in 1884. He was a lively and unorthodox teacher, and an equally original disciplinarian, who felt that he had failed if he had to punish an undergraduate. In 1895 he became a Delegate of the Press; he quickly gained the confidence of his colleagues, as the Secretary, Gell, never had, and succeeded him in 1898. In the next twenty years he so enlarged the organization that Price had created as to make it the largest publishing business in the world. He put together the tradition of popular scholarship at Oxford with the ever-growing London distributive success. Temperamentally unself-assertive and conservative, his dominant personality set its mark on a growth which seemed to him natural. He took decisions easily and without fuss, and trained his subordinates to do so too. His judgement, both of men and books, was so good that the Delegates became his coadjutors rather than directors.

The unique Oxford series were in the main his work. The Oxford Classical Texts, planned by Jowett, were modelled on Bywater's edition of Aristotle's *Ethics*, which became the archetype for the series. (The copy illustrated is that used as an undergraduate by Sir Ernest Barker, whose translation of Aristotle's *Politics*, published by the Press in 1946, is still widely used.) No fewer than ten more O.C.T.s were issued in 1900, the first year, and by 1911, when Bywater's great edition of Aristotle's *Poetics*, then as now and since the Middle Ages a text of special importance at Oxford, came out, there were seventy volumes in print.

The same formula was extended to the classics of English literature, and Birkbeck Hill's Boswell was followed by a whole series of scholarly texts; Beeching's Milton was the first of the flourishing series of Oxford English Texts. They also represented a new interest in the University in the academic study of modern English. Another aspect was represented by the first and still the most famous of the Press's deviation from scholarship towards popular publishing, the *Oxford Book of English Verse*. It was edited by Sir Arthur Quiller-Couch (1863–1944), one of Cannan's pupils and already a successful novelist, ballad-writer, and journalist. The idea may have stemmed from York Powell, but the form of Quiller-Couch's selection indicates that Cannan had a hand in it. It was based on two principles: first, that the *Golden Treasury*, its predecessor as the most popular anthology of English poetry, was narrow in the period covered (three and a half centuries) and extent (391 pages). Oxford India paper could provide the answer to the latter problem. The *Oxford Book of English Verse* was 1,168 pages long, and 'A.D. 1250–1900' after the title witnessed Quiller-Couch's successful introduction of the general reading public not only to old and new favourites but also to the masterpieces of early English poetry.

Cannan was not enthusiastic about the proposal from C. R. L. Fletcher (1857–1934), a Delegate since 1905, for a new school history of England written by himself. But he was disarmed when Fletcher introduced Rudyard Kipling as his collaborator. Together they produced a book which, as frankly propagandist as *Our Island Story*, was better history, which Kipling's twenty-three poems (including 'Big Steamers') made more memorable. 'What is it that has tempted Mr K. to leave his last and prostitute his genius to this petty political balderdash?' asked the *Weekly Times and Echo*, while the *Church Family Newspaper* hailed it as 'the chief literary event of Coronation Year'.

Long a best-seller, it survived for over forty years, a remarkable life-span for a school text.

F. H. Bradley (1846–1924), fellow of Merton College, disabled by chronic ill health, seldom left Oxford; over fifty years, unimpeded by teaching, he produced a series of books and articles which revolutionized English philosophy. *Ethical Studies* (1876), *The Principles of Logic* (1883), and *Appearance and Reality, a Metaphysical Essay* (1893) covered the main branches of philosophy, and *Essays on Truth and Reality*, published in the year in which he received the Order of Merit, was a distillation of his views. After a century of systematization in philosophy, personified by Mill, Comte, and Hegel, Bradley used Hegel's own ideas, particularly his monistic view of the universe, to establish the dominance of the individual mind: for Hegel's 'objective logic', he advanced the claims of subjective thought and sensation which have preoccupied the philosophy of this century. His influence, all-pervasive, can only be compared to Hume's.

THE EXPANSION OF THE LONDON BUSINESS
SIR HUMPHREY MILFORD

258. The young Humphrey Milford: a photograph.

259. *The English Hymnal*, 1906.

The World's Classics:

260. No. 1. Charlotte Brontë. *Jane Eyre*, 1901.

261. No. 484. Anthony Trollope. *The Way We Live Now*, 1941.

262. No. 542. Flora Thompson. *Lark Rise to Candleford*, 1954.

263. *Poems of Gerard Manley Hopkins*. Edited by Robert Bridges, 1918.

264. Oxford University Press General Catalogue, 1916.

By 1900 the Bound Book Business had grown into a complete publishing office. Under Frowde it had grown and expanded, in space (the offices were continually enlarged), and in the number and variety of books now published under the Oxford University Press imprint. It was said that only Cannan knew the difference between the Oxford University Press and the Clarendon Press, and nobody dared ask him what it was. In 1906 Frowde, the architect of this growth, was joined by Humphrey Milford (1877–1952), who was to succeed him in 1913. He had spent six years under Cannan, and although Cannan did not believe in teaching staff their business (a first-rate mind should be able to decide that), Milford and the Assistant Secretary, Cannan's eventual successor, R. W. Chapman, were thoroughly imbued with his methods. As with Cannan, a certain inarticulacy in Milford did not conceal the force of his character. He soon embarked on children's books, medical, and other educational books. The distinction between Oxford and London became harder and harder to draw.

In the year that Milford joined, two important additions were made to the list. The first of these was the *English Hymnal*. Formed in the reaction against the monotony of the Victorian favourite *Hymns Ancient and Modern*, it was, according to the preface, 'a collection of the best hymns in the English language, and is offered as a humble companion to the Book of Common Prayer'. Its editor, Percy Dearmer, and his coadjutors (notably Athelstan Riley and T. A. Lacey), had a fine sense not only for the history of English hymnody but also for simple, lively, singable English (many hymns came from the *Yattendon Hymnal*). The other notable innovation was the quality of the music edited by the young Ralph Vaughan Williams. His introductory essay gives the essence of his feeling for the Englishness of English music, which was echoed in his own beautiful settings.

The other event of 1906 was the acquisition of the World's Classics series from Grant Richards. Several pocket reprint series began in the first decade of the century, of which Richards's was one of the first. He began with *Jane Eyre*, and completed sixty-six volumes in the series before his financial difficulties obliged him to sell it. Oxford began with Anne Brontë and *The Tenant of Wildfell Hall*; since then the list has grown to 620 volumes. The smallest and most attractive of pocket editions, the World's Classics pioneered the revival of forgotten masterpieces and the introduction of foreign classics, notably Tolstoy's works, into English. One of its greatest triumphs was the revival of Trollope, under the inspiration of Michael Sadleir. *The Way We Live Now*, the longest and in some ways the greatest of all Trollope's novels, shows how elegantly a long text could be compressed into a small format. *Lark Rise to Candleford*, a more recent classic of a different side of Victorian life, first published by the Press in 1939–45, is another triumph in the same genre.

Gerard Manley Hopkins was the first major poet whose works were first published by the Press. They were edited after Hopkins's death by Robert Bridges, who had rightly gauged the moment. Hopkins's verbal rhythms brought a new freedom to English poetry. It was also a milestone in the progress of Oxford publishing, which had not hitherto concerned itself with new literary works. Hopkins was followed by Bridges himself, and by the now flourishing Oxford poetry list.

The final co-ordination of all the different strands of Oxford publishing and printing, the Sheldonian Theatre, the Clarendon Press, the Bible and Learned Presses, the Warehouses at Oxford and London, the Bound Book Business, the many parts succeeding and overlapping each other, now known to the world as the Oxford University Press, was achieved in the first *General Catalogue*, issued in November 1916. This was finally put in order by May Cannan, conscripted to the Press by her father to replace those away at the War. Its 576 pages began with the *Oxford University Roll of Service* 1914–16 and ended with the device of the second Oxford Press; the contents ranged from the notable series of pamphlets by Oxford historians examining the causes and the Allied case for the War to Uri's catalogue of the Bodleian oriental manuscripts, still in print after 128 years. It was a monument to the size and longevity of the Oxford Press.

RECENT FINE PRINTING

The *Testament of Beauty* [265] by Robert Bridges was a best-seller when it appeared, in the poet's eighty-fifth year, in 1929. It was published in two forms, an ordinary and a limited edition. The latter, a large quarto, was the first major use of a new large size of Stanley Morison's Bembo type, perhaps the most beautiful of his historic revivals.

Bruce Rogers went further back to Nicolas Jenson for the inspiration of the Centaur type in which the great lectern *Bible* [266], designed by him for the Press and printed at Oxford in 1935, was set. It is the largest and noblest of all the Bibles produced by the Press since 1675.

A slightly smaller but likewise typographically distinguished *Bible* [267] was printed for the Coronation of Queen Elizabeth II in 1953. A special limited edition of twenty-five copies on pre-War Oxford India paper was printed, and bound by hand. Fine bindings on Bibles, Prayer Books, and other works are a regular part of the Press's work. On one of these the Queen made the Coronation Oath.

The *New English Bible* dominated the English Bible market in recent times as the Revised Version did in 1881. The Vest Pocket Edition of the *New Testament* [268] was printed at Oxford in 1966, using a small but extremely legible type designed for it by Harry Carter, who combines the extreme manual dexterity required for cutting punches with a legendary knowledge of typographic history, recently evinced in his *History of the Oxford University Press*, whose archivist he also is.

Learned work still makes heavy demands on the printer, as it did in the seventeenth century. Exotic type is still in demand for oriental texts. One of the Press's most beautiful founts is the Tibetan type, acquired in 1884, and used recently for this experimental setting [269] of *Vishnaya Texts* (1952).

The text of the Greek New Testament, based on a vast number of manuscripts, has exercised compositors as well as editors from Fell and Mill to the present. The specimen page (1964) for a modern critical text [270] shows the full complexity which it now requires.

Perhaps no task is so difficult as the reproduction in typographic terms of an author's manuscript. T. S. Eliot's 'He do the police in several voices' from *The Waste Land: a facsimile and transcript* by Valerie Eliot, printed for Faber and Faber in 1971 [271], shows the original typescript, with comments and corrections by Ezra Pound and Vivien Eliot written in, over, up and down, and beside the text, requiring a patchwork of rules and different weights, and even a second colour.

Pictorial printing has been an increasing part of the printing business. *The Great Tournament Roll of Westminster* (1968) [272] shows the full elaboration of colour-printing required for the reproduction of medieval illumination.

In plain black and white, the facsimiles of *John Constable's Sketch-books of* 1813 *and* 1814 edited by Graham Reynolds and printed for Her Majesty's Stationery Office in 1973 [273], show with what accuracy fine-screen offset lithography can reproduce the soft lines of Constable's pencil.

Elegant typography has also been one of the strengths of the Press. *The Love Poems of John Donne* (1923) [274] met the exacting standard set by Sir Francis Meynell for the Nonesuch Press.

The simplicity of John Clare's *The Shepherd's Calendar* (1964) [275] sets off David Gentleman's vivid wood-cuts, subtly printed in a 'broken black', the darkest of brown ink, to give a sharper contrast with the text.

Finally, *Methods of Book Design* (1956) by Hugh Williamson (who learned the art at the Press) [276] is at once a classic manual of typography and a perfect example of its practice.

THE AMERICAN BRANCH

277. Photograph of Abraham Lincoln, 1861.

278. *The Book of Common Prayer*, 1867.

279. C. I. Scofield (ed.). *The Holy Bible. With introductions, annotations, subject chain references, and such word changes in the text as will help the reader*, 1909.

280. Samuel Eliot Morison & Henry Steele Commager. *The growth of the American republic*, 1930.

281. Samuel Eliot Morison. *The Oxford history of the American people*, 1965.

282. F. O. Matthiessen. *American Renaissance*, 1941.

283. Leo Marx. *The machine in the garden*, 1964.

284. Edmund Wilson. *Patriotic gore*, 1965.

285. Aldo Leopold. *A Sand County almanac*, 1966.

286. Wassily Leontief. *The structure of the American economy*, 1951.

287. Richard Ellmann (ed.). *The new Oxford book of American verse*, 1976.

288. Frederic W. Goudy. *The capitals from the Trajan column at Rome*, 1936.

The sale of Oxford books, and Bibles in particular, did not cease with the War of Independence: indeed, the first English Bibles printed on the American continent were not a commercial success; not until Isaiah Thomas's fine folio (1791) did America have a Bible that could be compared with those still imported from England. Oxford Bibles, directly or through the British and Foreign Bible Society, poured into the U.S.A. in the first half of the nineteenth century. One of them found its way to Illinois, an event still fresh in the mind of Abraham Lincoln when he inscribed this photograph: *For Mrs. Lucy G. Speed, from whose pious hand I accepted the present of an Oxford Bible twenty years ago. Washington D.C. October* 3, 1861. *A. Lincoln.*

In 1867 the Oxford Press printed its first *Book of Common Prayer* for the U.S. Episcopal Church, and by the end of the century the volume of business dictated the establishment of a branch of the Press in New York. On 3 June 1896 a meeting was held, attended by Price, Sir William Markby, Gell, and Frowde, with the Press's solicitor, at which it was decided to employ John Armstrong of Thomas Nelson (through whom the Press's books had hitherto been distributed) as manager, and to rent premises at 91 Fifth Avenue. The business grew and prospered. In 1909 the publication of the Scofield Reference Bible, a memorable work of biblical scholarship by the Revd. C. I. Scofield, created a sensation like that which attended the publication of the Revised Version.

In 1930 the Oxford University Press, New York, took an important step with the publication of Morison and Commager's *Growth of the American Republic.* Now in its sixth edition, this major textbook has formed the vision of their country for two generations of students. Admiral Morison's distinguished list of publications was crowned in 1965 with the *Oxford History of the American People.* Literature, as well as history, came to the Press's list, and F. O. Matthiessen's *American Renaissance*, a picture of expression in the age of Whitman and Emerson, has had an influential part in forming critical opinion. Marx's *Machine in the Garden*, a study of the impact of the machine age on a pastoral society in the nineteenth century, Edmund Wilson's *Patriotic Gore*, that famous evocation of the literature of the Civil War, and Aldo Leopold's *Sand County Almanac*, reflect different aspects of the history, society, and landscape of the nation, topics which have come to take an increasing part of the New York list.

Recently, Wassily Leontief's economic studies (for which he was awarded the Nobel Prize) have brought the Press distinction in a new field, and Richard Ellmann's *New Oxford Book of American Verse* (following Matthiessen's earlier selection) has provided a classic selection of the poetic line that runs from Anne Bradstreet to Leroi Jones.

Finally, the Oxford University Press in New York has shared the enthusiasm for fine typography and book design which has marked the work of the Press at Oxford itself. In 1936 it published the monograph on the Trajan Column by Frederic Goudy, the masterpiece and summation of a lifetime of work by that distinguished and prolific lettering artist, whose work has been the subject of a massive modern revival.

OTHER BRANCHES OVERSEAS

After the successful establishment of the 'Oxford University Press American Branch' similar branches were quickly opened in other parts of the English-speaking world.

The first was in Canada, where S. B. Gundy opened business at the 'Clarendon Building' [289] at 25 Richmond Street West, Toronto, in 1904. One of its early successes was another hymnal, *The Book of Common Praise* [290]; the stocks required in 1909 when it was published obliged Mr. Gundy 'to overflow into a neighbouring barber shop'. Still at Toronto but in new offices, the Press has since built up a notable list of Canadian literature, including Norah Story's *Oxford Companion to Canadian History and Literature* (1967) [291], which won the Governor-General's award.

Next came Australia in 1908. E. R. Bartholomew had visited Australia for the Press regularly before the offices in Cathedral Buildings, Melbourne, were taken. They too have been replaced by specially built offices [292], and in addition to British books published by the Press and other firms, the branch has now become vigorously involved with Australian academic writing. Uniquely, it has extended the Oxford lexicographic tradition to the most vigorous and versatile offshoots of the English language with the *Australian Pocket Oxford Dictionary* (ed. Grahame Johnston, 1976) [293].

In India, the Press quickly spread from its main base in Bombay (the warehouse a separate building adjoining the publishing offices) to Madras and Calcutta. The architect of this growth from 1912 was E. V. Rieu, later famous for his Penguin translation of Homer. With the aid of local staff (with whom he is seen in an early photograph) [294], Rieu early established a wide pattern of publishing, which includes school textbooks and even a series of atlases in the main languages and scripts, the classic texts of the history of the sub-continent, some fine colour-printed natural history books, the pick of Indian academic writing, and one classic, Jim Corbett's *Man Eaters of the Kumaon* [295], first printed in India in 1940, and many times in Britain from 1944 on. Rieu's successor, Geoffrey Cumberlege, subsequently became London Publisher, inaugurating a tradition by which the Indian branch became the training-ground for the management of the Press in Britain.

Since then branches have been opened at various times in Cape Town, Shanghai, Copenhagen, Paris, Leipzig, Wellington, Singapore, Karachi, Tokyo, Ibadan, Jakarta, Nairobi, Lusaka, Hong Kong, Kuala Lumpur, Addis Ababa, and Dacca. In Africa local publishing has included new studies of contemporary poetry, such as Jonathan Kariara and Ellen Kitonga's *Introduction to East African Poetry* (1976) [296], and records of recent archaeological exploration, such as Thurston Shaw's *Unearthing Igbo-Ikwu* (1977) [297]. The Far Eastern region, based on Kuala Lumpur, has built up a primacy in educational books in Malaysia and Hong Kong, and has liberally fostered the rapidly growing demand for the teaching of English as a second language all over the Far East. Japan has proved particularly enthusiastic, and the series of *Oxford Junior Workbooks* [298], recently published by Oxford University Press Kabushiki Kaisha, is amplified by a series of tape-cassettes. Besides this, there is the 'Oxford in Asia' series of reprints of the classic works of history and travel, of which Fanny Parks's *Wanderings of a Pilgrim in Search of the Picturesque* [299], originally published in 1850 and reprinted with an introduction and notes by Esther Chawner in 1975, is an example.

PUBLISHING IN MODERN TIMES

The last fifty years have seen growth in almost all the areas in which the Press has been active in the past. Classical texts and history have included M. Rostovtzeff's *Social and Economic History of the Roman Empire* (1927) [300]; Cyril Bailey's three-volume edition of Lucretius *De Rerum Natura* (1947), the sequel to his Oxford Classical Text (1900) [301]; A. W. Gomme's *Historical Commentary on Thucydides* (1944–56) [302], another lifetime's work; Sir W. D. Ross finally completed the Oxford translation of Aristotle, one of Cannan's great projects, in 1952.

In the sciences, the International Series of Monographs on Physics, founded in 1931 when refugees from Europe brought some brilliant scientists to the Oxford list, has included P. A. M. Dirac's *The Principles of Quantum Mechanics* [303]; other notable books number Cyril Hinshelwood's *Kinetics* (1926) [304], and J. Z. Young's *Introduction to the Study of Man* [305]. The Oxford Medical Series has also produced a series of distinguished clinical works. Oleg Polunin's series of botanical manuals, beginning with *Flowers of Europe: a field guide* [306], are both scholarly and immensely popular; their illustrations have set a new standard for the genre, an Oxford interest since the days of Morison (see 83).

In the philosophy list is R. G. Collingwood's original *Essay on Philosophical Method* (1933) [307], and the work of John Austin and Karl Popper; while in history the Oxford History of England has produced highly original work, notably R. C. K. Ensor's 1870–1914 volume (1936). The towering presence of Arnold Toynbee's *A Study of History* [308], published in ten volumes between 1934 and 1954, has stood out from the Oxford list for over forty years.

Oxford reference books have grown and multiplied. Sir Paul Harvey's *Companion to English Literature* (1932) [309] and the *Oxford Dictionary of Quotations* (1941) [310] are among the most outstanding. Books for educational purposes of all sorts are legion: H. A. Treble and K. M. King's *Everyday Life in Ancient Rome* (1930) [311] inaugurated a new genre, while the *Oxford Geography Project* (1974–5) [312] is a more recent and well-designed innovation.

Music has been strong since the inception of the Music Department under Hubert Foss in 1923. D. F. Tovey's *Essays in Musical Analysis* (1935–44) [313] and Percy Scholes's *Companion to Music* (1938) [314] are among its successes, which also number an increasing amount of new music. In the arts, F. Saxl and R. Wittkower's folio *British Art and the Mediterranean* (1948) [315] was an inspiration to those deprived of Greece and Italy for nearly ten years, and Johannes Wilde's *Art from Bellini to Titian* (1975) [316] is a monument of recent art history.

Children's books have become a larger and more significant part of the Press list, with a world reputation for good quality. Besides stories, non-fiction, and picture-books, poetry for children has been a speciality, evinced by the popularity of anthologies such as *All Day Long* [317], edited by Pamela Whitlock and with Joan Hassall's beautiful wood-engraved illustrations.

Children's games, folk-lore, nursery rhymes, and legends are another dimension of the juvenile world, reflected in the pioneering work of Iona and Peter Opie. Their *Lore and Language of School-Children* (1959) [318] has become the classic work on the subject.

Original works of literature were not included in the Press's publications until this century, but poets and playwrights writing in English from all over the world are now represented in a list which includes Christopher Fry's *The Lady's Not for Burning* (1950) [319], Edward Brathwaite's *Islands* (1969) [320], Peter Porter's *The Last of England* (1970) [321], Wole Soyinka's *Collected Plays* (1973) [322], and Athol Fugard's *Statements* (1974) [323], which includes 'Sizwe Bansi is Dead'.

English as a second language for the many countries where it has become the lingua franca is the fastest growing of all the different sides of the Press's business. A. S. Hornby's *Oxford Advanced Dictionary of Current English* [324], now in its third edition (1974), sells by the hundred thousand to serious students of English in every continent.

EPHEMERA

Visitors to the Press from its early days were offered a 'keepsake', a sheet of paper with their name and the date within an ornamental border printed on it; they were allowed to pull the press themselves on these occasions. Keepsakes are still produced for distinguished visitors, who are usually content to watch them printed [325, 326].

A different form of printing was required for the brief visit of Mr. and Mrs. Theodore Roosevelt on 7 June 1910 [327]. The Press's reception was planned down to the last minute, and the details circulated to all members.

The Press also prints the weekly *Oxford University Gazette* [328], the official journal of the University, flysheets announcing University business of all sorts, and examination papers not only for the University but for educational authorities all over the world, to whom learned accuracy and an unbroken record of security are important [329].

Special occasions demand special printing. The Coronation of Queen Elizabeth II was signalized by the printing of *The Form and Order of Service* [330] at Westminster Abbey on 2 June 1953, and the Queen's Silver Jubilee commemorated with a specially bound Bible [331].

EPILOGUE

On 12 October 1967, the day after his death, Stanley Morison's *John Fell: the University Press and the 'Fell' Types* [332] was published. He had been over forty years writing the book, which was set by hand in Fell's types and printed directly from them on part rag paper. It is probably the last book on this scale in which the Fell types will be used throughout for the actual printing, and it marks an epoch in the Press's life. Fell's legacy of types, the continuation of Laud's 'legacy' of the Press itself, has borne a fruit even greater than they intended. It is a foundation on which the Oxford University Press will build in the centuries to come.

APPENDIX: THE OXFORD ALMANACKS

The printing and sale of almanacs was one of the most lucrative of the privileges of the Stationers' Company that Fell hoped to invade in 1672. So with Aesop, Lily's Grammar, and the other school books, the partners printed two almanacs for 1673, a broadsheet and a pocket book. Both went the same way as the school books: in the composition with the Stationers, they were bought up and destroyed; a single copy of the sheet and two of the book almanac survive. But no obstruction was offered to a third form of almanac, a fine pictorial engraved calendar which by reason of its price would not compete with the main trade. A rolling-press was part of Fell's plans for the 'imprimerie', and an artist was at hand in Robert Streeter, who had just completed the magnificent painted ceiling for the Sheldonian Theatre. The first *Oxford Almanack* in 1674 was equally splendid, printed on four sheets and measuring 39 × 30 in. over all. Perhaps because of its cost or because too many were printed, there was no *Almanack* in 1675, but next year the regular series, on a single sheet measuring $23\frac{1}{2}$ × 20 in. began, and has continued ever since.

The earlier designs were clearly meant to take advantage of the skill of the engravers, David Loggan and Michael Burghers, whose work spans fifty years. Bred in the tradition of North European baroque, their designs are allegorical and emblematic, although Oxford buildings and figures appeared in the *Almanacks* from the start. Allegory came to an end with Michael Burghers; the University itself, or more exactly Dean Aldrich, who provided the inspiration and sometimes the original drawing for many of the *Almanacks*, seems to have been undeterred by the treasonable interpretations put by its Whig detractors upon them.

The new generation of engravers, beginning with George Vertue, turned to topography, and most of the major buildings and all the colleges were depicted often more than once during the eighteenth century. At the end of the century the employment of major artists, the Rookers, Dayes, and Turner, for the originals, turned the *Almanack* illustrations into artists' visions of Oxford, a tradition still maintained.

In the nineteenth century new printing processes, first the steel engraving, and then those dependent on photography, changed the image again. The original drawings of some early almanacs were reproduced in colour; new photographs were printed by collotype; the revival of artist's prints led to some etched views.

In recent times the Press's pioneering of advanced techniques in colour photolithography has produced a series of first-rate reproductions of views by contemporary artists, a reversion (but a colourful and vivid one) to the tradition of the eighteenth century.

1674 A vision of history, eng. R. White after Robert Streeter [333].

1676 Time and the Seasons, eng. M. Burghers and G. Edwards after Henry Aldrich (with Aldrich's original drawing) [334, 335].

1677 The first view of Oxford, eng. G. Edwards after designs selected by Obadiah Walker, who (significantly) inserted St. Cyprian's day, 9 December, in the calendar [336].

1683 Mathematicians, with Tom Tower,

Christ Church, in the background, eng. M. Burghers [337].

1700 Apollo, Mercury, and Minerva, eng. M. Burghers after prints belonging to Aldrich. The satirical interpretation put upon this in *Hieroglyphica Sacra Oxoniensia* (1700) accused the University and Aldrich in particular of crypto-Jacobitism [338].

1706 Figures round an oak tree, 'wherein is represented the Ld. Treasurer (Godolphin) playing at dice, and the Queen in a very disconsolate condition etc. If we may believe those who are suppos'd to understand the Meaning' (Hearne). Drawn and eng. M. Burghers. This too attracted a Whig squib on the same lines as in 1700 [339].

1715 Nicholas Hawksmoor's 'Forum Universitatis', drawn and eng. M. Burghers. For both Oxford and Cambridge, Hawksmoor planned a noble central piazza as the focal point of the University; neither came to fruition [340].

1720 Apollo on a plinth, surrounded by the Muses, with the Clarendon Building behind, eng. M. Burghers after Sir John Thornhill (with his original drawing) [341, 341A].

1724 Christ Church, drawn and eng. M. Burghers. Among the historic figures in the foreground, Fell and Aldrich can be seen on the right, behind Cardinal Wolsey, the founder [342].

1733 St. John's College, eng. Claude du Bosc after Green. The suffering figure of Laud appears on the left [343].

1742 Balliol College, eng. George Vertue. In the centre of the scene, at the back, is Duke Humfrey of Gloucester; in front on the left Bishop William Gray with a plan of the library he gave to the college [344].

1757 Allegory commemorating the addition to the Arundel marbles by the Countess of Pomfret, eng. J. Green after Samuel Wale [345].

1760 Dr. John Radcliffe conducted from the temple of Aesculapius by the Genius of Physic, his infirmary in the background, eng. B. Green after Wale, a print on silk [346].

1774 The Clarendon Building, drawn and eng. Edward and Michael Angelo Rooker (with the original drawing) [347, 347A].

1780 Friar Bacon's Study, with Folly Bridge, drawn and eng. by M. A. Rooker [348].

1799 View of Christ Church from the meadows, eng. James Basire after J. M. W. Turner, with the original drawing (his first *Almanack*) and plate [349, 350, 351].

1800 The Sheldonian Theatre and Clarendon Building, eng. Basire after Edward Dayes [352].

1804 View of Worcester College and Walton Street, towards the future site of the University Press, eng. Basire after J. M. W. Turner, with the original drawing [353, 354].

1814 The High Street, with the corner of Cat Street, between All Souls College and St. Mary's Church, eng. Basire after Hugh O'Neill [355].

1816 The Old Divinity School, next the Bodleian Library, eng. J. Skelton after J. Buckler [356].

1832 The new 'University Printing House', eng. Henry Le Keux, after F. Mackenzie [357].

1834 The arrival of the Vice-Chancellor for the University sermon at St. Mary's Church, eng. Le Keux after Mackenzie [358].

1850 The Martyrs' Memorial, eng. Radclyffe after Mackenzie. The Memorial, commemorating Latimer, Ridley, and Cranmer, was designed by Sir Gilbert Scott and built in 1841 [361].

1852 Oxford from the west, eng. Radclyffe after De Wint [362].

1860 The University Museum, drawn and eng. John Henry Le Keux [363].

1871 Balliol and Trinity Colleges, from a print of 1755, Woodbury type reproduction [364].

1878 Keble College chapel, etched by John Watkins after Alexander Macdonald [365].

1839 Oxford from the Castle Keep, eng. Le Keux after Peter de Wint [359].

1848 The Taylor Institution and the Ashmolean Museum, eng. W. Radclyffe after Mackenzie. Cockerell's new buildings for the University's art museum and modern languages institute were erected in 1841–5 [360].

1879 Balliol College, wood engraving by J. D. Cooper after Macdonald. William Butterfield was the architect of both Keble College and of the Balliol chapel [366].

1899 Duke Humfrey's library, the Bodleian Library, collotype from a photograph [367].

1904 The Press quadrangle, etching by William Monk [368].

1911 Magdalen Bridge and Tower, the first colour collotype, from a drawing by Edward Dayes (1792) eng. for the 1797 Almanack [369].

1922 Lady Margaret Hall, the first college for women (1878), collotype from a drawing by F. L. Griggs [370].

1943 Amen House after the blitz, August 1942, collotype from a drawing by Randolph Schwabe, with the original drawing [371, 371A].

1945 St. Giles's Fair, colour collotype with offset lithography from a drawing by Sir Muirhead Bone [372].

1949 Wolvercote Paper Mill, colour offset lithography from a drawing by Leonard Squirrell [373].

1972 View from the Upper Common Room, Queen's College, showing All Souls College with the Radcliffe Camera beyond, colour offset lithography from a painting by John Piper [374].

1973 Hertford College, with the quadrangle between the Bodleian Library, the Clarendon Building, and the Sheldonian Theatre, colour offset lithography from a painting by Alfred Daniels [375].

INDEX

Abbott, Evelyn, 46
Aeschylus, 39
Addison, Joseph, 40
Aesop, 20–1, 45, 60
Aldrich, Henry, 18, 25, 27–8, 52, 61–2
Aldus Manutius, 5, 55
Aleman, Mateo, 10
Alexander Gallus, *Doctrinale*, 4
Alfred, King, 1
Allestree, Richard, 14–15, 20–1, 32
Allot, Robert, 10
Amen House, 51, 54, 63
Anson, Sir William, 48
Anwykyll, John, 4
Apollonius Pergaeus, 28, 29–30
Aratus, 21–2
Armstrong, John, 57
Aristotle, 58
  Ethics, 2, 3, 5, 7, 53
  Poetics, 38–9, 53
  Politics, 53
Arnold, Thomas, 39
Arundel, 2nd Earl of, 22, 26, 30, 35
Austin, John, 59

Bacon, Sir Francis, 12–13, 22
Bailey, Cyril, 58
Baldwin, R., 31
Barker, Sir Ernest, 53
Barnes, Joseph, 6–8, 10
Bartholomew, E. R., 58
Basire, James, 62
Baskerville, John, 31, 34–5, 39
Baskett, John, 28, 31
  Mark, 31–2
Beeching, H. C., 53
Bekker, Immanuel, 39
Bell, F. J., 48
Bennett, Thomas, corrector and editor, 15, 20
  Thomas, bookseller, 28
Bensley, Thomas, 36–7, 38, 40, 41
Bentley, Richard, 39
Benzelius, Eric, 27
Bernard, Edward, 23, 24 n., 28–9
Beveridge, William, 20
Bible, Authorized (King James) Version, 7, 23–4, 36–7, 42, 43–4, 45–6, 50, 51, 55, 60
  New English, 55
  Revised Version, 51
  Scofield, 56–7
  Old Testament (Hebrew), 35–6
  New Testament (Greek), 23–4, 28, 30, 34–5, 41
    (Vulgate), 37
    (New English), 55
Bibliothèque Mazarine, 21
Bibliothèque Nationale, 25
Bignon, Jean-Paul, 25
Blackstone, Sir William, 33–5, 37, 47, 48
Blayney, Benjamin, 32, 42
Blore, Edward, 41
Boden, Joseph, 43
Bodley, Sir Thomas, 8
Bodoni, G. B., 37
Bologna, university of, 2
Bone, Sir Muirhead, 63
Book of Common Prayer, 23–4, 36–7, 56–7
Boswell, James, 36 n., 49, 53
Boyle, Robert, 12, 14
Bradley, F. H., 53–4
  Henry, 51–2
  James, 40
Bradshaw, Henry, 3
Brathwaite, E. R., 59
Bridges, Robert, 50, 54, 55
British and Foreign Bible Society, 42
Brittain, Thomas, & Sons, 44
Bronte, Anne, 54
  Charlotte, 54
Brown, Samuel, 11
Bruni, Leonardo, 2, 3, 5
Bryce, James, 46
Buckingham, Richard Grenville, 1st Duke of, 37
Buckler, J., 43, 62
Burges, Sir James Bland, 36
Burghers, Michael, 14, 22–3, 61–2
Burnet, Gilbert, 40
Burton, Robert, 9
Butler, Charles, 8, 10
Butterfield, William, 63
Bywater, Ingram, 49, 52, 53

Cadell, Thomas, 35
Caedmon, 26
Cambridge, university of, 2, 4, 6, 8–9, 11, 20, 38, 39
  press, 6, 8–9, 35, 38, 39, 42
Camden, William, 8, 10, 30–1
Campbell, Lewis, 46
Cannan, Charles, 53–4, 55, 58
  May, 55
Carbonel, William, 18–19
Carnan, Thomas, 32
Carter, H. G., xiii, 55
Cary, Lucius, Viscount Falkland, 12
Case, John, 7
Caslon, William I, 35, 37
  foundry, 43
Cat Street, 1, 2–3, 35
Cato, *Disticha*, 21
Caxton, William, 3, 4–5
Chandler, Richard, 35
Chapman, R. W., 54
Charles I, 8, 11, 12, 13
Charles II, 21
Charleton, Walter, 22–3
Charlett, Arthur, 28, 29, 31, 32
Chatterton, Thomas, 39
Chaucer, Geoffrey, 39, 46, 49–50
Chawner, Esther, 58
Chéron, Louis, 31
Chillingworth, William, 12
Cicero, 3, 18
Clare, John, 56
Clarendon, Edward Hyde, Earl of, 27–8, 44, 48
Clarke, Samuel, 14, 15, 20, 30
Clement I, 12, 20
Clerk Maxwell, James, 48
Cockerell, C. R., 62
Coke, Christopher, 3
Collingwood, R. G., 59
  Samuel, 38, 41, 42
Collins, F. H., 52
Cologne, 3, 4
Combe, Thomas, 43–4, 45–6, 47
  Mrs., 44
Commager, H. S., 56–7
Comte, Auguste, 54
Constable, John, 56
Cooke, Joshua, 36–7, 38, 41
Cooper, J. D., 63
Corbett, Jim, 58
Cottonian Library, 29

Coxe, Henry Octavius, 47
Craig, W. J., 51
Craigie, William, 51–2
Cremer, Acton, 23
Cripps, Henry, 9
Crowder, S., 31
Cumberlege, Geoffrey, 58
Cunradi, Christophorus, 26
Curtis, Thomas, 42
Cyprian, St., 25, 61

Daniel, C. H. O., 50
Daniels, Alfred, 63
Darwin, Charles, 48–9
Dasent, Sir George, 49
Dawson, William, 34, 36–7, 42
Dayes, Edward, 61–3
Dearmer, Percy, 54
Dedicus, Joannes, 5
Delaune, Thomas, 32
De Lorme, J.-L., 25
Demosthenes, 39
De Wint, Peter, 62
Didot, François-Ambroise and Pierre-François, 37
Digby, Sir John, 10
Dillenius, Johann, 32
Dindorf, Karl Wilhelm, 39
Dionysus Periegetes, 29
Dirac, P. A. M., 59
Dodart, Denis, 23
Dodgson, C. L. (Lewis Carroll), 47, 50
Dodsley, James, 35
D'Oili, Robert, 1
Dolben, John, 14–15
Donatus, *Ars minor*, 4
Donne, John, 56
Du Bosc, Claude, 62
Duns Scotus, 3

Edwards, George, 22–3, 44, 61
Eliot, T. S., 56
  Valerie, 56
  Vivien, 56
Elizabeth I, 6, 7
Elizabeth II, 55, 60
Ellis, Robinson, 46, 50
Ellmann, Richard, 56–7
Elmsley, Peter, the elder, 34–5, 41
  the younger, 41
Ensor, R. C. K., 51, 59
Essaeus, Henricus and Joannes, 26
Eton College, 10
Euclid, 23, 29, 45
Euripides, 38–9
Eyre, Charles, 32
  John, 32

Fell, John, 14–26, 27, 28, 31, 47, 51, 60, 62
  Samuel, 14
Figgins, Vincent, 37
Fletcher, C. R. L., 53–4
  James, 32
  Messrs., 35
Forrest, Edward, 12
Forshall, Josiah, 42
Foss, Hubert, 59
Fowler, H. W. and F. G., 52
François I, 10, 17
Frankfurt book-fair, 9–10
Frederick, Prince of Wales, 36
Freeman, E. A., 47–8
Frowde, Henry, 51, 54, 57
Fry, Christopher, 59
Fugard, Athol, 59
Furnivall, F. J., 52

Gaisford, Thomas, 38–9, 40, 41
Gale, Thomas, 28–9
Garamont, Claude, 10, 17–18
Gardner, Edward, 34, 41
  E. B., 34, 47, 51
Garland, A. H., 48
Gaza, Theodore, 5
Gell, Philip Lyttelton, 47, 52, 53, 57
Gentleman, David, 56
Gheeraerts, Marcus, 10
Gibson, Edmund, 29
  Strickland, 15 n.
Giraldus Cambrensis, 1
Gladstone, W. E., 50
Gomme, A. W., 58
Goudy, Frederick, 57
Granjon, Robert, 17
Graves, C. L., 46 n.
Gray, William, bishop of Ely, 3, 62
Green, B., 62
  J., 62
Gregory XIII, 17
Grenville, George, 34
  George, Marquis of Buckingham; Thomas; and William, Lord Grenville, 39
Griggs, F. L., 63
Grotius, Hugo, 14
Grundy, S. B., 57
Guy, Thomas, 23–4, 31

Hacket, John, 9
Hall, Edward Pickard, 45–6, 50
  Henry, 13
  John, 15, 19
Halley, Edmund, 28, 29–30
Halton, Timothy, 25
Hamilton, Archibald, 36–7
Handy, John, 35
Hanmer, Sir Thomas, 32–3, 36
Hardy, Sir Thomas Duffus, 40
Harmanszoon, Harman, 18
Hart, Horace, 50–1, 52
Hartel, Wilhelm, 25
Harvey, Sir Paul, 59
Hassall, Joan, 59
Haultin, Pierre, 10, 17
Hawkins, Thomas, 36
Hawksmoor, Nicholas, 27–8, 61
Hearne, Thomas, 23 n., 29 and n., 30–1
Hegel, Georg Wilhelm Friedrich, 54
Helmholtz, H. von, 46, 48
Henrietta Maria, Queen, 20
Henry VI, 2
Henry VIII, 30
Henry, Prince of Wales, 8
Her Majesty's Stationery Office, 56
Hertz, Heinrich, 48
Hesiod, 39
Heylyn, Peter, 9
Hickes, George, 26–7
Hill, George Birkbeck, 36 n., 49, 53
Hills, Henry, 24
Hinshelwood, Sir Cyril, 59
Hole, William, 8
Holman-Hunt, Sir William, 44
Homer, 17, 38–9, 46, 58
Hooker, Richard, 40
Hopkins, Gerard Manley, 54–5
Horman, William, 5 and n.
Hornby, A. S., 59
Hort, F. J. A., 51
Huddesford, George, 34
Hume, David, 54
Humfrey, Duke of Gloucester, 2, 62
Hyde, Thomas, 20–1, 26

Imprimerie Royale, 20, 22–3
Ingram, James, 40

Jackson, William, 31, 36–7, 41
James I, 8, 9
James, Thomas, 8
  M. R., 5 n.
Jenkins, Sir Leoline, 14–15, 18, 20, 21, 23–4, 25
Jenson, Nicolas, 55
Jewitt, Orlando, 40
Johnson, John, 15 n.
Johnson, Samuel, 27, 34–6, 49, 53
Johnston, Grahame, 58
Josephus, 29
Jowett, Benjamin, 46, 47, 48, 53
Junius, Francis, 15, 26–7

Kariara, Jonathan, 58
Keble, John, 40, 45
Keir, Peter, 38
Kennett, White, 28–9, 30, 40
Kennicott, Benjamin, 35–6
Ker, W. P., 49
Kettle, Tilly, 33
King, K. M., 59
  Richard, 59
King's College, Cambridge, 2
Kipling, Rudyard, 53–4
Kitchin, G. W., 46, 47
Kitonga, Ellen, 58
Kneller, Sir Godfrey, 14, 27
Kyrfoth, Charles, 5

Lacey, T. A., 54
Laguerre, Louis, 31
Lambeth Library, 29
Langbaine, Gerard, 11, 13–14
Langley, Thomas, 17
Latomus, Sigismundus, 9
Laud, William, 9, 11–12, 13, 14, 26, 39, 47, 60, 62
Leacroft, S., 35
Le Bé, Guillaume I and II, 18
Le Blon(d), C., 9
Lee, Sir Sidney, 36
Leeu, Gerard, 4
Leicester, Robert Dudley, Earl of, 6–7
Le Keux, Henry, 62
  John Henry, 63
Leland, John, 30
Le Neve, John, 40
Leontief, Wassily, 56–7
Leopold, Aldo, 56–7
Lichfield, Anne, 20
  John, 8–9, 10, 12
  Leonard I, 9, 11, 12, 13
  Leonard II, 20, 22
Liddell, H. G., 44–5, 47
Lightfoot, J. B., 51
Lily, William, 4, 5–6, 20–1, 60
Lincoln, Abraham, 56–7
Lister, Martin, 35–6
Lloyd, Charles, 41
  William, 32
Locke, John, 21
Loggan, David, 18, 21–3, 28, 61
Longfellow, Henry, 23
Longinus, 38–9
Lowth, Robert, 32–3, 36
Lucaris, Cyril, 12
Lucian, 52
Lucretius, 58
Ludolf, Heinrich Wilhelm, 28–9
Lye, Edward, 26–7
Lyndewood, William, *Constitutiones*, 3

Mabbe, James, 10
Macaulay, Thomas, 41
Macdonald, Alexander, 63
Mackenzie, F., 62, 63
Maclehose, James, 46
Macmillan, Alexander, 46, 47, 49, 51
Madden, Sir Frederic, 42
Maimonides, Moses, 13
Malalas, John, 11, 14, 22, 38–9
Mallarmé, Stéphane, 49
Markby, Sir William, 57
Markland, Jeremiah, 39
Marshall, Thomas, 15–18, 26, 30
Martin, Robert, 35
  William, 35
Marx, Leo, 56–7
Mary II, 18, 24
Masson, Gustave, 46
Matthiessen, F. O., 56–7
Maundrell, Henry, 28–9
Max Müller, Friedrich, 43, 52
Medici, Cardinal Ferdinand de', 17
Merry, W. W., 46
Meynell, Sir Francis, 56
Milford, Sir Humphrey, 54
Mill, John, 25, 28, 30, 31, 34, 39
  J. S., 54
Millais, Sir John Everett, 43–4
Miller, Simon, 22
Milton, John, 53
Mirk, John, *Festial*, 3
Monier-Williams, Sir Monier, 43
Monk, William, 63
Montgomery, Robert, 40–1
More, Sir Thomas, 30
Morison, Robert, 21–2, 59
  Samuel Eliot, 56–7
  Stanley, 55, 60
Morris, Richard, 46
Murray, Sir James, 51–2
Musgrave, Samuel, 38–9

Naghel, Frederic, 3
Nelson, Thomas, & Co., 57
Newman, John Henry, 44, 45
Newton, Sir Isaac, 13
Nicholls, Nicholas, 14
Nichols, John, 34–5
North, Frederick, Lord, 33, 37

O'Neill, Hugh, 62
Onions, C. T., 51–2
Opie, Iona and Peter, 59
Oughtred, William, 13
Ovid, 21, 45
OXFORD
  City
    Castle, 62
    Cat Street, 1, 2–3, 35, 62
    Friar Bacon's Study (Folly Bridge), 62
    Martyrs' Memorial, 63
    St. Mary's Church, 1, 2–3, 62
    St. Peter's Church, 3
  Halls and Colleges
    All Souls, 33, 48, 62–3
    Balliol, 3, 46–8, 62–3
    Brasenose, 9, 14, 15
    Christ Church, 9, 14, 15, 18, 19, 23, 39, 47, 61–2
    Corpus Christi, 9
    Jesus, 15
    Keble, 62, 63
    Lady Margaret Hall, 63
    Lincoln, 7, 15–17
    Magdalen, 4, 5, 8, 10, 39, 63
    Neville's Hall, 3
    New College, 7, 8
    Pembroke, 47
    Queen's, 15, 25, 63
    St. Alban Hall, 41
    St. Edmund Hall, 25, 30
    St. John's College, 62
    Trinity, 12, 63
    University, 28
    Wadham, 12
    Worcester, 50, 62
  University
    Architypographus, 14, 15, 20, 30
    Ashmolean Museum, 22, 41, 62
    Bodleian Library, 8, 11, 13, 26, 30, 39, 47, 55, 63; catalogues, 8, 10, 20–1, 43, 55; cold in, 8, 14, 21
    Chancellor, 1, 2, 6, 7, 11, 15, 31, 33, 37
    Convocation, 15, 20
    Indian Institute, 43
    Museum, 45, 62
    Radcliffe Camera and Infirmary, 62
    Royal Commission (1852) on, 34, 45–6
    Sheldonian Theatre, 14–15, 19, 33, 62, 63
    Stationers, 2–3
    Statutes, 1–2, 11
    Taylor Institution, 62
    Vice-Chancellor, 6, 15, 21, 25, 30, 34
Oxford Almanack, 21–2, 60–3
Oxford Movement, 40, 41, 44, 45
OXFORD UNIVERSITY PRESS
  Buildings
    first Printing House, 18–19
    Clarendon, 27–8, 62–3

Oxford University Press (*cont.*):
Buildings (*cont.*):
new University Printing House, 41, 62–3
Amen House, 51, 54, 63
Series
Clarendon Press, 46, 50
Oxford Classical Texts, 53
Oxford Classics, 51
Oxford English Texts, 49, 53
World's Classics, 54

Pafraet, Richard, 4
Page, William, 12
Pantin, Samuel, 41
Paris, F. S., 32
Parker, Joseph, 34, 39, 40, 41, 44
John Henry, 34, 41, 42
Peter, 23–4, 31
Parks, Fanny, 58
Pars, William, 35
Pattison, Mark, 46
Payne, John Thomas, 41
Thomas, 34–5, 41
Pearson, John, 25
Pecia system, 2
Peck, Francis, 29
Pembrey, J. C., 52
Perotti, Niccolò, 4
Perrault, Charles, 23
Pett, Phineas, 44–5
Philip and Mary, 6
Pickering, William, 41
Pickersgill, H. W., 38
Piper, John, 63
Pitt, Moses, 23–4
William, 36
Plantin, Christophe, 17, 22
Plato, 3, 39, 48
Plot, Robert, 22–3, 44
Pococke, Edward, 13, 14, 40
Polunin, Oleg, 59
Pomfret, Countess of, 35, 62
Pope, Alexander, 46
Popper, Karl, 59
Porson, Richard, 38–9
Porter, Peter, 59
Pound, Ezra, 56
Poussin, Nicolas, 22
Powell, Baden, 45
Powell, Frederick York, 49, 50
Price, Bartholomew, 43, 44, 47, 49, 53
Prideaux, Humphrey, 22, 24 and n., 35
Prince, Daniel, 34–5, 37, 41
Pritchard, Emmanuel, 21
Pusey, Edward Bouverie, 40, 43, 44
Pye, Henry James, 36

Quiller-Couch, Sir Arthur, 53

Radcliffe, Dr. John, 62
Radclyffe, W., 62
Rainsford, John, 19
Randolph, Thomas, 33–4, 37
Restraint of printing, 4–5, 8–9, 11, 24, 32, 33
Revett, Nicholas, 35
Reynbold, John, 3
Reynolds, Graham, 56
Richard III, 4
Richard de Bury, 7–8
Richards, Grant, 54
Richardson, Samuel, 33
Stephen, 34
Richelieu, Cardinal Armand de, 22
Rieu, E. V., 58
Riley, Athelstan, 54
Rivington, J. & J., 32
Robertson, Abraham, 40
Daniel, 41
Robinson, F. N., 50
Humphrey, 13
T., 13
Rogers, Bruce, 31, 55
Rood, Theodoric, 2, 3–4
Rooker, Edward and Michael Angelo, 61–2
Roosevelt, Mr. and Mrs. Theodore, 60
Roper, William, 30
Ross, Sir W. D., 58
Rostovtzeff, M., 58
Routh, Martin, 38–9, 40
Royal Commission on the Universities, 34, 45–6
Royal Society, 12–13
Rubens, Sir Peter Paul, 22
Rufinus of Aquileia, 3–4
Ruskin, John, 33
Russell, Richard, 32–3

Sadleir, Michael, 55
St. Albans printer, 4, 5
St. Jerome, 3–4
St. John Chrysostom, 7, 10
St. Mary the Virgin, Church of, 1, 2–3
St. Thomas Aquinas, 2
Sanderson, Robert, 10
Savile, Sir Henry, 10, 12
Saxl, F., 59
Scheffer, Johann, 22–3
Scholes, Percy, 59
Schwabe, Randolph, 63
Scofield, C. I., 56–7
Scolar, John, 5
Scott, Sir Gilbert, 62
Robert, bookseller, 20
Robert, lexicographer, 44–5
Secker, Thomas, 36
Sedgley, Richard, 28
Shakespeare, William, 39, 51
Shaw, Thurston, 58
Sheldon, Gilbert, 12, 14–15, 20, 21
Short, James, 9, 10
Sidney, Sir Philip, 7
Simmonds, William, 8
Simmons, J. S. G., 29 n.
Skeat, W. W., 49–50
Skelton, J., 62
Sloane, Sir Hans, 32
Smith, John, 8
Thomas, 29
Somner, William, 14
Sophocles, 39, 46
Soyinka, Wole, 59
Speed, Lucy G., 57
Spenser, Edmund, 46
Sprat, Thomas, 27, 52
Squirrell, Leonard, 63
Stacy, J. H., 43–4
Stanbridge, John, 4, 5
Stanhope, Charles, 3rd Earl, 37–8
Stationers' Company, 6, 11, 21, 24, 31–2, 60
Steel, Robert, 23–4
Stevens, Henry, of Vermont, 50
Story, Norah, 57
Streeter, Robert, 22, 60–1
Stubbs, William, 46, 48
Suidas, 39

Tait, Peter, 46
Tanner, Thomas, 26 n.
Tenniel, Sir John, 47
Ten Raem, Gerard, 4
Terence, 4
Terry, Thomas, 28
Theocritus, 39
Thomas, Thomas, 6
Thompson, Flora, 54–5
Thomson, Adam, 42
William, Lord Kelvin, 46
Thornborough, John, 10
Thornhill, Sir John, 31, 62
Thucydides, 39, 58
Thwaites, Edward, 26
Tolstoy, Leo, 55
Torelli, J., 40
Toup, Jonathan, 38–9
Tovey, D. F., 59
Toynbee, Arnold, 59
Treble, H. A., 59
Trench, R. C., 52

Trinitarian Bible Society, 42
Trollope, Anthony, 54–5
Turner, J. M. W., 61–2
  William (printer), 9, 10, 11
Types, printing, 15–18, 35, 50–1
  Anglo-Saxon and Gothic, 27–8
  exotic, 11, 13, 14, 18, 29, 55–6
  Fell, 15–18, 39, 50–1, 55
  Greek, 10, 16, 35, 39
Type-specimens (1693 and 1695), 18 (1768), 34–5
Tyrwhitt, Thomas, 38–9

Udall, Nicholas, 4
Ulfilas, 26
Uri, Joannes, 43, 55

Valla, Lorenzo, 4
Van Dijck, Abraham, 17, 18
  Christoffel, 17
Van Dyck, Sir Anthony, 11
Van Hoogenacker, Arend, 11
Van Mildert, William, 41
Van Waesberge, Jan, 17
Vaughan Williams, Ralph, 54
Veldener, Johann, 3
Vergetios, Angelos, 17
Verlaine, Paul, 49
Victorius, Petrus, 18
Vigfusson, Gudbrandt, 49
Vossius, Isaac, 26

Wake, William, 30
Wale, Samuel, 62
Walker, Obadiah, 24, 25, 62
Wallis, John, 13, 24 n., 28–9, 31, 52
Walpergen, Peter de, 17, 18, 19
Walpole, Horace, 28
Walton, Brian, 14
Wanley, Humfrey, 26–7, 29
Warton, Thomas, 35–6
Watkins, John, 62
Watts, Gilbert, 12–13
Waynflete, William of, 4
Wells, Edward, 28–9, 40
  William, 20
Westcott, B. F., 51
Westminster School, 45
Wharton, Henry, 11
Whatman, James, the younger, 35
White, R., 61
  Joseph, 40
Whitlock, Pamela, 59
Whittington, Robert, 4, 5–6
Whittock, N., 41
Wilde, Johannes, 59
Wilkes, John, 34
Wilkins, Sir Charles, 43
  David, 28, 30
  John, 12
William III, 24
William de Machlinia, 4
Williamson, Hugh, 56
Williamson, Sir Joseph, 14–15, 17, 25
Wilson, Andrew, 38
  Horace, 43
Wilson, Edmund, 56–7
Winchester, 7, 37
Wittkower, R., 59
Wolcot, John (Peter Pindar), 36
Wolfe, Reginald, 7
Wolsey, Cardinal Thomas, 62
Wolvercote, 19, 44, 47, 63
Wood, Anthony, 7 n., 20–1, 23
Woodyear, J., 35
Wordsworth, Charles, 44–5
Wright, T., and Gill, W., 32, 34, 37
Wynkyn de Worde, 5
Wyttenbach, Daniel, 38–9

Xenocrates, 9

Yate, Thomas, 14–15, 18–19, 21 and n., 22, 24, 25, 28
Young, J. Z., 59
  Patrick, 12
  Robert, 12

Zel, Ulrich, 4

PLATES

1

3

The first leaf of each of the duplicate quires of the Worcester Cathedral *pecia* manuscript, showing the close correspondence between them.

Reproduced from 'The *pecia* system in the medieval university' by Graham Pollard, in *Medieval scribes, manuscripts, and libraries: essays presented to N. R. Ker*, edd. M. B. Parkes and Andrew G. Watson (London, 1978).

Extat Augustinus de Civitate Dei, cũ Commentarijs Thomae de Valois et Nicolai Triveth Professorum Ordinis Praedicatorum, excussus per Petrũ Schoifer Moguntiae. 1473. folio.

racionis assignet Si inquam hec secundũ tradicionis supra exposite regulam con sequantur aduertimus deprecemur vt nobis et omnibus qui hec audiunt conce dat dominus fide quam suscepimus custo dia cursu consumato expectare iusticie reposi tam coronam : et inueniri inter eos qui resurgunt in vitam eternam. liberari vero a confusione et obprobrio eterno . per cristum dominum nostrum per quem ē deo patri omnipotēti cū spiritu sancto gloria et imperium in secula seculorum amen .

Rufini, ij omini huj

Explicit exposicio sancti Jeronimi in simbolo apostolorum ad papam laurē cium Impressa Oxonie Et finita Anno domini . M . cccc . lxviij . xvij . die decembris .

expositionis Auctor.

Vidi Novam Rhetoricã Fratri Laurentij Gulielmi de Saona, impressã in Villâ Sti. Albani. Anno. 1480. 4° G. 46. consul: etiam Joh. Arnoldũ de Chalcographiae Inventione, et Ber: Malinerot de Ortu, et progressu Typographiae 4°. H. 3. vide Aspinianũ de Templis. pag. 440. 441. ubi opinionem Jacobi Wimpfelingi citat et approbat, quod Ars Typographica inventa est a Joh: Gutenberg. Anno Chti. 1440.

amicorum esse inter se omnia.

This oon vyce age gyueth olde men thei be besyere to gete gode than nede is

Solū hoc vnū viciū affert hōibꝫ senec-tus. attēciores sūt ad rē oēs ꝙ̄ sat est.

Looke vp meryly

Experge frontem

I shall make hir as parched & blakk as a cole.

Tam excoctam atqꝫ atram reddam ꝙ̄ carbo est

There is no thynge bettir to a man than esynes meke nes or paciente

Facilitate nichil ē hōi meli⁹ neqꝫ clemēcia

He hath allwey ledd his lyfe in ese & welefare

Ille semper egit suam vitam in ocio in conuiuijs.

I haue woen my life to gete or to do muche for them

Illis vt ꝙ̄ plurimū facerem contriui in quirendo vitam meam

Now in myn olde age this thank I haue of them for my labour hate,

Nunc exacta etate hoc̄ fructi pro labore ab ijs fero odium.

¶ Prudentia politica subdiuidit᷑ alia architectonica .s. principalis q̄ est legispositiua. Alia est particularis pollitica nō h̄ns nomē ꝓprium sexto ethi. ca. nono. Alie sunt virtutes particulares annexe ⁊ ꝯtente sub prudētia particulari. ¶ Eubulia est circa agibilia cuius est inquirere ⁊ ꝯsiliare recte ⁊ dr̄ eē rectitudo ꝯsilii sexto ethi. ca. decio ⁊ prudentia est ostendere ⁊ ꝑcipere ⁊ sic differūt eubulia ⁊ prudētia ⁊ iste q̄ h̄nt eubuliā in cōsiliando neq; sunt veloces neq; tarde. Synosy est circa agibilia iudicans de ꝯsiliatis inuentis sexto ethi. ca. vndecimo ⁊ ille qui habet synosym dicitur sensatꝰ: q̄r scit bene iudicare de inuentis. ¶ Gnome est virtus bene iudicans de arduis soluꝫ ⁊ necessariis ⁊ per hoc differt a synesy ⁊ dr̄ talis epykeyes .i. iudicans recte in arduis sexto ethi. ca. duodecio. ¶ Eustochya est virtus bene ꝯsiliatiua: sꝫ velox. ⁊ i hoc differt ab eubulea sexto ethi. ca. duodecio. ¶ Solertia ē quedā eustochya i veniendi medium sine perscrutatiōe sexto ethi. ca. decimo.

¶ Explicitum est Joannis Dedici Oxoniensis in morali philosophia eruditissimi preclarū opusculuꝫ questionū / subtilissime discucientiū (licet sparsim cū quadā tamē dependētia) singulas materias in decē libris ethicorū Arestotilis inuestigatas / vti summa industria lucubranti patebit. Impressumq; in celeberima vniuersitate Oxoniensi per me Johannem Scolar in vicculo sancti Joannis Baptiste morā trahentē. Anno dn̄i. M. CCCCC. decimooctauo. Mensis vero Maij die decimoquinto.

¶ Cū priuilegio.

¶ Vetitum est per edictum sub sigillo cācellariatus ne quis in septennio hoc insigne opꝰ imprimat vel aliorum ductu impensis venditet in vniuersitate Oxonie: aut infra precinctum eiusdē: sub pena amissionis omniuꝫ librorum et quinq; librarū sterlingorum pro singulis sic venditis vbiubi impressi fuerint preter penā pretaxatam in decreto.

¶ Cornicum oculos configere noli.

7

¶ De heteroclitis nominibus.

¶ Editio Roberti Whittintoni lichfeldiensis Grammatice magistri: et prothouatis anglie in florentissima Oxoniensi achademia Laureati / de heteroclitis nominibus et gradibus comparatōnis.

¶ Tetrastichon eiusdem ad lectorem.

Protheos ve possis varios dinoscere vultus
Tyresie sexus ambiguosq; senis
Salmacidos ne vndis coeant heteroclita mixta
Hoc whittintoni voluito lector opus.

¶ Distichon eiusdem in zoilum.

Cornua rhinoceros / dentem ni zoile ponas
Sanguinolenta feret tela hecatebeletes.

8

10

2

IN ADVENTVM ILLVSTRISSIMI LECESTRENSIS COMITIS AD Collegium Lincolnienſe.

CARMEN GRATVLATORIVM.

COmiter hoc factum eſt a te (Comes optime) vt iſtis
hoſpes in anguſtis ædibus eſſe velis.
Quò minor hæc domus eſt, bonitas tua maior habenda eſt,
in tenui hoſpitio, gratior hoſpes eris.
O Comes es comis, merito Comes ergò vocaris,
dux tibi ſit Chriſtus, nobilitaſq; comes.
Oxoniæ, Patriæ, Eliſæ, Atlas, Neſtor, Achates,
Creſce, Vige, Perſta, Viribus, Arte, Fide.

OXONIÆ
Ex Ædibus IOSEPHI BARNES
tertio Idus Ianuarij.
1585.

SPECVLVM MORALIVM QVAESTIONVM IN VNIVERSAM ETHICEN Aristotelis, Authore Magistro IOHANNE CASO Oxoniensi, olim Collegij Diui Iohannis Præcursoris Socio.

SENECA LIB. II. EPIST. XVI. AD LVCILIVM.

¶ Illud ante omnia vide, vtrum in philosophia, an in ipsa vita profeceris: non est philosophia populare artificium, nec ostentationi paratum; non enim in verbis sed in rebus est.

¶ OXONIAE,

Ex officina Typographica IOSEPHI BARNESII *Celeberrimæ* Academiæ Oxoniensis Typographi,

Anno 1585.

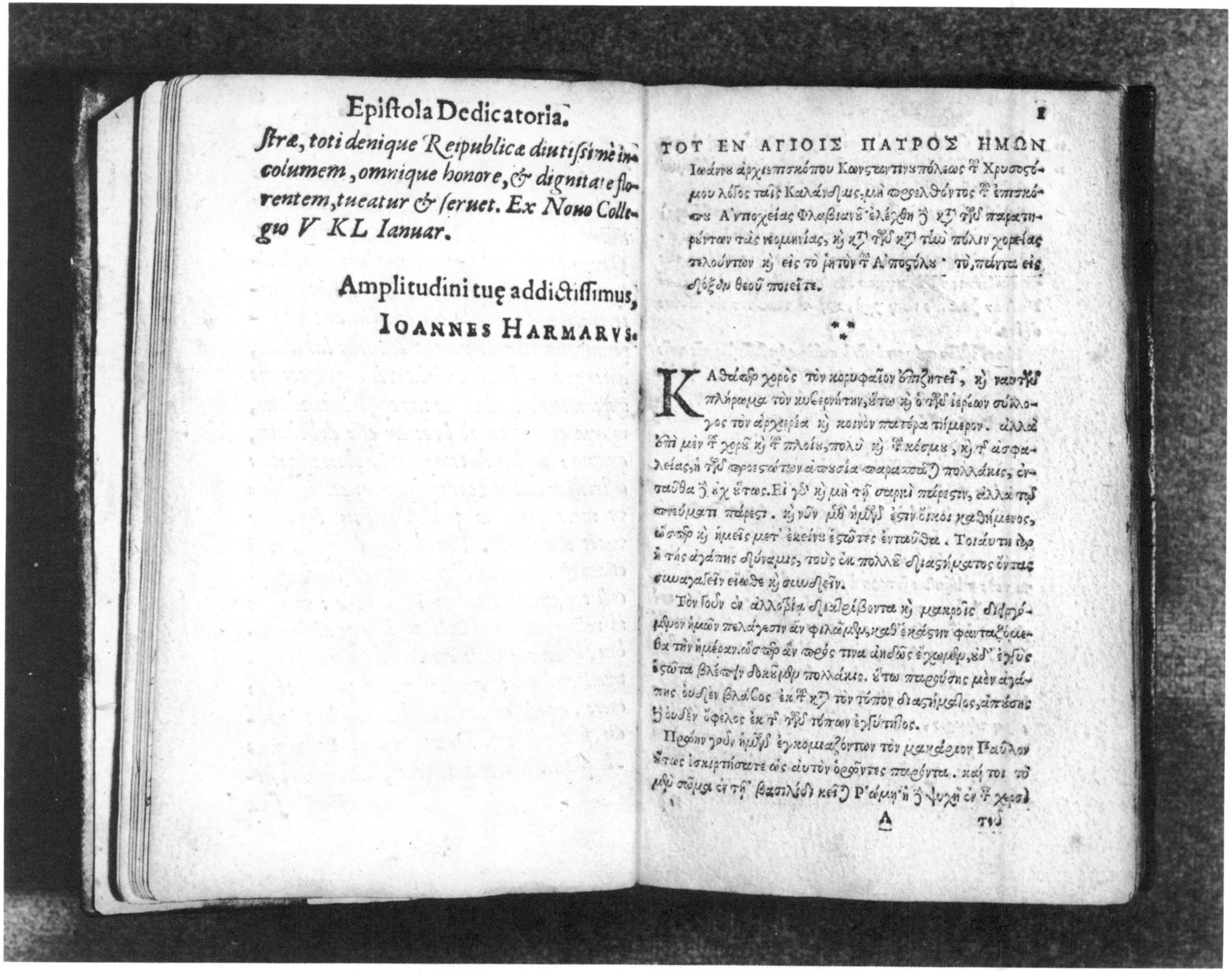

stræ, toti denique Reipublicæ diutissimè incolumem, omnique honore, & dignitate florentem, tueatur & seruet. Ex Nouo Collegio V KL Ianuar.

Amplitudini tuæ addictissimus,

IOANNES HARMARVS.

ΤΟΥ ΕΝ ΑΓΙΟΙΣ ΠΑΤΡΟΣ ΗΜΩΝ

Ἰωάννου ἀρχιεπισκόπου Κωνσταντινουπόλεως τοῦ Χρυσοστόμου λόγος ταῖς Καλάνδαις, μὴ παρελθόντος τοῦ ἐπισκόπου Ἀντιοχείας Φλαβιανοῦ· ἐλέχθη δὲ κατὰ τῶν παρατηρούντων τὰς νεομηνίας, καὶ κατὰ τῶν κατὰ τὴν πόλιν χορείας τελούντων· καὶ εἰς τὸ ῥητὸν τοῦ Ἀποστόλου· τό, πάντα εἰς δόξαν θεοῦ ποιεῖτε.

⁂

Καθάπερ χορὸς τὸν κορυφαῖον ἐπιζητεῖ, καὶ ναυτῶν πλήρωμα τὸν κυβερνήτην, οὕτω καὶ ὁ τῶν ἱερέων σύλλογος τὸν ἀρχιερέα καὶ κοινὸν πατέρα τήμερον. ἀλλὰ ἐπὶ μὲν τοῦ χοροῦ καὶ τοῦ πλοίου, πολὺ καὶ τοῦ κόσμου, καὶ τῆς ἀσφαλείας, ἡ τῶν προεστώτων ἀπουσία παραιρεῖται πολλάκις, ἐνταῦθα δὲ οὐχ οὕτως. Εἰ γὰρ καὶ μὴ τῇ σαρκὶ πάρεστιν, ἀλλὰ τῷ πνεύματι πάρεστι. καὶ νῦν μεθ' ἡμῶν ἐστιν οἴκοι καθήμενος, ὥσπερ καὶ ἡμεῖς μετ' ἐκείνου ἑστῶτες ἐνταῦθα. Τοιαύτη γὰρ ἡ τῆς ἀγάπης δύναμις, τοὺς ἐκ πολλοῦ διαστήματος ὄντας συναγαγεῖν εἴωθε καὶ συνδεῖν.

Τὸν γοῦν ἐν ἀλλοδημίᾳ διατρίβοντα καὶ μακροῖς διειργόμενον ἡμῶν πελάγεσιν ἂν φιλῶμεν, καθ' ἑκάστην φανταζόμεθα τὴν ἡμέραν. ὥσπερ ἂν πρός τινα ἀηδῶς ἔχωμεν, οὐδ' ἐγγὺς ἑστῶτα βλέπειν δοκοῦμεν πολλάκις. οὕτω παρούσης μὲν ἀγάπης οὐδὲν βλάβος ἐκ τοῦ κατὰ τὸν τόπον διαστήματος, ἀπούσης δὲ οὐδὲν ὄφελος ἐκ τῆς τῶν τόπων ἐγγύτητος.

Πρώην γοῦν ἡμῶν ἐγκωμιαζόντων τὸν μακάριον Παῦλον οὕτως ἐσκιρτήσατε ὡς αὐτὸν ὁρῶντες παρόντα. καίτοι τὸ μὲν σῶμα ἐν τῇ βασιλίδι κεῖται Ῥώμῃ· ἡ δὲ ψυχὴ ἐν τῇ χερσὶ

PHILOBIBLON

RICHARDI

DVNELMENSIS

ſive

DE AMORE LIBRORVM, ET INSTI-
TVTIONE BIBLIOTHECÆ,
tractatus pulcherrimus.

Ex collatione cum varijs manuſcriptis edi-
tio jam ſecunda;

cui

Acceſsit appendix de manuſcriptis Oxonienſibus.

Omnia hæc,
Opera & ſtudio T. I. Novi Coll. in alma Academia
Oxonienſi Socij.

B. P. N.
Non quæro quod mihi vtile eſt, ſed quod multis.

Oxoniæ,
Excudebat *Ioſephus Barneſius.* 1599.

for a swarme: which seldome ariseth the next day, vnlesse the weather be very pleasãt: but after two or three daies they will accept indifferent weather. I haue not knowne any stay after the fift day.

They sing both in triple time: the princesse thus 24 *The Bees musicke.*

with more or fewer notes, as she pleaseth. And sometime she taketh a higher key, specially toward their comming forth, and beginning the od minim in *A la mi re* shee tuneth the rest of hir notes in *C sol fa* thus,

But the Queene in a deeper voice thus,

continuing the same, some foure or fiue semibriefes, and sounding the end of every note in *C sol fa vt*. So that when they sing together, sometime they agree in a *perfect third*, sometime in a *Diapente*, & (if you respect the termination of the base) somtime in a *Diapasõ*. With these tunes answering one another, and some

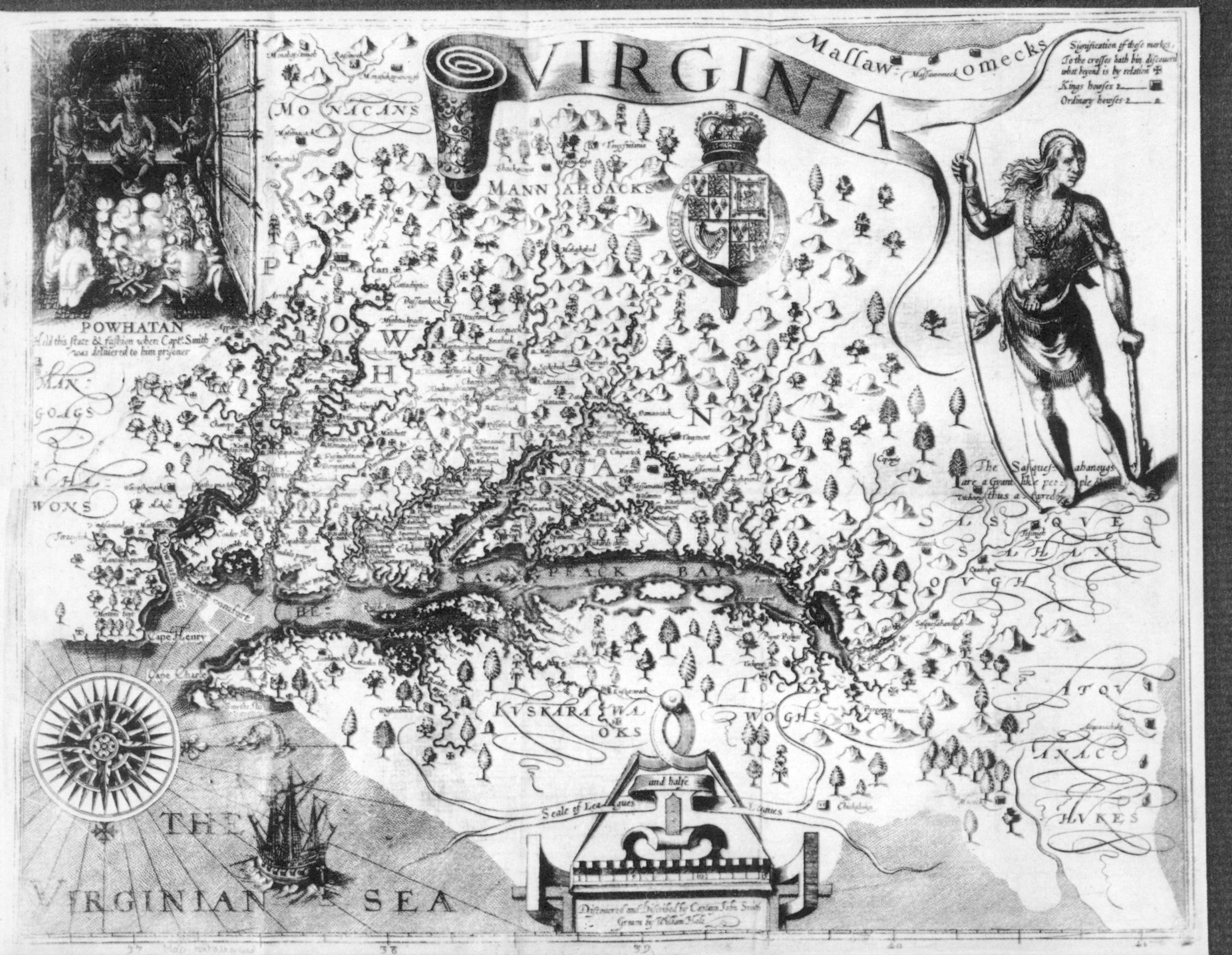
VIRGINIA
Massaw omecks
Signification of these markes
To the crosses hath bin discouerd what beyond is by relation
Kings howses
Ordinary howses
POWHATAN
Held this state & fashion when Capt. Smith was deliuered to him prisoner
MONACANS
MANNAHOACKS
POWHATAN
The Sasquesahanougs are a Gyant like people & thus a-tyred
KUSKARAWAOKS
TOCKWOGHS
SASQUESAHANOUGH
ATQUANACHUKES
THE VIRGINIAN SEA
Cape Henry
Cape Charles
Powhatan flu:
Scale of Leagues
and halfe
Discouered and Discribed by Captayn John Smith
Grauen by William Hole

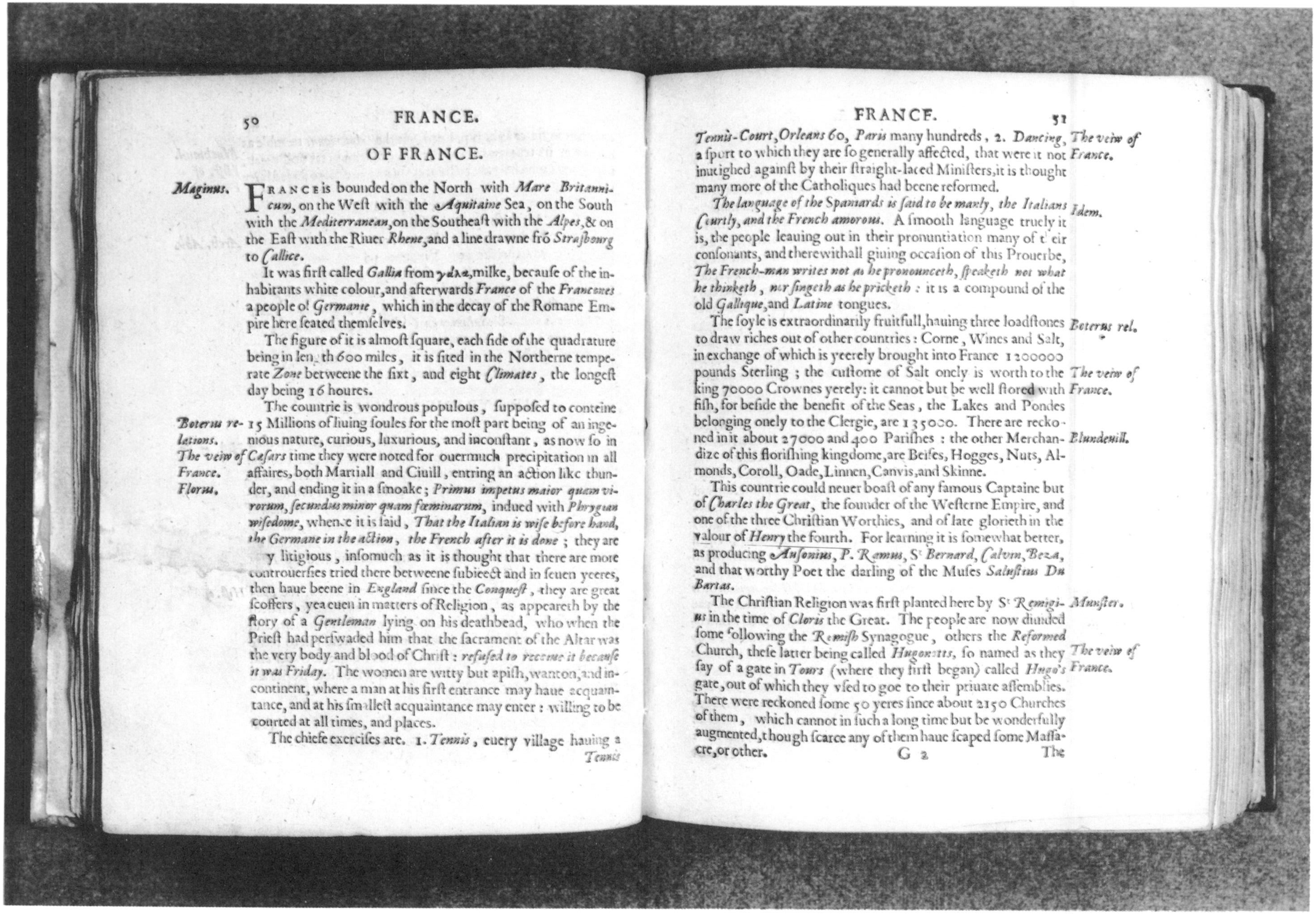

OF FRANCE.

Maginus.

FRANCE is bounded on the North with *Mare Britannicum*, on the West with the *Aquitaine* Sea, on the South with the *Mediterranean*, on the Southeast with the *Alpes*, & on the East with the Riuer *Rhene*, and a line drawne frō *Strasbourg* to *Callice*.

It was first called *Gallia* from γάλα, milke, because of the inhabitants white colour, and afterwards *France* of the *Francones* a people of *Germanie*, which in the decay of the Romane Empire here seated themselves.

The figure of it is almost square, each side of the quadrature being in length 600 miles, it is fited in the Northerne temperate *Zone* betweene the sixt, and eight *Climates*, the longest day being 16 houres.

Boterus relations. The veiw of France. Florus.

The countrie is wondrous populous, supposed to conteine 15 Millions of liuing soules for the most part being of an ingenious nature, curious, luxurious, and inconstant, as now so in *Cæsars* time they were noted for ouermuch precipitation in all affaires, both Martiall and Ciuill, entring an action like thunder, and ending it in a smoake; *Primus impetus maior quam virorum, secundus minor quam fœminarum*, indued with *Phrygian wisedome*, whence it is said, *That the Italian is wise before hand, the Germane in the action, the French after it is done*; they are very litigious, insomuch as it is thought that there are more controuersies tried there betweene subieect and in seuen yeeres, then haue beene in *England* since the *Conquest*, they are great scoffers, yea euen in matters of Religion, as appeareth by the story of a *Gentleman* lying on his deathbead, who when the Priest had perswaded him that the sacrament of the Altar was the very body and blood of Christ: *refused to receiue it because it was Friday*. The women are witty but apish, wanton, and incontinent, where a man at his first entrance may haue acquaintance, and at his smallest acquaintance may enter: willing to be courted at all times, and places.

The chiefe exercises are. 1. *Tennis*, euery village hauing a *Tennis*

Tennis-Court, *Orleans* 60, *Paris* many hundreds, 2. *Dancing*, a sport to which they are so generally affected, that were it not inueighed against by their straight-laced Ministers, it is thought many more of the Catholiques had beene reformed. *The veiw of France.*

The language of the Spaniards is said to be manly, the Italians Courtly, and the French amorous. A smooth language truely it is, the people leauing out in their pronuntiation many of their consonants, and therewithall giuing occasion of this Prouerbe, *The French-man writes not as he pronounceth, speaketh not what he thinketh, nor singeth as he pricketh*: it is a compound of the old *Gallique*, and *Latine* tongues. *Idem.*

Boterus rel. The veiw of France. Blundevill.

The soyle is extraordinarily fruitfull, hauing three loadstones to draw riches out of other countries: Corne, Wines and Salt, in exchange of which is yeerely brought into France 1200000 pounds Sterling; the custome of Salt onely is worth to the king 70000 Crownes yerely: it cannot but be well stored with fish, for beside the benefit of the Seas, the Lakes and Pondes belonging onely to the Clergie, are 135000. There are reckoned in it about 27000 and 400 Parishes: the other Merchandize of this florishing kingdome, are Beifes, Hogges, Nuts, Almonds, Coroll, Oade, Linnen, Canvis, and Skinne.

This countrie could neuer boast of any famous Captaine but of *Charles the Great*, the founder of the Westerne Empire, and one of the three Christian Worthies, and of late glorieth in the valour of *Henry* the fourth. For learning it is somewhat better, as producing *Ausonius*, *P. Ramus*, S[t] *Bernard*, *Calvin*, *Beza*, and that worthy Poet the darling of the Muses *Salustius Du Bartas*.

Munster. The veiw of France.

The Christian Religion was first planted here by S[t] *Remigius* in the time of *Cloris* the Great. The people are now diuided some following the *Remish* Synagogue, others the *Reformed* Church, these latter being called *Hugonotts*, so named as they say of a gate in *Tours* (where they first began) called *Hugo's* gate, out of which they vsed to goe to their priuate assemblies. There were reckoned some 50 yeres since about 2150 Churches of them, which cannot in such a long time but be wonderfully augmented, though scarce any of them haue scaped some Massacre, or other.

G 2 The

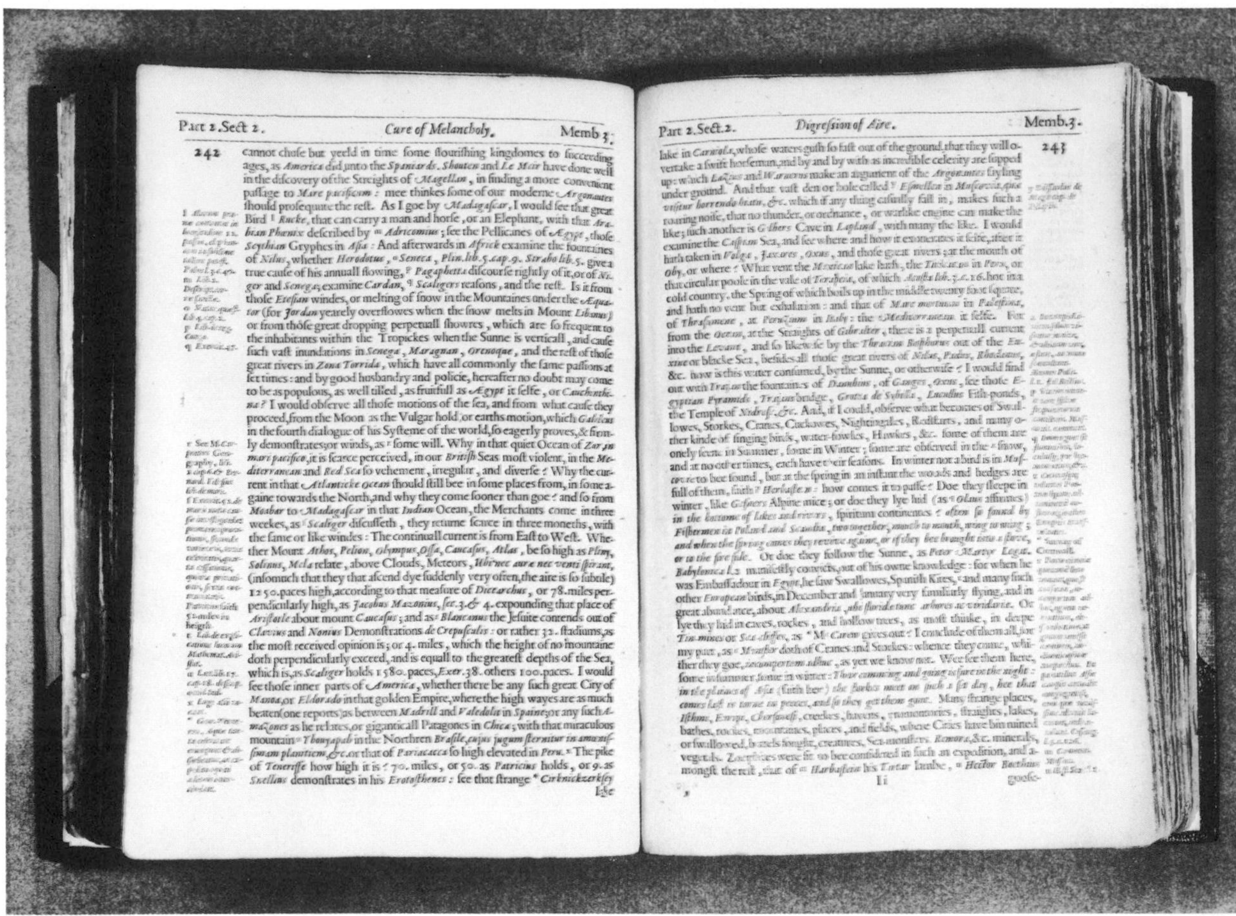

Part 2. Sect 2. *Cure of Melancholy.* Memb 3.

242 cannot chuse but yeeld in time some flourishing kingdomes to succeeding ages, as *America* did unto the *Spaniards*. *Shouten* and *Le Mair* have done well in the discovery of the Streights of *Magellan*, in finding a more convenient passage to *Mare pacificum*: mee thinkes some of our moderne *Argonautes* should prosequute the rest. As I goe by *Madagascar*, I would see that great Bird [l] *Rucke*, that can carry a man and horse, or an Elephant, with that *Arabian Phœnix* described by [m] *Adricomius*; see the Pellicanes of *Ægypt*, those *Scythian* Gryphes in *Asia*: And afterwards in *Africk* examine the fountaines of *Nilus*, whether *Herodotus*, [o] *Seneca*, *Plin. lib. 5. cap. 9.* *Strabo lib. 5.* give a true cause of his annuall flowing, [p] *Pagaphetta* discourse rightly of it, or of *Niger* and *Senega*; examine *Cardan*, [q] *Scaligers* reasons, and the rest. Is it from those *Etesian* windes, or melting of snow in the Mountaines under the *Æquator* (for *Jordan* yearely overflowes when the snow melts in Mount *Libanus*) or from those great dropping perpetuall showres, which are so frequent to the inhabitants within the Tropickes when the Sunne is verticall, and cause such vast inundations in *Senega*, *Maragnan*, *Orenoque*, and the rest of those great rivers in *Zona Torrida*, which have all commonly the same passions at set times: and by good husbandry and policie, hereafter no doubt may come to be as populous, as well tilled, as fruitfull as *Ægypt* it selfe, or *Cauchinchina*? I would observe all those motions of the sea, and from what cause they proceed, from the Moon as the Vulgar hold, or earths motion, which *Galileus* in the fourth dialogue of his Systeme of the world, so eagerly proves, & firmly demonstrates; or winds, as [r] some will. Why in that quiet Ocean of *Zur in mari pacifico*, it is scarce perceived, in our *British* Seas most violent, in the *Mediterranean* and *Red Sea* so vehement, irregular, and diverse? Why the current in that *Atlanticke Ocean* should still bee in some places from, in some againe towards the North, and why they come sooner than goe? and so from *Moabar* to *Madagascar* in that *Indian* Ocean, the Merchants come in three weekes, as [s] *Scaliger* discusseth, they returne scarce in three moneths, with the same or like windes: The continuall current is from East to West. Whether Mount *Athos*, *Pelion*, *Olympus*, *Ossa*, *Caucasus*, *Atlas*, be so high as *Pliny*, *Solinus*, *Mela* relate, above Clouds, Meteors, *Ubi nec auræ nec venti spirant*, (insomuch that they that ascend dye suddenly very often, the aire is so subtile) 1250. paces high, according to that measure of *Dicearchus*, or 78. miles perpendicularly high, as *Jacobus Mazonius*, *sec. 3. & 4.* expounding that place of *Aristotle* about mount *Caucasus*; and as [t] *Blancanus* the Jesuite contends out of *Clavius* and *Nonius* Demonstrations *de Crepusculis*: or rather 32. stadiums, as the most received opinion is; or 4. miles, which the height of no mountaine doth perpendicularly exceed, and is equall to the greatest depths of the Sea, which is, as *Scaliger* holds 1580. paces, *Exer. 38.* others 100. paces. I would see those inner parts of *America*, whether there be any such great City of *Manoa*, or *Eldorado* in that golden Empire, where the high wayes are as much beaten (one reports) as between *Madrill* and *Valedolit* in *Spaine*; or any such *Amazones* as he relates, or giganticall Patagones in *Chica*; with that miraculous mountain [w] *Ybouyapab* in the Northren *Brasile*, *cujus jugum sternitur in amœnissimam planitiem*, &c. or that of *Pariacacca* so high elevated in *Peru*. [x] The pike of *Teneriffe* how high it is? 70. miles, or 50. as *Patricius* holds, or 9. as *Snellius* demonstrates in his *Eratosthenes*: see that strange * *Cirknickzerksey* lake

Part 2. Sect. 2. *Digression of Aire.* Memb. 3.

243 lake in *Carniola*, whose waters gush so fast out of the ground, that they will overtake a swift horseman, and by and by with as incredible celerity are supped up: which *Lazius* and *Warnerus* make an argument of the *Argonautes* sayling under ground. And that vast den or hole called [y] *Esmellen* in *Muscovia*, *quæ visitur horrendo hiatu*, &c. which if any thing casually fall in, makes such a roaring noise, that no thunder, or ordnance, or warlike engine can make the like; such another is *Gilbers* Cave in *Lapland*, with many the like. I would examine the *Caspian* Sea, and see where and how it exonerates it selfe, after it hath taken in *Volga*, *Jaxartes*, *Oxus*, and those great rivers; at the mouth of *Oby*, or where? What vent the *Mexican* lake hath, the *Titicaca* in *Peru*, or that circular poole in the vale of *Terapeia*, of which *Acosta lib. 3. c. 16.* hot in a cold country, the Spring of which boils up in the middle twenty foot square, and hath no vent but exhalation: and that of *Mare mortuum* in *Palestina*, of *Thrasumene*, at *Peruzium* in *Italy*: the [z] *Mediterranean* it selfe. For from the *Ocean*, at the Straights of *Gibralter*, there is a perpetuall current into the *Levant*, and so likewise by the *Thracian Bosphorus* out of the *Euxine* or blacke Sea, besides all those great rivers of *Nilus*, *Padus*, *Rhodanus*, &c. how is this water consumed, by the Sunne, or otherwise? I would find out with *Trajan* the fountaines of *Danubius*, of *Ganges*, *Oxus*, see those *Egyptian Pyramids*, *Trajans* bridge, *Grotta de Sybilla*, *Lucullus* Fish-ponds, the Temple of *Nidrose*, &c. And, if I could, observe what becomes of Swallowes, Storkes, Cranes, Cuckowes, Nightingales, Redstarts, and many other kinde of singing birds, water-fowles, Hawkes, &c. some of them are onely seene in Summer, some in Winter; some are observed in the [a] snow, and at no other times, each have their seasons. In winter not a bird is in *Muscovie* to bee found, but at the spring in an instant the woods and hedges are full of them, saith [b] *Herbastein*: how comes it to passe? Doe they sleepe in winter, like *Gesners* Alpine mice; or doe they lye hid (as [c] *Olaus* affirmes) *in the bottome of lakes and rivers*, spiritum continentes? *often so found by Fishermen in Poland and Scandia, two together, mouth to mouth, wing to wing; and when the spring comes they revive againe, or if they bee brought into a stove, or to the fire side.* Or doe they follow the Sunne, as *Peter Martyr Legat. Babylonica l. 2.* manifestly convicts, out of his owne knowledge: for when he was Embassadour in *Egypt*, he saw Swallowes, Spanish Kites, [e] and many such other *European* birds, in December and January very familiarly flying, and in great abundance, about *Alexandria*, *ubi floridæ tunc arbores ac viridaria*. Or lye they hid in caves, rockes, and hollow trees, as most thinke, in deepe *Tin-mines* or *Sea-cliffes*, as * Mr *Carew* gives out? I conclude of them all, for my part, as [f] *Munster* doth of Cranes and Storkes: whence they come, whither they goe, *incompertum adhuc*, as yet we know not. Wee see them here, some in summer, some in winter: *Their comming and going is sure in the night: in the plaines of Asia (saith hee) the Storkes meet on such a set day, hee that comes last is torne in peeces, and so they get them gone.* Many strange places, *Isthmi*, *Euripi*, *Chersonesi*, creekes, havens, promontories, straights, lakes, bathes, rockes, mountaines, places, and fields, where Cities have bin ruined or swallowed, battels fought, creatures, Sea-monsters, *Remora*, &c. minerals, vegetals. Zoophites were fit to bee considered in such an expedition, and amongst the rest, that of [m] *Harbastein* his *Tartar* lambe, [n] *Hector Boethius* goose-

Ii

18

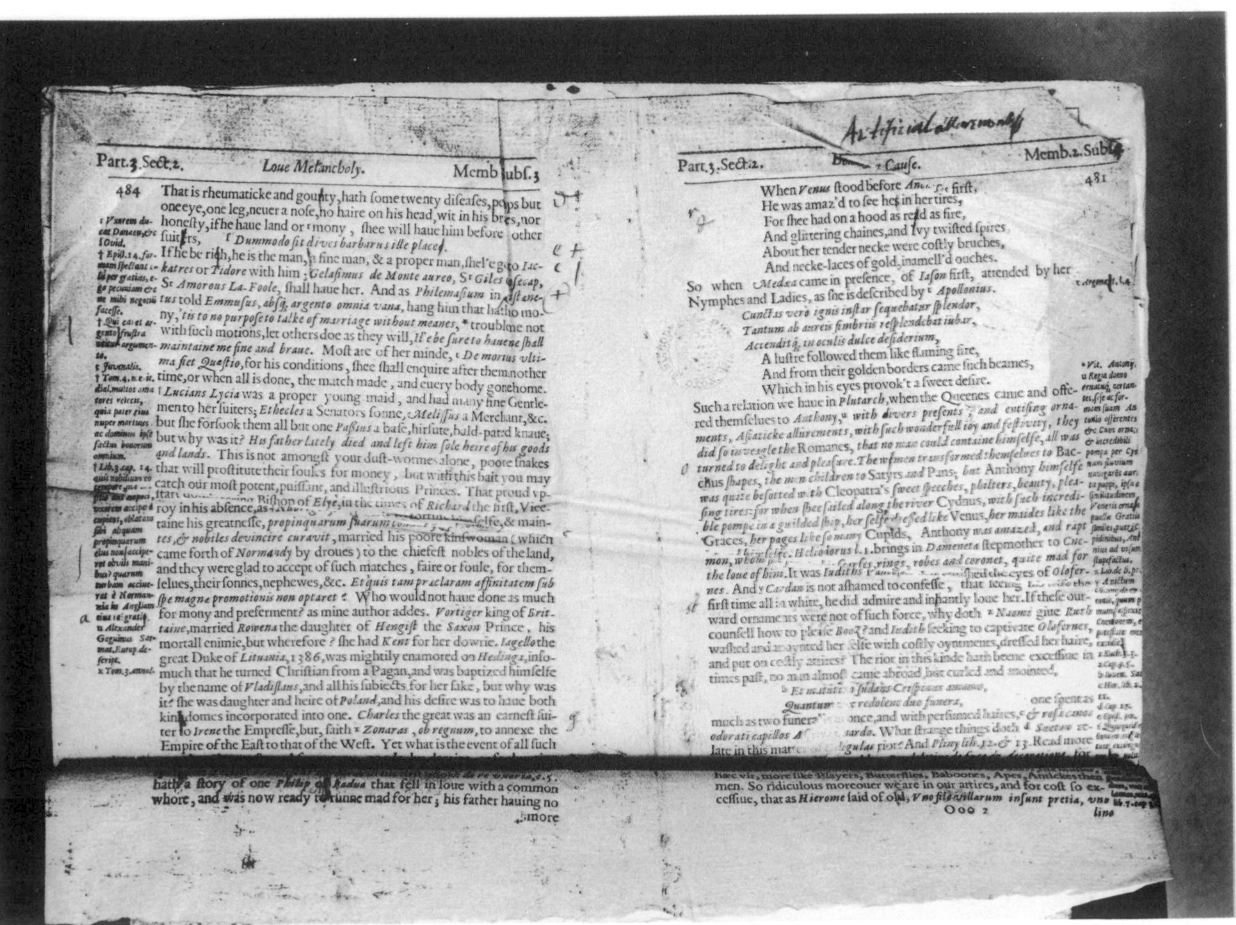

Part. 3. Sect. 2. *Loue Melancholy.* Memb. Subs. 3

484 That is rheumaticke and gouty, hath some twenty diseases, pops but one eye, one leg, neuer a nose, no haire on his head, wit in his bres, nor honesty, if he haue land or [r] mony, shee will haue him before other suitors, [f] *Dummodo sit dives barbarus ille placet.* If he be rich, he is the man, a fine man, & a proper man, she'l e go to *Jackatres* or *Tidore* with him; *Gelasimus de Monte aureo*, Sr *Giles Goosecap*, Sr *Amorous La-Foole*, shall haue her. And as *Philemasium* in *Aristænetus* told *Emmusus*, *absq; argento omnia vana*, hang him that hath no mony, *'tis to no purpose to talke of marriage without meanes*, * trouble me not with such motions, let others doe as they will, *I'le be sure to haue one shall maintaine me fine and braue.* Most are of her minde, [t] *De moribus ultima fiet Quæstio*, for his conditions, shee shall enquire after them another time, or when all is done, the match made, and euery body gone home. † *Lucians Lycia* was a proper young maid, and had many fine Gentlemen to her suiters; *Ethecles* a Senators sonne, *Melissus* a Merchant, &c. but she forsook them all but one *Passius* a base, hirsute, bald-pated knaue; but why was it? *His father lately died and left him sole heire of his goods and lands.* This is not amongst your dust-wormes alone, poore snakes that will prostitute their soules for money, but with this bait you may catch our most potent, puissant, and illustrious Princes. That proud vpstart [illegible] Bishop of *Elye*, in the times of *Richard* the first, Viceroy in his absence, as [illegible] taine his greatnesse, *propinquarum suarum* [illegible] selfe, & maintes, & *nobiles devincire curavit*, married his poore kinswoman (which came forth of *Normandy* by droues) to the chiefest nobles of the land, and they were glad to accept of such matches, faire or foule, for themselues, their sonnes, nephewes, &c. *Et quis tam præclaram affinitatem sub spe magnæ promotionis non optaret?* Who would not haue done as much for mony and preferment? as mine author addes. *Vortiger* king of *Brittaine*, married *Rowena* the daughter of *Hengist* the *Saxon* Prince, his mortall enimie, but wherefore? she had *Kent* for her dowrie. *Iagello* the great Duke of *Lituania*, 1386, was mightily enamored on *Hedinga*, insomuch that he turned Christian from a Pagan, and was baptized himselfe by the name of *Vladislaus*, and all his subiects for her sake, but why was it? she was daughter and heire of *Poland*, and his desire was to haue both kingdomes incorporated into one. *Charles* the great was an earnest suiter to *Irene* the Empresse, but, saith [x] *Zonaras*, *ob regnum*, to annexe the Empire of the East to that of the West. Yet what is the event of all such

[illegible]

hath a story of one *Philip* of *Padua* that fell in loue with a common whore, and was now ready to runne mad for her; his father hauing no more

Part. 3. Sect. 2. [illegible] *Cause.* Memb. 2. Subs.

481

When *Venus* stood before *An[illegible]* first,
He was amaz'd to see her in her tires,
For shee had on a hood as red as fire,
And glittering chaines, and Ivy twisted spires,
About her tender necke were costly bruches,
And necke-laces of gold, inamell'd ouches.

So when *Medæa* came in presence, of *Iason* first, attended by her Nymphes and Ladies, as she is described by [t] *Apollonius*.

Cunctas verò ignis instar sequebatur splendor,
Tantum ab aureis fimbriis resplendebat iubar,
Accenditq; in oculis dulce desiderium,

A lustre followed them like flaming fire,
And from their golden borders came such beames,
Which in his eyes provok't a sweet desire.

Such a relation we haue in *Plutarch*, when the Queenes came and offered themselues to *Anthony*, [u] *with divers presents, and entising ornaments, Asiaticke allurements, with such wonderfull ioy and festivity, they did so inveagle the* Romanes, *that no man could containe himselfe, all was turned to delight and pleasure. The women transformed themselues to Bacchus shapes, the men children to* Satyrs and Pans; *but* Anthony *himselfe was quite besotted with* Cleopatra's *sweet speeches, philters, beauty, pleasing tires: for when shee sailed along the river* Cydnus, *with such incredible pompe in a guilded ship, her selfe dressed like* Venus, *her maides like the* Graces, *her pages like so many* Cupids, Anthony *was amazed, and rapt* [illegible] *himselfe.* *Heliodorus l. 1.* brings in *Demeneta* stepmother to *Cnemon*, *whom* [illegible] *scarfes, rings, robes and coronet, quite mad for the loue of him.* It was *Iudiths* [illegible] ravished the eyes of *Olofernes*. And [y] *Cardan* is not ashamed to confesse, that seeing [illegible] the first time all in white, he did admire and instantly loue her. If these outward ornaments were not of such force, why doth [z] *Naomi* giue *Ruth* counsell how to please *Booz*? and *Iudith* seeking to captivate *Olofernes*, washed and anoynted her selfe with costly oyntments, dressed her haire, and put on costly attires? The riot in this kinde hath beene excessiue in times past, no man almost came abroad but curled and anointed,

[b] *Et matutino sudans Crispinus amomo,*
Quantum vix redolent duo funera,

one spent as much as two funerals at once, and with perfumed haires, [c] *& rosa canos odorati capillos Assyriaque nardo.* What strange things doth [d] *Suetonius* relate in this matter of *Caligulas* riot? And *Pliny lib. 12. & 13.* Read more

[illegible]

hæc vir, more like Players, Butterflies, Baboones, Apes, Antickes than men. So ridiculous moreouer we are in our attires, and for cost so excessiue, that as *Hierome* said of old, *Uno filo villarum insunt pretia, uno lino*

Ooo 2

18A

Λιθοθεωρικός, siue nihil, aliquid, omnia, antiquorum sapientum viuis coloribus depicta Philosophico-Theologicè: autore Ioanne Thornburg Episcopo Wigorniensi. Oxoniæ apud Ioannem Lichfield & Iacobum Short in 8.

Logonomia Anglica, qua gentis sermo facilius addiscitur, conscripta ab Alexandro Gil Paulinæ Scholæ Magistro primario Londini in 4.

Conradi Gesneri Tigurini Historiæ Animalium Liber I. II. III. IV. & V. Ambstelodami apud Henricum Laurentium in fol.

Prodromus dissertationum Cosmographicarum, continens Mysterium Cosmographicum de admirabili proportione orbium cælestium, deq; causis cælorum numeri, magnitudinis, &c. autore Ioan. Keplero Mathematico. Francof. apud Gotofredum Tampach in fol.

Eiusdem Apologia pro suo opere Harmonices mundi, aduersus demonstrationem Analyticam Roberti de Fluctibus, ibid. in fol.

Epitome Astronomiæ Copernicanæ libri V. VI. VII. eodem autore, ibid. in 8.

Dominici BaudI Orationes quæ extant omnes, ex Bibliotheca Iani RutgersI. Lugduni Batauorum apud Iacobum Marcum in 8.

Thesauri Latinitatis puræ comparandæ Principia Ioannis Brentij: quibus præter nomina substantiua Germanica accesserunt Gallica, annexis simul in fine verbis Latinis, Gallicis, & Germanicis. Argentinæ apud Ioannem Carolum in 8.

Grammatica Gallica noua Samuelis Bernhardi. Argentinæ apud Paulum Ledertz in 8.

Maturini Corderij Colloquiorum scholasticorum libri quinque, ibid. in 8.

Catechismus B. Lutheri est parua Biblia, idque ostenditur præcipuis Scripturæ sacræ dictis doctrinæ Christianæ sedem & fundamentum continenib. à Ioan. Gisenio SS. Th. Doctore, ibid. in 8.

Eiusdem pia & perspicua Catechismi B. Lutheri defensio contra Iesuitas & Zuinglio-Caluinianos, ibid. apud Paul. Ledertz & Casp. Chemlinum in 8.

Μωροσοφία, id est, stulta sapientia, & sapiens stultitia, opusculum ex varijs autoribus collectum à Gaspare Ens liber I. & II. Coloniæ apud Petrum Brackel in 12.

Prima linguæ Græcæ rudimenta, in quibus tum recte legendi ratio, tum declinationum & coniugationum Paradigmata exhibentur, Ambstelodami apud Henr. Laurentiũ in 8.

Diophanti Alexandrini Arithmeticorum libri VI. & de numeris multangulis liber vnus: autore Claudio Gaspare Bacheto Meziriaco Sebusiano V.C. Parisijs apud Sebast. Cramoisij in fol.

Francisci de Verulamio, summi Angliæ Cancellarij, instauratio magna. Londini apud Ioannem Billium in fol.

Prælectiones in Philippicam de pace Demosthenis, Andreæ Dounai Professoris Regij Cantabrigiæ Græci, ibid. in 8.

Causa Regia, siue, de autoritate & dignitate Principum Christianorum dissertatio aduersus Robertum Bellarminum, ibid. in 4.

Strena Catholica, seu, explicatio breuis & dilucida noui fidelitatis iuramenti, ib. in 8.

Sodalis

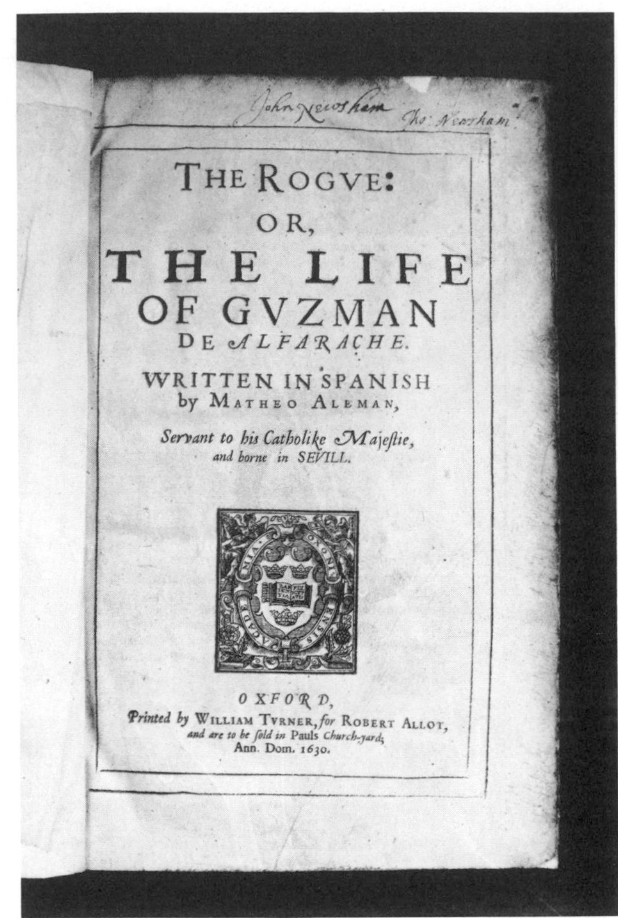

THE ROGVE:
OR,
THE LIFE
OF GVZMAN
DE ALFARACHE.

WRITTEN IN SPANISH
by MATHEO ALEMAN,

Servant to his Catholike Majestie,
and borne in SEVILL.

OXFORD,
Printed by WILLIAM TVRNER, *for* ROBERT ALLOT,
and are to be sold in Pauls *Church-yard,*
Ann. Dom. 1630.

20

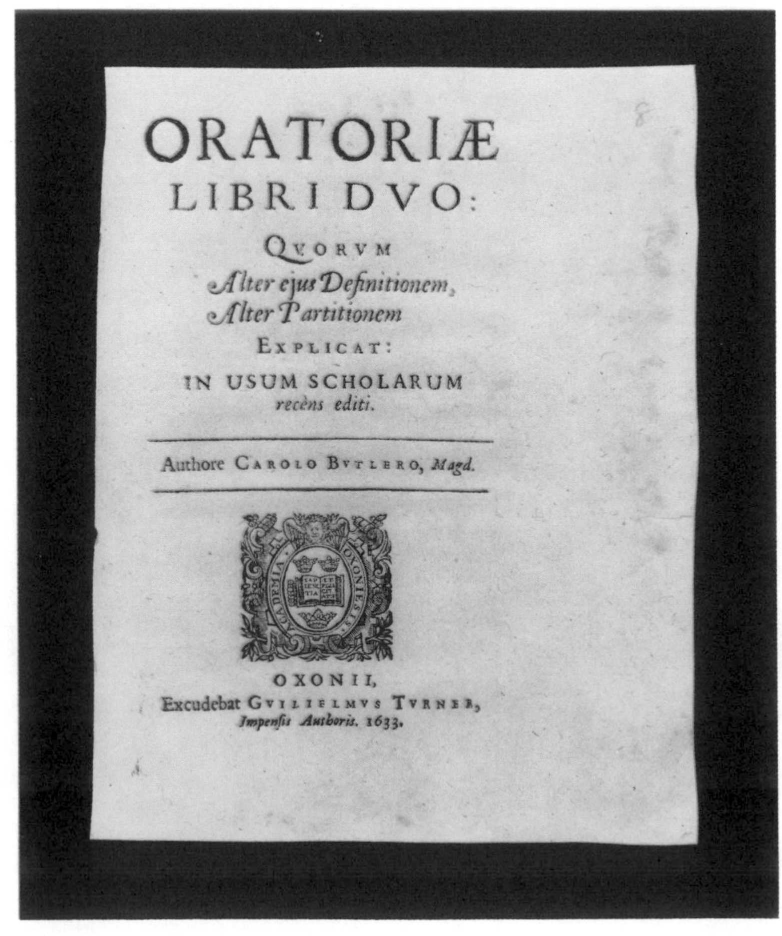

ORATORIÆ
LIBRI DVO:

QVORVM
Alter ejus Definitionem,
Alter Partitionem
EXPLICAT:

IN USUM SCHOLARUM
recens editi.

Authore CAROLO BVTLERO, *Magd.*

OXONII,
Excudebat GVILIELMVS TVRNER,
Impensis Authoris. 1633.

21

22

MVNIFICENTIA SAVILII IN CELEBERRIMAM VNIVERSITATEM OXONIENSEM.

Lecturas duas in *Geometria* & *Astronomia* cæterisq; scientijs *Mathematicis* fundavit in perpetuum; & earundem Professores publicos trecentarum & viginti librarum stipendio annuo locupletavit.

Bibliothecam Mathematicam privatam in prælectorum suorum vsum iuxta scholas Mathematicas instruxit.

Cistæ, quam ipse instituit Mathematicam centum libras donavit.

Novarum scholarum fabricæ centum & viginti libras dedit.

BIBLIOTHECAM BODLEIANAM plurimis cum typis excusis tum manuscriptis libris rarioribus ornavit.

Officinam Vniversitatis Typographicam literis græcis innumeris, literarumq; matricibus (monimento insigni) ditavit.

Tandemq; testamentô

Almæ Vniversitati, prælectoribus suis, cistæq; Mathematicæ annuum quadraginta librarum reditum legavit.

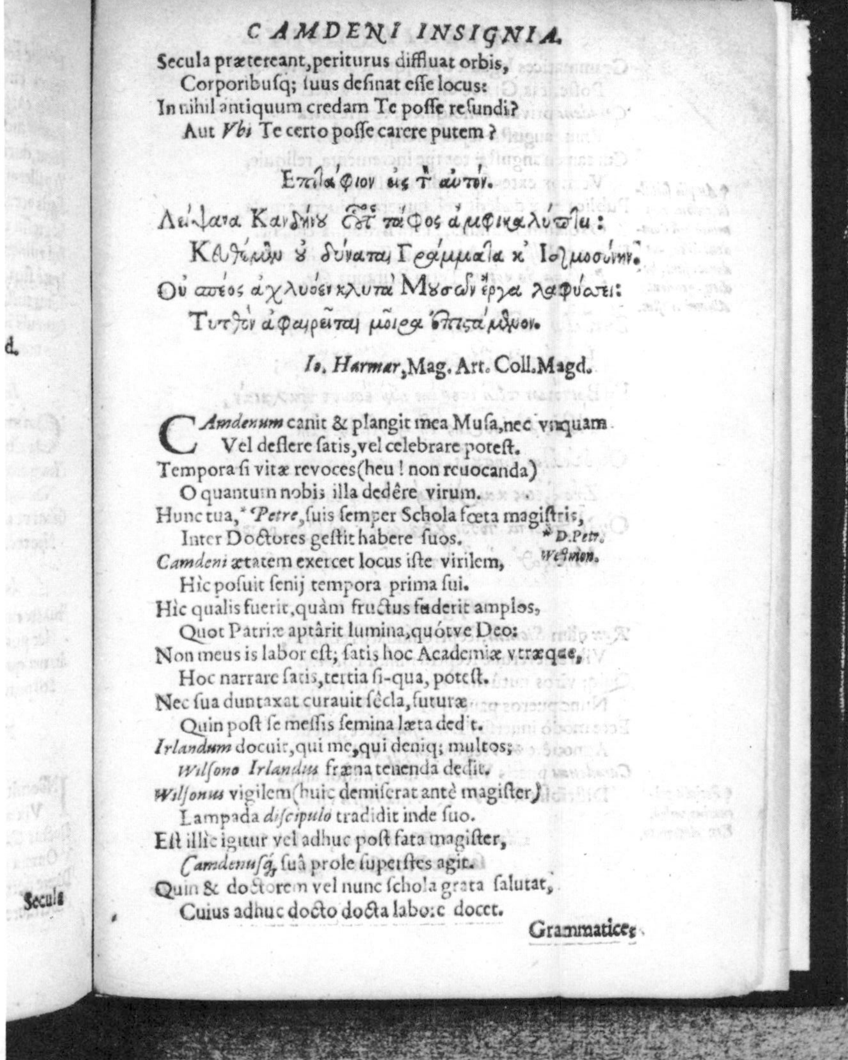

CAMDENI INSIGNIA.

Secula prætereant, periturus diffluat orbis,
Corporibusq; suus desinat esse locus:
In nihil antiquum credam Te posse resundi?
Aut *Vbi* Te certo posse carere putem?

Ἐπιτάφιον εἰς τὸν αὐτόν.

Λείψανα Καμδήνου σῶμα τάφος ἀμφικαλύπτει:
Καθελεῖν οὐ δύναται Γράμματα καὶ Ἰδμοσύνην.
Οὐ τοῖος ἀχλυόεν κλυτὰ Μουσάων ἔργα λαφύσσει:
Τοῦτον ἀφαιρεῖται μοῖρα ἐπιστάμενον.

Io. Harmar, Mag. Art. Coll. Magd.

Camdenum canit & plangit mea Musa, nec vnquam
Vel deflere satis, vel celebrare potest.
Tempora si vitæ revoces (heu! non reuocanda)
O quantum nobis illa dedêre virum.
Hunc tua, * *Petre*, suis semper Schola fœta magistris,
Inter Doctores gestit habere suos.
Camdeni ætatem exercet locus iste virilem,
Hìc posuit senij tempora prima sui.
Hìc qualis fuerit, quàm fructus fuderit amplos,
Quot Patriæ aptârit lumina, quótve Deo:
Non meus is labor est; satis hoc Academiæ vtræque,
Hoc narrare satis, tertia si-qua, potest.
Nec sua duntaxat curauit sécla, futuræ
Quin post se messis semina læta dedit.
Irlandum docuit, qui me, qui deniq; multos;
Wilsono Irlandus fræna tenenda dedit,
Wilsonus vigilem (huic demiserat antè magister)
Lampada *discipulo* tradidit inde suo.
Est illic igitur vel adhuc post fata magister,
Camdenusq; suâ prole superstes agit.
Quin & doctorem vel nunc schola grata salutat,
Cuius adhuc docto docta labore docet.

* D. Petr. Westmon.

Grammatices

Breviars.

אגרתא דיהודא שליחא אחוהי
דיעקוב אפסקופא :

יהודא עבדא דישוע משיחא
אחא דין דיעקוב לעממא קריא
דבאלהא אבא רחימין בישוע
משיחא נטירין. רחמא ושלמא
בחובא נסגא לכון. חביבי כד
כלה יציפותא עבד־אנא למכתב
לכון על חיא דילן דגוא אננקי
איתלי למכתב לכון כד מפיס
אנא דאגונא תעבדון חלף ה
הימנותא אידא דחדא זבן א
אשתלמת לקדישא : קנו גיר
אנשין מעלנותא אילין דמן
שוריא קדמי אתכתבו בחויבא
הנא אנשא רשיעא דלטיבותה
דאלהא מהפכין לטנפותא וכהו
דאיתוהי בלחודוהי מרא אלהא
מרן ישוע משיחא כפרין.

א א ב ג ג ד ד ה ה ה ו ז ח ט י י
כ כ ך ל ל ל מ מ ם ם נ נ ן ס ע
פ ף צ ץ ק ק ר ש ש ש ת ת א.

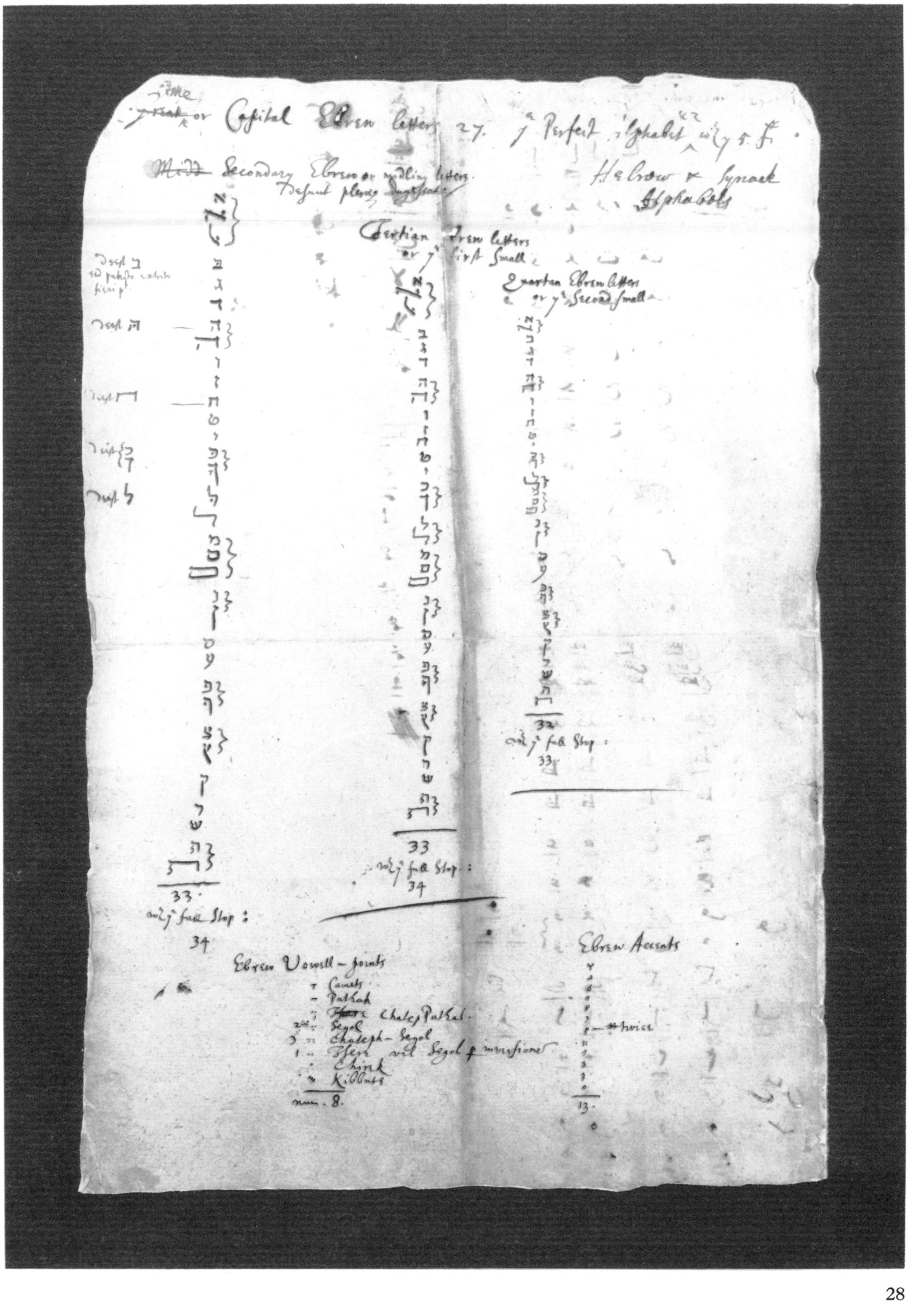

Prime or Capital Ebrew letters 27. ye Perfect Alphabet with ye 5. F.

Secondary Ebrew or midling letters.

Tertian Ebrew letters or ye first Small

Quartan Ebrew letters or ye Second Small

Hebrew & Syriack Alphabets

33

and ye full Stop :

34

33

and ye full Stop :

34

32

and ye full Stop :

33

Ebrew Vowell-points

Camets

Pathah

Chateph Pathah

Segol

Chateph-Segol

Tsere vel Segol

Chirek

Kibbuts

num. 8.

Ebrew Accents

twice

13.

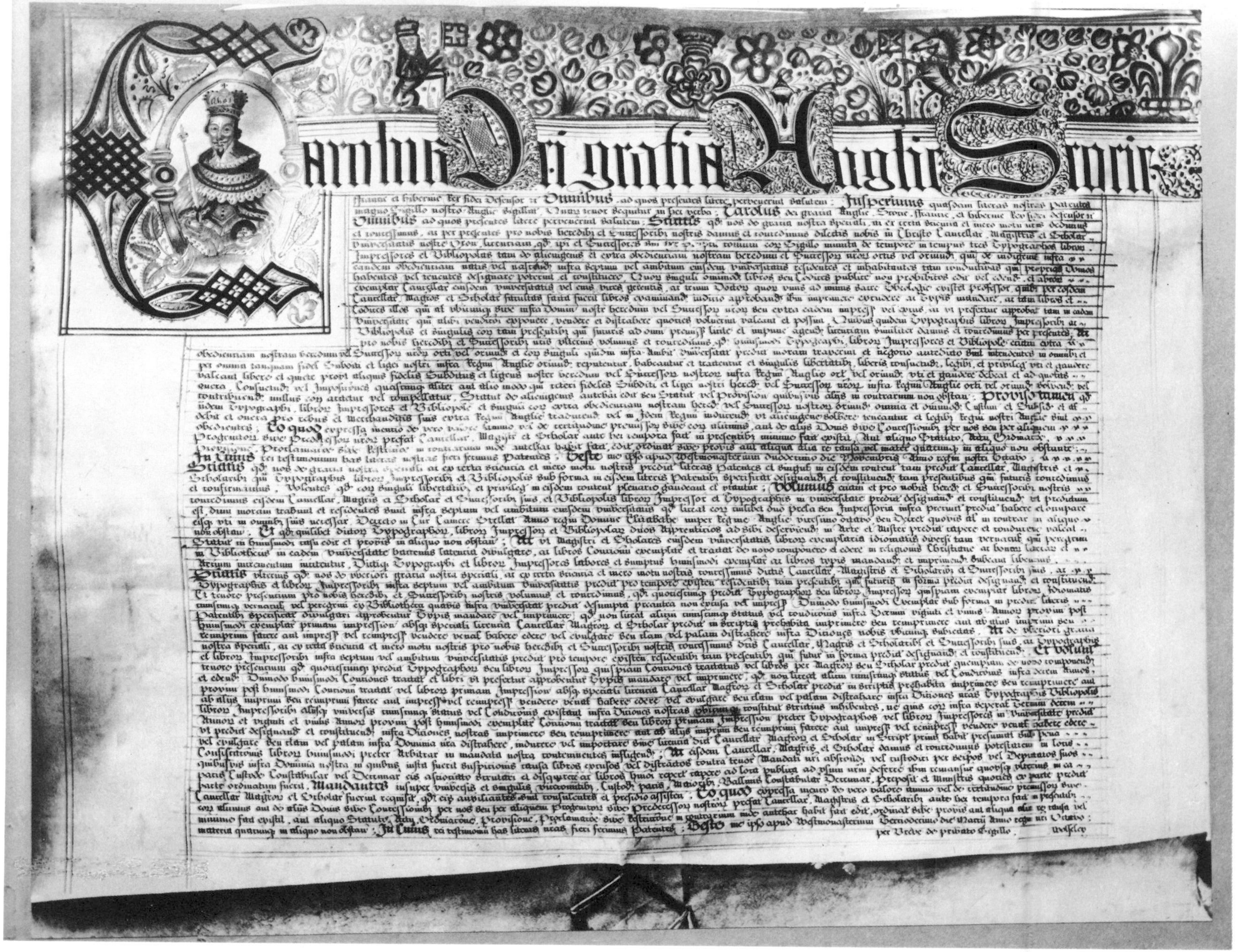

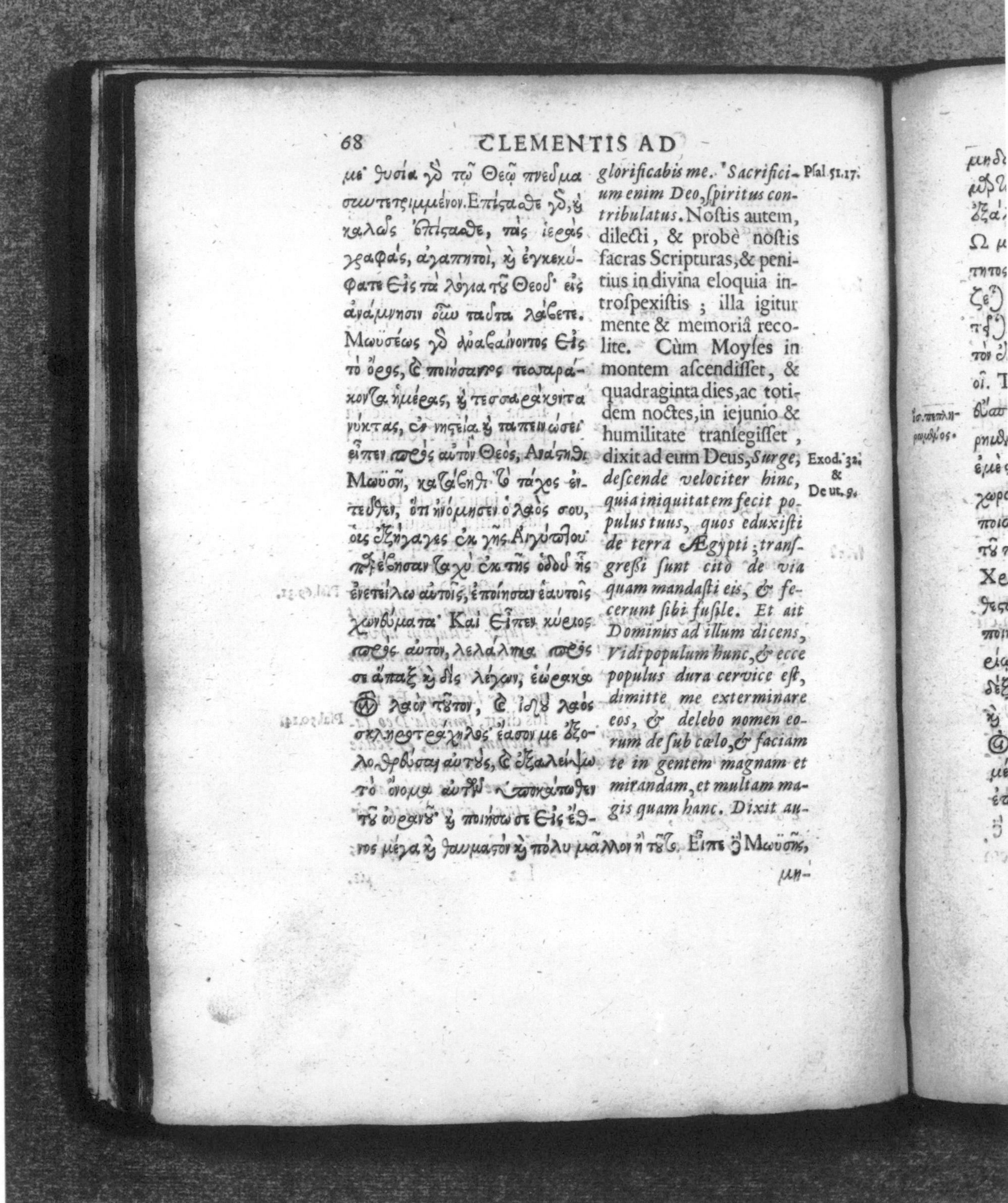

με· θυσία γὰρ τῷ Θεῷ πνεῦμα συντετριμμένον. Ἐπίστασθε γάρ, καὶ καλῶς ἐπίστασθε, τὰς ἱερὰς γραφάς, ἀγαπητοί, καὶ ἐγκεκύφατε εἰς τὰ λόγια τοῦ Θεοῦ· εἰς ἀνάμνησιν οὖν ταῦτα λάβετε. Μωϋσέως γὰρ ἀναβαίνοντος εἰς τὸ ὄρος, καὶ ποιήσαντος τεσσαράκοντα ἡμέρας, καὶ τεσσαράκοντα νύκτας, ἐν νηστείᾳ καὶ ταπεινώσει εἶπεν πρὸς αὐτὸν Θεός, Ἀνάστηθι Μωϋσῆ, κατάβηθι τὸ τάχος ἐντεῦθεν, ὅτι ἠνόμησεν ὁ λαός σου, οὓς ἐξήγαγες ἐκ γῆς Αἰγύπτου· παρέβησαν ταχὺ ἐκ τῆς ὁδοῦ ἧς ἐνετείλω αὐτοῖς, ἐποίησαν ἑαυτοῖς χωνεύματα· Καὶ εἶπεν Κύριος πρὸς αὐτόν, λελάληκα πρὸς σε ἅπαξ καὶ δὶς λέγων, ἑώρακα τὸν λαὸν τοῦτον, καὶ ἰδοὺ λαὸς σκληροτράχηλος· ἔασόν με ἐξολοθρεῦσαι αὐτούς, καὶ ἐξαλείψω τὸ ὄνομα αὐτῶν ὑποκάτωθεν τοῦ οὐρανοῦ· καὶ ποιήσω σε εἰς ἔθνος μέγα καὶ θαυμαστὸν καὶ πολὺ μᾶλλον ἢ τοῦτο. Εἶπε δὲ Μωϋσῆς, μη-

glorificabis me. *Sacrificium enim Deo, ſpiritus contribulatus.* Noſtis autem, dilecti, & probè noſtis ſacras Scripturas, & penitius in divina eloquia introſpexiſtis; illa igitur mente & memoriâ recolite. Cùm Moyſes in montem aſcendiſſet, & quadraginta dies, ac totidem noctes, in iejunio & humilitate tranſegiſſet, dixit ad eum Deus, *Surge, deſcende velociter hinc, quia iniquitatem fecit populus tuus, quos eduxiſti de terra Ægypti; tranſgreſſi ſunt citò de via quam mandaſti eis, & fecerunt ſibi fuſile. Et ait Dominus ad illum dicens, Vidi populum hunc, & ecce populus dura cervice eſt, dimitte me exterminare eos, & delebo nomen eorum de ſub cælo, & faciam te in gentem magnam et mirandam, et multam magis quam hanc. Dixit au-*

Pſal. 51.17.

Exod. 32. & Deut. 9.

THE

RELIGION OF

PROTESTANTS

A SAFE VVAY

TO SALVATION.

OR

AN ANSVVER TO A BOOKE ENTITLED MERCY AND TRVTH, Or, Charity maintain'd by Catholiques, Which pretends to prove the Contrary.

By WILLIAM CHILLINGWORTH Master *of Arts of the University of* OXFORD.

Isaac. Casauben. in Epist. ad Card. *Perron*. Regis IACOBI nomine scriptâ,

Rex arbitratur, rerum absolutè necessariarum ad salutem, non magnum esse numerum. Quare existimat ejus Majestas, nullam ad ineundam concordiam breviorem viam fore, quàm si diligentèr separentur necessaria à non necessariis, & ut de necessariis conveniat, omnis opera insumatur: in non necessariis libertati Christianæ locus detur. Simpliciter necessaria Rex appellat, quæ vel expresse verbum Dei præcipit credenda faciendave, vel ex verbo Dei necessariâ consequentiâ vetus Ecclesia elicuit.---*Si* ad decidendas hodiernas Controversias hæc distinctio adhiberetur, & jus divinum à positivo seu Ecclesiastico candidè separaretur; non videtur de iis quæ sunt absolutè necessaria, inter pios & moderatos viros, longa aut acris contentio futura. Nam & pauca illa sunt, ut modò dicebamus, & fere ex æquo omnibus probantur, qui se Christianos dici postulant. Atq; istam distinctionem *Serenissi.* Rex tanti putat esse momenti ad minuendas Controversias, quæ hodie Ecclesiam Dei tantopere exercent, ut omnium pacis studiosorum judicet officium esse, diligentissimè hanc explicare, docere, urgere.

OXFORD
Printed by LEONARD LICHFIELD, Printer to the UNIVERSITY.

Anno Salutis M.DC.XXXVIII.

ARTIVS C PLATONE PHILOSOPHIÆ PRINCEPS
QVOD FELICITER VORTAT REIP: LITERARIÆ
V.C FRAN: DE VERVLAMIO PHILOSOPHIÆ LIBERTATIS
ASSERTOR AVDAX, SCIENTIARV REPARATOR FELIX
MVNDI MENTISQ MAGNVS ARBITER INCLYTI
PP AVG: clↄ Iↄc XXVI.

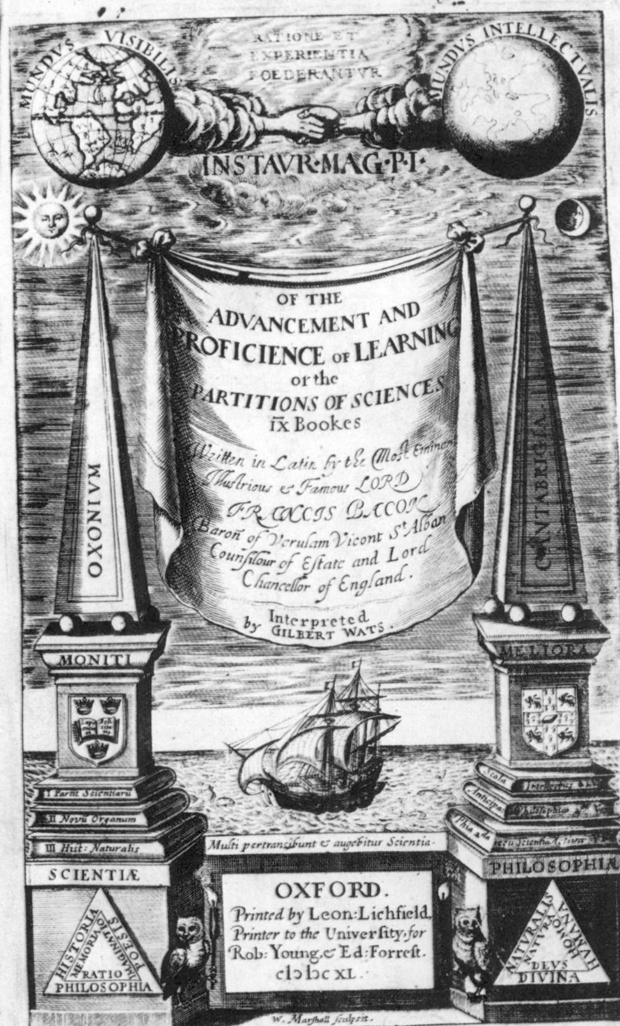
MVNDVS VISIBILIS
RATIONE ET EXPERIENTIA FOEDERANTVR
MVNDVS INTELLECTVALIS
INSTAVR·MAG·P·I·
OF THE ADVANCEMENT AND PROFICIENCE OF LEARNING or the PARTITIONS OF SCIENCES IX Bookes
Written in Latin by the Most Eminent Illustrious & Famous LORD FRANCIS BACON Baron of Verulam Vicont St Alban Counsellour of Estate and Lord Chancellor of England.
Interpreted by GILBERT WATS.
OXONIVM
CANTABRIGIA
MONITI
MELIORA
I Partit Scientiaru
II Novu Organum
III Hist: Naturalis
SCIENTIÆ
PHILOSOPHIA
Multi pertransibunt & augebitur Scientia.
OXFORD.
Printed by Leon: Lichfield, Printer to the University for Rob: Young & Ed: Forrest.
clↄ Iↄc XL.
HISTORIA MEMORIA
POESIS IMAGINATIO
RATIO PHILOSOPHIA
NATVRALIS HVMANA
DEVS DIVINA
W. Marshall sculpsit.

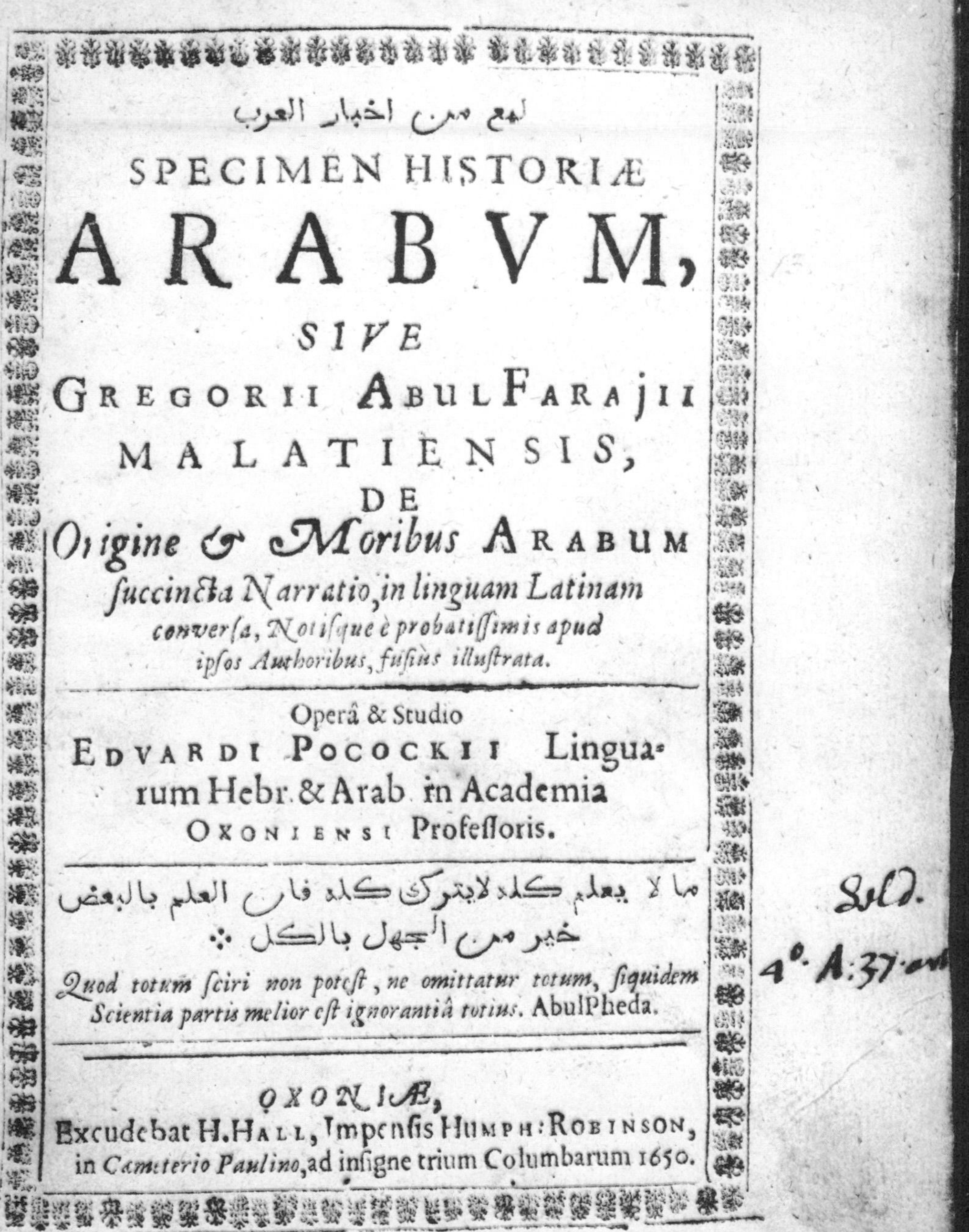

لمع من اخبار العرب

SPECIMEN HISTORIÆ

ARABVM,

SIVE

GREGORII ABUL FARAJII

MALATIENSIS,

DE

Origine & Moribus ARABUM

succincta Narratio, in linguam Latinam conversa, Notisque è probatissimis apud ipsos Authoribus, fusius illustrata.

Operâ & Studio

EDVARDI POCOCKII Linguarum Hebr. & Arab. in Academia OXONIENSI Professoris.

ما لا يعلم كله لا يترك كله فان العلم بالبعض
خير من الجهل بالكل ∴

Quod totum sciri non potest, ne omittatur totum, siquidem Scientia partis melior est ignorantiâ totius. AbulPheda.

OXONIÆ,

Excudebat H. HALL, Impensis HUMPH: ROBINSON, in *Cæmeterio Paulino*, ad insigne trium Columbarum 1650.

Johannis Wallisii, SS. Th. D.
GEOMETRIÆ PROFESSORIS
SAVILIANI in Celeberrimâ
Academia OXONIENSI,

DE
ANGVLO CONTACTVS
ET SEMICIRCULI
Disquisitio Geometrica.

OXONII,
Typis LEON: LICHFIELD Academiæ Typographi,
Impensis THO: ROBINSON. *Anno* 1656.

37

Arab. punsons of letters 86
of vowels &c. 20
wanting

for ... diacrit: points are wanting.

Wanting in ye punsons, of ye Brevier ~~middle~~ ~~font~~ of Hebr.

ב ה ל
ד ל
ן ן ה

• Non pareile Hebrew without points
Punsons perfect except ה which is broken

Non pareile Hebrew matrices without points
perfect excepting ה which is wanting

Arab matrices

45
42
47
45
179

Wanting of ye Arab. Matrices ...

to cast a compleat font of Hebrew lrs of that body of 200lb weight or thereabouts which is comonly called & knowne by the name of Brevier and with the poynts & accents fitted thereto out of the matrices of the sayd university, & according to a proof thereof to him the sayd Nicholas delivered at the sealing hereof togither with the matrices in number 115 for the safe custody & restitution thereof togither with the sayd font of letters by him to be cast, & that in the meane time they shall not be made use of to any other purpose then is expressed in these presents

It the sayd Nicholas Nicholls doth covenant & grant &c. to supply the defects of the punchions & matrices of the university by making new ones of the same kind & body when any are wanting & to justify all of them in a workman like fashion. & to deliver the sayd font of lrs by him so cast as aforesayd & the matrices of the Univty by him received togither with such other punsons or matrices as shall be by him made as aforesayd into the hands of such pson or psons as shall be appoynted by the sayd Ger. Langb. or by any other to be appoynted by the sayd Chan: mrs & schs. to receive the same at the now dwelling house of the sayd Nich. N. in Aldersgate street London at or before the 1 day of July.

It the sayd Ger: Langbaine in behalf of the sayd Ch: &c doth promise to pay unto the sayd N. N. for the letter so by him to be cast as is above sayd after the rate of eight pence the pound. And for every new punson & matrice by the sayd N. N. made & added ... [illegible]

Dec. 7. 1657

Sr

I thank you for communicating so much of yr intentions for an Oriental Dictionary & the specimen of it you sent me, that to Mr Pocock I sent by his servt on friday last. I have not seen him here this moneth, he has not been well of late. pray God restore him to his health. I desire you returne my respects to yr fellow labourers in this work Mr Castell & Mr Thurch[illegible]. that you should adde my name to the number of those that doe approve the undertaking I shall be glad of an opportunity to further the carrying on of the worke, is the least thing of a thousand you could desire, or I graunt.

For my judgment upon the severall particulars of yr paper I dare not be peremptory. I like the maine designe well; but

1 your characters are not well matched to print together, the Arabick being of a much bigger body then the rest. by which both the grace of the work is impaired, & there will be a losse of paper for it will often happen that either one line must be kept [illegible] context for a word in the Arabick or else the rest must be confusedly jumbled togither.

2 The grammars will be very neary to accompany the worke.

3. For the Latine Index I should think it not so necessary, as an alphabeticall Index to the severall languages, such as that of Stephanus, or Scapula to their Greek lexica. And this might well enough supply most of what is to be expected from those Concordances you have thought upon. The Hebrew & Greek being already well enough performed by Buxtorf, Stephanus, & Kircher, & the rest I think would be of more trouble & charges, then benefit being [illegible]. I cannot stay to adde the reasons of all I say, the maine is the hazard of rendring an impression.

Wee have in yr publ: library (which it may not be amisse for you to see) Mr Bedwells additions in MSS. to Munsters Chaldee Dictionary, done in MS. interleaved & bound up with the printed copy of Munster. And in like method a Lexicon Harmonicum by Mr Wm Lamplugh, who lived in London about 20 years agoe. his method is this, he has bound up Buxtorfs Epitome interleaved with his owne MSS. additions, of the severall words in other languages derived from those Hebrew roots.

I doe purpose to drive hard for the setting up of yr learned presse. the Vice-chancellor hath promised me to call a meeting to that purpose on munday next. But you shall not be ready for you yet. Pray God blesse you in yr labours. I am

Yr very loving friend Gerard Langbaine.

Qu: Coll: Oxon
Dec. 7. 1657.

40

42

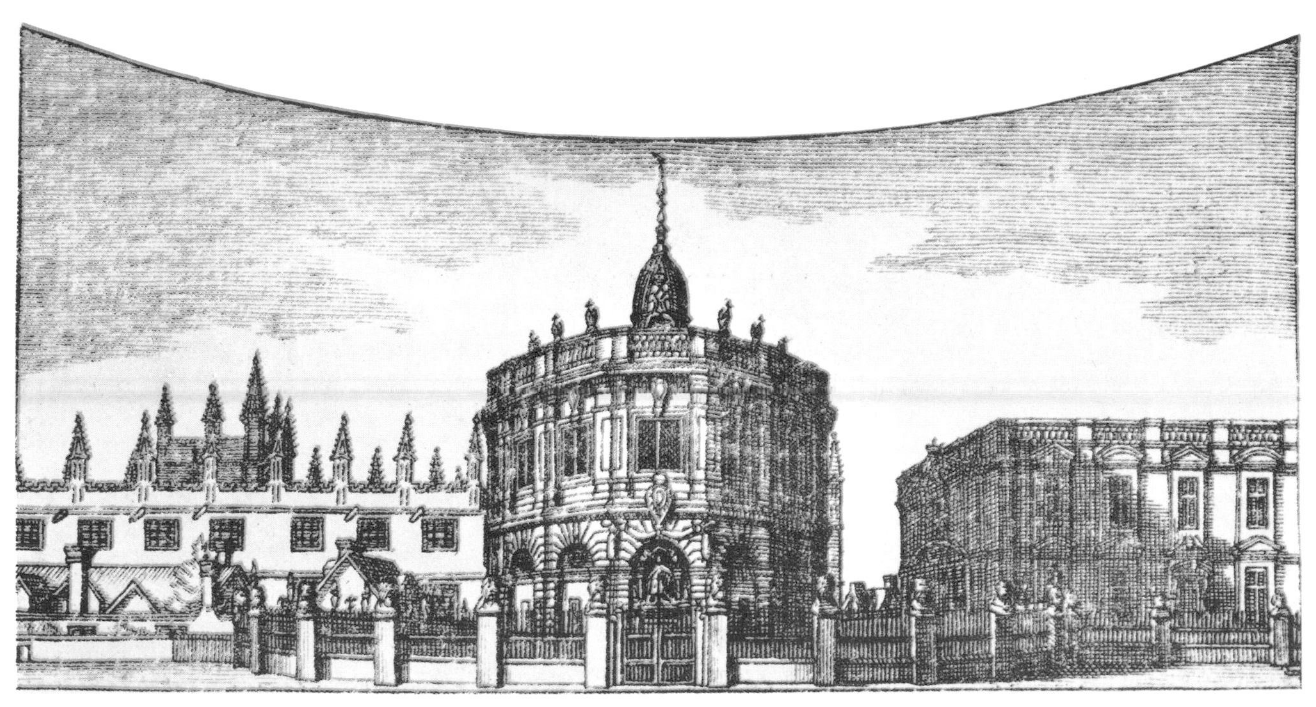

44

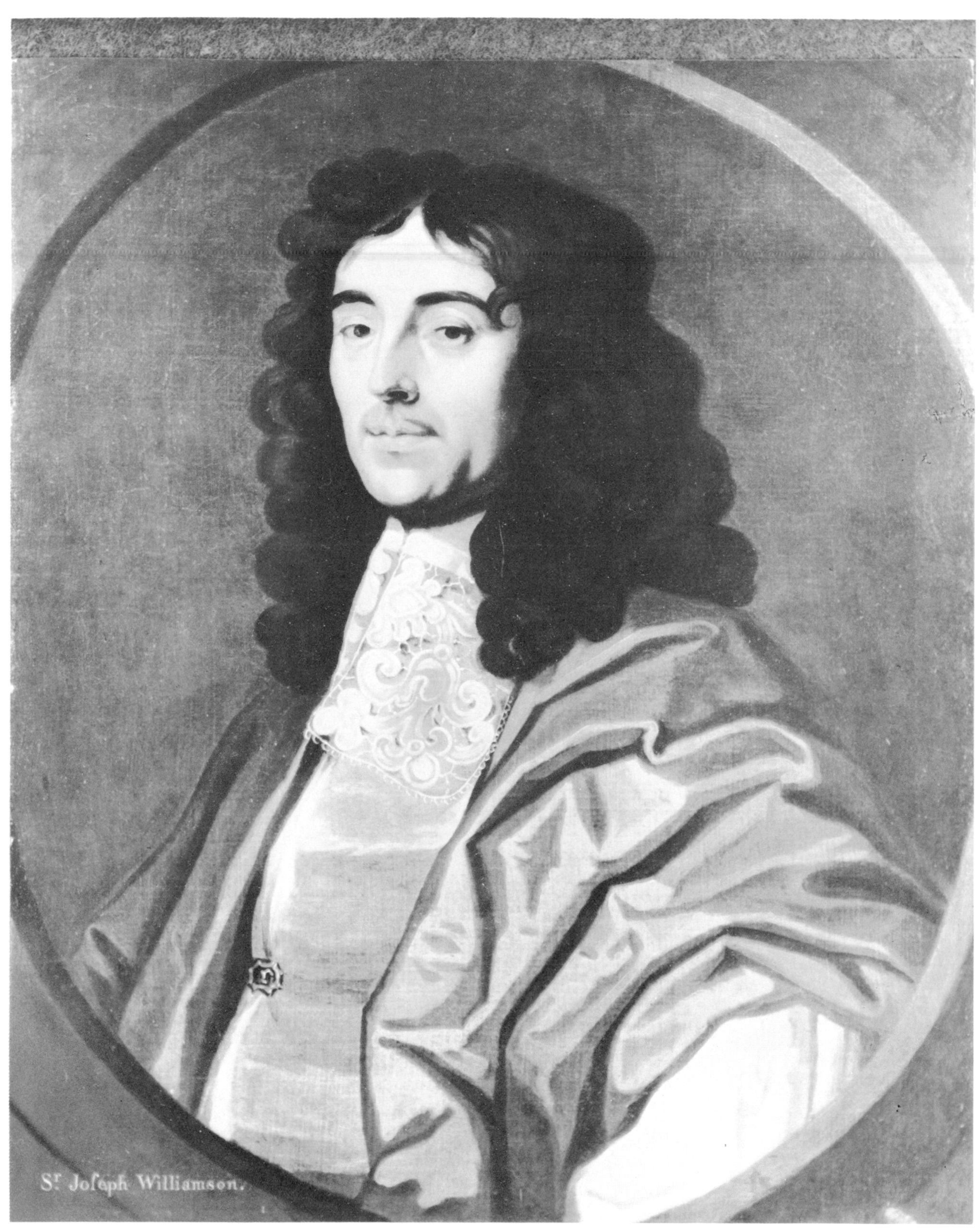
Sr. Joseph Williamson.

46

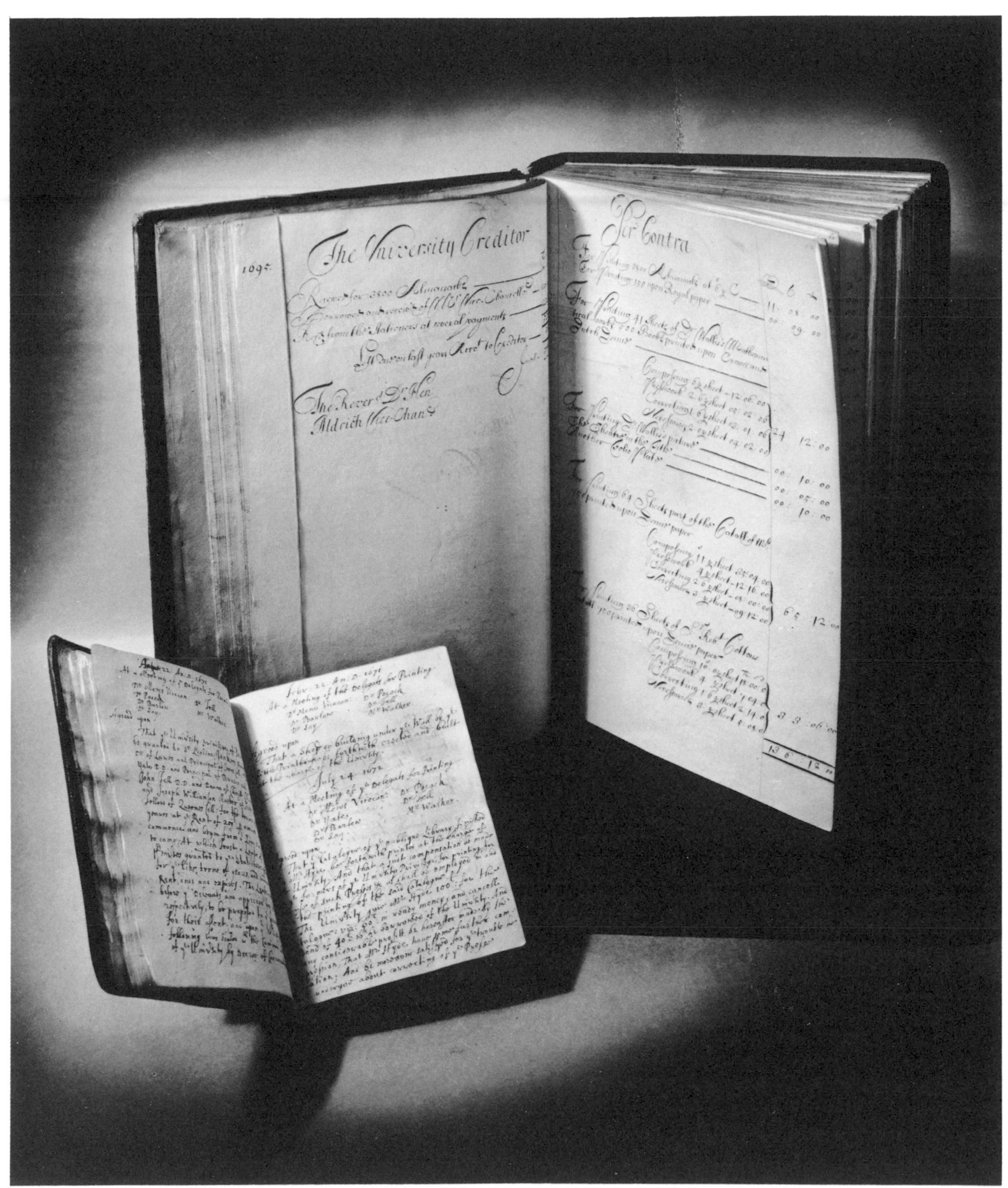
1695
The University Creditor
Per Contra

Dordrecht. April 2/12. 1670 / (122)

Rev. Sr,

Willing to give a satisfactory account of your commission about Types,
I thought best to wave transaction by writing, & wait for a seasonable opportunity to treat wth ye Letter-founders in their own houses. And to
that end, I made a journey lately to Amsterdam on purpose: where I
quickly understood yt this last winter had sent Van Dyke & Voskens,
the two best Artists in this Country, to their graves. Both have left sons, with
whom I treated: & from ye son of Van Dyke have sent such Greek & Latin Letters
as you desired, with ye respective prices of each, set down by his own direction. By
ye plainer account adjoyned to ye Greek I suppose ye shorter, placed by ye Latin,
will be easily understood. A guilder consisteth of 20. stuyvers, whereof 11. are now
worth an English shilling. Voskens his prices were lower, but Greek Median he
had none, neither complete Latin Matrices: onely offered to cast upon very civill
termes; but utterly refuseth to conform to ye size of your letters, wch are much
lower (& consequently will be dearer) then those used here. Van Dyke offers
Types or Matrices upon ye conditions now intimated; wch I thought fit
to send wth a Specimen of ye severall letters, that you may, wth ye advice of your Artists, judge both of the commodity & price. The Latin in
mine eyes seem good. Other median Greek I cannot yet hear off to be sold, in
Amsterdam. The other sorts of Greek now sent, are onely to gratify curi-
osity, yet are vendible also. If you please to deal for any of these, & judge your founders maste[rs]
of their profession, I should think Matrices would best serve your occasi[on]
partly, because of ye difficulty to reconcile ye Dutch casting-instrumen[ts]
to ye size of your low letters; & chiefly, because these founders know not
what you mean by a Fount, being use to sell by ye pounds. They ask m[e]
whether you intend letters to furnish one, two or three Formes together
& soy [?], to a compleat Case of Brevier are requisite, 180. pounds Roman,
50. pounds Cursyf, or Italick. Wherein I may further be servi-
able, be pleased to command

Worthy Sr Your obliged servant
Tho. Marshall.

Mr Bressy [?] presents his best respects & thankfulness for yor inspection over his son.

brevier letters in Holland worth 24 Stivers the pound.

Perle 42 Stivers the pound.

Median Greek 1 guilder, one shilling ten pence the pound

To prevent mistakes ye prices of ye Latin letters stand thus.

			Matrices	Types cast upon English size	
Latin	Brevier	Roman	225 guilders	24 stuyvers	the pound.
		Italick or Cursyf	150 guilders	24 stuyvers	
	Nonpareil	Roman	250 guilders	42 stuyvers	
		Italick or Cursyf	250 guilders	42 stuyvers	
Greek Median in number 410 [?]			600 guilders		

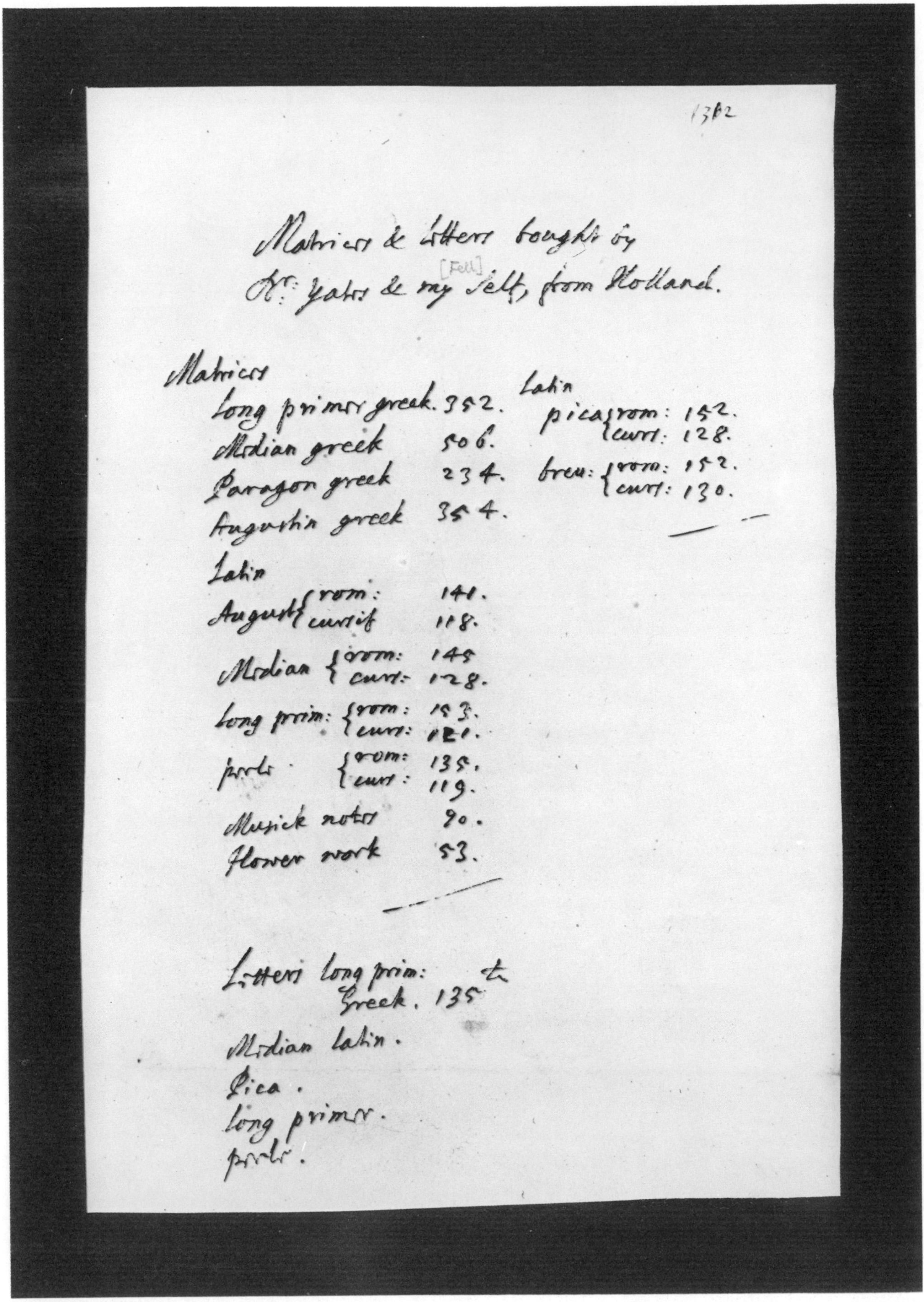

1382

Matrices & Letters bought by
Mr: Yates & my [Fell] self, from Holland.

Matrices

Long primer greek.	352.	Latin	
Median greek	506.	pica {rom:	152.
Paragon greek	234.	{curs:	128.
Augustin greek	354.	brev: {rom:	152.
		{curs:	130.

Latin

August {rom:		141.
{cursif		118.
Median {rom:		145
{curs:		128.
Long prim: {rom:		153.
{curs:		121.
perle {rom:		135.
{curs:		119.
Musick notes		90.
Flower work		53.

Letters long prim:
Greek. 135 [lb]

Median latin.
Pica.
long primer.
perle.

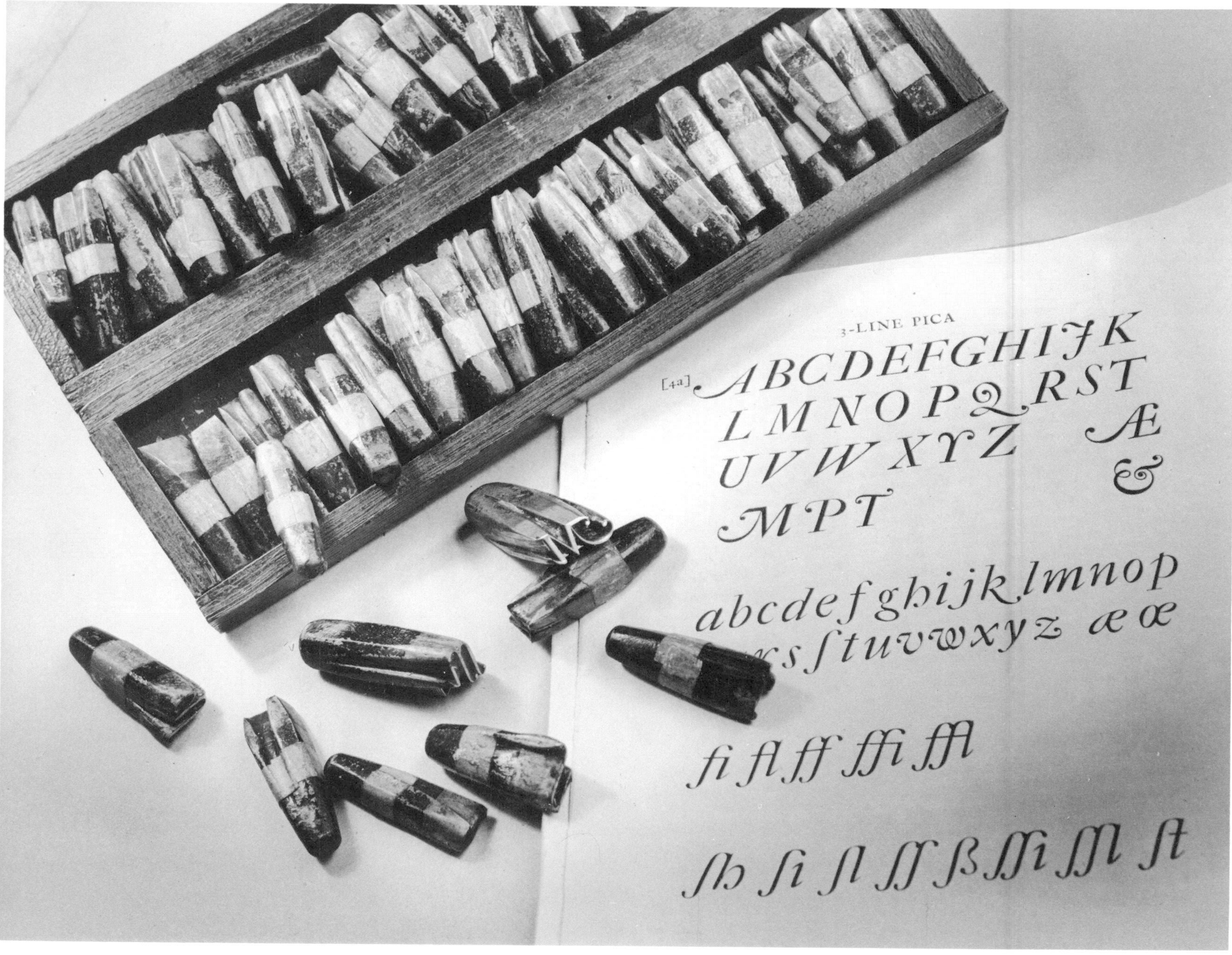

3-LINE PICA
[4a] ABCDEFGHIJK
LMNOPQRST
UVWXYZ Æ
&
MPT
abcdefghijklmnop
ſtuvwxyz æ œ
ﬁ ﬂ ﬀ ﬃ ﬄ
ſb ſi ſl ſſ ß ſſi ſſl ſt

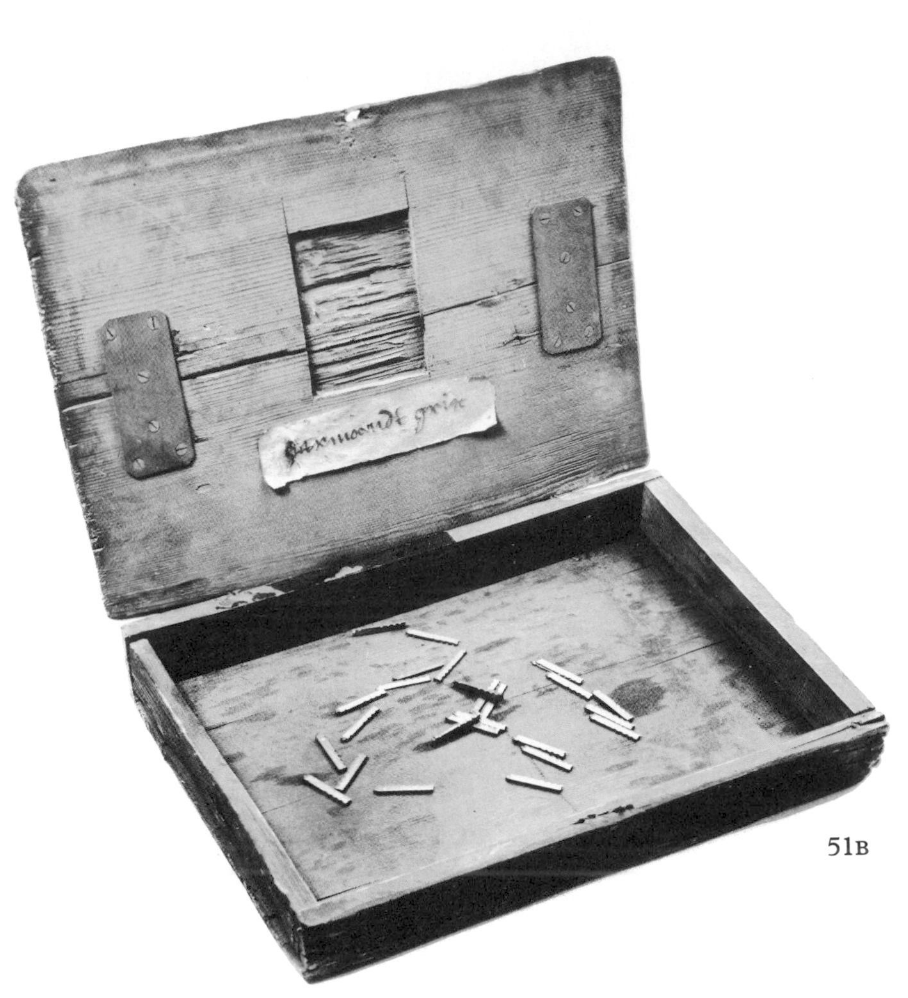

51B

52

comme s'esbahissant, luy demandoit la cause pourquoy au lieu qu'au-
parauant il se tenoit si priué de luy, maintenant il ne demandoit qu'à
fuir & se cacher. 30 Et comme Adam se taisoit, se sentant coulpable en
sa conscience de ce qu'il auoit transgressé le commandement de son
Createur, Dieu luy dit, Vray est, que i'auoye pourueu à toutes choses qui
vous seroyent expedientes : i'auoye donné ordre que deussiez mener vne
vie heureuse & exempte de tous maux, comment vous ne deussiez
estre aucunement solicitez en vos esprits de fascherie ne de soin quel-
conque: & toutes choses qui sont bonnes pour vser, & pour donner
plaisir, vous venoyent d'elles mesmes par ma seule prouidence, & sans
que vous y deussiez employer aucun trauail: & en iouïssant d'icelles, la
vieillesse ne vous eust point soudainement surprins ny opprimez, & eus-
siez vescu fort longuement. 31 Mais tu as eu en moquerie ceste mienne

A SPECIMEN OF THE TYPES ATTRIBUTABLE TO

PETER DE WALPERGEN

CUT FOR THE UNIVERSITY OF OXFORD

1676–1702

4-line Pica Capitals

ABCDEFGHI
JKLMNOPQ
RSTUVWXY
ΓΔΘΛΞΠΣΦ

2-line Pica Capitals

ABCDEFGHIJKLMN
OPQRSTUVWXYZÆ

Double-Pica Greek Titling Capitals

ΑΒΓΔΕΖΗΘΙΚΛΜΝΞΟΠΡΣ
ΤΥΦΧΨΩ

Pica Black Letter

And I, even I Artaxerxes the king, do make a decree to all the treasurers which are beyond the river, that whatsoever Ezra the priest, the scribe of the law of the God of heaven, shall require of you, it be done speedily.
ABCDEFGHIJKLMNOPQRSTUVWXYZ

Astronomical & Mathematical Signs

♈♉♊♋♌♍♎♏♐♑♒♓ ☌☍ ☉☽♂♀☿ — = □ √

2-line Double-Pica Music

3-line Pica Roman

Man that is born
of a woman is of
few days and full
of trouble *†§‖¶)
ABCDEFGHIJK

3-line Pica Italic

*He cometh forth
like a flower and
is cut down: asisus
Et st A Q M J &*

Double-Pica Roman

As first, it is reason he be thought a Master of words, that could with one word appease a mutiny in his Army; which was thus. æœctll&ffiffifl.,;:!)]
ABCDEFGH ABCDEFGH 1234567890

Double-Pica Italic

The Romanes when their Generalls did speake in their Army did use the word Milites; but when the Magistrates spake to the people, they did use the word Quirites: ij fr & ß ABCDEFGHIJKLMNO

English Syriac

Great Primer Roman

The Souldiers were in tumult, and seditiously prayed to bee cassiered: not that they soe meant, but by expostulation thereof, to drawe Cæsar to other Conditions; wherein he being Resolute ABCDEFGHIJKLMNOPQRSTU VWXYZ ABCDEF 1234567890 éàèìòù §‖†✠&

Great Primer Italic

After some silence he began his speech, Ego, Quirites, which did admit them already cassiered; wherewith they were so crossed, surprized & confused, as they would not suffer him to goe on in his speech. ÆDMP ABC DEFG abcdefghijklmnopqrstuvwxyz

Pica Roman

The second speech was thus: Cæsar did extreamely affect the name of King; and some were set on, as he passed by, in popular acclamation to salute him King; whereupon finding the cry weake and poore; he put it off thus, in a kind of Jest, as if they had mistaken his surname; ABC ABCDEFGHIJKL MNOPQRSTUVWXYZÆ

Pica Italic

Non Rex sum, sed Cæsar, a speech that if it be searched, the life and fulnesse of it, can scarce be expressed: For first it was a refusall of the name, but yet not serious: againe it did signifie an infinite confidence and magnanimity. & ABCDEFGHIJ KLMNOPQRSTUVWXYZÆ

Pica Armenian

Pica Coptic

English Samaritan

Peter de Walpergen, a German from Frankfurt, was engaged by John Fell as typefounder to the press set up in the Sheldonian Theatre in 1668, from which the present University Press is descended. Walpergen, who had previously served the Dutch East India Company as letter-cutter and typefounder in Java, came to Oxford in 1676 and died here in 1702. As the servant of Dr. Fell, Bishop of Oxford and Dean of Christ Church, he cut punches, made matrices, and cast type in a workroom in the Dean's Lodging, was listed as a *Janitor* of the college and sometimes waited on the Dean at table. In later years he was repeatedly cited in the University Chancellor's Court for debt.

Besides the types shown above, which are believed to be wholly the work of Walpergen, the Double Pica and Great Primer Greeks of Fell's press were supplemented with a large number of ligatures by him; and he cut additional characters for the Arabic type of the University, adapting it for the Turkish, Persian, and Malay languages. He replaced missing letters in the University's types for Hebrew and Anglo-Saxon, and reformed the Roman and Italic on *English* body by recutting 19 of the letters. Matrices for Walpergen's Double Pica and Great Primer Roman and Italic belonged to the James' typefoundry in London in the 18th cent., and the Double Pica was much used by London printers. After Fell's death in 1686 Walpergen continued to work in Oxford, and sold punches and matrices to the University. He also cut a music-type of more modern fashion for the account of himself and a partner. The punches and matrices for the types shown on this sheet are kept at the University Press.

Printed in Great Britain, at the University Press, Oxford, by Vivian Ridler, Printer to the University

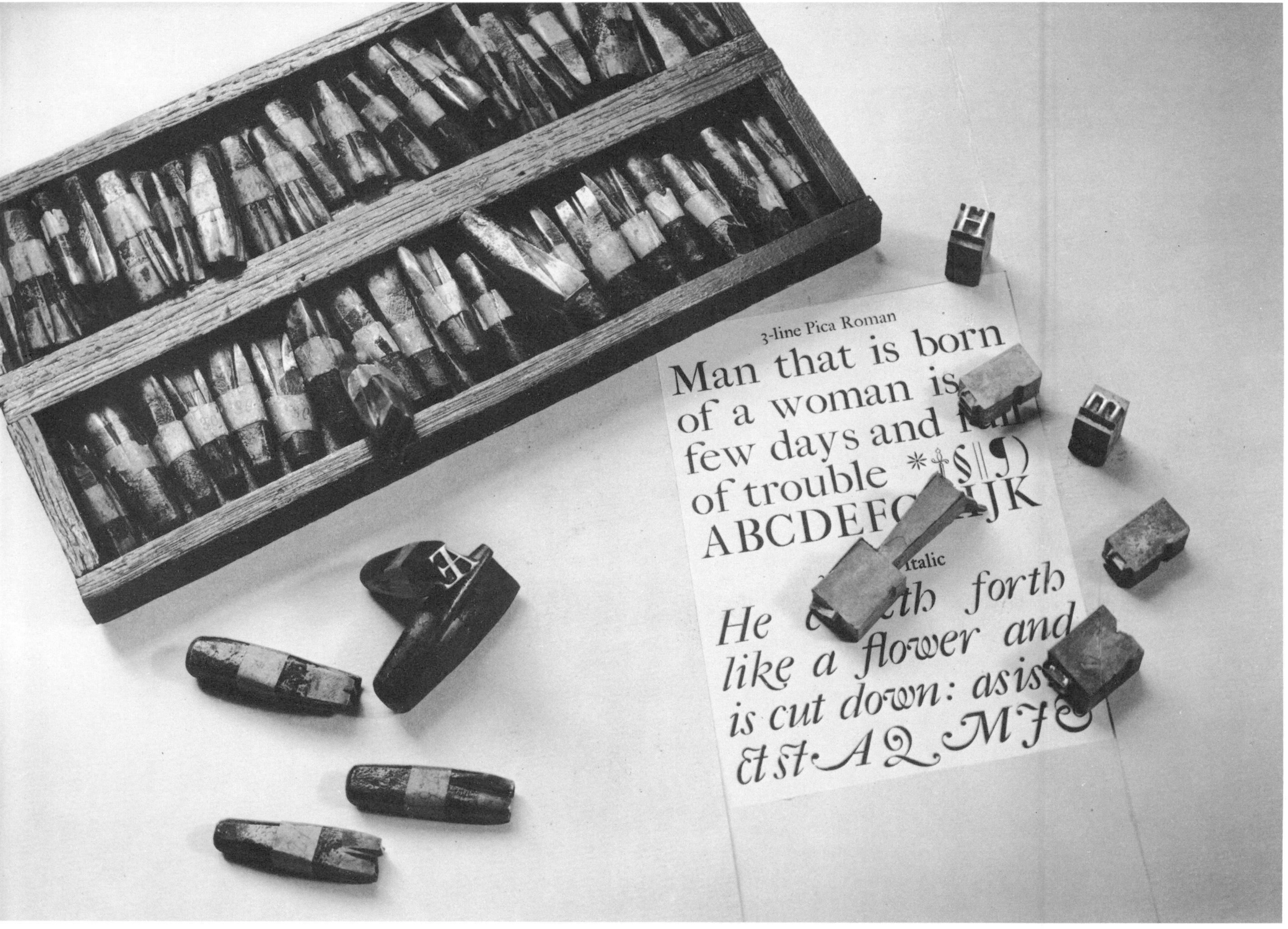
3-line Pica Roman
Man that is born
of a woman is
few days and
of trouble
ABCDEF
Italic
He
forth
like a flower and
is cut down: as
Et st A Q M

56

ENGLISH SYRIAC
Synopsis of the sorts.
Aleph
Beth
Gamal
Daleth
He
Waw
Zain
Ḥeth
Ṭeth
Yodh
Kaf
Lamadh
Mim
Nun
Semkath
'E
Pe

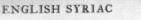

MUSIC TYPES
Cut by Peter de Walpergen

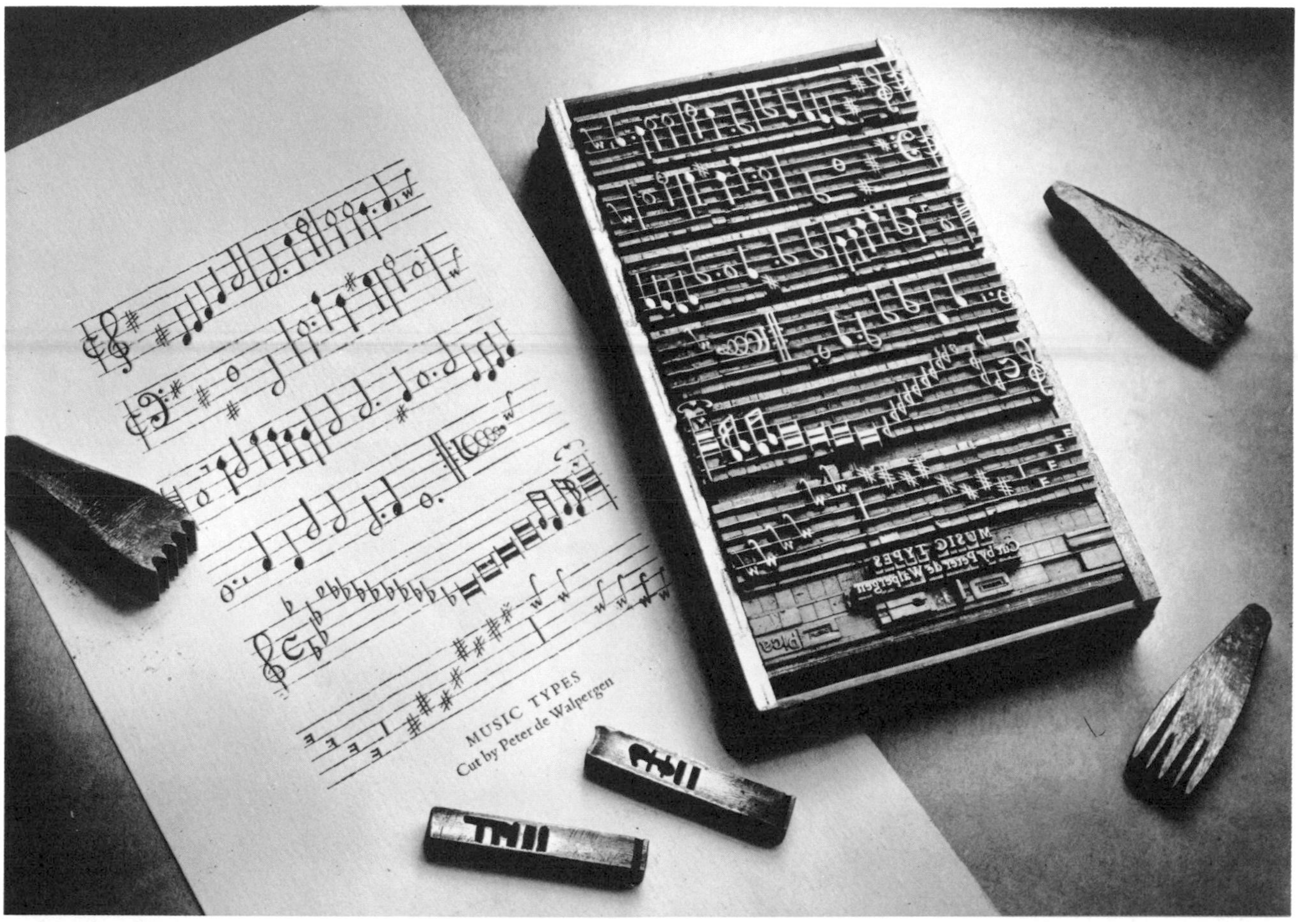

58

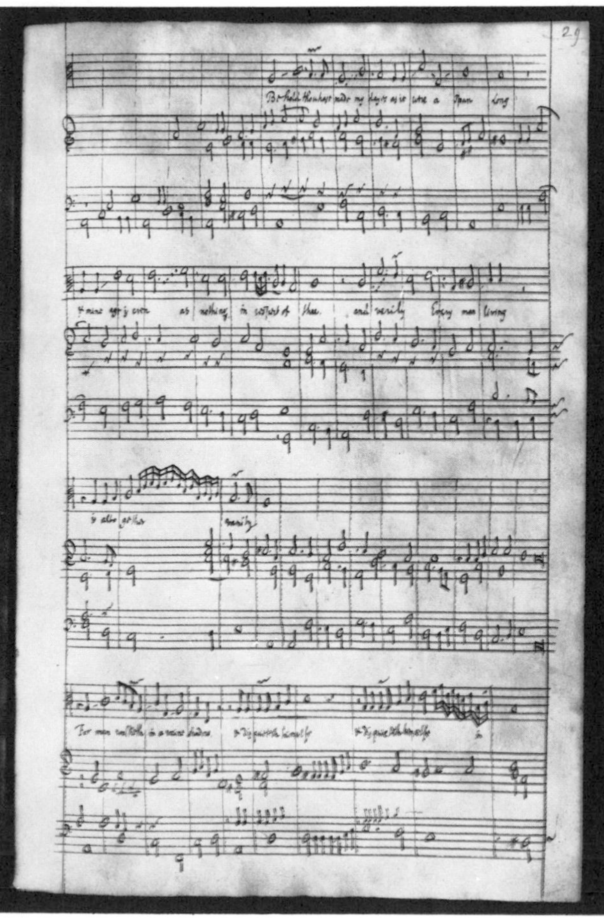

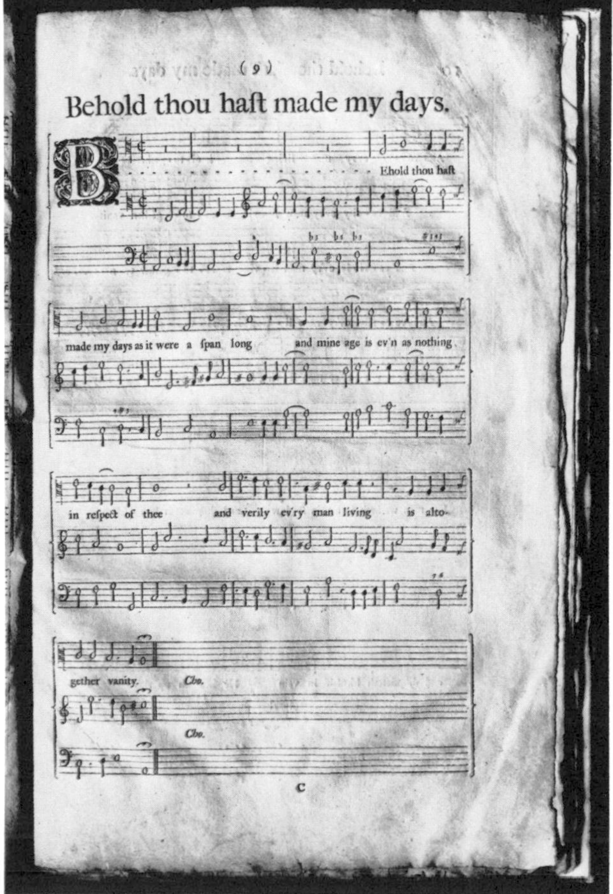

Behold thou haſt made my days.
Ehold thou haſt
made my days as it were a ſpan long
and mine age is ev'n as nothing
in reſpect of thee
and verily ev'ry man living
is alto-
gether vanity.
Cho.
Cho.
C

59

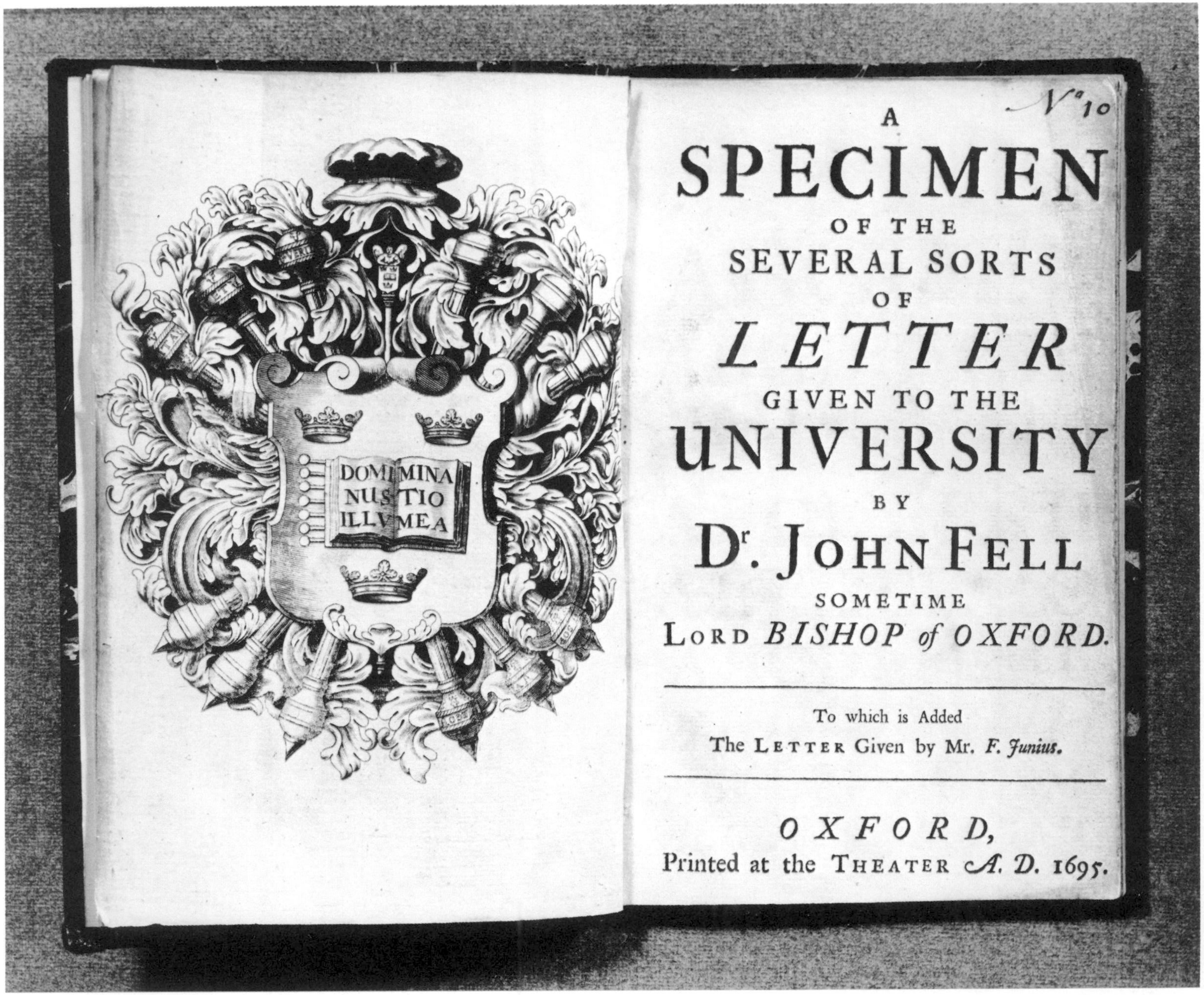

A

SPECIMEN

OF THE

SEVERAL SORTS

OF

LETTER

GIVEN TO THE

UNIVERSITY

BY

D[r]. JOHN FELL

SOMETIME

LORD *BISHOP of OXFORD.*

To which is Added

The LETTER Given by Mr. *F. Junius.*

OXFORD,

Printed at the THEATER *A. D.* 1695.

To enter all Bookes as ours.

Orders of the Councell observed

Correctors. not to intermeddle in any thing, but to mind his busines.

How to make use of Sr H. as we doe in the Hyle or otherwise:

Mr Whistler to cut armes etc.

wt advantage to print of every sort great ~~[illegible]~~ [illegible]

To write to Dr Marshall to know wt paper and the price of it Riccai illustracon of Italy is printed on.

who to keepe acct. & money

Fields 4to Bible	old test.	P pp. 63
Common pray – 13.	new test.	T. 19
Apocrypha. 16	Psal gay.	H. 8
Cambridg 4to ~~Bible~~	common pray.	H. ~~[illegible]~~
	old test —	Ppp. 39
. 77 Sheetes.	Apocrypha –	I. 11
	new testam	M. 13
	Sing. Psal.	G. 7.
London fol. Bibles in ye chappells }	old test. } Apocrypha } new testam }	Y. yyy 95.

A Dictionary.

wt quantity & wt sortes of Paper to be bought presently

wt rate Presse work & composers for 3000. wt price for 2000 wt price for 1000. etc

To know ye price of composing of a sheet. wt presse work of every Reame. when great numbers are to be printed.

wt Plates to be cut for every Booke wee shall print

wt Paper to print Schoole Bookes on, whether a Fools cap. or a Pott.

wt Letter at the Theater may be made use of

Whether to build any roome under the wall of the Theater for composing & Presse. wch I think is absolutely necessary.

If we print the Catalogue to doe it in a Large Letter, Large Paper & a Large margent, and on Paper will beare Inke.

~~[illegible] the [illegible] or [illegible] Reading [illegible] Orders of the Councell, and [illegible] in the opinion of Councell [illegible] to our [illegible] [illegible]~~ by them.

A Designe to cut for a large Almanack on a Brasse plate

write to Mr Marshall about a letter for a fol. Bible, Paper, Allmanacks for Almanackes and Bibles.

For Oyle. Linseed Turpentine. Lampblack. Vermilion. To provide some quantity of Each at London. and to set Joe shall have money upon account for this purpose

Then wt sorte on wt paper, and of wt edition, and wt Letter are to be put to print Tully offices. Ovid. Virgil. Florus. Erasmus – Horace Iuvenall & Persius.

wt workes to put in forward & keep men upon

not to say Printed for the University [illegible] all [illegible] to be [illegible]

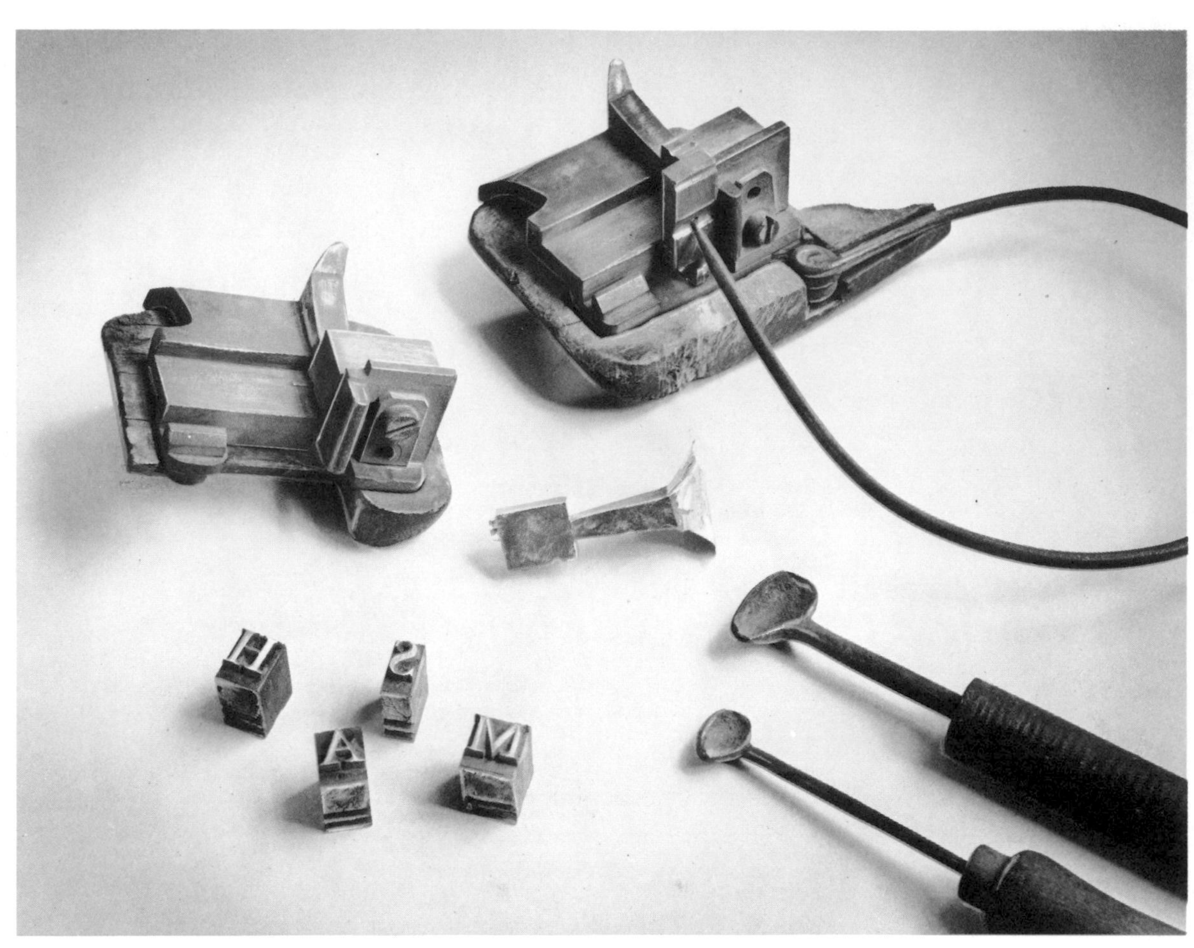

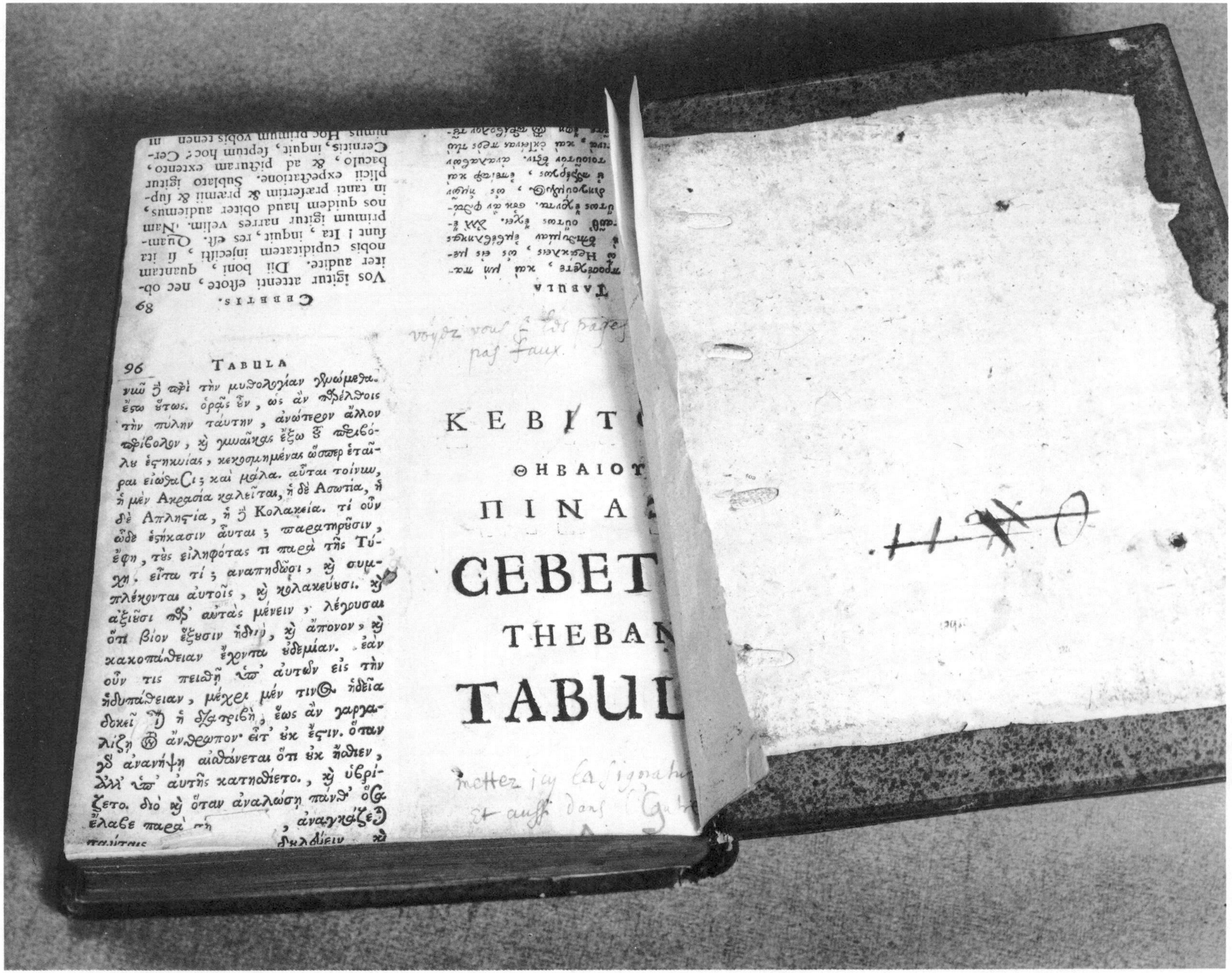

An Account of the Matrices, Punchions, &c. given by Bishop FELL *to the University of* Oxford.

XXVIII Boxes of Matrices.

THe I. Box, Great Primer Roman Matrices 121.
II. Double Pica Roman Matr. 123.
III. Pica Greek Matr. 506.
IV. Augustin Greek Matr. 354.
V. Long Primer Greek Matr. 352.
VI. Great Primer Greek Matr. 456.
VII. Long Primer Italick Matr. 121.
VIII. Small Pica Italick Matr. 128.
IX. Long Primer Roman Matr. 153.
X. Pica Roman Matr. 145.
XI. Brevier Roman Matr. 152.
XII. Great Brass Roman Capital Matr. 40.
XIII. Augustin Roman Matr. 141.
XIV. Black English Matr. 73.
XV. Small Pica Roman Matr. 152.
XVI. Coptick Matr. 135.
XVII. Augustin Italick Matr. 126.
XVIII. Pica Italick Matr. 129.
XIX. Non-pariel Italick Matr. 130.
XX. Non-pariel Roman Matr. 135.
XXI. XXII. Paragon Greek Matr. 235.
XXIII. Syriack Matr. 121.
XXIV. Double Pica Italick Matr. 83.
XXV. Great Canon Matr. 204.
XXVI. Brevier Italick Matr. 130.
XXVII. Musick Matr. 70.
[Pica Roman and Italick Matrices, bought by the University An. 1692.]

A Paper

Matrices, Punchions, &c.

A Paper of Great Primer Italick Matrices 124.
A Paper of Samaritan Matr. 31.
The 12 Signs and Astronomical Figures, Matr. 26.
A Paper of Flower Matrices.
[A Paper of Matrices for Mathematicks.]
A Paper of Great Primer Roman and Italick, cut by Mr. Nicols, not good.

Punchions, seal'd up in an Earthen Pott.

For the Double Pica Roman and Italick, and some for the Double Pica Greek.
For the Great Primer Roman and Italick, and some for the Great Primer Greek.
For the Great Brass Roman Capitals.
For the Black English.
For the Coptick.
For the Syriack.
For the Samaritan.
For the Cannon Roman and Italick.
For the Astronomical Signs and Figures.
[For Pica Roman and Italick.]

1 Small Anvil.
4 Hammers.
28 Moulds.
1 Engine to make brass Rules, with a plane.
1 Wyer Sieve.
332 Dressing Sticks.
2 Great Vices.
2 Hand Vices.
21 Great Files.
10 Douzen of Small Files.
1 Pair of Sheers.
2 Iron Potts.

4 Dressing

ARTICLES

Agreed upon by the

WORKMEN

OF THE

UNIVERSITY Printing-House, *OXFORD*,

Whose Names are hereunto Subscribed the First Day of *March*, in the Year of our Lord 17 11/12. for the more effectual carrying on the Contribution, begun the First Day of *March*, in the Year of our Lord 170 7/8. for the Purposes herein after mentioned, *Viz.*

I. THAT Yearly, upon the First Day of *March*, at Nine of the Clock in the Forenoon, the said Workmen, or the Major Part of them, shall Assemble in the Printing-house of the said University, or in such other Place as they shall Agree upon, and shall then and there Choose Two of the said Workmen to be Key-keepers of the Chest herein after mentioned, (One whereof shall be always a *Compositor*, and the other a *Pressman*) and every of the said Workmen, so long as he shall continue in *Oxford*, shall Pay to the *Compositor*, or in his Absence, to the *Pressman*, for the Time being, the Sum of One Shilling, upon *Saturday* in every Third Week for ever: And likewise at each of the Three usual Reckonings in the Year; *viz. Christmas*, *Easter*, and the *Wake-goose*, every of the said Workmen, during the Time aforesaid, shall Pay to the said *Compositor*, or in his Absence, to the said *Pressman*, for the Time being, the further Sum of One Shilling, over and above the Payments aforesaid.

II. That the Key-keepers for the Time being, shall Summon the Workmen to Assemble at such Time and Place in *Oxford*, as they shall think fit; and upon the First Day of *March*, in every Year, at Nine of the Clock in the Forenoon, the said Key-keepers shall, before such of the said Work-men as shall think fit to be Present, Make a true Account of all Money, which in the preceding Year shall have come to their Hands, or been Paid by reason of these Presents, and of what Money shall have been Lent that Year out of the Stock of the said Workmen, and to whom, and what Increase hath been made of the said Stock that Year, by Interest, or otherwise; and of what Morts shall have been Paid, or other Disbursments made; and shall deliver all Money, and all Papers, Writings and Securities, which shall then be in their Hands, to the succeeding Key-keepers, who shall be chosen that Day.

III. That upon the First Day of *March* in every Year, at Nine of the Clock in the Forenoon, the said Workmen, or the Major Part of them, shall Elect one other of the said Workmen, to be an Assistant to the said Key-keepers for the Year ensuing; and the said Assistant shall make an exact Register or Entry of all Money that Day Paid, or to be Paid by the former Key-keepers, to the New-elected Key-keepers; and of all Money which shall be Lent out during the following Year, and to whom; and of all Increase which shall be made of the Stock of the said Workmen that Year, and of all Morts which shall be Paid, and other Disbursments in that Year; and the said Assistant shall likewise give up his Accounts upon the First Day of *March*, in the Year following his Election; which Accounts of the Key-keepers and Assistant, being approved of by the Workmen then present, or the Major Part of them, shall be Subscribed and Allowed by them.

IV. That a Chest shall be kept for the Use of the said Workmen, in such Place as they, or the Major Part of them shall think fit; and all the Money Contributed or Paid to the said Key-keepers, by reason of these Presents, and all Securities, Papers, Writings, and Accounts concerning the same, shall be kept therein; and there shall be always Two Locks, and Two Keys to the said Chest, and the Keys thereof shall from Time to Time, be kept by the said Key-keepers; and the said Two Locks shall not at any Time be opened, but in the Presence of the said Key-keepers, or of such Person, or Persons, as they shall respectively Depute for that Purpose.

V. That if any of the said Workmen shall refuse or Neglect to Pay any Sum, herein before agreed to be Paid by him, longer than the *Saturday* next, after that the same ought to be Paid as aforesaid; then every Person, so Refusing or Neglecting, shall for every such Refusal or Neglect, Pay the further Sum of One Shilling to the Key-keepers, for the Time being, or to One of them.

VI. That nothing concerning these Presents, shall be done or transacted, without the Consent of the Workmen, or the Major Part of them, whereof the Overseer for the Time being, having first Subscribed these Presents, shall be One; and every of the said Workmen who shall be absent, may Depute any Person to Vote in their stead, touching all Matters concerning these Presents.

VII. That all Money paid into the Chest, and all Interest arising therefrom, shall be appropriated only to the Use and Benefit of the Widows and Orphans (if any) of the said Workmen; and the Sum which shall become Payable to the Widow, and Children of every of the said Workmen who shall die, shall be Paid in Three Days next after the Death of the said Workman, and shall be Proportionable to the Number of Years the deceased Workman shall have Paid to the said Chest; to which end the Table Annexed to these Presents is Calculated, which Table and Explanation thereof, with these Articles, shall always be kept in the said Chest, that all Persons concern'd, may have Recourse thereunto, as often as Occasion shall Require; and all the said Workmen are hereby Obliged to Observe the same; and the Money which shall become Payable to the Widow and Children of every the said Workmen who shall die, shall be Paid in the Manner following, (that is to say) If the deceased Workman shall leave a Widow and no Child, then the Money shall be Paid only to the Widow; and if he shall leave any Child or Children and no Widow, then the same shall be Paid to the said Child or Children, equally between them; and if he shall leave a Widow and any Child or Children, then the said Money shall be Paid in such Proportions as the Surviving Workmen, or the Major Part of them at any Meeting shall direct; and in Case any such deceased Workman shall leave no Child nor Widow, then the Sum which shall become Payable at his Death, shall be paid to such Person or Persons as the deceased Workman shall in his Life-time direct to Receive the same; and for want of such Direction, then for the defraying the Charges of the Sickness and Interment of such Workman; and the Residue thereof shall be Paid to such Person or Persons, being of Kin to the said deceased Workman, as the said Workmen, or the Major Part of them, shall direct.

VIII. That as often as there shall be such a Sum of Money in the Chest, as the said Workmen, or the Major Part of them shall adjudge sufficient to answer the Charges hereby agreed to be Paid out of the same, and other incident Charges; the said Workmen, or the Major Part of them, may lend the Remainder to Interest unto any of the said Workmen (provided the Sum so Lent, do not exceed one Half of the Principal Money by him or them Paid into the said Chest) they repaying it again Weekly, in such Proportion, as the whole may be received within a Year after; and the Residue may be Lent to any other Person upon good Security for Payment thereof. And all Securities which shall be taken for any Sum so to be Lent out, shall be taken in the Names of the Key-keepers for the Time being; and the Sum so to be Lent out, and the Interest thereof shall be Repaid at such Time as the said Workmen, or the Major Part of them, shall appoint; and for want thereof, the Security for the same shall be put in Suit.

IX. If any of the said Workmen, who shall have Borrowed Money out of the said Chest, shall die before the same shall be Repaid; then so much thereof, as shall remain Unpaid, shall be deducted out of the Money which at his Death shall become Payable to his Widow, or Orphans, or other Persons, who, according to the true Meaning hereof, ought to receive the same.

X. That if any of the said Workmen shall leave *Oxford*, they may nevertheless continue Contributors, and have the Benefit of these Presents: Provided, That during their Absence from *Oxford*, they do Pay unto the Key-keepers, for the Time being, Quarterly, the Sum of Four Shillings and Three Pence, upon the First Day of *June*, or within one Month after; The First Day of *September*, or within one Month after; The First Day of *December*, or within one Month after; And the First Day of *March*; And do also Pay one Shilling at each of the said Three usual Reckonings, viz. *Christmas*, *Easter*, and the *Wake-goose*: Or such Workman so leaving *Oxford*, may, if he shall think fit, withdraw Four Parts in Five (the Whole being divided into Five Parts) of all the Principal Money which he shall have Paid into the said

A

said Chest; but one Fifth Part thereof is hereby agreed, in that Case, to be Reserved towards the Discharge of former Payments, by Reason of these Presents.

XI. That every Person who shall hereafter have a Place in the Printing-house, in the University of *Oxford*, shall be Obliged, within Three Months after that he shall have such Place, to Subscribe and Seal these Articles, and to Conform himself in all things thereunto.

XII. That every Person Smouting in the said Printing-house, and Receiving Copy-money, shall Pay out of his Copy-money Two Pence a Week to the said Chest, for the Increase of the Stock in the said Chest, so long as he shall continue Smouting; but if such Smouter shall have a Place in the said Printing-house, he shall then be Obliged forthwith to Subscribe and Seal these present Articles, and to Conform himself thereunto, as aforesaid.

XIII. That every of the said Workmen shall be obliged to Observe and Perform all, and every Article which at any Time hereafter shall be agreed upon by the said Workmen, or the Major Part of them, as fully, as if the same were inserted in these Presents.

XIV. That every of the said Workmen shall, in all Things, Conform to these Articles; and upon Neglect or Refusal thereof, shall Undergo such Penalties as the Workmen Subscribing these Presents, or the Major Part of them, shall from Time to Time Inflict.

XV. That the Workmen may Elect Trustees, if they please, to see that the Cash is duly apply'd; and to Oblige all manner of Conformity to these Presents.

We whose Names are hereunto Affix'd, do Approve of, and Promise in all Things to Conform to the foregoing Articles, under the Penalties in them respectively Mentioned, and in Testimony thereof, we have hereunto Set our Hands and Seals the Day and Year above-mentioned.

Lewis Thomas.	*John Rance.*	*Rich. Wilmott.*	*Charles Combes, Jun.*
Charles Combes.	*Charles Garrett.*	*John Garrett.*	*Francis Stephens.*
Edw. Price.	*Thomas Richardson.*	*Tho. Farmer.* †	*Tho. Branson.*
Alexander Ashburn. †	*George Webb.*	*Richard Ridge.*	*John Bull.*
Thomas Tayler. †	*St. John Litchfield.*	*Tho. Darrack.*	*Tho. Cooke.*
Richard Green.			

The Yearly ACCOUNTS.

		l. s. d.
March 1. 1707.	THE Collection for the Chest began.	
1708.	Receiv'd this Year	11. 02. 09.
	Paid Mr. *Tho. Farmer's* Mort, and other Disbursments	02. 17. 00.
	Remain'd in the Chest	08. 05. 09.
1709.	Receiv'd this Year	16. 08. 06.
	Remain'd in the Chest	24. 14. 03.
1710.	Receiv'd this Year	15. 01. 00.
	Remain'd in the Chest	39. 15. 03.
1711.	Receiv'd this Year	17. 10. 06.
	For Interest this Year	01. 07. 00.
	In all	58. 12. 09.
	Paid Mr. *Ashburn's* Mort 06. 02. 06. Other Disbursments 00. 11. 00.	06. 13. 06.
	Remain'd in the Chest	51. 19. 03.
1712.	Receiv'd this Year	22. 05. 06.
	For Interest this Year	03. 12. 09.
	In all	77. 17. 06.
	Paid Mr. *Tayler's* Mort 08. 00. 00. Other Disbursments 04. 02. 02.	12. 02. 02.
	Remain'd in the Chest	65. 15. 04.
	Receiv'd this Year	14. 06. 06.
1713.	For Interest this Year	02. 08. 06.
	In all	82. 10. 04.
	Disbursments	08. 17. 02.
	Remain'd in the Chest	73. 13. 02.
1714.	Receiv'd this Year	17. 00. 04.
	For Interest this Year	00. 13. 06.
	In all	91. 07. 00.
	Disbursments	00. 15. 00.
	Remain'd in the Chest	90. 12. 00.
1715.	Receiv'd this Year	18. 09. 00.
	For Interest this Year	01. 14. 06.
	In all	110. 15. 06.
	Disbursments	04. 10. 00.
	Remain'd in the Chest	106. 05. 06.
	Now at Interest	24. 17. 00.
	Cash in the Chest	81. 08. 06.
	Total as above	106. 05. 6.

The TABLE.

Years.	l.	s.	d.	Years.	l.	s.	d.
I.	1	10	00	XIII.	21	10	00
II.	3	00	00	XIV.	23	00	00
III.	5	00	00	XV.	25	00	00
IV.	6	10	00	XVI.	26	10	00
V.	8	00	00	XVII.	28	00	00
VI.	10	00	00	XVIII.	30	00	00
VII.	11	10	00	XIX.	32	10	00
VIII.	13	00	00	XX.	36	00	00
IX.	15	00	00	XXI.	40	00	00
X.	16	10	00	XXII.	44	00	00
XI.	18	00	00	XXIII.	46	00	00
XII.	20	00	00	XXIV.	48	00	00

The TABLE Explain'd.

EVery Member Paying Twenty Shillings Yearly, will have Thirty Shillings the First Year, Three Pounds the Second, and Five Pounds the Third Year, Paid at his Death; and in the same Manner to the Eighteenth Year inclusive: But the Three following Years are Advanced more than the former Proportion, to make the Two and Twentieth Year Double to what any Member hath Paid in: And so it is to continue in all the succeeding Years. If One Payment be made in any of the intermediate Quarters, the Benefit of that Quarter is Allowed.

THis Design has been so Beneficial and Useful to the Members of it, (after so many Years Experience) that they have been prevail'd with to Publish their Articles, which are drawn up according to Law, as well to Obviate what Objections might be made, as to Encourage all Persons whose Families entirely depend upon them for their Subsistence, to use the same, or some such Method; for want of which, the Poor Widows and Children are often left in bad Circumstances.

The TABLE, at one View, shews what a considerable Advantage will arise in a few Years, from so small a Sum as Twenty Shillings Annually Contributed, which is a little above a Groat a Week; and no Person hardly is so Indigent, but can spare that, even out of his Ordinary Expences, if he has the least Regard for his Posterity: The longer a Man lives, the greater is the Benefit; for then the Widow may have such a Sum as to put her Self and Children in some comfortable way of a Livelihood again, which would never have happened, but by this Method.

Besides, There is a continual Advantage to the Contributors in their Life-time, for they may Borrow out of this Fund, in Proportion to what they have Contributed, and Repay it at the easie Rate of Twelve Pence a Week; This has been thought by judicious Persons (and Experience has Confirm'd it) to be as great Benefit, or rather better, than so much Money given; for it hath caus'd such an Industry towards the latter end of the Payments especially, that thereby they have been enabled to lay down a Sum, in order to Borrow again.

It might be made more Extensive and Useful, if Gentlemen and Magistrates would Encourage the Forming of such Societies, by being Trustees of them: If the Masters and Wardens of Incorporated Companies, all Master-Workmen, of what Occupation or Manufactory soever, would Engage all those under them to Contribute, and to Countenance the Thing the more, be Members themselves; it would be Productive of Variety of good Effects: Such as the Promoting of Industry, a Relief to many Widows and Orphans, and an Ease to all the Kingdom of a great Burden that now lies heavy upon it, for want of some such good Design afoot: For next to Imploying the People, to put them in a Way of Saving for their Families, would be the greatest Charity.

Mr. JOHN BASKETT, Printer to the Kings most Excellent Majesty, and to the University of *Oxford*, }
Mr. LEWIS THOMAS. } TRUSTEES.

PRÆFATIO.

AD ineuntis Anni auspicia, quo tempore frequenti studio pubes Academica, limina obsidere, nuncupare vota, gratulationibus certare, pro more solenni habet: turpissimum mihi videtur, nullas liberalis animi persolvisse vices, & in hac Xeniorum palæstrâ, vacuas, pessimeque vi-

A 4 ctas

71

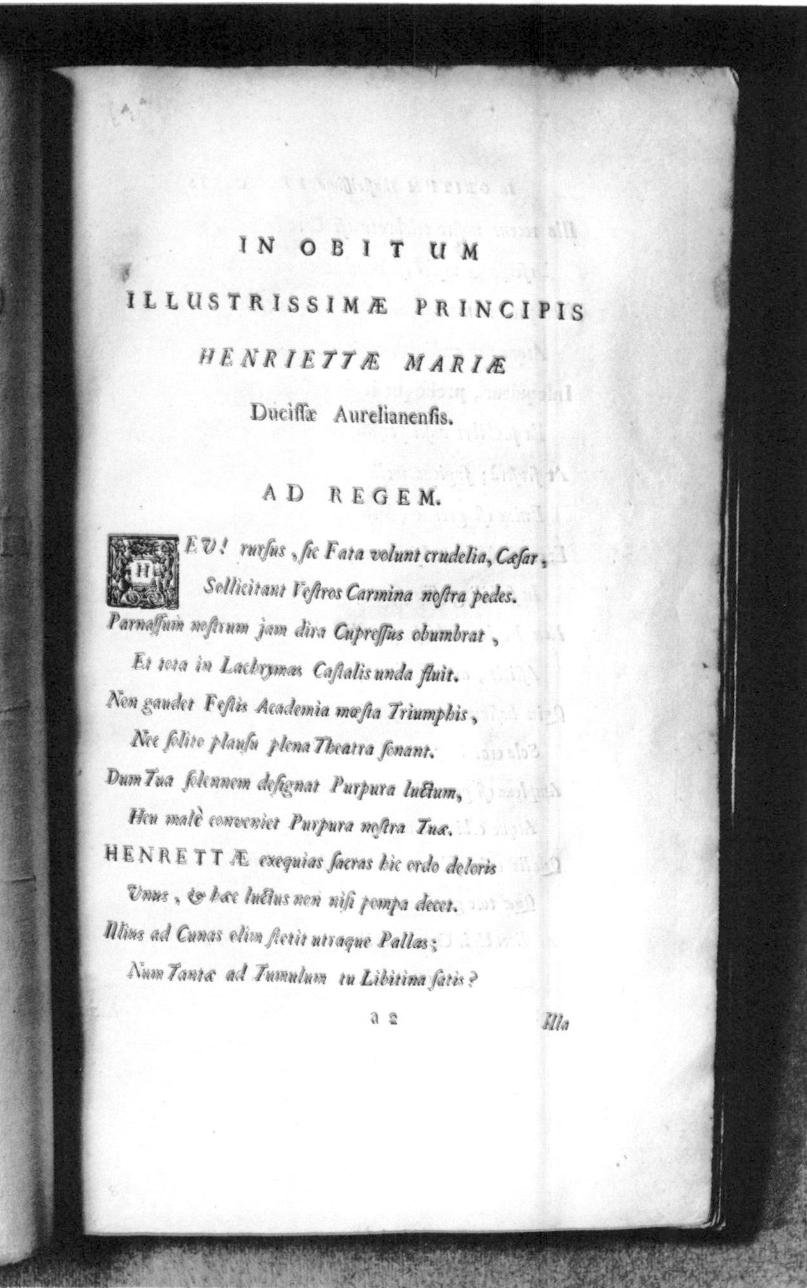
IN OBITUM

ILLUSTRISSIMÆ PRINCIPIS

HENRIETTÆ MARIÆ

Ducissæ Aurelianensis.

AD REGEM.

HEU! rursus, sic Fata volunt crudelia, Cæsar,
Sollicitant Vestros Carmina nostra pedes.
Parnassum nostrum jam dira Cupressus obumbrat,
Et tota in Lachrymas Castalis unda fluit.
Non gaudet Festis Academia mæsta Triumphis,
Nec solito plausu plena Theatra sonant.
Dum Tua solennem designat Purpura luctum,
Heu malè conveniet Purpura nostra Tuæ.
HENRETTÆ exequias sacras hic ordo doloris
Unus, & hæc luctus non nisi pompa decet.
Illius ad Cunas olim stetit utraque Pallas;
Num Tantæ ad Tumulum tu Libitina satis?

a 2 Illa

72

ΣΥΝΟΔΙΚΟΝ
SIVE
PANDECTÆ CANONUM
SS. APOSTOLORUM,
ET
CONCILIORUM
AB
Ecclesia GRÆCA receptorum;

NEC NON

Canonicarum SS. Patrum Epistolarum:
Unà cum SCHOLIIS ANTIQUORUM singulis eorum annexis,
Et SCRIPTIS aliis huc spectantibus;
QUORUM PLURIMA
E
BIBLIOTHECÆ BODLEIANÆ

Aliarumque MSS. Codicibus nunc primum edita: reliqua cum iisdem MSS. summâ fide & diligentiâ collata.

Totum Opus in duos TOMOS divisum

GUILIELMUS BEVEREGIUS Ecclesiæ Anglicanæ Presbyter,
Recensuit, Prolegomenis munivit, & Annotationibus auxit.

OXONII,
E THEATRO SHELDONIANO.
Sumptibus Guilielmi Wells & Roberti Scott Bibliop. *LOND.*

M. DC. LXXII.

siam redierit. Qui Clericum autem, qui suam amisit patriam ex necessitate quadam receperit, culpari nequit.

Canon XXI.

Clericos vel Laicos, Episcopos aut Clericos accusantes, non indiscriminatim, ac citra inquisitionem admittere ad accusationem, nisi eorum existimatio prius examinata fuerit.

Bals. Quære vi. Can. ii. Syn. & præsentis Canonis disces interpretationem.

Zonar. Sexto quoque secundæ Synodi Canone idem statuitur. Quæ in eum igitur scripsimus, ad hujus quoque Canonis explicationem satis superque sufficiunt.

Arist. *Clericus vel Laicus, qui Episcopum temere accusat non admittendus.*

Oportet existimationem eorum, qui Episcopos aut Clericos accusant, examinare, & non sine probatione eos ad accusationem admittere, sive Clerici sint ii qui accusant, sive Laici. Ne forte ejecti sint, aut excommunicati, aut criminum aliquorum accusati, & nondum compertum sit illos vitio vacare; aut aliter vitâ culpatâ, & à religione aliena. Multi enim hujusmodi Ecclesiasticum confundere & evertere volentes ordinem, calumniosas contra inculpatos & orthodoxos Episcopos Clericosque accusationes consarcinant.

Canon XXII.

Non licere Clericis post mortem propris Episcopi res, quæ ad ipsum pertinent, rapere, quemadmodum & adsumentibus, prohibitum est: aut qui hoc fecerint, de proprio gradu in periculum venire.

Bals. Præsens Canon deponi jubet Clericos, qui post mortem proprii Episcopi res, quæ ad illum pertinent, rapiunt; & non solùm ipsos, sed & reliquos, qui eorum sibi custodiam vendicant; Metropolitanos scilicet, & alios, apud quos mortuus est Episcopus, qui etiam παραλαμβάνοντες, hoc est, adsumentes, dicuntur. Tunc autem dicitur Episcopus res habere, & de iis disponere ac testari potest, quando, ut vult xl. Canon Apostolicus, cùm primùm fuit electus, quæ sunt sua propria, & quæ Episcopatus, descripsit. Nisi enim ita fecerit, omnia quæ sunt ejus ad Ecclesiam pertinebunt. Descriptione autem factâ, ut dictum est, si intestatus moritur Episcopus existimo quòd secundùm leges cognati ejus, qui ab intestato vocantur, ei succedent. Etsi enim nonnulli ex lxxxi. Can. Syn. Carth. dixerunt esse in potestate succedentis Episcopi, ut bona ejus qui mortuus est intestatus, ut voluerit, administret: sed mihi videtur, quòd ex eo Canone statuens debere eum, qui intestato Episcopo succedit, Episcopum, descriptionem facere ejus voto congruentem, ostenditur maximè debere fieri secundùm leges rerum defuncti successionem. Hoc enim si fecerit, ejus voto convenientem descriptionem faciet. Quære etiam xxiv. Can. Antioch. Syn. & Syn. in Trul. Can. xxxv.

Zonar. Quadragesimus quoque sanctorum Apostolorum Canon, quænam Episcopi propriæ possessiones, quæque Deo dicatæ sint, notum omnino ac testatum esse decernit; Episcopòque, quod ad proprias possessiones attinet, illas testamento cuicunque libitum fuerit legandi potestatem facit. Eadem Antiochenæ Synodi quarto & vigesimo Canone constituta. Hoc etiam Canone, quæ

[Greek column:] κλησίαν ἐπιμέλθοι. [illegible]

ΚΑΝΩΝ κα΄.

[illegible]

ΒΑΛΣ. [illegible]

ΖΩΝΑΡ. [illegible]

ΑΡΙΣΤ. [illegible]

ΚΑΝΩΝ κβ΄.

[illegible]

ΒΑΛΣ. [illegible]

ΖΩΝΑΡ. [illegible]

(+) Books begun to be printed at the Theater in Oxford.

The Councils gr: l. 2 Vol: fol:

The history of the University in Latin fol: with cutts.

Catalogue of the Bodley-library fol:

Catalogue of the MS. fol:

Dr. Morisons herbal in latin fol: with cutts.

The Arundel Marbles with their Explication in fol: together with a Discourse of Mr. Lidiats upon the Epocha, & others of like nature with cutts.

A Treatise concerning the Soul, latin in 4.o by Dr. Willis.

Aratus with the Scholia of Theon. Eratosthen: &c gr: 8.o

We purpose to Print, if we may be encouraged.

1. The greek Bible in a royal folio, to wch: pur=:pose we have procured the use of the Alexan=:drian MS. out of his Maties: library, with others of good note from diverse Places; & have of our own several copies of venerable Antiquity never yet collated.

HISTORIA

ET

ANTIQUITATES

UNIVERSITATIS

OXONIENSIS

Duobus Voluminibus Comprehensæ.

OXONII,

E THEATRO SHELDONIANO.

M. DC. LXXIV.

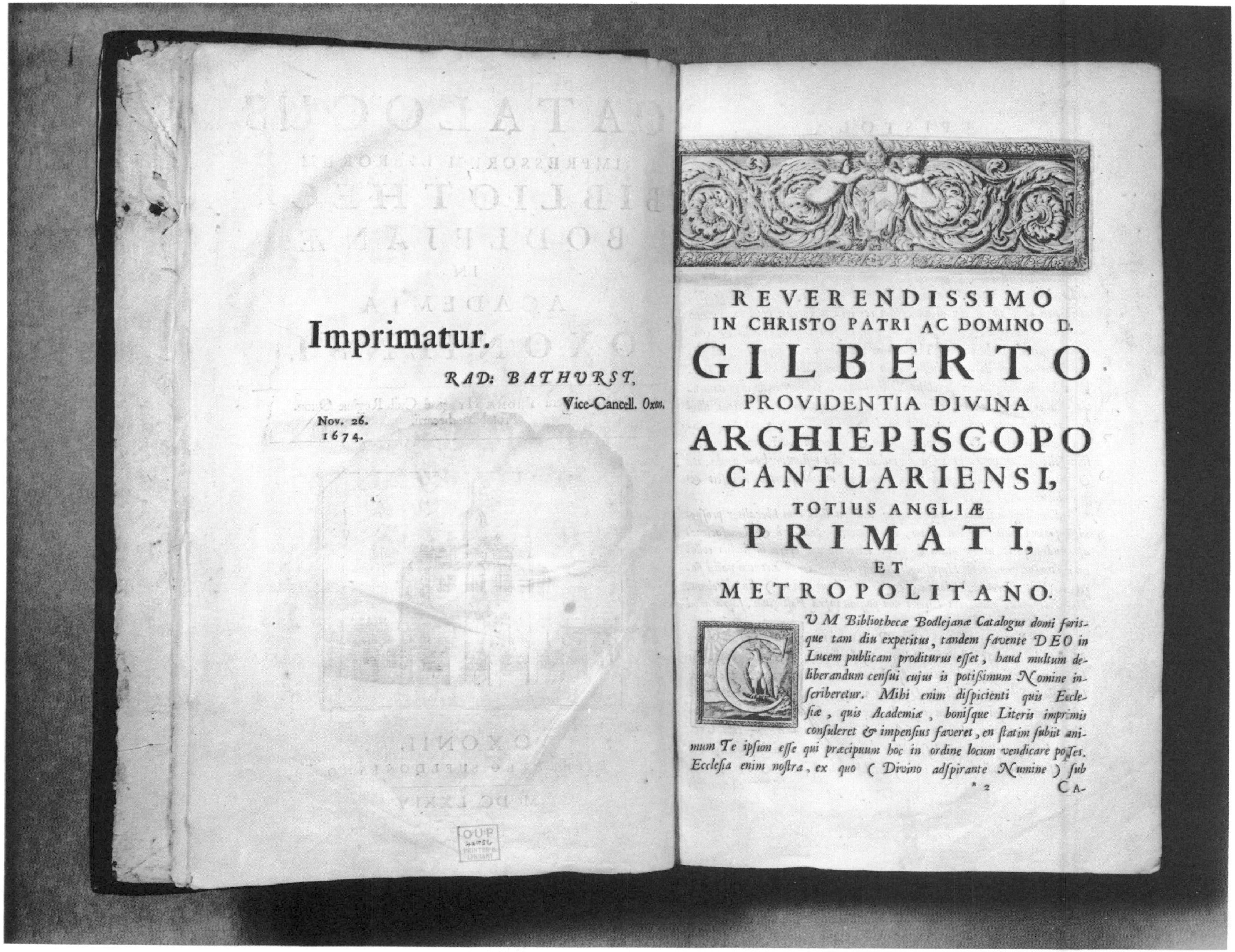

Imprimatur.

RAD: BATHURST,
Vice-Cancell. Oxon.

Nov. 26.
1674.

REVERENDISSIMO
IN CHRISTO PATRI AC DOMINO D.

GILBERTO

PROVIDENTIA DIVINA

ARCHIEPISCOPO
CANTUARIENSI,

TOTIUS ANGLIÆ

PRIMATI,

ET

METROPOLITANO.

CUM Bibliothecæ Bodlejanæ Catalogus domi forisque tam diu expetitus, tandem favente DEO in Lucem publicam proditurus esset, haud multum deliberandum censui cujus is potissimum Nomine inscriberetur. Mihi enim dispicienti quis Ecclesiæ, quis Academiæ, bonisque Literis imprimis consuleret & impensius faveret, en statim subiit animum Te ipsum esse qui præcipuum hoc in ordine locum vendicare posses. Ecclesia enim nostra, ex quo (Divino adspirante Numine) sub

* 2 CA-

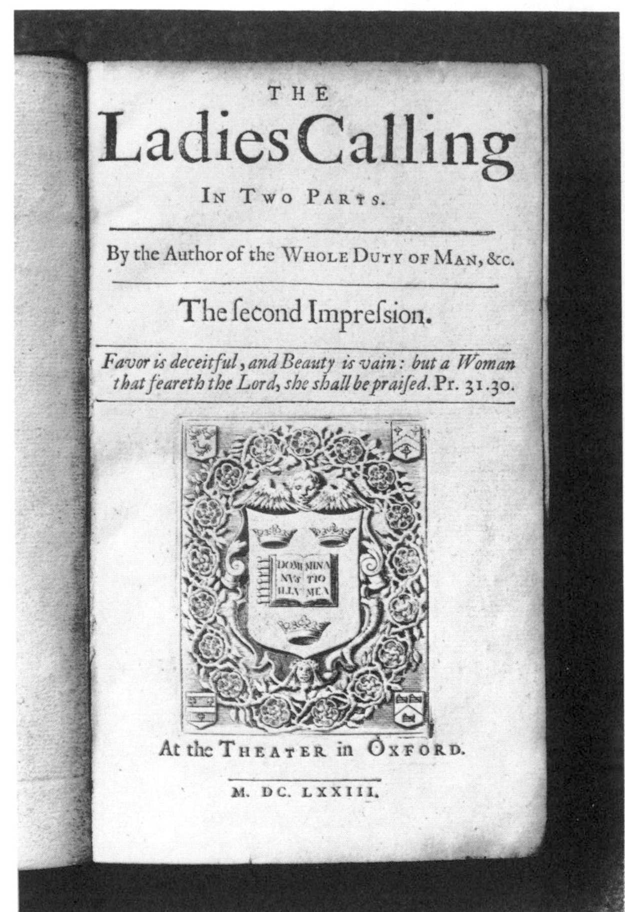

THE

Ladies Calling

IN TWO PARTS.

By the Author of the WHOLE DUTY OF MAN, &c.

The ſecond Impreſsion.

Favor is deceitful, and Beauty is vain: but a Woman that feareth the Lord, she shall be praiſed. Pr. 31. 30.

At the THEATER in OXFORD.

M. DC. LXXIII.

30 THE LADIES CALLING. PART I.

compliſhment of their ſex, 1 Pet. 3. 4. where after the mention of all the exquiſit and coſtly deckings of art, this one *ornament of a meek and quiet ſpirit*, is confronted to them, with this eminent atteſtation, that it is *in the ſight of God of great price*, and therefore to all who will not enter diſpute with God, and conteſt his judgment, it muſt be ſo too. Now tho Meekneſs be in it ſelf a ſingle entire vertu, yet it is diverſifi'd, according to the ſeveral faculties of the ſoul, over which it has influence; ſo that there is a Meekneſs of Underſtanding, a Meekneſs of the Will, and a Meekneſs of the Affections; all which muſt concur to make up the Meek and quiet ſpirit.

3. AND firſt for the Meekneſs of the Underſtanding, it conſiſts in a pliableneſs to conviction, and is directly oppoſite to that ſullen adherence obſervable in too many; who judg of tenets not by their conformity to truth and reaſon, but to their prepoſſeſſions, and tenaciouſly retain'd opinions, only becauſe they (or ſome in whom they confide) have once own'd them; and certainly ſuch a temper is of all others the moſt obſtructive to Wiſdom. This puts them upon the chance of a Lottery, and what they firſt happen to draw, determines them meerly upon the priviledg of its precedency, ſo that had *Mahomet* firſt ſeiz'd them, his tenure would have bin as indefeſable, as Chriſts now. How great the force of ſuch prejudices are, we may ſee by the oppoſitions it rais'd againſt Chriſtian doctrine in groſs at its firſt promulgation,

SECT. II. *Of Meekneſs.* 31

tion; the *Jews* blind Zeal for the Traditions of their Fathers, engaging them in the murder even of that very Meſſias whom thoſe Traditions had taught them to expect, and after in the perſecution of that doctrine which his Reſurrection had ſo irrefragably atteſted. And to juſtifie the propriety of this obſervation, to thoſe I now write to, 'tis expreſly affirm'd, *Acts* 13. 50. That they made uſe of the zeal of the female Proſelites for that purpoſe. *The* Jews *ſtirred up the devout and honorable women, and rais'd a perſecution againſt* Paul *and* Barnabas. So that 'tis no unſeaſonable advice to ſuch, to be ſure they ſee well their way before they run too fierce a carriere in it; otherwiſe the greateſt heat without light, does but reſemble that of the bottomleſs pit, where flames and darkneſs do at once cohabit.

4. BUT whilſt I decry this prejudicate ſtifneſs, I intend not to plead for its contrary extreme, and recommend a too eaſie flexibility; which is a temper of equal, if not more ill conſequence then the former. The adhering to one opinion can expoſe but to one error, but a mind that lies open to the effluxes of all new tenets, may ſucceſſively entertain a whole ocean of deluſions; and to be thus yielding, is not a Meekneſs but Servileneſs of Underſtanding. Indeed 'tis ſo great a weakneſs of mind, that the Apoſtle ſinks it ſomwhat below the impotence of women, and reſembles it to that of children, *Eph.* 4. 14. yet it ſeems the folly of ſome women had levell'd them with children

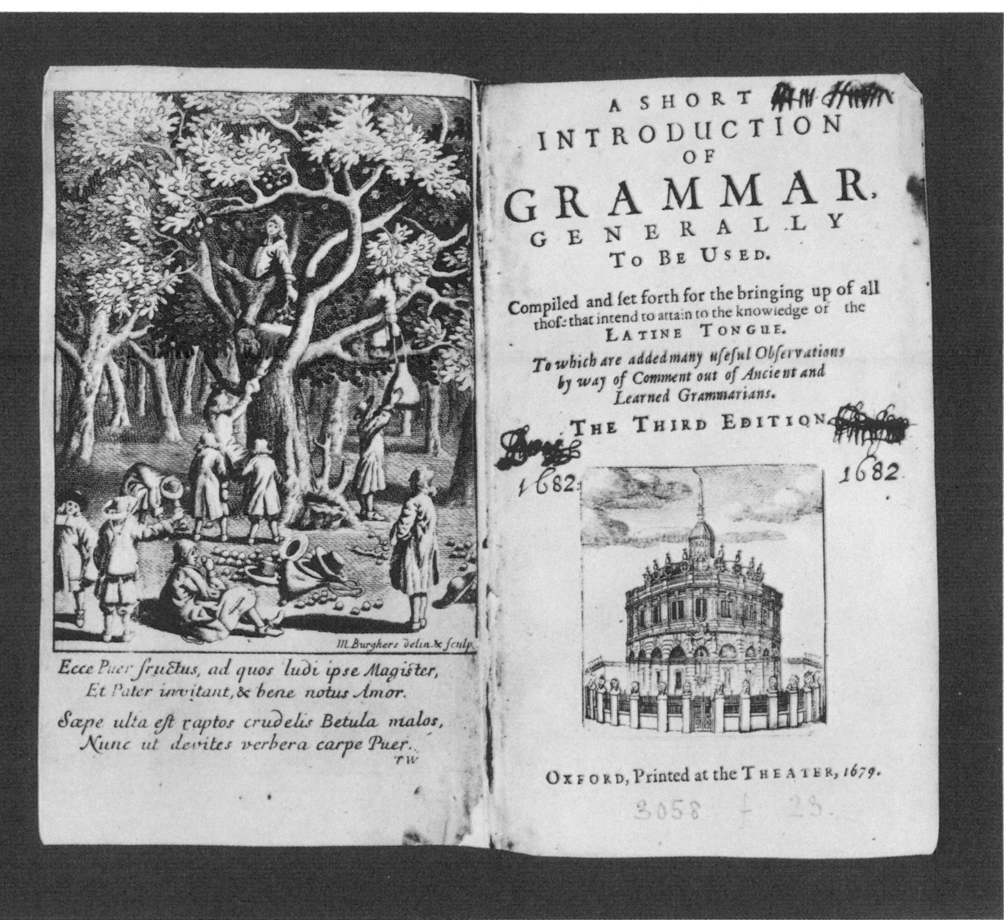

M. Burghers delin. & sculp.

Ecce Puer fructus, ad quos ludi ipse Magister,
Et Pater invitant, & bene notus Amor.

Sæpe ulta est raptos crudelis Betula malos,
Nunc ut devites verbera carpe Puer.
TW

A SHORT
INTRODUCTION
OF
GRAMMAR,
GENERALLY
To Be Used.

Compiled and set forth for the bringing up of all those that intend to attain to the knowledge of the
LATINE TONGUE.

To which are added many useful Observations by way of Comment out of Ancient and Learned Grammarians.

THE THIRD EDITION

1682. 1682

OXFORD, Printed at the THEATER, 1679.

78

79

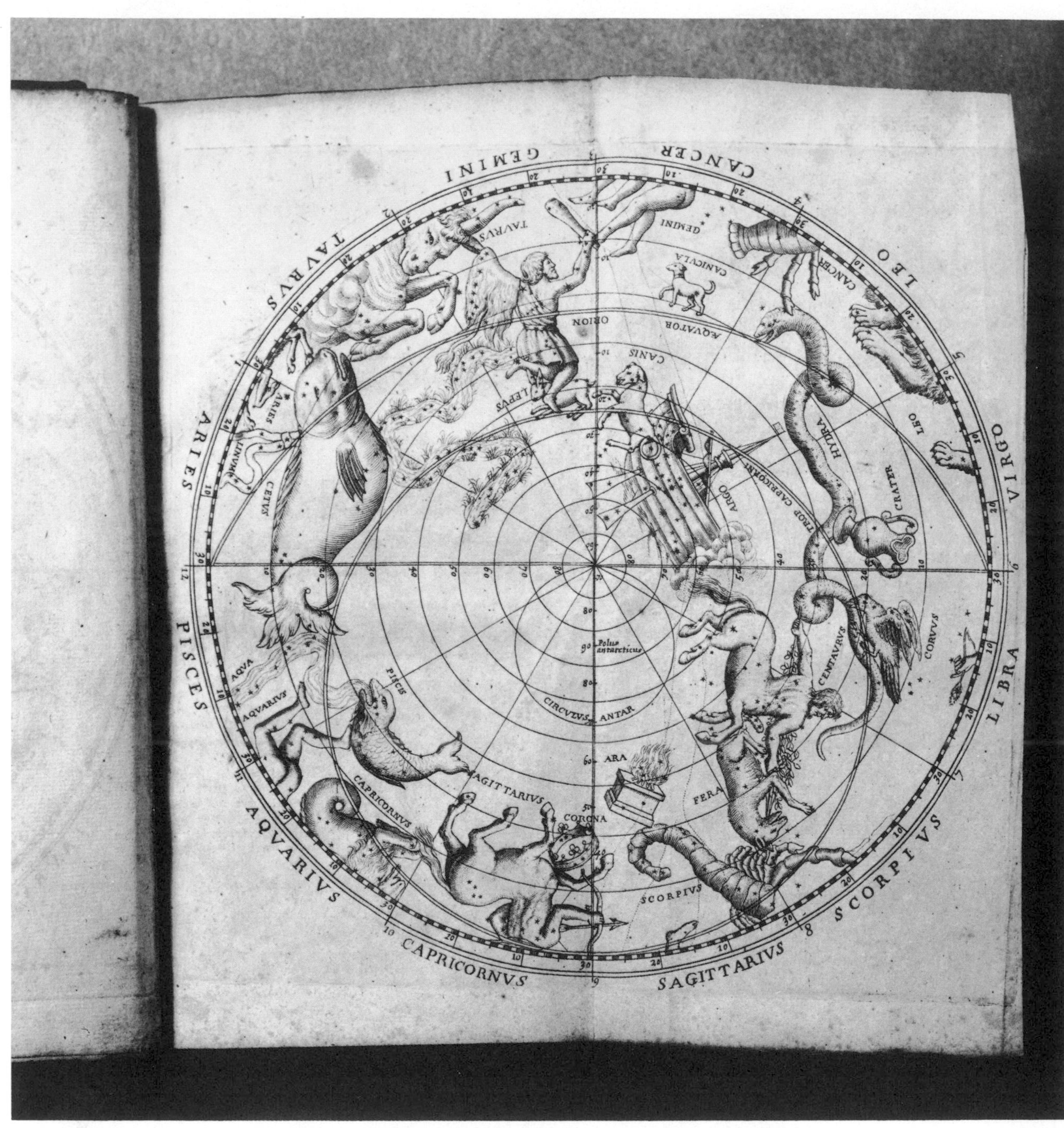
GEMINI
CANCER
LEO
VIRGO
LIBRA
SCORPIVS
SAGITTARIVS
CAPRICORNVS
AQVARIVS
PISCES
ARIES
TAVRVS
TAVRVS
GEMINI
CANICVLA
CANCER
ORION
AQVATOR
CANIS
LEPVS
HYDRA
LEO
CRATER
ARGO
CORVVS
CENTAVRVS
Polus antarcticus
CIRCVLVS ANTAR
ARA
FERA
CORONA
SAGITTARIVS
CAPRICORNVS
PISCES
AQVA
AQVARIVS
CETVS
ARIES
SCORPIVS

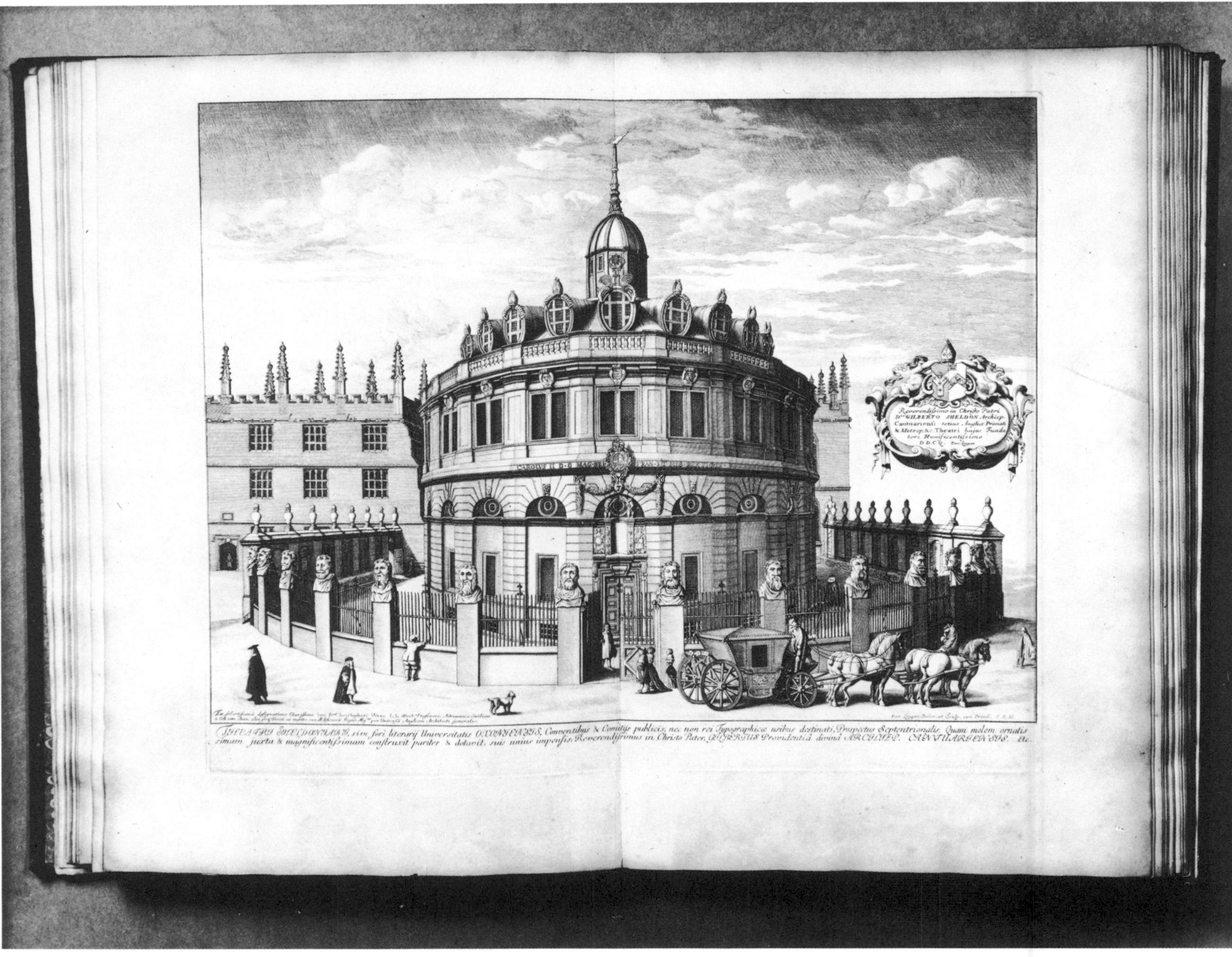
Reverendissimo in Christo Patri
Dno GILBERTO SHELDON Archiep.
Cantuariensi totius Angliæ Primati
& Metrop. &c. Theatri hujus Funda
tori Munificentissimo
D.D.C.Q. Dav. Loggan
THEATRI SHELDONIANI, sive, fori literarij Universitatis OXONIENSIS, Conventibus & Comitijs publicis, nec non rei Typographicæ usibus destinati, Prospectus Septentrionalis. Quam molem ornatissimam juxta & magnificentissimam construxit pariter & dotavit, suis unius impensis, Reverendissimus in Christo Pater, GILBERTUS Providentiâ divinâ ARCHIEP. CANTUARIENSIS. &c.

THE OXFORD ALMANACK 1674.

Dec: 13: 1699. At a meeting at Mr Vice-Chancellor's Lodgings, present Mr Vice-Chan: Dr Halton Provost of Queens, Dr Edwards princ: of Jesus, and Dr Charlett Master of University there was an Account setled with Mrs Morrison as under written.

Expences in printing the second Vol: of Dr Morrisons Herbal

	li	s	d
Composing 173 sheets at 10s a sheet	86	10	00
The presse-work at 5s a sheet	43	05	00
Necessaries 3s a sheet	25	19	00
Correcting 5s a sheet	43	05	00
297 Reams of paper at 16s p Ream	237	12	00
39 Reams of Royal paper at 38s p Ro.	74	02	00
For working 166 plates at ye rolling-press 750 printed on each plate at 2s p hundred	124	10	00
For Graveing plates as appeares by Mr Vice-Chanr Accounts	280	06	00
	921	09	00

Allowed Mr Jacob Bobart 350: 00: 00

For printing 30 sheets over again 52: 10: 00

There is moreover due to the University 4 p pound, which ariseth thus

		li	s	d
Poundage	For printing	31	02	00
	For Correcting	08	12	00
	For paper	62	04	00
	For working ye plates	24	18	00
	For graveing ye plates	57	04	00
		184	00	00

There is due to the University for the former Volume	405	00	00
The expences of the last Vol	921	09	00
The Poundage	184	00	00
In all	1510	09	00

Memorand. It was likewise agreed Mrs Morrison being present That she should pay to Mr Vice-Chanr 405li: 00s: 00d Then to take 100 li worth of the Herbal, And when she hath disposed of them to pay 50 more to the University, the other 50 to keep for her own use: And so on till the University be satisfied the above mentioned Debt of 1510li. 09s. 00d.

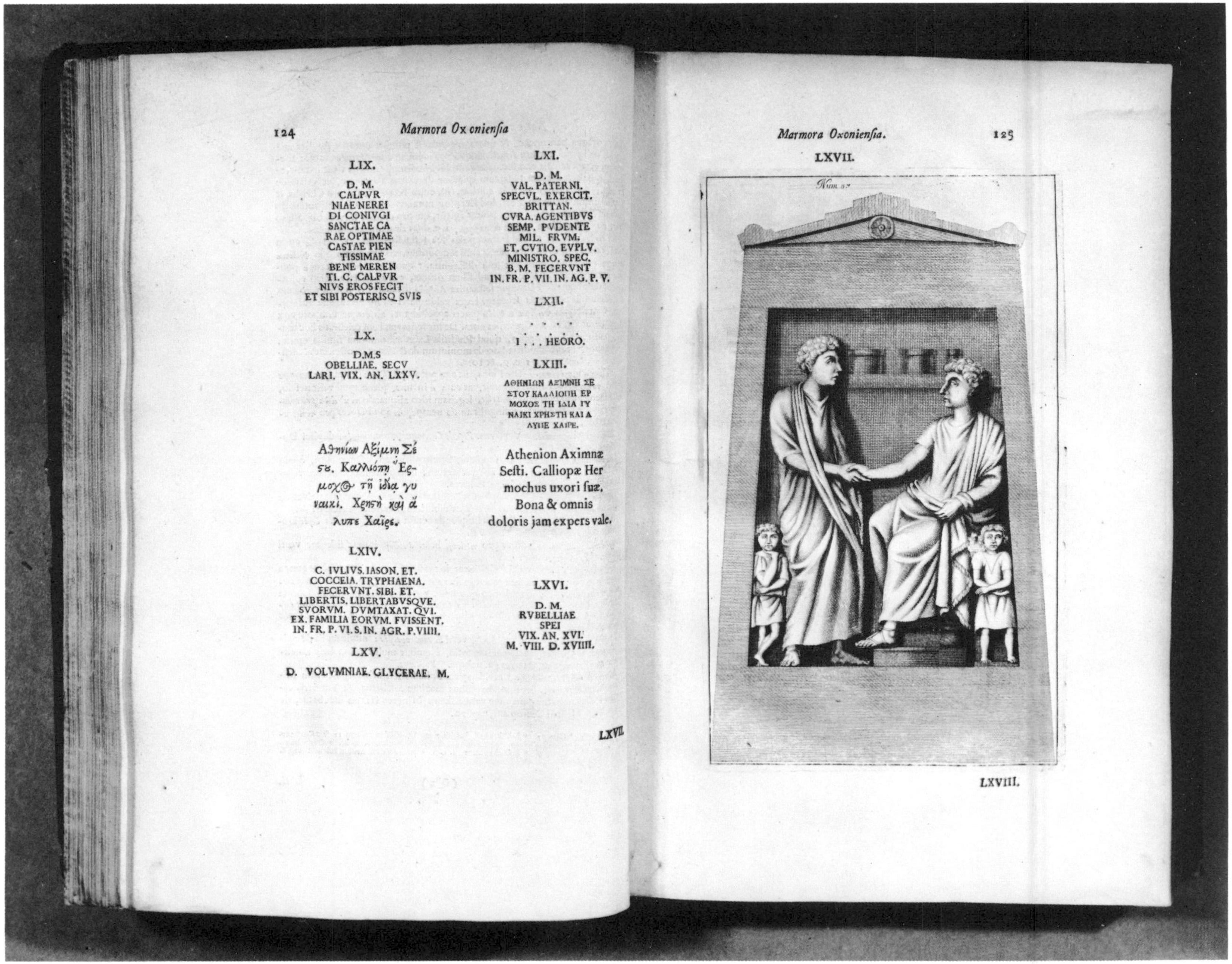

LIX.

D. M.
CALPVR
NIAE NEREI
DI CONIVGI
SANCTAE CA
RAE OPTIMAE
CASTAE PIEN
TISSIMAE
BENE MEREN
TI. C. CALPVR
NIVS EROS FECIT
ET SIBI POSTERISQ SVIS

LX.

D.M.S
OBELLIAE. SECV
LARI. VIX. AN. LXXV.

Ἀθηνίων Ἀξίμνῃ Σέ
ϛε. Καλλιόπῃ Ἑρ-
μοχος τῇ ἰδίᾳ γυ
ναικὶ. Χρηστὴ καὶ ἄ
λυπε Χαῖρε.

LXIV.

C. IVLIVS. IASON. ET.
COCCEIA. TRYPHAENA.
FECERVNT. SIBI. ET.
LIBERTIS. LIBERTABVSQVE.
SVORVM. DVMTAXAT. QVI.
EX. FAMILIA EORVM. FVISSENT.
IN. FR. P. VI. S. IN. AGR. P. VIIII.

LXV.

D. VOLVMNIAE. GLYCERAE. M.

LXI.

D. M.
VAL. PATERNI.
SPECVL. EXERCIT.
BRITTAN.
CVRA. AGENTIBVS
SEMP. PVDENTE
MIL. FRVM.
ET. CVTIO. EVPLV.
MINISTRO. SPEC.
B. M. FECERVNT
IN. FR. P. VII. IN. AG. P. V.

LXII.

. . . .
I . . . HEORO.

LXIII.

ΑΘΗΝΙΩΝ ΑΞΙΜΝΗ ΣΕ
ΣΤΟΥ ΚΑΛΛΙΟΠΗ ΕΡ
ΜΟΧΟΣ ΤΗ ΙΔΙΑ ΓΥ
ΝΑΙΚΙ ΧΡΗΣΤΗ ΚΑΙ Α
ΛΥΠΕ ΧΑΙΡΕ.

Athenion Aximnæ
Sesti. Calliopæ Her
mochus uxori suæ.
Bona & omnis
doloris jam expers vale.

LXVI.

D. M.
RVBELLIAE
SPEI
VIX. AN. XVI.
M. VIII. D. XVIIII.

LXVII.

LXVII.

Num. 37

LXVIII.

238 *The Natural History*

though fed only with a single *spring* rising in a piece of ground call'd *Ramsall*, between *Enston* and *Ludston*. The natural *Rock* is about 10 foot high, and so many in bredth; some few *shelves* of lead *d d*, and the top stones only having been added (easily to be distinguisht by their *dryness*) which have advanced it in all about 14 foot high.

54. In the *half pace* just before the *Compartment e e e*, upon turning one of the *cocks* at *f* rises a *chequer hedge* of *water*, as they call it, *g g g g*; and upon turning *another*, the two side *columns* of *water h h*, which rise not above the height of the natural *rock*; and of a *third*, the middle *column i*, which ascending into the *turn* of the *Arch*, and returning not again, is received into hidden *pipes* provided for that purpose: Into *one* whereof, terminated in a very small *Cistern* of *water* behind a *stone* of the *rock*, and having a *mouth* and *Languet* just above its surface, the *air* being forced into it by the approaches of the *water*, a noise is made near resembling the *notes* of a *Nightingale*: But when that *pipe* is filled there is then no more singing, till the *water* has past away by another *pipe* in the lower part of the *rock*, which when almost done, there is heard a *noise* somwhat like the sound of a *drum*, performed by the rushing in of *air* into the hollow of the *pipe*, which is large, and of *copper*, to supply the place of the *water* now almost gon out; which don, the *Nightingale* may be made to sing again.

55. From the turned *roof* of the *rock*, by help of the brass *instrument k*, and turn of a cock in one of the *closets* above, they can let down a *canopy* of *water l l*; from the top also they can throw *arched spouts* of *water* crossing one another, and dashing against the walls, opposite to those of their rise, as at *m n* and *o p*; and *others* that rise out, and enter in again to the *roof* at some distance, never falling down at all at *q r* and *s t*. Which falls of *water* may be also delicatly seen, turning the back upon them as well as looking forward, by help of a Looking-glass placed in the wall opposite to them, which could not be possibly represented in the *Cut*. And some of these *waters* (I must not say which) being often used by way of *sport* to wet the *Visitants* of the *Grot*, that they might not avoid it by running up the *stairs*, and so out into the *Grove*, by turning a cock in another of the *Closets*, they can let fall water so plentifully in the *door u u*, that most *people* rather

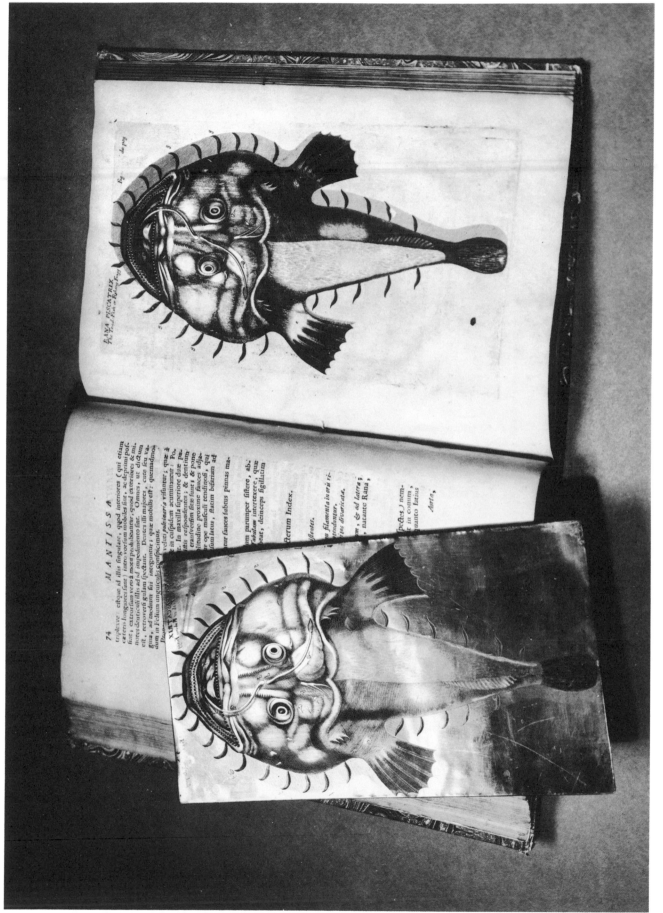
74 MANTISSA
RANA PISCATRIX
The Toad-Fish or Fishing Frogg

THE HISTORY OF LAPLAND

WHEREIN

Are ſhewed the Original, Manners, Habits, Marriages, Conjurations, &c. of that People.

WRITTEN

By JOHN SCHEFFER, *Profeſſor of Law and Rhetoric at* Upſal *in* Sweden.

At the THEATER in *OXFORD.*

M. DC. LXXIV.

And are to be ſold by GEORGE WEST and AMOS CURTEIN.

380

Aula D. Johannis Bap. vulgo Aula Glocestriensis.

D occiduam Vici Stockwelliani partem, in parochiâ S. Nicolai, alias Divi Thomæ Martyris, superest usq; hodie maxima veteris Musarum habitaculi pars, quod ...

15

117

Sr.

I am very glad to find that the great hast
which you made in your iourny, had also good
speed; and that you had the desirable welcome
added, of finding my Lord in so good health.
He continues to be very obliging, in retaining our
concernes in his thoughts; and since you tell me that
he approves of an attempt of an Edition of the Bible
we shall think upon it with more courage then we
did. The truth is, Mr. Principal & my self, have
had long debates upon that head; for as it is certain
that we can never carry on our Expensive business of
printing without the help of Subscriptions; so it seems
evident to us that nothing can be so usefull, as beni=
classicall Authors wherein Scholars are concernd; to pro=
=pose also such an universal book as will be acceptable
to all conditions not only of men, but the Women likewise.
and doubtless what you recommended to us, the setting
out an English bible, with all the advantages of print &
paper, & exterior ornaments, and the accession of practi=
=call annotations fitted for the use of every Christian
reader, had advantages beyond any other design
that we can think of: But the difficulty to have it
creditably don; & then owned by such a Character &
approbation as would give it countenance; stuck
with us. To obviate this we have thought of Sixe
Doctors, men of learning & reputation, whom we verily think
we can engage, to share the task of making Notes; And
have perswaded the Doctor of the Chair, to undertake
the reviewing of the whole, when it is don: which I confess
is a Point gaind so much beyond expectation; (for you
know with what unwillingness he is brought to work)

that I begin to hope; we shall meet with no ob=
=struction that will be insuperable. I pray Sr.
consider whither this cast which we have made
be admirable; or what may be altered from, or ad=
=ded to it. The Persons we have in designation are
Dr. Pocock, Dr. Marshall, Dr. Jully, Dr. Marsh,
Dr. Lloyd of Reading, & Dr. Hall. Upon my
Lords, & your direction we shall go on to
modell the affair. This Afternoon I shall
be at a meeting of the heads of houses, where
I shall see what may be don about your
course at St. Maries. Sr. I wish you
all health & remain

Your

Most affectionate

Ap: 11. J. Fell.

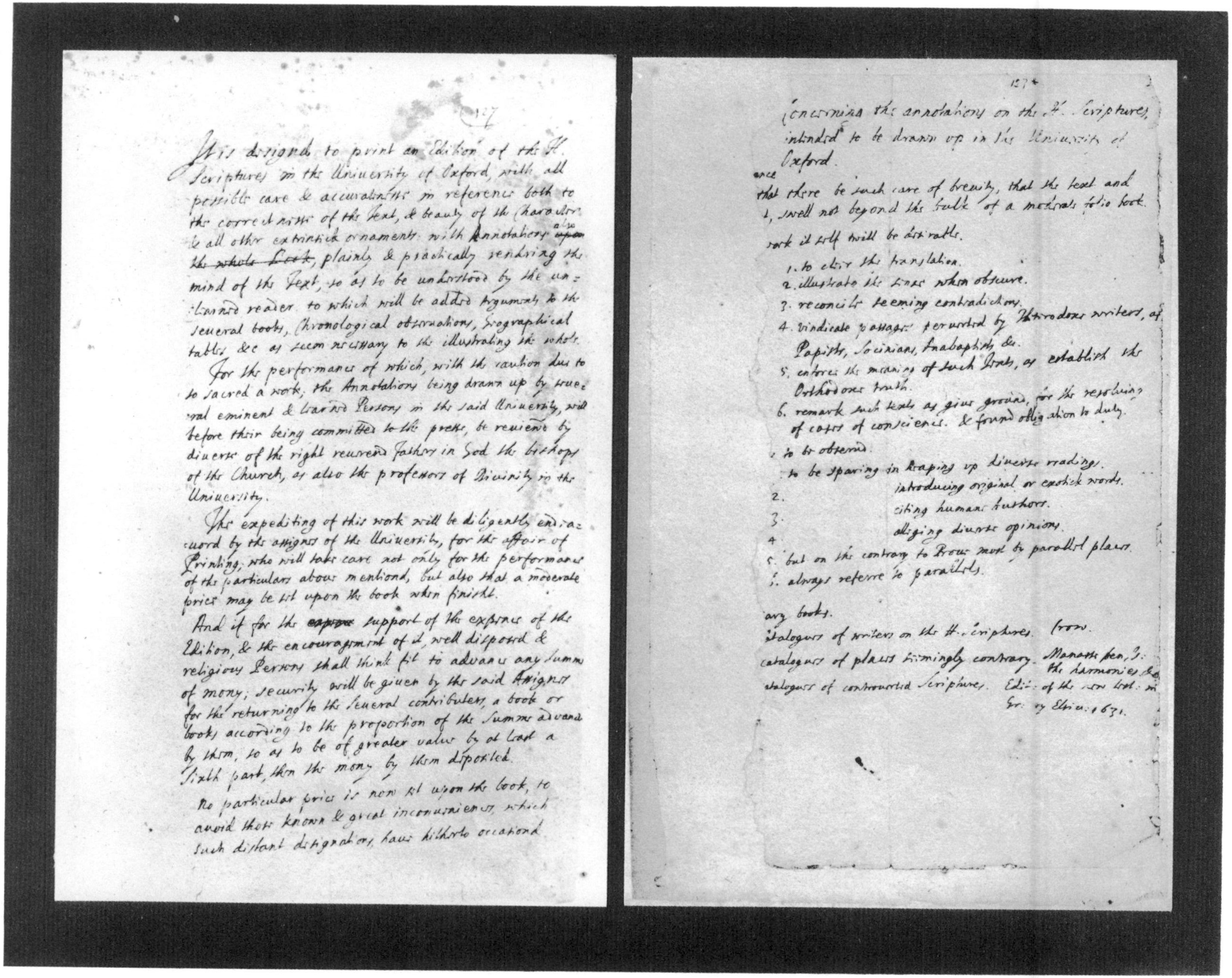

127

It is designed to print an Edition of the H. Scriptures in the University of Oxford, with all possible care & accurateness in reference both to the correctness of the text, & beauty of the Characters & all other extrinsick ornaments: with Annotations ~~upon the whole Book~~ also, plainly & practically rendring the mind of the Text, so as to be understood by the unlearned reader. to which will be added Arguments to the severall books, Chronological observations, Geographical tables &c as seem necessary to the illustrating the whole.

For the performance of which, with the caution due to so sacred a work, the Annotations being drawn up by severall eminent & learned Persons in the said University, will before their being committed to the presse, be reviewed by diverse of the right reverend fathers in God the bishops of the Church, as also the professors of Divinity in the University.

The expediting of this work will be diligently endeavoured by the assignes of the University, for the affair of Printing; who will take care not only for the performance of the particulars above mentiond, but also that a moderate price may be set upon the book when finisht.

And if for the ~~expence~~ support of the expence of the Edition, & the encouragement of it, well disposed & religious Persons shall think fit to advance any summ of mony; security will be given by the said Assignes for the returning to the severall contributers, a book or books according to the proportion of the summe advanced by them, so as to be of greater value by at least a sixth part, then the mony by them deposited.

No particular price is now set upon the book, to avoid those known & great inconveniences, which such distant designations have hitherto occasiond.

127*

Concerning the annotations on the H. Scriptures, intended to be drawn up in the University of Oxford.

...ance that there be such care of brevity, that the text and ..., swell not beyond the bulk of a moderate folio book.

...rork it self will be desirable.

1. to clear the translation.
2. illustrate the lines when obscure.
3. reconcile seeming contradictions.
4. vindicate passages perverted by Heterodoxe writers, as Papists, Socinians, Anabaptists &c.
5. enforce the meaning of such texts, as establish the Orthodoxe truth.
6. remark such texts as give ground, for the resolving of cases of conscience. & found obligation to duty.

... to be observed.

... to be sparing in heaping up diverse readings.
2. introducing original or exotick words.
3. citing humane Authors.
4. alleging diverse opinions.
5. but on the contrary to bestow most by parallel places.
6. always referre to parallels.

...ary books.

...atalogues of writers on the H. Scriptures. from
catalogues of places seemingly contrary. Manasse ben I.
...atalogues of controverted Scripture. the harmonies &c Edi. of the new test. in Gr. by Elzev. 1631.

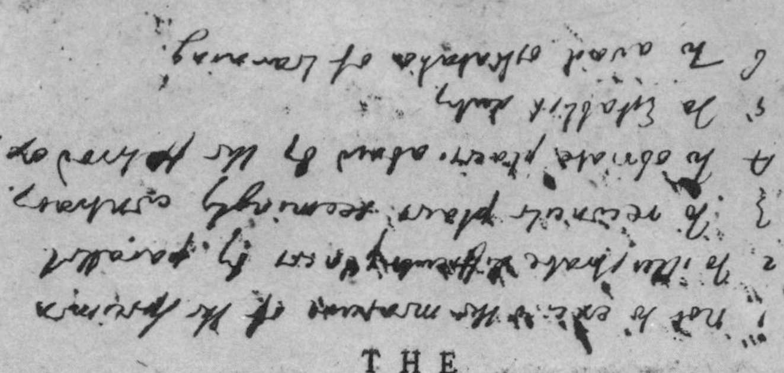

THE FIRST BOOK OF *MOSES* Called *GENESIS.*

CHAP. I.

1 The creation of heaven and earth, 3 of the light, 6 of the firmament, 9 of the earth separated from the waters, 11 and made fruitful, 14 of the sun, moon and stars, 20 of fish and fowl, 24 of beasts and cattel, 26 of man in the image of God. 29 Also the appointment of food.

IN * the [b] beginning God created the [c] heaven
and the earth.
2 And the earth was without form, and
void; and darkness *was* upon the face of
the deep; and the [d] Spirit of God [e] moved
upon the face of the waters.
3 And [f] God said, * Let there be light:
and there was light.
4 And God saw the light, [g] that *it was* good: and
God divided † the light from the darkness.
5 And God called the light Day, and the darkness he called Night: † and the [h] evening and the
morning were the first day.
6 ¶ And God said, * Let there be a † firmament
in the midst of the waters; and let it divide the waters from the waters.
7 And God made the firmament; and divided the
waters which *were* under the † firmament, from the [i] waters which *were* above the firmament: and it was so.
8 And God called the firmament Heaven: and
the evening and the morning were the second day.
9 ¶ And [k] God said, * Let the waters under the
heaven be gathered together unto one place; and let
the [l] dry-land appear: and it was so.
10 And God called the dry-land Earth, and the gathering together of the waters called he Seas: and
God saw that *it was* good.
11 And God said, Let the earth [m] bring forth † grass,
the herb yielding seed, *and* the fruit-tree yielding
fruit after his kind, whose seed *is* in it self, upon the
earth: and it was so.
12 And the earth brought forth grass, *and* herb
yielding seed after his kind; and the tree yielding
fruit, whose seed *was* in it self, after his kind: and
God saw that *it was* good.
13 And the evening and the morning were the
third day.
14 ¶ And God said, Let there be * lights in the
firmament of the heaven, to divide † the [n] day from
the night: and let them be for [o] signs, and for [p] seasons, and for daies, and [q] years.
15 And let them be for lights in the firmament
of the heaven, to give [r] light upon the earth: and it
was so.
16 And God made two [s] great lights; the greater
light, to rule the day, and the lesser light to rule
the night: *he made* the stars also.
17 And God set them in the firmament of the
heaven, to give light upon the earth,
18 And † to rule over the day and over the night,
and to divide the light from the darkness: and God
saw that *it was* good.
12 And the evening and the morning were the
fourth day.
20 And God said, * Let the waters bring forth
abundantly the [t] moving creature that hath † life,
and fowl *that* may flie above the earth in the † o-
pen firmament of heaven.
21 And God created great whales, and every
living creature that moveth, which the waters brough
forth abundantly after their kind, and every winged
fowl after his kind: and God saw that *it was* good.
22 And God blessed them, saying, * Be fruitful,
and multiply, and fill the waters in the seas, and
let fowl multiply in the earth.
23 And the evening and the morning were the

* Psal. 33.6. & 136.5. Acts 14.15. and 17.24. Heb. 11.3. * 2 Cor. 4.6. † Heb. between the light and between the darkness. † Heb. and the evening was, and the morning was, &c. * Psal. 136.5. Jer. 10.12. and 51.15. † Heb. expansion. * Psal. 33.7. & 136.6. Job 38.8. † Heb. tender grass. * Deut. 4.19. Psal. 136.7. † Heb. between the day, and between the night. † Heb. for the rule of the day &c. * Jer. 51.35. 2 Esd. 6.47. † Or, creepeth. † Heb. soul † Heb. face of the firmament of heaven. * Chap. 8.17. 9.1.

GENESIS] The title of this first book of Moses seemeth to be borrowed from the Greek Interpreters of the old Testament, who for *These are the generations of the heavens and of the earth* translated, Chap. 2. 4. thus, *This is the book of Genesis* (that is, of the generation or original) *of heaven and earth*. The same word is also in the beginning of the new Testament. §. *Verse* I. *In the beginning*] The world was not from eternity, but made in the *beginning of the Creation which God created*, Mar. 13. 19. 2. Pet. 3. 4. Heb. 1. 10. That is, when as yet there was nothing but God himself, who onely is eternal, he first created heaven and earth. §. ibid. *The heaven and the earth*] The world and all things therein were made by the Lord of heaven and earth, Acts 17. 24. §. II. *Spirit of God*] The holy Ghost, to whom is here ascribed a personal work, as Acts 13. 2. and 16. 6 7. 1 Cor. 12. 11. and particularly Gods work of Creation, as Job 33. 4. and 26. 13. Psa. 33. 6. §. Ibid. *Moved*] Hovered or brooded, as a fowl over her eggs to hatch them, or over her young to cherish them. See Deut. 32. 11. Where the same Heb. word is used, and compare Mat. 3. 16. Such was the powerful over-shadowing of the Spirit of God in the wonderful conception of Christ [Luke 1. 35.] and such is the efficacy of his mighty power in the regeneration of those that are born of the Spirit, Psal. 51. 10. Eph. 1. 19. §. III. *God said*] God made the world by his word [Psa. 33 6. Heb. 11. 3.] and by his son, who is also called the Word of God [Rev. 19. 13. 1. 40. 5. 7.] were all things created [Col. 1. 16. Heb. 1. 2.] And this *Word*, by whom all things were made, *was in the beginning* with God, and the same *was God*, John 1. 1. 2, 3. §. Ibid. *Light*] The first thing that God commanded to appear in the creation of the world, was Light: and the first work of his spirit in forming the new Creature, is to enlighten the understanding with knowledg, after the image of him that created. See 2 Cor. 4. 6. Col. 3. 10 §. IV. If it were expedient to inquire after the creation of the Angels of light [2 Cor. 11. 14] and the heavenly mansions of the saints in light [Col. 1. 12.] it would seem reasonable to refer it to this first day. See Job 38. 4, 7. §. V. *The evening and the morning*] See Dan. 8. 14, 26. in Heb. and 2 Cor. 11. 25. so the Sabbaths and Passover began in the evening, Lev. 23. 32. Exod. 12. 18. *v.* 7. *Waters above the firmament*] which are bound up in the clouds [Job 26. 8.] from whence they are poured out, Psal. 77. 17. Of these waters see further Psal. 148. 4. and 104. 3. and 18. 11. as also chap. 7. 11. and 8. 2. and 2 Sam. 21. 10. §. IX. *Gathered together into one place*] called sea [*v.* 10] which is the common storehouse, from whence all rivers are derived, and whether they return again, Eccl. 1. 7. §. Ibid *Dry land*] fenced by Gods decree against the inundation of the sea, Job. 28. 8, 11. Psal. 104. 9. See John 1. 9. Heb. 11. 29. Mat. 23. 15. Gr. §. XI. *Bring forth grass*] spring with, send or shoot forth sprouts. See Joel 2. 22. Heb. XIV. *The day*] called artificial, which consisteth of twelve hours [John 11. 9.] and so is distinct from the natural [*v.* 19.] which containeth four and twenty hours. §. Ibid. *Signes*] of weather [Mat. 16. 2.] and other events, Mat. 24. 29. The extraordinary Signs of Gods displesure are dreadful [Luke 21. 11. 25] but Astrologers observations from the ordinary signs of heaven, we are commanded not to fear, Jer. 10. 2. §. Ibid. *Seasons*] such are those of the year [chap. 8. 22.] to teach man providence in laying up in the summer and harvest [Pro. 6. 6. 7. 8.] and such are the solemn seasons for divine worship [Psal 104. 19] to teach him regularity in devotion [Num. 9. 23. and 28 2.] which at certain seasons is not to be neglected, Isa. 66. 23. §. Ibid *Daies and years*] that men by numbring the daies of the years of their lives [2 Sam. 19. 34. Heb.] may more punctually apply their hearts [Psal. 90. 12.] to attend their religious and worldly callings. See Psal. 81. 3. and 55. and Exod. 20. 9. Psal. 104. 22. 23. §. XV. *Light*] which implieth also heat and influence, Psal. 19 6 Deut. 33. 14. §. XVI. *Great lights*] namely the sun and moon [Psal. 136. 7, 8. 9.] great in appearance efficacy and service. §. XX. *Moving creature*] See Psal. 104. 25.

v. 26

THE HOLY

BIBLE,

Containing the

Old Teſtament

And the New;

Tranſlated out of the Original Tongues, and with the former Tranſlations diligently compared and reviſed

BY

His *Majeſties* ſpecial Command.

Appointed to be read in Churches.

OXFORD.

At the THEATER 1675.

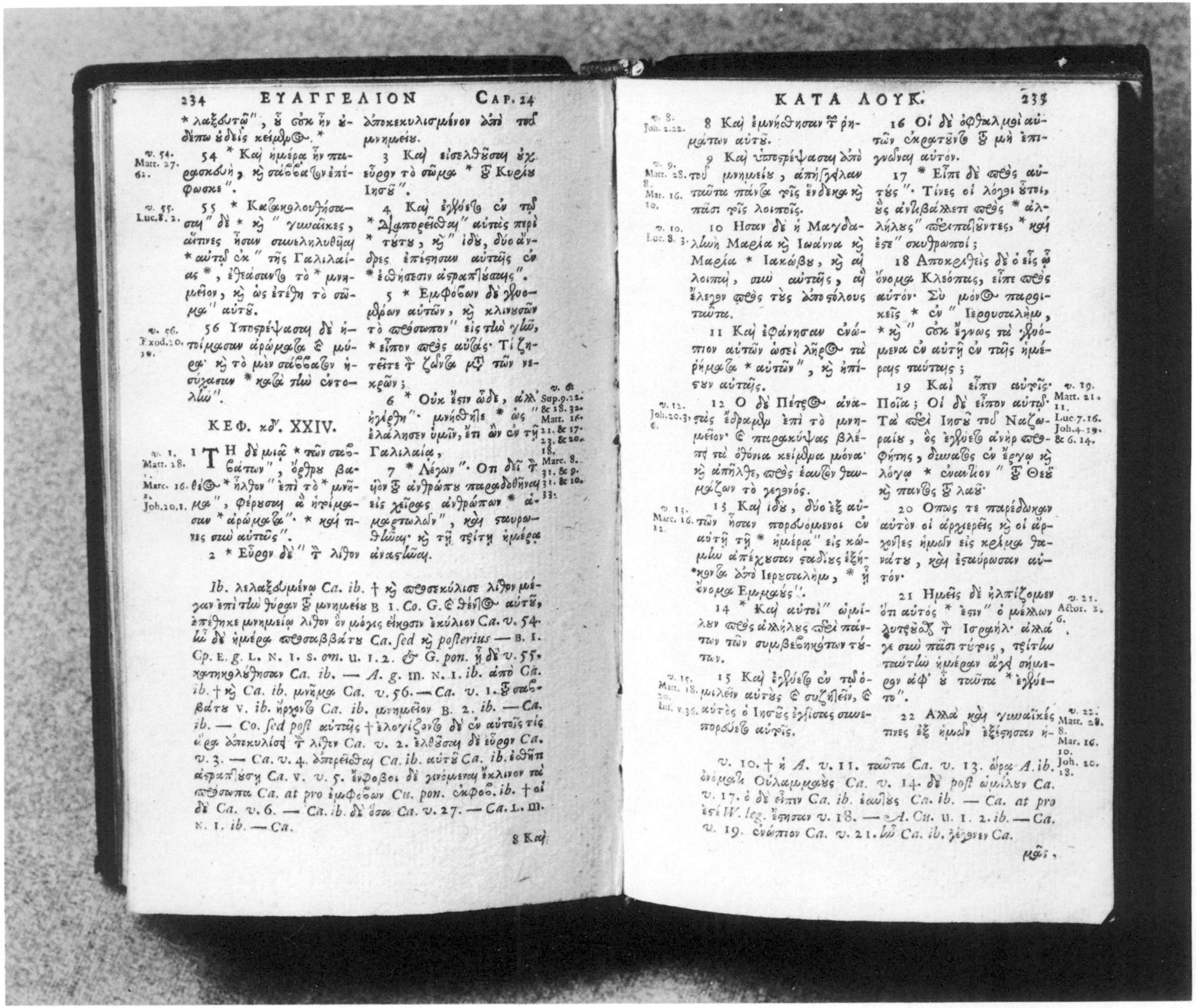

*λαξευτῷ", οὗ οὐκ ἦν οὐ-
δέπω οὐδεὶς κείμενος.*

v. 54. Matt. 27. 62.

54 *Καὶ ἡμέρα ἦν πα-
ρασκευὴ, καὶ σάββατον ἐπέ-
φωσκε".

v. 55. Luc. 8. 2.

55 *Κατακολουθήσα-
σαι" δὲ *καὶ" γυναῖκες,
αἵτινες ἦσαν συνεληλυθυῖαι
*αὐτῷ ἐκ" τῆς Γαλιλαί-
ας*, ἐθεάσαντο τὸ *μνη-
μεῖον, καὶ ὡς ἐτέθη τὸ σῶμα" αὐτοῦ.

v. 56. Exod. 20. 10.

56 Ὑποστρέψασαι δὲ ἡ-
τοίμασαν ἀρώματα καὶ μύ-
ρα· καὶ τὸ μὲν σάββατον ἡ-
σύχασαν *κατὰ τὴν ἐντο-
λήν".

ΚΕΦ. κδʹ. XXIV.

v. 1. Matt. 28. 1. Marc. 16. 2. Joh. 20. 1.

1 Τῇ δὲ μιᾷ *τῶν σαβ-
βάτων", ὄρθρου βα-
θέος *ἦλθον" ἐπὶ τὸ *μνῆ-
μα", φέρουσαι ἃ ἡτοίμα-
σαν *ἀρώματα"· *καί τι-
νες σὺν αὐταῖς".
2 *Εὗρον δὲ" τὸν λίθον
ἀποκεκυλισμένον ἀπὸ τοῦ
μνημείου.
3 Καὶ εἰσελθοῦσαι οὐχ
εὗρον τὸ σῶμα *τοῦ Κυρίου
Ἰησοῦ".
4 Καὶ ἐγένετο ἐν τῷ
*διαπορεῖσθαι" αὐτὰς περὶ
*τούτου, καὶ" ἰδοὺ, δύο ἄν-
δρες ἐπέστησαν αὐταῖς ἐν
*ἐσθήσεσιν ἀστραπτούσαις".
5 *Ἐμφόβων δὲ γενο-
μένων αὐτῶν, καὶ κλινουσῶν
τὸ πρόσωπον" εἰς τὴν γῆν,
*εἶπον πρὸς αὐτάς· Τί ζη-
τεῖτε τὸν ζῶντα μετὰ τῶν νεκρῶν;

v. 6. Sup. 9. 22. & 18. 32. Matt. 16. 21. & 17. 23. & 20. 18. Marc. 8. 31. & 9. 31. & 10. 33.

6 *Οὐκ ἔστιν ὧδε, ἀλλ'
ἠγέρθη"· μνήσθητε *ὡς"
ἐλάλησεν ὑμῖν, ἔτι ὢν ἐν τῇ
Γαλιλαίᾳ,
7 *Λέγων"· Ὅτι δεῖ τὸν
υἱὸν τοῦ ἀνθρώπου παραδοθῆναι
εἰς χεῖρας ἀνθρώπων *ἁ-
μαρτωλῶν", καὶ σταυρω-
θῆναι· καὶ τῇ τρίτῃ ἡμέρᾳ
ἀναστῆναι.

Ib. λελαξευμένῳ *Ca. ib.* † καὶ προσεκύλισε λίθον μέγαν ἐπὶ τὴν θύραν τοῦ μνημείου B 1. *Co.* G. καὶ θέντος αὐτοῦ, ἐπέθηκε μνημείῳ λίθον ὃν μόγις εἴκοσιν ἐκύλιον *Ca.* v. 54. ἦν δὲ ἡμέρα προσαββάτου *Ca. sed* καὶ *posterius* — B. 1. Cp. E. g. L. N. 1. S. *om.* u. 1. 2. & G. *pon.* ἡ δὲ v. 55. κατηκολούθησαν *Ca. ib.* — *A.* g. m. N. 1. *ib.* ἀπὸ *Ca. ib.* † καὶ *Ca. ib.* μνῆμα *Ca.* v. 56. — *Ca.* v. 1. τοῦ σαββάτου v. *ib.* ἤρχοντο *Ca. ib.* μνημεῖον B. 2. *ib.* — *Ca. ib.* — Co. *sed post* αὐταῖς † ἐλογίζοντο δὲ ἐν αὐταῖς τίς ἄρα ἀποκυλίσει τὸν λίθον *Ca.* v. 2. ἐλθοῦσαι δὲ εὗρον *Ca.* v. 3. — *Ca.* v. 4. ἀπορεῖσθαι *Ca. ib.* αὐτοῦ *Ca. ib.* ἐσθῆτι ἀστραπτούσῃ *Ca.* v. v. 5. ἔμφοβοι δὲ γενόμεναι ἔκλινον τὰ πρόσωπα *Ca. at pro* ἐμφόβων *Cu. pon.* ἐκφοβ. *ib.* † αἱ δὲ *Ca.* v. 6. — *Ca. ib.* δὲ ὅσα *Ca.* v. 27. — *Ca.* L. m. N. 1. *ib.* — *Ca.*

8 Καὶ

v. 8. Joh. 2. 22.

8 Καὶ ἐμνήσθησαν τῶν ῥη-
μάτων αὐτοῦ.

v. 9. Matt. 28. 8. Mar. 16. 10.

9 Καὶ ὑποστρέψασαι ἀπὸ
τοῦ μνημείου, ἀπήγγειλαν
ταῦτα πάντα τοῖς ἕνδεκα καὶ
πᾶσι τοῖς λοιποῖς.

v. 10. Luc. 8. 3.

10 Ἦσαν δὲ ἡ Μαγδα-
ληνὴ Μαρία καὶ Ἰωάννα καὶ
Μαρία *Ἰακώβου, καὶ αἱ
λοιπαὶ, σὺν αὐταῖς, αἳ
ἔλεγον πρὸς τοὺς ἀποστόλους
ταῦτα.
11 Καὶ ἐφάνησαν ἐνώ-
πιον αὐτῶν ὡσεὶ λῆρος τὰ
ῥήματα *αὐτῶν", καὶ ἠπί-
στουν αὐταῖς.

v. 12. Joh. 20. 3, 6.

12 Ὁ δὲ Πέτρος ἀνα-
στὰς ἔδραμεν ἐπὶ τὸ μνη-
μεῖον· καὶ παρακύψας βλέ-
πει τὰ ὀθόνια κείμενα μόνα·
καὶ ἀπῆλθε, πρὸς ἑαυτὸν θαυ-
μάζων τὸ γεγονός.

v. 13. Marc. 16. 12.

13 Καὶ ἰδοὺ, δύο ἐξ αὐ-
τῶν ἦσαν πορευόμενοι ἐν
αὐτῇ τῇ *ἡμέρᾳ" εἰς κώ-
μην ἀπέχουσαν σταδίους ἑξή-
κοντα ἀπὸ Ἱερουσαλὴμ, *ᾗ
ὄνομα Ἐμμαούς".
14 *Καὶ αὐτοὶ" ὡμί-
λουν πρὸς ἀλλήλους περὶ πάντων τῶν συμβεβηκότων τού-
των.

v. 15. Matt. 18. 20. Inf. v. 36.

15 Καὶ ἐγένετο ἐν τῷ ὁ-
μιλεῖν αὐτοὺς καὶ συζητεῖν, καὶ
αὐτὸς ὁ Ἰησοῦς ἐγγίσας συνε-
πορεύετο αὐτοῖς.
16 Οἱ δὲ ὀφθαλμοὶ αὐ-
τῶν ἐκρατοῦντο τοῦ μὴ ἐπι-
γνῶναι αὐτόν.
17 *Εἶπε δὲ πρὸς αὐ-
τούς"· Τίνες οἱ λόγοι οὗτοι,
οὓς ἀντιβάλλετε πρὸς *ἀλ-
λήλους" περιπατοῦντες, *καί
ἐστε" σκυθρωποί;
18 Ἀποκριθεὶς δὲ ὁ εἷς ᾧ
ὄνομα Κλεόπας, εἶπε πρὸς
αὐτόν· Σὺ μόνος παροι-
κεῖς *ἐν" Ἱερουσαλὴμ,
*καὶ" οὐκ ἔγνως τὰ γενό-
μενα ἐν αὐτῇ ἐν ταῖς ἡμέ-
ραις ταύταις;

v. 19. Matt. 21. 11. Luc. 7. 16. Joh. 4. 19. & 6. 14.

19 Καὶ εἶπεν αὐτοῖς·
Ποῖα; Οἱ δὲ εἶπον αὐτῷ·
Τὰ περὶ Ἰησοῦ τοῦ Ναζω-
ραίου, ὃς ἐγένετο ἀνὴρ προφήτης, δυνατὸς ἐν ἔργῳ καὶ
λόγῳ *ἐναντίον" τοῦ Θεοῦ
καὶ παντὸς τοῦ λαοῦ·
20 Ὅπως τε παρέδωκαν
αὐτὸν οἱ ἀρχιερεῖς καὶ οἱ ἄρ-
χοντες ἡμῶν εἰς κρίμα θα-
νάτου, καὶ ἐσταύρωσαν αὐ-
τόν.

v. 21. Actor. 1. 6.

21 Ἡμεῖς δὲ ἠλπίζομεν
ὅτι αὐτός *ἐστιν" ὁ μέλλων
λυτροῦσθαι τὸν Ἰσραήλ· ἀλλά
γε σὺν πᾶσι τούτοις, τρίτην
ταύτην ἡμέραν ἄγει σήμε-
ρον ἀφ' οὗ ταῦτα *ἐγένε-
το".

v. 22. Matt. 28. 8. Mar. 16. 10. Joh. 20. 18.

22 Ἀλλὰ καὶ γυναῖκές
τινες ἐξ ἡμῶν ἐξέστησαν ἡ-

v. 10. † ἡ *A.* v. 11. ταῦτα *Ca.* v. 13. ὥρᾳ *A. ib.* ὀνόματι Οὐλαμμαοὺς *Ca.* v. 14. δὲ *post* ὡμίλουν *Ca.* v. 17. ὁ δὲ εἶπεν *Ca. ib.* ἑαυτοὺς *Ca. ib.* — *Ca. at pro* ἐστε *W. leg.* ἔστησαν v. 18. — *A. Cu.* u. 1. 2. *ib.* — *Ca.* v. 19. ἐνώπιον *Ca.* v. 21. ἦν *Ca. ib.* γέγονεν *Ca.*

μᾶς,

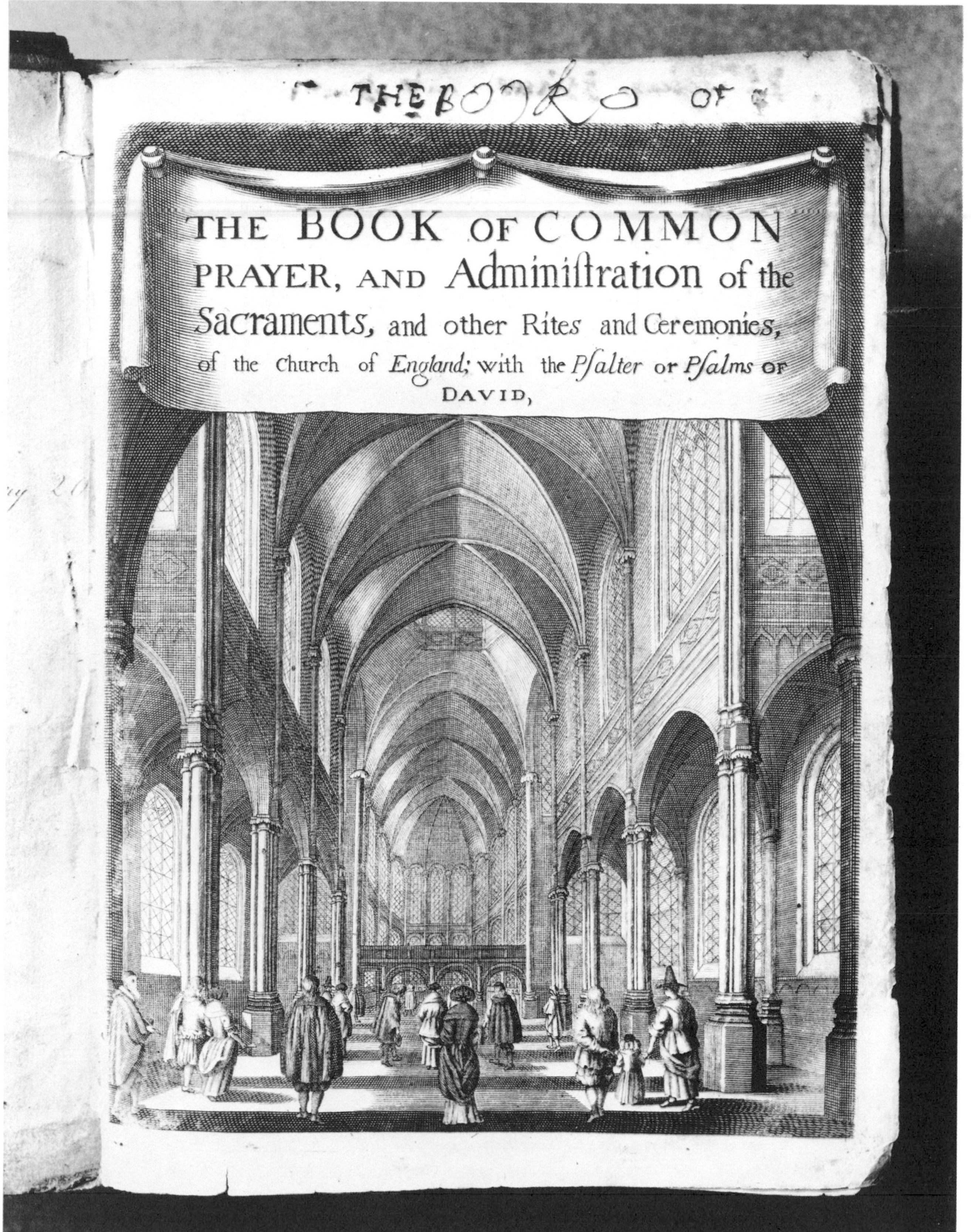
THE BOOK OF COMMON PRAYER, AND Administration of the Sacraments, and other Rites and Ceremonies, of the Church of England; with the Psalter or Psalms OF DAVID,

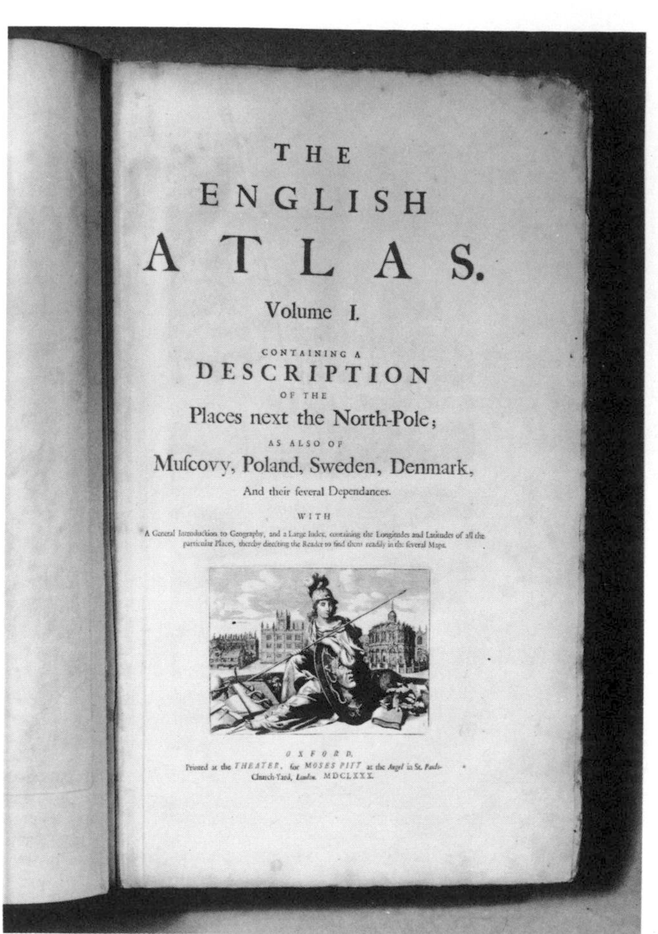

THE

ENGLISH

ATLAS.

Volume I.

CONTAINING A

DESCRIPTION

OF THE

Places next the North-Pole;

AS ALSO OF

Muſcovy, Poland, Sweden, Denmark,

And their ſeveral Dependances.

WITH

A General Introduction to Geography, and a Large Index, containing the Longitudes and Latitudes of all the particular Places, thereby directing the Reader to find them readily in the ſeveral Maps.

OXFORD,

Printed at the *THEATER*, for *MOSES PITT* at the *Angel* in St. *Pauls*-Church-Yard, *London*. MDCLXXX.

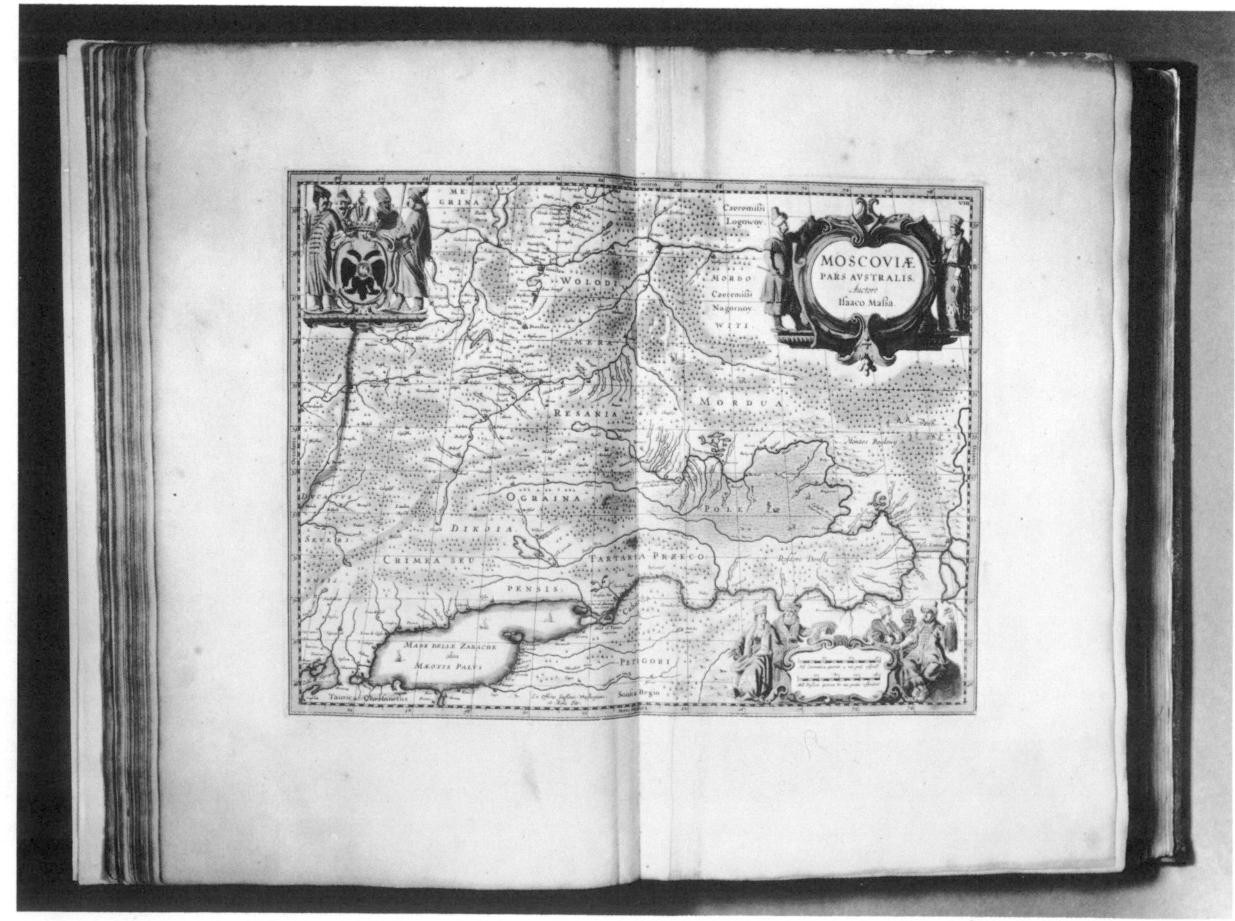

98

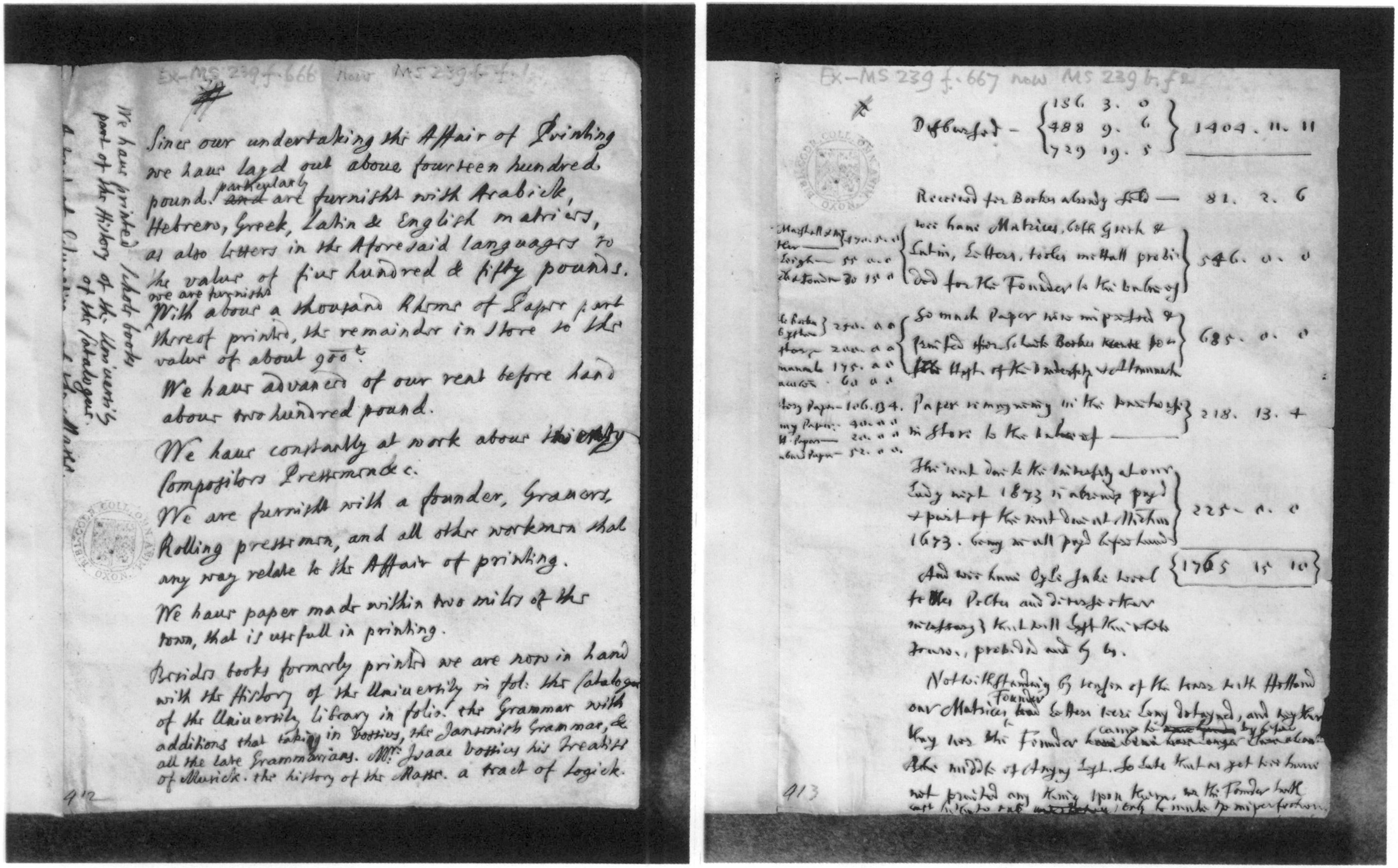

#

Since our undertaking the Affair of Printing we have layd out above fourteen hundred pound. particularly we are furnisht with Arabick, Hebrew, Greek, Latin & English matrices, as also letters in the Aforesaid languages to the value of five hundred & fifty pounds.

we are furnisht With about a thousand Rheme of Paper part thereof printed, the remainder in Store to the value of about 900^l.

We have advanced of our rent before hand about two hundred pound.

We have constantly at work about thirty Compositors Pressmen &c.

We are furnisht with a founder, Gravers, Rolling pressmen, and all other workmen that any way relate to the Affair of printing.

We have paper made within two miles of the town, that is usefull in printing.

Besides books formerly printed we are now in hand with the History of the University in fol: the Catalogue of the University Library in folio: the Grammar with additions that taking in Vossius, the Jansenist Grammar, & all the late Grammarians. Mr Isaac Vossius his Treatise of Musick. the history of the Mass. a tract of Logick.

We have printed Schole books
part of the History of the University
of the Catalogue.
A [illegible] of [illegible] and the Mass.

412

#

Disbursed –	156. 3. 0 488. 9. 6 729. 19. 5		1404. 11. 11
	Received for Books already sold —		81. 2. 6
[illegible]	Wee have Matrices, both Greek & Latin, Letters, tooles mettall provided for the Founder to the value of		546. 0. 0
[illegible]	So much Paper now imprinted & printed [illegible] Books [illegible] the History of the University [illegible]		685. 0. 0
[illegible]	Paper remaining in the [illegible] in Store to the value of —		218. 13. 4
	The rent due to the University at our Lady next 1673 is already payd & part of the rent due at Mich. 1673. being in all payd before hand		225. 0. 0
			1765 15 10

And wee have Oyle, [illegible] wood [illegible] and diverse other [illegible] which will [illegible] provided and [illegible].

Notwithstanding by reason of the warre with Holland our Matrices and Letters were long delayed, and [illegible] [illegible] the Founder came to us by [illegible] the middle of [illegible] that we yet have not printed any thing upon them, [illegible] the Founder hath [illegible] only to make up imperfections.

413

16

An account of the state of the Press in the University of Oxford as it now stands, January 9. 1679/80 |Print. 14 Jan.

IN the Year 1672, several persons members of the University of *Oxford*, namely *John* Bishop of *Oxford*, Sir *Joseph Williamson*, Sir *Leoline Jenkins*, and Dr *Thomas Tate*, taking into consideration the disabilities of the Press as constituted at *Oxford*, to supply the occasions of the University, in printing Books of ancient learning, and principal use in Divinity and other Sciences: and in receiving and vending the modern productions of learned men in their several faculties, both within and out of the University; and lastly in preventing foraign Universities, and Cities; such as are *Lions*, *Paris*, *Geneva*, *Antwerp*, *Bruxels*, *Leiden*, *Amsterdam*, &c. to impose their Wares upon us, and oblige us to receive not only Books at their prizes, but opinions from their dictates: to redeem the state of Learning, and that of the Press from these and like inconveniences, undertook the charge of the Press in the aforesaid University: and at the Expence of above five thousand pounds, furnisht from *Germany*, *France*, and *Holland*, an Imprimery with all the necessaries thereof, and pursued the undertaking so vigorously as in the short compass of time which has intervened; to have engag'd in the stock of Printing, besides the aforesaid summe, upwards of ten thousand pounds; and besides several Books actually prepared for the Press, to have Printed many considerable books. Such as are

In *FOLIO.*

THE Synodicon or Canons of ancient Councils with their Scholia, Greek *&* Latin *in* 2 *Vol.*
The Catalogue of printed Books in the University Library.
The History of the University. Lat.
The description of Colleges and public Buildings in the University, in perspective.
The History of Lapland.
The Marbles, Arundel and others in the University. Lat.
The Natural History of Oxford-shire.
Dr. Pococks Commentarys on the lesser Prophets; whereof a part is now in the Press.
Iamblichus of the Ægyptian Mysteries, Greek *&* Latin.
Dr. Charletons description of Animals. Lat.
St. Cyprians works; now in the Press. Lat.
Josephus Gr. *&* Lat. *now in the Press.*
The great Universal Herbal of Dr. Morison; now in the Press. Lat.
Jo. Scotus de Divisione Naturæ; not yet extant, now in the Press. Lat.
The great Atlas, in 12. *Volumes, on Imperial paper, now in the Press.*
A large English Bible, now in the Press.

In *QUARTO.*

SEveral English Bibles.
Dr. Willis de anima Brutorum. Lat.
His Pharmaceutice Rationalis 2 *Vol.* Lat.
The description of the more rare Plants of Sicily, Malta, Italy, &c. by P. Boccone. Lat.
Four controversial Dialogues, by Dr. Cole.
A Tract of Maimonides Heb. *&* Lat. *of the Tything for the poor, &c.*
The History of the Jacobits, &c. by Jos. Abudacnus Lat.
Edw. Earl of Clarendon against Mr. Hobbs.
The Benefits of our Savior to Mankind.
Dr. Salls Votum pro Pace. Lat.
A discourse of Convex Glasses.

In *OCTAVO.*

THO. Lidiats Chronological Canons. Lat.
Dr. Vossius de poematum cantu. Lat.
De Sibyllinis Oraculis. Lat.
Dr. Mayow de Spiritu nitro-Aereo, &c. Lat.
Dr Brevints Saul and Samuel, or the new waies of Salvation, &c.
*A Paraphrase and Annot. on the Epistles of St.*Paul,*&c.*
The Ladies Calling.
The Government of the Tongue.
The Art of Contentment.
The Lively Oracles.
Xenophon Cyr. Poed. Gr.
A Dissertation of Free-Schools. by C. Wase.
Epictetus Ench. & Theophrastus Charact. Gr. *&* Lat.
The Certainty of Christian Faith, by D. Whitby.
Herodians History, Gr. *&* Lat.
Zosimus History, Gr. *&* Lat.
Aratus with Schol. Gr.
Nemesius de Nat. Hom. Gr. *&* Lat.
Quintilians Declam. Lat.
The History of West Barbary.
Homers Iliads Gr. *with the Schol.*
Theocrit. Gr. *with the Schol.*
Suetonius, lives of Cesars, Lat.
The state of the Greek Church, by Tho. Smith.
Mr. Oughtreds Mathematical Tracts, not before extant.
Plinies Epistles, Lat.
Demetrius Phalereus, de Elocut. Gr. *&* Lat.
Pachymerius Logic. Gr. *&* Lat.
Reflexions on the Council of Trent, by H. Luzancy.
Greek Psalter, according to the Alexandrian Copy.

In *TWELVES.*

NEw Testament Gr. *with the Various readings.*
Dr. Cole, de Secretione. Lat.
Grotius, de Veritate, &c. Lat.
St. Clements Epist. Gr. *&* Lat.
Cornelius Nepos, Lat.
Grammatica Rationis. Lat.
Ars Rationis. Lat.
Lilies Grammar with Notes. Lat.
Of the Education of Gentlemen.
Depth and Mystery of the Roman Mass, by Dr. Brevint.
The Christian Sacrifice, &c.
Maximus Tyrius Gr. *&* Lat.
B. Andrews Devotions Gr. *&* Lat.
Dr. Willis Pharmac. Rat. 2 *Vol.* Lat.
Archimedes his Arenarius Gr. *&* Lat.
Justins History. Lat.
Dr. Salls Defence of the Catholic Religion of the Church of Eng
Sallusts History. Lat.
M. Aurel. Antoninus Gr. *&* Lat.
Faustinus' works, Lat.

Books prepared for the Press.

A Volume of the ancient English Historians never yet Printed.
A Saxon Lexicon, the work of Mr. Junius, not yet Printed.
His Etymologicon, not yet Printed.
Several of the ancient Greek Mathematicians.
The Coptic Gospels and Psalter.
The Saxon Chronology.
Lactantius Instit. &c.
Orosius Hist.
Jo. Antioch. Gr. *&* Lat. *never yet Printed.*

With many others almost fitted for the Press.

Ex dono Reverend Johan: Oxon Episcopi

R King

Sancti Cæcilii CYPRIANI OPERA

RECOGNITA & ILLUSTRATA

Per

JOANNEM OXONIENSEM Episcopum.

Accedunt

ANNALES CYPRIANICI,

SIVE

Tredecim Annorum, quibus S. Cyprianus inter Christianos versatus est, brevis historia Chronologice delineata

Per JOANNEM CESTRIENSEM.

OXONII

E THEATRO SHELDONIANO Anno CIƆ IƆC LXXXII.

218

lacet.

sculp.

E R R A T A.

Pag. 1, lin. 2. dele comma, post *Poëtica*. lin. 5. lege modum. Pag. 2. lin. 22. lean. P. 4. l. 6. æfre. l. 20. Adam. l. 23. Adames. P. 6. l. 8. adde punctum, post willan. P. 7. l. 13. heardmode. P. 8. l. 5. englas. l. 18. waldan. P. 9. l. 1. nid bedd. l. 11. befælled. P. 10. l. 9. onclinesse. P. 11. l. 19. pro wora worda reponitur ad oram Manuscripti wraðra worda. P. 14. l. 4. Cwæð. l. 20. læste. l. 21. idesa. P. 15. l. 17. þearf. P. 17. l. 12. bræcon. P. 21. l. 6. beþeahton. l. 17. hear hleoðrade. P. 23. l. 19. Ongunnon. P. 25. l. 9. mundum. l. 15. wineleas. P. 26. l. 3. anum. P. 30. l. 6. dohte. l. 12. wæter. P. 31. l. 6. þara. l. 17. hrofgefor. P. 32. l. 9. wætres. P. 33. l. 4. sincende. P. 36. l. 14. à. P. 37. l. 3. rærde. l. 25. somed. P. 40. l. 24. mæg. P. 42. l. 24. wunden. P. 43. l. 19. fæðm. P. 46. l. 7. feasceaft. l. 20. led. P. 48. l. 4. heofon. hyrste gerim. P. 50. l. 9. agen. l. 22. agan. P. 53. l. 24. laste. freonda feasceaft. l. 25. weran usser her. aldor dema. P. 62. l. 9. gedæde. P. 64. l. 8. lete. P. 66. l. 14. hreowan. P. 69. l. 19. sceolde. l. 23. heard hand plega. P. 70. l. 3. ꝥ he siððor for. l. 11. polcnum. l. 13. magum. P. 71. l. 20. æfter. P. 74. l. 4. gihðum. P. 76. l. 10. Gesamnode. P. 80. l. 2. wa. P. 82. l. 13. weorde. þa of roderum wæs. P. 84. l. 25. Agæf. P. 85. l. 6. onget. l. 23. dele alterum nyde. P. 89. l. 24. æðelingas. P. 92. l. 11. ðis is se ðeorstræ ham. l. 13. wulres. P. 98. l. 12. fæste gebunden. P. 100. l. 3. becom. p. 103. l. 19. gesceafta.

Pag. 1,

C Æ D M O N I S

Paraphrasis poëtica,

Genesios ac præcipuarum sacræ paginæ historiarum.

Us is riht micel. ðæt we rodera weard. wereda wuldor cining. wordum herigen. modum lufien. he is mægna sped. heafod ealra heah gesceafta. frea ælmihtig. Næs him fruma æfre. or geworden. ne nu ende cymþ. ecean drihtnes. ac he bið á rice. ofer heofen stolas. heagum þrymmum. soðfæst ⁊ swið feorom. swegl-bosmas heold. þa wæron gesette. wide ⁊ side. þurh geweald godes. wuldres bearnum. gasta weardum. Hæfdon gleam ⁊ dream. ⁊ heora ordfruman. engla þreatas. beorhte blisse. wæs heora blæd micel. þegnas þrymfæste. þeoden heredon. sægdon lustum lof. heora lif-frean. demdon drihtenes dugeþum. wæron swiðe gesælige. synna ne cuþon. firena fremman. ac hie on friðe lifdon. ece mid heora aldor. elles ne ongunnon. ræran on roderum. nymþe riht ⁊ soð. ærðon engla weard. for oferhygde. dæl on gedwilde. noldon dreogan leng. heora selfra ræd. ac hie of siblufan. godes ahwurfon. Hæfdon gielp micel. ꝥ hie wið drihtne. dælan meahton. wuldor-fæstan wic.. werodes þrymme. sid ⁊ swegl-torht. him þær sar gelamp. æfst ⁊ oferhygd. ⁊ þæs engles mod. þe þone unræd. ongan ærest fremman. wefan ⁊ weccean. þa he worde cwæð. niþes ofþyrsted. ꝥ he on norð dæle. (2) ham ⁊ heahsetl. heofena rices. agan wolde. þa wearð yrre god. ⁊ þam werode wrað. þe he ær wurðode.

wlite

103

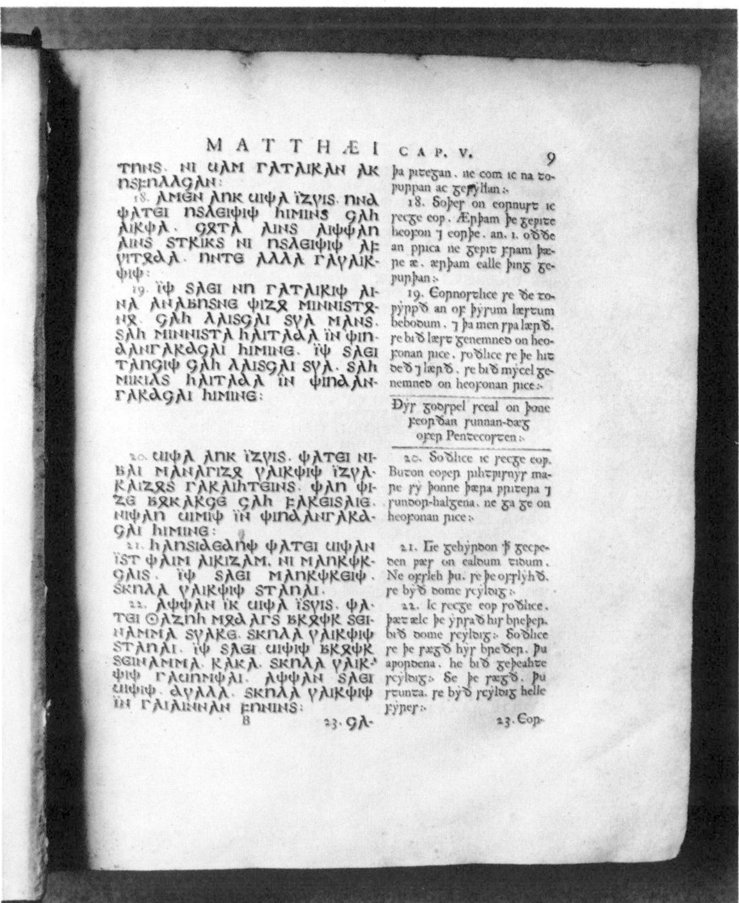

tins. ni qam gatairan ak
usfulljan:
18. Amen auk qiþa izwis. und
þatei usleiþiþ himins jah
airþa. jota ains aiþþau
ains striks ni usleiþiþ af
witoda. unte alla gawair-
þiþ:
19. iþ saei nu gatairiþ ai-
na anabusne þizo minnisto-
no. jah laisjai swa mans.
sah minnista haitada in þiu-
dangardjai himine. iþ saei
taujiþ jah laisjai swa. sah
mikils haitada in þiudan-
gardjai himine:
20. qiþa auk izwis. þatei ni-
bai managizo wairþiþ izwa-
raizos garaihteins. þau þi-
ze bokarje jah Fareisaie.
niþ qimiþ in þiudangarda-
jai himine:
21. hausideduþ þatei qiþan
ist þaim airizam. ni maurþr-
jais. iþ saei maurþreiþ.
skula wairþiþ stauai.
22. aþþan ik qiþa izwis. þatei hvazuh modags broþr seinamma swarei. skula wairþiþ
stauai. iþ saei qiþiþ broþr
seinamma. raka. skula wairþiþ gaqumþai. aþþan saei
qiþiþ. dwala. skula wairþiþ
in gaiainnan funins:

23. Ja-

þa witegan. ne com ic na towurpan ac gefyllan:

18. Soþes on eornust ic secge eow. Ærþam þe gewite heofon ⁊ eorþe. an. i. oððe an prica ne gewit fram þære æ. ærþam ealle þing gewurþan:

19. Eornostlice se ðe towyrpð an of þysum læstum bebodum. ⁊ þa men swa lærð. se bið læst genemned on heofonan rice. soðlice se þe hit deð ⁊ lærð. se bið mycel genemned on heofonan rice:

Ðys godspel sceal on þone feorðan sunnan-dæg ofer Pentecosten:

20. Soðlice ic secge eow. Buton eower rihtwisnys mare sy þonne þæra writera ⁊ sundor-halgena. ne ga ge on heofonan rice:

21. Ge gehyrdon ꝥ gecweden wæs on ealdum tidum. Ne ofsleh þu. se þe ofslyhð. se byð dome scyldig:

22. Ic secge eow soðlice. þæt ælc þe yrsað his breþer. bið dome scyldig: Soðlice se þe sægð hys breðer. þu aworpena. he bið geþeahte scyldig: Se þe sægð. þu stunta. se byð scyldig helle fyres:

23. Eor-

104

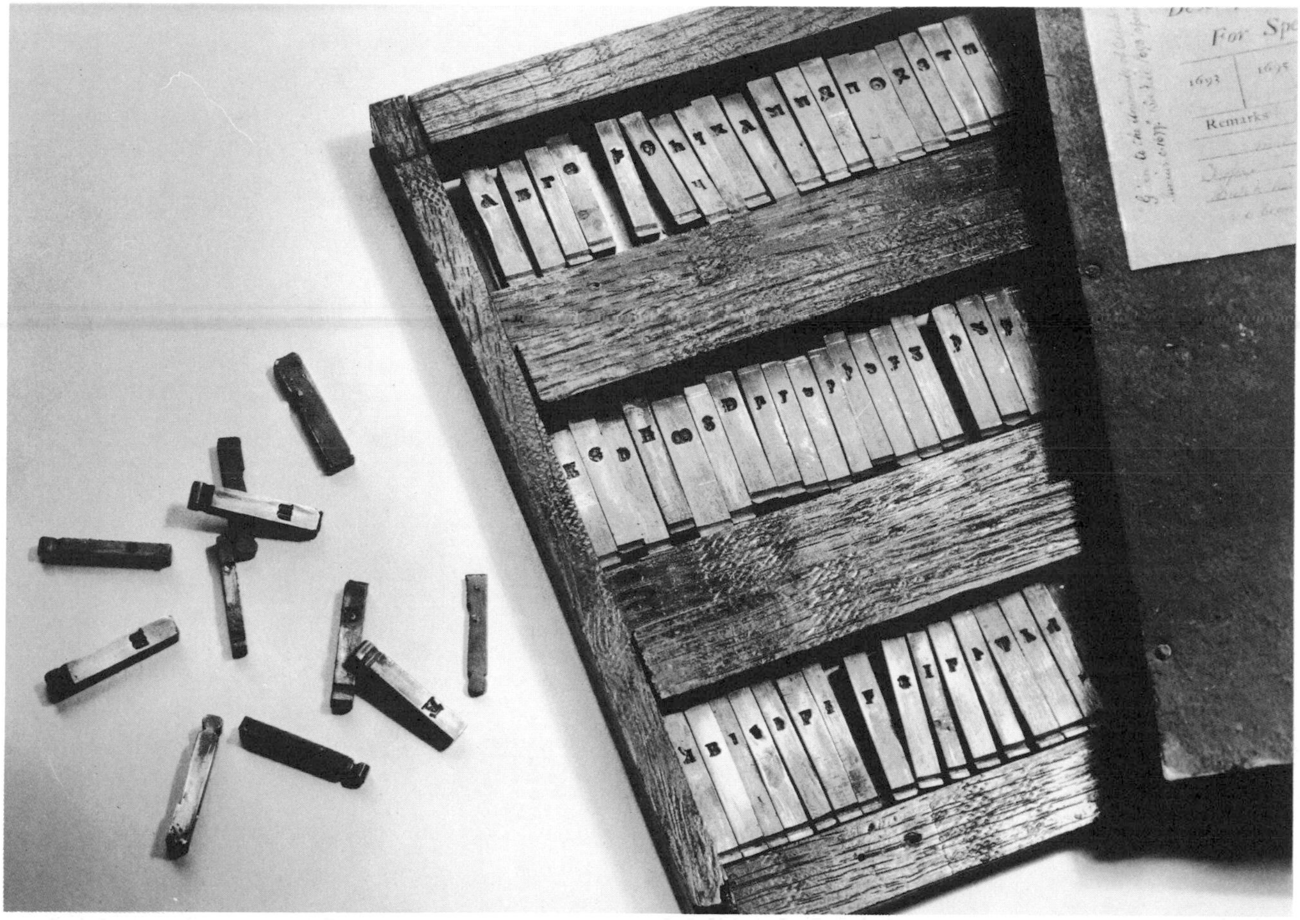

105

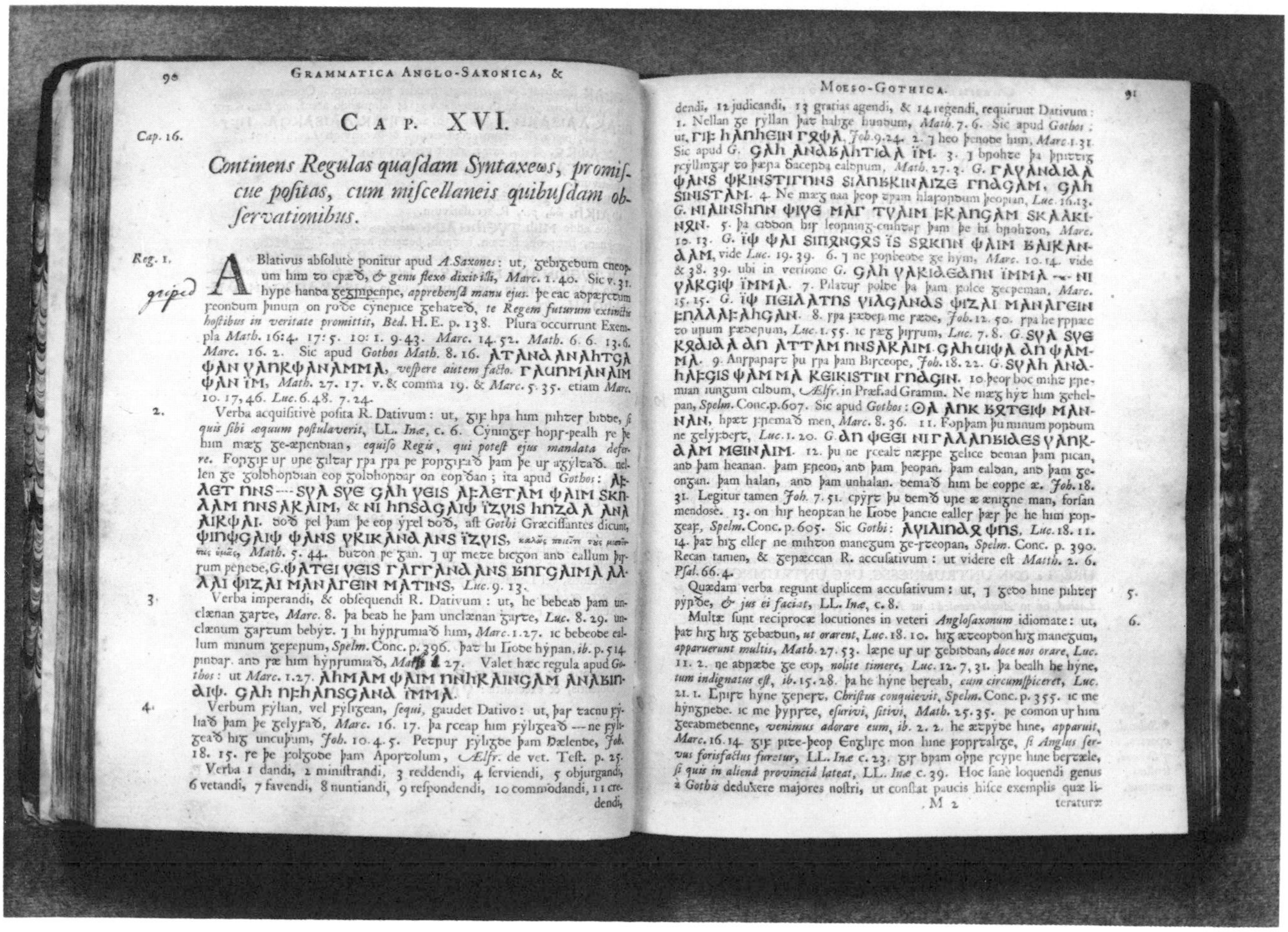

106

GEORGIUS HICKES S.T.P.
Non ita pridem Collegii Lincoln. in Academia Oxon. Socius, ex Canonico Ecclesiæ Cathedr. Wigorn. factus Decanus Octobris die 15. AD 1683.

Linguarum Vett.
SEPTENTRIONALIUM
THESAURUS
GRAMMATICO-CRITICUS
ET
ARCHÆOLOGICUS.
Auctore *GEORGIO HICKESIO*, S.T.P.

OXONIÆ.

E THEATRO SHELDONIANO, *An. Dom.* MDCCV.

FRANCISCI JUNII

FRANCISCI FILII

ETYMOLOGICUM

ANGLICANUM.

EX

Autographo deſcripſit & acceſſionibus permultis auctum edidit

EDWARDUS LYE A. M. Eccleſiæ Parochialis de *Yardley-Haſtings* in agro *Northamptonienſi* Rector.

PRÆMITTUNTUR

VITA AUCTORIS

ET

GRAMMATICA ANGLO-SAXONICA.

—— *Antiquam exquirite Matrem.* Virg.

Grammatica eſt clavis, quæ librorum ſenſum reſerat. Præf. Ælfrici Grammaticæ præfix.

OXONII:

E THEATRO SHELDONIANO,

MDCCXLIII.

Henry Aldrich, D.D.
Dean of Christ=Church.
1689.

The Second Book.

Thy tongue deviseth mischiefs, like a sharp Rasor, working deceitfully:
Thou lovest all devouring words, o thou deceitful tongue. Psal. 52. 2. 4.
The words of his mouth were smoother than Butter, but War was in his
heart: his words were softer than oyl, yet were they drawn Swords. Ps. 55. 21.

Affairs in Scotl. after the Kings return thence relating chiefly to the composing a Liturgy and Canons.

It was towards ye end of the year 1633, when the King returned from Scotland, having left it to the care of some of the Bps there, to provide such a Liturgy, & such a Book of Canons, as might best suit the nature, & humour of the better sort of that people; to which the rest would easily submit; and that, as fast as they made them ready, they should transmit them to the Arch-Bp of Canterbury, to whose assistance the King joyned the Bishop of London, & Dr Wren, who, by that time, was become Bp of Norwich, a man of a severe sowr nature, but very learned, & particularly versed in the old Liturgies of the Greek, & Latin Churches. And after his Majtie should be this way certified of what was so sent, he would recomend, & injoyn the practice, and use of both to that his Native Kingdom. The Bps there had somewhat to do before they went about the preparing the Canons, & ye Liturgy. What had passed, at the Kings being there in Parliament, had left bitter inclinations, & unruly spirits in many of the most popular Nobility; who watched only for an opportunity to enflame ye people, and were well enough contented to see combustible matter every day gathered together, to contribute to that fire. The promoting so many Bps to be of the Privy-Council, and to sit in the Courts of Justice, seemed at first wonderfully to facilitate all that was in design, and to create an affection, & reverence towards the Church at least an application to, & dependance upon the greatest Church-men.

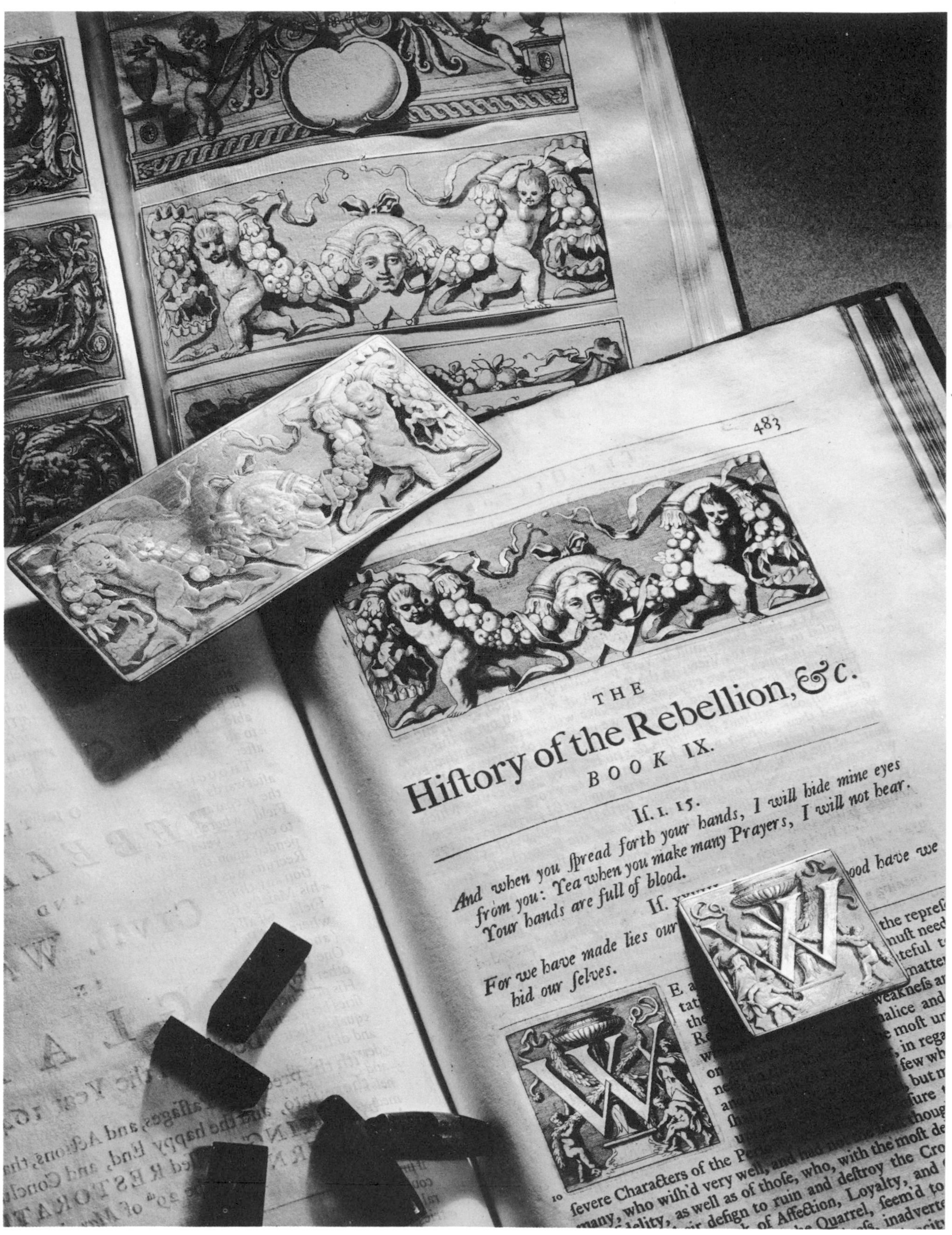
483
THE
History of the Rebellion, &c.
BOOK IX.
If. I. 15.
And when you spread forth your hands, I will hide mine eyes
from you: Yea when you make many Prayers, I will not hear.
Your hands are full of blood.
bid our selves.

Edward Earle of CLARENDON Lord High CHANCELLOR of England
and Chancellor of the University of Oxford. An.o Dni 1667.

THE
HISTORY
OF THE
REBELLION and CIVIL WARS
IN
ENGLAND,
Begun in the Year 1641.

With the precedent Paſſages, and Actions, that contributed thereunto, and the happy End, and Concluſion thereof by the KING's bleſſed RESTORATION, and RETURN upon the 29th of *May*, in the Year 1660.

Written by the Right Honourable
EDWARD Earl of CLARENDON,
Late Lord High Chancellour of *England*, Privy Counſellour in the Reigns of King CHARLES the Firſt and the Second.

Κτῆμα ἐς ἀεί. *Thucyd.*
Ne quid Falſi dicere audeat, ne quid Veri non audeat. Cicero.

VOLUME THE FIRST.

OXFORD,
Printed at the THEATER, *An. Dom.* MDCCII.

Anno Domini MDCCV. *Jun.* die 12. in Theatro *Sheldoniano* apud *Oxonienſes* ſub Prelo ſunt libri ſequentes.

NOvum Teſtamentum Græce, cum variis Lectionibus, &c. Fol.

An Expoſition of *Daniel's* Prophecy of LXX. Weeks, with Chronological Tables of thoſe Weeks and other matters relating to the ſame; by the Right Reverend Father in God, *William* Lord Biſhop of *Worceſter*. 4to.

Archæologia Britannica; Containing ſome Account, additional to what has been hitherto publiſhed, of the Ancienteſt Languages, Cuſtoms and Monuments of the *Britiſh* Iſles: From Obſervations and Collections in Travels through *Wales*, *Cornwall*, *Baſſe Bretagne*, *Ireland* and *Scotland*. By *Edward Lhwyd* A. M. Keeper of the *Aſhmolean Muſæum*. Vol. I. of the Languages. Fol. This Tome contains I. Some Obſervations in general, relating to the alteration of Languages. II. The various Dialects of the *Britiſh* and ancient *Scotiſh* Languages compar'd. III. A ſhort Grammar and Vocabulary of the *Corniſh*. IV. The Roman names of Perſons and Places in *Britain*, parallel'd with *Britiſh* names yet remaining, and partly interpreted. V. An examination how far the *Britiſh* Tongue agrees with the *Greek* and *Latin*. VI. The *Britiſh*, *Celtic* and *Teutonic*, compar'd with Obſervations as to the Origin of the *Britains*. VII. A Catalogue of *Britiſh* MSS. VIII. A Grammar of the *Iriſh* (or ancient *Scotiſh*) with a Catalogue of MSS. in that Language. IX. An *Iriſh-Engliſh* Dictionary: and laſtly the *Iriſh* Language collated with the *Cantabrian*, *Celtic* and *Teutonic*; with an Enquiry into the Origin of the Ancient *Scots* and *Picts*.

Joſippon, ſeu *Joſephi Ben-Gorionis* Hiſtoriæ Judaicæ Libri ſex integri hactenus inediti, nunc primum ex Hebræo in Latinum tranſlati, & Notis illuſtrati, opera & ſtudio *Joannis Gagnier* A. M. 4to.

Novum Teſtamentum Græce cum Var. Lect. 8vo.

Jo. Erneſti Grabe Diſſertationes tres de verſione LXX Interpretum. 4to.

Athenagoræ Athenienſis, Philoſophi Chriſtiani, Opera. Ex vetuſtis Exemplaribus recenſuit, Adnotationibuſque *Geſneri*, *Suffridi*, *Kortholtii*, *Langi*, *Rechenbergi*, *Stephani*, aliorum, ſuas qualeſcunque adjecit *Edv. Dechair* A. M. è Coll. *Linc.*

Sophoclis Ajax Flagellifer, & Electra Gr. Lat. cum Scholiis antiquis & Annott. per *Th. Johnſon Etonenſem.*

Introductio ad Veram Phyſicam: ſeu Lectiones Phyſicæ habitæ in Schola Naturalis Philoſophiæ Academiæ *Oxonienſis*. Quibus accedunt *Chriſtiani Hugenii* Theoremata de Vi Centrifuga & Motu Circulari demonſtrata. Per *Jo. Keill* A. M. & Reg. Soc. Socium. Editio ſecunda Emendatior & Auctior. 8vo.

Nuper etiam ex eodem Typographéo prodierunt,

The Hiſtory of the Rebellion and Civil Wars in *England*, Begun in the Year 1641. Written by the Right Honourable *Edward* Earl of *Clarendon*, &c. In three Volumes, Fol.

Linguarum Veterum Septentrionalium Theſaurus Grammatico-Criticus & Archæologicus; necnon, de Linguarum iſtarum Uſu & Dignitate diſſertatio Epiſtolaris: Opera & ſtudio *Georgii Hickeſii*, S. T. P. Accedunt *Andreæ Fountaine* Equitis Aurati Numiſmata *Saxonica*, & *Humphredi Wanley* Librorum Veterum Septentrionalium, tam eorum qui in Anglia excuſi ſunt, quam qui in membranis ſcripti nondum eduntur, Catalogus, quam fieri licuit, locupletiſſimus.

Dionyſii Halicarnaſſenſis opera omnia Gr. & Lat. Fol. duobus Voluminibus comprehenſa. Curâ *J. Hudſon* Bibl. Bodl. Præfecti.

R. Moſis Maimonidis Tractatus Duo: I. De Doctrina Legis, ſive Educatione Puerorum. II. De natura & ratione pœnitentiæ apud Hebræos. Latinè reddidit, notiſque illuſtravit *Robertus Clavering*, A. M. Coll. Univ. Soc. 4to.

The *Engliſh Euclide*, being the Firſt Six Elements of Geometry, Tranſlated out of the Greek, with Annotations and uſeful Supplements; by *Edmund Scarburgh* A. M.

De Bibliorum Textu Hebraico, & Verſionibus Græca & Latina Vulgata Libri IV. Auctore *Humfredo Hodio* S. T. P. & Ling. Græc. Profeſ. Fol.

Marci Antonini Imperatoris τῶν εἰς ἑαυτὸν libri XII. Gr. & Lat. cum Annotationibus. 8vo.

M. Juniani Juſtini Hiſtoriarum ex Trogo Pompejo libri XLIV. MSS. Codicum Collatione recogniti, Annotationibuſque illuſtrati, per *Tho. Hearne*, A. M. ex Aul. S. Edm. 8vo.

S. P. N. Cyrilli Hieroſolymorum Archiepiſcopi opera, quorum quædam nunc primum ex Codd. MSS. edidit, reliqua cum Codd. MSS. contulit, emendavit, notiſque illuſtravit *Tho. Milles* S. T. B. ex Æde Chriſti. Fol.

Euclidis Opera quæ ſuperſunt omnia, Gr. & Lat. Fol. Ex recenſione *Davidis Gregorii* M. D. Aſtronomiæ Profeſſoris Saviliani, & R. S. S.

Novum Teſtamentum, una cum Scholiis Græcis, operâ *Joh. Gregorii* Archidiac. Glouc. Fol.

S. Irenæi Libri quinque adverſus Hæreſes, quorum Latinam verſionem antiquam è Codicibus MSS. emendavit, &c. *Joan. Erneſtus Grabe*. Fol.

Eutropii Breviarium Hiſtoriæ Romanæ, cum Pæanii Metaphraſi Græca. Meſſala Corvinus de Auguſti Progenie. Julius Obſequens de Prodigiis. Anonymi Oratio Funebris Gr. Lat. in Imp. Conſtant. Conſtantini M. fil. cum variis Lectionibus & Annotationibus, per *T. Hearne*, A. M. 8vo.

Xenophontis opera omnia Græce & Latine cum variis Lectionibus, ſex Voluminibus. 8vo.

A Preſervative againſt *Socinianiſm*: in 4. Parts, by Dr. *Edwards* Princip. of Jeſus Coll. in *Oxf.* 4to.

Aſtronomiæ Phyſicæ & Geometricæ Elementa, Auctore *Davide Gregorio* M. D. Aſtronomiæ Profeſſore Saviliano *Oxoniæ*, & R. S. S. Fol.

A general View of Ancient and Preſent Geography, together with a Sett of Maps, by *Edw. Wells* S. T. P.

Sir *Robert Cottons*'s Catalogue of MSS.

Librorum Manuſcriptorum Angliæ & Hiberniæ Catalogus, cum Indicibus Accuratiſſimis. Fol.

Dr. *Pocok*'s Commentary on Micah, Malachy, and Joel. Fol.

Hiſtoria Plantarum Oxonienſis: per *Robertum Moriſonum* M. D. & *Jac. Bobartium*. 2 Vol. Fol.

Joannis Walliſii nuper Geometriæ Prof. Savil. Operum Tomus III^{us}. Fol.

Geographiæ Veteris Scriptores Græci Minores (cum Interpretatione Latina, Diſſertationibus Cl. *Dodwelli*, ac Annotationibus) duobus Voluminibus comprehenſi, opera ac cura *Joan. Hudſon* Biblioth. Bodl. Præfecti.

C. Plinii Cæcilii Secundi Epiſtolæ & Panegyricus cum variis Lectionibus & Annotationibus. Accedit Vita Plinii ordine Chronologico digeſta, per *T. Hearne*, A. M. 8vo.

Sancti Juſtini Philoſophi & Martyris Apologia prima pro Chriſtianis ad Antoninum Pium; cum Latina Joannis Langi verſione, quamplurimis in locis correcta, &c. edita à *Joan. Erneſto Grabe*. Ejuſdem Apologia ſecunda cura *Hugonis Hutchin* A. M. ex Æd. Chr. 8vo.

Aſtronomiæ Cometicæ Synopſis, autore *Edm. Halleio* Geometriæ Profeſſore Saviliano.

Prelo parantur.

Geographorum Græcorum minorum Volumen tertium. Auctorum nomina & ſeriem in ſingulis Voluminibus ſiſtit pagina proxime excipiens *H. Dodwelli* Diſſertationes ſecundo Volumini præfixas. 8vo.

Apollonii Pergæi libri duo περὶ λόγου ἀποτομῆς ex Arabico in Latinum converſi, per *E. Hallejum* Geom. Prof. Savil.

Verſio LXX Viralis juxta exemplar Alexandrinum cum var. Lectt. Annott. & locis Parallelis, Fol. per *Jo. Erneſtum Grabe*.

Livii Opera cum Variis Lectionibus Chronologia & Notis &c. Accurante *T. Hearne* A. M.

Sir *John Spelman*'s Life of King *Ælfred* the Great, from the Original Copy, with ſeveral additions from MSS. &c. by Mr. *Hearne*.

Quintiliani Inſtitutiones Oratoriæ & Hermogenis Rhetorice cum Notis & var. Lect. 2 Vol. 8vo.

Rogandi ſunt viri docti & bonarum artium Fautores, qui libros, quotquot è Theatro Oxonienſi *in poſterum prodibunt, in charta Regia vel majori impreſſos habere malint quam communi, ut nomina ſua ad* Joannem Hall *Typographei* Sheldoniani *cuſtodem mature mittere velint.*

PHRASES
ET
MODI LOQUENDI
Communiores.

Глава а҃.		Cap. I.
Ѡ Сочиненїи предлога.		*De Constructione Præpositionum.*
Где ты былъ.	(1)	Ubi fuisti?
ꙋ брата моево, ꙋ сестрѣ твоеи.		Apud meum fratrem, apud sororem tuam.
ѿ кꙋди придешъ.	(2)	Unde venis?
ѿ батꙋшки, ѿ матꙋшки.		à patre, à matre.
изъ агленскои землы привозѧтъ сꙋкно.	(3)	Ex Anglia advehunt pannum.
давноли ты съ москвы.		Diune è Moscovia discessisti?

Cap. I.

Von der Construction der Praeposition.

(1) Wo seyd ihr gewesen? bey meinen bruder, bey deiner schwester. (2) Wo kombt ihr her? vom vatter: von der mutter. (3) Aus England bringen sie tuch. Wie lange ist es dass ihr ans der Moscau kommen.

G — БУЕ-

GUIL. COMES PEMBROCH ACAD CANC

POSTERIS, ET ÆTERNITATI SACRUM.
THOMÆ BODLÆI QUICQUID MORTALE TABELLA,
INGENTEMQUE ANIMAM BIBLIOTHECA REFERT.

GUIL. LAUD ARCHIEP CANT ACAD CANC

KENELMUS DIGBY EQUES AURATUS

IOANNES SELDENUS ARMIGER

CATALOGI
LIBRORUM
MANUSCRIPTORUM
ANGLIÆ
ET
HIBERNIÆ
IN UNUM COLLECTI,
CUM
INDICE ALPHABETICO.

OXONIÆ,
E THEATRO SHELDONIANO,
An. Dom. MDCXCVII.

A

JOURNEY

FROM

Aleppo to *Jeruſalem*

At Eaſter *A.D.* 1697.

By *Hen.Maundrell* M. A. late Fellow of *Exeter* Coll. and Chaplain to the Factory at *Aleppo*.

OXFORD

Printed at the THEATER, *An. Dom.* MDCCIII.

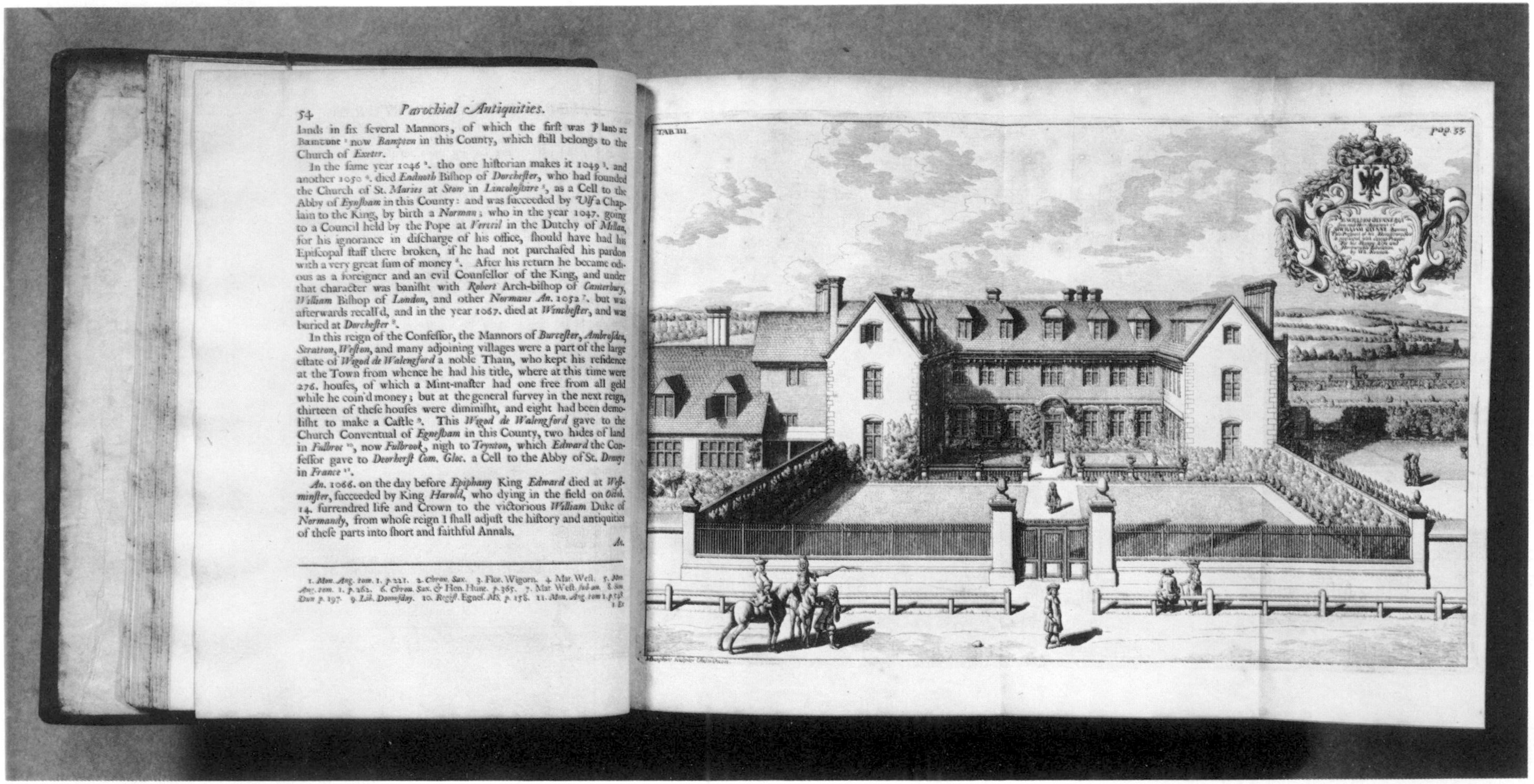

54 *Parochial Antiquities.*

lands in six several Mannors, of which the first was ꝥ land at Bamtune [1] now *Bampton* in this County, which still belongs to the Church of *Exeter*.

In the same year 1046 [2]. tho one historian makes it 1049 [3]. and another 1050 [4]. died *Ednoth* Bishop of *Dorchester*, who had founded the Church of St. *Maries* at *Stow* in *Lincolnshire* [5], as a Cell to the Abby of *Eynsham* in this County: and was succeeded by *Ulf* a Chaplain to the King, by birth a *Norman*; who in the year 1047. going to a Council held by the Pope at *Vercil* in the Dutchy of *Millan*, for his ignorance in discharge of his office, should have had his Episcopal staff there broken, if he had not purchased his pardon with a very great sum of money [6]. After his return he became odious as a foreigner and an evil Counsellor of the King, and under that character was banisht with *Robert* Arch-bishop of *Canterbury*, *William* Bishop of *London*, and other *Normans An.* 1052 [7]. but was afterwards recall'd, and in the year 1067. died at *Winchester*, and was buried at *Dorchester* [8].

In this reign of the Confessor, the Mannors of *Burcester*, *Ambrosden*, *Stratton*, *Weston*, and many adjoining villages were a part of the large estate of *Wigod de Walengford* a noble Thain, who kept his residence at the Town from whence he had his title, where at this time were 276. houses, of which a Mint-master had one free from all geld while he coin'd money; but at the general survey in the next reign, thirteen of these houses were diminisht, and eight had been demolisht to make a Castle [9]. This *Wigod de Walengford* gave to the Church Conventual of *Egnesham* in this County, two hides of land in *Fulbroc* [10], now *Fulbrook*, nigh to *Tryston*, which *Edward* the Confessor gave to *Deorherst Com. Gloc.* a Cell to the Abby of St. *Denys* in *France* [11].

An. 1066. on the day before *Epiphany* King *Edward* died at *Westminster*, succeeded by King *Harold*, who dying in the field on *Octob.* 14. surrendred life and Crown to the victorious *William* Duke of *Normandy*, from whose reign I shall adjust the history and antiquities of these parts into short and faithful Annals.

An.

1. *Mon. Ang. tom.* 1. *p.* 221. 2. *Chron. Sax.* 3. Flor. Wigorn. 4. Mat. West. 5. *Mon. Ang. tom.* 1. *p.* 262. 6. *Chron. Sax.* & Hen. Hunt. *p.* 365. 7. Mat. West. *sub an.* 8. *Sim. Dun p.* 197. 9. *Lib. Doomsday.* 10. *Regist.* Egnes. *MS. p.* 158. 11. *Mon. Ang. tom* 1. *p.* 548

TAB. III

pag. 55.

A NEW MAP of the TERRAQUEOUS GLOBE according
to the Ancient Discoveries and most general Divisions of it into CONTINENTS and OCEANS
Dedicated To his Highness WILLIAM Duke of Gloucester

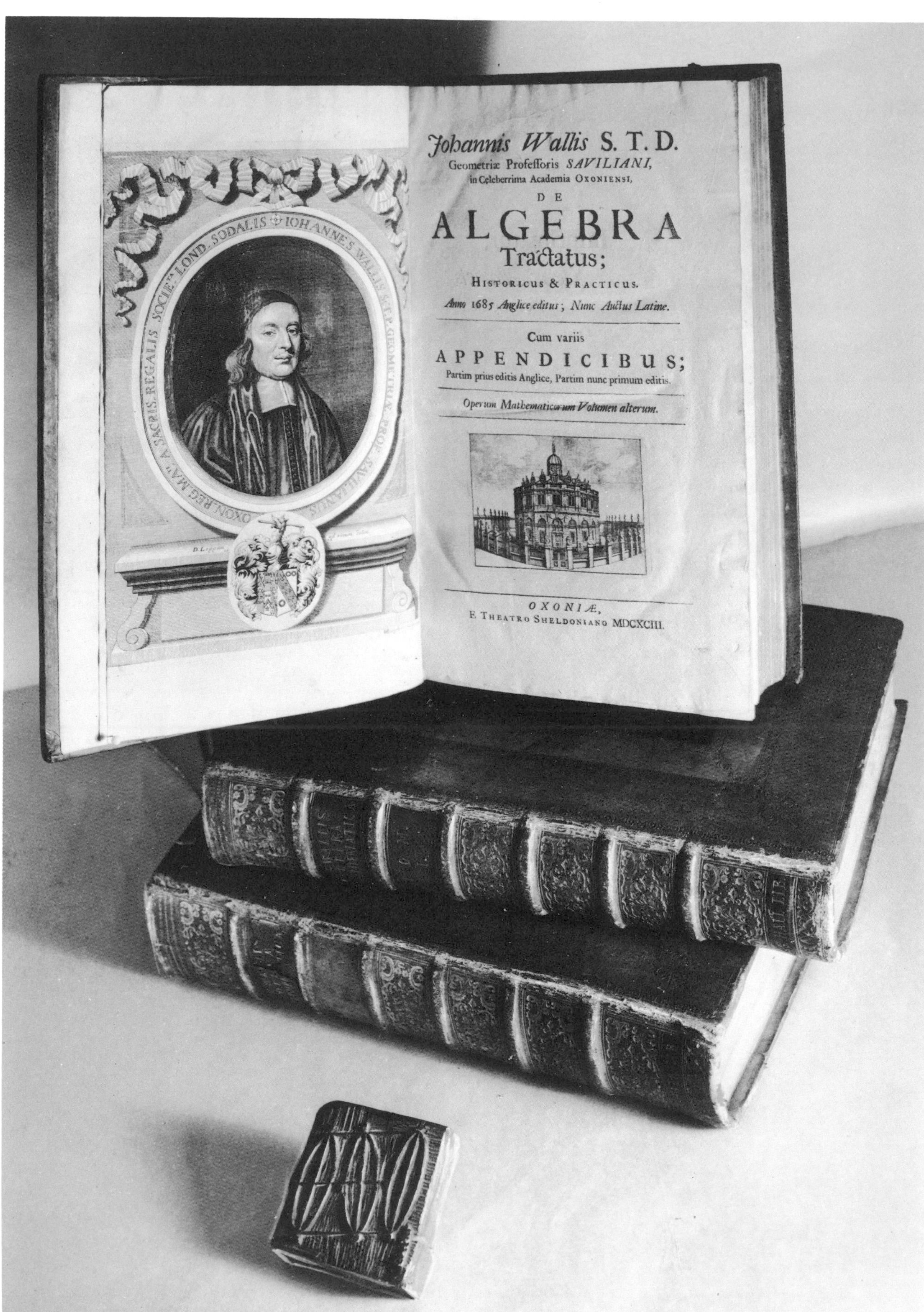
Johannis Wallis S. T. D.
Geometriæ Professoris SAVILIANI,
in Celeberrima Academia Oxoniensi,
DE
ALGEBRA
Tractatus;
Historicus & Practicus.
Anno 1685 Anglice editus; Nunc Auctus Latine.
Cum variis
APPENDICIBUS;
Partim prius editis Anglice, Partim nunc primum editis.
Operum Mathematicorum Volumen alterum.
OXONIÆ,
E Theatro Sheldoniano MDCXCIII.

Liber Bibliothecæ Savilianæ
ex dono Editoris.

APOLLONII PERGÆI CONICORUM LIBRI OCTO,

ET

SERENI ANTISSENSIS DE SECTIONE CYLINDRI & CONI LIBRI DUO.

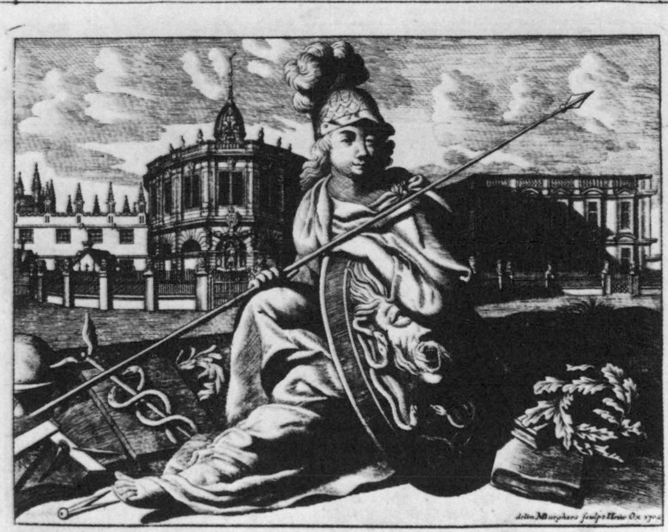

OXONIÆ,

E THEATRO SHELDONIANO, An. Dom. MDCCX.

HOC EST

NOVUM TESTAMENTUM

ÆGYPTIUM vulgo COPTICUM

Ex MSS. BODLEJANIS descripsit,

Cum Vaticanis et Parisiensibus contulit,

et in Latinum sermonem convertit

DAVID WILKINS

Ecclesiæ Anglicanæ Presbyter.

OXONII,

E Theatro Sheldoniano Typis et Sumptibus Academiæ, 1716.

ⲈⲨⲀⲄⲄⲈⲖⲒⲞⲚ

ⲔⲀⲦⲀ

ⲘⲀⲦⲐⲈⲞⲚ.

Ⲕⲉⲫ. ⲁ̅.

EVANGELIUM

Secundum

MATTHÆUM.

Cap. I.

Liber generationis Jesu Christi filii David, filii Abraham.

2. Abraham autem genuit Isaac, Isaac autem genuit Jacob, Jacob autem genuit Judam & fratres ejus.

3. Judas autem genuit Phares & Zaram ex Thamar, Phares autem genuit Esrom, Esrom autem genuit Aram.

4. Aram autem genuit Aminadab, Aminadab autem genuit Nasson, Nasson autem genuit Salmon.

5. Salmon autem genuit Boes ex Ræchab, Boes autem genuit Jubed ex Ruth, Jubed autem genuit Jesse.

6. Jesse autem genuit David Regem, David autem genuit Solomon ex illa Uriæ.

7. Solomon autem genuit Roboam, Roboam autem genuit Abiam, Abia autem genuit Asaph.

8. Asaph autem genuit Josaphat, Josaphat autem genuit Joram, Joram autem genuit Oziam.

9. Ozias autem genuit Joatham, Joatham autem genuit Achaz, Achaz autem genuit Ezekiam.

10. Ezekias autem genuit Manasse, Manasse autem genuit Amos, Amos autem genuit Josiam.

11. Josias autem genuit Jechoniam & fratres ejus circa transportationem in Babylon.

12. Post transportationem in Babylon Jechonias autem genuit Salathiel, Salathiel autem genuit Zorobabel.

13. Zorobabel autem genuit Abiud, Abiud autem genuit Eliakim,

A

Η ΚΑΙΝΗ
ΔΙΑΘΗΚΗ.
NOVUM
TESTAMENTUM.

CUM LECTIONIBUS VARIANTIBUS
MSS Exemplarium, Verſionum, Editionum, SS Patrum & Scriptorum Eccleſiaſticorum; & in eaſdem NOTIS.

ACCEDUNT
Loca Scripturæ PARALLELA, aliaque ἐξηγητικὰ, & APPENDIX ad Variantes Lectiones.

PRÆMITTITUR DISSERTATIO,
In qua de Libris N. T. & Canonis Conſtitutione agitur: Hiſtoria S. Textus N. Fœderis ad noſtra uſque tempora deducitur: Et quid in hac EDITIONE *præſtitum ſit, explicatur.*

STUDIO ET LABORE
JOANNIS MILLII S. T. P.

OXONII,
E THEATRO SHELDONIANO, M DCC VII.

ΤΟ
ΚΑΤΑ ΜΑΡΚΟΝ
ΑΓΙΟΝ ΕΥΑΓΓΕΛΙΟΝ.

ΚΕΦΑΛΑΙΟΝ Α'. 1.

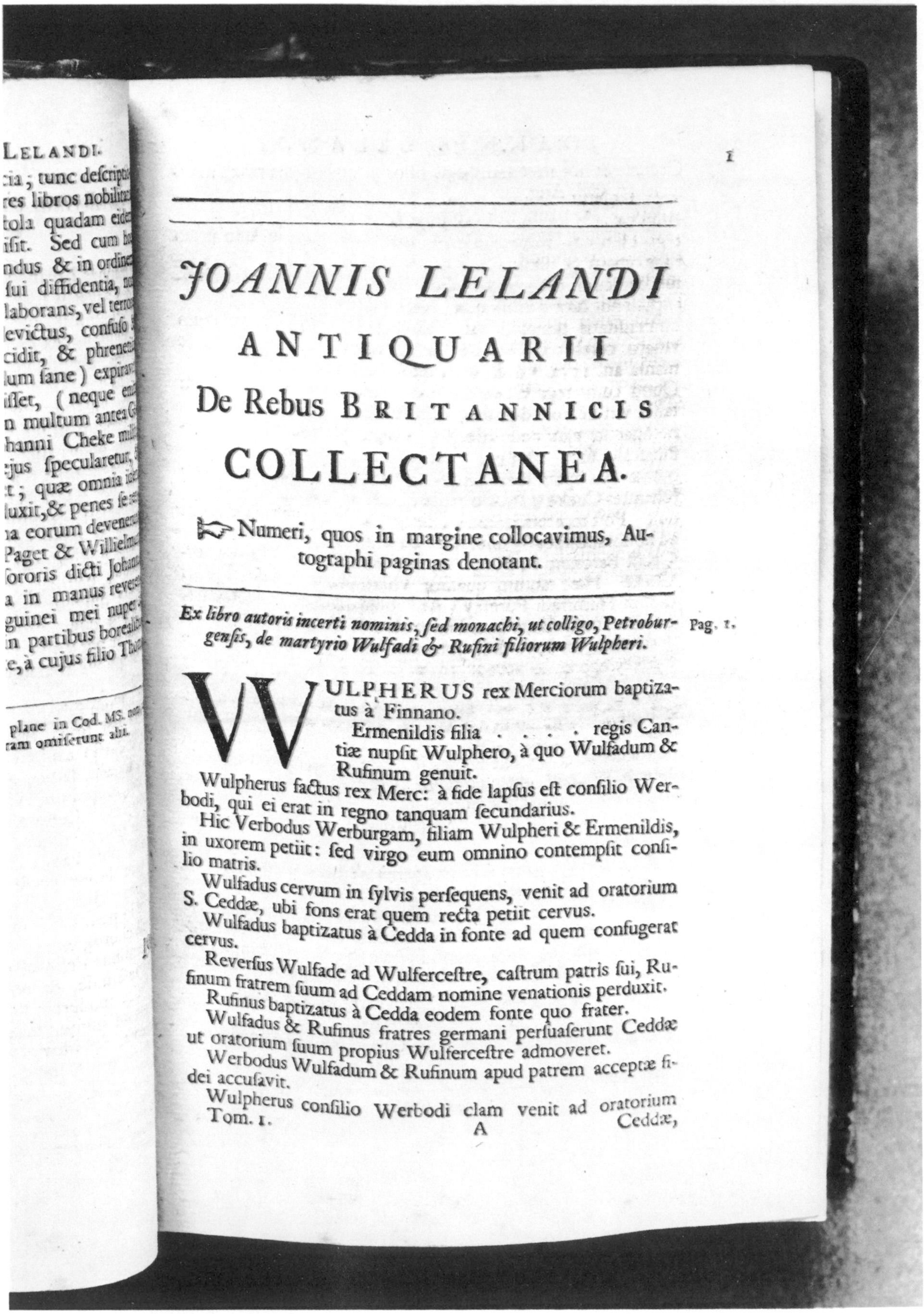

JOANNIS LELANDI ANTIQUARII De Rebus BRITANNICIS COLLECTANEA.

☞ Numeri, quos in margine collocavimus, Autographi paginas denotant.

Ex libro autoris incerti nominis, sed monachi, ut colligo, Petroburgensis, de martyrio Wulfadi & Rufini filiorum Wulpheri. Pag. 1.

WULPHERUS rex Merciorum baptizatus à Finnano.

Ermenildis filia . . . . regis Cantiæ nupsit Wulphero, à quo Wulfadum & Rufinum genuit.

Wulpherus factus rex Merc: à fide lapsus est consilio Werbodi, qui ei erat in regno tanquam secundarius.

Hic Verbodus Werburgam, filiam Wulpheri & Ermenildis, in uxorem petiit: sed virgo eum omnino contempsit consilio matris.

Wulfadus cervum in sylvis persequens, venit ad oratorium S. Ceddæ, ubi fons erat quem recta petiit cervus.

Wulfadus baptizatus à Cedda in fonte ad quem confugerat cervus.

Reversus Wulfade ad Wulfercestre, castrum patris sui, Rufinum fratrem suum ad Ceddam nomine venationis perduxit.

Rufinus baptizatus à Cedda eodem fonte quo frater.

Wulfadus & Rufinus fratres germani persuaserunt Ceddæ ut oratorium suum propius Wulfercestre admoveret.

Werbodus Wulfadum & Rufinum apud patrem acceptæ fidei accusavit.

Wulpherus consilio Werbodi clam venit ad oratorium Ceddæ,

Tom. I. A

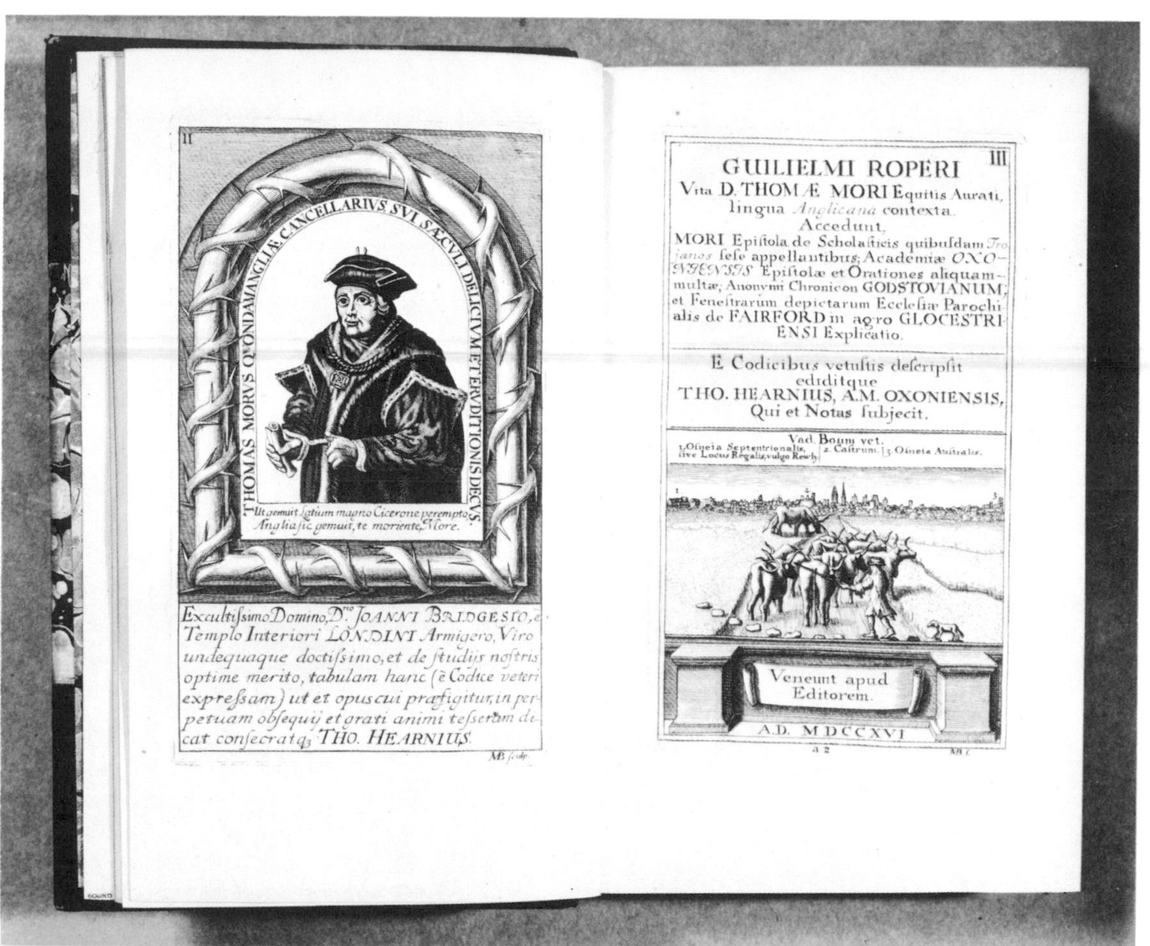

126

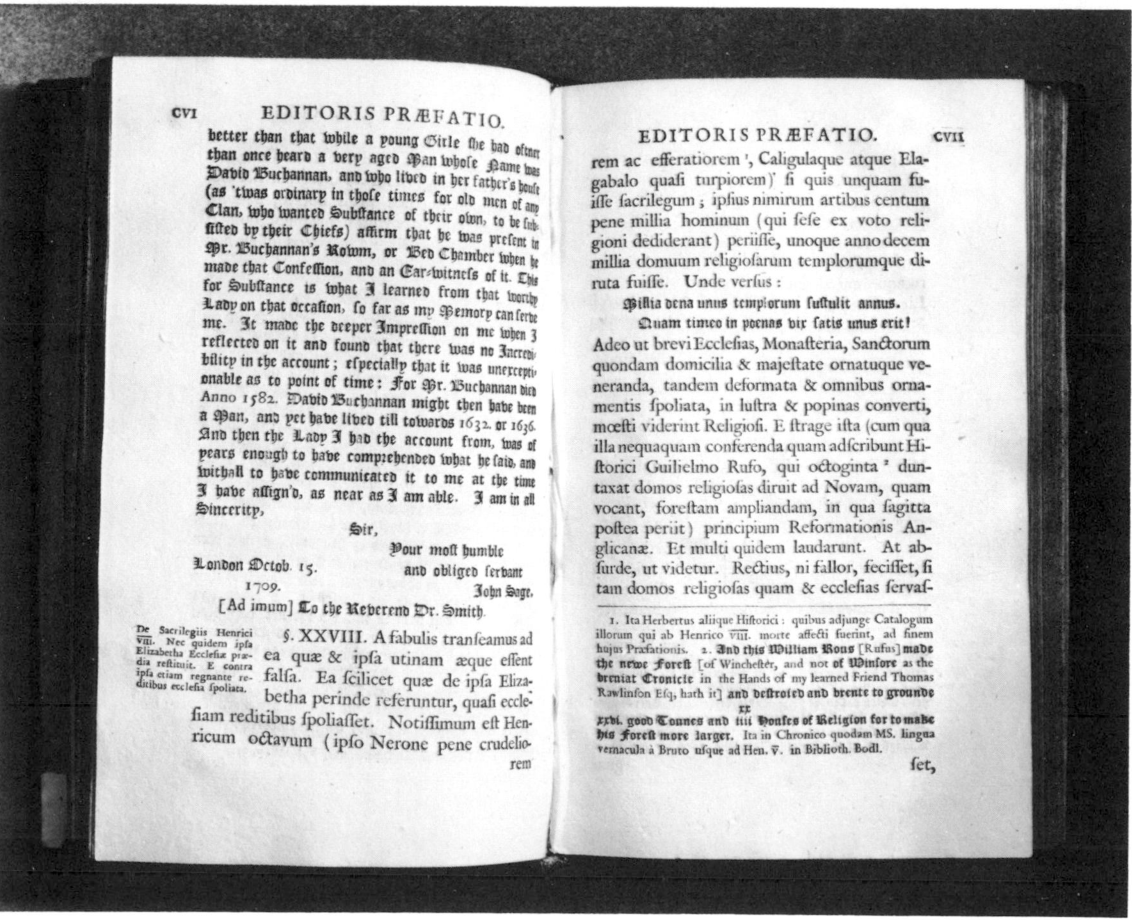

CVI EDITORIS PRÆFATIO.

better than that while a young Girle she had ofttner than once heard a very aged Man whose Name was David Buchannan, and who lived in her father's house (as 'twas ordinary in those times for old men of any Clan, who wanted Substance of their own, to be subsisted by their Chiefs) affirm that he was present in Mr. Buchannan's Rowm, or Bed Chamber when he made that Confession, and an Ear-witness of it. This for Substance is what I learned from that worthy Lady on that occasion, so far as my Memory can serve me. It made the deeper Impression on me when I reflected on it and found that there was no Incredibility in the account; especially that it was unexceptionable as to point of time: For Mr. Buchannan died Anno 1582. David Buchannan might then have been a Man, and yet have lived till towards 1632. or 1636. And then the Lady I had the account from, was of years enough to have comprehended what he said, and withall to have communicated it to me at the time I have assign'd, as near as I am able. I am in all Sincerity,

Sir,

Your most humble and obliged servant

London Octob. 15. 1709.

John Sage.

[Ad imum] To the Reverend Dr. Smith.

De Sacrilegiis Henrici VIII. Nec quidem ipsa Elizabetha Ecclesiæ prædia restituit. E contra ipsa etiam regnante reditibus ecclesia spoliata.

§. XXVIII. A fabulis transeamus ad ea quæ & ipsa utinam æque essent falsa. Ea scilicet quæ de ipsa Elizabetha perinde referuntur, quasi ecclesiam reditibus spoliasset. Notissimum est Henricum octavum (ipso Nerone pene crudeliorem

EDITORIS PRÆFATIO. CVII

rem ac efferatiorem [1], Caligulaque atque Elagabalo quasi turpiorem) si quis unquam fuisse sacrilegum; ipsius nimirum artibus centum pene millia hominum (qui sese ex voto religioni dediderant) periisse, unoque anno decem millia domuum religiosarum templorumque diruta fuisse. Unde versus:

Millia dena unus templorum sustulit annus.
Quam timeo in poenas vix satis unus erit!

Adeo ut brevi Ecclesias, Monasteria, Sanctorum quondam domicilia & majestate ornatuque veneranda, tandem deformata & omnibus ornamentis spoliata, in lustra & popinas converti, mœsti viderint Religiosi. E strage ista (cum qua illa nequaquam conferenda quam adscribunt Historici Guilielmo Rufo, qui octoginta [2] duntaxat domos religiosas diruit ad Novam, quam vocant, forestam ampliandam, in qua sagitta postea periit) principium Reformationis Anglicanæ. Et multi quidem laudarunt. At absurde, ut videtur. Rectius, ni fallor, fecisset, si tam domos religiosas quam & ecclesias servas-

1. Ita Herbertus aliique Historici: quibus adjunge Catalogum illorum qui ab Henrico VIII. morte affecti fuerint, ad finem hujus Præfationis. 2. And this William Rous [Rufus] made the newe Forest [of Winchester, and not of Winsore as the breviat Cronicle in the Hands of my learned Friend Thomas Rawlinson Esq; hath it] and destroied and brente to grounde xx xxvi. good Tounes and iiii Houses of Religion for to make his Forest more larger. Ita in Chronico quodam MS. lingua vernacula à Bruto usque ad Hen. V. in Biblioth. Bodl.

set,

Printed by Jn. Baskett at the Clarendon Printing-house in OXFORD

THE

HOLY BIBLE,

CONTAINING THE

Old TESTAMENT and the New:

Newly Tranſlated out of the

ORIGINAL TONGUES:

And with the former TRANSLATIONS

Diligently Compared and Reviſed.

By His Majeſty's Special Command.

Appointed to be Read in CHURCHES.

OXFORD:

Printed by *JOHN BASKETT*, Printer to the King's moſt Excellent Majeſty, for GREAT BRITAIN; and to the UNIVERSITY. MDCCXVII.

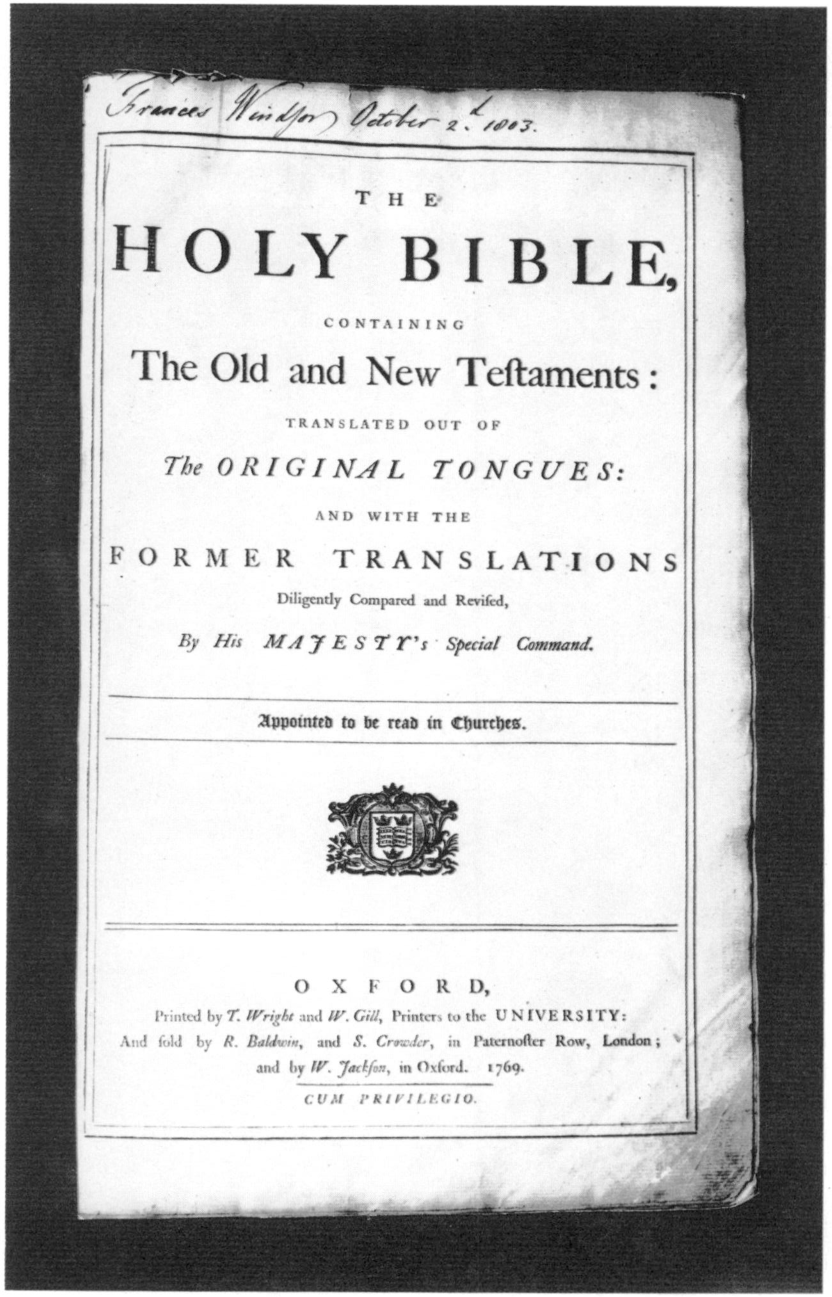

Frances Windsor October 2d. 1803.

THE

HOLY BIBLE,

CONTAINING

The Old and New Teſtaments:

TRANSLATED OUT OF

The ORIGINAL TONGUES:

AND WITH THE

FORMER TRANSLATIONS

Diligently Compared and Reviſed,

By His MAJESTY's Special Command.

Appointed to be read in Churches.

OXFORD,

Printed by *T. Wright* and *W. Gill*, Printers to the UNIVERSITY:
And ſold by *R. Baldwin*, and *S. Crowder*, in Paternoſter Row, London;
and by *W. Jackſon*, in Oxford. 1769.

CUM PRIVILEGIO.

131

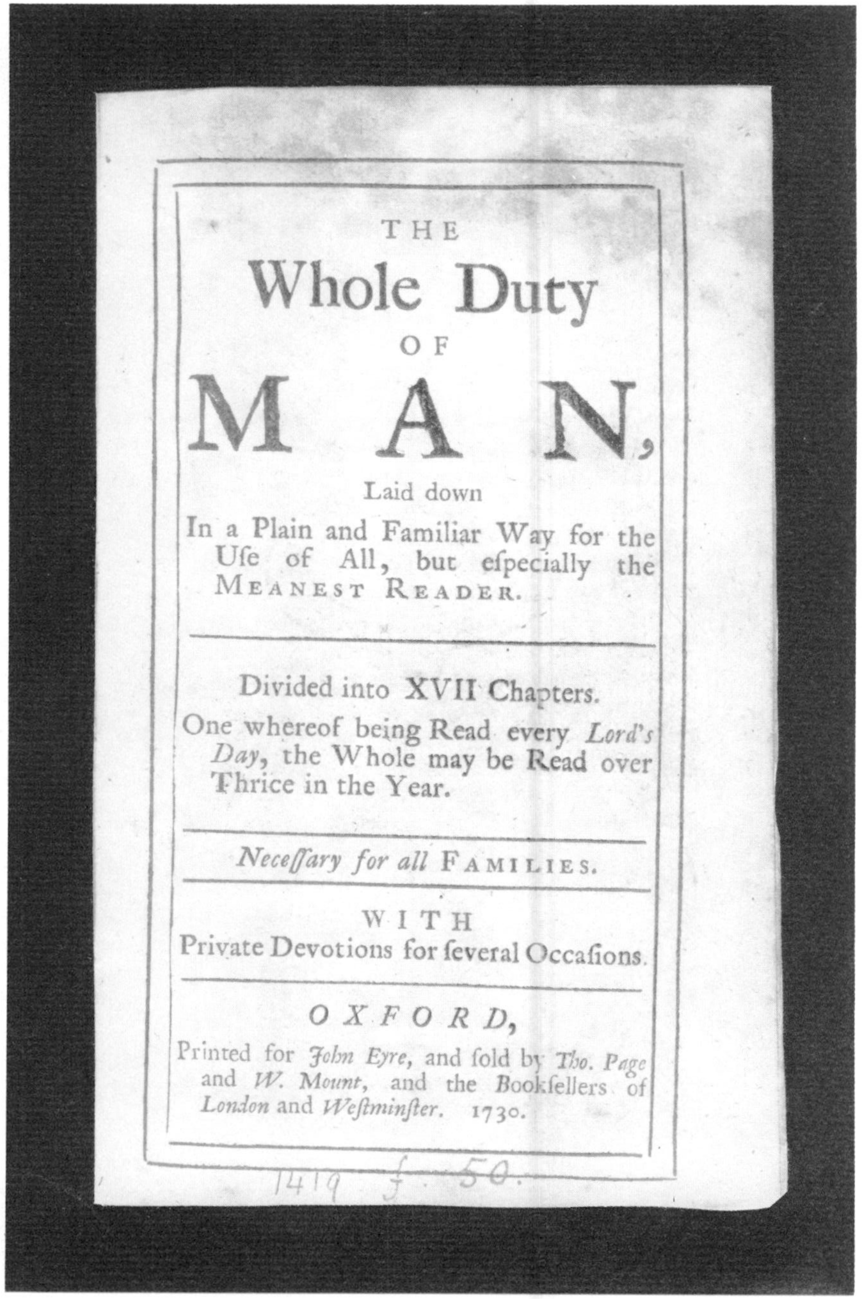

THE

Whole Duty

OF

MAN,

Laid down

In a Plain and Familiar Way for the Uſe of All, but eſpecially the MEANEST READER.

Divided into XVII Chapters.

One whereof being Read every *Lord's Day*, the Whole may be Read over Thrice in the Year.

Neceſſary for all FAMILIES.

WITH

Private Devotions for ſeveral Occaſions.

OXFORD,

Printed for *John Eyre*, and ſold by *Tho. Page* and *W. Mount*, and the Bookſellers of *London* and *Weſtminſter*. 1730.

1419 f. 50.

132

Byssus.
TAB. I.
Fig. 2.
3
4
5
6.
7.
8.
9.
10.
11.
12. A.
12. B.
13.
14.
15. B.
15. A.
a
16.
17.
18.
19. A. 19. B.
20.

A DISSERTATION

CONCERNING THE USE

OF SEA WATER

IN DISEASES OF THE GLANDS, &c.

TO WHICH IS ADDED

AN EPISTOLARY DISSERTATION

TO R. FREWIN, M. D.

BY RICHARD RUSSELL, M.D. & F.R.S.

Θάλασσα κλύζει πάντα τ᾽ ἀνθρώπων κακά.

Eurip. Iphigen. in Taur.

OXFORD,

Printed at the THEATRE: and Sold by JAMES FLETCHER in the *Turl*, and J. and J. RIVINGTON in St. *Paul's* Church-Yard, *London*. MDCCLIII.

72 THE TEMPEST.

And the particular accidents gone by
Since I came to this Iſle: and in the morn
I'll bring you to your ſhip; and ſo to *Naples*.
Where I have hope to ſee the nuptials
Of theſe our dear-beloved ſolemniz'd;
And thence retire me to my *Milan*, where
Every third thought ſhall be my grave.
Alon. I long
To hear the ſtory of your life, which muſt
Take the ear ſtrangely.
Pro. I'll deliver all,
And promiſe you calm ſeas, auſpicious gales,
And ſail ſo expeditious, it ſhall catch
Your royal fleet far off: My *Ariel*, chick,
That is thy charge: Then to the elements
Be free, and fare thou well! Pleaſe you, draw near.
[*Exeunt omnes.*

EPI-

EPILOGUE.

Spoken by *Proſpero.*

NOW my charms are all o'er-thrown,
And what ſtrength I have's mine own;
Which is moſt faint: and now 'tis true
I muſt be here confin'd by you,
Or ſent to Naples. *Let me not,*
Since I have my Dukedom got,
And pardon'd the deceiver, dwell
In this bare iſland by your ſpell;
But releaſe me from my bands,
With the help of your good hands.
Gentle breath of yours my ſails
Muſt fill, or elſe my project fails,
Which was to pleaſe. For now I want
Spirits t' enforce, art to enchant;
And my ending is deſpair,
Unleſs I be reliev'd by prayer;
Which pierces ſo, that it aſſaults
Mercy it ſelf, and frees all faults.
As you from crimes would pardon'd be,
Let your indulgence ſet me free.

VOL. I. K

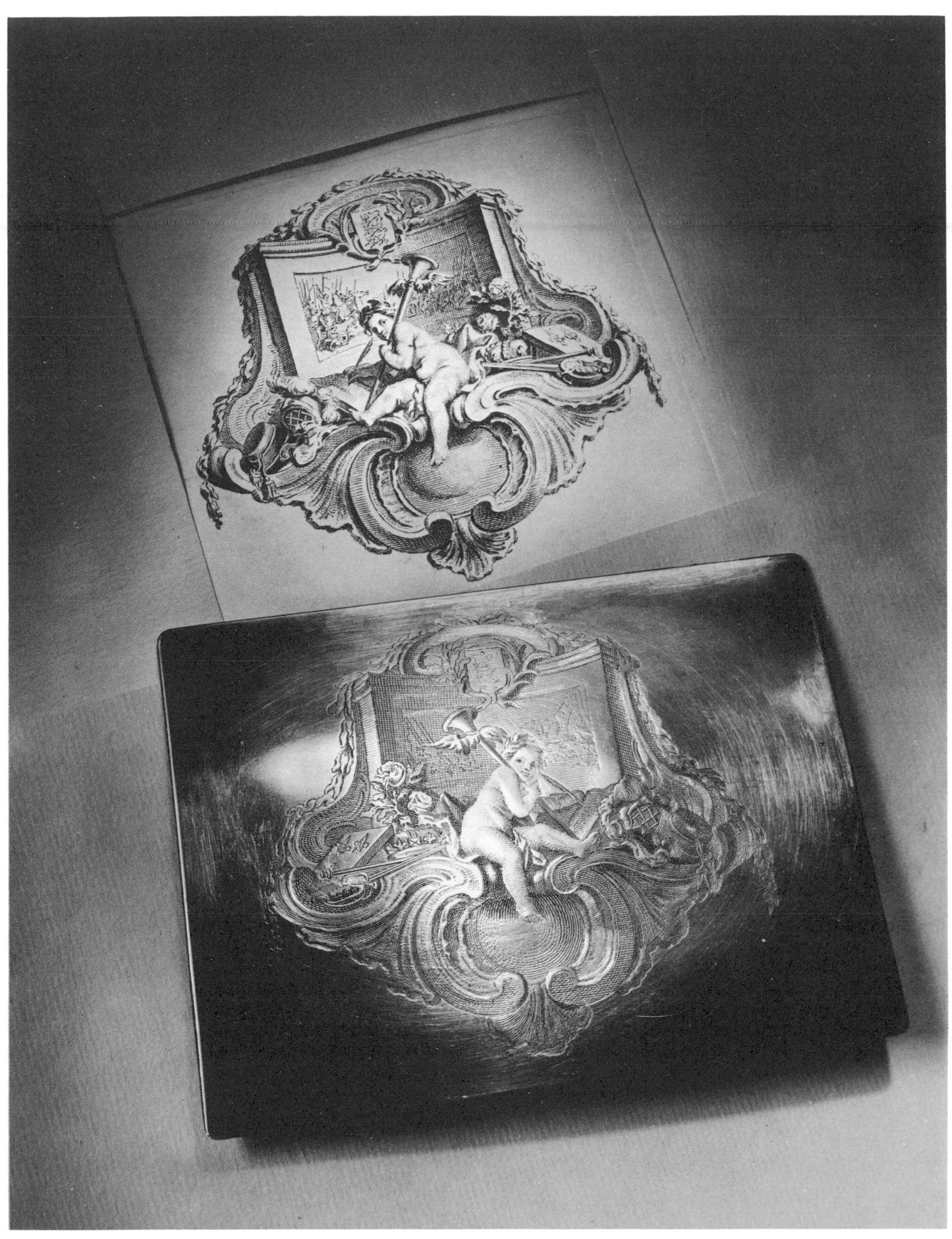

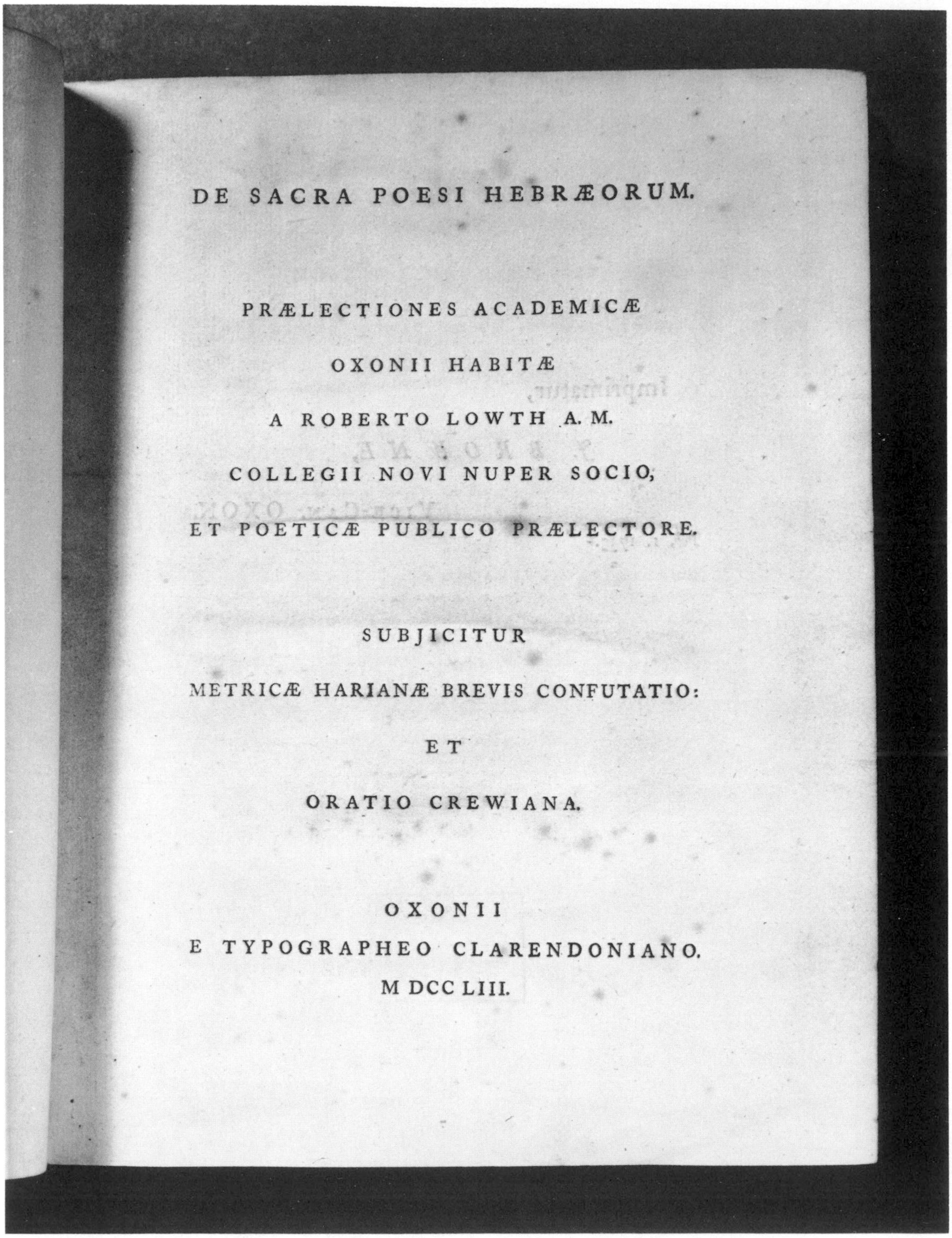

DE SACRA POESI HEBRÆORUM.

PRÆLECTIONES ACADEMICÆ

OXONII HABITÆ

A ROBERTO LOWTH A. M.

COLLEGII NOVI NUPER SOCIO,

ET POETICÆ PUBLICO PRÆLECTORE.

SUBJICITUR

METRICÆ HARIANÆ BREVIS CONFUTATIO:

ET

ORATIO CREWIANA.

OXONII

E TYPOGRAPHEO CLARENDONIANO.

M DCC LIII.

10 Febr. 1756.

Sir.

You say p. 2. that you are informed "that the Prices of Printing have in general "been much reduced of late Years." I am not sure of this. For the many Years I have been concerned in Business, they have not much varied. Journeymen have raised theirs upon us.

You say in several Places, that you at Oxford find not a Corrector; Gentlemen generally with you, chusing to correct their own Work. So they frequently do with us: Nevertheless, we find a Corrector of the Press necessary, in order to sweep-out, if I may so express myself, the grosser Faults of the Compositor, the cleanest of which must make some, and often make what they call Outs and Doubles; that is, Omissions of Words and Passages, and Repetition of both, through Inattention. The Corrector of the Press takes Care to make the Proof conformable to ye Copy, and to correct Typographical Errors, the last of which few Gentlemen are so well able to do, as those who are used to ye Press; and this shortens an Author's Labour, and makes his final Revising pleasant to him: and will be a means of ascertaining the Value of any Corrections or Alterations, which the Author makes from his first Copy; for the Compositor is obliged in his Price of Composing, to make his Proof conformable to the Copy from which he composes. If you engage with an able Overseer, this may be one of his Offices; & I should think your best way is to purchase his whole time at a handsome Salary; instead of allowing him so much in every Sheet. He will in this Case be wholly Yours; and a middle Man between the Delegates, his Masters, and the Workmen: He will by your Direction and Consent, buy in Ink, and other necessary Materials, and charge them to you at prime Cost only, and you will know what you are about. Our Correctors of the Press generally read the Proofs twice, tho' the Author himself revises his Work. There are many Conveniencies to the Principals, that will accrue from the Establishing of an Overseer, who shall be able to attend to Typographical Errors, and at the same time to ye general Management and be between the Masters and Workmen (who will be always for encroaching) which are too obvious to need farther Enforcing. On ye whole then of this Article, I think you the Masters, should, as ye London Printers do, reckon at the Rate of 2d. in the Shilling for the Press Corrector, of what is paid the Compositor; and this will be a Saving that will go towards the Salary of your Overseer, and allow it to be the handsomer. As Work increases, Help allowed him at his Discretion, in ye Warehouse, will enable him to bestow ye usefullest Part of his time, where it will be most useful.

In the Calculation of Prices p. 4 it is to be observed, that that Calculation is made as we in Town reckon to Booksellers. The Masters generally expect something more Profit from Gentlemen of Ability, than they do from Men in Trade, who are to subsist by their Business: But this alters not the Case between ye Workmen and their Principals; I only mention it, therefore, for your Observations on particular Occasions, as such may offer. Since, if you treat Booksellers and Men of Fortune alike, the former will think they have Reason to be dissatisfied; and such Gentlemen will have an Advantage from your Press, which they will not always have from the London Press.

REVEREND SIR,

YOUR eminent station in this place, and the character you have deservedly maintained of integrity, learning, and public spirit, have determined me to apply myself to you, with regard to a complaint of no small importance, which I find myself under the disagreeable necessity of making. And as the object of this complaint is a trust, wherein the honour and interest of the whole university seem to me to be deeply concerned, I shall make no apology for laying the same before the members of convocation also; since their advice and concurrence will be requisite, to minister effectual redress.

It is now almost two years ago, since I had the unexpected honour to be nominated a delegate for printing; an employment by no means to be coveted in the most flourishing state of the press, but much less so at a period of time when it was notoriously reduced to a very deplorable condition. I thought myself however obliged to the gentlemen concerned in the nomination, for this mark of their confidence and good opinion, and therefore accepted the trust; little dreaming of the difficulties it has since been my lot to encounter.

When I came to consider the weight and extent of the charge, thus suddenly cast upon me, I perceived myself bound, both in point of reputation and duty, to learn in some little degree the nature of the business I had undertaken: for without a competent knowledge of the constitution of the press in general, and the university press in particular, I presumed it would be impossible to understand the causes of its present decline, so as to prepare the way for a speedy and lasting restorative. I saw that the credit of the place was intimately connected with this enquiry: that all seminaries of learning had made it their particular care to raise and support the character of their learned press; being sensible that it was principally from this outward fruit, that posterity or foreign nations could judge of their internal merit: that other less respectable universities, even in our own island, were daily extending their fame by this and by similar methods: while the *Oxford* press, which was once the foremost in this laudable contention, was languishing in a lazy obscurity, and barely reminding us of it's existence, by now and then slowly bringing forth a programma, a sermon printed by request, or at best a *Bodleian* catalogue. Individuals, it is true, had at times, very nobly contributed

A 2

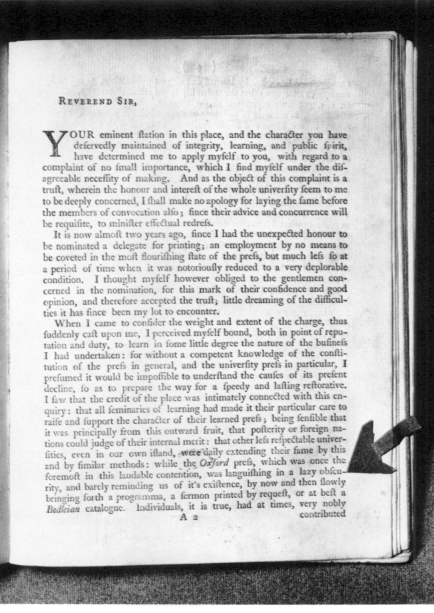

Orders of the Delegates of the Press

Friday Jan 24th 1758 — At a meeting of the Delegates of the Press in the Delegates Room
Present

Dr. Randolph Vicechancellor
Dr. Leigh, Dr. Niblett, Dr. Gower, Dr. Blackstone } Sworn
Mr. Eyre Sen. Proctor, Mr. Lernoult Jun. Proctor, Mr. Owen, Mr. Bridle Esq. } Sworn

Three years account of the Press to Michaelmas 1757 were examined and signed.

Ordered, That Copies of the Royal Charters 12 Nov. 8 Car. I – 13 March 8 Car. I or so much of them or any other as relates to the University Press — Copies of the University Statute de Typographis Universitatis — of such Parts of the Acts 17 Car. 2. c. 4 – 8 Ann. c. 19. 10 Ann. c. 19 & 12 Ann. Sess. 2. c. 9 as relate to the University Press — together with the new Statute De Delegatorum Preli nominatione et munere be fairly transcribed in Order of Time in a Book to be kept by the Registrar of the University for the Perusal of the Delegates or any Delegate of the Press.

Adjourned to Wednesday Feb. 1st at 11 o'Clock in the morning.

Hen. Fisher Registrar.

At a meeting of the Delegates of the Press in the Delegates Room
Present

The same as attended on January the 24th.

Wednesday Feb. 1st 1758 — Ordered, that a New Register in Folio be provided by the University Registrar, at one end of which shall be entered the Resolutions of the Delegacy and at the other End shall be kept a General Cash account, of the gross Summs received and disbursed on account of the Press by their authority and Direction, to be laid before the Delegates of Accounts at the end of the year.

Resolved, that this Delegacy take into Consideration the Revenues of the Press at their next meeting.

Adjourned to Thursday Feb. 9th at ten o'Clock in the morning

Henry Fisher Registrar.

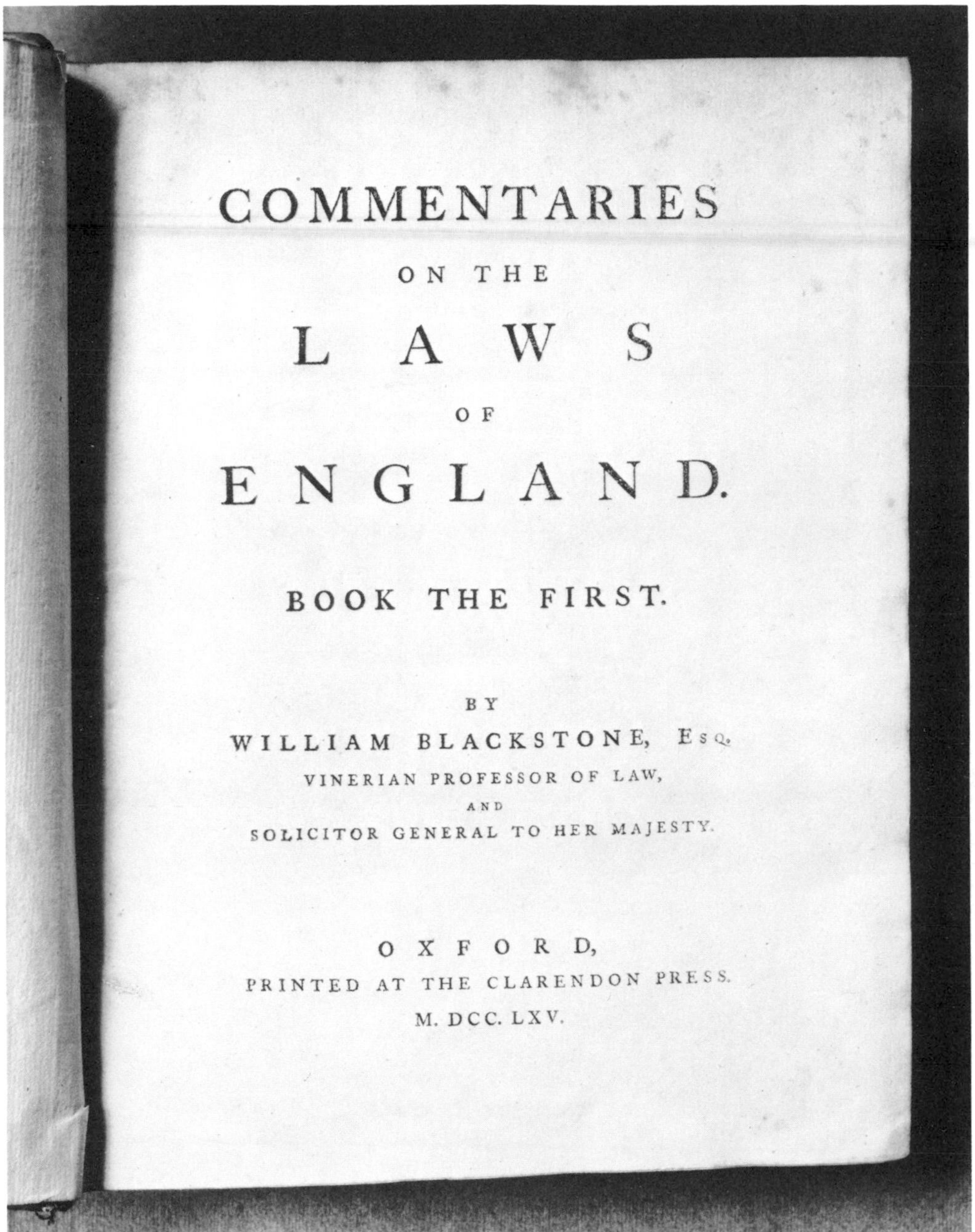

COMMENTARIES

ON THE

LAWS

OF

ENGLAND.

BOOK THE FIRST.

BY

WILLIAM BLACKSTONE, Esq.

VINERIAN PROFESSOR OF LAW,

AND

SOLICITOR GENERAL TO HER MAJESTY.

OXFORD,

PRINTED AT THE CLARENDON PRESS.

M. DCC. LXV.

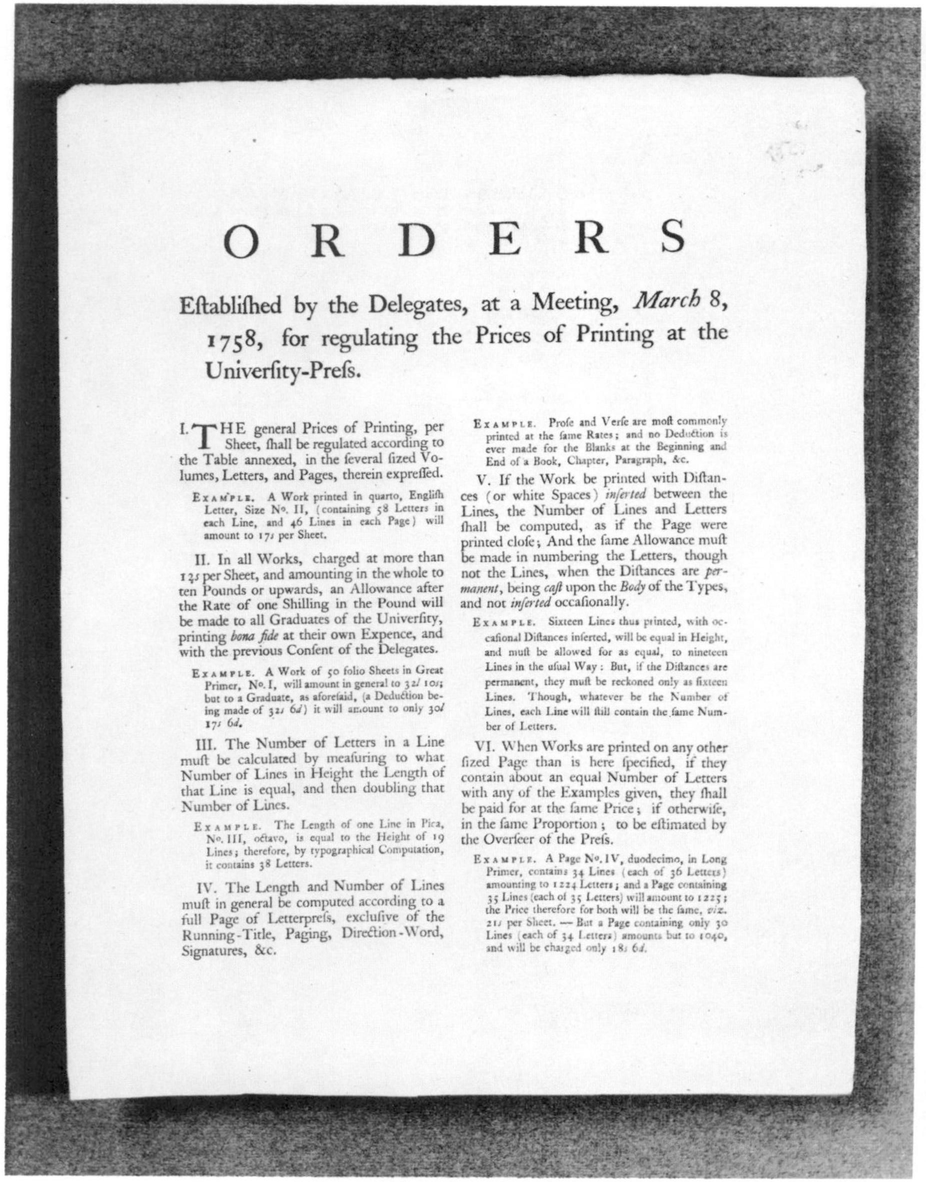

O R D E R S

Eftablifhed by the Delegates, at a Meeting, *March* 8, 1758, for regulating the Prices of Printing at the Univerfity-Prefs.

I. THE general Prices of Printing, per Sheet, fhall be regulated according to the Table annexed, in the feveral fized Volumes, Letters, and Pages, therein expreffed.

EXAMPLE. A Work printed in quarto, Englifh Letter, Size N°. II, (containing 58 Letters in each Line, and 46 Lines in each Page) will amount to 17*s* per Sheet.

II. In all Works, charged at more than 12*s* per Sheet, and amounting in the whole to ten Pounds or upwards, an Allowance after the Rate of one Shilling in the Pound will be made to all Graduates of the Univerfity, printing *bona fide* at their own Expence, and with the previous Confent of the Delegates.

EXAMPLE. A Work of 50 folio Sheets in Great Primer, N°. I, will amount in general to 32*l* 10*s*; but to a Graduate, as aforefaid, (a Deduction being made of 32*s* 6*d*) it will amount to only 30*l* 17*s* 6*d*.

III. The Number of Letters in a Line muft be calculated by meafuring to what Number of Lines in Height the Length of that Line is equal, and then doubling that Number of Lines.

EXAMPLE. The Length of one Line in Pica, N°. III, octavo, is equal to the Height of 19 Lines; therefore, by typographical Computation, it contains 38 Letters.

IV. The Length and Number of Lines muft in general be computed according to a full Page of Letterprefs, exclufive of the Running-Title, Paging, Direction-Word, Signatures, &c.

EXAMPLE. Profe and Verfe are moft commonly printed at the fame Rates; and no Deduction is ever made for the Blanks at the Beginning and End of a Book, Chapter, Paragraph, &c.

V. If the Work be printed with Diftances (or white Spaces) *inferted* between the Lines, the Number of Lines and Letters fhall be computed, as if the Page were printed clofe; And the fame Allowance muft be made in numbering the Letters, though not the Lines, when the Diftances are *permanent*, being *caft* upon the *Body* of the Types, and not *inferted* occafionally.

EXAMPLE. Sixteen Lines thus printed, with occafional Diftances inferted, will be equal in Height, and muft be allowed for as equal, to nineteen Lines in the ufual Way: But, if the Diftances are permanent, they muft be reckoned only as fixteen Lines. Though, whatever be the Number of Lines, each Line will ftill contain the fame Number of Letters.

VI. When Works are printed on any other fized Page than is here fpecified, if they contain about an equal Number of Letters with any of the Examples given, they fhall be paid for at the fame Price; if otherwife, in the fame Proportion; to be eftimated by the Overfeer of the Prefs.

EXAMPLE. A Page N°. IV, duodecimo, in Long Primer, contains 34 Lines (each of 36 Letters) amounting to 1224 Letters; and a Page containing 35 Lines (each of 35 Letters) will amount to 1225; the Price therefore for both will be the fame, *viz.* 21*s* per Sheet. — But a Page containing only 30 Lines (each of 34 Letters) amounts but to 1040, and will be charged only 18*s* 6*d*.

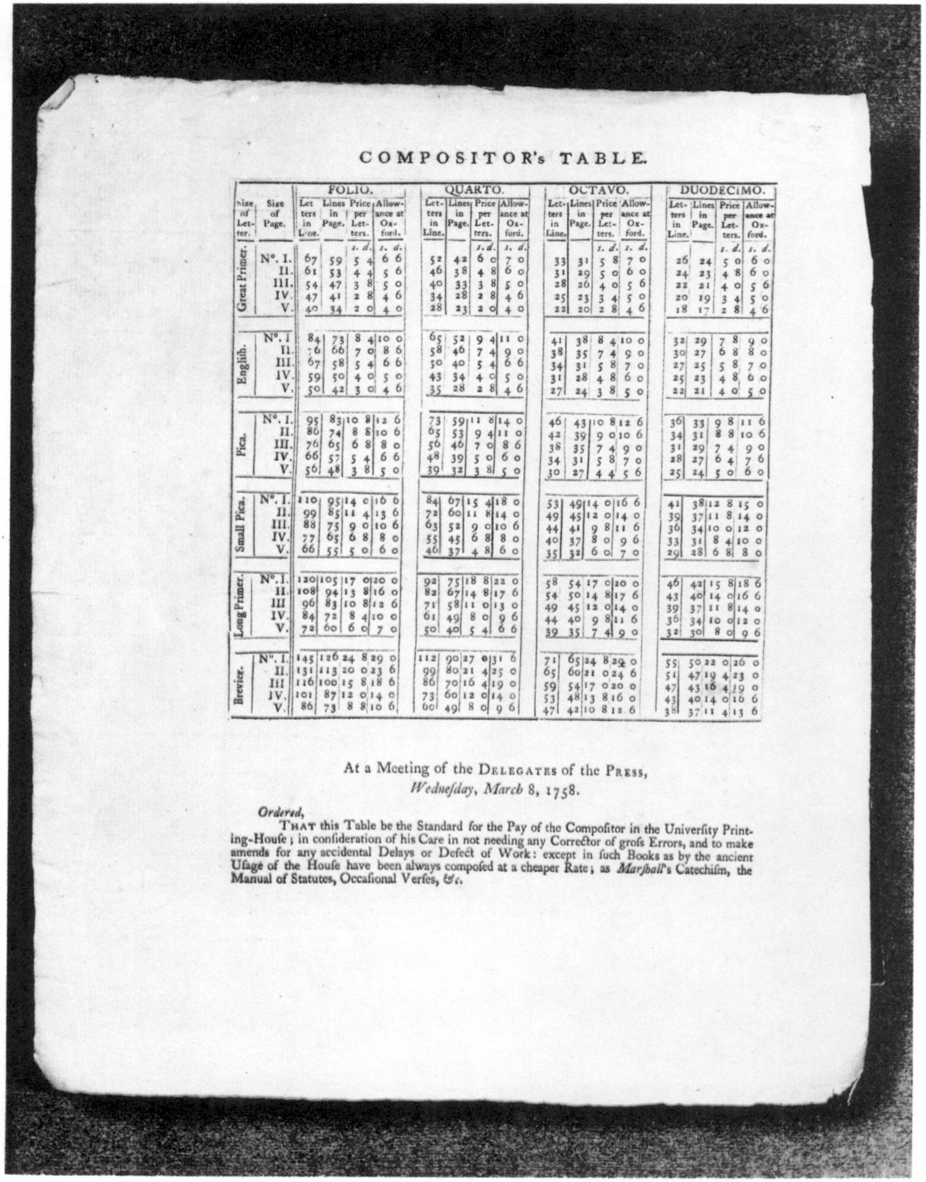

COMPOSITOR's TABLE.

Size of Letter.	Size of Page.	FOLIO.				QUARTO.				OCTAVO.				DUODECIMO.			
		Letters in Line.	Lines in Page.	Price per Letters.	Allowance at Oxford.	Letters in Line.	Lines in Page.	Price per Letters.	Allowance at Oxford.	Letters in Line.	Lines in Page.	Price per Letters.	Allowance at Oxford.	Letters in Line.	Lines in Page.	Price per Letters.	Allowance at Oxford.
				s. d.	*s. d.*			*s. d.*	*s. d.*			*s. d.*	*s. d.*			*s. d.*	*s. d.*
Great Primer.	N°. I.	67	59	5 4	6 6	52	42	6 0	7 0	33	31	5 8	7 0	26	24	5 0	6 0
	II.	61	53	4 4	5 6	46	38	4 8	6 0	31	29	5 0	6 0	24	23	4 8	6 0
	III.	54	47	3 8	5 0	40	33	3 8	5 0	28	26	4 0	5 6	22	21	4 0	5 6
	IV.	47	41	2 8	4 6	34	28	2 8	4 6	25	23	3 4	5 0	20	19	3 4	5 0
	V.	40	34	2 0	4 0	28	23	2 0	4 0	22	20	2 8	4 6	18	17	2 8	4 6
English.	N°. I	84	73	8 4	10 0	65	52	9 4	11 0	41	38	8 4	10 0	32	29	7 8	9 0
	II.	76	66	7 0	8 6	58	46	7 4	9 0	38	35	7 4	9 0	30	27	6 8	8 0
	III.	67	58	5 4	6 6	50	40	5 4	6 6	34	31	5 8	7 0	27	25	5 8	7 0
	IV.	59	50	4 0	5 0	43	34	4 0	5 0	31	28	4 8	6 0	25	23	4 8	6 0
	V.	50	42	3 0	4 6	35	28	2 8	4 6	27	24	3 8	5 0	22	21	4 0	5 0
Pica.	N°. I.	95	83	10 8	12 6	73	59	11 8	14 0	46	43	10 8	12 6	36	33	9 8	11 6
	II.	86	74	8 8	10 6	65	53	9 4	11 0	42	39	9 0	10 6	34	31	8 8	10 6
	III.	76	65	6 8	8 0	56	46	7 0	8 6	38	35	7 4	9 0	31	29	7 4	9 0
	IV.	66	57	5 4	6 6	48	39	5 0	6 0	34	31	5 8	7 0	28	27	6 4	7 6
	V.	56	48	3 8	5 0	39	32	3 8	5 0	30	27	4 4	5 6	25	24	5 0	6 0
Small Pica.	N°. I.	110	95	14 0	16 6	84	67	15 4	18 0	53	49	14 0	16 6	41	38	12 8	15 0
	II.	99	85	11 4	13 6	72	60	11 8	14 0	49	45	12 0	14 0	39	37	11 8	14 0
	III.	88	75	9 0	10 6	63	52	9 0	10 6	44	41	9 8	11 6	36	34	10 0	12 0
	IV.	77	65	6 8	8 0	55	45	6 8	8 0	40	37	8 0	9 6	33	31	8 4	10 0
	V.	66	55	5 0	6 0	46	37	4 8	6 0	35	32	6 0	7 0	29	28	6 8	8 0
Long Primer.	N°. I.	120	105	17 0	20 0	92	75	18 8	22 0	58	54	17 0	20 0	46	42	15 8	18 6
	II.	108	94	13 8	16 0	82	67	14 8	17 6	54	50	14 8	17 6	43	40	14 0	16 6
	III	96	83	10 8	12 6	71	58	11 0	13 0	49	45	12 0	14 0	39	37	11 8	14 0
	IV.	84	72	8 4	10 0	61	49	8 0	9 6	44	40	9 8	11 6	36	34	10 0	12 0
	V.	72	60	6 0	7 0	50	40	5 4	6 6	39	35	7 4	9 0	32	30	8 0	9 6
Brevier.	N°. I.	145	126	24 8	29 0	112	90	27 0	31 6	71	65	24 8	29 0	55	50	22 0	26 0
	II.	131	113	20 0	23 6	99	80	21 4	25 0	65	60	21 0	24 6	51	47	19 4	23 0
	III	116	100	15 8	18 6	86	70	16 4	19 0	59	54	17 0	20 0	47	43	16 4	19 0
	IV.	101	87	12 0	14 0	73	60	12 0	14 0	53	48	13 8	16 0	43	40	14 0	16 6
	V.	86	73	8 8	10 6	60	49	8 0	9 6	47	42	10 8	12 6	38	37	11 4	13 6

At a Meeting of the DELEGATES of the PRESS,
Wednefday, March 8, 1758.

Ordered,

THAT this Table be the Standard for the Pay of the Compofitor in the Univerfity Printing-Houfe; in confideration of his Care in not needing any Corrector of grofs Errors, and to make amends for any accidental Delays or Defect of Work: except in fuch Books as by the ancient Ufage of the Houfe have been always compofed at a cheaper Rate; as *Marfhall's* Catechifm, the Manual of Statutes, Occafional Verfes, *&c.*

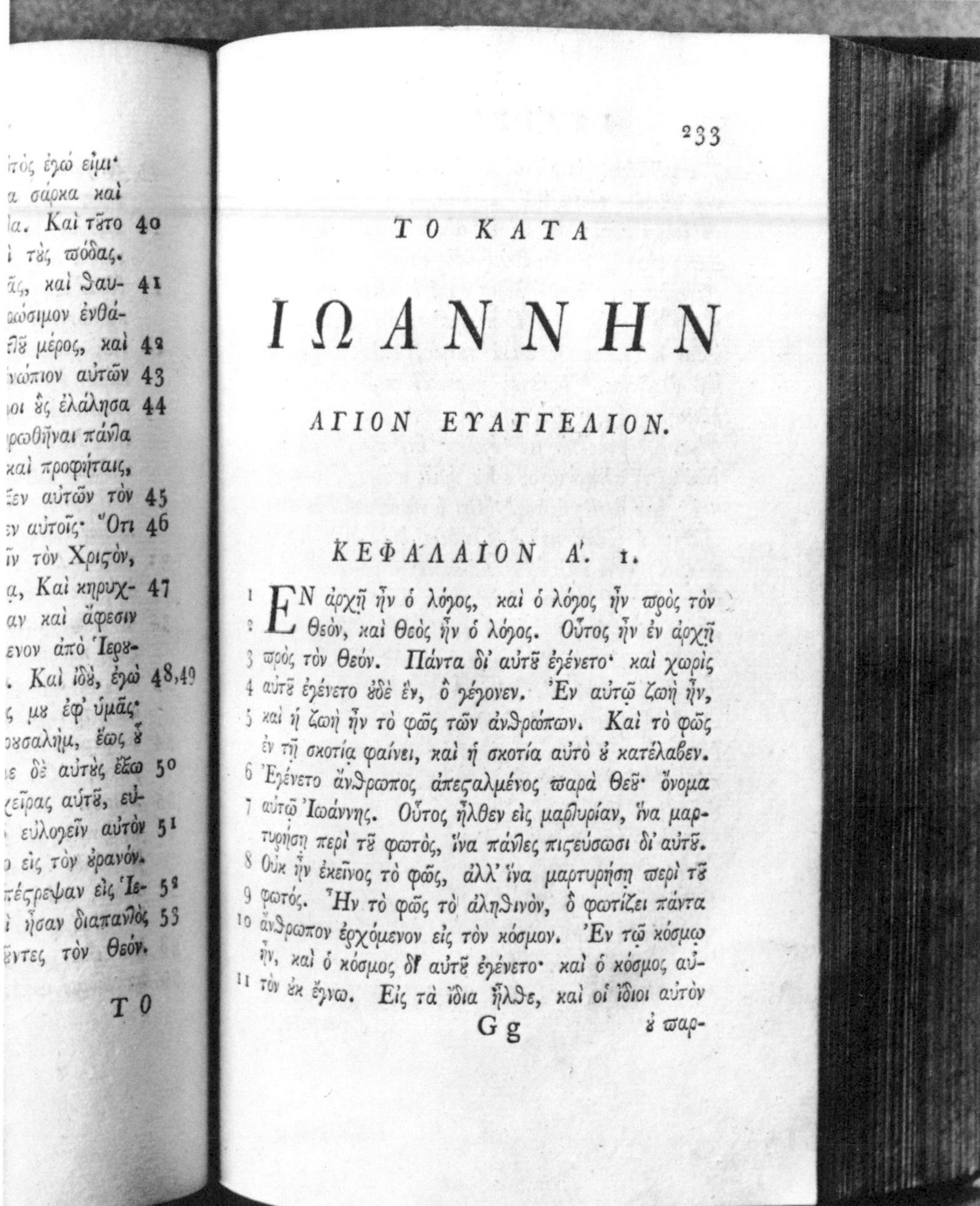

ΤΟ ΚΑΤΑ

ΙΩΑΝΝΗΝ

ΑΓΙΟΝ ΕΥΑΓΓΕΛΙΟΝ.

ΚΕΦΑΛΑΙΟΝ Α΄. 1.

1 ΕΝ ἀρχῇ ἦν ὁ λόγος, καὶ ὁ λόγος ἦν πρὸς τὸν
2 Θεὸν, καὶ Θεὸς ἦν ὁ λόγος. Οὗτος ἦν ἐν ἀρχῇ
3 πρὸς τὸν Θεόν. Πάντα δι' αὐτοῦ ἐγένετο· καὶ χωρὶς
4 αὐτοῦ ἐγένετο οὐδὲ ἓν, ὃ γέγονεν. Ἐν αὐτῷ ζωὴ ἦν,
5 καὶ ἡ ζωὴ ἦν τὸ φῶς τῶν ἀνθρώπων. Καὶ τὸ φῶς
ἐν τῇ σκοτίᾳ φαίνει, καὶ ἡ σκοτία αὐτὸ οὐ κατέλαβεν.
6 Ἐγένετο ἄνθρωπος ἀπεσταλμένος παρὰ Θεοῦ· ὄνομα
7 αὐτῷ Ἰωάννης. Οὗτος ἦλθεν εἰς μαρτυρίαν, ἵνα μαρτυρήσῃ περὶ τοῦ φωτὸς, ἵνα πάντες πιστεύσωσι δι' αὐτοῦ.
8 Οὐκ ἦν ἐκεῖνος τὸ φῶς, ἀλλ' ἵνα μαρτυρήσῃ περὶ τοῦ
9 φωτός. Ἦν τὸ φῶς τὸ ἀληθινὸν, ὃ φωτίζει πάντα
10 ἄνθρωπον ἐρχόμενον εἰς τὸν κόσμον. Ἐν τῷ κόσμῳ
ἦν, καὶ ὁ κόσμος δι' αὐτοῦ ἐγένετο· καὶ ὁ κόσμος αὐ-
11 τὸν οὐκ ἔγνω. Εἰς τὰ ἴδια ἦλθε, καὶ οἱ ἴδιοι αὐτὸν

Gg οὐ παρ-

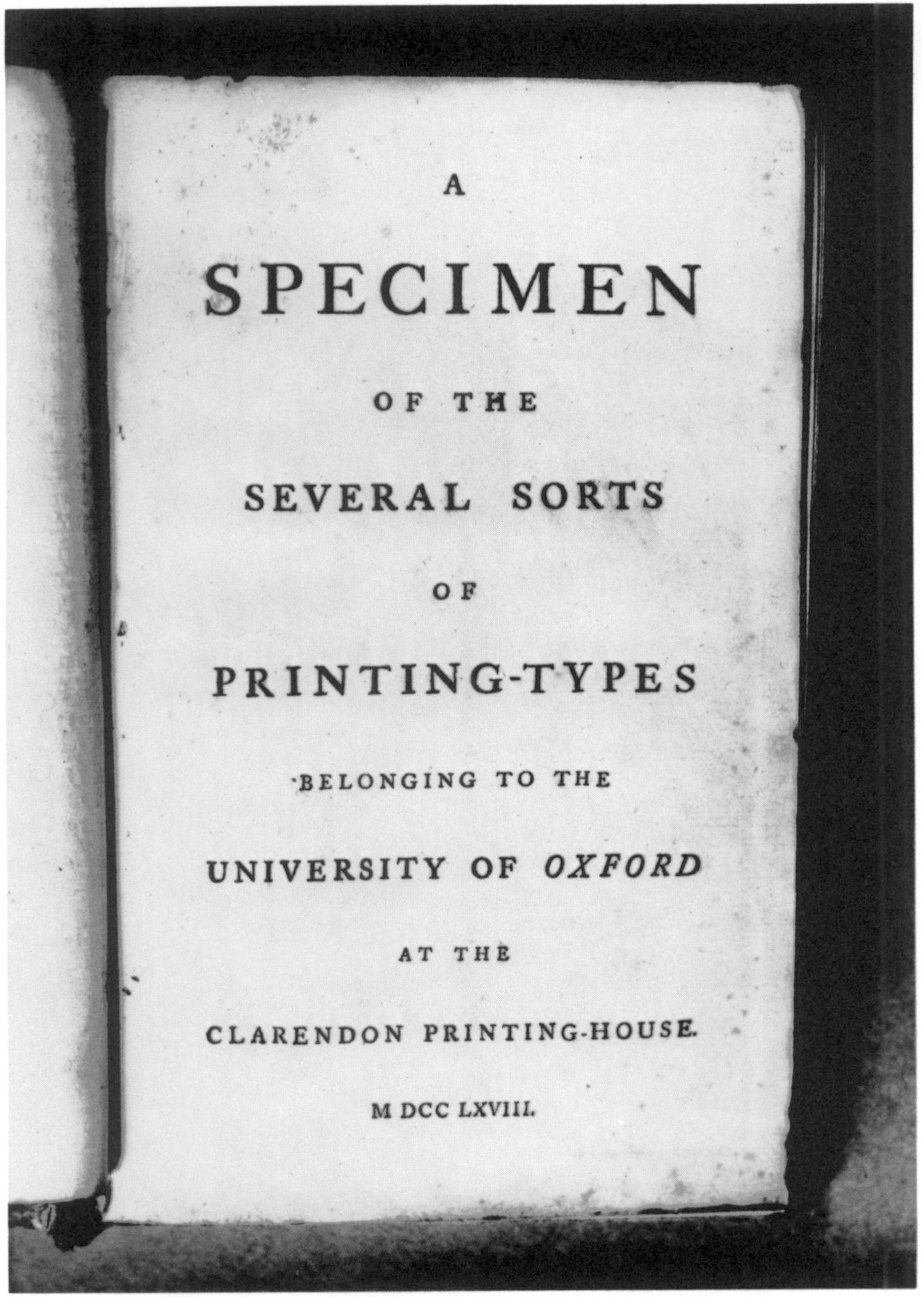

A

SPECIMEN

OF THE

SEVERAL SORTS

OF

PRINTING-TYPES

BELONGING TO THE

UNIVERSITY OF *OXFORD*

AT THE

CLARENDON PRINTING-HOUSE.

M DCC LXVIII.

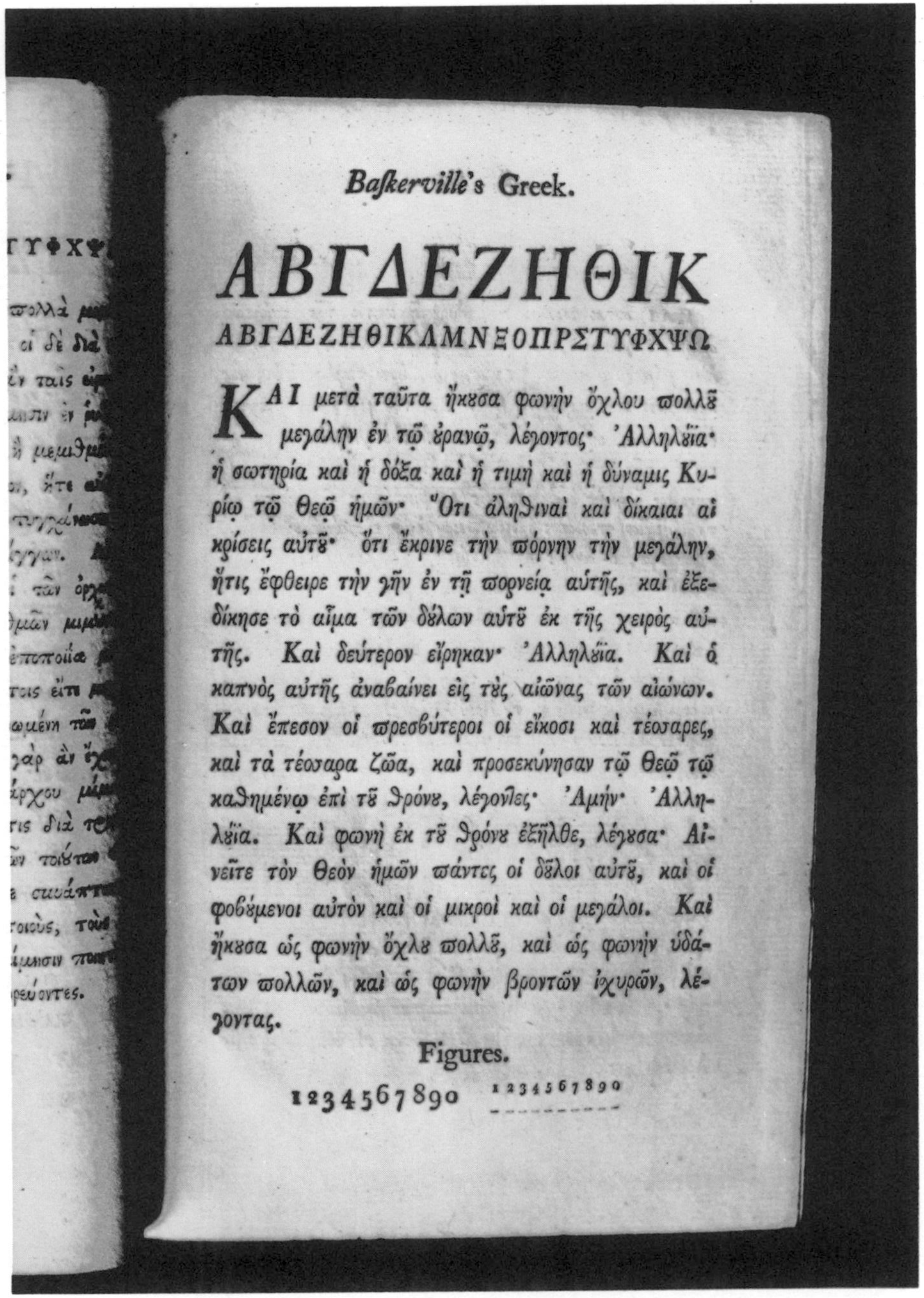

Baskerville's Greek.

ΑΒΓΔΕΖΗΘΙΚ

ΑΒΓΔΕΖΗΘΙΚΛΜΝΞΟΠΡΣΤΥΦΧΨΩ

ΚΑΙ μετὰ ταῦτα ἤκουσα φωνὴν ὄχλου πολλοῦ μεγάλην ἐν τῷ οὐρανῷ, λέγοντος· Ἀλληλούϊα· ἡ σωτηρία καὶ ἡ δόξα καὶ ἡ τιμὴ καὶ ἡ δύναμις Κυρίῳ τῷ Θεῷ ἡμῶν· Ὅτι ἀληθιναὶ καὶ δίκαιαι αἱ κρίσεις αὐτοῦ· ὅτι ἔκρινε τὴν πόρνην τὴν μεγάλην, ἥτις ἔφθειρε τὴν γῆν ἐν τῇ πορνείᾳ αὐτῆς, καὶ ἐξεδίκησε τὸ αἷμα τῶν δούλων αὐτοῦ ἐκ τῆς χειρὸς αὐτῆς. Καὶ δεύτερον εἴρηκαν· Ἀλληλούϊα. Καὶ ὁ καπνὸς αὐτῆς ἀναβαίνει εἰς τοὺς αἰῶνας τῶν αἰώνων. Καὶ ἔπεσον οἱ πρεσβύτεροι οἱ εἴκοσι καὶ τέσσαρες, καὶ τὰ τέσσαρα ζῶα, καὶ προσεκύνησαν τῷ Θεῷ τῷ καθημένῳ ἐπὶ τοῦ θρόνου, λέγοντες· Ἀμήν· Ἀλληλούϊα. Καὶ φωνὴ ἐκ τοῦ θρόνου ἐξῆλθε, λέγουσα· Αἰνεῖτε τὸν Θεὸν ἡμῶν πάντες οἱ δοῦλοι αὐτοῦ, καὶ οἱ φοβούμενοι αὐτὸν καὶ οἱ μικροὶ καὶ οἱ μεγάλοι. Καὶ ἤκουσα ὡς φωνὴν ὄχλου πολλοῦ, καὶ ὡς φωνὴν ὑδάτων πολλῶν, καὶ ὡς φωνὴν βροντῶν ἰσχυρῶν, λέγοντας.

Figures.

1234567890 1234567890

MARMORA

OXONIENSIA

OXONII

E TYPOGRAPHEO CLARENDONIANO.

IMPENSIS ACADEMIAE.

MDCCLXIII.

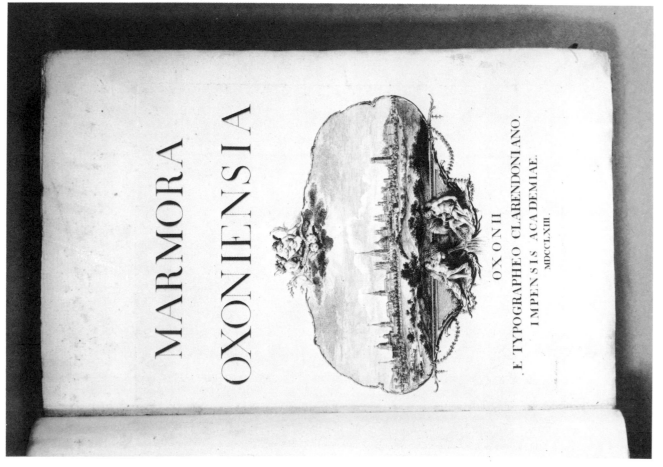

148

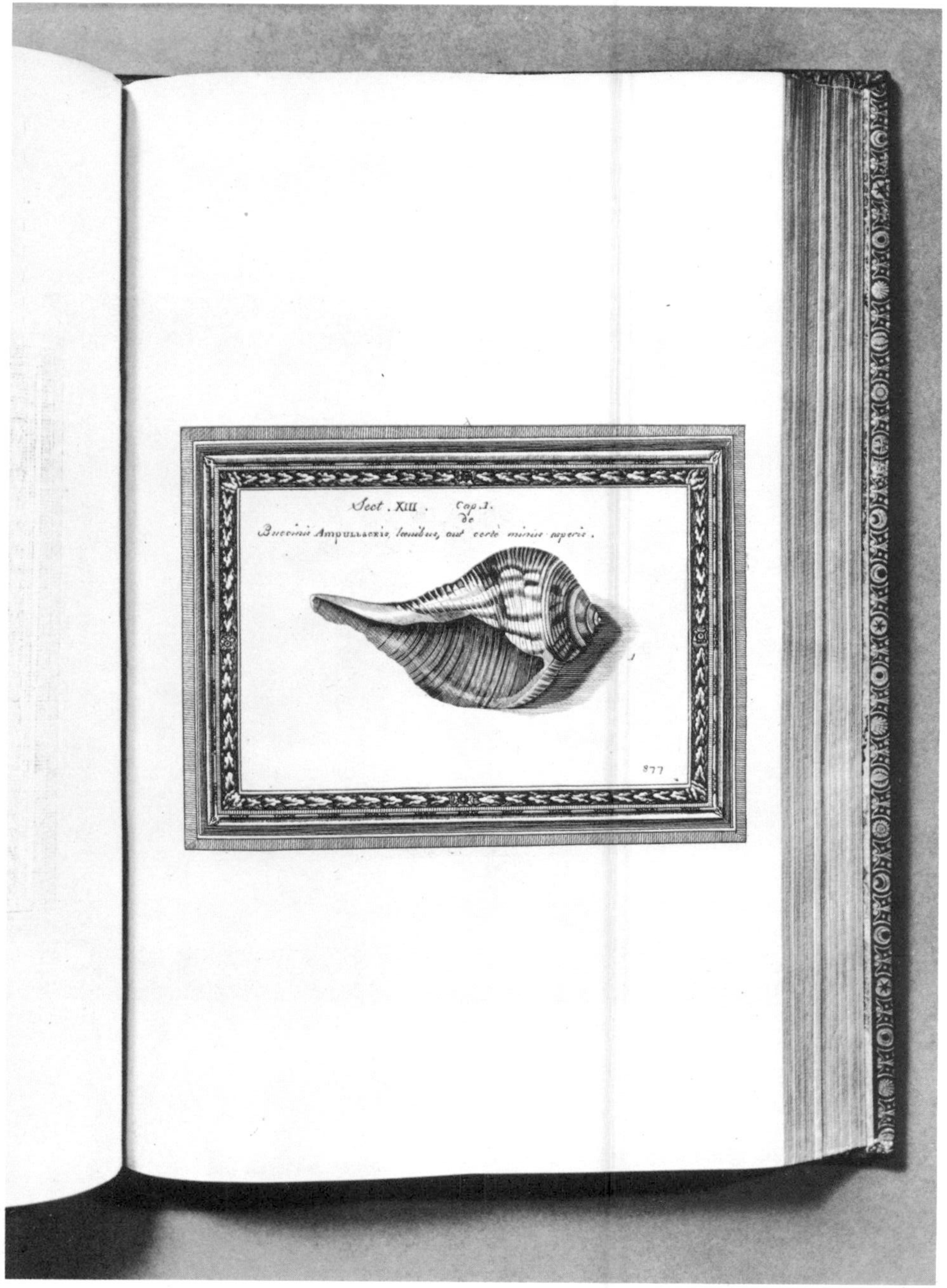

Sect. XIII. Cap. I.
de
Buccinis Ampullaceis, laevibus, aut certe minus asperis.

877

149

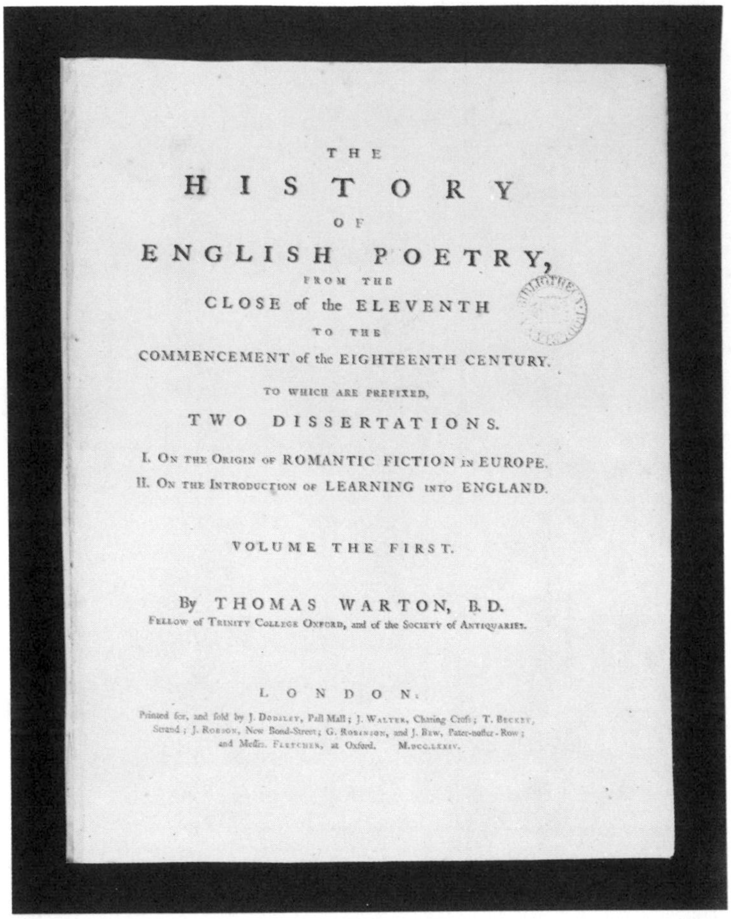

THE

HISTORY

OF

ENGLISH POETRY,

FROM THE

CLOSE of the ELEVENTH

TO THE

COMMENCEMENT of the EIGHTEENTH CENTURY.

TO WHICH ARE PREFIXED,

TWO DISSERTATIONS.

I. ON THE ORIGIN OF ROMANTIC FICTION IN EUROPE.

II. ON THE INTRODUCTION OF LEARNING INTO ENGLAND.

VOLUME THE FIRST.

By THOMAS WARTON, B.D.

FELLOW of TRINITY COLLEGE OXFORD, and of the SOCIETY of ANTIQUARIES.

LONDON:

Printed for, and fold by J. DODSLEY, Pall Mall; J. WALTER, Charing Crofs; T. BECKET, Strand; J. ROBSON, New Bond-Street; G. ROBINSON, and J. BEW, Pater-nofter-Row; and Meffrs. FLETCHER, at Oxford. M.DCC.LXXIV.

150

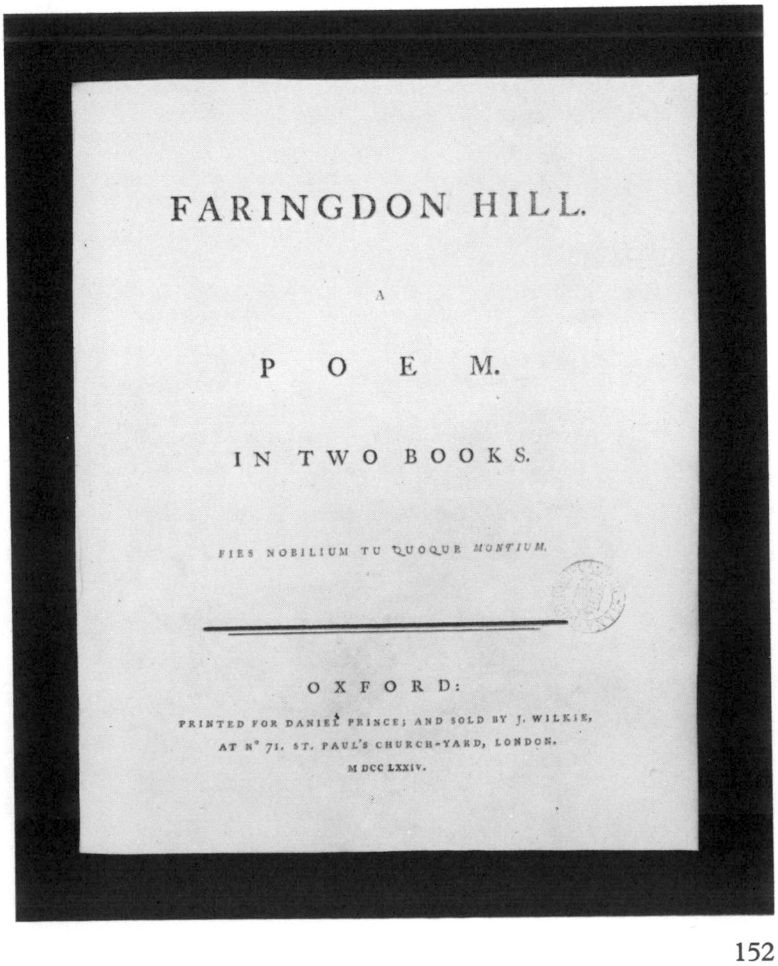

FARINGDON HILL.

A

POEM.

IN TWO BOOKS.

FIES NOBILIUM TU QUOQUE *MONTIUM.*

OXFORD:

PRINTED FOR DANIEL PRINCE; AND SOLD BY J. WILKIE, AT N° 71. ST. PAUL'S CHURCH-YARD, LONDON. M DCC LXXIV.

152

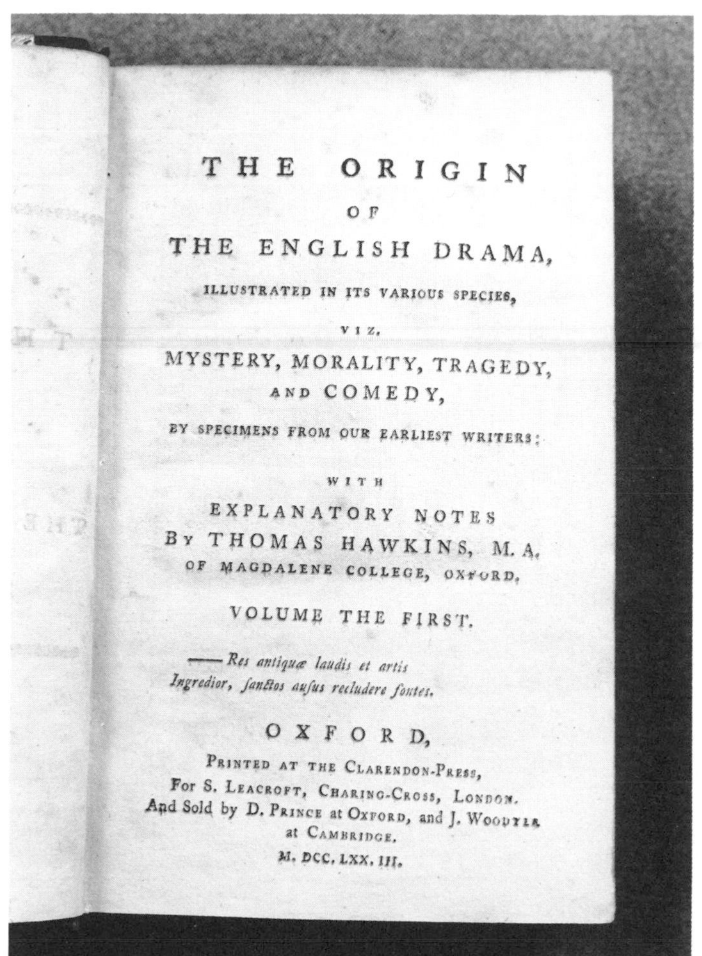

THE ORIGIN

OF

THE ENGLISH DRAMA,

ILLUSTRATED IN ITS VARIOUS SPECIES,

VIZ.

MYSTERY, MORALITY, TRAGEDY,

AND COMEDY,

BY SPECIMENS FROM OUR EARLIEST WRITERS:

WITH

EXPLANATORY NOTES

BY THOMAS HAWKINS, M. A.

OF MAGDALENE COLLEGE, OXFORD.

VOLUME THE FIRST.

—— *Res antiquæ laudis et artis*
Ingredior, sanctos ausus recludere fontes.

OXFORD,

PRINTED AT THE CLARENDON-PRESS,
For S. LEACROFT, CHARING-CROSS, LONDON.
And Sold by D. PRINCE at OXFORD, and J. WOODYER at CAMBRIDGE.
M. DCC. LXX. III.

151

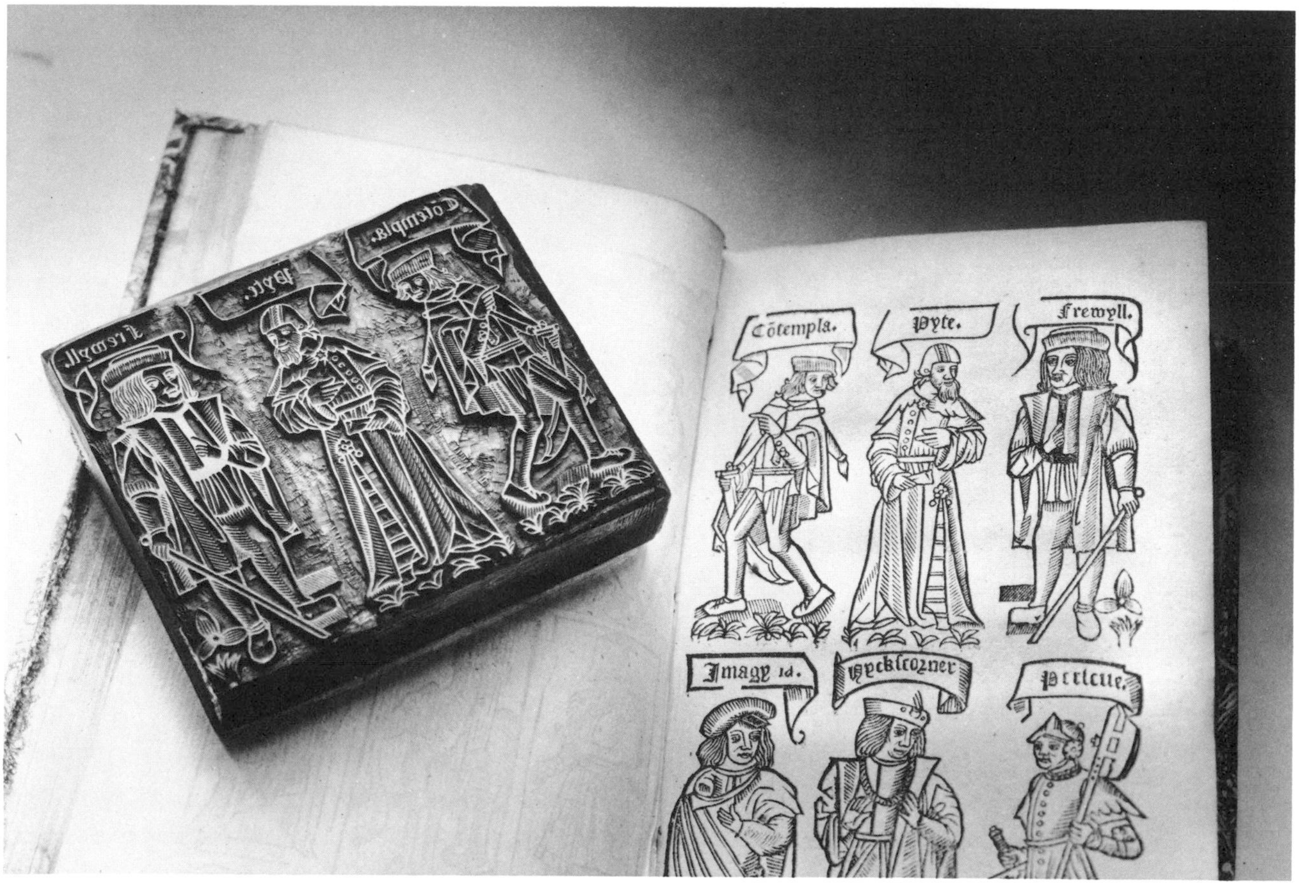

151A

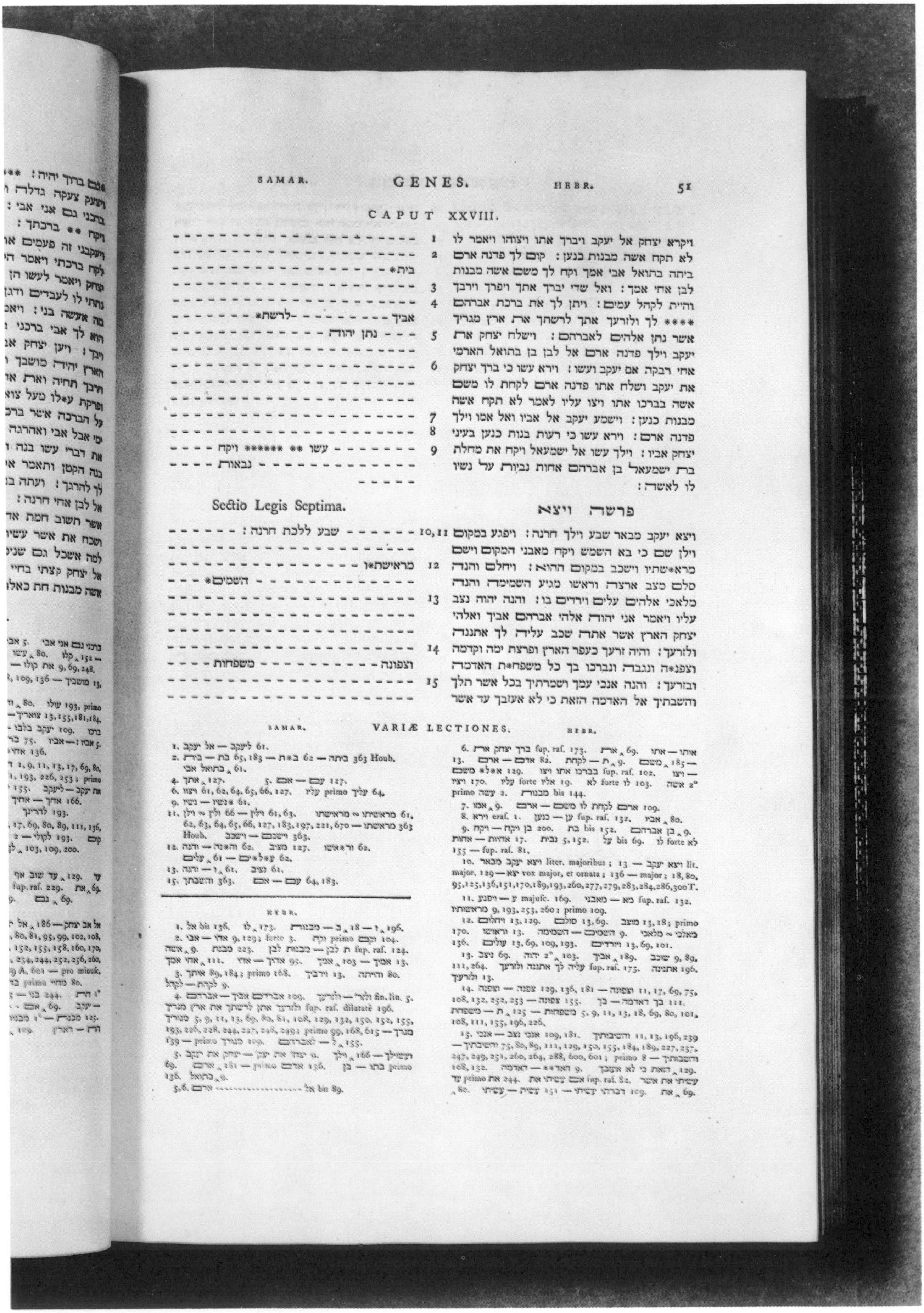

CAPUT XXVIII.

SAMAR.		HEBR.
- -	1	ויקרא יצחק אל יעקב ויברך אתו ויצוהו ויאמר לו
- -	2	לא תקח אשה מבנות כנען : קום לך פדנה ארם
בית* - - - - - - - - - - - - - - - - - - -		ביתה בתואל אבי אמך וקח לך משם אשה מבנות
- -	3	לבן אחי אמך : ואל שדי יברך אתך ויפרך וירבך
- -	4	והיית לקהל עמים : ויתן לך את ברכת אברהם
אביך - - - - - - - - - - -לרשת* - - - - - - -		**** לך ולזרעך אתך לרשתך ארת ארץ מגריך
- - - נתן יהודה - - - - - - - - - - - - - -	5	אשר נתן אלהים לאברהם : וישלח יצחק ארת
- -		יעקב וילך פדנה ארם אל לבן בן בתואל הארמי
- -	6	אחי רבקה אם יעקב ועשו : וירא עשו כי ברך יצחק
- -		את יעקב ושלח אתו פדנה ארם לקחת לו משם
- -		אשה בברכו אתו ויצו עליו לאמר לא תקח אשה
- -	7	מבנות כנען : וישמע יעקב אל אביו ואל אמו וילך
- -	8	פדנה ארם : וירא עשו כי רעות בנות כנען בעיני
- - - - - - - - עשו ** ****** ויקח - - - -	9	יצחק אביו : וילך עשו אל ישמעאל ויקח את מחלת
- - - - - - - - - - - - - - - נבאות - - - -		בת ישמעאל בן אברהם אחות נביות על נשיו
- - - - - -		לו לאשה :

Sectio Legis Septima.		פרשה ויצא
- - - - - - שבע ללכת חרנה : - - - - - - -	10, 11	ויצא יעקב מבאר שבע וילך חרנה : ויפגע במקום
- -		וילן שם כי בא השמש ויקח מאבני המקום וישם
- מראישת*ו	12	מרא*שתיו וישכב במקום ההוא : ויחלם והנה
- - - - - - - - - - - - - - - - - השמים* - - -		סלם מצב ארצה וראשו מגיע השמימה והנה
- -	13	מלאכי אלהים עלים וירדים בו : והנה יהוה נצב
- -		עליו ויאמר אני יהוה אלהי אברהם אביך ואלהי
- -		יצחק הארץ אשר אתה שכב עליה לך אתננה
- -	14	ולזרעך : והיה זרעך כעפר הארץ ופרצת ימה וקדמה
וצפונה - - - - - - - - - - - - - משפחות - - - -		וצפנ*ה ונגבה ונברכו בך כל משפח*ת האדמה
- -	15	ובזרעך : והנה אנכי עמך ושמרתיך בכל אשר תלך
- -		והשבתיך אל האדמה הזאת כי לא אעזבך עד אשר

VARIÆ LECTIONES.

SAMAR.

1. ליעקב — אל יעקב 61.
2. בירת — בת 65, 183 — ב*ת 62 — ביתה 363 Houb. ‸בתואל אבי 61.
4. ‸אתך 127. 5. עם — אם 127.
6. ויצו ויצוו 61, 62, 64, 65, 66, 127. עליו primo עליך 64.
9. נשיו — נשיו* 61.
11. וילן ∾ ולין 66 — וילין 61, 63. מראישתו ∾ מראישתיו 61, 62, 63, 64, 65, 66, 127, 183, 197, 221, 670 — מראשתו 363 Houb. וישכב — וישכבם 363.
12. והנה — והא*נה 62. מציב 127. ור*אשו 62. ‸עלים 61 — ע*ל*ים 62.
13. והנה — ‸ו 61. נציב 61.
15. והשבתך 363. אם — עם 64, 183.

HEBR.

1. אל bis 136. ‸לו 173. מבנורת — ‸ב 18 — ‸ו 196.
2. אבי — אחי 9, 129; forte 3. וקח primo וקם 104. ‸אשה 9. מבנת 223. לבן — מבנות ת fup. raf. 124. ‸אחי אמך 111. אחי — אחיך 95. ‸אמך 103 — אמיך 13.
3. אותך 89, 184; primo 168. וירביך 13. והייתה 80. לקהל — לקרת 9.
4. אברהם — אברהם אביך 109. ולזרעך — ולזר' fin. lin. 5. ולזרעך אתך לרשתך את ארץ מגריך fup. raf. dilatatè 196. מגוריך 5, 9, 11, 13, 69, 80, 81, 108, 129, 132, 150, 152, 155, 193, 226, 228, 244, 247, 248, 249; primo 99, 168, 615 — מגרך 159 — primo מגורך 109. לאברהם — ‸ל 155.
5. וישלך — ‸וילך 166 — יצחק את יעקב — יצח' את יעק' 9. ‸ארם 181 — primo אדם 136. בן — בתו primo 136. ‸בתואל 9.
5, 6. ארם - - - - - - - - - - - - - - - - - אל bis 89.
6. ברך יצחק ארת fup. raf. 173. ‸ארת 69. אתו — אותו 13. ארם — אדם 82. לקחת — ‸ת 9. ‸משם 185 — משם *א*ל* 129. בברכו אתו ויצו fup. raf. 102. ויצו — ויציו 170. עליו forte אליו 19. לא forte לו 103. אשה 2° primo עשה 2. מבנורת bis 144.
7. ‸אמו 9. ארם — ארם לקחת לו משם 109.
8. וירא eraf. 1. כנען — ען fup. raf. 132. ‸אביו 80.
9. ויקח — בן ויקח 200. בת bis 152. ‸בן אברהם 9. אחות — אחיות 17. נבית 5, 152. על bis 69. לא forte לו 155 — fup. raf. 81.
10. ויצא יעקב מבאר liter. majoribus; 13 — ויצא יעקב lit. major. 129 — יצא vox major, et ornata; 136 — major; 18, 80, 95, 125, 136, 151, 170, 189, 193, 260, 277, 279, 283, 284, 286, 300 T.
11. ויפגע — ע majufc. 169. מאבני — מא fup. raf. 132. מראשותיו 9, 193, 253, 260; primo 109.
12. ויחלום 13, 129. סולם 13, 69. מוצב 13, 18; primo 170. וראושו 13. השמימה — השמים 9. מלאכי ∾ מאלכי 136. עולים 13, 69, 109, 193. ויורדים 13, 69, 101.
13. ניצב 69. יהוה 2° ‸ 103. ‸אביך 189. שוכב 9, 89, 111, 264. עליה לך אתננה ולזרעך fup. raf. 173. אתנינה 196. ולזרעך 13.
14. וצפנה — צפנה 129, 136, 181 — וצפונה 11, 17, 69, 75, 108, 132, 252, 253 — צפונה 155. בך — בך דאדמה 111. משפחת — ‸ת 125 — משפחות 5, 9, 11, 13, 18, 69, 80, 101, 108, 111, 155, 196, 226.
15. אנכי — אנכי נצב 109, 181. והשיבותיך 11, 13, 196, 239 — והשיבתיך 75, 80, 89, 111, 129, 150, 155, 184, 189, 227, 237, 247, 249, 251, 260, 264, 288, 600, 601; primo 8 — והשבותיך 108, 132. האדמה — האד** 9. ‸הזאת כי לא אעזבך 129. עד primo את 244. את עשיתי אם fup. raf. 82. עשיתי את אשר ‸ 80. עשיתי — עשית 151 — דברתי עשיתי 109. ‸את 69.

Memorandum of an Agreement for nine years from Lady-Day 1780. *propofed to be entered into between the Univerfity of Oxford, and William Jackfon, of the fame place, for himfelf and for Mr. Archibald Hamilton, of Fleet Street, London, Printers, viz.*

I. THAT one moiety of the Clarendon Printing-Houfe, lately leafed out to Meffrs. Wright and Gill, heretofore appropriated to the purpofe of printing Bibles and Common Prayers, fhall be jointly occupied by the contracting parties for the above term, for their common convenience, and the advantage of carrying on bufinefs.

II. That the faid Parties fhall be jointly concerned, during the abovefaid term, in Bibles and Common Prayers, and fuch other Books within the prerogative of the Univerfity, as fhall be from time to time agreed upon between the Delegates and the faid William Jackfon and Archibald Hamilton.

III. That the faid William Jackfon and Archibald Hamilton, being appointed Printers to the Univerfity during the term of agreement, fhall under this agreement, with the concurrence and approbation of the Delegates of the Prefs for the time being, tranfact the whole bufinefs, to the beft of their abilities, for the mutual benefit of the Univerfity and themfelves, making no charge for any fuch fervice; the Univerfity on their part making no charge for rent of fo much of the Clarendon Printing-Houfe as fhall be jointly occupied for this purpofe, nor for their privilege of printing. And that the faid William Jackfon and Archibald Hamilton fhall be paid for printing, from the joint ftock, at the fame price allowed them in their late partnerfhip with Meffrs. Wright and Gill; thofe prices to be fpecified, deducting (as with them) 12l. 10s. *per cent.* for the ufe of the materials. The prices for printing any other Books befides

A Bibles

OXFORD, March 1, 1800.

A CATALOGUE OF BIBLES, COMMON PRAYER BOOKS, &c.

Printed at the Clarendon Press by Dawson, Bensley, and Cooke,
Printers to the University;

And Sold by W. Dawson, at the Bible Warehouse, Pater-noster Row, London:

WITH A SCHEME OF THE PRICES.

The Trade to have delivered 112 Copies on full Payment for 96; and no further Allowance will be made.

	Nominal Price.	7.	14.	28.	56.	112.
	£. s. d.	£. s. d.	£. s. d.	£. s. d.	£. s. d.	£. s. d.
BIBLES.						
Super *Royal* Folio, Double Pica Letter	3 13 6	22 1 0	44 3 0	88 4 0	176 8 0	352 16 0
Folio, Medium, fine Paper, Pica Letter, with Dr. Blayney's Marginal References	1 18 0	11 8 0	22 16 0	45 12 0	91 4 0	182 8 0
Folio, Demy Paper, Ditto, Ditto	1 8 0	8 8 0	16 16 0	33 12 0	67 4 0	134 8 0
Royal Quarto, fine Wove Paper, Ditto, Ditto	2 0 0	12 0 0	24 0 0	48 0 0	96 0 0	192 0 0
Service to Ditto	0 3 6	1 1 0	2 2 0	4 4 0	8 8 0	16 16 0
Large Quarto, Medium Paper, Pica Letter, with Dr. Blayney's Marginal References	1 0 0	6 0 0	12 0 0	24 0 0	48 0 0	96 0 0
Service to Ditto	0 2 6	0 15 0	1 10 0	3 0 0	6 0 0	12 0 0
Psalms to Ditto	0 1 2	0 7 0	0 14 0	1 8 0	2 16 0	5 12 0
Small Quarto, Long Primer Letter, Demy Paper	0 13 6	4 1 0	8 2 0	16 4 0	32 8 0	64 16 0
Service to Ditto	0 2 4	0 14 0	1 8 0	2 16 0	5 12 0	11 4 0
Psalms to Ditto	0 0 8	0 4 0	0 8 0	0 16 0	1 12 0	3 4 0
Large Octavo, Brevier Letter, with Marginal References	0 9 0	2 14 0	5 8 0	10 16 0	21 12 0	43 4 0
Apocrypha to Ditto	0 1 3	0 7 6	0 15 0	1 10 0	3 0 0	6 0 0
Service to Ditto	0 1 3	0 7 6	0 15 0	1 10 0	3 0 0	6 0 0
Psalms to Ditto	0 0 8	0 4 0	0 8 0	0 16 0	1 12 0	3 4 0
Octavo, Brevier Letter	0 5 6	1 13 0	3 6 0	6 12 0	13 4 0	26 8 0
Apocrypha to Ditto	0 1 2	0 7 0	0 14 0	1 8 0	2 16 0	5 12 0
Service to Ditto	0 1 2	0 7 0	0 14 0	1 8 0	2 16 0	5 12 0
Psalms to Ditto	0 0 7	0 3 6	0 7 0	0 14 0	1 8 0	2 16 0
Octavo Royal, fine Wove Paper, Brevier Letter	0 11 0	3 6 0	6 12 0	13 4 0	26 8 0	52 16 0
Apocrypha to Ditto	0 2 4	0 14 0	1 8 0	2 16 0	5 12 0	11 4 0
Minion Letter, Crown Octavo	0 4 6	1 7 0	2 14 0	5 8 0	10 16 0	21 12 0
Apocrypha to Ditto	0 1 0	0 6 0	0 12 0	1 4 0	2 8 0	4 16 0
Service to Ditto	0 0 8	0 4 0	0 8 0	0 16 0	1 12 0	3 4 0
Psalms to Ditto	0 0 6	0 3 0	0 6 0	0 12 0	1 4 0	2 8 0
Nonpareil Letter, 12mo.	0 3 0	0 18 0	1 16 0	3 12 0	7 4 0	14 8 0
Apocrypha to Ditto	0 0 11	0 5 6	0 11 0	1 2 0	2 4 0	4 8 0
Service to Ditto	0 0 8	0 4 0	0 8 0	0 16 0	1 12 0	3 4 0
Psalms to Ditto	0 0 5	0 2 6	0 5 0	0 10 0	1 0 0	2 0 0
Nonpareil, *Inferior*, 12mo.	0 2 4	0 14 0	1 8 0	2 16 0	5 12 0	11 4 0
Twenty-fours, *Nonpareil* Letter	0 3 0	0 0 0	1 16 0	3 12 0	7 4 0	14 8 0
Ditto, *Pearl* Letter	0 3 0	0 0 0	1 16 0	3 12 0	7 4 0	14 8 0
12mo. *Pocket Size*, printed on Whatman's thin wove Fool's Cap, with the best Ink, and hotpressed	0 6 0	1 16 0	3 12 0	7 4 0	14 8 0	28 16 0
Folio, Welch, *fine Demy*	2 12 6	15 15 0	31 10 0	63 0 0	126 0 0	252 0 0
Ditto, Ditto, *Common Paper*	1 15 0	10 10 0	21 0 0	42 0 0	84 0 0	168 0 0
Testaments.						
Pica Letter, Octavo	0 2 4	0 14 0	1 8 0	2 16 0	5 12 0	11 4 0
Long Primer Letter, Ditto	0 1 6	0 9 0	0 18 0	1 16 0	3 12 0	7 4 0
Brevier, or *Oxford* 12mo.	0 1 0	0 6 0	0 12 0	1 4 0	2 8 0	4 16 0
Ditto, fine Paper	0 1 4	0 8 0	0 16 0	1 12 0	3 4 0	6 8 0
Twenty-fours, *Nonpareil* Letter	0 1 0	0 6 0	0 12 0	1 4 0	2 8 0	4 16 0
Common Prayers.						
Folio, *Royal* Paper, Double Pica Letter	1 11 6	9 9 0	18 18 0	37 16 0	75 12 0	151 4 0
Psalms to Ditto	0 4 6	1 7 0	2 14 0	5 8 0	10 16 0	21 12 0
Ditto, fine *Medium* Paper, Ditto	1 1 0	6 6 0	12 12 0	25 4 0	50 8 0	100 16 0
Psalms to Ditto	0 3 6	1 1 0	2 2 0	4 4 0	8 8 0	16 16 0
Ditto, thick *Demy* Paper, Ditto	0 12 0	3 12 0	7 4 0	14 8 0	28 16 0	57 12 0
Psalms to Ditto	0 2 6	0 15 0	1 10 0	3 0 0	6 0 0	12 0 0
Quarto, fine *Royal* Paper, Great Primer Letter	0 14 0	4 4 0	8 8 0	16 16 0	33 12 0	67 4 0
Psalms to Ditto	0 2 6	0 15 0	1 10 0	3 0 0	6 0 0	12 0 0
Ditto, *Demy* Paper, Ditto	0 7 0	2 2 0	4 4 0	8 8 0	16 16 0	33 12 0
Psalms to Ditto	0 1 2	0 7 0	0 14 0	1 8 0	2 16 0	5 12 0
Octavo Royal, Long Line, fine Wove Paper, Great Primer Letter	0 8 0	2 8 0	4 16 0	9 12 0	19 4 0	38 8 0
Psalms to Ditto, Long Primer Letter	0 1 8	0 10 0	1 0 0	2 0 0	4 0 0	8 0 0
Ditto, *Long Line* Ditto, *Demy* Paper, Ditto	0 4 0	1 4 0	2 8 0	4 16 0	9 12 0	19 4 0
Psalms to Ditto, Long Primer	0 0 10	0 5 0	0 10 0	1 0 0	2 0 0	4 0 0
Ditto Royal, *Pica* Letter, fine Wove Paper	0 5 6	1 13 0	3 6 0	6 12 0	13 4 0	26 8 0
Psalms to Ditto	0 1 8	0 10 0	1 0 0	2 0 0	4 0 0	8 0 0
Ditto, *Pica* Letter, *Demy* Paper	0 2 8	0 16 0	1 12 0	3 4 0	6 8 0	12 16 0
Psalms to Ditto	0 0 10	0 5 0	0 10 0	1 0 0	2 0 0	4 0 0
Long Line, *Long Primer* Letter, *fine* Wove Demy Paper, hotpressed	0 7 6	2 5 0	4 10 0	9 0 0	18 0 0	36 0 0
Ordination Service to bind with Prayer, Long Primer, fine	0 0 6	0 3 0	0 6 0	0 12 0	1 4 0	2 8 0
Psalms to Ditto	0 1 6	0 9 0	0 18 0	1 16 0	3 12 0	7 4 0
Ditto, *Ditto*, *fine Crown* Paper	0 4 6	1 7 0	2 14 0	5 8 0	10 16 0	21 12 0
Ordination service to bind with Prayer, Ditto, Crown	0 0 6	0 3 0	0 6 0	0 12 0	1 4 0	2 8 0
Psalms to Ditto	0 1 0	0 6 0	0 12 0	1 4 0	2 8 0	4 16 0
Brevier Letter, 12mo.	0 1 4	0 8 0	0 16 0	1 12 0	3 4 0	6 8 0
Psalms to Ditto	0 0 5	0 2 6	0 5 0	0 10 0	1 0 0	2 0 0
Minion, *Long Line*, fine Post Paper, a very handsome Impression, printed with the best Ink	0 2 6	0 15 0	1 10 0	3 0 0	6 0 0	12 0 0
Psalms to Ditto	0 0 6	0 3 0	0 6 0	0 12 0	1 4 0	2 8 0
Minion Letter, fine *Fool's Cap*, 24° size, a fine Impression, printed with the best Ink	0 2 2	0 13 0	1 6 0	2 12 0	5 4 0	10 8 0
Psalms to Ditto	0 0 5	0 0 0	0 5 0	0 10 0	1 0 0	2 0 0
Ditto Letter, Columns, 12mo.	0 1 1	0 6 6	0 13 0	1 6 0	2 12 0	5 4 0
Psalms to Ditto	0 0 4	0 2 0	0 4 0	0 8 0	0 16 0	1 12 0
Ditto, *fine* Wove Demy	0 1 10	0 11 0	1 2 0	2 4 0	4 8 0	8 16 0
Psalms to Ditto	0 0 7	0 3 6	0 7 0	0 14 0	1 8 0	2 16 0
Twenty-fours, Columns, Nonpareil Letter, fine Royal Paper	0 1 4	0 0 0	0 16 0	1 12 0	3 4 0	6 8 0
Psalms to Ditto	0 0 5	0 0 0	0 5 0	0 10 0	1 0 0	2 0 0
Ditto, Columns, Nonpareil Letter	0 0 9	0 0 0	0 9 0	0 18 0	1 16 0	3 12 0
Psalms to Ditto	0 0 3	0 0 0	0 3 0	0 6 0	0 12 0	1 4 0
Thirty-two's, *Pearl* Letter, Long Lines, Thin Post	0 1 10	0 0 0	1 2 0	2 4 0	4 8 0	8 16 0
Psalms to Ditto	0 0 8	0 0 0	0 8 0	0 16 0	1 12 0	3 4 0
Ditto, *Nonpareil* Ditto, *Long Lines*, no Offices, *very small*, fine Paper, and best Ink	0 1 4	0 0 0	0 16 0	1 12 0	3 4 0	6 8 0
The Five Offices; to which is now added an *Appendix*, containing useful Directions for the due Discharge of the same; and other Articles relative to the Ministerial Function	0 1 6	0 9 0	0 18 0	1 16 0	3 12 0	7 4 0
The Ordination Service; the same size as the Five Offices, and may be bound up with the same, or separate	0 1 6	0 9 0	0 18 0	1 16 0	3 12 0	7 4 0
The Catechism set forth in the Book of Common Prayer, briefly explained by Notes grounded upon Holy Scripture	0 0 5	0 2 6	0 5 0	0 10 0	1 0 0	2 0 0
The Psalter, to which are added the Collects, with References to the Epistles and Gospels; *printed chiefly for the use of the Society for promoting Christian Knowledge*	0 0 6	0 3 0	0 6 0	0 12 0	1 4 0	2 8 0

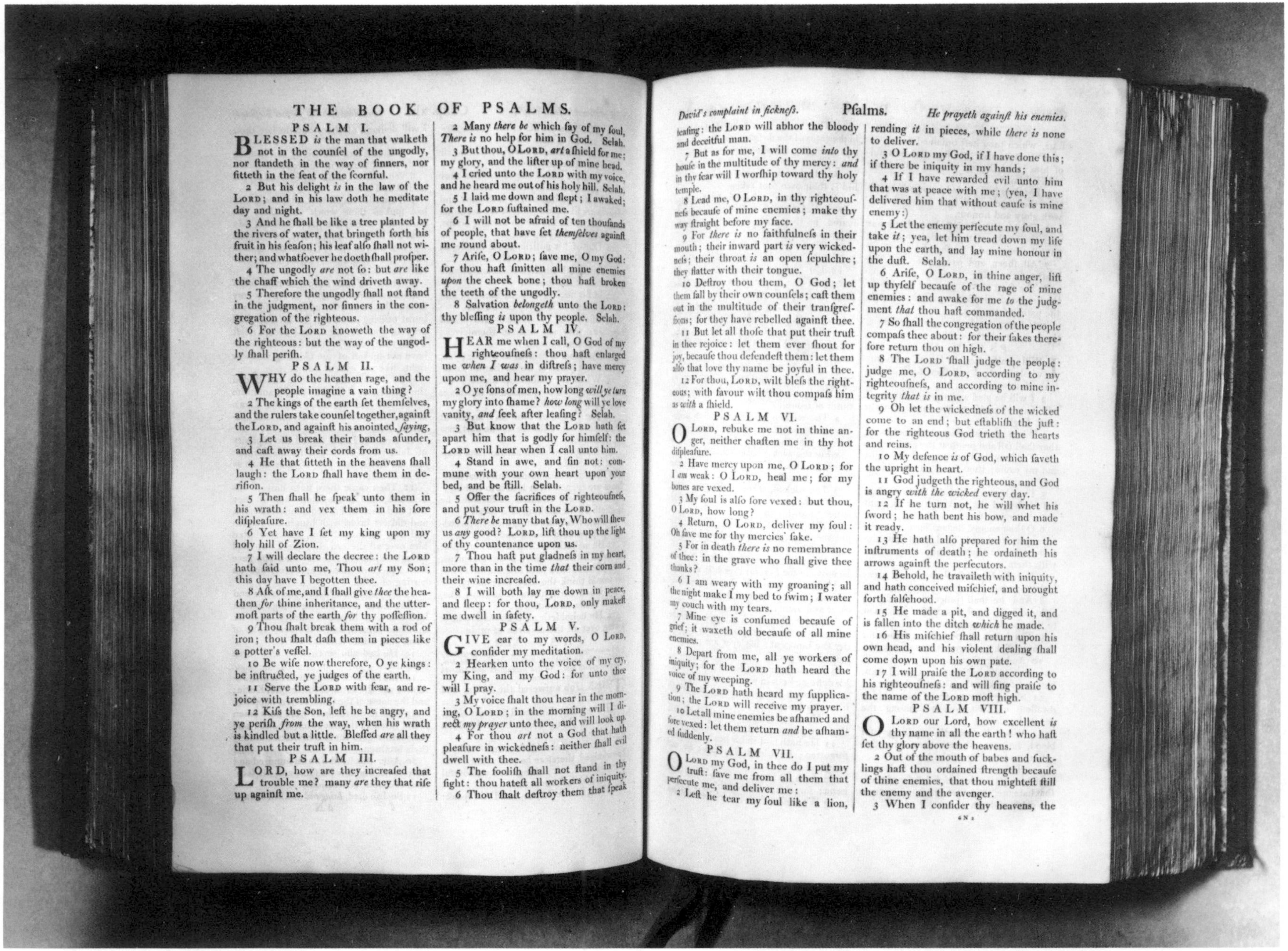

THE BOOK OF PSALMS.

PSALM I.

BLESSED *is* the man that walketh not in the counsel of the ungodly, nor standeth in the way of sinners, nor sitteth in the seat of the scornful.

2 But his delight *is* in the law of the LORD; and in his law doth he meditate day and night.

3 And he shall be like a tree planted by the rivers of water, that bringeth forth his fruit in his season; his leaf also shall not wither; and whatsoever he doeth shall prosper.

4 The ungodly *are* not so: but *are* like the chaff which the wind driveth away.

5 Therefore the ungodly shall not stand in the judgment, nor sinners in the congregation of the righteous.

6 For the LORD knoweth the way of the righteous: but the way of the ungodly shall perish.

PSALM II.

WHY do the heathen rage, and the people imagine a vain thing?

2 The kings of the earth set themselves, and the rulers take counsel together, against the LORD, and against his anointed, *saying*,

3 Let us break their bands asunder, and cast away their cords from us.

4 He that sitteth in the heavens shall laugh: the LORD shall have them in derision.

5 Then shall he speak unto them in his wrath: and vex them in his sore displeasure.

6 Yet have I set my king upon my holy hill of Zion.

7 I will declare the decree: the LORD hath said unto me, Thou *art* my Son; this day have I begotten thee.

8 Ask of me, and I shall give *thee* the heathen *for* thine inheritance, and the uttermost parts of the earth *for* thy possession.

9 Thou shalt break them with a rod of iron; thou shalt dash them in pieces like a potter's vessel.

10 Be wise now therefore, O ye kings: be instructed, ye judges of the earth.

11 Serve the LORD with fear, and rejoice with trembling.

12 Kiss the Son, lest he be angry, and ye perish *from* the way, when his wrath is kindled but a little. Blessed *are* all they that put their trust in him.

PSALM III.

LORD, how are they increased that trouble me? many *are* they that rise up against me.

2 Many *there be* which say of my soul, *There is* no help for him in God. Selah.

3 But thou, O LORD, *art* a shield for me; my glory, and the lifter up of mine head.

4 I cried unto the LORD with my voice, and he heard me out of his holy hill. Selah.

5 I laid me down and slept; I awaked; for the LORD sustained me.

6 I will not be afraid of ten thousands of people, that have set *themselves* against me round about.

7 Arise, O LORD; save me, O my God: for thou hast smitten all mine enemies *upon* the cheek bone; thou hast broken the teeth of the ungodly.

8 Salvation *belongeth* unto the LORD: thy blessing *is* upon thy people. Selah.

PSALM IV.

HEAR me when I call, O God of my righteousness: thou hast enlarged me *when I was* in distress; have mercy upon me, and hear my prayer.

2 O ye sons of men, how long *will ye turn* my glory into shame? *how long* will ye love vanity, *and* seek after leasing? Selah.

3 But know that the LORD hath set apart him that is godly for himself: the LORD will hear when I call unto him.

4 Stand in awe, and sin not: commune with your own heart upon your bed, and be still. Selah.

5 Offer the sacrifices of righteousness, and put your trust in the LORD.

6 *There be* many that say, Who will shew us *any* good? LORD, lift thou up the light of thy countenance upon us.

7 Thou hast put gladness in my heart, more than in the time *that* their corn and their wine increased.

8 I will both lay me down in peace, and sleep: for thou, LORD, only makest me dwell in safety.

PSALM V.

GIVE ear to my words, O LORD, consider my meditation.

2 Hearken unto the voice of my cry, my King, and my God: for unto thee will I pray.

3 My voice shalt thou hear in the morning, O LORD; in the morning will I direct *my prayer* unto thee, and will look up.

4 For thou *art* not a God that hath pleasure in wickedness: neither shall evil dwell with thee.

5 The foolish shall not stand in thy sight: thou hatest all workers of iniquity.

6 Thou shalt destroy them that speak

leasing: the LORD will abhor the bloody and deceitful man.

7 But as for me, I will come *into* thy house in the multitude of thy mercy: *and* in thy fear will I worship toward thy holy temple.

8 Lead me, O LORD, in thy righteousness because of mine enemies; make thy way straight before my face.

9 For *there is* no faithfulness in their mouth; their inward part *is* very wickedness; their throat *is* an open sepulchre; they flatter with their tongue.

10 Destroy thou them, O God; let them fall by their own counsels; cast them out in the multitude of their transgressions; for they have rebelled against thee.

11 But let all those that put their trust in thee rejoice: let them ever shout for joy, because thou defendest them: let them also that love thy name be joyful in thee.

12 For thou, LORD, wilt bless the righteous; with favour wilt thou compass him as *with* a shield.

PSALM VI.

O LORD, rebuke me not in thine anger, neither chasten me in thy hot displeasure.

2 Have mercy upon me, O LORD; for I *am* weak: O LORD, heal me; for my bones are vexed.

3 My soul is also sore vexed: but thou, O LORD, how long?

4 Return, O LORD, deliver my soul: Oh save me for thy mercies' sake.

5 For in death *there is* no remembrance of thee: in the grave who shall give thee thanks?

6 I am weary with my groaning; all the night make I my bed to swim; I water my couch with my tears.

7 Mine eye is consumed because of grief; it waxeth old because of all mine enemies.

8 Depart from me, all ye workers of iniquity; for the LORD hath heard the voice of my weeping.

9 The LORD hath heard my supplication; the LORD will receive my prayer.

10 Let all mine enemies be ashamed and sore vexed: let them return *and* be ashamed suddenly.

PSALM VII.

O LORD my God, in thee do I put my trust: save me from all them that persecute me, and deliver me:

2 Lest he tear my soul like a lion,

rending *it* in pieces, while *there is* none to deliver.

3 O LORD my God, if I have done this; if there be iniquity in my hands;

4 If I have rewarded evil unto him that was at peace with me; (yea, I have delivered him that without cause is mine enemy:)

5 Let the enemy persecute my soul, and take *it*; yea, let him tread down my life upon the earth, and lay mine honour in the dust. Selah.

6 Arise, O LORD, in thine anger, lift up thyself because of the rage of mine enemies: and awake for me *to* the judgment *that* thou hast commanded.

7 So shall the congregation of the people compass thee about: for their sakes therefore return thou on high.

8 The LORD shall judge the people: judge me, O LORD, according to my righteousness, and according to mine integrity *that is* in me.

9 Oh let the wickedness of the wicked come to an end; but establish the just: for the righteous God trieth the hearts and reins.

10 My defence *is* of God, which saveth the upright in heart.

11 God judgeth the righteous, and God is angry *with the wicked* every day.

12 If he turn not, he will whet his sword; he hath bent his bow, and made it ready.

13 He hath also prepared for him the instruments of death; he ordaineth his arrows against the persecutors.

14 Behold, he travaileth with iniquity, and hath conceived mischief, and brought forth falsehood.

15 He made a pit, and digged it, and is fallen into the ditch *which* he made.

16 His mischief shall return upon his own head, and his violent dealing shall come down upon his own pate.

17 I will praise the LORD according to his righteousness: and will sing praise to the name of the LORD most high.

PSALM VIII.

O LORD our Lord, how excellent *is* thy name in all the earth! who hast set thy glory above the heavens.

2 Out of the mouth of babes and sucklings hast thou ordained strength because of thine enemies, that thou mightest still the enemy and the avenger.

3 When I consider thy heavens, the

6 N 2

THE BOOK OF

COMMON PRAYER,

AND ADMINISTRATION OF

THE SACRAMENTS,

AND OTHER

RITES AND CEREMONIES OF THE CHURCH,

ACCORDING TO THE USE OF

The Church of England:

TOGETHER WITH

THE PSALTER OR PSALMS OF DAVID,

POINTED AS THEY ARE TO BE SUNG OR SAID IN CHURCHES;

AND THE

FORM OR MANNER OF MAKING, ORDAINING, AND CONSECRATING

OF

BISHOPS, PRIESTS, AND DEACONS.

OXFORD.

PRINTED BY DAWSON, BENSLEY, AND COOKE,

PRINTERS TO THE UNIVERSITY;

AND SOLD AT THE OXFORD BIBLE WAREHOUSE, PATERNOSTER ROW, LONDON.

1799.

CUM PRIVILEGIO. PRICE [illegible] UNBOUND.

A general Statement of the Partnership Account from Decr. 31. 1809 to Decr. 31st. 1810.

Bills & Notes	6466..5..3
Book Debts	12472..2..5
Printed Stock	31,137..15..6
Printing Materials	4389..3..8¾
Paper in the Warehouse	2729..7..9¾
Drawback not yet recd	674..5..9
Ditto	183..1..3
	58,052..1..8½

The University	½	29,026..–..10¾
Thos. Bensley	⅜	10,884..15..3¾
Joshua Cooke		10,884..15..3¾
S. Collingwood	⅛	2418..16..8¾
Edd. Gardner		2418..16..8¾
Joseph Parker		2418..16..8¾
		58,052..1..8½

Examined & approved
Errors excepted

1811
May 25th –

John Cole Vice Chr.
T. Bensley.
Jos. Cooke
Saml. Collingwood
For Mr. Gardner – T. Bensley.
Jos. Parker

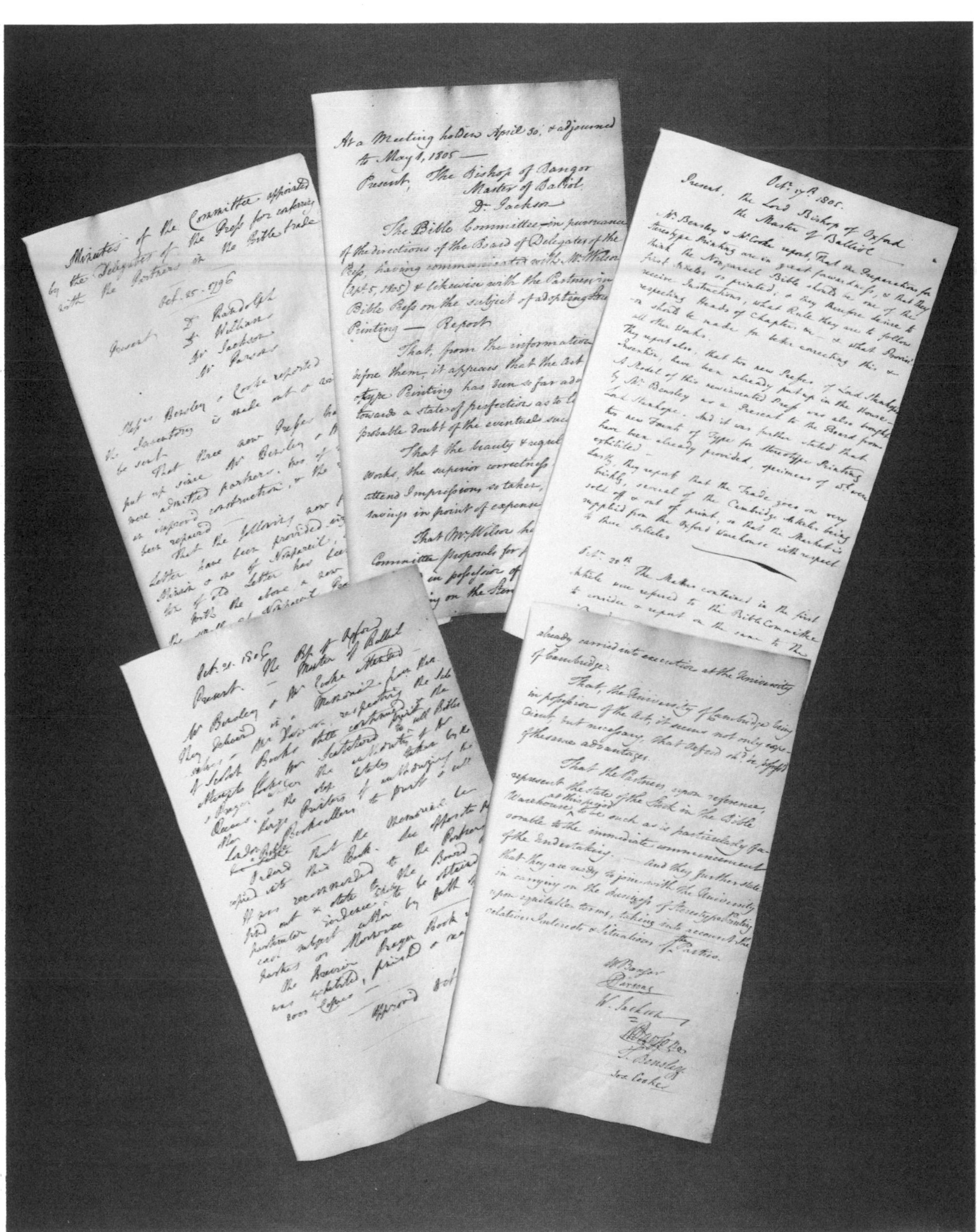

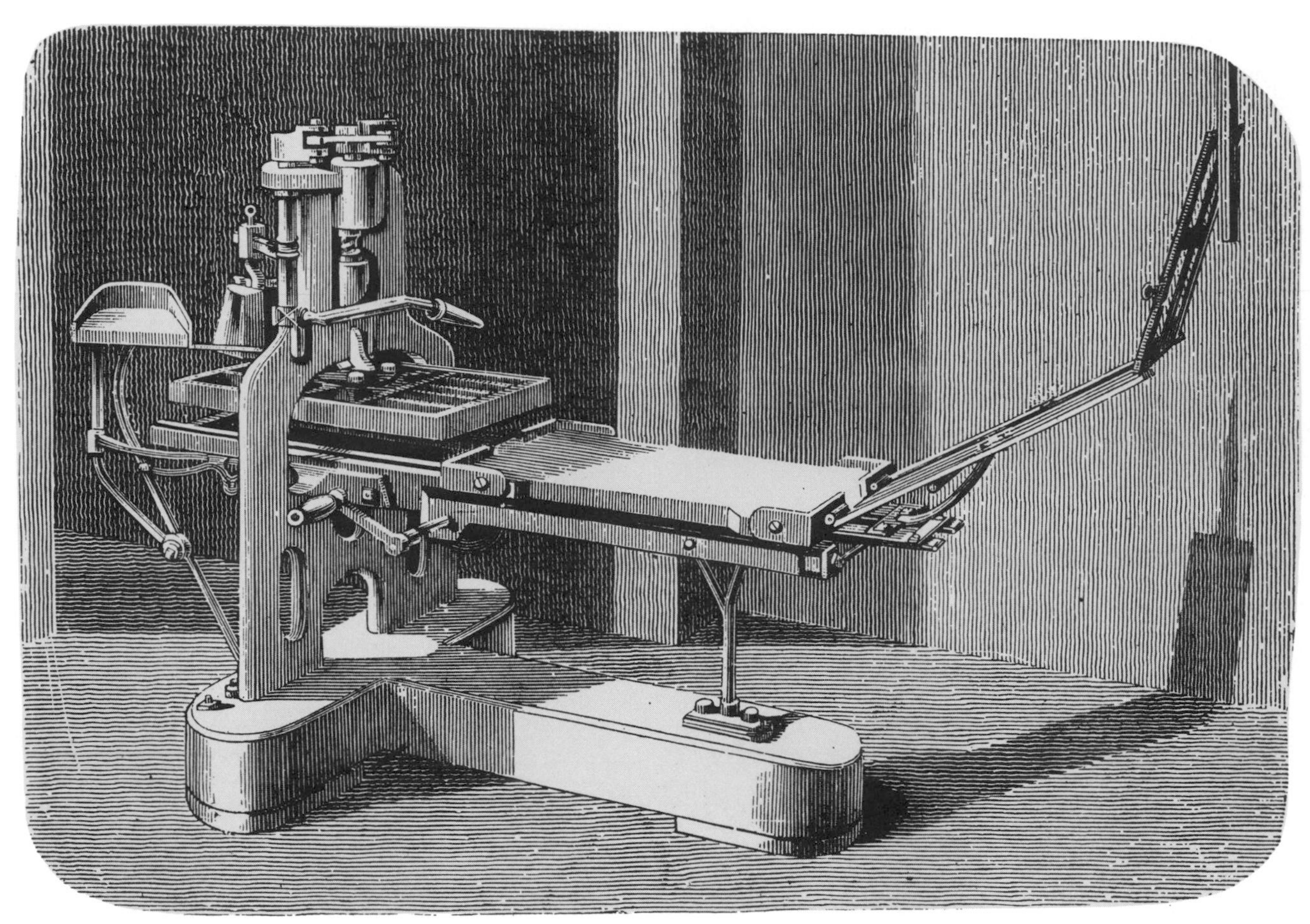

161

THE BOOK

OF

COMMON PRAYER,

AND ADMINISTRATION OF

THE SACRAMENTS,

AND OTHER

RITES AND CEREMONIES OF THE CHURCH,

ACCORDING TO THE USE OF THE

United Church of England and Ireland:

TOGETHER WITH

THE PSALTER

OR

PSALMS OF DAVID,

POINTED AS THEY ARE TO BE SUNG OR SAID IN CHURCHES.

STEREOTYPE EDITION.

OXFORD:

Printed at the Clarendon Press,

BY DAWSON, BENSLEY, AND COOKE,

PRINTERS TO THE UNIVERSITY;

And sold by W. DAWSON, at the Oxford Bible Warehouse,

Paternoster Row, London.

[Cum Privilegio.] 1806. [Price 1s. 4d. in Sheets.]

162

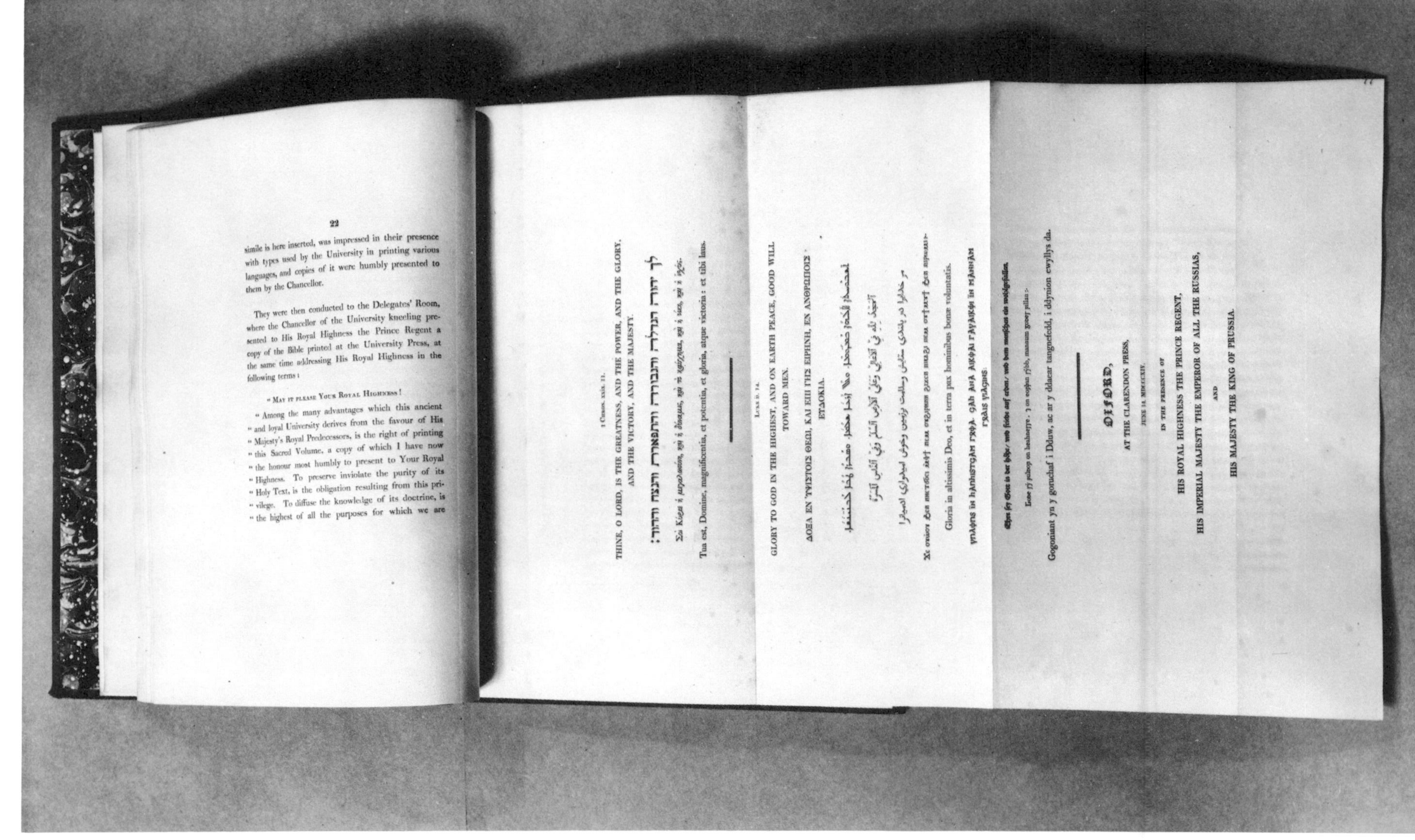

22

simile is here inserted, was impressed in their presence with types used by the University in printing various languages, and copies of it were humbly presented to them by the Chancellor.

They were then conducted to the Delegates' Room, where the Chancellor of the University kneeling presented to His Royal Highness the Prince Regent a copy of the Bible printed at the University Press, at the same time addressing His Royal Highness in the following terms:

"May it please Your Royal Highness!

"Among the many advantages which this ancient "and loyal University derives from the favour of His "Majesty's Royal Predecessors, is the right of printing "this Sacred Volume, a copy of which I have now "the honour most humbly to present to Your Royal "Highness. To preserve inviolate the purity of its "Holy Text, is the obligation resulting from this pri- "vilege. To diffuse the knowledge of its doctrine, is "the highest of all the purposes for which we are

1 Chron. xxix. 11.

THINE, O LORD, IS THE GREATNESS, AND THE POWER, AND THE GLORY, AND THE VICTORY, AND THE MAJESTY.

לך יהוה הגדלה והגבורה והתפארת והנצח וההוד׃

Σοὶ Κύριε ἡ μεγαλωσύνη, καὶ ἡ δύναμις, καὶ τὸ καύχημα, καὶ ἡ νίκη, καὶ ἡ ἰσχύς.

Tua est, Domine, magnificentia, et potentia, et gloria, atque victoria: et tibi laus.

Luke ii. 14.

GLORY TO GOD IN THE HIGHEST, AND ON EARTH PEACE, GOOD WILL TOWARD MEN.

ΔΟΞΑ ΕΝ ὙΨΙΣΤΟΙΣ ΘΕΩΙ, ΚΑΙ ΕΠΙ ΓΗΣ ΕΙΡΗΝΗ, ΕΝ ΑΝΘΡΩΠΟΙΣ ΕΥΔΟΚΙΑ.

Gloria in altissimis Deo, et in terra pax hominibus bonæ voluntatis.

Ehre sey Gott in der Höhe, und Friede auf Erden, und den Menschen ein Wohlgefallen.

Gogoniant yn y goruchaf i Dduw, ac ar y ddaear tangnefedd, i ddynion ewyllys da.

OXFORD,

AT THE CLARENDON PRESS.

JUNE 14 MDCCCXIV.

IN THE PRESENCE OF

HIS ROYAL HIGHNESS THE PRINCE REGENT,

HIS IMPERIAL MAJESTY THE EMPEROR OF ALL THE RUSSIAS,

AND

HIS MAJESTY THE KING OF PRUSSIA.

LIBER NONUS.

De Temporibus Consulum Romanorum.

ΛΟΓΟΣ ΕΝΝΑΤΟΣ.

Χρόνων Ὑπάτων Ῥώμης.

Respublica Romana à Consulibus primum administrata fuit, per annos CCCCLXIV, usque ad Julium Cæsarem Dictatorem. Hic natus non erat, sed, matre mense nono mortua, dissectaque, ex utero ejus exertus est: unde Cæsar dictus, quod Romanis, *Dissectio*, sonat. Adultus tandem, virque strenuus factus, cum Pompeio Magno, Crassoque, Triumvir creatus est. Post Crassum vero à Persis captum, occisumque, Cæsar Dictator, cum copiis suis, in regionibus Occidentalibus bellum prosecutus est: donec à Senatu, Pompeioque Magno, genero suo, Consulatu, sive Triumviratu exutus, ægre hoc ferens, in Romanos arma sumpsit. Ascitis itaque sibi Romanorum hostibus, Senatui, Pompeioque Magno bellum intulit: Romaque occupata, Senato-

Τὰ οὖν Ῥωμαίων πράγματα πρῶτον διῳκεῖτο ὑπὸ τῶν ὑπάτων, [1] ἐπὶ ἔτη υξδ', ἕως Καίσαρος Ἰουλίου τοῦ Δικτάτορος· ὃς οὐκ ἐγεννήθη, ἀλλὰ τῆς αὐτοῦ μητρὸς τελευτησάσης τῷ ἐννάτῳ μηνὶ, ἀνέκειραν αὐτὴν, καὶ ἐξέβαλον αὐτὸν βρέφος, [2] διὸ Καῖσαρ ἐλέγετο· (Καῖσαρ λέγεται Ῥωμαϊστὶ, ἡ ἀνατομή.) Ἀνατραφεὶς δὲ, καὶ ἀνδρεῖος γενόμενος, προεβλήθη Τριομβυράτωρ, μετὰ Πομπηΐου Μάγνου, καὶ Κράσσου· ὑπὸ γὰρ τῶν τριῶν τούτων ἐδιῳκεῖτο τὰ Ῥωμαίων. Ὁ δὲ Καῖσαρ ὁ Δικτάτωρ, μετὰ τὸ φονευθῆναι τὸν Κράσσον, [1] παραληφθέντα ὑπὸ Περσῶν πολέμῳ ἐν τοῖς Περσικοῖς μέρεσιν, ἔμεινε πολεμῶν μετὰ τοῦ πλήθους αὐτοῦ ἐν τοῖς μέρεσι τῆς δύσεως. Καὶ [2] διαδεχθεὶς τῆς ὑπατείας, ἤτοι τῆς Τριομβυρατορίας, κατὰ δοκιμασίαν τινὰ τῆς συγκλήτου Ῥώμης, καὶ Πομπηΐου Μάγνου, [3] τοῦ αὐτοῦ πενθεροῦ, ὁ αὐτὸς Καῖσαρ Ἰούλιος λυπηθεὶς, ἐτυράννησε Ῥωμαίους· καὶ προστρεψάμενος τοὺς κατὰ Ῥωμαίων πολεμίους, ἐπεστράτευσε μετὰ τῆς συγ-

1. ἐπὶ ἔτη υξδ'.] De Consulatus duratione, à Regibus scilicet expulsis, ad C. J. Cæsarem Dictatorem, magna est inter auctores opinionum diversitas. Chr. Alex. auctor annos enumerat tantum CCCXCIII. Eusebius, CCCCLXXIII. Excerptiones Chronologicæ ad Florum, an. DLXII. quod incidit in an. ab urb. Cond. DCCVI. vid. Scal. de Emend. Temp.

2. διὸ Καῖσαρ ἐλέγετο.] Ita etiam Cedrenus, Chr. Alexandr. Glycas, & Constantinus Manasses, qui tamen etiam alias nominis rationes profert. Zonaras vero vulgatam hanc nominis hujus rationem falsam esse asserit, his verbis, Tom. 2. Ἐλέγετο δὲ Καῖσαρ, ὥς τινες οἴονται, οὐχ ὅτι δὴ τάχα τῆς μητρὸς αὐτοῦ ἐν τῷ τίκτειν θανούσης, καὶ αὐτὸς διὰ ἀνατομῆς προαχθείη εἰς φῶς· οὐκ ἀληθὲς δὲ τοῦτό ἐστι. Deinde ad hoc confirmandum, Matrem eum, ad virilem usque ætatem, habuisse affirmat: rectissime. Hujus rei testem habemus Suetonium, in J. Cæsares, cap. 26. *Eodem temporis spatio matrem primo, deinde filiam, nec multo post nepiem amisit.* Sed & ante J. Cæsarem multi etiam alii fuerunt Cæsares: quorum catalogum nobis exhibet Jo. Glandorpius, in *Notitia familiæ Caii Julii Cæsaris* &c. J. Cæsar itaque Cæsareæ quidem dignitatis auctor fuit; nominis non item. Licet autem probabile satis sit, primum Cæsarem ab istiusmodi casu nomen habuisse, nostro tamen hoc competere non posse manifestum est. Vide Is. Causabon. in Sueton.

1. παραληφθέντα ὑπὸ Περσῶν] omnino scribendum Πάρθων: Crassus enim bello Parthico interiit.

2. διαδεχθεὶς τῆς ὑπατείας, ἤτοι τῆς Τριομβ.] Hæc vertit Chr. Alex. Interpres; *Consulatu, seu Triumviratu donatus*, male. Διαδέχομαι enim hic passive, improprie licet, pro, διάδοχον ἔχων ponitur. Ita etiam infra frequentius, ut in Valentiniano Imp. Ἡ μόνον δὲ ἐβασίλευσεν, εὐθέως διεδέξατο τὸν αὐτὸν ἔπαρχον Σαλλούστιον, &c. In Zenone etiam Imp. Ὁ δὲ βασιλεὺς Ζήνων πεισθεὶς, διεδέξατο αὐτὸν ἐκ τῆς ἀρχῆς τοῦ μαγίστρου, καὶ ἐποίησεν αὐτὸν στρατηλάτην ἀνατολῆς. Atque huic interpretationi suffragatur Florus, lib. 4. *De successione Cæsaris Senatus, id est, Pompeius, agitabat, nec ille abnuebat, si ratio sui proximis comitiis haberetur. Consulatus absenti, quem decem tribuni plebis, favente Pompeio, nuper decreverant, tum, dissimulante eodem, negabatur. Veniret, & peteret more majorum: ille contra flagitare decreta, ac, nisi in fide permanerent, non se remittere exercitum. Ergo ut in hostem decernitur.* Apud Chr. Alex. vero Τελουμβιράτωρ scribitur, *Triumvir*; & Τελουμβιρατορία, Triumviratus p. 438. Noster infra etiam habet, Τελομβουρεία.

3. τοῦ αὐτοῦ πενθεροῦ] reponendum γαμβροῦ: Pompeius enim J. Cæsaris filiam, Juliam, uxorem habuit. Sed & Cæsar etiam Pompeii filiam in matrimonium petierat. Vide Sueton. in Julio, cap. 27.

res

ΕΥΡΙΠΙΔΟΥ

ΕΚΑΒΗ.

ΙΑΜΒΟΙ.

ΗΚΩ, νεκρῶν κευθμῶνα καὶ σκότου πύλας
Λιπὼν, ἵν᾽ Ἅιδης χωρὶς ᾤκισαι θεῶν,
Πολύδωρος, Ἑκάβης παῖς γεγὼς τῆς Κισσέως,
Πριάμου τε πατρός· ὅς μ᾽, ἐπεὶ Φρυγῶν πόλιν
Κίνδυνος ἔσχε δορὶ πεσεῖν Ἑλληνικῷ,
Δείσας ὑπεξέπεμψε Τρωϊκῆς χθονὸς,
Πολυμήστορος πρὸς δῶμα Θρηκίου ξένου,
Ὃς τὴν ἀρίστην Χεῤῥονησίαν πλάκα
Σπείρει, φίλιππον λαὸν εὐθύνων δορί.
Πολὺν δὲ σὺν ἐμοὶ χρυσὸν ἐκπέμπει λάθρα
Πατὴρ, ἵν᾽, εἴποτ᾽ Ἰλίου τείχη πέσοι,
Τοῖς ζῶσιν εἴη παισὶ μὴ σπάνις βίου.
Νεώτατος δ᾽ ἦν Πριαμιδῶν, ὃ καί με γῆς
Ὑπεξέπεμψεν· οὔτε γὰρ φέρειν ὅπλα,
Οὔτ᾽ ἔγχος, οἷός τ᾽ ἦν, νέῳ βραχίονι.
Ἕως μὲν οὖν γῆς ὄρθ᾽ ἔκειθ᾽ ὁρίσματα,
Πύργοι τ᾽ ἄθραυστοι Τρωϊκῆς ἦσαν χθονὸς,
Ἕκτωρ τ᾽ ἀδελφὸς οὑμὸς ηὐτύχει δορὶ,
Καλῶς παρ᾽ ἀνδρὶ Θρηκὶ, πατρῴῳ ξένῳ,
Τροφαῖσιν, ὥς τις πτόρθος, ηὐξόμην τάλας.

Ἐπεὶ

Goulstoniana repetendas designaverat, quibus, ut in illa, ita in hac nostra Auctorum adscribuntur nomina.

Hæc itaque nobis in manus tradita sunt futuræ Editionis subsidia ab ipso exarata. Nec vero eorum eadem prorsus erat ratio. Etenim Græcum textum ita ad amussim castigatum dederat, ut in eo vix unicum punctum immutandum fuerit. Latinam Versionem non item: quanquam et illam quoque sedulo procuraverat; sed in resecandis tam multis, et in immutandis non tantum vocabulis quamplurimis, sed et toto habitu et ductu orationis, erant nonnulla, ad interpunctionem et ea quæ cursivis literis imprimenda erant spectantia, quæ Virum longe omnium accuratissimum effugerunt; quæque ipse proculdubio, si quando Versionem Latinam Græco textui subjectam viderit, inter imprimendum emendaturus erat. In his igitur corrigendis nobis aliquid licere arbitrabamur; nec vero aliam ob causam, quam ut interpunctio et imprimendi ratio magis sibi constaret, et Græcis aptius responderet. Si quædam etiam nunc restet discrepantia, ignoscat Lector. Sed hæc leviora.

Restabant adhuc pauca, in quibus dubii hærebamus, ubi scilicet clausulam aliquam antiquæ Versionis calamo in transversum ducto deleverat TYRWHITTUS, aliam de suo non suffecerat. Etenim illi solenne erat, sicubi Græca corrupta esse judicaverit, nulla autem iis emendandis auctoritas daretur, ex Latina interpretatione manifestum facere, quo modo illa emendari, et quo

sensu intelligi voluit. Hæc igitur de quibus loquimur partim sunt ea, in quibus Græca corrupta esse judicavit, atque adeo in iis reddendis liberiore calamo usurus erat; partim, in quibus Latinam Versionem per se vel vitiosam vel saltem minus elegantem esse arbitrabatur: sed quicquid voluit certe rem in medio reliquerat.

Singulatim autem hæc proponenda sunt, ita ut simul intelligat Lector cujusmodi fuerint, et quænam ipsi consilia in rebus tam incertis ceperimus.

Ac primo, locum illum quem indicavimus p. 51. Animadversiones Tyrwhittianæ Græce ex conjectura emendatum exhibent, subjecta nova interpretatione Latina; exinde igitur illud quod deerat supplevimus.

Alterum p. 62. Græce itidem emendaverat TYRWHITTUS, parum quidem fidenter, nec Latinam interpretationem dederat; suffecimus eam quæ ex Græcis ab illo emendatis luculenter se offerebat, quanquam ipse eam non diserte posuerat.

In 3^tio loco p. 63. obscurissimo sane, non tam emendationem Græci textus, quam meditationem quandam de suo proposuerat, quam tamen cum nihil aliud ad manum erat, Græcis manifeste vitiosis, Latine vertimus, et suo in loco suffecimus: quod et in alio fere consimili p. 93. καὶ εἶναι Ἰκάδιον &c. iterum fecimus: quin et in his pariter duobus satis liquebat quibus verbis reddenda essent ea quæ TYRWHITTUS excogitaverat.

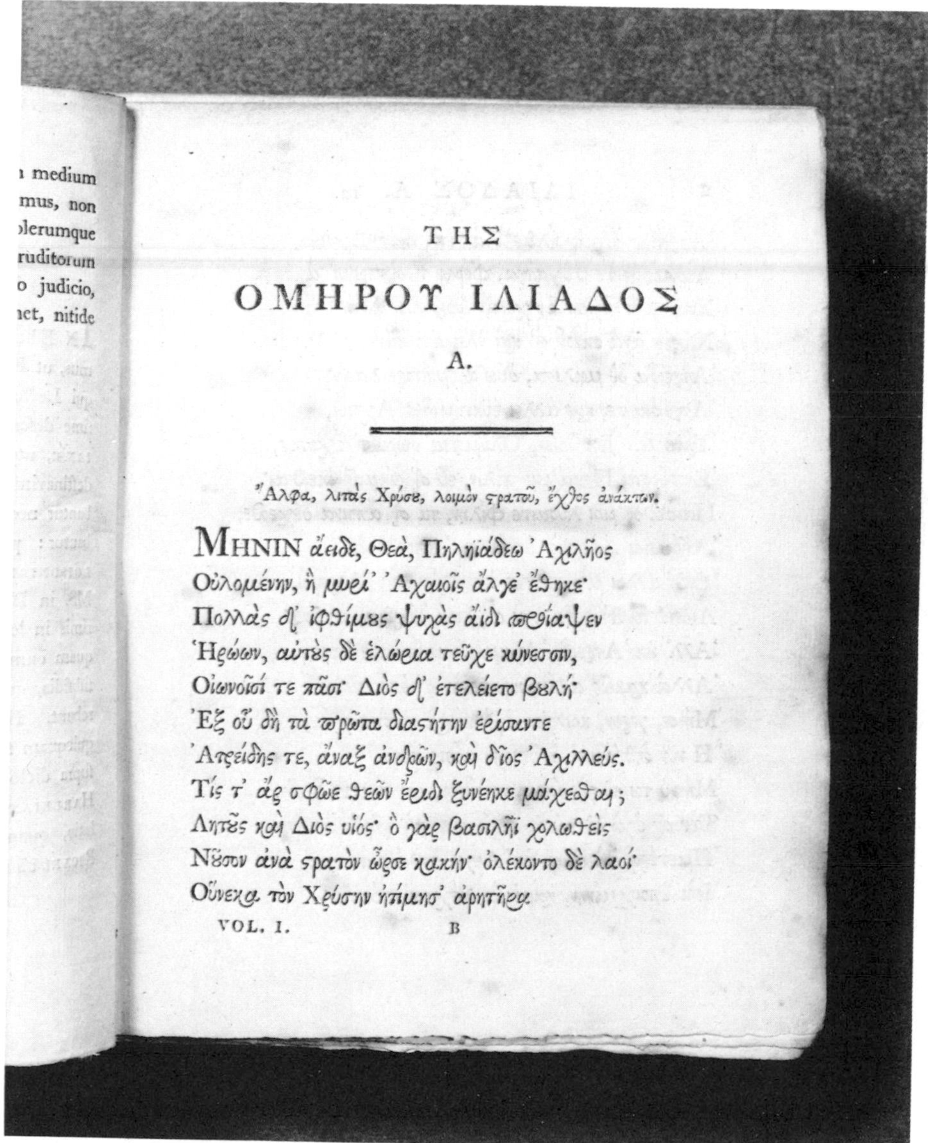

ΤΗΣ

ΟΜΗΡΟΥ ΙΛΙΑΔΟΣ

Α.

Ἄλφα, λιτὰς Χρύσε, λοιμὸν στρατοῦ, ἔχθος ἀνάκτων.

ΜΗΝΙΝ ἄειδε, Θεὰ, Πηληϊάδεω Ἀχιλῆος
Οὐλομένην, ἣ μυρί' Ἀχαιοῖς ἄλγε' ἔθηκε·
Πολλὰς δ' ἰφθίμους ψυχὰς Ἄϊδι προΐαψεν
Ἡρώων, αὐτοὺς δὲ ἑλώρια τεῦχε κύνεσσιν,
Οἰωνοῖσί τε πᾶσι· Διὸς δ' ἐτελείετο βουλή·
Ἐξ οὗ δὴ τὰ πρῶτα διαστήτην ἐρίσαντε
Ἀτρείδης τε, ἄναξ ἀνδρῶν, καὶ δῖος Ἀχιλλεύς.
Τίς τ' ἄρ σφῶε θεῶν ἔριδι ξυνέηκε μάχεσθαι;
Λητοῦς καὶ Διὸς υἱός· ὁ γὰρ βασιλῆϊ χολωθεὶς
Νοῦσον ἀνὰ στρατὸν ὦρσε κακήν· ὀλέκοντο δὲ λαοί·
Οὕνεκα τὸν Χρύσην ἠτίμησ' ἀρητῆρα

VOL. I. B

POETÆ MINORES

GRÆCI.

PRÆCIPUA LECTIONIS VARIETATE

ET

INDICIBUS LOCUPLETISSIMIS

INSTRUXIT

THOMAS GAISFORD, A. M.

ÆDIS CHRISTI ALUMNUS,

NECNON

GRÆCÆ LINGUÆ PROFESSOR REGIUS.

VOL. IV.

OXONII,

E TYPOGRAPHEO CLARENDONIANO.

MDCCCXX.

172

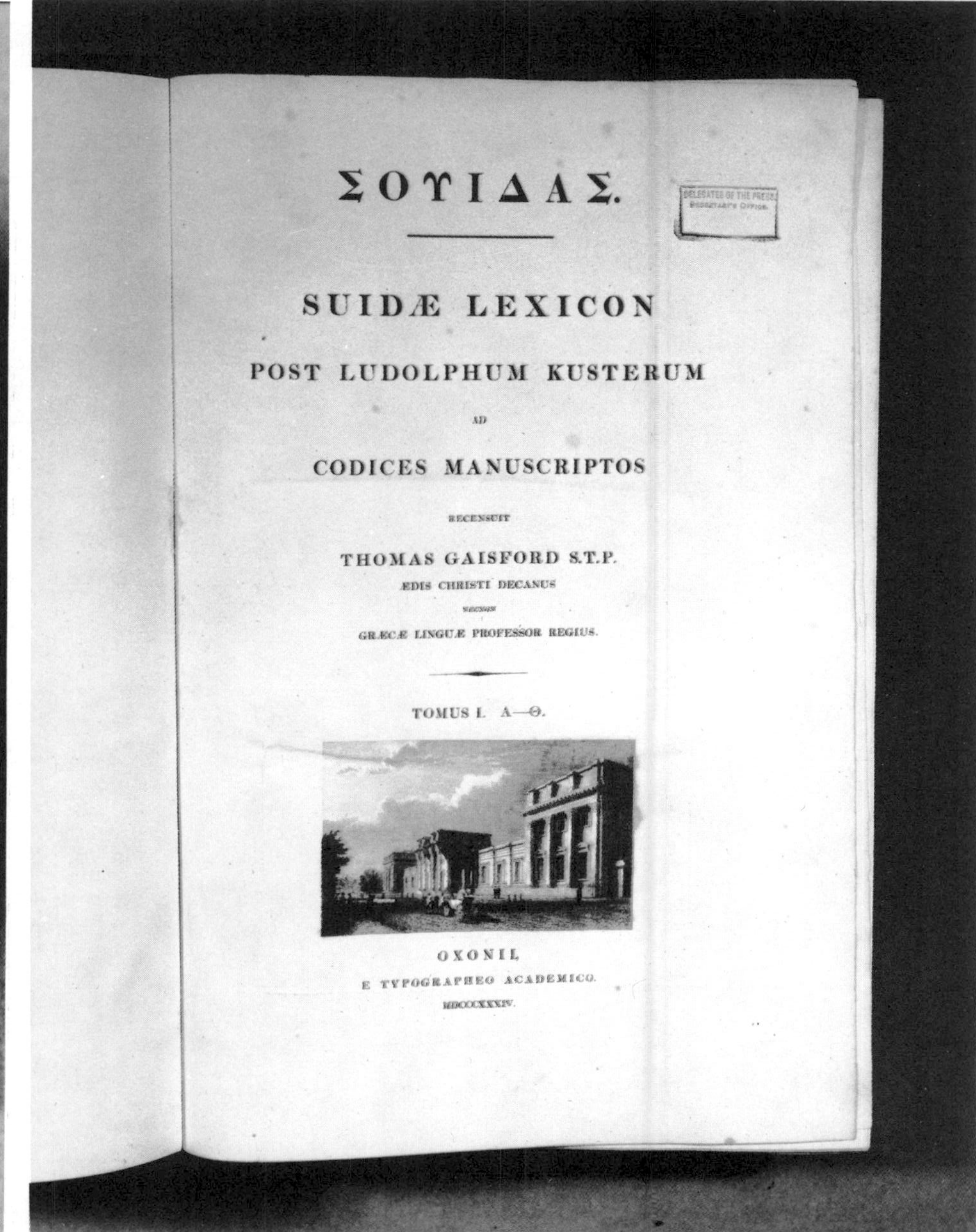

ΣΟΥΙΔΑΣ.

SUIDÆ LEXICON

POST LUDOLPHUM KUSTERUM

AD

CODICES MANUSCRIPTOS

RECENSUIT

THOMAS GAISFORD S.T.P.

ÆDIS CHRISTI DECANUS

NECNON

GRÆCÆ LINGUÆ PROFESSOR REGIUS.

TOMUS I. Α—Θ.

OXONII,

E TYPOGRAPHEO ACADEMICO.

MDCCCXXXIV.

173

EDVARDUS POCOCK, S.T.P.
Ædis Christi Canonicus.
Linguarum Heb. et Arab.
In Academia Oxoniensi Professor.

SPECIMEN
HISTORIÆ ARABUM;

AUCTORE EDVARDO POCOCKIO.

ACCESSIT

HISTORIA *VETERUM* ARABUM
EX ABU'L FEDA:

CURA ANTONII I. SYLVESTRE DE SACY.

EDIDIT JOSEPHUS WHITE, S.T.P.
ÆDIS CHRISTI CANONICUS,
LINGUARUM HEB. ET ARAB. IN ACAD. OXON. PROFESSOR.

OXONII,
E TYPOGRAPHEO CLARENDONIANO.
MDCCCVI.

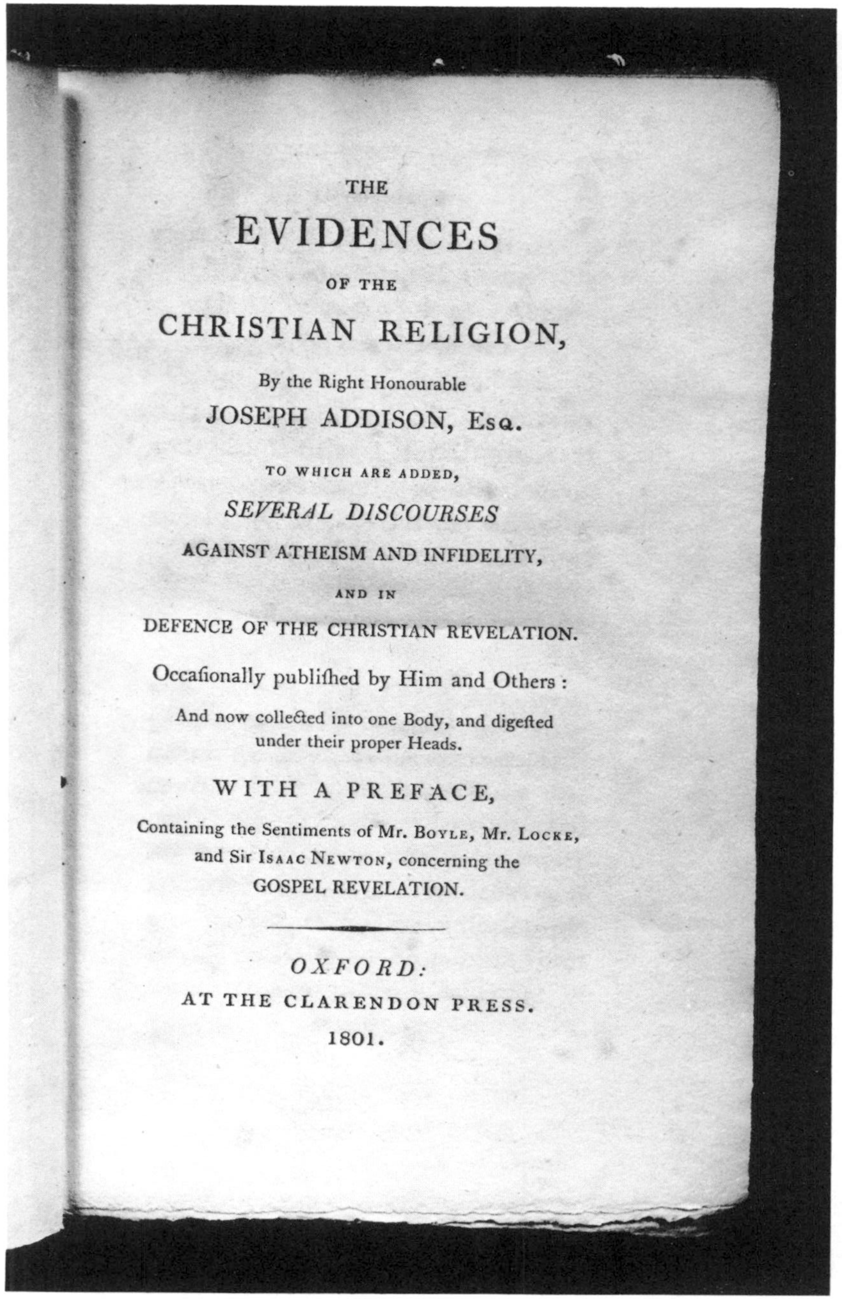

THE

EVIDENCES

OF THE

CHRISTIAN RELIGION,

By the Right Honourable

JOSEPH ADDISON, Esq.

TO WHICH ARE ADDED,

SEVERAL DISCOURSES

AGAINST ATHEISM AND INFIDELITY,

AND IN

DEFENCE OF THE CHRISTIAN REVELATION.

Occafionally publifhed by Him and Others:

And now collected into one Body, and digefted under their proper Heads.

WITH A PREFACE,

Containing the Sentiments of Mr. Boyle, Mr. Locke, and Sir Isaac Newton, concerning the GOSPEL REVELATION.

OXFORD:

AT THE CLARENDON PRESS.

1801.

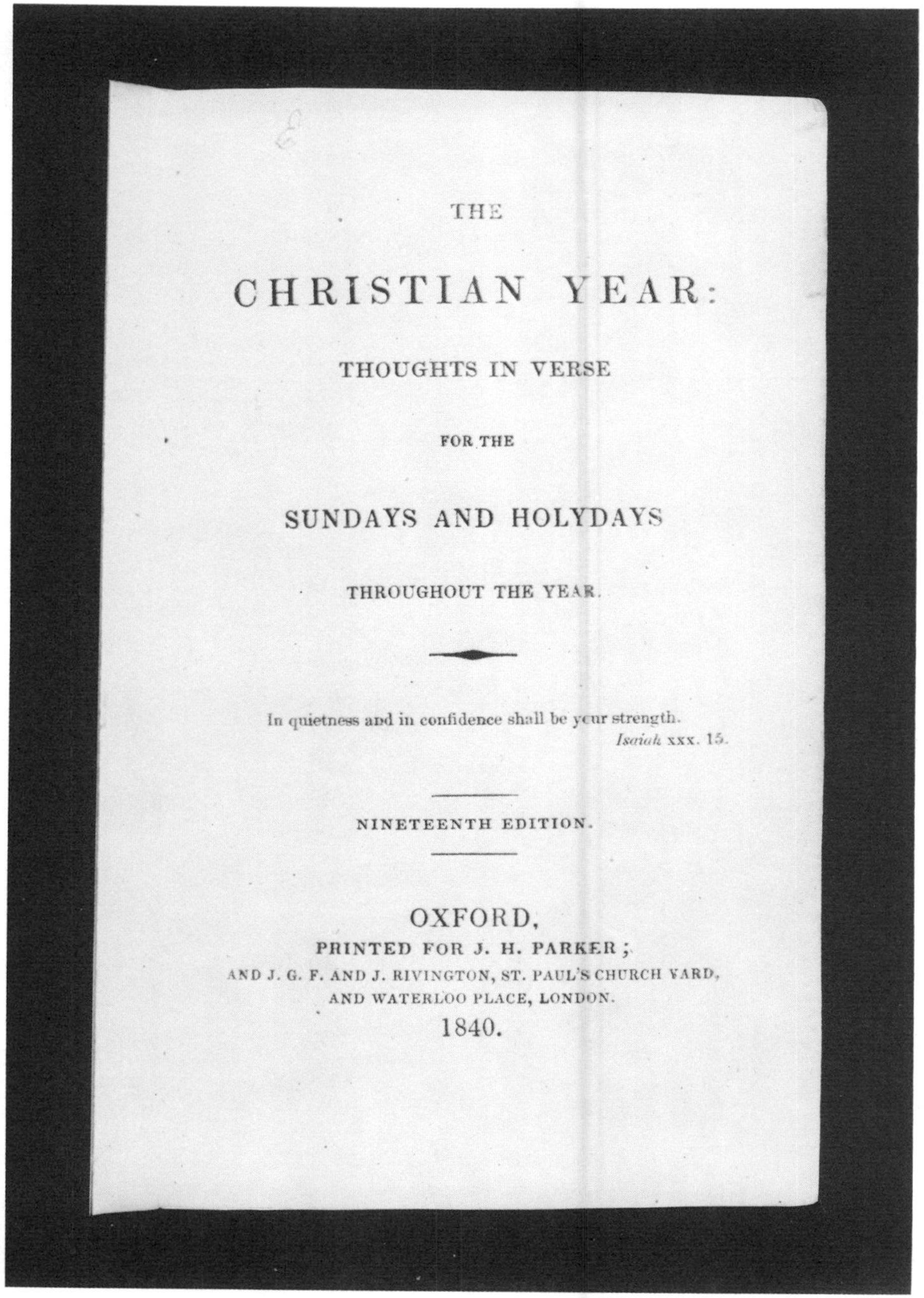

THE

CHRISTIAN YEAR:

THOUGHTS IN VERSE

FOR THE

SUNDAYS AND HOLYDAYS

THROUGHOUT THE YEAR.

In quietness and in confidence shall be your strength.
Isaiah xxx. 15.

NINETEENTH EDITION.

OXFORD,

PRINTED FOR J. H. PARKER;

AND J. G. F. AND J. RIVINGTON, ST. PAUL'S CHURCH YARD,

AND WATERLOO PLACE, LONDON.

1840.

MEMORIALS OF OXFORD.

EAST END OF THE CATHEDRAL.

Christ Church.

In presenting to the public these Memorials of Oxford, instead of following the chronological order of precedence usually adopted, we commence our labours with Christ Church.

This princely establishment is unquestionably worthy of our first attention on several distinct accounts. Its

B

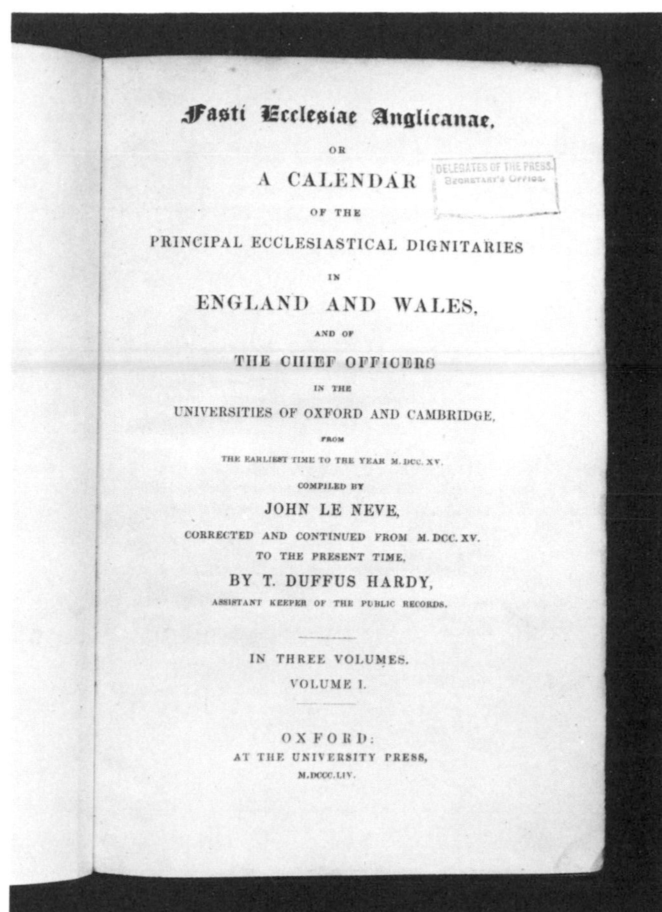

Fasti Ecclesiae Anglicanae,

OR

A CALENDAR

OF THE

PRINCIPAL ECCLESIASTICAL DIGNITARIES

IN

ENGLAND AND WALES,

AND OF

THE CHIEF OFFICERS

IN THE

UNIVERSITIES OF OXFORD AND CAMBRIDGE,

FROM

THE EARLIEST TIME TO THE YEAR M. DCC. XV.

COMPILED BY

JOHN LE NEVE,

CORRECTED AND CONTINUED FROM M. DCC. XV.

TO THE PRESENT TIME,

BY T. DUFFUS HARDY,

ASSISTANT KEEPER OF THE PUBLIC RECORDS.

IN THREE VOLUMES.

VOLUME I.

OXFORD:

AT THE UNIVERSITY PRESS,

M.DCCC.LIV.

185

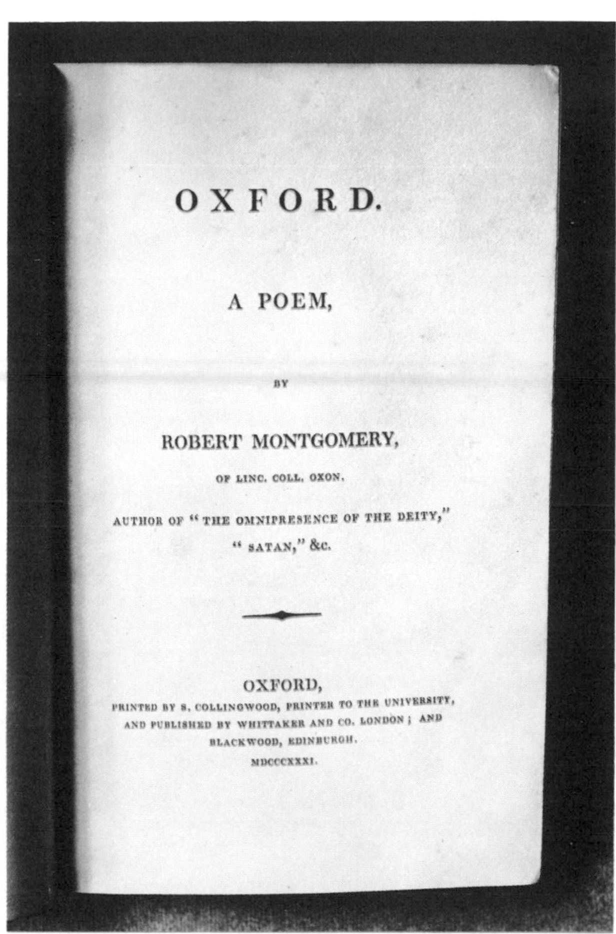

OXFORD.

A POEM,

BY

ROBERT MONTGOMERY,

OF LINC. COLL. OXON.

AUTHOR OF "THE OMNIPRESENCE OF THE DEITY," "SATAN," &c.

OXFORD,

PRINTED BY S. COLLINGWOOD, PRINTER TO THE UNIVERSITY,
AND PUBLISHED BY WHITTAKER AND CO. LONDON; AND
BLACKWOOD, EDINBURGH.

MDCCCXXXI.

186

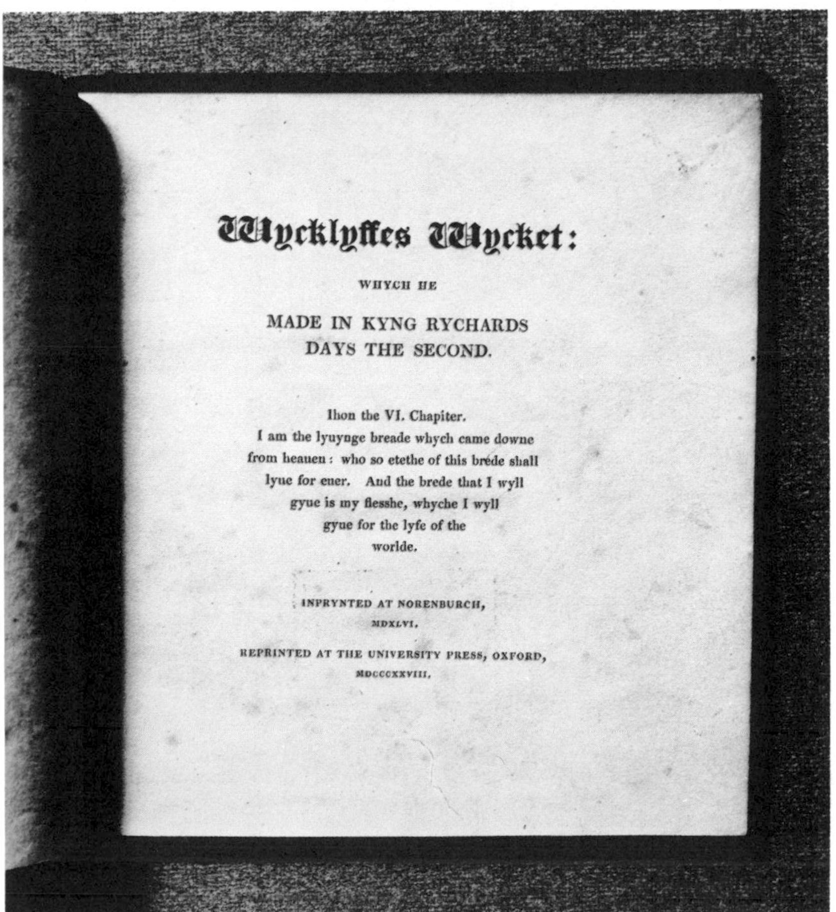

Wycklyffes Wycket:

WHYCH HE

MADE IN KYNG RYCHARDS
DAYS THE SECOND.

Ihon the VI. Chapiter.
I am the lyuynge breade whych came downe
from heauen: who so etethe of this brede shall
lyue for euer. And the brede that I wyll
gyue is my flesshe, whyche I wyll
gyue for the lyfe of the
worlde.

INPRYNTED AT NORENBURCH,

MDXLVI.

REPRINTED AT THE UNIVERSITY PRESS, OXFORD,

MDCCCXXVIII.

187

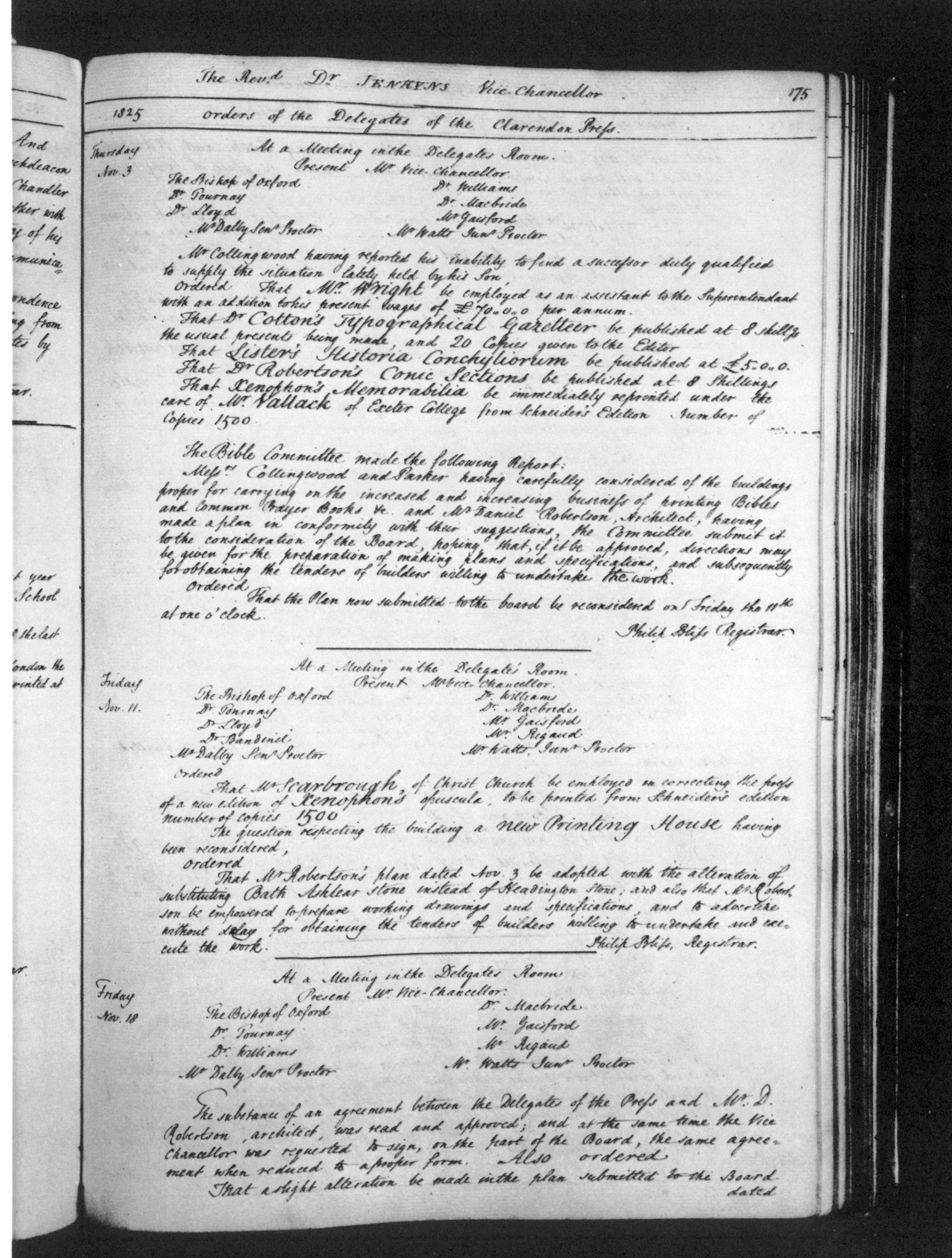

The Rev.d Dr. JENKYNS Vice-Chancellor. 175

1825 orders of the Delegates of the Clarendon Press.

Thursday Nov. 3

At a Meeting in the Delegates Room.
Present Mr. Vice-Chancellor

The Bishop of Oxford — Dr. Williams
Dr. Tournay — Dr. Macbride
Dr. Lloyd — Mr. Gaisford
Mr. Dalby Sen.r Proctor — Mr. Watts Jun.r Proctor

Mr. Collingwood having reported his inability to find a successor duly qualified to supply the situation lately held by his Son,
Ordered That Mr. Wright be employed as an assistant to the Superintendant with an addition to his present wages of £70..0..0 per annum.
That Dr. Cotton's Typographical Gazetteer be published at 8 shill.gs the usual presents being made, and 20 Copies given to the Editor
That Lister's Historia Conchyliorum be published at £5..0..0.
That Dr. Robertson's Conic Sections be published at 8 Shillings
That Xenophon's Memorabilia be immediately reprinted under the care of Mr. Vallack of Exeter College from Schneider's Edition. Number of Copies 1500.

The Bible Committee made the following Report:
Mess.rs Collingwood and Parker having carefully considered of the buildings proper for carrying on the increased and increasing business of printing Bibles and Common Prayer Books &c. and Mr. Daniel Robertson, Architect, having made a plan in conformity with their suggestions, the Committee submit it to the consideration of the Board, hoping that, if it be approved, directions may be given for the preparation of making plans and specifications, and subsequently for obtaining the tenders of builders willing to undertake the work.
Ordered
That the Plan now submitted to the board be reconsidered on Friday the 11th at one o'clock.

Philip Bliss Registrar.

Friday Nov. 11.

At a Meeting in the Delegates' Room
Present Mr. Vice-Chancellor.

The Bishop of Oxford — Dr. Williams
Dr. Tournay — Dr. Macbride
Dr. Lloyd — Mr. Gaisford
Dr. Bandinel — Mr. Rigaud
Mr. Dalby Sen.r Proctor — Mr. Watts, Jun.r Proctor

Ordered
That Mr. Scarbrough, of Christ Church be employed in correcting the proofs of a new edition of Xenophon's opuscula, to be printed from Schneider's edition number of copies 1500
The question respecting the building a New Printing House having been reconsidered,
Ordered
That Mr. Robertson's plan dated Nov. 3 be adopted with the alteration of substituting Bath Ashlear stone instead of Headington stone; and also that Mr. Robertson be empowered to prepare working drawings and specifications, and to advertise without delay for obtaining the tenders of builders willing to undertake and execute the work.

Philip Bliss, Registrar.

Friday Nov. 18

At a Meeting in the Delegates Room
Present Mr. Vice-Chancellor.

The Bishop of Oxford — Dr. Macbride
Dr. Tournay — Mr. Gaisford
Dr. Williams — Mr. Rigaud
Mr. Dalby Sen.r Proctor — Mr. Watts Jun.r Proctor

The substance of an agreement between the Delegates of the Press and Mr. D. Robertson, architect, was read and approved; and at the same time the Vice Chancellor was requested to sign, on the part of the Board, the same agreement when reduced to a proper form. Also ordered
That a slight alteration be made in the plan submitted to the Board dated

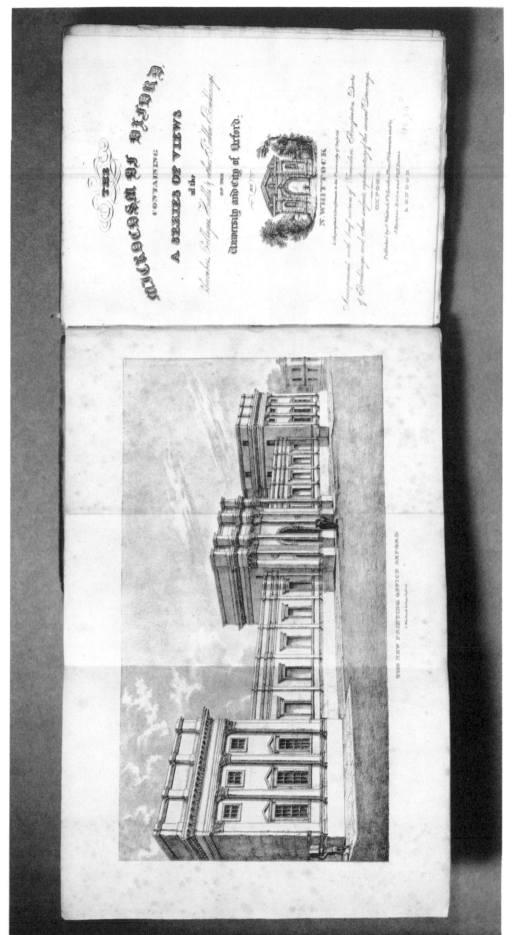

THE NEW PRINTING OFFICE OXFORD

N. Whittock, Lithog. Oxford.

THE

MICROCOSM OF OXFORD,

CONTAINING

A SERIES OF VIEWS

of the

Churches, Colleges, Halls & other Public Buildings

OF THE

University and City of Oxford.

BY

N. WHITTOCK

Lithographist & Draftsman to the University of Oxford.

Accompanied with brief notices of Founders, Benefactors, Dates of Buildings, and other subjects explanatory of the several Drawings.

OXFORD.

Published by N. Whittock, No. 11 London Place, St. Clements and by J. Bumpus, Holborn and Geo. H. Davis

LONDON.

ἐφ' ὑμᾶς· ὑμεῖς δὲ καθίσατε ἐν τῇ πόλει
Ἱερουσαλὴμ, ἕως οὗ ἐνδύσησθε δύναμιν ἐξ
ὕψους.
[u] Ἐξήγαγε δὲ αὐτοὺς ἔξω ἕως εἰς Βηθα- 50
νίαν· καὶ ἐπάρας τὰς χεῖρας αὐτοῦ, εὐλόγη-
σεν αὐτούς. [x] καὶ ἐγένετο ἐν τῷ εὐλογεῖν 51
αὐτὸν αὐτοὺς, διέστη ἀπ' αὐτῶν, καὶ ἀνεφέ-
ρετο εἰς τὸν οὐρανόν. καὶ αὐτοὶ προσκυν- 52
ήσαντες αὐτὸν, ὑπέστρεψαν εἰς Ἱερουσαλὴμ
μετὰ χαρᾶς μεγάλης· καὶ ἦσαν διαπαντὸς ἐν 53
τῷ ἱερῷ, αἰνοῦντες καὶ εὐλογοῦντες τὸν Θεόν.
Ἀμήν.

u Act. 1. 12.
x Marc. 16. 19. Act. 1. 9.

ΤΟ ΚΑΤΑ ΙΩΑΝΝΗΝ
ΑΓΙΟΝ ΕΥΑΓΓΕΛΙΟΝ.

[y] ἘΝ ἀρχῇ ἦν ὁ λόγος, καὶ ὁ λόγος ἦν πρὸς 1
τὸν Θεὸν, καὶ Θεὸς ἦν ὁ λόγος. οὗτος ἦν ἐν 2
ἀρχῇ πρὸς τὸν Θεόν. [z] Πάντα δι' αὐτοῦ ἐγέ- 3
νετο, καὶ χωρὶς αὐτοῦ ἐγένετο οὐδὲ ἓν ὃ γέγονεν. ἐν αὐτῷ ζωὴ ἦν, καὶ ἡ ζωὴ ἦν τὸ φῶς 4
τῶν ἀνθρώπων, [a] καὶ τὸ φῶς ἐν τῇ σκοτίᾳ 5
φαίνει, καὶ ἡ σκοτία αὐτὸ οὐ κατέλαβεν.
[b] Ἐγένετο ἄνθρωπος ἀπεσταλμένος παρὰ 6
Θεοῦ, ὄνομα αὐτῷ Ἰωάννης. οὗτος ἦλθεν εἰς 7
μαρτυρίαν, ἵνα μαρτυρήσῃ περὶ τοῦ φωτὸς,
ἵνα πάντες πιστεύσωσι δι' αὐτοῦ. οὐκ ἦν 8
ἐκεῖνος τὸ φῶς, ἀλλ' ἵνα μαρτυρήσῃ περὶ τοῦ

y 10. 33, 36. 1 Joh. 1. 1, 2. Apoc. 19. 13.
z 5. 26. et 8. 12. et 9. 5. et 12. 46. Eph. 3. 9. Col. 1. 17. Heb. 1. 2. 1 Joh. 5. 11.
a 3. 19.
b Matt. 3. 1. Marc. 1. 2, &c. Luc. 3. 3. et 7. 27. Act. 13. 24.

9 φωτός. [c] ἦν τὸ φῶς τὸ ἀληθινὸν, ὃ φωτίζει
πάντα ἄνθρωπον ἐρχόμενον εἰς τὸν κόσμον.
10 [d] ἐν τῷ κόσμῳ ἦν, καὶ ὁ κόσμος δι' αὐτοῦ
11 ἐγένετο, καὶ ὁ κόσμος αὐτὸν οὐκ ἔγνω. εἰς
τὰ ἴδια ἦλθε, καὶ οἱ ἴδιοι αὐτὸν οὐ παρέλα-
12 βον. [e] ὅσοι δὲ ἔλαβον αὐτὸν, ἔδωκεν αὐτοῖς
ἐξουσίαν τέκνα Θεοῦ γενέσθαι, τοῖς πιστεύ-
13 ουσιν εἰς τὸ ὄνομα αὐτοῦ· [f] οἳ οὐκ ἐξ αἱμά-
των, οὐδὲ ἐκ θελήματος σαρκὸς, οὐδὲ ἐκ θελήματος ἀνδρὸς, ἀλλ' ἐκ Θεοῦ ἐγεννήθησαν.
14 [g] Καὶ ὁ λόγος σὰρξ ἐγένετο, καὶ ἐσκήνωσεν
ἐν ἡμῖν, καὶ ἐθεασάμεθα τὴν δόξαν αὐτοῦ,
δόξαν ὡς μονογενοῦς παρὰ πατρὸς, πλήρης
χάριτος καὶ ἀληθείας.
15 [h] Ἰωάννης μαρτυρεῖ περὶ αὐτοῦ, καὶ κέ-
κραγε λέγων, Οὗτος ἦν ὃν εἶπον, Ὁ ὀπίσω
μου ἐρχόμενος, ἔμπροσθέν μου γέγονεν· ὅτι
16 πρῶτός μου ἦν. [i] καὶ ἐκ τοῦ πληρώματος αὐτοῦ ἡμεῖς πάντες ἐλάβομεν καὶ χάριν ἀντὶ
17 χάριτος· [k] ὅτι ὁ νόμος διὰ Μωσέως ἐδόθη, ἡ
χάρις καὶ ἡ ἀλήθεια διὰ Ἰησοῦ Χριστοῦ ἐγέ-
18 νετο. [l] Θεὸν οὐδεὶς ἑώρακε πώποτε· ὁ μονο-
γενὴς υἱὸς, ὁ ὢν εἰς τὸν κόλπον τοῦ πατρὸς,
19 ἐκεῖνος ἐξηγήσατο. [m] Καὶ αὕτη ἐστὶν ἡ μαρ-
τυρία τοῦ Ἰωάννου, ὅτε ἀπέστειλαν οἱ Ἰου-
δαῖοι ἐξ Ἱεροσολύμων ἱερεῖς καὶ Λευΐτας, ἵνα
20 ἐρωτήσωσιν αὐτὸν, Σὺ τίς εἶ; [n] καὶ ὡμολό-
γησε, καὶ οὐκ ἠρνήσατο· καὶ ὡμολόγησεν,
21 Ὅτι οὐκ εἰμὶ ἐγὼ ὁ Χριστός. [o] καὶ ἠρώτησαν
αὐτὸν, Τί οὖν; Ἠλίας εἶ σύ; καὶ λέγει,
Οὐκ εἰμί. Ὁ προφήτης εἶ σύ; καὶ ἀπεκρίθη,

c 3. 19. et 8. 12. et 9. 5. et 12. 46.
d Heb. 1. 2.
e Rom. 8. 15. Gal. 3. 26. 2 Pet. 1. 4. 1 Joh. 5. 1.
f 3. 5. Jac. 1. 18. 1 Pet. 1. 23.
g Matt. 1. 16. et 17. 2. Luc. 1. 31. et 2. 7. 1 Pet. 1. 17. Col. 1. 19. et 2. 3, 9.
h ver. 26, &c. et 3. 31. Matt. 3. 11. Marc. 1. 7. Luc. 3. 16.
i Col. 1. 19. et 2. 9.
k Exod. 20. 1, &c. Deut. 5. 6, &c.
l 6. 46. Exod. 33. 20. Deut. 4. 12. 1 Joh. 4. 12. 1 Tim. 6. 16. Matt. 11. 27. Luc. 10. 22.
m 5. 33.
n 3. 28. Act. 13. 25.
o Deut. 18. 15.

Before CHRIST cir. 1892.

didst thou tell me, neither yet heard
I *of it*, but to day.
27 And Abraham took sheep and
oxen, and gave them unto Abimelech; and both of them [f] made a covenant.
28 And Abraham set seven ewe
lambs of the flock by themselves.
29 And Abimelech said unto Abraham, [g] What *mean* these seven ewe
lambs which thou hast set by themselves?
30 And he said, For *these* seven ewe
lambs shalt thou take of my hand,
that [h] they may be a witness unto me,
that I have digged this well.
31 Wherefore he [i] called that place
|| Beer-sheba; because there they sware
both of them.
32 Thus they made a covenant at
Beer-sheba: then Abimelech rose up,
and Phichol the chief captain of his
host, and they returned into the land
of the Philistines.
33 ¶ And *Abraham* planted a || grove
in Beer-sheba, and [k] called there on
the name of the LORD, [l] the everlasting God.
34 And Abraham sojourned in the
Philistines' land many days.

f ch. 26. 31. g ch. 33. 8. h ch. 31. 48, 52. i ch. 26. 33. || That is, *The well of the oath.* cir. 1891. || Or, *tree.* k ch. 4. 26. l Deut. 33. 27. Is. 40. 28. Rom. 16. 26. 1 Tim. 1. 17.

CHAP. XXII.

1 Abraham is tempted to offer Isaac. 3 He giveth proof of his faith and obedience. 11 The angel stayeth him. 13 Isaac is exchanged with a ram. 14 The place is called Jehovah-jireh. 15 Abraham is blessed again. 20 The generation of Nahor unto Rebekah.

AND it came to pass after these
things that [a] God did tempt A-
braham, and said unto him, Abraham: and he said, † Behold, *here* I
am.
2 And he said, Take now thy son,
[b] thine only *son* Isaac, whom thou
lovest, and get thee [c] into the land of
Moriah; and offer him there for a
burnt offering upon one of the mountains which I will tell thee of.
3 ¶ And Abraham rose up early in
the morning, and saddled his ass, and
took two of his young men with him,
and Isaac his son, and clave the wood
for the burnt offering, and rose up,
and went unto the place of which
God had told him.
4 Then on the third day Abraham
lifted up his eyes, and saw the place
afar off.
5 And Abraham said unto his
young men, Abide ye here with the
ass; and I and the lad will go yon-
der and worship, and come again to
you.
6 And Abraham took the wood of
the burnt offering, and [d] laid *it* upon
Isaac his son; and he took the fire in
his hand, and a knife; and they went
both of them together.
7 And Isaac spake unto Abraham
his father, and said, My father: and
he said, † Here *am* I, my son. And
he said, Behold the fire and the
wood: but where *is* the || lamb for a
burnt offering?
8 And Abraham said, My son, God
will provide himself a lamb for a
burnt offering: so they went both of
them together.
9 And they came to the place which
God had told him of; and Abraham
built an altar there, and laid the wood
in order, and bound Isaac his son,
and [e] laid him on the altar upon the
wood.
10 And Abraham stretched forth his
hand, and took the knife to slay his
son.
11 And the angel of the LORD called unto him out of heaven, and said,
Abraham, Abraham: and he said,
Here *am* I.
12 And he said, [f] Lay not thine
hand upon the lad, neither do thou
any thing unto him: for [g] now I know
that thou fearest God, seeing thou
hast not withheld thy son, thine only
son from me.
13 And Abraham lifted up his eyes,
and looked, and behold behind *him* a
ram caught in a thicket by his horns:
and Abraham went and took the ram,
and offered him up for a burnt offering in the stead of his son.
14 And Abraham called the name of
that place || Jehovah-jireh: as it is
said *to* this day, In the mount of the
LORD it shall be seen.
15 ¶ And the angel of the LORD
called unto Abraham out of heaven
the second time,
16 And said, [h] By myself have I
sworn, saith the LORD, for because
thou hast done this thing, and hast
not withheld thy son, thine only *son*:
17 That in blessing I will bless thee,
and in multiplying I will multiply
thy seed [i] as the stars of the heaven,
[k] and as the sand which *is* upon the

1872. *Jos. Ant.* a 1 Cor. 10. 13. Heb. 11. 17. James 1. 12. 1 Pet. 1. 7. † Heb. *Behold me.* b Heb. 11. 17. c 2 Chron. 3. 1.

Before CHRIST cir. 1872. d John 19. 17. † Heb. *Behold me.* || Or, *kid.* e Heb. 11. 17. Jam. 2. 21. f 1 Sam. 15. 22. Mic. 6. 7, 8. g ch. 26. 5. Jam. 2. 22. || That is, *The LORD will see, or, provide.* h Ps. 105. 9. Ecclus. 44. 21. Luke 1. 73. Heb. 6. 13, 14. i ch. 15. 5. Jer. 33. 22. k ch. 13. 16.

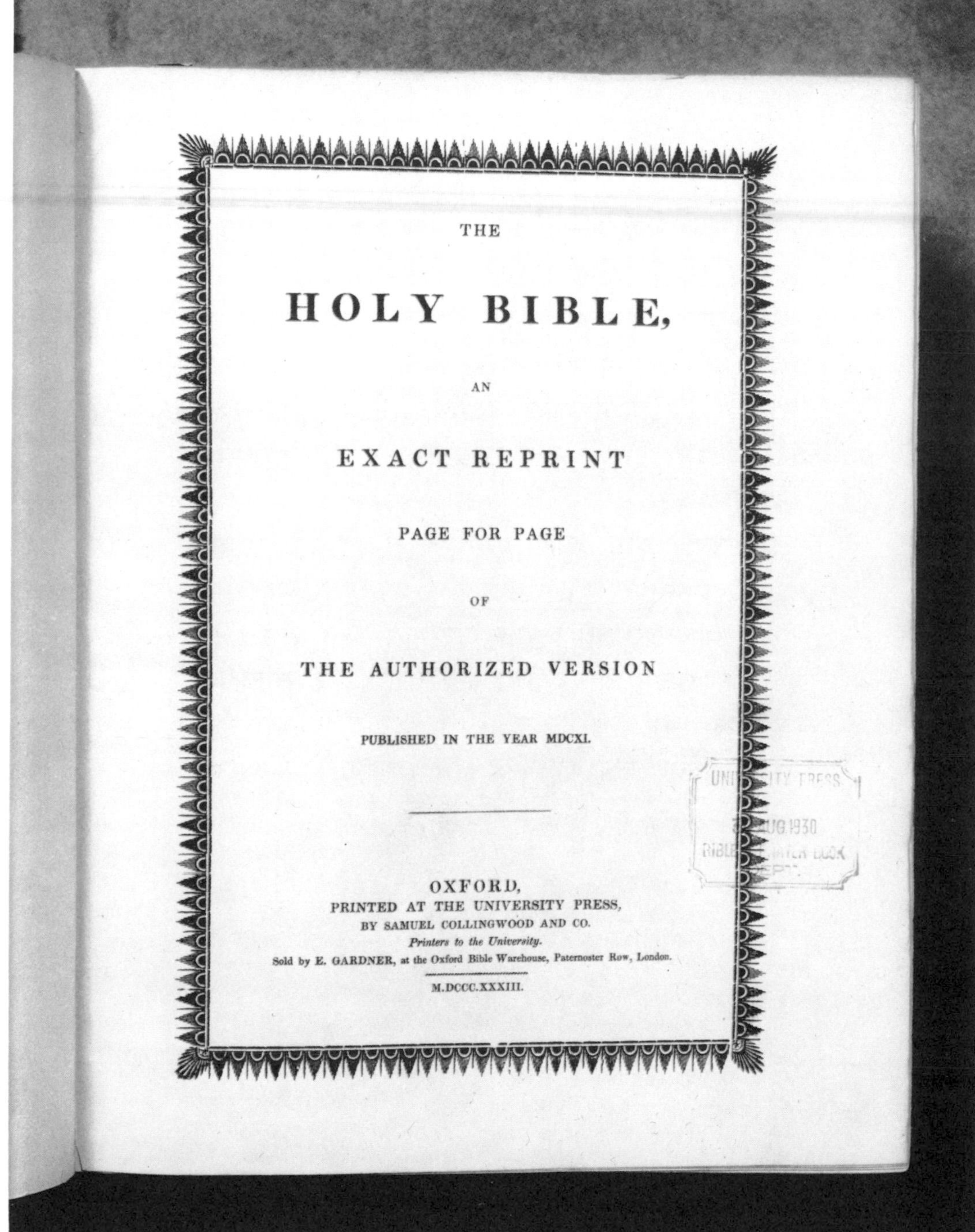

THE

HOLY BIBLE,

AN

EXACT REPRINT

PAGE FOR PAGE

OF

THE AUTHORIZED VERSION

PUBLISHED IN THE YEAR MDCXI.

OXFORD,
PRINTED AT THE UNIVERSITY PRESS,
BY SAMUEL COLLINGWOOD AND CO.
Printers to the University.
Sold by E. GARDNER, at the Oxford Bible Warehouse, Paternoster Row, London.

M.DCCC.XXXIII.

[42]तदाचार्य्येणोक्तं। भद्रं [43]कृतं [31]भवद्भिर् [44]यद् [36]अहं [45]जानामि तद् अहं [24]युष्मान् [46]अध्यापयिष्यामि। इति [47]कथयित्वा स तेषाम् [48]उपवेशनार्थम् [49]आसनानि [50]दापितवान् ॥ तेषु [51]विद्यार्थिषु [52]सुखम् [53]उपविष्टेषु वेदगर्भो विद्यागर्भं [54]स्वपुत्रम् [55]अवदत्। विद्यागर्भ [56]त्वम् [57]एतेषां सर्व्वेषां विद्यार्थिनां [58]निवासार्थं [59]प्रत्येकम् [60]मठं [61]दर्शयित्वा [62]देहि ॥ ततो विद्यागर्भो [63]गुरोर् [64]यथानिदेशं [65]तथानुष्ठितवान् ॥

अथ परेद्युः [66]प्रातः स्नात्वा [67]कृताह्निकः स आचार्य्यः [68]सपुत्रः पाठशालां [69]समेत्योपविष्टः ॥ तदा पुत्रेण [70]समाहूताः सर्व्वे [71]छात्राः पाठशालाम् आगताः ॥ तत आचर्य्यस् तान् [72]अपृच्छत्। [73]केषां किं शास्त्रम् [74]अध्ययनीयं? ॥ [75]केचित् प्रत्यूचुः। [76]अस्माकं वेदाः [77]पठनीयाः ॥ केचिद् ऊचुः। [76]अस्माभिः [78]स्मृतयोऽ[79]ध्येतव्याः ॥ केचिद् ऊचुः। वयं [80]तर्कान् [1]अध्येष्यामहे ॥ आचा-

42) for तदा आचार्य्येण उक्तं, r. 4. r. 5. r. 199. 43) p. 138. *b.* 44) r. 174. 45) p. 123. 46) 2d future, p. 88. 47) p. 144. *c.* 48) उपवेशन, "sitting down," p. 177. *c.* 49) acc. pl. neut. p. 32. 50) "He gave," p. 142. *a.* 51) locative absolute, r. 189. 52) p. 151. *a.* 53) p. 139. *i.* p. 174. 54) p. 53. r. 83. 55) 1st pret. of root *vad.* 56) p. 51. 57) r. 79. 58) p. 177. *c.* 59) "to each one," r. 171. *b.* 60) मठ, "a cell or student's apartment." 61) p. 144. *c.* p. 126. 62) p. 118. 63) gen. c. p. 35. Vis. changed to *r* by r. 27. *a.* 64) "according to the order," r. 171. *b.* 65) "he performed," root *sthā*, with prep. *anu* (p. 173.), see also p. 142. *a.* 66) प्रातर्, "in the morning," r. 31. 67) कृताह्निक, "having performed his daily prayers, or religious observances," r. 159. 68) r. 161. 69) "having arrived at," root *i*, with *sam* and *ā*, r. 166. p. 144. *a.* 70) p. 139. *e.* 71) छात्र, "a scholar." 72) r. 90. *a.* p. 111. 73) r. 186. *a.* 74) p. 113. p. 147. *b.* 75) p. 54. r. 85. 76) r. 215. and p. 50. 77) "are to be read," nom. pl. m. root पठ्. 78) nom. pl. of स्मृति, "law," as delivered by Manu and other legislators, p. 34. 79) p. 146. *a.* 80) acc. pl. of तर्क, "logical treatise." 1) 2d fut. ātm. of *i*, with *adhi*, p. 79. *e.*

RIG-VEDA-SANHITA,

THE

SACRED HYMNS OF THE BRAHMANS;

TOGETHER WITH THE

COMMENTARY OF SAYANACHARYA.

EDITED BY

DR. MAX MÜLLER.

VOLUME I.

PUBLISHED UNDER THE PATRONAGE OF

THE HONOURABLE THE EAST-INDIA-COMPANY.

LONDON,
W. H. ALLEN AND CO.,
BOOKSELLERS TO THE HONOURABLE THE EAST-INDIA-COMPANY,
7, LEADENHALL STREET.
1849.

1850

A
B
M
F
G
H
I
K
L
D
C

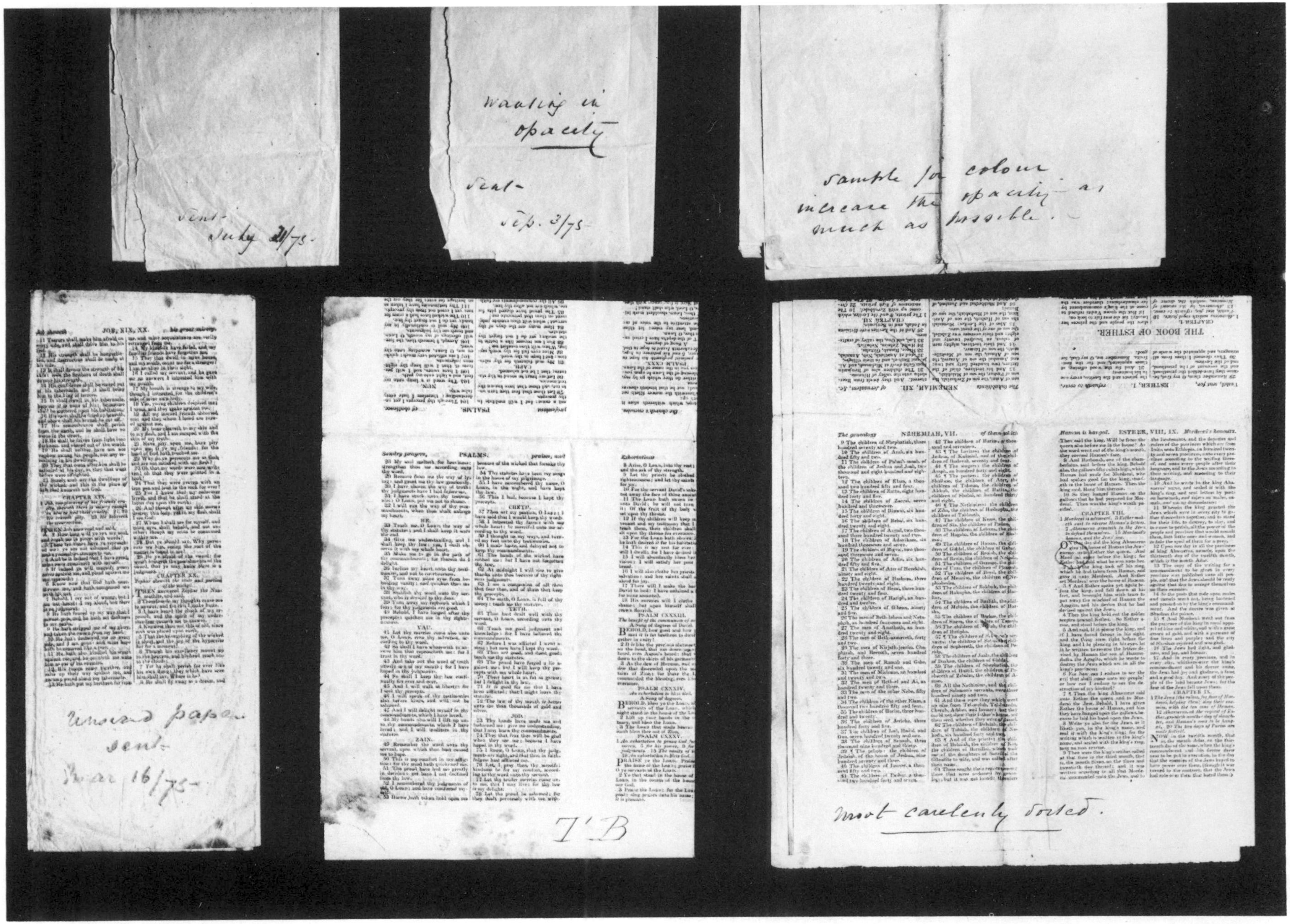

Sent-
July 21/75-

Wanting in
opacity

Sent-
Sep. 3/75

Sample for colour
increase the opacity as
much as possible.

Unsized paper
sent-
Mar 16/75-

T'B

Most carelessly sorted.

206

206A

A

GREEK-ENGLISH LEXICON

BASED ON

THE GERMAN WORK OF FRANCIS PASSOW.

BY

HENRY GEORGE LIDDELL, M.A.,
STUDENT OF CHRIST CHURCH;

AND

ROBERT SCOTT, M.A.,
SOMETIME STUDENT OF CHRIST CHURCH, AND LATE FELLOW OF BALLIOL COLLEGE.

OXFORD:
AT THE UNIVERSITY PRESS.
M.DCCC.XLIII.

ἀλεκτρῠοπώλης, ου, ὁ, = ἀλεκτρυονοπώλης, Lob. Phryn. 669.

ἀλεκτρῠοπωλητήριον, τό, *a poultry-market*, Phryn. (Com.) Cron. 4.

ἀλεκτρῠών, όνος, ὁ, ἡ, *a cock, hen*, Theogn. 862, etc.: ὁ ἀλ. ᾄδει 'tis cock-crow, Plat. Symp. 223 C.

ἀλέκτωρ, *ορος*, ὁ, *a cock, house-cock*, Pind. O. 12. 20, Simon. 130, etc. (akin to ἄλεκτρος, *the sleepless*.)

ἀλέκτωρ, ορος, ἡ, (α privat., λέγω) = ἄλεκτρος.

'ΑΛΕ'ΚΩ, less usu. form for ἀλέξω, *to ward off, avert*, τινί τι Anth.: hence comes the Homeric aor. med. ἀλέξασθαι, *to ward off from oneself, repel*, ἀλέξω, and ἄλκω.

ἀλέλαιον, τό, (ἅλς) *salted oil*, Hipp.

ἀλέματος, Dor. for ἠλέματος, Call. Cer. Cal. 90.

ἄλεν, Dor. and Ep. 3 pl. aor. 2 pass. from εἴλω, for ἐάλησαν, *they drew back, retired*, Il. 22. 12.

ἀλέν, v. ἀλείς.

ἀλεξαίθριος, ον, (ἀλέξω, αἴθρη) *skreening from the chill air*, Soph. Fr. 120.

'Αλεξανδρίζω, *to be like Alexander*, Ath.

'Αλεξανδριστής, ὁ, *a partisan of Alexander*, Plut.

'Αλεξανδροκόλαξ, ακος, ὁ, *a flatterer of Alexander*, Ath.

ἀλέξανδρος, ον, (ἀνήρ) *defending men*, πόλεμος Epigr. ap. Diod. 11. 4. II. *the usu. name of Paris* in Il.

'Αλεξανδρώδης, ες, (εἶδος) *Alexander-like*, Menand. p. 211.

ἀλεξανεμία, ἡ, *shelter from wind*, Polyb. Maii 2. 451: from

ἀλεξάνεμος, ον, *keeping off the wind, sheltering from it*, Od. 14. 529. [ξᾰ]

ἀλεξέω, = ἀλέξω, in pres. only Pind. O. 13. 12: for several tenses from it v. sub ἀλέξω.

ἀλέξημα, ατος, τό, *a defence, guard, help*, Aesch. Pr. 479: ἀλ. τινος or πρός τι, defence *against*.., Plut., and Dion. H.

ἀλεξήνωρ, ορος, ὁ, ἡ, (ἀνήρ) *aiding man*, esp. as epith. of Hephaistos and Aesculapius.

ἀλέξησις, εως, ἡ, *a keeping off, resistance*, Hdt. 9. 18: *a helping*, Hipp.

ἀλεξήτειρα, ἡ, Nonn., fem. from

ἀλεξητήρ, ῆρος, ὁ, *one who keeps off, a helper, guardian*, ἀλ. μάχης one who keeps the fight off the rest, a champion, Il. 20. 396: λοιμοῦ a protector from plague, Ap. Rh.: as Adj., ἀλ. θυμός Opp. Ep. word, used however by Xen. Oec. 4. 3. Hence

ἀλεξητήριος, ία, ιον, *fit* or *able to keep off, defend* or *help*, esp. as epith. of the gods, like Lat. *Averrunci*, Aesch. Theb. 8, Eur. H. F. 464: τὸ ἀλεξητήριον, sc. φάρμακον, *a help, remedy, medicine*, Hipp.: *a protection*, Xen.: *an amulet*, Theophr.

ἀλεξητικός, ή, όν, = ἀλεξητήριος.

ἀλεξήτωρ, ορος, ὁ, = ἀλεξητήρ, of Zeus, Soph. O. C. 143.

ἀλεξιάρη, ἡ, (ἀρά) *she that keeps off a curse*, or (from Ἄρης) *she that guards from death and ruin*, Hes. Op. 462, ἀλ. ῥάμνος a wand that served as an amulet, Nic. [ᾰρ]

ἀλεξιβέλεμνος, ον, (βέλεμνον) *keeping off darts*, Anth.

ἀλεξίγαμος, ον, *keeping off, shunning marriage*, Βάκχαι Nonn.

ἀλεξίκᾰκος, ον, *keeping off ill* or *mischief*, Il. 10. 20.

ἀλεξίλογος, ον, *promoting* or *supporting discourse*, γράμματα Critias Fr. 1. 9, dub.

ἀλεξίμβροτος, ον, *protecting mortals*, λόγχη Pind. N. 8. 51, πομπαί sacred processions to shield men from ill, Pind. P. 5. 122.

ἀλεξίμορος, ον, *warding off fate* or *death*, Soph. O. T. 164.

ἀλέξιμος, ον, = ἀλεξητήριος, Nic.

ἀλέξιον, τό, = ἀλεξητήριον, Nic.

ἄλεξις, εως, ἡ, *help*, Aristid.

ἀλεξιφάρμᾰκος, *keeping off poison, acting as an antidote*, Hipp.: τὸ ἀλεξιφάρμακον an antidote, Lat. *remedium*, Plat.: in gen. *a remedy*.

'ΑΛΕ'ΞΩ, or ἀλεξέω, q. v., fut. ἀλεξήσω, fut. med. ἀλεξήσομαι: aor. act. opt. ἀλεξήσειε Od., aor. inf. med. ἀλέξασθαι, part. ἀλεξάμενος, conj. ἀλεξώμεσθα, as if from ἀλέκω, Hom.:—to this must be referred the poet. aor. 2 ἤλαλκον, rarely ἄλαλκον, inf. ἀλαλκεῖν, as if from ἄλκω, Hom. *To ward* or *keep off, turn away* or *aside*, hence *to defend, assist, aid*:—Construct., c. dat. pers. et acc. rei, separately or together, as ἀλ. τινι *to help* one, Il. 3. 9, Ζεὺς τόγ' ἀλεξήσειε Od. 3. 346, but most freq. ἀλ. Δαναοῖς κακὸν ἦμαρ, ἀλλήλοις πόνον ἀλέξειν Il.: in Hdt. oft. absol.: cf. ἄλαλκε. Med. ἀλέξασθαί τινα, *to keep one off from oneself, defend oneself against* him, Lat. *defendere*, Il. 13. 475, Hdt. 7. 207, also ἀλέξασθαι περί τινι or τινος Ap. Rh.: also c. dat. instrum. Soph. O. T. 171, where Buttm. holds ἀλέξεται for fut., Ellendt for pres. Soph. is the only one of Trag. who has the word, and Xen. the chief authority in Att. prose.

ἀλέομαι, contr. ἀλεῦμαι (Theogn. 575), a defect. Med., whose Act. is only found in the form ἀλεύω: hence opt. ἀλέοιτο Il., part. ἀλεύμενος Simon. Amorg. 61: but chiefly used by Hom. in aor., as 3 sing. ἠλεύατο or ἀλεύατο Il., inf. ἀλέασθαι Il., ἀλεύασθαι Hes.; conj. ἀλέηται Od., also ἀλεύεται Od. 14. 400; opt. ἀλέαιτο Od.; imperat. ἄλευαι Il., ἀλέασθε Od., etc. *To avoid, shun*, usu. c. acc. rei, ἀλ. βέλος, θάνατον, etc., Hom., rarely c. acc. pers. as Od. 9. 274: also c. inf. *to avoid doing, omit to* do, Il. 23. 340, Od. 14. 400: absol. *to escape, flee*, Il. 5. 28, Od. 20. 305: *to neglect*, Hes. Op. 732: cf. ἀλεῦ.

ἀλεός, όν, Dor. for ἠλεός, Orph.

ἀλεότης, ητος, ἡ, (ἀλής) *an assemblage, assembly*, like ἄθροισις, Gal.

ἀλεόφρων, ον, gen. ονος, = Homer's φρένας ἠλεός.

ἀλεπίδωτος, ον, *without scales*, Opp. [ῐ]

ἀλέπιστος, ον, (λεπίζω) *without scales*, Archestr. ap. Ath. 311 B. II. *unpeeled*: of flax, *not hackled*.

ἄλεσις, εως, ἡ, (ἀλέω) *a grinding*.

ἀλεστέον, verb. Adj. from ἀλέω, *one must grind*, Diosc.

ἀλεστής, οῦ, ὁ, *a miller*, dub. in Joseph.

ἄλεται, Ep. for ἄληται, conj. aor. 2 of ἅλλομαι, *to leap*, Spitzn. Il. 11. 192.

ἀλέτης, ου, ὁ, *a grinder*, ἀλ. ὄνος a mill-stone, Xen. An. 1. 5, 5.

ἄλετος, ὁ, *a grinding, bruising, pounding*, Plut. II. = ἄλητον, ἄλευρον, late.

ἀλετρεύω, εύσω, strengthd. from ἀλέω, *to grind*, Od. 7. 104.

ἀλετρίβᾰνος, ὁ, (τρίβω) *that which grinds* or *pounds, a pestle*, Ar. Pac. 259, etc. [ᾰλ, ῐ]

ἀλετρίς, ίδος, ἡ, *a female slave who grinds corn*, Lat. *molitrix*, γυνὴ ἀλετρίς Od. 20. 105. 2. at Athens, *one of the noble maidens who prepared the meal* for the offering-cakes. II. *an insect found in mills*.

ἀλετών, ῶνος, ὁ, *a grinding place, mill*, Ath.

ἀλεῦ, or ἄλευ, prob. shortened for ἀλέου, imperf. from ἀλέομαι, *avoid! cease!* Aesch. Pr. 568.

ἀλευρίτης, ου, ὁ, *of wheaten flour* (ἄλευρον), Diph. Siphn. ap. Ath. 115 C.

ἀλευρομαντεῖον, τό, *divination from flour*, Oenom. ap. Euseb.

ἀλευρόμαντις, εως, ὁ, *one that divines from flour*, epith. of Apollo, Lob. Aglaoph. 2. 815.

ἄλευρον, τό, (ἀλέω) *wheaten flour*, in gen. *fine meal* or *flour*, usu. in plur., distinguished from ἄλφιτα Hdt. 7. 119, Plat., etc.

ἀλευροποιέω, *to make wheaten flour*.

ἀλευρότησις, εως, ἡ, (ἄλευρον) *a flour sieve*. II. *the flour sifted*, Gramm.

ἀλευρώδης, ες, *like flour*, Gal.

ἀλεύω, (ἄλη, ἀλέα I.) Act. very rare: *to remove, keep far away*, Aesch. Suppl. 528, Theb. 87, 141; fut. ἀλεύσω Soph. Fr. 825: the Med. ἀλεύομαι, = ἀλέομαι, in pres., Hes. Op. 533, the other forms v. sub ἀλέομαι.

'ΑΛΕ'Ω, f. έσω, imperf. ἤλουν: perf. act. Att. ἀλήλεκα, perf. pass. ἀλήλεσμαι Thuc. 4. 26, (where however Bekk. ἀλήλεμαι) Hdt. 7. 23, later ἤλεσμαι Diosc. *To grind, bruise, pound*, like ἀλέθω and ἀλήθω, κατὰ πυρὸν ἄλεσσαν Od. 20. 109: βίος ἀληλεμένος *a civilised* life, in which one uses ground corn and not raw fruits, v. Meineke ad Amph. Gynaecom. 1. (perh. akin to ἔλω, ὀλαί, οὐλαί, Lat. *mola, molere*, Buttm. Lexil. voc. εἰλεῖν 8.)

ἀλέω, = ἀλεύω, only used in Med. ἀλέομαι, q. v.

ἀλεωρή, ἡ, Att. ἀλεωρά, (ἀλέα, ἀλέομαι) *an avoiding, shunning, escaping*, Il. 24. 216: hence *a means of escape, defence, shelter, from* a person or thing, e. g. δηΐων ἀνδρῶν Il. 12. 57, of a breastplate, Il. 15. 533: absol. *a defence against* an enemy, *help, succour*, Hdt. 9. 6: *shelter*, Opp.

ἀλέως, Adv. from ἀλής, Hipp.

ἌΛΗ, ἡ, (ἀλάομαι) *a wandering* or *roaming* without home or hope of rest, Od.: also of the motion of ghosts, Soph. Fr. 693. 2. metaph. *a wandering of mind, distraction*, Lat.

GRÆCÆ GRAMMATICÆ

RUDIMENTA

IN USUM SCHOLARUM.

EDITIO QUINTA.

OXONII:

E TYPOGRAPHEO ACADEMICO.

MDCCCXLIV.

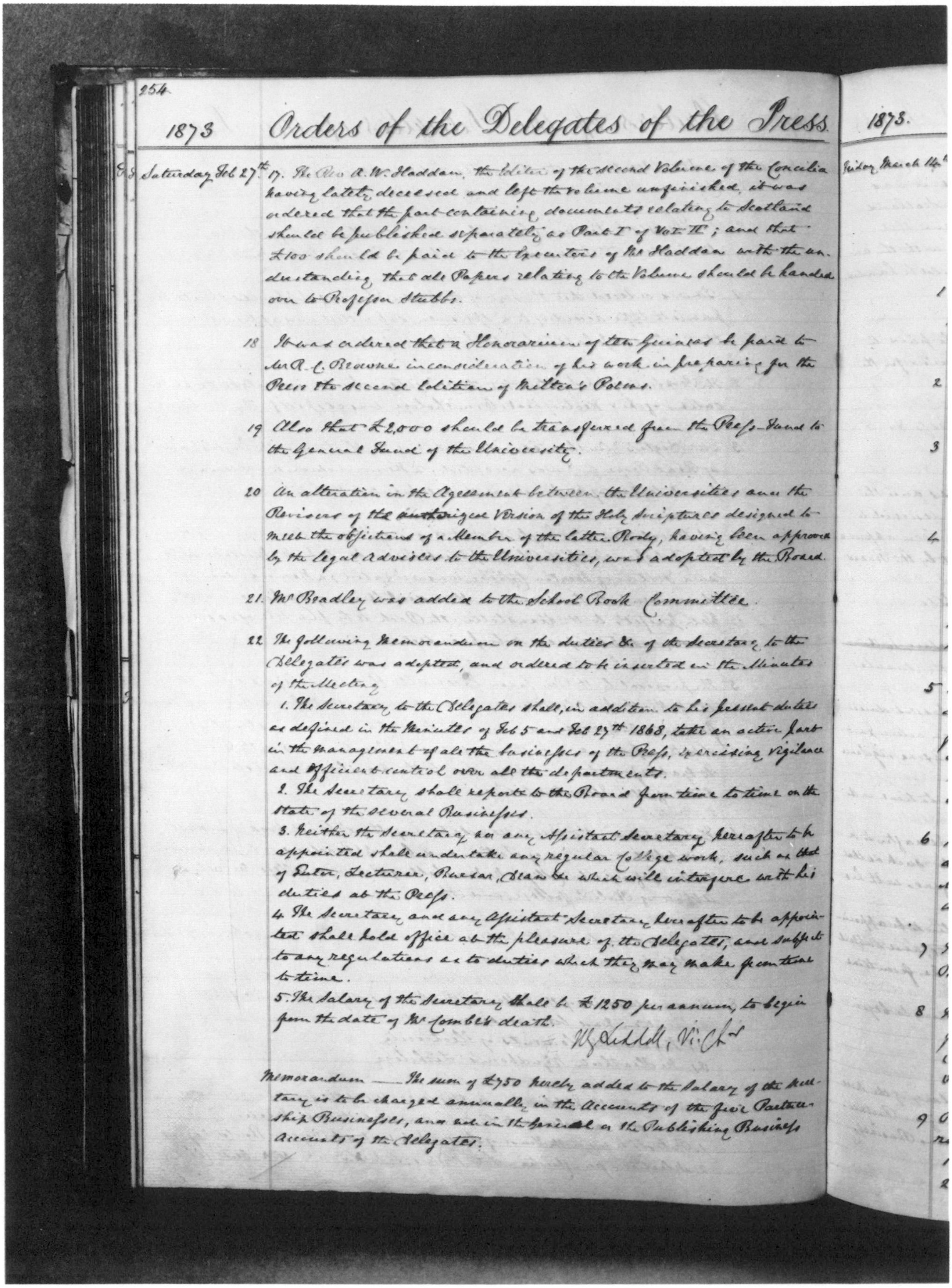

254

1873 Orders of the Delegates of the Press

Saturday Feb 27th

17. The Rev A. W. Haddan, the Editor of the Second Volume of the Concilia having lately deceased and left the volume unfinished, it was ordered that the part containing documents relating to Scotland should be published separately as Part I of Vol. II; and that £100 should be paid to the Executors of Mr Haddan with the understanding that all Papers relating to the Volume should be handed over to Professor Stubbs.

18 It was ordered that a Honorarium of ten Guineas be paid to Mr R. C. Browne in consideration of his work in preparing for the Press the second Edition of Milton's Poems.

19 Also that £2,000 should be transferred from the Press-Fund to the General Fund of the University.

20 An alteration in the Agreement between the Universities and the Revisers of the ~~authorized~~ Version of the Holy Scriptures designed to meet the objections of a Member of the latter Body, having been approved by the legal advisers to the Universities, was adopted by the Board.

21. Mr Bradley was added to the School Book Committee.

22 The following Memorandum on the duties &c of the Secretary to the Delegates was adopted, and ordered to be inserted in the Minutes of the Meeting

1. The Secretary to the Delegates shall, in addition to his present duties as defined in the Minutes of Feb 5 and Feb 27th 1868, take an active part in the management of all the businesses of the Press, exercising vigilance and efficient control over all the departments.

2. The Secretary shall report to the Board from time to time on the state of the several Businesses.

3. Neither the Secretary nor any Assistant Secretary hereafter to be appointed shall undertake any regular College work, such as that of Tutor, Lecturer, Bursar, Dean &c which will interfere with his duties at the Press.

4. The Secretary and any Assistant Secretary hereafter to be appointed shall hold office at the pleasure of the Delegates, and subject to any regulations as to duties which they may make from time to time.

5. The Salary of the Secretary shall be £1250 per annum, to begin from the date of Mr Combe's death.

H. G. Liddell, Vi. Chr

Memorandum — The sum of £750 hereby added to the Salary of the Secretary is to be charged annually in the Accounts of the five Partnership Businesses, and not in the General or the Publishing Business Accounts of the Delegates.

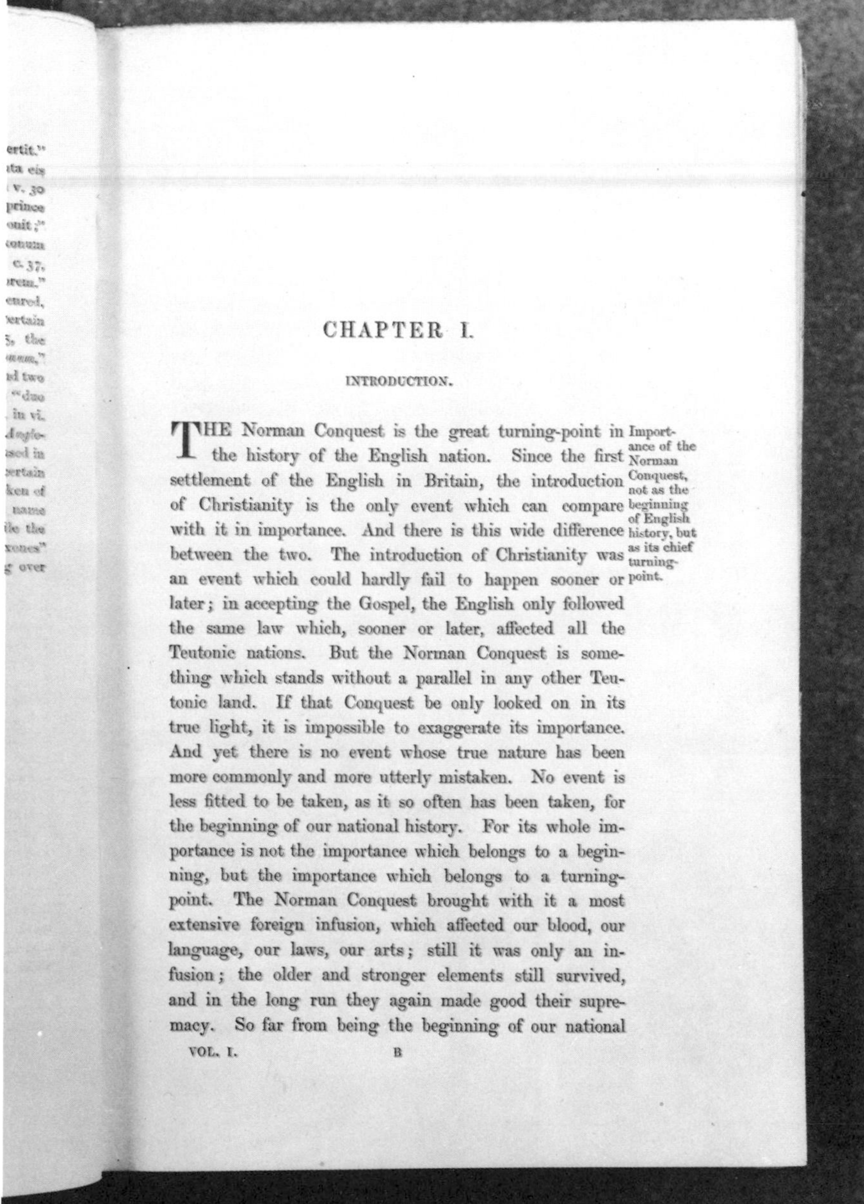

CHAPTER I.

INTRODUCTION.

Importance of the Norman Conquest, not as the beginning of English history, but as its chief turning-point.

THE Norman Conquest is the great turning-point in the history of the English nation. Since the first settlement of the English in Britain, the introduction of Christianity is the only event which can compare with it in importance. And there is this wide difference between the two. The introduction of Christianity was an event which could hardly fail to happen sooner or later; in accepting the Gospel, the English only followed the same law which, sooner or later, affected all the Teutonic nations. But the Norman Conquest is something which stands without a parallel in any other Teutonic land. If that Conquest be only looked on in its true light, it is impossible to exaggerate its importance. And yet there is no event whose true nature has been more commonly and more utterly mistaken. No event is less fitted to be taken, as it so often has been taken, for the beginning of our national history. For its whole importance is not the importance which belongs to a beginning, but the importance which belongs to a turning-point. The Norman Conquest brought with it a most extensive foreign infusion, which affected our blood, our language, our laws, our arts; still it was only an infusion; the older and stronger elements still survived, and in the long run they again made good their supremacy. So far from being the beginning of our national

VOL. I. B

THE

DIALOGUES OF PLATO

Translated into English

WITH ANALYSES AND INTRODUCTIONS

BY

B. JOWETT, M.A.

MASTER OF BALLIOL COLLEGE

REGIUS PROFESSOR OF GREEK IN THE UNIVERSITY OF OXFORD

IN FOUR VOLUMES

VOL. I

Oxford

AT THE CLARENDON PRESS

M DCCC LXXI

Clarendon Press Series

A TREATISE

ON

ELECTRICITY AND MAGNETISM

BY

JAMES CLERK MAXWELL, M.A.

LLD. EDIN., F.R.SS. LONDON AND EDINBURGH

HONORARY FELLOW OF TRINITY COLLEGE,

AND PROFESSOR OF EXPERIMENTAL PHYSICS

IN THE UNIVERSITY OF CAMBRIDGE

VOL. I

Oxford

AT THE CLARENDON PRESS

1873

Clarendon Press Series

PRINCIPLES

OF THE

ENGLISH LAW OF CONTRACT

BY

SIR WILLIAM R. ANSON, BART., M.A., B.C.L.

OF THE INNER TEMPLE, BARRISTER AT LAW

VINERIAN READER OF ENGLISH LAW

FELLOW OF ALL SOULS' COLLEGE, OXFORD

Oxford

AT THE CLARENDON PRESS

1879

JOHANNES MÜLLER

ON CERTAIN VARIATIONS

IN THE

VOCAL ORGANS

OF THE

PASSERES

THAT HAVE HITHERTO ESCAPED NOTICE

THE TRANSLATION

BY

F. JEFFREY BELL, B.A.

EXHIBITIONER OF MAGDALEN COLLEGE, OXFORD

EDITED, WITH AN APPENDIX

BY

A. H. GARROD, M.A., F.R.S.

FELLOW OF ST. JOHN'S COLLEGE, CAMBRIDGE

Oxford

AT THE CLARENDON PRESS

M DCCC LXXVIII

228, 229, 230, 231

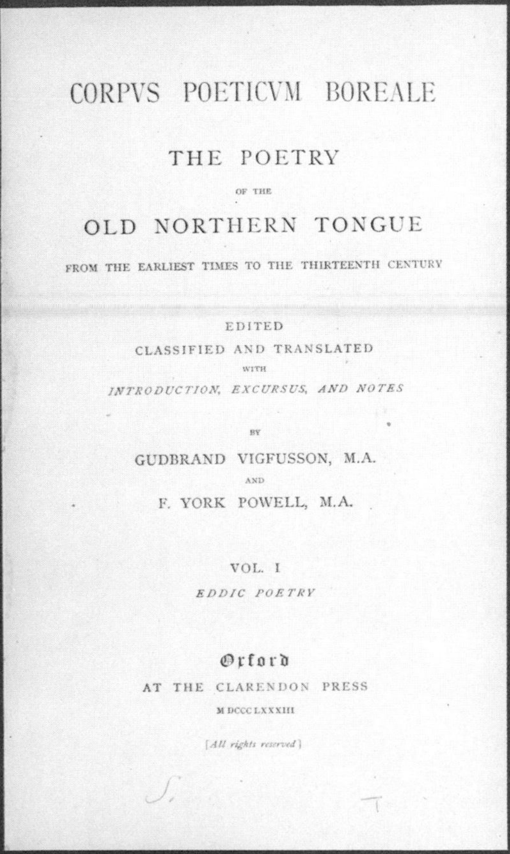

CORPVS POETICVM BOREALE

THE POETRY

OF THE

OLD NORTHERN TONGUE

FROM THE EARLIEST TIMES TO THE THIRTEENTH CENTURY

EDITED

CLASSIFIED AND TRANSLATED

WITH

INTRODUCTION, EXCURSUS, AND NOTES

BY

GUDBRAND VIGFUSSON, M.A.

AND

F. YORK POWELL, M.A.

VOL. I

EDDIC POETRY

Oxford

AT THE CLARENDON PRESS

M DCCC LXXXIII

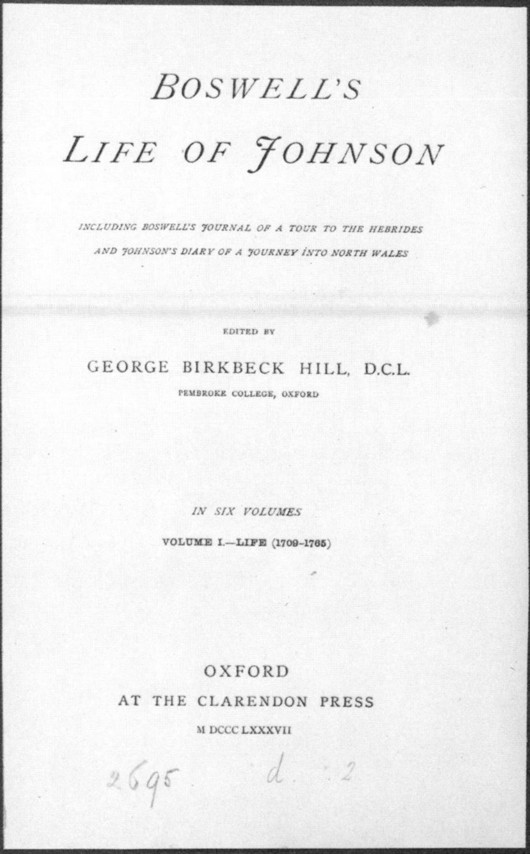

BOSWELL'S

LIFE OF JOHNSON

INCLUDING BOSWELL'S JOURNAL OF A TOUR TO THE HEBRIDES

AND JOHNSON'S DIARY OF A JOURNEY INTO NORTH WALES

EDITED BY

GEORGE BIRKBECK HILL, D.C.L.

PEMBROKE COLLEGE, OXFORD

IN SIX VOLUMES

VOLUME I.—LIFE (1709–1765)

OXFORD

AT THE CLARENDON PRESS

M DCCC LXXXVII

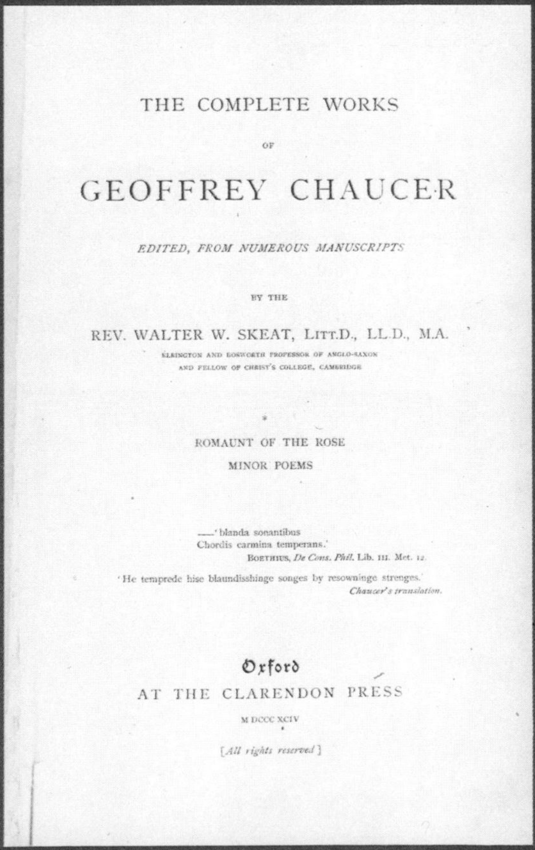

THE COMPLETE WORKS

OF

GEOFFREY CHAUCER

EDITED, FROM NUMEROUS MANUSCRIPTS

BY THE

REV. WALTER W. SKEAT, LITT.D., LL.D., M.A.

ELRINGTON AND BOSWORTH PROFESSOR OF ANGLO-SAXON

AND FELLOW OF CHRIST'S COLLEGE, CAMBRIDGE

ROMAUNT OF THE ROSE

MINOR POEMS

——'blanda sonantibus
Chordis carmina temperans.'

BOETHIUS, *De Cons. Phil.* Lib. III. Met. 12.

'He temprede hise blaundisshinge songes by resowninge strenges.'

Chaucer's translation.

Oxford

AT THE CLARENDON PRESS

M DCCC XCIV

232, 233, 234

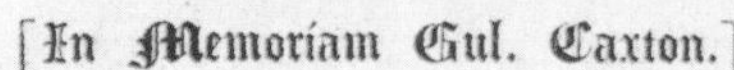
[In Memoriam Gul. Caxton.]

The

Holy Bible,

containing the

Old and New Testaments:

Translated out of the Original Tongues: and with the former
Translations diligently compared and revised,
by His Majesty's special Command.

Appointed to be read in Churches.

Oxford:
Printed at the University Press.
London: Henry Frowde,
Oxford University Press Warehouse, 7, Paternoster Row.
New York: 42, Bleecker Street.

Minion 16mo. JUNE 30, 1877. Cum Privilegio.

V.

VIVAMUS, mea Lesbia, atque amemus,
Rumoresque senum seueriorum
Omnes unius aestimemus assis.

Soles occidere et redire possunt:
Nobis cum semel occidit breuis lux,
Nox est perpetua una dormienda.

Da mi basia mille, deinde centum,
Dein mille altera, dein secunda centum,
Deinde usque altera mille, deinde centum.

Dein, cum milia multa fecerimus,
Conturba*b*imus illa, ne sciamus,
Aut ne quis malus inuidere possit,
Cum tantum sciat esse basiorum.

V.

Carmen in quatuor strophas diuisi monente Ribbeckio. Quarta stropha 4 *uersuum est, non ut ceterae trium.*

AD LESBIAM *ABDGHLLa*^{1}*L*^{2} *ab*. *Spatium unius uersus in OV.*

3. extimemus *BCDGLa*^{1}*V ab* axis *BCVLa*^{1} *a m. pr. bc* asses *b*^{2}.

4. ocidere *Ob*^{2} ridere *H*.

5. Nobiscum *G et codices plerique; correxerunt Itali.* Nobis, cum *editiones pleraeque; interpunctionem cum Klotzio deleui.*

7. my *b*^{2} mihi *AHLLa*^{1} *ab* baxia *H* bassia *La*^{1} *b* mile *H*.

8. *om A* Deinde mi altera da secunda centum *G, et sic, sed sine spatiis BCHLa*^{1}*La*^{2}*V Phillippensis Riccardianus abc, ed. Pr.* Deinde me altera da secunda centum *D* Deinde (dein *b*^{2}) mille altera deinde s. centum *LOb*^{2} Deinde mille altera da s. c. *b* *Hinc in* A *suspicor scriptum fuisse* Dein (dein) ml' altera da secunda centum Dein (*ed. Pr.*) mille altera da s. c. *Calpurnius Guar. Sillig.* Dein m. a. dein s. c. *Puccius Ald. uulgo et Lachm.* Deinde mi altera mille, deinde centum, *Heysius.*

9. *om V* mile *Ha.*

10. Deinde *ABCDGHLLa*^{1}*La*^{2}*OV bab*^{2} Dein *bc ex correctione Italorum* multa milia *A* multa alia mille *b*.

11. Conturbauimus *ABCDGHLa*^{1} *a m. pr. OV a* Conturbabemus *b* Contribuamus *b*^{2} Conturbabimus *bc corr. La*^{1}.

nesciamus *codices omnes sinceri* ne sciamus *b, ed. Pr.*

Post u. 11 *unum uersum excidisse, uu.* 12, 13 *delendos esse tamquam spurios, ut carmen quatuor strophas contineat, trium singulam uersuum, censet Th. Maurer in Nou. Mus. Rhen. XIV. p.* 323.

12. At *V*.

13. tantus *CGHO* tantu *La*^{1}. *Scriptum fuerat in* A tantusciat sciet *Buechelerus ex Priap. LII.* 12, 'Cum tantum sciet esse mentularum.' bassiorum *b* *Versum delent Ribbeckius, G. Richterus in Mus. Rhen. XIX.* 363.

RACHEL! babe, whoſe frolic ſmile
Might a ſtoic's frown beguile,
Thou ſmall quinteſſential thing,
That doſt heaven to mortals bring,
Cradled from the world's alarms
In a mother's tender arms,
Stretch thy dimpled hands and crow—
Voiceleſs love finds paſſage ſo.

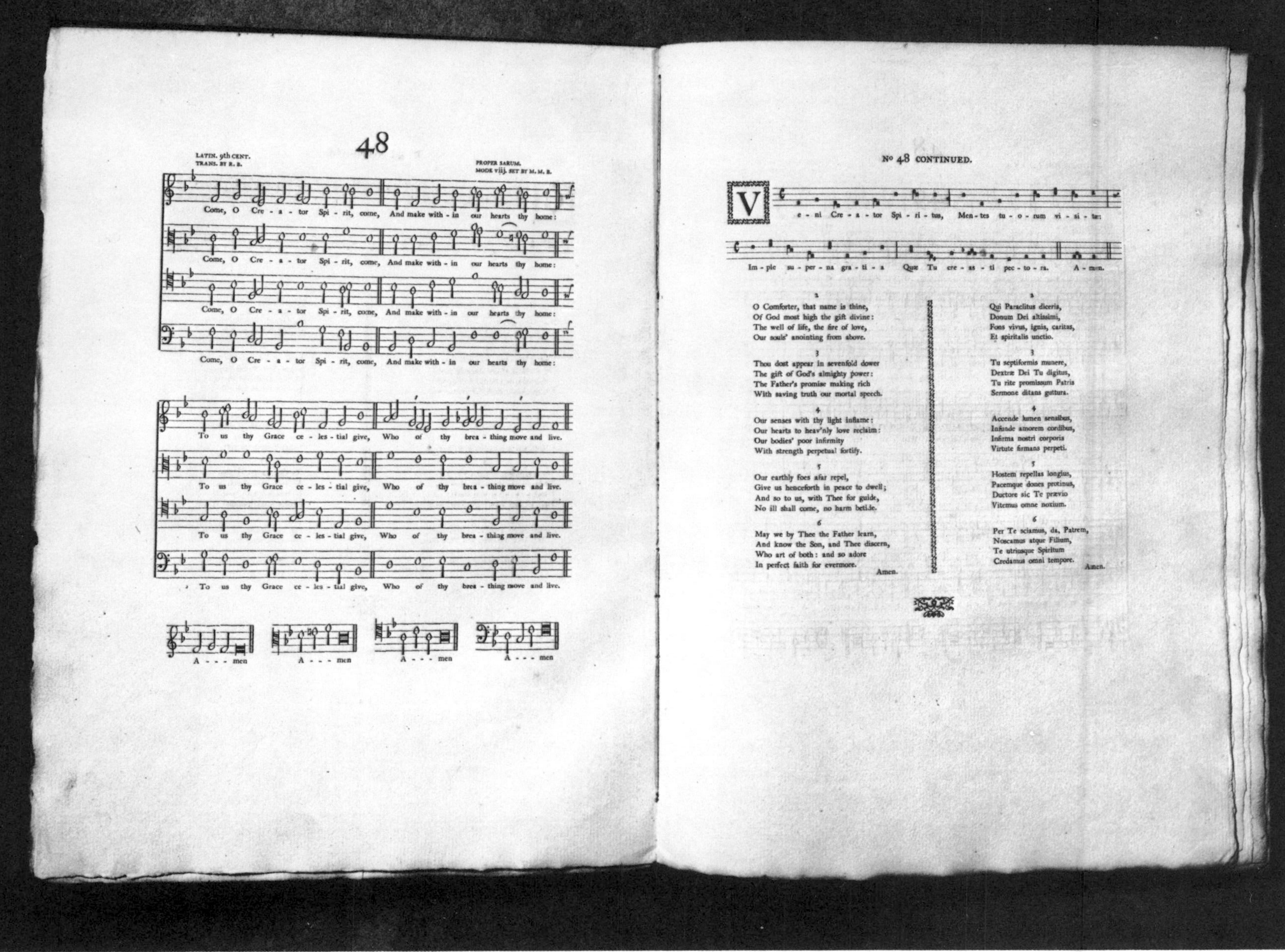

2

O Comforter, that name is thine,
Of God most high the gift divine:
The well of life, the fire of love,
Our souls' anointing from above.

2

Qui Paraclitus diceris,
Donum Dei altissimi,
Fons vivus, ignis, caritas,
Et spiritalis unctio.

3

Thou dost appear in sevenfold dower
The gift of God's almighty power:
The Father's promise making rich
With saving truth our mortal speech.

3

Tu septiformis munere,
Dextræ Dei Tu digitus,
Tu rite promissum Patris
Sermone ditans guttura.

4

Our senses with thy light inflame:
Our hearts to heav'nly love reclaim:
Our bodies' poor infirmity
With strength perpetual fortify.

4

Accende lumen sensibus,
Infunde amorem cordibus,
Infirma nostri corporis
Virtute firmans perpeti.

5

Our earthly foes afar repel,
Give us henceforth in peace to dwell;
And so to us, with Thee for guide,
No ill shall come, no harm betide.

5

Hostem repellas longius,
Pacemque dones protinus,
Ductore sic Te prævio
Vitemus omne noxium.

6

May we by Thee the Father learn,
And know the Son, and Thee discern,
Who art of both: and so adore
In perfect faith for evermore.
Amen.

6

Per Te sciamus, da, Patrem,
Noscamus atque Filium,
Te utriusque Spiritum
Credamus omni tempore.
Amen.

Prefatory Notes

(*See p.* 114.)

F THE READER of these Prefatory Notes shall ask, as he reasonably may, why the *Century of Oxford Typography* with which we are here concerned begins at 1693 and ends at 1794, the answer is that no printed *Specimen* of types was issued by the Oxford Press before the earlier and none after the later date—or, at any rate, if any were issued no copies are known. In those days, as in these, a Printing House issued Type *Specimens* in order that authors might be able to choose suitable characters in which their works could be printed; while a Type Foundry issued impressions from Types to show what characters it had to sell. The Oxford Press has been from early times both Printing House and Type Foundry, but its *Specimens* were issued probably for the first reason only.

The earliest Oxford printing was executed with characters brought from Cologne; and when FELL and JUNIUS in the seventeenth century were seeking for types for the University Press, they sent to 'Germany, France, and Holland' for them[1]. Type-founding was not authorized in England before 1637; and

[1] This is Dr. Fell's own statement. See his report drawn up in 1679, Gutch, *Collectanea Curiosa* (Clarendon Press, 1781), vol. i. p. 271.

The following is from p. 278 of the *Calendar of State Papers, Domestic*, relating to the year 1672: '*June* 26, 1672. . . . the Dean of Christ Church' [Dr. Fell] 'requests that you would recommend

according

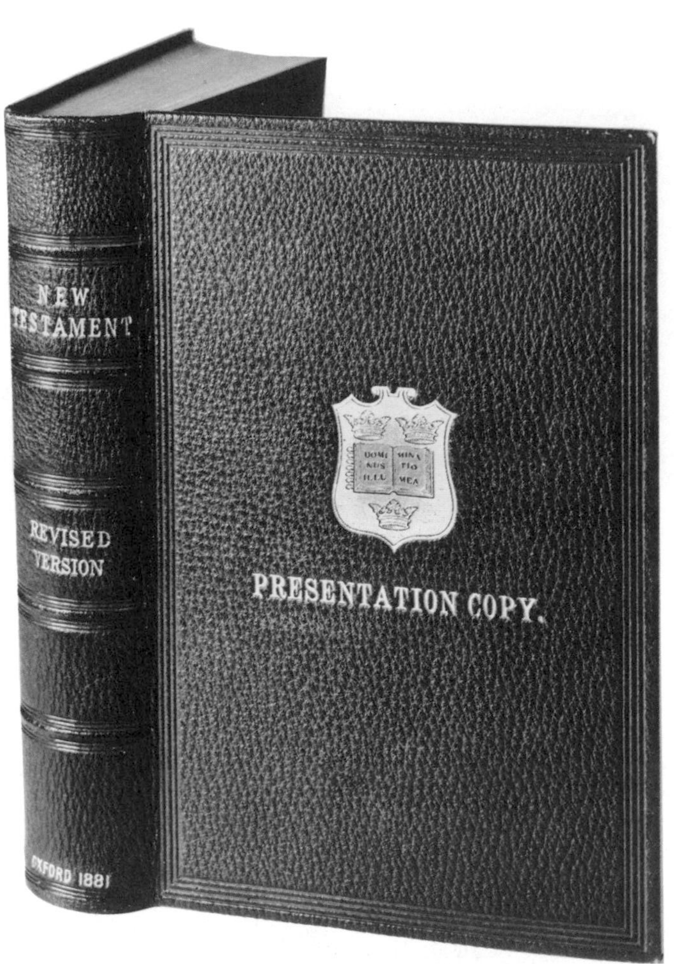

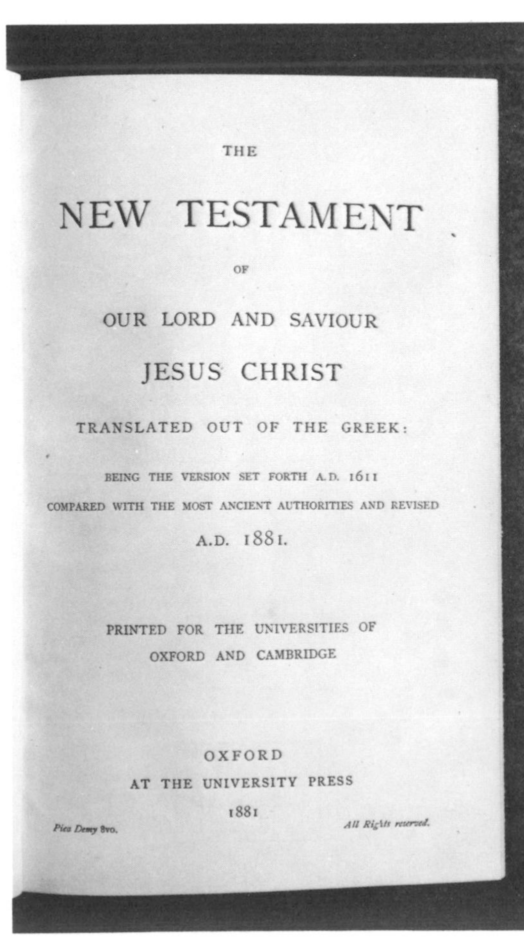

THE

NEW TESTAMENT

OF

OUR LORD AND SAVIOUR

JESUS CHRIST

TRANSLATED OUT OF THE GREEK:

BEING THE VERSION SET FORTH A.D. 1611

COMPARED WITH THE MOST ANCIENT AUTHORITIES AND REVISED

A.D. 1881.

PRINTED FOR THE UNIVERSITIES OF
OXFORD AND CAMBRIDGE

OXFORD
AT THE UNIVERSITY PRESS
1881

Pica Demy 8vo. *All Rights reserved.*

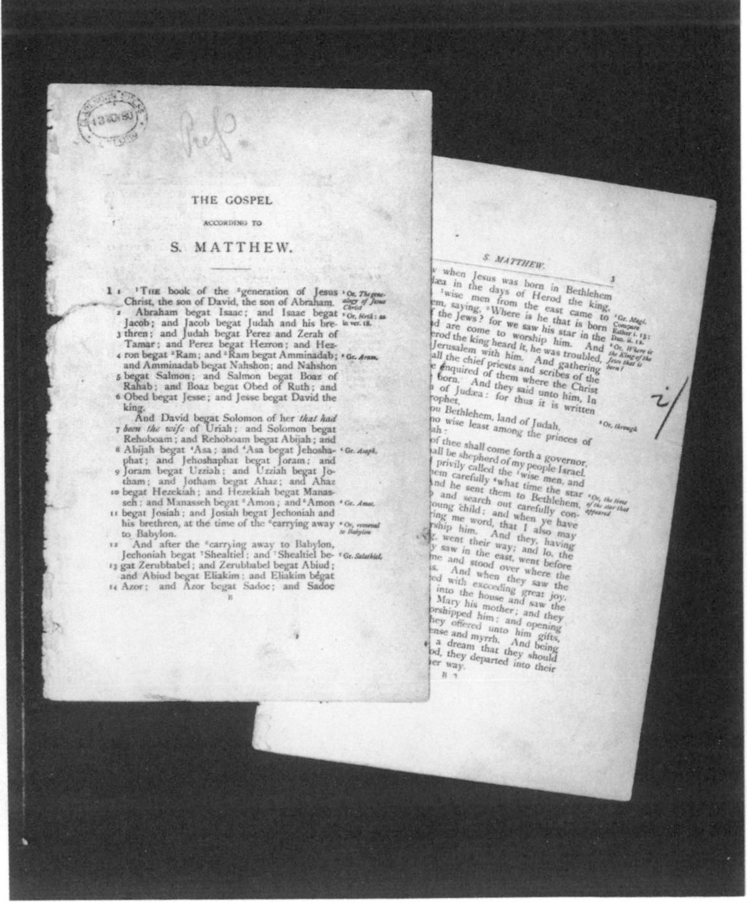

THE GOSPEL

ACCORDING TO

S. MATTHEW.

1 1 [1]The book of the [2]generation of Jesus
Christ, the son of David, the son of Abraham.
2 Abraham begat Isaac; and Isaac begat
Jacob; and Jacob begat Judah and his bre-
3 thren; and Judah begat Perez and Zerah of
Tamar; and Perez begat Hezron; and Hez-
4 ron begat [3]Ram; and [3]Ram begat Amminadab;
and Amminadab begat Nahshon; and Nahshon
5 begat Salmon; and Salmon begat Boaz of
Rahab; and Boaz begat Obed of Ruth; and
6 Obed begat Jesse; and Jesse begat David the
king.
And David begat Solomon of her *that had*
7 *been the wife* of Uriah; and Solomon begat
Rehoboam; and Rehoboam begat Abijah; and
8 Abijah begat [4]Asa; and [4]Asa begat Jehoshaphat; and Jehoshaphat begat Joram; and
9 Joram begat Uzziah; and Uzziah begat Jotham; and Jotham begat Ahaz; and Ahaz
10 begat Hezekiah; and Hezekiah begat Manasseh; and Manasseh begat [5]Amon; and [5]Amon
11 begat Josiah; and Josiah begat Jechoniah and
his brethren, at the time of the [6]carrying away
to Babylon.
12 And after the [6]carrying away to Babylon,
Jechoniah begat [7]Shealtiel; and [7]Shealtiel be-
13 gat Zerubbabel; and Zerubbabel begat Abiud;
and Abiud begat Eliakim; and Eliakim begat
14 Azor; and Azor begat Sadoc; and Sadoc

B

[1] *Or, The genealogy of Jesus Christ*
[2] *Or, birth: as in ver. 18.*
[3] *Gr. Aram.*
[4] *Gr. Asaph.*
[5] *Gr. Amos.*
[6] *Or, removal to Babylon*
[7] *Gr. Salathiel.*

S. MATTHEW.

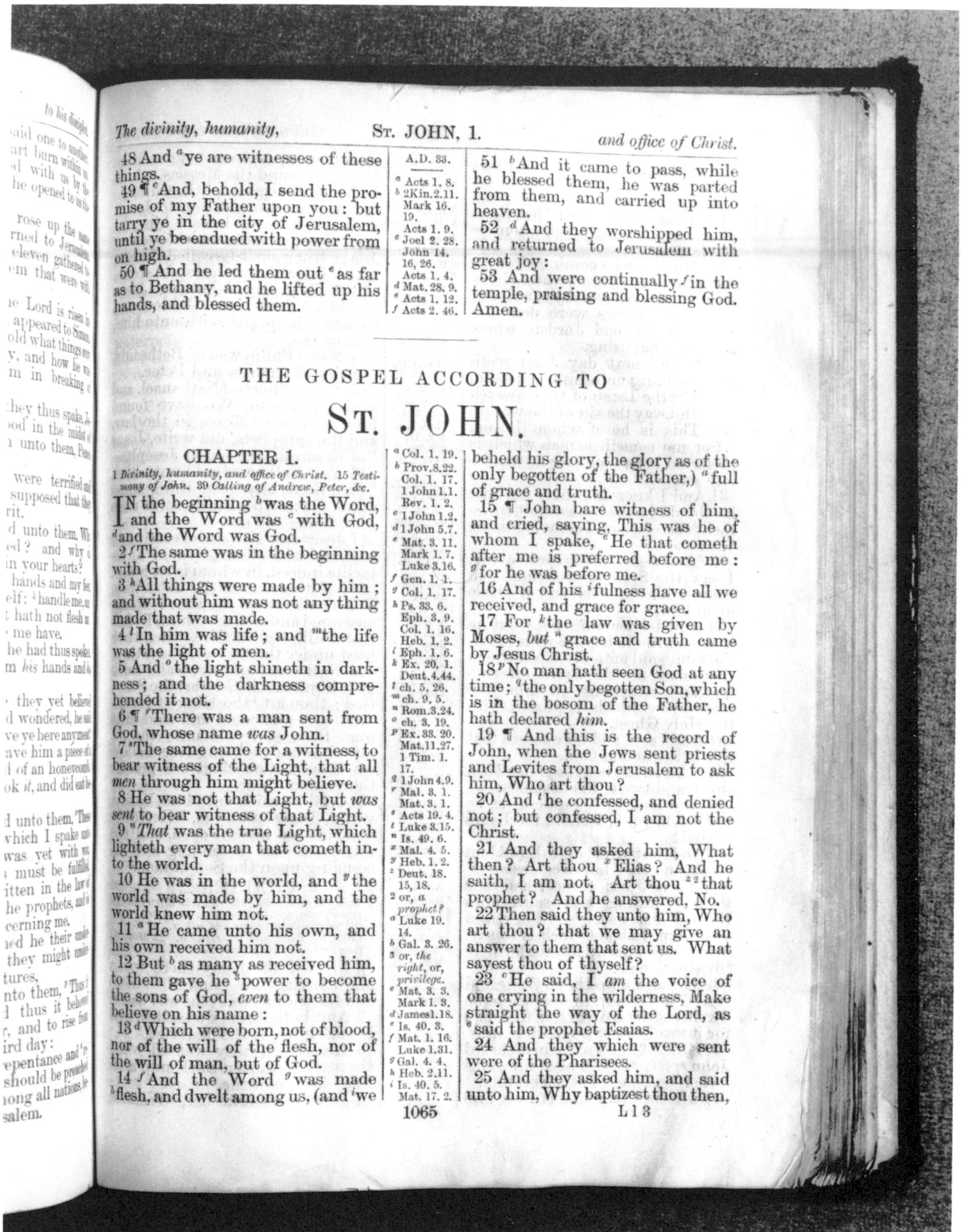

48 And [a]ye are witnesses of these
things.
49 ¶ [c]And, behold, I send the promise of my Father upon you: but
tarry ye in the city of Jerusalem,
until ye be endued with power from
on high.
50 ¶ And he led them out [e]as far
as to Bethany, and he lifted up his
hands, and blessed them.
51 [b]And it came to pass, while
he blessed them, he was parted
from them, and carried up into
heaven.
52 [d]And they worshipped him,
and returned to Jerusalem with
great joy:
53 And were continually [f]in the
temple, praising and blessing God.
Amen.

A.D. 33.

[a] Acts 1. 8.
[b] 2Kin.2.11. Mark 16. 19. Acts 1. 9.
[c] Joel 2. 28. John 14. 16, 26. Acts 1. 4.
[d] Mat. 28. 9.
[e] Acts 1. 12.
[f] Acts 2. 46.

THE GOSPEL ACCORDING TO ST. JOHN.

CHAPTER 1.

1 Divinity, humanity, and office of Christ. 15 Testimony of John. 39 Calling of Andrew, Peter, &c.

IN the beginning [b]was the Word,
and the Word was [c]with God,
[d]and the Word was God.
2 [f]The same was in the beginning
with God.
3 [h]All things were made by him;
and without him was not any thing
made that was made.
4 [l]In him was life; and [m]the life
was the light of men.
5 And [o]the light shineth in darkness; and the darkness comprehended it not.
6 ¶ [r]There was a man sent from
God, whose name *was* John.
7 [s]The same came for a witness, to
bear witness of the Light, that all
men through him might believe.
8 He was not that Light, but *was*
sent to bear witness of that Light.
9 [u]*That* was the true Light, which
lighteth every man that cometh into the world.
10 He was in the world, and [y]the
world was made by him, and the
world knew him not.
11 [a]He came unto his own, and
his own received him not.
12 But [b]as many as received him,
to them gave he [3]power to become
the sons of God, *even* to them that
believe on his name:
13 [d]Which were born, not of blood,
nor of the will of the flesh, nor of
the will of man, but of God.
14 [f]And the Word [g]was made
[h]flesh, and dwelt among us, (and [i]we
beheld his glory, the glory as of the
only begotten of the Father,) [a]full
of grace and truth.
15 ¶ John bare witness of him,
and cried, saying, This was he of
whom I spake, [e]He that cometh
after me is preferred before me:
[g]for he was before me.
16 And of his [i]fulness have all we
received, and grace for grace.
17 For [k]the law was given by
Moses, *but* [n]grace and truth came
by Jesus Christ.
18 [p]No man hath seen God at any
time; [q]the only begotten Son, which
is in the bosom of the Father, he
hath declared *him*.
19 ¶ And this is the record of
John, when the Jews sent priests
and Levites from Jerusalem to ask
him, Who art thou?
20 And [t]he confessed, and denied
not; but confessed, I am not the
Christ.
21 And they asked him, What
then? Art thou [x]Elias? And he
saith, I am not. Art thou [z][2]that
prophet? And he answered, No.
22 Then said they unto him, Who
art thou? that we may give an
answer to them that sent us. What
sayest thou of thyself?
23 [c]He said, I *am* the voice of
one crying in the wilderness, Make
straight the way of the Lord, as
[e]said the prophet Esaias.
24 And they which were sent
were of the Pharisees.
25 And they asked him, and said
unto him, Why baptizest thou then,

[a] Col. 1. 19.
[b] Prov.8.22. Col. 1. 17. 1 John 1.1. Rev. 1. 2.
[c] 1 John 1.2.
[d] 1 John 5.7.
[e] Mat. 3. 11. Mark 1. 7. Luke 3.16.
[f] Gen. 1. 1.
[g] Col. 1. 17.
[h] Ps. 33. 6. Eph. 3. 9. Col. 1. 16. Heb. 1. 2.
[i] Eph. 1. 6.
[k] Ex. 20. 1. Deut.4.44.
[l] ch. 5. 26.
[m] ch. 9. 5.
[n] Rom.3.24.
[o] ch. 3. 19.
[p] Ex. 33. 20. Mat.11.27. 1 Tim. 1. 17.
[q] 1 John 4.9.
[r] Mal. 3. 1. Mat. 3. 1.
[s] Acts 19. 4.
[t] Luke 3.15.
[u] Is. 49. 6.
[x] Mal. 4. 5.
[y] Heb. 1. 2.
[z] Deut. 18. 15, 18.
[2] or, *a prophet?*
[a] Luke 19. 14.
[b] Gal. 3. 26.
[3] or, *the right*, or, *privilege*.
[c] Mat. 3. 3. Mark 1. 3.
[d] James1.18.
[e] Is. 40. 3.
[f] Mat. 1. 16. Luke 1.31.
[g] Gal. 4. 4.
[h] Heb. 2.11.
[i] Is. 40. 5. Mat. 17. 2.

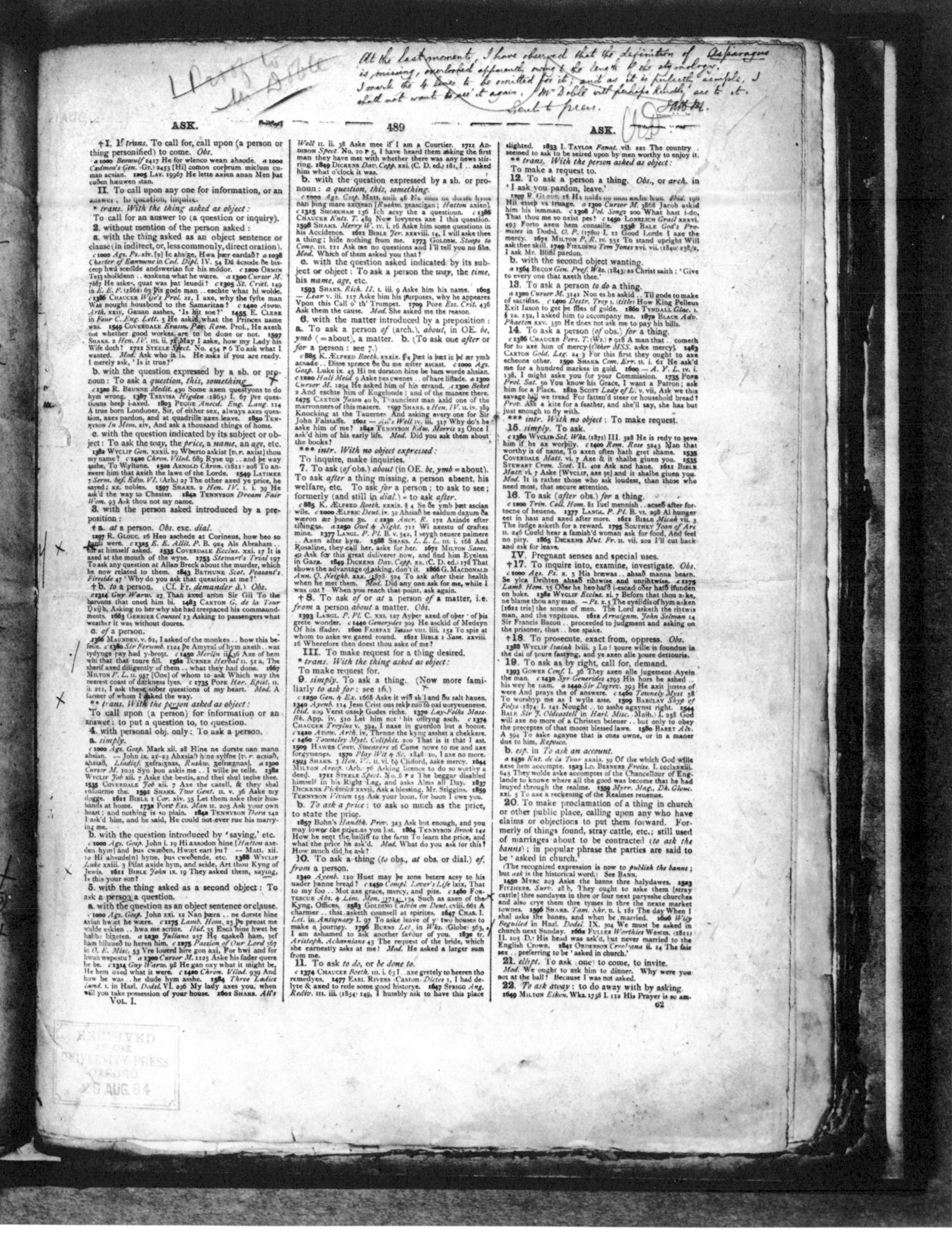

At the last moment, I have observed that the definition of Asparagus is missing, overlooked apparently owing to the length of the etymology. I mark the 4 lines to be omitted for it; and as it is perfectly simple, I shall not want to see it again. Mr Doble will perhaps kindly see to it. JAHM.

Sent to press.

†I. 1. *trans.* To call for, call upon (a person or thing personified) to come. *Obs.*

a 1000 *Beowulf* 2417 He for wlenco wean ahsode. a 1000 *Cædmon's Gen.* (Gr.) 2453 [Hi] comon corþrum miclum cuman acsian. 1205 LAY. 19967 He lette axien anan Men þat cuðen hæuwen stan.

II. To call upon any one for information, or an answer; to question, inquire.

* *trans. With the thing asked as object:*

To call for an answer to (a question or inquiry).

2. without mention of the person asked:

a. with the thing asked as an object sentence or clause (in indirect, or, less commonly, direct oration).

c 1000 *Ags. Ps.* xiv. [2] Ic ahsige, Hwa þær eardað? a 1038 *Charter of Eanwene* in *Cod. Dipl.* IV. 54 Ðá ácsode ðe biscеop hwá sceólde andswerian for his módor. c 1200 ORMIN Te33 sholldenn .. asskenn what he wære. a 1300 *Cursor M.* 7887 He askes, quat was þat leuedi? c 1305 *St. Criet.* 149 in *E. E. P.* (1862) 63 Þis gode man .. eschte what hi wolde. c 1386 CHAUCER *Wife's Prol.* 21, I axe, why the fyfte man Was nought housbond to the Samaritan? c 1420 *Avow. Arth.* xxiv, Gauan asshes, 'Is hit soe?' 1455 E. CLERE in *Four C. Eng. Lett.* 5 He askid what the Princes name was. 1549 COVERDALE *Erasm. Par. Rom.* Prol., He axeth not whether good workes are to be done or not. 1597 SHAKS. 2 *Hen. IV*, III. ii. 71 May I aske, how my Lady his Wife doth? 1711 STEELE *Spect.* No. 454 ¶ 6 To ask what I wanted. *Mod.* Ask who it is. He asks if you are ready. I merely ask, 'Is it true?'

b. with the question expressed by a sb. or pronoun: To ask a *question, this, something.*

c 1320 R. BRUNNE *Medit.* 430 Some axen questyons to do hym wrong. 1387 TREVISA *Higden* (1865) I. 67 Þre questiouns beeþ i-axed. 1803 PEGGE *Anecd. Eng. Lang.* 114 A true born Londoner, Sir, of either sex, always axes question, axes pardon, and at quadrille axes leave. 1850 TENNYSON *In Mem.* xiv, And ask a thousand things of home.

c. with the question indicated by its subject or object: To ask the *way*, the *price*, a *name*, an *age*, etc.

1382 WYCLIF *Gen.* xxxii. 29 Wherto askist [*v.r.* axist] thou my name? c 1420 *Chron. Vilod.* 689 Ryse up .. and þe way asshe, To Wyltone. 1502 ARNOLD *Chron.* (1811) 208 To answere him that axith the lawe of the Lorde. 1549 LATIMER 7 *Serm. bef. Edw. VI.* (Arb.) 27 The other axed ye price, he sayed: xx. nobles. 1597 SHAKS. 2 *Hen. IV*, I. i. 39 He ask'd the way to Chester. 1842 TENNYSON *Dream Fair Wom.* 93 Ask thou not my name.

3. with the person asked introduced by a preposition:

†a. *at* a person. *Obs.* exc. *dial.*

1297 R. GLOUC. 16 Heo aschede at Corineus, how heo so hardi were. c 1325 *E. E. Allit. P.* B. 924 Als Abraham .. hit at himself asked. 1535 COVERDALE *Ecclus.* xxi. 17 It is axed at the mouth of the wyse. 1753 *Stewart's Trial* 197 To ask any question at Allan Breck about the murder, which he now related to them. 1843 BETHUNE *Scot. Peasant's Fireside* 47 'Why do you ask that question at me?'

†b. *to* a person. (Cf. Fr. *demander à.*) *Obs.*

c 1314 *Guy Warw.* 27 Than axed anon Sir Gii To the barouns that oned him bi. 1483 CAXTON *G. de la Tour* D vij b, Asking to her why she had trespaced his commaundments. 1663 GERBIER *Counsel* 13 Asking to passengers what weather it was without doores.

c. *of* a person.

1366 MAUNDEV. v. 61, I asked of the monkes .. how this befelle. c 1380 *Sir Ferumb.* 1124 Þe Amyral of hym axeth .. wat tydynge þay had y-broȝt. c 1450 *Merlin* ii. 36 Axe of hem whi that that toure fill. 1562 TURNER *Herbal* II. 51 a, The sherif axed diligently of them .. what they had done. 1667 MILTON *P. L.* II. 957 [One] of whom to ask Which way the neerest coast of darkness lyes. c 1735 POPE *Hor. Epist.* II. ii. 211, I ask these sober questions of my heart. *Mod.* A farmer of whom I asked the way.

** *trans. With the person asked as object:*

To call upon (a person) for information or an answer: to put a question to, to question.

4. with personal obj. only: To ask a person.

a. *simply.*

c 1000 *Ags. Gosp.* Mark xii. 28 Hine ne dorste nan mann ahsian. — John ix. 21–23 Ahxsiað hine sylfne [*v.r.* acsiað, ahxiað, *Lindisf.* ȝefraiȝnas, *Rushw.* ȝefræȝnas]. a 1300 *Cursor M.* 1031 Syn þou askis me .. I wille þe telle. 1382 WYCLIF *Job* xii. 7 Aske the bestis, and thei shul teche thee. 1535 COVERDALE *Job* xii. 7 Axe the catell, & they shal enfourme the. 1591 SHAKS. *Two Gent.* II. v. 36 Aske my dogge. 1611 BIBLE 1 *Cor.* xiv. 35 Let them aske their husbands at home. 1732 POPE *Ess. Man* II. 205 Ask your own heart; and nothing is so plain. 1842 TENNYSON *Dora* 142 I ask'd him, and he said, He could not ever rue his marrying me.

b. with the question introduced by 'saying,' etc.

c 1000 *Ags. Gosp.* John i. 19 Hi axsodon hine [*Hatton* axeden hym] and þus cwæðen, Hwæt eart þu? — Matt. xii. 10 Hi ahsude[n] hyne, þus cweðende, etc. 1388 WYCLIF *Luke* xxiii. 3 Pilat axide hym, and seide, Art thou Kyng of Jewis. 1611 BIBLE *John* ix. 19 They asked them, saying, Is this your son?

5. with the thing asked as a second object: To ask a person a question.

a. with the question as an object sentence or clause.

c 1000 *Ags. Gosp.* John xxi. 12 Nan þæra .. ne dorste hine axian hwæt he wære. c 1175 *Lamb. Hom.* 25 Þe preost me walde eskien .. hwa me scriue. *Ibid.* 35 Esca hine hwet he habbe biȝeten. a 1230 *Juliana* 257 He easkeð ham, ȝef ham biluueð to heren him. c 1275 *Passion of Our Lord* 567 in *O. E. Misc.* 53 Vre louerd hire gon axi, For hwi and for hwan wepestu? a 1300 *Cursor M.* 1125 Aske his fader quere he be. c 1314 *Guy Warw.* 98 He gan oxy what it might be, He hem oxed what it were. c 1420 *Chron. Vilod.* 939 And how he was .. he dude hym asshe. 1584 *Three Ladies Lond.* I. in Hazl. *Dodsl.* VI. 296 My lady axes you, when will you take possession of your house. 1602 SHAKS. *All's Well* II. ii. 38 Aske mee if I am a Courtier. 1711 ADDISON *Spect.* No. 10 ¶ 5, I have heard them asking the first man they have met with whether there was any news stirring. 1849 DICKENS *Dav. Copp.* xxi. (C. D. ed.) 181, I .. asked him what o'clock it was.

b. with the question expressed by a sb. or pronoun: *a question, this, something.*

c 1000 *Ags. Gosp.* Matt. xxii. 46 Ne dorste ænig man þing mare axiȝean [*Rushw.* geasciȝan; *Hatton* axien]. c 1315 SHOREHAM 136 Ich acsy the a questioun. c 1386 CHAUCER *Knts. T.* 489 Now lovyeres axe I this question. 1598 SHAKS. *Merry W.* IV. i. 16 Aske him some questions in his Accidence. 1611 BIBLE *Jer.* xxxviii. 14, I will aske thee a thing; hide nothing from me. 1773 GOLDSM. *Stoops to Conq.* III. 111 Ask me no questions and I'll tell you no fibs. *Mod.* Which of them asked you that?

c. with the question asked indicated by its subject or object: To ask a person the *way*, the *time*, his *name*, *age*, etc.

1593 SHAKS. *Rich. II*, I. iii. 9 Aske him his name. 1605 — *Lear* v. iii. 117 Aske him his purposes, why he appeares Vpon this Call o' th' Trumpet. 1709 POPE *Ess. Crit.* 436 Ask them the cause. *Mod.* She asked me the reason.

6. with the matter introduced by a preposition: a. To ask a person *of* (arch.), *about*, in OE. *be*, *ymb* (= about), a matter. b. (To ask one *after* or *for* a person: see 7.)

c 885 K. ÆLFRED *Boeth.* xxxix. § 4 Þæt is þæt ic þé ær ymb acsade .. Ðisse spræce ðe ðu me æfter ascast. c 1000 *Ags. Gosp.* Luke ix. 45 Hi ne dorston hine be þam worde ahsian. c 1220 *Hali Meid.* 9 Aske þes cwenes .. of hare liflade. a 1300 *Cursor M.* 1204 He asked him of his errand. c 1300 *Beket* 2 And eschte him of Engelonde; and of the manere there. 1475 CAXTON *Jason* 40 b, Thauncient man axid one of the marronners of this matere. 1597 SHAKS. 2 *Hen. IV*, II. iv. 389 Knocking at the Tauernes And asking every one for Sir John Falstaffe. 1601 — *All's Well* IV. iii. 317 Why do's he aske him of me? 1842 TENNYSON *Edw. Morris* 23 Once I ask'd him of his early life. *Mod.* Did you ask them about the books?

*** *intr. With no object expressed:*

To inquire, make inquiries.

7. To ask (*of* obs.) *about* (in OE. *be, ymb* = about). To ask *after* a thing missing, a person absent, his welfare, etc. To ask *for* a person; to ask to see; formerly (and still in *dial.*) = to ask *after*.

c 885 K. ÆLFRED *Boeth.* xxxix. § 4 Se ðe ymb þæt ascian wile. c 1000 ÆLFRIC *Deut.* iv. 32 Ahsiað be ealdum dagum ða wæron ær þonne ȝe. c 1230 *Ancr. R.* 172 Axinde efter tiðinges. a 1250 *Owl & Night.* 711 Wi axestu of craftes mine. 1377 LANGL. *P. Pl.* B. v. 542, I seygh neuere palmere .. Axen after hym. 1588 SHAKS. *L. L. L.* III. i. 168 And Rosaline, they call her, aske for her. 1671 MILTON *Sams.* 40 Ask for this great deliverer now, and find him Eyeless in Gaza. 1849 DICKENS *Dav. Copp.* xx. (C. D. ed.) 178 That shows the advantage of asking, don't it. 1866 G. MACDONALD *Ann. Q. Neighb.* xxx. (1878) 524 To ask after their health when he met them. *Mod.* Did any one ask for me, while I was out? When you reach that point, ask again.

†8. To ask *of* or *at* a person *of* a matter, i.e. *from* a person *about* a matter. *Obs.*

1393 LANGL. *P. Pl.* C. xxi. 127 Ayþer axed of oþer of þis grete wonder. c 1440 *Generydes* 309 He asckid of Medeyn Of his ffader. 1600 FAIRFAX *Tasso* VIII. liii. 152 To spie at whom to aske we gazed round. 1611 BIBLE 1 *Sam.* xxviii. 16 Wherefore then doest thou aske of me?

III. To make request for a thing desired.

* *trans. With the thing asked as object:*

To make request for.

9. *simply.* To ask a thing. (Now more familiarly *to ask for*: see 16.)

c 1250 *Gen. & Ex.* 1668 Aske it wið skil and ðu salt hauen. 1340 *Ayenb.* 114 Jesu Crist ous tekþ zuo to oxi uoryeuenesse. *Ibid.* 209 Verst oxseþ Godes riche. 1370 *Lay-Folks Mass-Bk.* App. iv. 510 Let him not his offryng asch. c 1374 CHAUCER *Troylus* v. 594, I naxe in guerdon but a boone. c 1420 *Avow. Arth.* iv, Thenne the kyng asshet a chekkere. c 1460 *Towneley Myst. Coliphiz.* 200 That is it that I ast. 1509 HAWES *Conv. Swearers* 26 Come nowe to me and axe forgyuenes. 1570 *Play Wit & Sc.* (1848) 10, I axe no more. 1593 SHAKS. 3 *Hen. VI*, II. vi. 69 Clifford, aske mercy. 1644 MILTON *Areop.* (Arb.) 76 Asking licence to do so worthy a deed. 1711 STEELE *Spect.* No. 6 ¶ 2 The beggar disabled himself in his Right Leg, and asks Alms all Day. 1837 DICKENS *Pickwick* xxvii, Ask a blessing, Mr. Stiggins. 1859 TENNYSON *Vivien* 155 Ask your boon, for boon I owe you.

b. *To ask a price*: to ask so much as the price, to state the price.

1857 Bohn's *Handbk. Prov.* 323 Ask but enough, and you may lower the price as you list. 1864 TENNYSON *Brook* 142 How he sent the bailiff to the farm To learn the price, and what the price he ask'd. *Mod.* What do you ask for this? How much did he ask?

10. To ask a thing (*to* obs., *at* obs. or dial.) *of*, *from* a person.

1340 *Ayenb.* 110 Huet may þe zone betere acsy to his uader þanne bread? c 1450 *Compl. Lover's Life* lxix, That to my foo .. Mot axe grace, mercy, and pite. c 1460 FORTESCUE *Abs. & Lim. Mon.* (1714) 134 Such as axen of the Kyng, Offices. 1583 GOLDING *Calvin on Deut.* cviii. 661 A charmer .. that asketh counsell at spirites. 1647 CHAS. I. *Let.* in *Antiquary* I. 97 To aske leave of ye two houses to make a journey. 1796 BURNS *Let.* in *Wks.* (Globe) 563, I am ashamed to ask another favour of you. 1830 tr. *Aristoph. Acharnians* 43 The request of the bride, which she earnestly asks at me! *Mod.* He asked a larger sum from me.

11. To ask *to do*, or *be done to*.

c 1374 CHAUCER *Boeth.* III. i. 63 I .. axe gretely to heeren tho remedyes. 1477 EARL RIVERS (Caxton) *Dictes* 1, I had delyte & axed to rede some good historye. 1647 SPRIGG *Ang. Rediv.* III. iii. (1854) 149, I humbly ask to have this place slighted. 1833 I. TAYLOR *Fanat.* vii. 221 The country .. seemed to ask to be seized upon by men worthy to enjoy it.

** *trans. With the person asked as object:*

To make a request to.

12. To ask a person a thing. *Obs.*, or *arch.* in 'I ask you pardon, leave.'

1297 R. GLOUC. 16 He nolde no mon asche leue. *Ibid.* 190 Hii esseþ vs truage. a 1300 *Cursor M.* 3868 Jacob askid him his lemman. c 1308 *Pol. Songs* 200 What hast i-do, That thou me so oxist pes? c 1450 LONELICH *Grail* xxxvi. 493 Forto axen hem consaille. 1538 BALE *God's Promises* in Dodsl. *O. P.* (1780) I. 11 Good Lorde I axe the mercy. 1671 MILTON *P. R.* IV. 551 To stand upright Will ask thee skill. 1749 FIELDING *Tom Jones* XVI. vii. (1840) 238/2, I ask Mr. Blifil pardon.

b. with the second object wanting.

a 1564 BECON *Gen. Pref. Wks.* (1843) 22 Christ saith: 'Give to every one that axeth thee.'

13. To ask a person *to do* a thing.

a 1300 *Cursor M.* 3141 Nou es he askid .. Til gode to make of sacrifise. c 1400 *Destr. Troy* 1. (*title*) How King Pelleus Exit Iason to get þe flles of golde. 1860 TYNDALL *Glac.* I. § 22. 152, I asked him to accompany me. 1872 BLACK *Adv. Phaeton* xxv. 350 He does not ask me to pay his bills.

14. To ask a person (*of* obs.) *for* a thing.

c 1386 CHAUCER *Pers. T.* (Wr.) ¶ 918 A man that .. cometh for to axe him of mercy [*Other MSS.* aske mercy]. 1483 CAXTON *Gold. Leg.* 24/3 For this first they ought to axe echeone other. 1590 SHAKS. *Com. Err.* II. i. 61 He ask'd me for a hundred markes in gold. 1600 — *A. Y. L.* IV. i. 138, I might aske you for your Commission. 1735 POPE *Prol. Sat.* 50 You know his Grace, I want a Patron; ask him for a Place. 1810 SCOTT *Lady of L.* v. vii, Ask we this savage hill we tread For fatten'd steer or household bread? *Prov.* Ask a kite for a feather, and she'll say, she has but just enough to fly with.

*** *intr. With no object*: To make request.

15. *simply.* To ask.

c 1380 WYCLIF *Sel. Wks.* (1871) III. 328 He is redy to ȝeve him if he ax worþily. c 1400 *Rom. Rose* 5243 Man that worthy is of name, To axen often hath gret shame. 1535 COVERDALE *Matt.* vi. 7 Axe & it shalbe giuen you. 1535 STEWART *Cron. Scot.* II. 402 Ask and haue. 1611 BIBLE *Matt.* vi. 7 Aske [WYCLIF, axe ȝe] and it shalbe giuen you. *Mod.* It is rather those who ask loudest, than those who need most, that secure attention.

16. To ask (*after* obs.) *for* a thing.

c 1200 *Trin. Coll. Hom.* 81 Iuel mennish .. acseð after fortocne of heuene. 1377 LANGL. *P. Pl.* B. vi. 298 Al hunger eet in hast and axed after more. 1611 BIBLE *Micah* vii. 3 The iudge asketh for a reward. 1795 SOUTHEY *Joan of Arc* II. 246 Could hear a famish'd woman ask for food, And feel no pity. 1865 DICKENS *Mut. Fr.* II. vii. 202 I'll cut back and ask for leave.

IV. Pregnant senses and special uses.

†17. To inquire into, examine, investigate. *Obs.*

c 1000 *Ags. Ps.* x. 5 His bræwas .. ahsað manna bearn. Se ylca Drihten ahsað rihtwise and unrihtwise. c 1175 *Lamb. Hom.* 35 Oðer he heo hafð i-escad oðer hafð ifunden on boke. 1382 WYCLIF *Ecclus.* xi. 7 Beforn that thou aske, ne blame thou any man. — *Ps.* x. 5 The eyelidis of hym asken [1611 trie] the sones of men. The Lord asketh the riȝtwis man, and the vnpitous. 1612 *Arraignm. John Selman* 14 Sir Francis Bacon .. proceeded to judgment and asking on the prisoner, thus .. hee spake.

†18. To prosecute, exact from, oppress. *Obs.*

1388 WYCLIF *Isaiah* lviii. 3 Lo! ȝoure wille is foundun in the dai of ȝoure fastyng, and ye axen alle ȝoure dettouris.

19. To ask as by right, call for, demand.

1393 GOWER *Conf.* I. 36 They axen alle jugement Ayein the man. c 1430 *Syr Generides* 4795 His hors he ashed .. his wey he nam. a 1440 *Sir Degrev.* 393 He axit justes of were And prays the of answere. c 1460 *Towneley Myst.* 58 To worshyp me as I wylle asse. 1509 BARCLAY *Shyp of Folys* (1874) I. 141 Nought .. to asshe agaynst right. 1544 BALE *Sir J. Oldcastell* in *Harl. Misc.* (Malh.) I. 258 God will axe no more of a Christen beleuer .. but only to obey the preceptes of that moost blessed lawe. 1580 BARET *Alv.* A 594 To aske agayne that is ones owne, or in a maner due to him, *Reposco.*

b. *esp.* in *To ask an account.*

a 1450 *Knt. de la Tour* xxxix. 59 Of the which God wille axse hem accompte. 1523 LD. BERNERS *Froiss.* I. ccclxxxiii. 645 They wolde aske accomptes of the Chancellour of Englande to knowe where all the good was become that he had leuyed through the realme. 1559 *Myrr. Mag., Dk. Glouc.* xxi. 5 To axe a reckening of the Realmes reuenue.

20. To make proclamation of a thing in church or other public place, calling upon any who have claims or objections to put them forward. Formerly of things found, stray cattle, etc.; still used of marriages about to be contracted (*to ask the banns*); in popular phrase the parties are said to be 'asked in church.'

(The recognized expression is now to *publish the banns*; but *ask* is the historical word.) See BANN.

1450 MYRC 203 Aske the banns thre halydawes. 1523 FITZHERB. *Surv.* 28 b, They ought to aske them [stray cattle] thre sondayes in thre or four next parysshe churches and also crye them thre tymes in thre the nexte market townes. 1596 SHAKS. *Tam. Shr.* II. i. 181 The day When I shal aske the banes, and when be married. 1606 *Wily Beguiled* in Hazl. *Dodsl.* IX. 304 We must be asked in church next Sunday. 1662 FULLER *Worthies* Westm. (1811) II. 105 D.) His head was ask'd, but never married to the English Crown. 1841 ORDERSON *Creol'ana* ii. 14 The fair sex .. preferring to be 'asked in church.'

21. *ellipt.* To ask (one) to come, to invite.

Mod. We ought to ask him to dinner. Why were you not at the ball? Because I was not asked.

22. *To ask away*: to do away with by asking.

1649 MILTON *Eikon.* Wks. 1738 I. 112 His Prayer is so am-

VOL. I. 62

SPELLING (*continued*).

élite	*naïveté*
en masse	*ne plus ultra*
en passant	*pari passu*
ex cathedra	*plébiscite*
garçon	*de quoi vivre*
grand monde	*raison d'être*
habitué	*sansculotte*
in propria persona	*sans cérémonie*
	sine qua non
lapsus linguae	*sotto voce*
mêlée	*tête à tête*
mot	*vis-à-vis*

The digraphs *æ* and *œ* should be separate in Latin and Greek words, as Aeneid, Aeschylus, Caesar, Oedipus; and in English, as mediaeval. In Old-English and in French names, however, it is incorrect to separate the letters, as Ælfred, Cædmon, manœuvre.

A or An.

a European	a unanimous
a ewe	a uniform
a ewer	a union
a hospital	a universal
a humble	a useful
an heir, -loom	an honour, -able
an herb, -al	an hotel
an heroic	an hour, -glass
an historical[1]	

[1] 'Nobody says so now, except old men—pedants chiefly.'—Dr. J. H. MURRAY. (But for various reasons 'an historical,' &c., have been retained.—H. H.)

CONTRACTIONS.

Ain't, don't, haven't, shan't, shouldn't, 'tis, won't, *to be close up*.

ETC. only to be used in small cap. lines, in titles, where ampersand would not range. Otherwise always print &c.; and 'Longmans & Co.'

8vo, 4to, 12mo, &c., should not be treated as contractions.

Print Scripture references as follows:—

Old Testament.

Gen. xi. 17	1 Kings	Eccles.	Amos
Exod.	2 Kings	Song of Sol.	Obad.
Lev.	1 Chron.		Jonah
Num.	2 Chron.	Isa.	Mic.
Deut.	Ezra	Jer.	Nahum
Joshua	Nehem.	Lam.	Hab.
Judges	Esther	Ezek.	Zeph.
Ruth	Job	Dan.	Hag.
1 Sam.	Ps.	Hos.	Zech.
2 Sam.	Prov.	Joel	Mal.

New Testament.

Matt.	2 Cor.	1 Tim.	2 Pet.
Mark	Gal.	2 Tim.	1 John
Luke	Eph.	Titus	2 John
John	Phil.	Philem.	3 John
Acts	Col.	Heb.	Jude
Rom.	1 Thess.	Jas.	Rev.
1 Cor.	2 Thess.	1 Pet.	

Apocrypha.

1 Esdras	Wisd. of Sol.	Susanna
2 Esdras	Ecclus.	Bel and Dragon.
Tobit	Baruch	Pr. of Manasses.
Judith	Song of Three Childr.	1 Macc.
Rest of Esth.		2 Macc.

Present &c. after *as if & as though* (*It looks as if we are winning* or *shall win*).

Me &c. for *my* &c. in gerund construction (*Instead of me being dismissed*).

Between . . . or for *between . . . &* (*The choice is between glorious death or shameful life*).

Almost quite, rather unique, more preferable.

Aggravating for annoying.

Individual for person.

Any very bad hyphening (*the ruling-class, my wooden-leg*).

Rev. Jones; *the hon. Smith.*

ILLOGICALITIES. The spread of education adds to the writer's burdens by multiplying that pestilent fellow the critical reader. No longer can we depend on an audience that will be satisfied with catching the general drift & obvious intention of a sentence & not trouble itself to pick holes in our wording; the words used must nowadays actually yield on scrutiny the desired sense; to plead that anyone could see what you meant, or so to write as to need that plea, is not now permissible; all our pet illogicalities will have to be cleared away by degrees.

If Milton might be excused or even commended for calling Eve fairest of her daughters, the modern newspaper man must not expect pardon for similar conduct. *Sir Ernest Cassel's Christmas gift to the hospitals of £50,000 is only the latest of many acts of splendid munificence by which he has benefited his fellows before now.* If it is the latest of them, says the pestilent one, it is one of them; if one of them, it was given before now; but it is in fact given now, not before now; which is absurd.

Take, again, the following comment on a quotation the commentator thinks unjustified: *Were ever finer lines perverted to a meaner use?* We know well enough what he is trying to do—to emphasize the meanness of the use—; it is in expressing the emphasis that he has gone wrong; it has escaped him that *Never were lines perverted to a meaner use* is made weaker, not stronger, if changed to *never were fine lines* &c., & that again is further weakened, not strengthened, by a change of *fine* to *finer*; everything that narrows the field of rivals for the distinction of meanest perversion, as *fine & finer* do progressively, has an effect contrary to what was intended; it may be worth while to insert *fine* in spite of that, since it adds a qualification of importance; but the change to *finer* weakens the force without adding to the accuracy. Richard III says *Was ever woman in this humour won?*; to have said *Princess*, or *prouder Princess*, instead of *woman* would have made the marvel less & not greater.

Another common, & more conspicuous, illogicality is the unintended anticlimax. *Masters, it is already proved that you are little better than false knaves, & it will go near to be thought so shortly.* Dogberry felt no uneasiness about putting it that way, & some writers seem to agree with him:—*A scepticism about the result of military operations which must have had & probably has had a damping effect upon the soldier* (If it must have had, it certainly, not probably, has had)./*It will, I think, delight the reader as if it were something told by Meadows Taylor; indeed the mysterious 'sadhu' who figures in it, & the account of the fight with the yellow leopard, are not unworthy of the suggested comparison* (Not unworthy, quotha? but *indeed* led us to expect *more than worthy*, a climax instead of an anticlimax).

The abandonment of blind confidence in *much less* is another compliment that will have to be paid to the modern reader's logic. It is still usual to give no hearing to *much more* before deciding for its more popular rival; sometimes a loose but illogical excuse is to be found in the general effect of the context, sometimes even that is wanting; these two varieties appear

πολιτικὴν ἐφίεσθαι καὶ τί τὸ πάντων ἀκρότατον τῶν πρακτῶν
ἀγαθῶν. ὀνόματι μὲν οὖν σχεδὸν ὑπὸ τῶν πλείστων ὁμολο- 2
γεῖται· τὴν γὰρ εὐδαιμονίαν καὶ οἱ πολλοὶ καὶ οἱ χαρίεντες λέγουσιν, τὸ δ' εὖ ζῆν καὶ τὸ εὖ πράττειν ταὐτὸν ὑπο-
λαμβάνουσι τῷ εὐδαιμονεῖν· περὶ δὲ τῆς εὐδαιμονίας, τί
ἐστιν, ἀμφισβητοῦσι καὶ οὐχ ὁμοίως οἱ πολλοὶ τοῖς σοφοῖς
ἀποδιδόασιν. οἱ μὲν γὰρ τῶν ἐναργῶν τι καὶ φανερῶν, οἷον 3
ἡδονὴν ἢ πλοῦτον ἢ τιμήν, ἄλλοι δ' ἄλλο—πολλάκις δὲ
καὶ ὁ αὐτὸς ἕτερον· νοσήσας μὲν γὰρ ὑγίειαν, πενόμενος δὲ
πλοῦτον· συνειδότες δ' ἑαυτοῖς ἄγνοιαν τοὺς μέγα τι καὶ
ὑπὲρ αὐτοὺς λέγοντας θαυμάζουσιν. ἔνιοι δ' ᾤοντο παρὰ τὰ
πολλὰ ταῦτα ἀγαθὰ ἄλλο τι καθ' αὑτὸ εἶναι, ὃ καὶ τούτοις
πᾶσιν αἴτιόν ἐστι τοῦ εἶναι ἀγαθά. ἁπάσας μὲν οὖν ἐξετάζειν 4
τὰς δόξας ματαιότερον ἴσως ἐστίν, ἱκανὸν δὲ τὰς μάλιστα
ἐπιπολαζούσας ἢ δοκούσας ἔχειν τινὰ λόγον. μὴ λανθανέτω δ' 5
ἡμᾶς ὅτι διαφέρουσιν οἱ ἀπὸ τῶν ἀρχῶν λόγοι καὶ οἱ ἐπὶ
τὰς ἀρχάς. εὖ γὰρ καὶ ὁ Πλάτων ἠπόρει τοῦτο καὶ ἐζήτει, πότε-
ρον ἀπὸ τῶν ἀρχῶν ἢ ἐπὶ τὰς ἀρχάς ἐστιν ἡ ὁδός, ὥσπερ
1095ᵇ ἐν τῷ σταδίῳ ἀπὸ τῶν ἀθλοθετῶν ἐπὶ τὸ πέρας ἢ ἀνάπαλιν.
ἀρκτέον μὲν γὰρ ἀπὸ τῶν γνωρίμων, ταῦτα δὲ διττῶς· τὰ
μὲν γὰρ ἡμῖν τὰ δ' ἁπλῶς. ἴσως οὖν ἡμῖν γε ἀρκτέον ἀπὸ
τῶν ἡμῖν γνωρίμων. διὸ δεῖ τοῖς ἔθεσιν ἦχθαι καλῶς τὸν 6
περὶ καλῶν καὶ δικαίων καὶ ὅλως τῶν πολιτικῶν ἀκουσόμε-
νον ἱκανῶς. ἀρχὴ γὰρ τὸ ὅτι, καὶ εἰ τοῦτο φαίνοιτο ἀρ- 7
κούντως, οὐδὲν προσδεήσει τοῦ διότι· ὁ δὲ τοιοῦτος ἔχει ἢ
λάβοι ἂν ἀρχὰς ῥᾳδίως. ᾧ δὲ μηδέτερον ὑπάρχει τούτων,
ἀκουσάτω τῶν Ἡσιόδου·

---

17. ἀγαθόν Mᵇ Γ 27. τοῖσδε Lᵇ 28. πᾶσι τοῦ εἶναι ἀγαθὰ αἴτιόν ἐστιν Kᵇ Mᵇ 32. ὁ om. Lᵇ 1095ᵇ 1. ἐπὶ τῶν σταδίων Lᵇ Γ 2. γὰρ Kᵇ Mᵇ : οὖν Lᵇ Γ 3. γε om. Lᵇ Γ 4. ἤθεσιν Lᵇ Mᵇ Asp. 6. εἰ τοῦτο] ἐν τούτοις pr. Kᵇ 7. ἔχει] ἔχοι Lᵇ : ἢ ἔχοι Mᵇ

οὗτος μὲν πανάριστος ὃς αὐτὸς πάντα νοήσῃ,
ἐσθλὸς δ' αὖ κἀκεῖνος ὃς εὖ εἰπόντι πίθηται.
ὃς δέ κε μήτ' αὐτὸς νοέῃ μήτ' ἄλλου ἀκούων
ἐν θυμῷ βάλληται, ὁ δ' αὖτ' ἀχρήιος ἀνήρ.

V. Ἡμεῖς δὲ λέγωμεν ὅθεν παρεξέβημεν. τὸ γὰρ ἀγαθὸν 3
καὶ τὴν εὐδαιμονίαν οὐκ ἀλόγως ἐοίκασιν ἐκ τῶν βίων
2 ὑπολαμβάνειν οἱ μὲν πολλοὶ καὶ φορτικώτατοι τὴν ἡδονήν·
διὸ καὶ τὸν βίον ἀγαπῶσι τὸν ἀπολαυστικόν. τρεῖς γάρ εἰσι
μάλιστα οἱ προύχοντες, ὅ τε νῦν εἰρημένος καὶ ὁ πολιτικὸς
3 καὶ τρίτος ὁ θεωρητικός. οἱ μὲν οὖν πολλοὶ παντελῶς ἀν-
δραποδώδεις φαίνονται, βοσκημάτων βίον προαιρούμενοι,
τυγχάνουσι δὲ λόγου διὰ τὸ πολλοὺς τῶν ἐν ταῖς ἐξουσίαις
4 ὁμοιοπαθεῖν Σαρδαναπάλλῳ. οἱ δὲ χαρίεντες καὶ πρακτικοὶ
τιμήν· τοῦ γὰρ πολιτικοῦ βίου σχεδὸν τοῦτο τέλος. φαίνεται δ' ἐπιπολαιότερον εἶναι τοῦ ζητουμένου· δοκεῖ γὰρ ἐν
τοῖς τιμῶσι μᾶλλον εἶναι ἢ ἐν τῷ τιμωμένῳ, τἀγαθὸν δὲ
5 οἰκεῖόν τι καὶ δυσαφαίρετον εἶναι μαντευόμεθα. ἔτι δ' ἐοί-
κασι τὴν τιμὴν διώκειν ἵνα πιστεύσωσιν ἑαυτοὺς ἀγαθοὺς
εἶναι· ζητοῦσι γοῦν ὑπὸ τῶν φρονίμων τιμᾶσθαι, καὶ παρ'
οἷς γινώσκονται, καὶ ἐπ' ἀρετῇ· δῆλον οὖν ὅτι κατά γε
6 τούτους ἡ ἀρετὴ κρείττων. τάχα δὲ καὶ μᾶλλον ἄν τις
τέλος τοῦ πολιτικοῦ βίου ταύτην ὑπολάβοι. φαίνεται δὲ
ἀτελεστέρα καὶ αὕτη· δοκεῖ γὰρ ἐνδέχεσθαι καὶ καθεύδειν
ἔχοντα τὴν ἀρετὴν ἢ ἀπρακτεῖν διὰ βίου, καὶ πρὸς τούτοις
κακοπαθεῖν καὶ ἀτυχεῖν τὰ μέγιστα· τὸν δ' οὕτω ζῶντα 1096ᵃ
οὐδεὶς ἂν εὐδαιμονίσειεν, εἰ μὴ θέσιν διαφυλάττων. καὶ
περὶ μὲν τούτων ἅλις· ἱκανῶς γὰρ καὶ ἐν τοῖς ἐγκυκλίοις

---

18. προέχοντες Kᵇ 22. ὁμοπαθεῖν pr. Kᵇ 26. εἶναι om. Lᵇ Γ 27. πιστεύωσιν Lᵇ Asp. εἶναι ἀγαθούς Kᵇ Mᵇ 31. δὲ] δὴ Lᵇ: γὰρ pr. Kᵇ 32. καὶ ante καθεύδειν om. Kᵇ 1096ᵃ 3. καὶ om. Lᵇ Mᵇ Γ

120. *To the Virginian Voyage*

YOU brave heroic minds
Worthy your country's name,
That honour still pursue;
Go and subdue!
Whilst loitering hinds
Lurk here at home with shame.

Britons, you stay too long:
Quickly aboard bestow you,
And with a merry gale
Swell your stretch'd sail
With vows as strong
As the winds that blow you.

Your course securely steer,
West and by south forth keep!
Rocks, lee-shores, nor shoals
When Eolus scowls
You need not fear;
So absolute the deep.

And cheerfully at sea
Success you still entice
To get the pearl and gold,
And ours to hold
Virginia,
Earth's only paradise.

Where nature hath in store
Fowl, venison, and fish,
And the fruitfull'st soil
Without your toil
Three harvests more,
All greater than your wish.

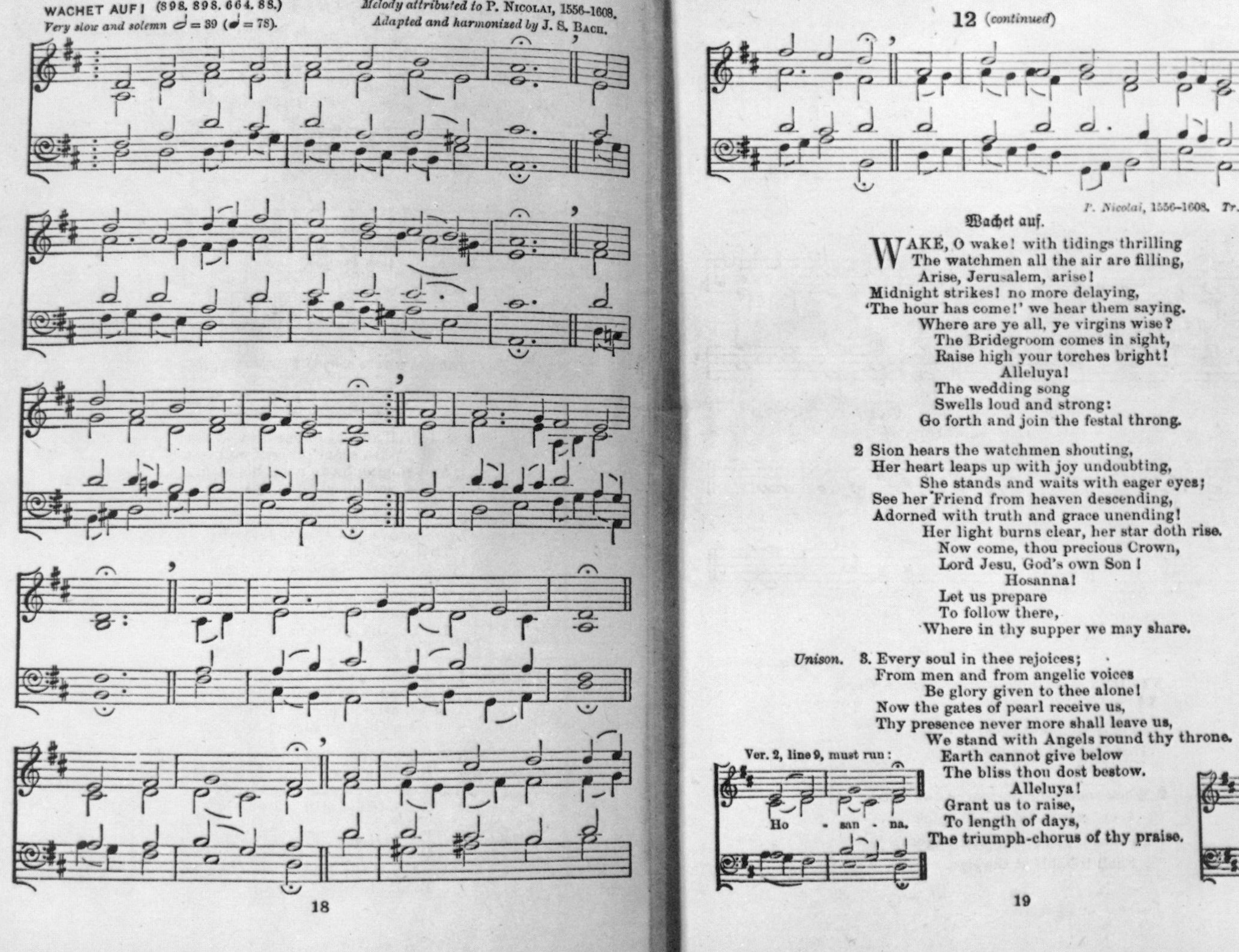
THE CHRISTIAN YEAR
12
WACHET AUF! (898. 898. 664. 88.)
Very slow and solemn 𝅗𝅥. = 39 (♩ = 78).
Melody attributed to P. Nicolai, 1556–1608.
Adapted and harmonized by J. S. Bach.
18
ADVENT
12 (continued)
P. Nicolai, 1556–1608. Tr. F. C. B.
Wachet auf.
WAKE, O wake! with tidings thrilling
The watchmen all the air are filling,
Arise, Jerusalem, arise!
Midnight strikes! no more delaying,
'The hour has come!' we hear them saying.
Where are ye all, ye virgins wise?
The Bridegroom comes in sight,
Raise high your torches bright!
Alleluya!
The wedding song
Swells loud and strong:
Go forth and join the festal throng.
2 Sion hears the watchmen shouting,
Her heart leaps up with joy undoubting,
She stands and waits with eager eyes;
See her Friend from heaven descending,
Adorned with truth and grace unending!
Her light burns clear, her star doth rise.
Now come, thou precious Crown,
Lord Jesu, God's own Son!
Hosanna!
Let us prepare
To follow there,
Where in thy supper we may share.
Unison. 3. Every soul in thee rejoices;
From men and from angelic voices
Be glory given to thee alone!
Now the gates of pearl receive us,
Thy presence never more shall leave us,
We stand with Angels round thy throne.
Earth cannot give below
The bliss thou dost bestow.
Alleluya!
Grant us to raise,
To length of days,
The triumph-chorus of thy praise.
Ver. 2, line 9, must run:
Ho - san - na.
A - men.
19

2 OXFORD UNIVERSITY PRESS

The Outbreak of the War

Twelfth Impression (third edition, revised October 1914) of the first Oxford Book on the W

Why We are at War: Great Britain's Case, by Members of the Ox Faculty of Modern History: E. BARKER, H. W. C. DAVIS, C. R. L. FLETCH ARTHUR HASSALL, L. G. WICKHAM LEGG, F. MORGAN. With an appendix the original documents, including the authorized English translation of the White Book issued by the German Government, selections from the Ambassadors' dispatches, from the Russian Orange Book and from the Belgian Grey Book. Third edition revised, twelfth impression. 8vo ($8\frac{1}{2} \times 5\frac{1}{2}$). Paper cover, 2s. net; cloth, 2s. 6d. net. *At the Clarendon Press.*

Translations of *Why We are at War.*

8vo ($8\frac{1}{2} \times 5\frac{1}{2}$), on thin paper for convenience of postage, paper cover, 2s. net each.
French: *Pourquoi l'Angleterre a pris les Armes.* 2 fr. 50.
Italian: *Perchè la Gran Brettagna combatte.* 2 lire 50.
Swedish: *Hvarför England Deltager I Kriget.* 2 kronor.
Danish: *Grundene til Englands Deltagelse I Krigen.* 2 kroner.
Spanish: *Por qué estamos en guerra: La Justificación de la Gran Bretaña.* 2.50 pesetas.
German: *Warum wir Krieg führen: Grossbritanniens Rechtsstandpunkt.* 2 fr. 50.

The German White Book: an exact reprint with facsimile title-pages of the English translation issued by the German Government, August 1914. Reprinted from *Why We are at War.* 8vo (9×6). Paper cover, 6d. net. *At the Clarendon Press.*

Published November 26, 1914, the well-known American lawyer's presentation of the Case.

The Double Alliance *v.* the Triple Entente, by J. M. BECK. Oxford Pamphlets No. 31. Fcap 8vo ($7 \times 4\frac{1}{2}$), pp. 44. Paper, 3d. net. *At the Clarendon Press.*

Published September 1915, an account prepared from official and other records.

The Thirteen Days, July 23–August 4, 1914, a Chronicle and Interpretation by WILLIAM ARCHER. 8vo ($8\frac{1}{2} \times 5\frac{1}{2}$), pp. 244, 3s. 6d. net. *At the Clarendon Press.*

Published July 1915, an elaborate review of the policy of Sir Edward Grey not only in 1914 but in his whole tenure of the Foreign Office since 1906. By Professor GILBERT MURRAY.

The Policy of Sir Edward Grey; the Twelve Days; the Eight Years. 8vo ($8\frac{1}{2} \times 5\frac{1}{2}$), pp. 128. Paper cover, 1s. 6d. net. *At the Clarendon Press.*

Published August 1915, the famous Italian historian's demonstration that 'The European War was decided on at Potsdam in the evening of July 29, 1914'.

Who Wanted the European War? by GUGLIELMO FERRERO. Translated by permission from the Italian *Chi ha voluto la Guerra?* 1915. 8vo ($8\frac{1}{2} \times 5\frac{1}{2}$), pp. 40. Paper cover, 8d. net. *At the Clarendon Press.*

Who Caused the War, being a study of the diplomatic negotiations by EDWARD KYLIE, University of Toronto. 1915. Crown 8vo ($8 \times 5\frac{1}{2}$), pp. 88. 6d. net. *Oxford University Press, London.*

Professor SANDAY'S 'Attempt at Synthesis'

The Meaning of the War for Great Britain and Germany; the British Case; the German Case; An attempt at Synthesis. By WILLIAM SANDAY. 1915. 8vo ($8\frac{1}{2} \times 5\frac{1}{2}$), pp. 124. Paper cover, 1s. 6d. net; cloth (9×6), 2s. net. *At the Clarendon Press.*

Oxford Pamphlets, 1914–15. Crown 8vo. *At the Clarendon Press.*

Series I (Nos. 1–5). Paper boards, 1s. net.

The Deeper Causes of the War, by W. SANDAY. 3d. net.
To the Christian Scholars of Europe and America: A Reply from Oxford to the German 'Address to Evangelical Christians' (here reprinted). 2d. net.
The Responsibility for the War, by W. G. S. ADAMS. 2d. net.
Great Britain and Germany, by SPENSER WILKINSON. 2d. net.
'Just for a Scrap of Paper', by ARTHUR HASSALL. 1d. net.

Series VI (No. 26). Paper boards, 1s. net.

August 1914: The Coming of the War, by SPENSER WILKINSON.

THE WAR 1916 3

Histories of the Belligerents

The Evolution of Prussia, The Making of an Empire. By J. A. R. MARRIOTT and C. GRANT ROBERTSON. 1915. Crown 8vo ($7\frac{1}{2} \times 5\frac{1}{4}$), pp. 460, with eight maps. 5s. net. *At the Clarendon Press.*

The Balkans: A History of Bulgaria, Serbia, Greece, Rumania, Turkey, by NEVILL FORBES, A. J. TOYNBEE, D. MITRANY, D. G. HOGARTH. 1915. Cr. 8vo ($7\frac{1}{2} \times 5\frac{1}{4}$), pp. 408, with three maps. 5s. net. *At the Clarendon Press.*

The Balkan Wars, 1912–13, by J. G. SCHURMAN. Second edition, 1915, with a preface tracing the change in the Balkan situation up to Nov. 26, 1914. Crown 8vo ($8 \times 5\frac{1}{4}$), pp. 144. 4s. 6d. net. *Princeton University Press.*

Nationalism and War in the Near East, by a DIPLOMATIST, with a Preface by LORD COURTNEY OF PENWITH. 1915. Royal 8vo (10×7), pp. xxvi, 428 + 6. 12s. 6d. net. *Carnegie Endowment for International Peace.*

A Short History of Russia, by LUCY CAZALET. 1915. Crown 8vo ($7\frac{1}{2} \times 5\frac{1}{2}$), pp. 88, with eight illustrations and a map. 2s. *At the Clarendon Press.*

The Triple Alliance to 1914

Oxford Pamphlets. Series II (Nos. 6–10). Paper boards, 1s. net.

The Germans, their Empire, and how they have made it, by C. R. L. FLETCHER. 2d. net.
The Germans, their Empire, and what they covet, by C. R. L. FLETCHER. 2d. net.
Might is Right, by Sir WALTER RALEIGH. 2d. net.
Austrian Policy since 1867, by MURRAY BEAVEN. 3d. net.
Italian Policy since 1870, by KEITH FEILING. 2d. net.

German History and Ideals

Oxford Pamphlets. Series VIII (Nos. 31–35). Paper boards, 1s. net.

The Double Alliance versus *The Triple Entente*, by JAMES M. BECK. 3d. net.
The Germans in Africa, by EVANS LEWIN. 3d. net.
All for Germany, or The World's Respect Well Lost, by E. BARKER. 2d. net.
Germany, The Economic Problem, by C. GRANT ROBERTSON. 2d. net.
German Sea-Power, by C. S. TERRY. 3d. net.

Oxford Pamphlets. Series XIV (Nos. 61–65). Paper boards, 1s. net.

Through German Eyes, by E. A. SONNENSCHEIN. 2d. net.
Idols of Peace and War, by E. A. SONNENSCHEIN. 3d. net.
German Philosophy and the War, by J. H. MUIRHEAD. 2d. net.
Outlines of Prussian History to 1871, by E. F. ROW. 2d. net.
The Man of Peace, by ROY NORTON. 2d. net.
Fighting a Philosophy, by WILLIAM ARCHER. 2d. net.

Oxford Pamphlets (Nos. 20, 83)

Nietzsche and Treitschke: The Worship of Power in Modern Germany, by E. BARKER. 2d. net.
Bombastes in the Shades, by LAURENCE BINYON. 4d. net.

Oxford Pamphlets (Nos. 37, 40, 76)

Poland, Prussia, and Culture, by LUDWIK EHRLICH. 3d. net.
North Sleswick under Prussian Rule, 1864–1914, by W. R. PRIOR. 2d. net.
Alsace-Lorraine, by F. Y. ECCLES. 2d. net.

Submerged Nationalities of the German Empire, by ERNEST BARKER. 1915. 8vo (9×6), pp. 64, with a map. Paper cover, 8d. net. *At the Clarendon Press.*

The War Spirit of Germany, by GEORGE M. WRONG, University of Toronto. 1915. 8vo ($8 \times 5\frac{1}{2}$), pp. 28. Paper cover, 6d. net. *Oxford University Press, London.*

England and Germany, 1740–1914, by B. E. SCHMITT. 1916. Demy 8vo ($8\frac{3}{4} \times 5\frac{1}{2}$), pp. 534, with two sketch-maps. 8s. 6d. net. *Princeton University Press.*

B 2

THE TESTAMENT OF BEAUTY

A POEM

IN FOUR BOOKS

BY

ROBERT BRIDGES

POET LAUREATE

OXFORD

AT THE CLARENDON PRESS

1929

BOOK I

INTRODUCTION

Mortal Prudence, handmaid of divine Providence,
hath inscrutable reckoning with Fate and Fortune:
We sail a changeful sea through halcyon days and storm,
and when the ship laboureth, our stedfast purpose
trembles like as the compass in a binnacle.
Our stability is but balance, and wisdom lies
in masterful administration of the unforeseen.

'Twas late in my long journey, when I had clomb to where
the path was narrowing and the company few,
a glow of childlike wonder enthral'd me, as if my sense
had come to a new birth purified, my mind enrapt
re-awakening to a fresh initiation of life;
with like surprise of joy as any man may know
who rambling wide hath turn'd, resting on some hill-top
to view the plain he has left, and see'th it now out-spredd
mapp'd at his feet, a landscape so by beauty estranged
he scarce wil ken familiar haunts, nor his own home,
maybe, where far it lieth, small as a faded thought.

[1]

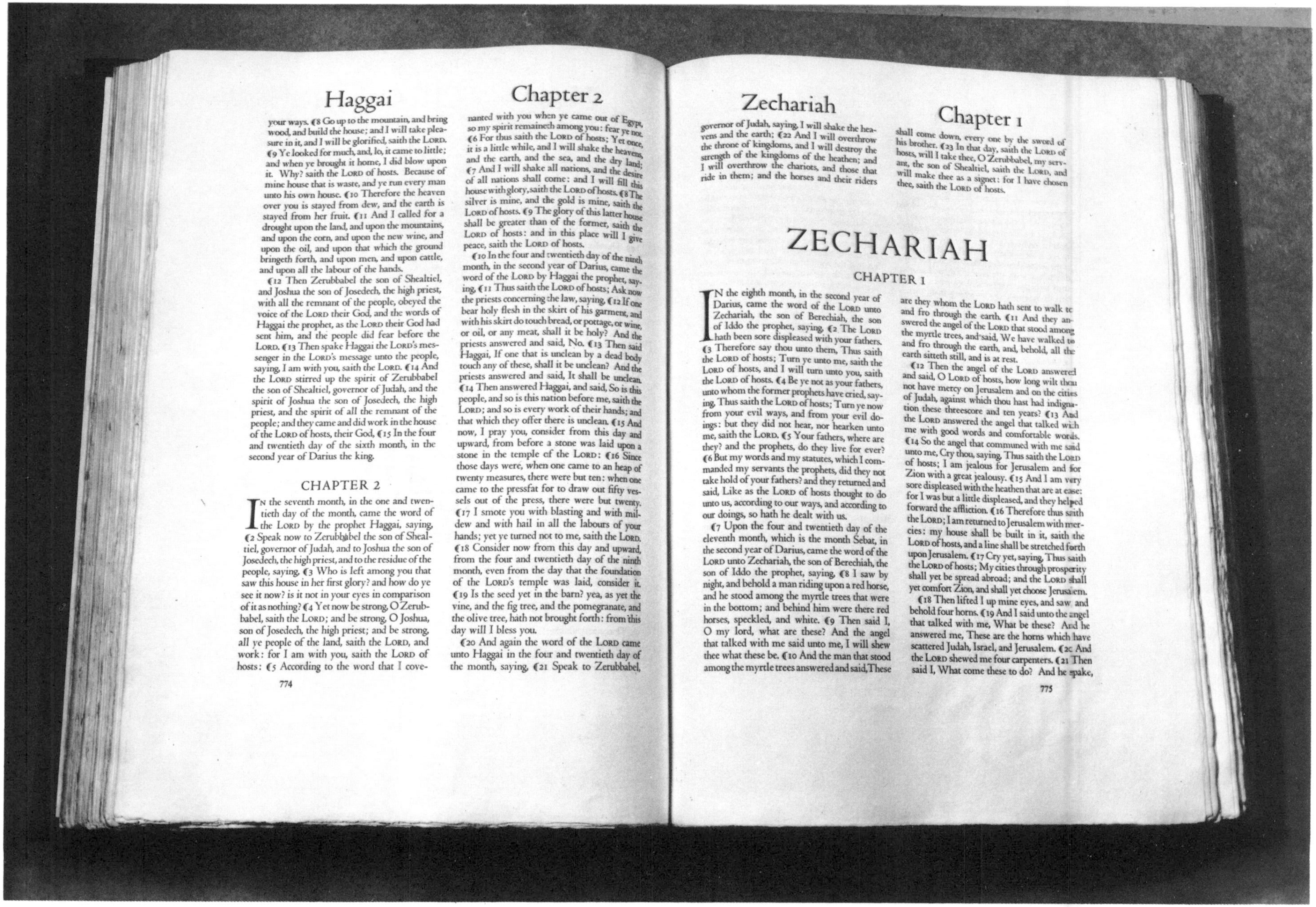

your ways. ❡8 Go up to the mountain, and bring wood, and build the house; and I will take pleasure in it, and I will be glorified, saith the LORD. ❡9 Ye looked for much, and, lo, it came to little; and when ye brought it home, I did blow upon it. Why? saith the LORD of hosts. Because of mine house that is waste, and ye run every man unto his own house. ❡10 Therefore the heaven over you is stayed from dew, and the earth is stayed from her fruit. ❡11 And I called for a drought upon the land, and upon the mountains, and upon the corn, and upon the new wine, and upon the oil, and upon that which the ground bringeth forth, and upon men, and upon cattle, and upon all the labour of the hands.

❡12 Then Zerubbabel the son of Shealtiel, and Joshua the son of Josedech, the high priest, with all the remnant of the people, obeyed the voice of the LORD their God, and the words of Haggai the prophet, as the LORD their God had sent him, and the people did fear before the LORD. ❡13 Then spake Haggai the LORD's messenger in the LORD's message unto the people, saying, I am with you, saith the LORD. ❡14 And the LORD stirred up the spirit of Zerubbabel the son of Shealtiel, governor of Judah, and the spirit of Joshua the son of Josedech, the high priest, and the spirit of all the remnant of the people; and they came and did work in the house of the LORD of hosts, their God, ❡15 In the four and twentieth day of the sixth month, in the second year of Darius the king.

CHAPTER 2

IN the seventh month, in the one and twentieth day of the month, came the word of the LORD by the prophet Haggai, saying, ❡2 Speak now to Zerubbabel the son of Shealtiel, governor of Judah, and to Joshua the son of Josedech, the high priest, and to the residue of the people, saying, ❡3 Who is left among you that saw this house in her first glory? and how do ye see it now? is it not in your eyes in comparison of it as nothing? ❡4 Yet now be strong, O Zerubbabel, saith the LORD; and be strong, O Joshua, son of Josedech, the high priest; and be strong, all ye people of the land, saith the LORD, and work: for I am with you, saith the LORD of hosts: ❡5 According to the word that I covenanted with you when ye came out of Egypt, so my spirit remaineth among you: fear ye not. ❡6 For thus saith the LORD of hosts; Yet once, it is a little while, and I will shake the heavens, and the earth, and the sea, and the dry land; ❡7 And I will shake all nations, and the desire of all nations shall come: and I will fill this house with glory, saith the LORD of hosts. ❡8 The silver is mine, and the gold is mine, saith the LORD of hosts. ❡9 The glory of this latter house shall be greater than of the former, saith the LORD of hosts: and in this place will I give peace, saith the LORD of hosts.

❡10 In the four and twentieth day of the ninth month, in the second year of Darius, came the word of the LORD by Haggai the prophet, saying, ❡11 Thus saith the LORD of hosts; Ask now the priests concerning the law, saying, ❡12 If one bear holy flesh in the skirt of his garment, and with his skirt do touch bread, or pottage, or wine, or oil, or any meat, shall it be holy? And the priests answered and said, No. ❡13 Then said Haggai, If one that is unclean by a dead body touch any of these, shall it be unclean? And the priests answered and said, It shall be unclean. ❡14 Then answered Haggai, and said, So is this people, and so is this nation before me, saith the LORD; and so is every work of their hands; and that which they offer there is unclean. ❡15 And now, I pray you, consider from this day and upward, from before a stone was laid upon a stone in the temple of the LORD: ❡16 Since those days were, when one came to an heap of twenty measures, there were but ten: when one came to the pressfat for to draw out fifty vessels out of the press, there were but twenty. ❡17 I smote you with blasting and with mildew and with hail in all the labours of your hands; yet ye turned not to me, saith the LORD. ❡18 Consider now from this day and upward, from the four and twentieth day of the ninth month, even from the day that the foundation of the LORD's temple was laid, consider it. ❡19 Is the seed yet in the barn? yea, as yet the vine, and the fig tree, and the pomegranate, and the olive tree, hath not brought forth: from this day will I bless you.

❡20 And again the word of the LORD came unto Haggai in the four and twentieth day of the month, saying, ❡21 Speak to Zerubbabel,

governor of Judah, saying, I will shake the heavens and the earth; ❡22 And I will overthrow the throne of kingdoms, and I will destroy the strength of the kingdoms of the heathen; and I will overthrow the chariots, and those that ride in them; and the horses and their riders shall come down, every one by the sword of his brother. ❡23 In that day, saith the LORD of hosts, will I take thee, O Zerubbabel, my servant, the son of Shealtiel, saith the LORD, and will make thee as a signet: for I have chosen thee, saith the LORD of hosts.

ZECHARIAH

CHAPTER 1

IN the eighth month, in the second year of Darius, came the word of the LORD unto Zechariah, the son of Berechiah, the son of Iddo the prophet, saying, ❡2 The LORD hath been sore displeased with your fathers. ❡3 Therefore say thou unto them, Thus saith the LORD of hosts; Turn ye unto me, saith the LORD of hosts, and I will turn unto you, saith the LORD of hosts. ❡4 Be ye not as your fathers, unto whom the former prophets have cried, saying, Thus saith the LORD of hosts; Turn ye now from your evil ways, and from your evil doings: but they did not hear, nor hearken unto me, saith the LORD. ❡5 Your fathers, where are they? and the prophets, do they live for ever? ❡6 But my words and my statutes, which I commanded my servants the prophets, did they not take hold of your fathers? and they returned and said, Like as the LORD of hosts thought to do unto us, according to our ways, and according to our doings, so hath he dealt with us.

❡7 Upon the four and twentieth day of the eleventh month, which is the month Sebat, in the second year of Darius, came the word of the LORD unto Zechariah, the son of Berechiah, the son of Iddo the prophet, saying, ❡8 I saw by night, and behold a man riding upon a red horse, and he stood among the myrtle trees that were in the bottom; and behind him were there red horses, speckled, and white. ❡9 Then said I, O my lord, what are these? And the angel that talked with me said unto me, I will shew thee what these be. ❡10 And the man that stood among the myrtle trees answered and said, These are they whom the LORD hath sent to walk to and fro through the earth. ❡11 And they answered the angel of the LORD that stood among the myrtle trees, and said, We have walked to and fro through the earth, and, behold, all the earth sitteth still, and is at rest.

❡12 Then the angel of the LORD answered and said, O LORD of hosts, how long wilt thou not have mercy on Jerusalem and on the cities of Judah, against which thou hast had indignation these threescore and ten years? ❡13 And the LORD answered the angel that talked with me with good words and comfortable words. ❡14 So the angel that communed with me said unto me, Cry thou, saying, Thus saith the LORD of hosts; I am jealous for Jerusalem and for Zion with a great jealousy. ❡15 And I am very sore displeased with the heathen that are at ease: for I was but a little displeased, and they helped forward the affliction. ❡16 Therefore thus saith the LORD; I am returned to Jerusalem with mercies: my house shall be built in it, saith the LORD of hosts, and a line shall be stretched forth upon Jerusalem. ❡17 Cry yet, saying, Thus saith the LORD of hosts; My cities through prosperity shall yet be spread abroad; and the LORD shall yet comfort Zion, and shall yet choose Jerusalem.

❡18 Then lifted I up mine eyes, and saw, and behold four horns. ❡19 And I said unto the angel that talked with me, What be these? And he answered me, These are the horns which have scattered Judah, Israel, and Jerusalem. ❡20 And the LORD shewed me four carpenters. ❡21 Then said I, What come these to do? And he spake,

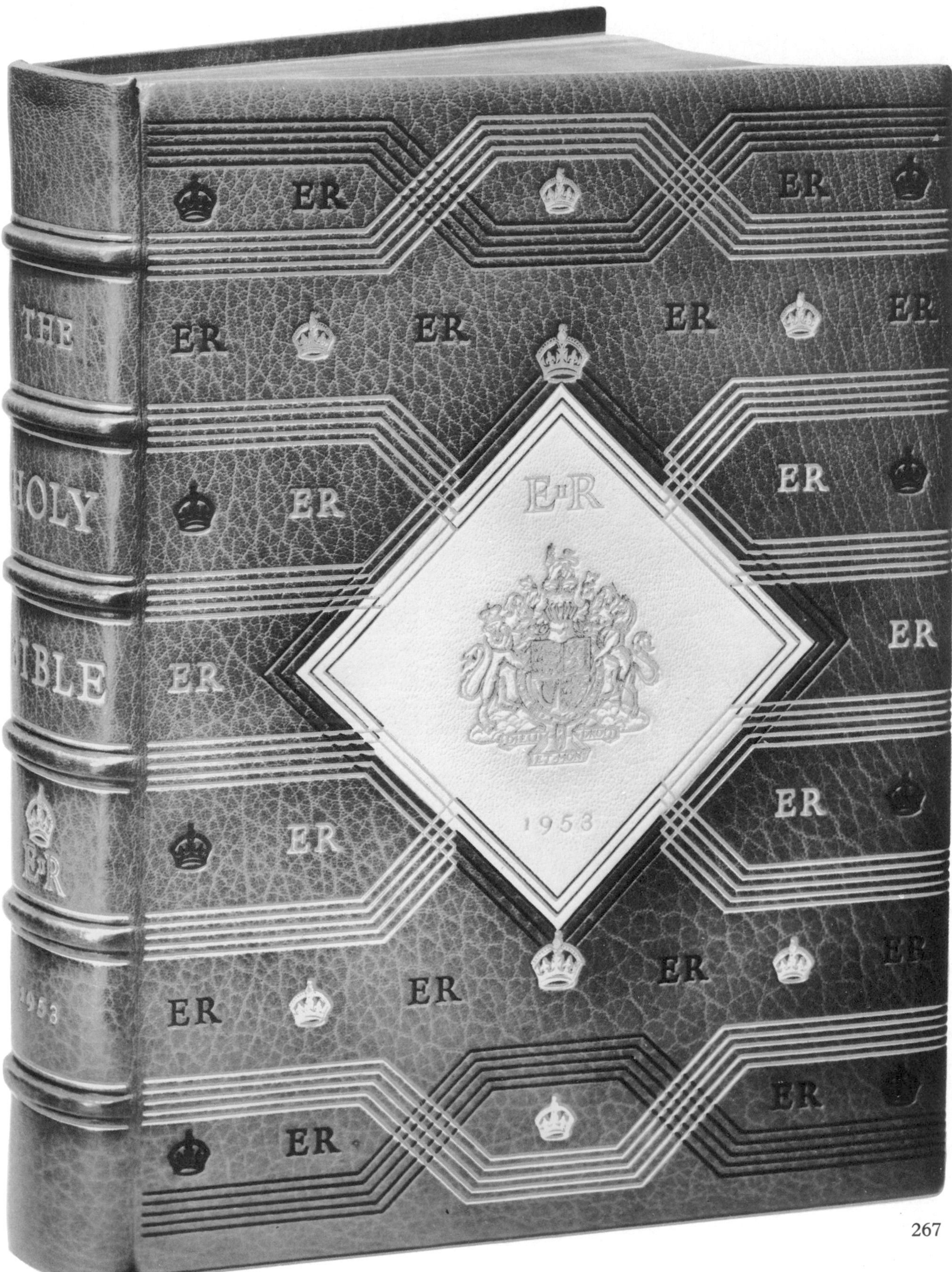

267

THE

HOLY BIBLE

CONTAINING THE

OLD AND NEW TESTAMENTS

TRANSLATED OUT OF THE ORIGINAL TONGUES
AND WITH THE FORMER TRANSLATIONS
DILIGENTLY COMPARED AND REVISED BY
HIS MAJESTY'S SPECIAL COMMAND

APPOINTED TO BE READ IN CHURCHES

CUM PRIVILEGIO

OXFORD : AT THE UNIVERSITY PRESS
LONDON : GEOFFREY CUMBERLEGE
OXFORD UNIVERSITY PRESS · AMEN HOUSE · EC4

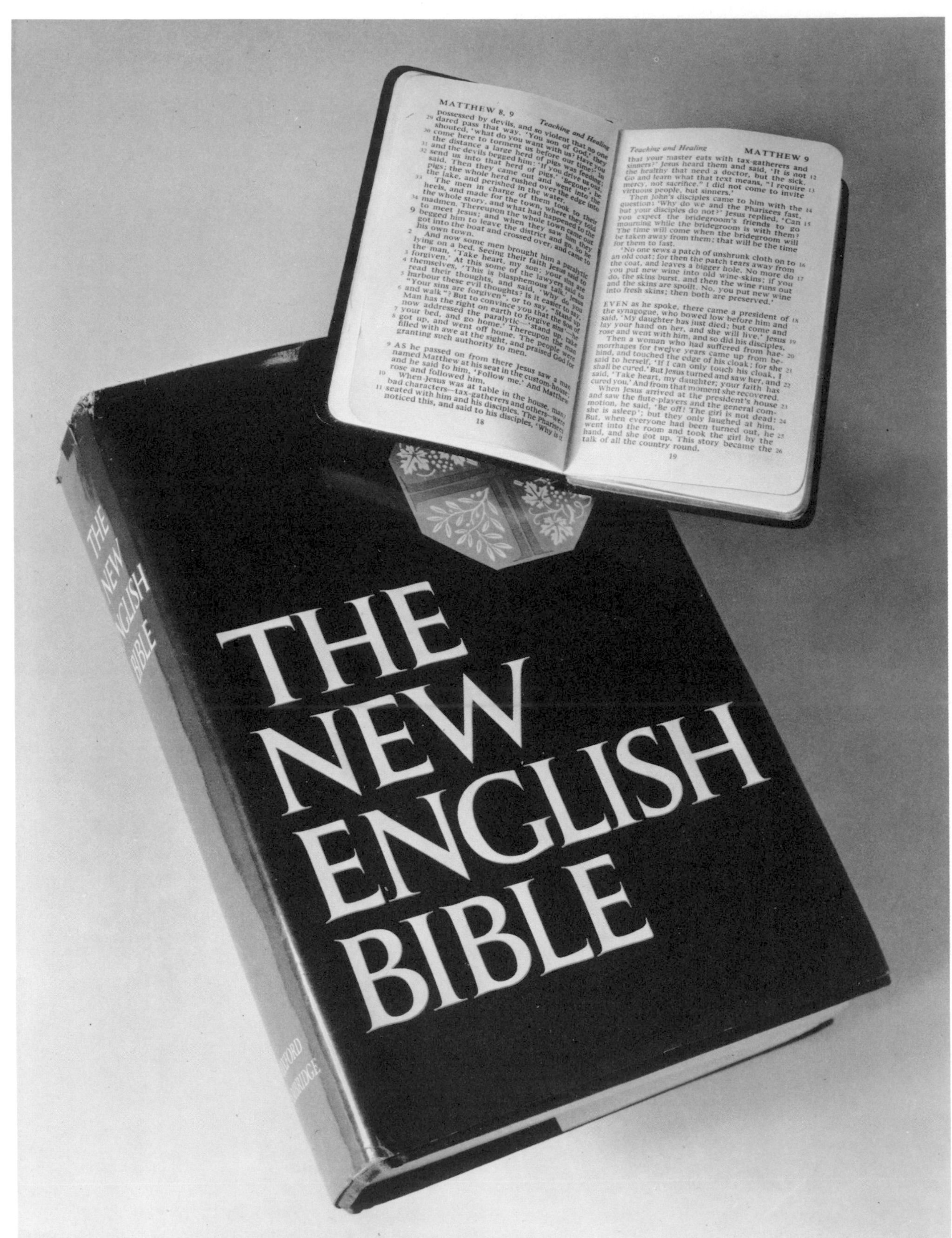
MATTHEW 8, 9
Teaching and Healing
18
Teaching and Healing
MATTHEW 9
19
THE NEW ENGLISH BIBLE
THE NEW ENGLISH BIBLE
THE NEW ENGLISH BIBLE

I

VINAYA TEXTS

81

Ch. 73. xii. 2a, Ch. 73. vii, frag. A. 6 and frag. 3, Poṭhī; 46·5 c.×11·5 c.: foll. 24, numbered ཀ 4, 6, 7, 10, 12–15, 20, 23–24, 27–28, 32–33, 36, 43, 52, 54, 63–64, 70–71; ll. 7: *dbu-can*, some damaged.

འཕགས་པ་[མི་འམ་ཅིའི་རྒྱལ་པོ་སྡོང་པོས་ཞུས་པ]་ཞེས་བྱ་བ་ཐེག་པ་ཆེན་པོའི་མདོ། *Ḥphags-pa-*[*mi-ḥam-ciḥi-rgyal-po-Sdoṅ-pos-źus-pa*]*-źes-bya-ba-theg-pa-chen-poḥi-mdo/* (*Ārya-*[*druma-kinnara-rāja-paripṛcchā*]*-nāma-mahāvāna-sūtra*)

Part of a Mahāyāna-sūtra.

Druma-kinnara-rāja-paripṛcchā, Mdo, Csoma, xii; Beckh, xiv; Nanjio, 161. Compare *Mahā-druma-kinnara-rāja-paripṛcchā*, Nanjio, 161, 162 (161 = *Mahā-druma-kinnara-rāja-paripṛcchā-ratna-tathā-gata-samādhi*).

On the excellencies and qualities of the Bodhisattvas, &c. The Bodhisattva Lhaḥi-cod-pan (Devamukuṭa) taught by the Sthavira Mahākāśyapa (fol. 10), by Bhagavat. Bhagavat and a Mahārāja, Prince Nirmalacakṣus (Dri-ma-myed-paḥi-mig); Bhagavat and Śāriputra; rain of flowers; '*bhagavan-maṇḍala-cakra*', and question of Śāriputra thereon.

The same hand as **125 b.**

Fol. 52. Ten *dharmas* to abandon womanhood.

Fol. 33. Kinnara-rāja (Sdoṅ-po)—32 purifications of gift.

Fol. 28. Kinnara-rāja.

Fol. 24. Lhaḥi-cod-pan inquires whether Sdoṅ-po, the chief interlocutor Kinnara-rāja, attains the Ratnākara-samādhi.

Fol. 70. Bhagavat, the King Ajātaśatru, and the Kinnara-rāja (Sdoṅ-po). On *bodhi-citta*, verso, l. 3:

. . . སླས་དང་བཅས་བུ་དང་བཅས་གཡོག་དང་བཅས་པས་འདིར་བྱང་ཆུབ་ཏུ་སེམས་བསྐྱེད་ནས།།དེ་དག་ཐམས་ཅད . . .

82

Ch. 03. 25, Poṭhī; 54 c.×7·3 c.: fol. 1, numbered 1; ll. 4: *dbu-can*: two holes, red circle, four lines yellow.

[དགའ་བོའི་མདོ།།] [*Dgaḥ-boḥi-mdo/*] ([*Nandika-sūtra*]) (*Nan-ti-ka-su-tra*) (ནན་ཏི་ཀ་སུ་ཏྲ)

Title and beginning of the Sūtra.

Bkaḥ-ḥgyur, Mdo, Csoma, xxvi. 425; Beckh, xxviii. 354.

Nandika asks བཅོམ་ལྡན་འདས . . . . སངས་རྒྱས་ཀྱིས་མཁྱེན་གཟིགས་ཏེ། གང་འདི་དགེ་བསྙེན་དག་གི་བསླབ་པ་ལྔ་བཤད་པ་དེ་དག་ལས། དགེ་བསྙེན་གྱིས་གལ་ན་ཉམས་པར་སྨིན་པ་ཅིར་འགྱུར།

Compare for the topic *Śikṣā-samuccaya*, p. 175. Dgaḥ-bo is a character in **47, 50, 176, 269.**

83

Ch. 77. xv. 1, Poṭhī; 44 c.×20 c.: fol. 1, unnumbered; ll. 12: *dbu-can.*

Bhagavat and Subhūti.

84 (*see* **165 d**)

85

Ch. 9. i, frag. 45, Poṭhī; 38 c.×8·5 c.: fol. a, unnumbered; ll. 13: *dbu-med.*

[ཤེས་རབ་ཀྱི་ཕ་རོལ་ཏུ་ཕྱིན་པ།] [*Śes-rab-kyi-pha-rol-tu-phyin-pa*]/ ([*Prajñā-pāramitā*])

Bhagavat teaches Śāriputra; the *Prajñā* and the *Prajñā-caryā* (*śes-rab-kyi-spyod-pa*) of a Bodhisattva.

Begins: ཤཱ་རི་བུ་དེ་ལ་ཤེས་རབ་ཞེས་བྱ་བ་ནི། །འདི་ལྟ་སྟེ། དགེ་བི་ཆོས་ཐམས་ཅད་རབ་ཏུ་རྟོགས་པ་གང་ཡིན་པ་དེ་ནི

[TIBETAN]

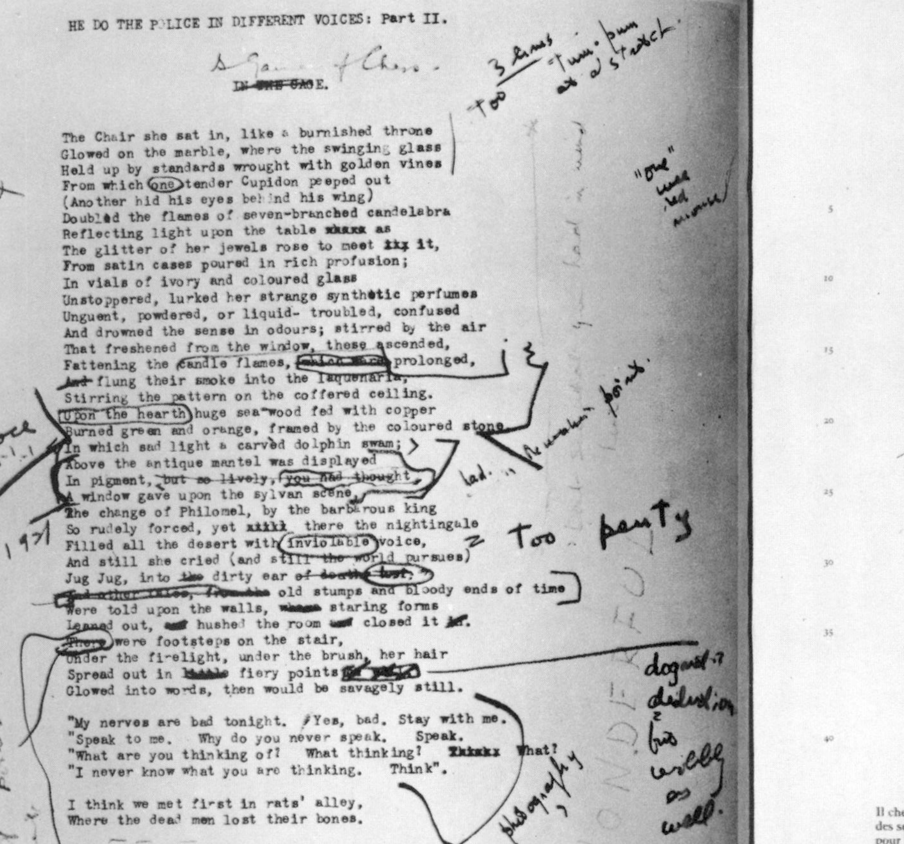

HE DO THE POLICE IN DIFFERENT VOICES: Part II.

~~IN THE CAGE.~~

The Chair she sat in, like a burnished throne
Glowed on the marble, where the swinging glass
Held up by standards wrought with golden vines
From which one tender Cupidon peeped out
(Another hid his eyes behind his wing)
Doubled the flames of seven-branched candelabra
Reflecting light upon the table ~~where~~ as
The glitter of her jewels rose to meet ~~it,~~ it,
From satin cases poured in rich profusion;
In vials of ivory and coloured glass
Unstoppered, lurked her strange synthetic perfumes
Unguent, powdered, or liquid- troubled, confused
And drowned the sense in odours; stirred by the air
That freshened from the window, these ascended,
Fattening the candle flames, ~~which were~~ prolonged,
~~And~~ flung their smoke into the laquenaria,
Stirring the pattern on the coffered ceiling.
Upon the hearth huge sea-wood fed with copper
Burned green and orange, framed by the coloured stone,
In which sad light a carvèd dolphin swam;
Above the antique mantel was displayed
In pigment, ~~but so lively,~~ you had thought,
A window gave upon the sylvan scene,
The change of Philomel, by the barbarous king
So rudely forced, yet ~~still~~ there the nightingale
Filled all the desert with inviolable voice,
And still she cried (and still the world pursues)
Jug Jug, into ~~the~~ dirty ear ~~of death;~~ lust.
~~And other tales, from the~~ old stumps and bloody ends of time
Were told upon the walls, ~~where~~ staring forms
Leaned out, ~~and~~ hushed the room ~~and~~ closed it ~~in~~.
~~There~~ were footsteps on the stair,
Under the fi-elight, under the brush, her hair
Spread out in ~~little~~ fiery points ~~of will,~~
Glowed into words, then would be savagely still.

"My nerves are bad tonight. Yes, bad. Stay with me.
"Speak to me. Why do you never speak. Speak.
"What are you thinking of? What thinking? ~~Think~~ What?
"I never know what you are thinking. Think".

I think we met first in rats' alley,
Where the dead men lost their bones.

"What-is-that-noise?"

The wind under the door.

"What is that noise now? What is the wind doing?"

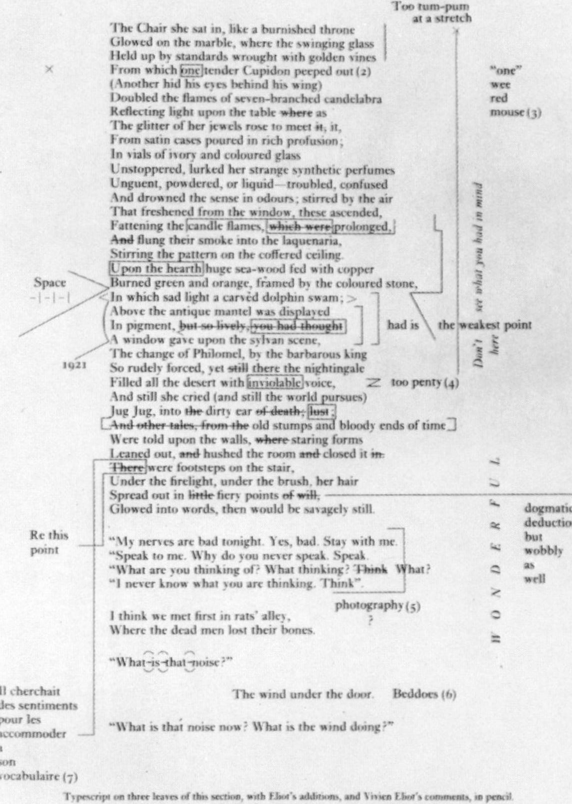

HE DO THE POLICE IN DIFFERENT VOICES: Part II.

A Game of Chess.
~~IN THE CAGE.~~ (1)

3 lines
Too tum-pum
at a stretch

The Chair she sat in, like a burnished throne
Glowed on the marble, where the swinging glass
Held up by standards wrought with golden vines
From which one tender Cupidon peeped out (2)
(Another hid his eyes behind his wing)
Doubled the flames of seven-branched candelabra
Reflecting light upon the table ~~where~~ as
The glitter of her jewels rose to meet ~~it,~~ it,
From satin cases poured in rich profusion;
In vials of ivory and coloured glass
Unstoppered, lurked her strange synthetic perfumes
Unguent, powdered, or liquid—troubled, confused
And drowned the sense in odours; stirred by the air
That freshened from the window, these ascended,
Fattening the candle flames, ~~which were~~ prolonged,
~~And~~ flung their smoke into the laquenaria,
Stirring the pattern on the coffered ceiling.
Upon the hearth huge sea-wood fed with copper
Burned green and orange, framed by the coloured stone,
In which sad light a carvèd dolphin swam; >
Above the antique mantel was displayed
In pigment, ~~but so lively,~~ ~~you had thought~~
A window gave upon the sylvan scene,
The change of Philomel, by the barbarous king
So rudely forced, yet ~~still~~ there the nightingale
Filled all the desert with inviolable voice,
And still she cried (and still the world pursues)
Jug Jug, into ~~the~~ dirty ear ~~of death;~~ lust.
~~And other tales, from the~~ old stumps and bloody ends of time
Were told upon the walls, ~~where~~ staring forms
Leaned out, ~~and~~ hushed the room ~~and~~ closed it ~~in~~.
~~There~~ were footsteps on the stair,
Under the firelight, under the brush, her hair
Spread out in ~~little~~ fiery points ~~of will,~~
Glowed into words, then would be savagely still.

"My nerves are bad tonight. Yes, bad. Stay with me.
"Speak to me. Why do you never speak. Speak.
"What are you thinking of? What thinking? ~~Think~~ What?
"I never know what you are thinking. Think".

I think we met first in rats' alley,
Where the dead men lost their bones.

"What-is-that-noise?"

The wind under the door. Beddoes (6)

"What is that noise now? What is the wind doing?"

"one"
wee
red
mouse (3)

Space
-|-|-|

1921

had is the weakest point

Don't see what you had in mind here

too penty (4)

W O N D E R F U L

dogmatic
deduction
but
wobbly
as
well

Re this
point

photography (5)
?

Il cherchait
des sentiments
pour les
accommoder
a
son
vocabulaire (7)

Typescript on three leaves of this section, with Eliot's additions, and Vivien Eliot's comments, in pencil. Pound's criticism is in pencil and in ink. Line 16: laquenaria] laquearia

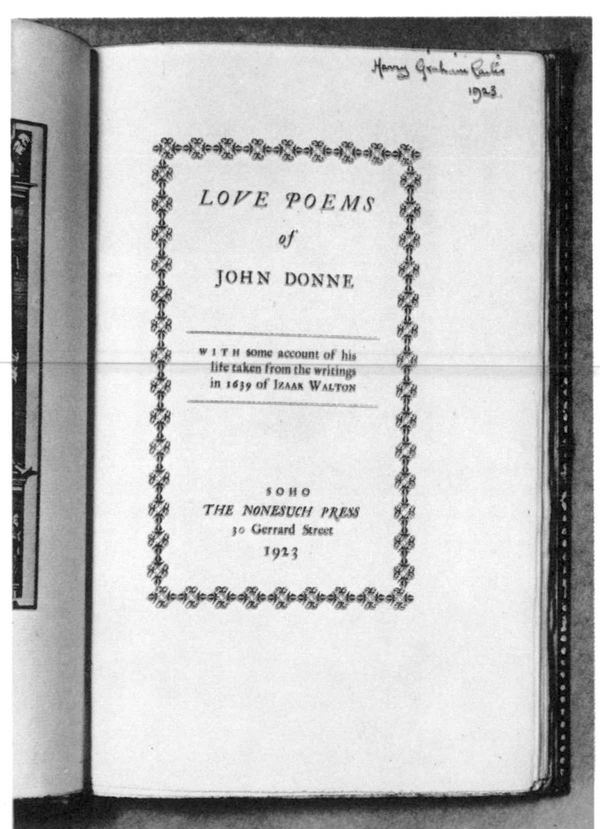

LOVE POEMS
of
JOHN DONNE

WITH some account of his
life taken from the writings
in 1639 of IZAAK WALTON

SOHO
THE NONESUCH PRESS
30 Gerrard Street
1923

274

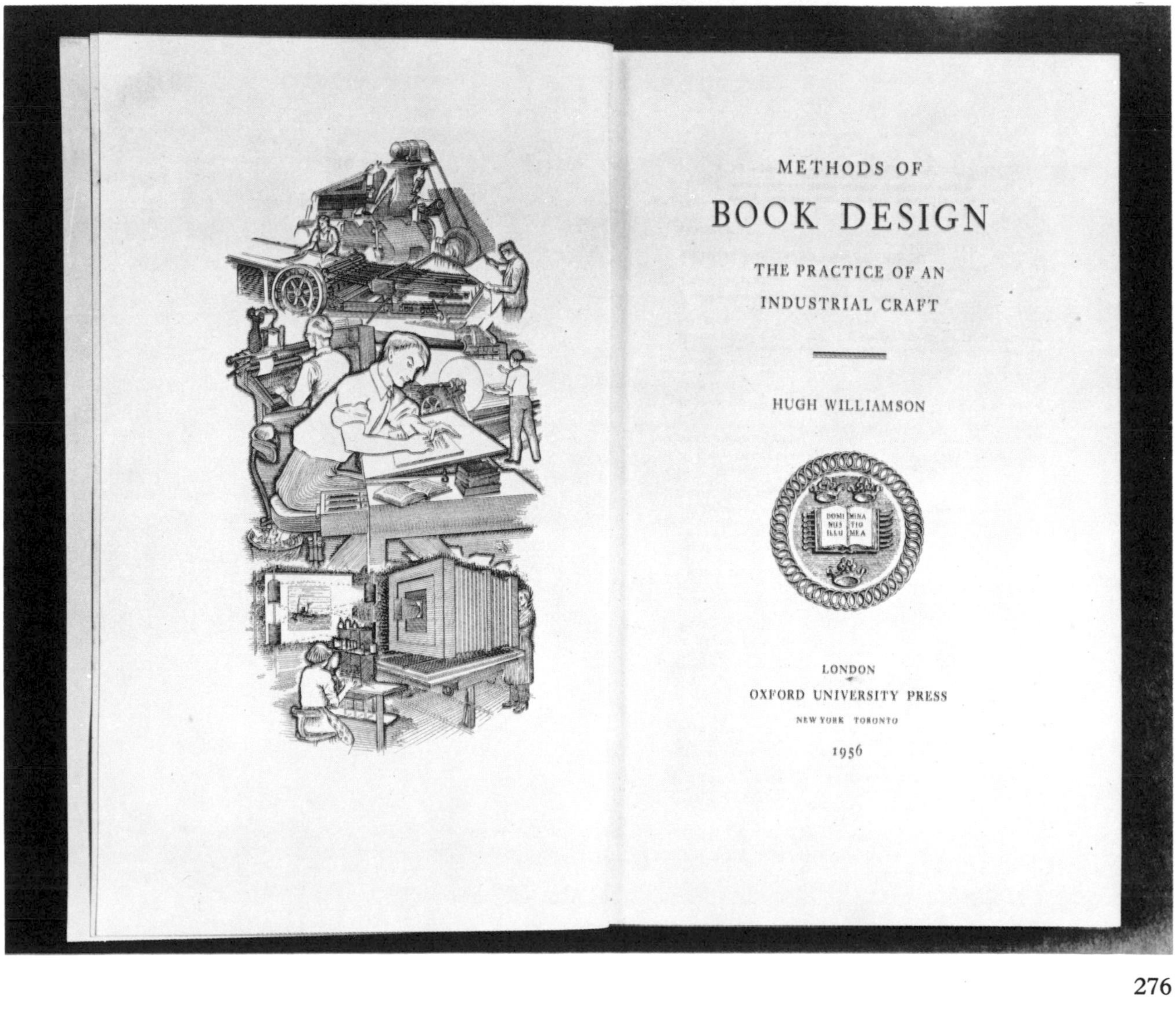

METHODS OF
BOOK DESIGN
THE PRACTICE OF AN
INDUSTRIAL CRAFT

HUGH WILLIAMSON

DOMI NA
NUS TIO
ILLU MEA

LONDON
OXFORD UNIVERSITY PRESS
NEW YORK TORONTO
1956

276

For Mrs. Lucy G. Speed, from whose pious hand I ac-
cepted the present of an Oxford Bible twenty years ago.
Washington, D.C. October 3, 1861
A. Lincoln

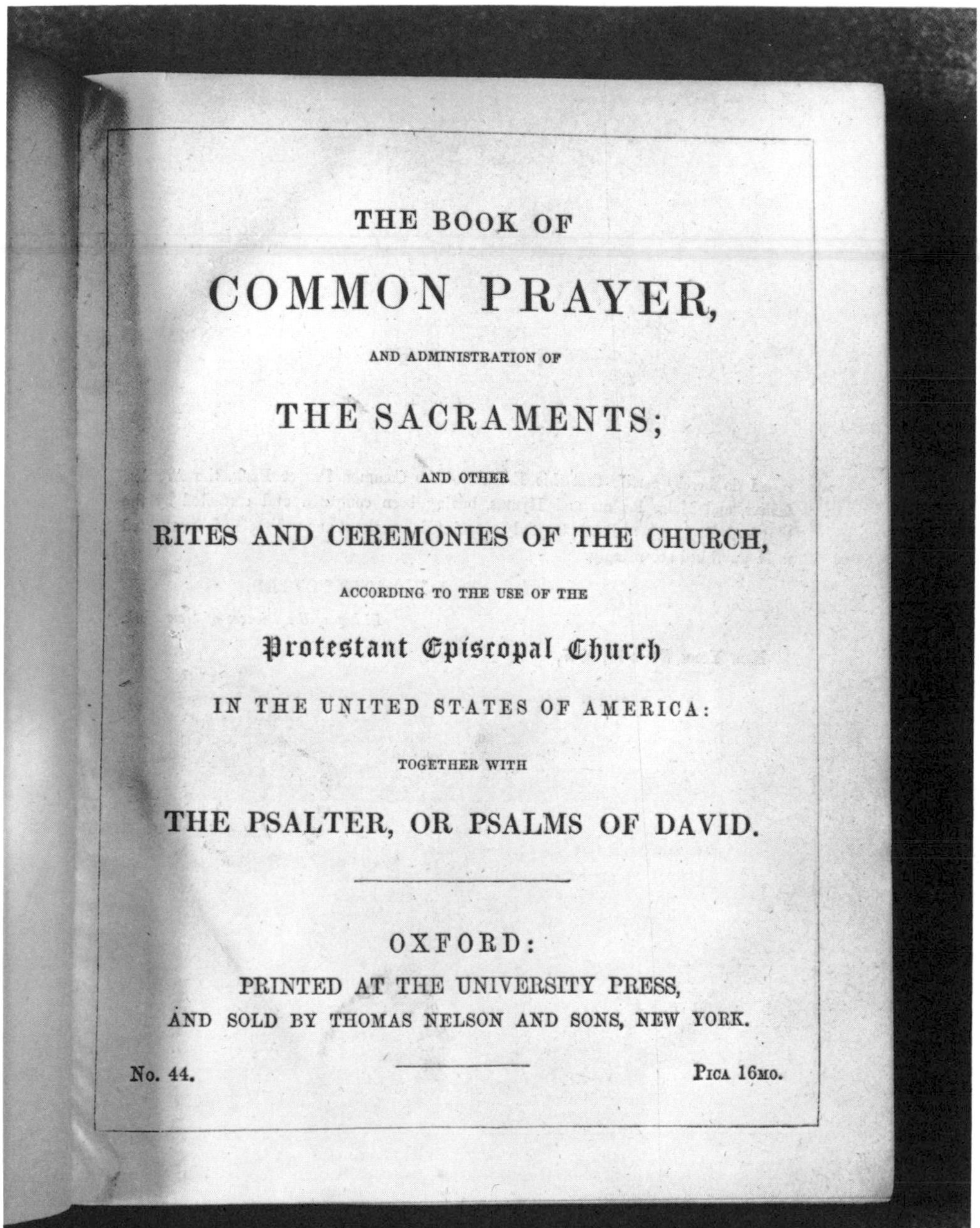

THE BOOK OF

COMMON PRAYER,

AND ADMINISTRATION OF

THE SACRAMENTS;

AND OTHER

RITES AND CEREMONIES OF THE CHURCH,

ACCORDING TO THE USE OF THE

Protestant Episcopal Church

IN THE UNITED STATES OF AMERICA:

TOGETHER WITH

THE PSALTER, OR PSALMS OF DAVID.

OXFORD:
PRINTED AT THE UNIVERSITY PRESS,
AND SOLD BY THOMAS NELSON AND SONS, NEW YORK.

No. 44. PICA 16MO.

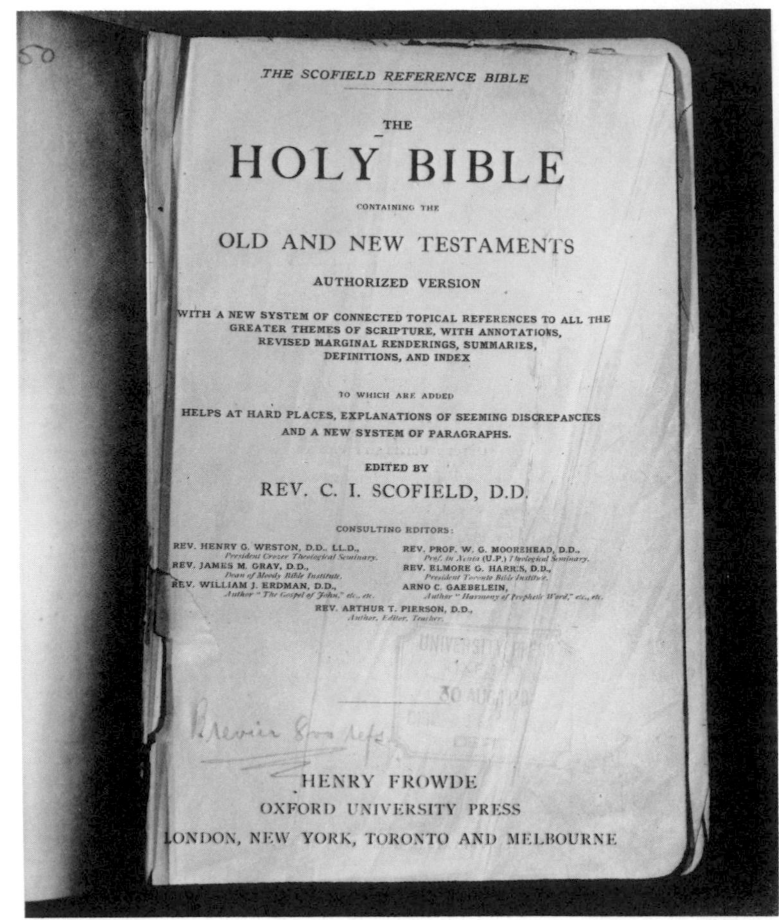

THE SCOFIELD REFERENCE BIBLE

THE

HOLY BIBLE

CONTAINING THE

OLD AND NEW TESTAMENTS

AUTHORIZED VERSION

WITH A NEW SYSTEM OF CONNECTED TOPICAL REFERENCES TO ALL THE GREATER THEMES OF SCRIPTURE, WITH ANNOTATIONS, REVISED MARGINAL RENDERINGS, SUMMARIES, DEFINITIONS, AND INDEX

TO WHICH ARE ADDED

HELPS AT HARD PLACES, EXPLANATIONS OF SEEMING DISCREPANCIES AND A NEW SYSTEM OF PARAGRAPHS.

EDITED BY

REV. C. I. SCOFIELD, D.D.

CONSULTING EDITORS:

REV. HENRY G. WESTON, D.D., LL.D., *President Crozer Theological Seminary.*
REV. PROF. W. G. MOOREHEAD, D.D., *Prof. in Xenia (U.P.) Theological Seminary.*
REV. JAMES M. GRAY, D.D., *Dean of Moody Bible Institute.*
REV. ELMORE G. HARRIS, D.D., *President Toronto Bible Institute.*
REV. WILLIAM J. ERDMAN, D.D., *Author "The Gospel of John," etc., etc.*
ARNO C. GAEBELEIN, *Author "Harmony of Prophetic Word," etc., etc.*
REV. ARTHUR T. PIERSON, D.D., *Author, Editor, Teacher.*

HENRY FROWDE
OXFORD UNIVERSITY PRESS
LONDON, NEW YORK, TORONTO AND MELBOURNE

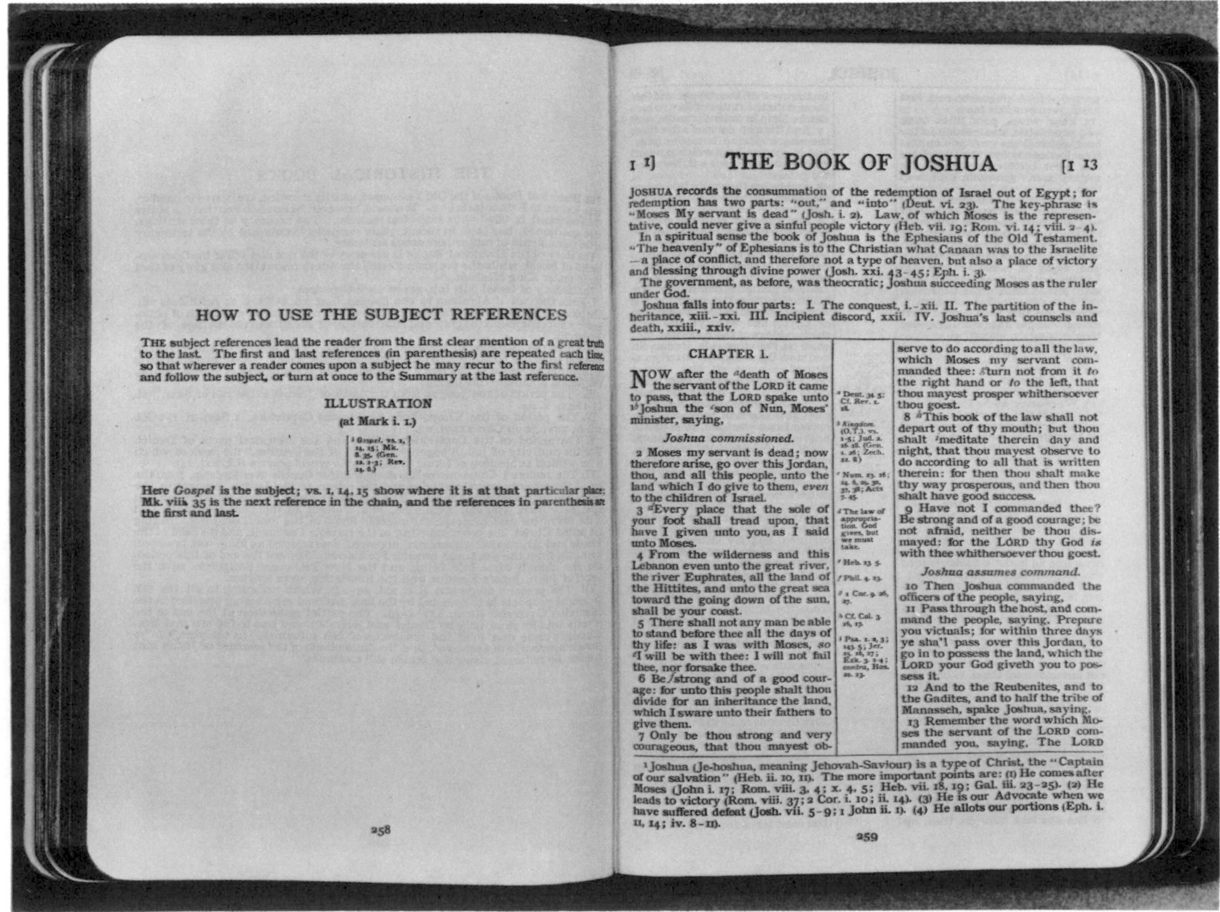

HOW TO USE THE SUBJECT REFERENCES

THE subject references lead the reader from the first clear mention of a great truth to the last. The first and last references (in parenthesis) are repeated each time, so that wherever a reader comes upon a subject he may recur to the first reference and follow the subject, or turn at once to the Summary at the last reference.

ILLUSTRATION

(at Mark i. 1.)

[1] *Gospel*, vs. 1, 14, 15; Mk. 8. 35. (Gen. 12. 1-3; Rev. 14. 6.)

Here *Gospel* is the subject; vs. 1, 14, 15 show where it is at that particular place; Mk. viii. 35 is the next reference in the chain, and the references in parenthesis are the first and last.

258

1 1] THE BOOK OF JOSHUA [1 13

JOSHUA records the consummation of the redemption of Israel out of Egypt; for redemption has two parts: "out," and "into" (Deut. vi. 23). The key-phrase is "Moses My servant is dead" (Josh. i. 2). Law, of which Moses is the representative, could never give a sinful people victory (Heb. vii. 19; Rom. vi. 14; viii. 2-4).

In a spiritual sense the book of Joshua is the Ephesians of the Old Testament. "The heavenly" of Ephesians is to the Christian what Canaan was to the Israelite—a place of conflict, and therefore not a type of heaven, but also a place of victory and blessing through divine power (Josh. xxi. 43-45; Eph. i. 3).

The government, as before, was theocratic; Joshua succeeding Moses as the ruler under God.

Joshua falls into four parts: I. The conquest, i.-xii. II. The partition of the inheritance, xiii.-xxi. III. Incipient discord, xxii. IV. Joshua's last counsels and death, xxiii., xxiv.

CHAPTER 1.

NOW after the [a]death of Moses the servant of the LORD it came to pass, that the LORD spake unto [1b]Joshua the [c]son of Nun, Moses' minister, saying,

Joshua commissioned.

2 Moses my servant is dead; now therefore arise, go over this Jordan, thou, and all this people, unto the land which I do give to them, *even* to the children of Israel.

3 [d]Every place that the sole of your foot shall tread upon, that have I given unto you, as I said unto Moses.

4 From the wilderness and this Lebanon even unto the great river, the river Euphrates, all the land of the Hittites, and unto the great sea toward the going down of the sun, shall be your coast.

5 There shall not any man be able to stand before thee all the days of thy life: as I was with Moses, *so* [e]I will be with thee: I will not fail thee, nor forsake thee.

6 Be [f]strong and of a good courage: for unto this people shalt thou divide for an inheritance the land, which I sware unto their fathers to give them.

7 Only be thou strong and very courageous, that thou mayest observe to do according to all the law, which Moses my servant commanded thee: [g]turn not from it *to* the right hand or *to* the left, that thou mayest prosper whithersoever thou goest.

8 [h]This book of the law shall not depart out of thy mouth; but thou shalt [i]meditate therein day and night, that thou mayest observe to do according to all that is written therein: for then thou shalt make thy way prosperous, and then thou shalt have good success.

9 Have not I commanded thee? Be strong and of a good courage; be not afraid, neither be thou dismayed: for the LORD thy God *is* with thee whithersoever thou goest.

Joshua assumes command.

10 Then Joshua commanded the officers of the people, saying,

11 Pass through the host, and command the people, saying, Prepare you victuals; for within three days ye shall pass over this Jordan, to go in to possess the land, which the LORD your God giveth you to possess it.

12 And to the Reubenites, and to the Gadites, and to half the tribe of Manasseh, spake Joshua, saying,

13 Remember the word which Moses the servant of the LORD commanded you, saying, The LORD

[a] Deut. 34. 5; Cf. Rev. 1. 18.
[b] *Kingdom* (O.T.). vs. 1-5; Jud. 2. 16-18. (Gen. 1. 26; Zech. 12. 8)
[c] Num. 13. 16; 14. 6, 29, 30, 37, 38; Acts 7. 45.
[d] The law of appropriation. God gives, but we must take.
[e] Heb. 13. 5.
[f] Phil. 4. 13.
[g] 1 Cor. 9. 26, 27.
[h] Cf. Col. 3. 16, 17.
[i] Psa. 1. 2, 3; 143. 5; Jer. 15. 16, 17; Ezk. 3. 1-4; *contra*, Hos. 10. 13.

[1] Joshua (Je-hoshua, meaning Jehovah-Saviour) is a type of Christ, the "Captain of our salvation" (Heb. ii. 10, 11). The more important points are: (1) He comes after Moses (John i. 17; Rom. viii. 3, 4; x. 4, 5; Heb. vii. 18, 19; Gal. iii. 23-25). (2) He leads to victory (Rom. viii. 37; 2 Cor. i. 10; ii. 14). (3) He is our Advocate when we have suffered defeat (Josh. vii. 5-9; 1 John ii. 1). (4) He allots our portions (Eph. i. 11, 14; iv. 8-11).

259

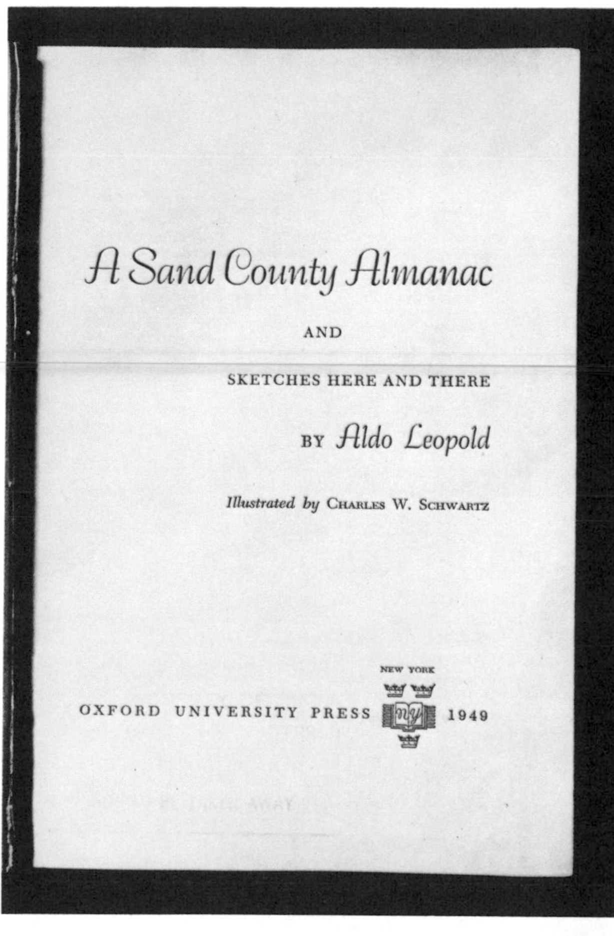

A Sand County Almanac

AND

SKETCHES HERE AND THERE

BY *Aldo Leopold*

Illustrated by CHARLES W. SCHWARTZ

NEW YORK

OXFORD UNIVERSITY PRESS 1949

285

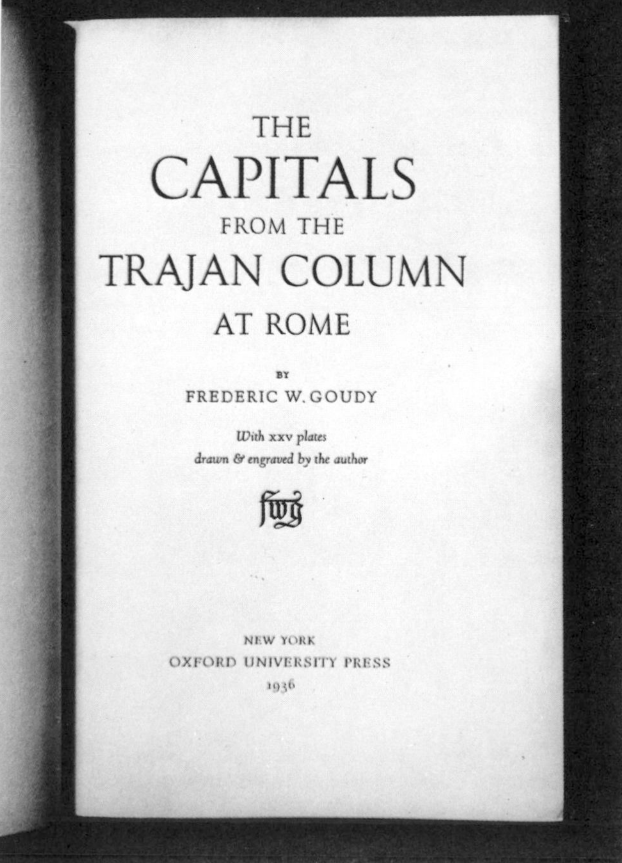

THE

CAPITALS

FROM THE

TRAJAN COLUMN

AT ROME

BY

FREDERIC W. GOUDY

With xxv plates
drawn & engraved by the author

fwg

NEW YORK
OXFORD UNIVERSITY PRESS
1936

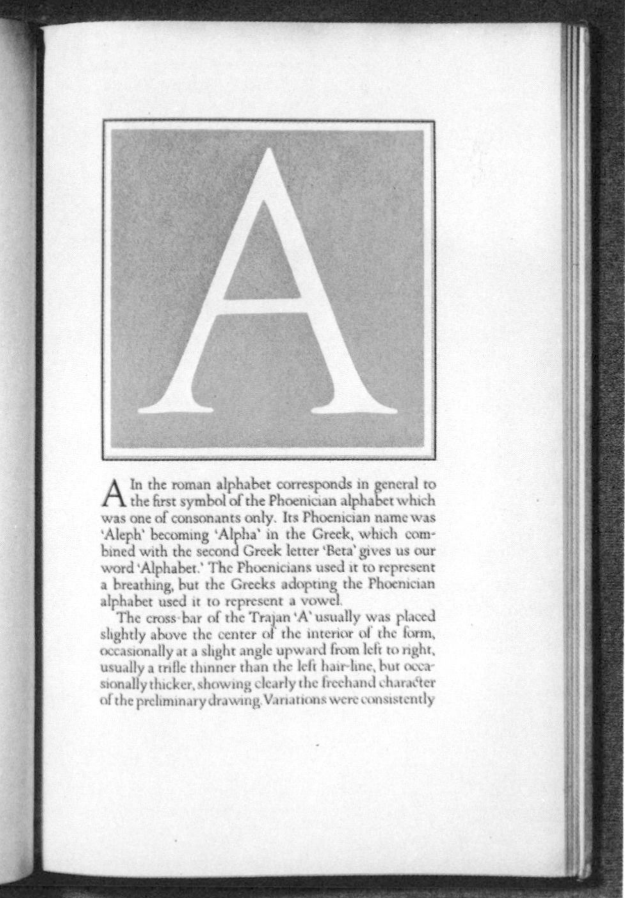

A In the roman alphabet corresponds in general to the first symbol of the Phoenician alphabet which was one of consonants only. Its Phoenician name was 'Aleph' becoming 'Alpha' in the Greek, which combined with the second Greek letter 'Beta' gives us our word 'Alphabet.' The Phoenicians used it to represent a breathing, but the Greeks adopting the Phoenician alphabet used it to represent a vowel.

The cross-bar of the Trajan 'A' usually was placed slightly above the center of the interior of the form, occasionally at a slight angle upward from left to right, usually a trifle thinner than the left hair-line, but occasionally thicker, showing clearly the freehand character of the preliminary drawing. Variations were consistently

288

CLARENDON
BUILDING
OXFORD UNIVERSITY PRESS
OXFORD BIBLES

292

294

way a general definition of the operator $\partial/\partial t$ in which there is, of course, a considerable amount of indefiniteness, owing not only to the arbitrary phases of the representation but also to the fact that we can take different sets of q's to be diagonal and will then in general get different results. We are interested, however, in only one of the operators $\partial/\partial t$, this being the one that is given when the phases of the representation do not depend explicitly on t, so that when a time displacement δt is applied to a state, the $q_{t+\delta t}$-representative of the displaced state is the same function of its variables $q'_{t+\delta t}$ that the q_t-representative of the undisplaced state is of its variables q'_t. Thus to obtain the q_t-representative of the displaced state we must substitute $t-\delta t$ for t in the q_t-representative of the undisplaced state, considered as a function of the $n+1$ variables $q'_1, q'_2, \ldots q'_n, t$. There is now complete analogy with the x-displacement case, so that (42) follows in the same way as (37). The validity of (42) shows that the operator $\partial/\partial t$ defined by a representation with phases not explicitly dependent on t is independent of which set of q's are diagonal in the representation. If we have one representation giving a $\partial/\partial t$ operator that satisfies (42), we can obtain another by making any canonical transformation for which the transformation function does not involve t.

From (41) and (42) we obtain

$$i\hbar\frac{\partial\psi}{\partial t} = H\psi. \tag{43}$$

This may be regarded as an alternative way of expressing the equations of motion of the system. Expressed in terms of representatives, it gives us *

$$i\hbar\frac{\partial}{\partial t}(q'_t|) = \int (q'_t|H|q''_t)\,dq''_t\,(q''_t|), \tag{44}$$

an equation which shows how the representative $(q'_t|)$ of a state, considered as a function of the $n+1$ variables $q'_1, q'_2, \ldots q'_n, t$, varies with t. When the q_r have conjugate momenta p_r, it reduces to the ordinary differential equation

$$i\hbar\frac{\partial}{\partial t}(q'_t|) = H\Big(q'_t, -i\hbar\frac{\partial}{\partial q'_t}\Big)(q'_t|). \tag{45}$$

This equation was discovered by Schrödinger and is known as *Schrödinger's wave equation*. It is very useful in applications of

* The case of continuous q''s is taken for definiteness, the usual modifications in the notation being required for the discrete case.

quantum mechanics since its solutions have an immediate physical interpretation, the square of the modulus of any solution giving the probability of the q's having specified values for one particular state throughout all time. It is called a wave equation because in many elementary examples, as will be seen in the next chapter, its solutions are of the form of waves moving through q-space. For this same reason the solutions are called *wave functions*, even also in those examples where they have no resemblance to waves.

When the Hamiltonian does not involve the time explicitly, the wave equation in the form (45) or in the more general form (44) will have solutions that vary periodically with the time, according to the law

$$(q'|) = (q'|)_0 e^{-iW't/\hbar}, \tag{46}$$

where W' is a number and $(q'|)_0$ is independent of t. The equation that $(q'|)_0$ must satisfy is

$$W'(q'|)_0 = \int (q'|H|q'')\,dq''(q''|)_0$$
$$= H\Big(q', -i\hbar\frac{\partial}{\partial q'}\Big)(q'|)_0.$$

But this is just the equation for determining the eigenvalues of H, namely, equation (29) with H for f. Thus W' is an eigenvalue of H or energy-level of the system and $(q'|)_0$ is an eigenfunction of H.

§ 38. Heisenberg's Matrices

In the preceding section we dealt with a q_t-representation, defined by observables q_t that are the values at time t of a set of dynamical variables q. We saw that if the phases of the representation are suitably chosen, then Schrödinger's equation holds, in the form (44) or (45), in which case the representation may conveniently be called a Schrödinger representation. The condition for the phases is such that, when a state is given a time-displacement δt, the $q_{t+\delta t}$-representative of the displaced state is the same function of its variables $q'_{t+\delta t}$ as the q_t-representative of the undisplaced state is of its variables q'_t. This condition will hold in an analogous form for observables. If we take an observable ξ_t which is the value at time t of a dynamical variable ξ, then the displaced observable will be $\xi_{t+\delta t}$. We shall then have that the $q_{t+\delta t}$-representative of the displaced observable, namely $(q'_{t+\delta t}|\xi_{t+\delta t}|q''_{t+\delta t})$, is the same function of its variables $q'_{t+\delta t}, q''_{t+\delta t}$ as the q_t-representative of the undisplaced observable, namely $(q'_t|\xi_t|q''_t)$, is of its variables q'_t, q''_t. This means simply that the form of the

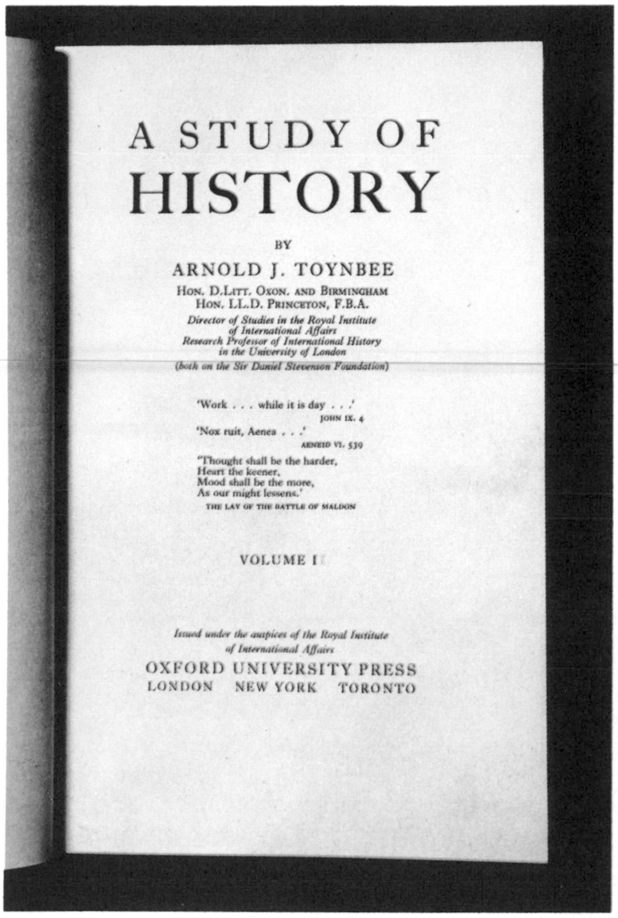

A STUDY OF

HISTORY

BY

ARNOLD J. TOYNBEE

HON. D.LITT. OXON. AND BIRMINGHAM
HON. LL.D. PRINCETON, F.B.A.

Director of Studies in the Royal Institute of International Affairs
Research Professor of International History in the University of London
(both on the Sir Daniel Stevenson Foundation)

'Work . . . while it is day . . .'
JOHN IX. 4

'Nox ruit, Aenea . . .'
AENEID VI. 539

'Thought shall be the harder,
Heart the keener,
Mood shall be the more,
As our might lessens.'
THE LAY OF THE BATTLE OF MALDON

VOLUME I

Issued under the auspices of the Royal Institute of International Affairs

OXFORD UNIVERSITY PRESS
LONDON NEW YORK TORONTO

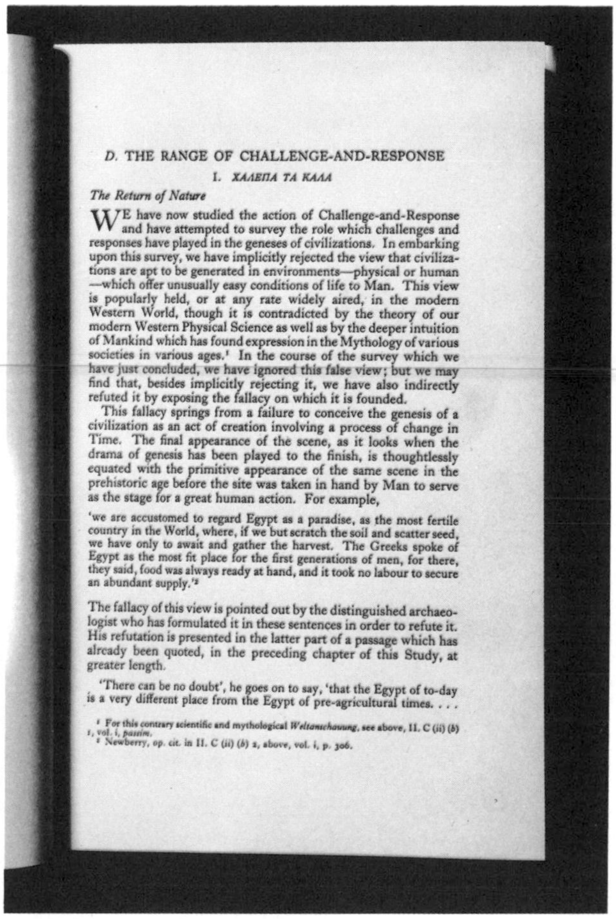

D. THE RANGE OF CHALLENGE-AND-RESPONSE

I. *ΧΑΛΕΠΑ ΤΑ ΚΑΛΑ*

The Return of Nature

WE have now studied the action of Challenge-and-Response and have attempted to survey the role which challenges and responses have played in the geneses of civilizations. In embarking upon this survey, we have implicitly rejected the view that civilizations are apt to be generated in environments—physical or human—which offer unusually easy conditions of life to Man. This view is popularly held, or at any rate widely aired, in the modern Western World, though it is contradicted by the theory of our modern Western Physical Science as well as by the deeper intuition of Mankind which has found expression in the Mythology of various societies in various ages.[1] In the course of the survey which we have just concluded, we have ignored this false view; but we may find that, besides implicitly rejecting it, we have also indirectly refuted it by exposing the fallacy on which it is founded.

This fallacy springs from a failure to conceive the genesis of a civilization as an act of creation involving a process of change in Time. The final appearance of the scene, as it looks when the drama of genesis has been played to the finish, is thoughtlessly equated with the primitive appearance of the same scene in the prehistoric age before the site was taken in hand by Man to serve as the stage for a great human action. For example,

'we are accustomed to regard Egypt as a paradise, as the most fertile country in the World, where, if we but scratch the soil and scatter seed, we have only to await and gather the harvest. The Greeks spoke of Egypt as the most fit place for the first generations of men, for there, they said, food was always ready at hand, and it took no labour to secure an abundant supply.'[2]

The fallacy of this view is pointed out by the distinguished archaeologist who has formulated it in these sentences in order to refute it. His refutation is presented in the latter part of a passage which has already been quoted, in the preceding chapter of this Study, at greater length.

'There can be no doubt', he goes on to say, 'that the Egypt of to-day is a very different place from the Egypt of pre-agricultural times. . . .

[1] For this contrary scientific and mythological *Weltanschauung*, see above, II. C (ii) (*b*) 1, vol. i, *passim*.
[2] Newberry, *op. cit.* in II. C (ii) (*b*) 2, above, vol. i, p. 306.

308

THE OXFORD COMPANION TO ENGLISH LITERATURE

COMPILED AND EDITED BY
SIR PAUL HARVEY

FOURTH EDITION
REVISED BY
DOROTHY EAGLE

OXFORD
AT THE CLARENDON PRESS

309

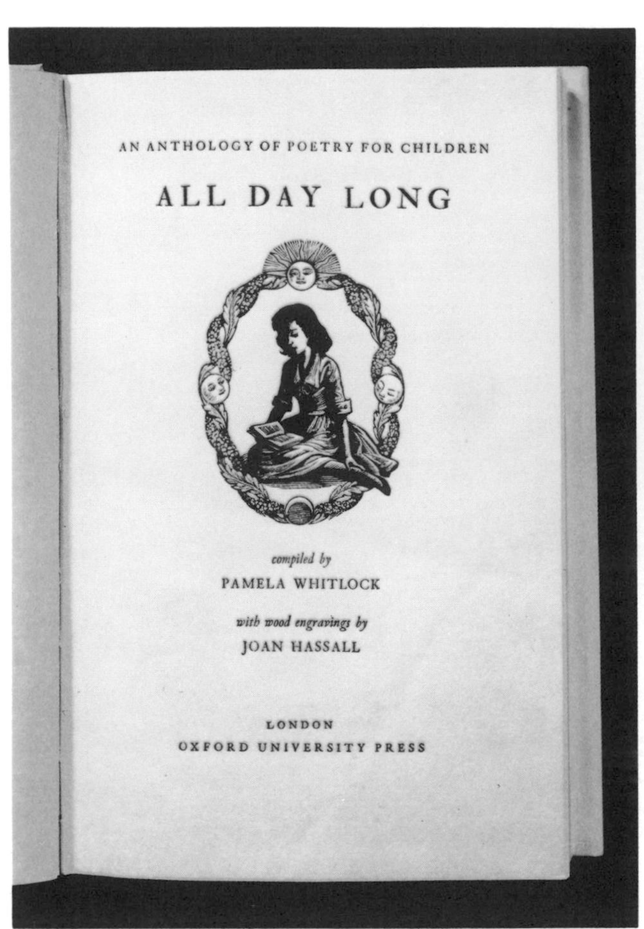
AN ANTHOLOGY OF POETRY FOR CHILDREN

ALL DAY LONG

compiled by
PAMELA WHITLOCK

with wood engravings by
JOAN HASSALL

LONDON
OXFORD UNIVERSITY PRESS

317

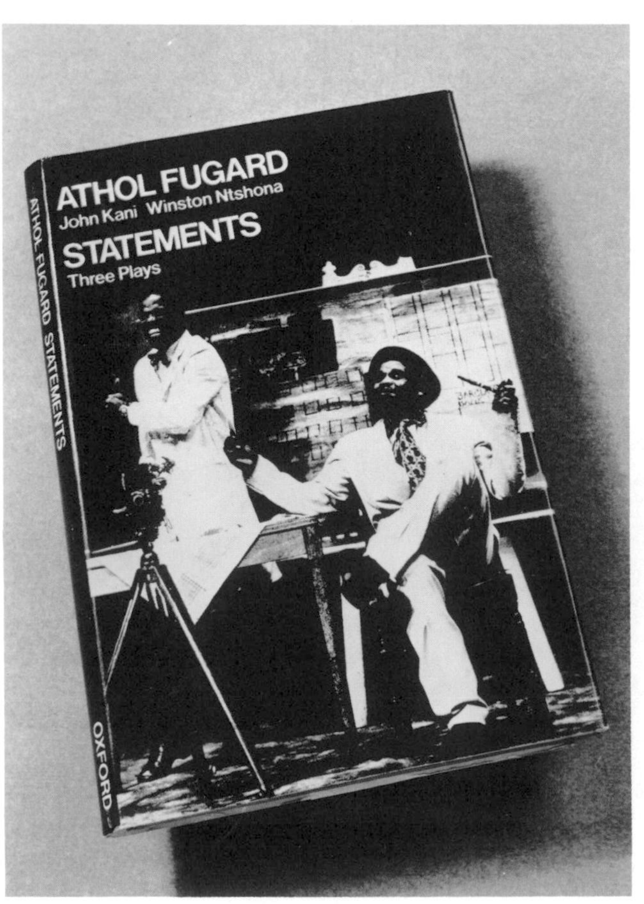

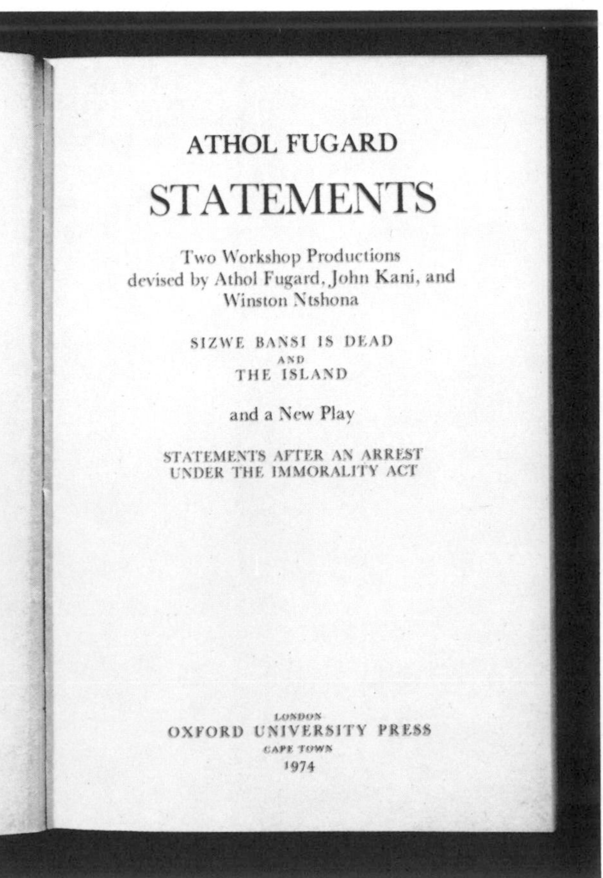
ATHOL FUGARD

STATEMENTS

Two Workshop Productions
devised by Athol Fugard, John Kani, and
Winston Ntshona

SIZWE BANSI IS DEAD
AND
THE ISLAND

and a New Play

STATEMENTS AFTER AN ARREST
UNDER THE IMMORALITY ACT

LONDON
OXFORD UNIVERSITY PRESS
CAPE TOWN
1974

323

The Noble Art and Myſtery of PRINTING was firſt Invented by JOHN
London, in the YEAR of our LORD 1471.
Mr. John Lloyd.
OXFORD:
Printed at the CLARENDON Printing-Houſe, July 5. 1722.
1440: And brought into ENGLAND by JOHN ISLIP, of
The Noble Art and Myſtery of PRINTING was firſt
Invented by John Guttenbergh in the
Dorothy Olliffe.
Her BOOK, 171
The Noble Art and Myſtery of PRINTING was firſt Invented by JOHN
GUTTEMBERG, a soldier, at Harlem, Holland,
in the YEAR 1440: And brought into ENGLAND by JOHN ISLIP,
of London, in the YEAR of our LORD 1471.
A keepsake for members of the Double Crown Club and the Gezelschap Nonpareil, Amsterdam
OXFORD:
Printed at the UNIVERSITY PRINTING HOUSE, 28 June 1957.
Richard Jordan 1756
Richard Jordan 1756
His Book
William Rowney.
June 30. 1660.
On Friday June 28
A.D. M.dcccc.vii
Dr. Samuel Langhorne Clemens
Visited the University Preſs, Oxford
and
This Keepsake was Printed
in his Presence

Visit of Mr. and Mrs. Roosevelt to the University Press, Oxford

TUESDAY, JUNE 7, 1910

PROGRAMME OF CONDENSED TOUR AND PRESENTATION

As Mr. ROOSEVELT has only half an hour to spare for his visit to the Press, the workpeople are requested to refrain from all demonstration until after the presentation; and should remain in their places in the Quadrangle until after the departure of the Visitors. Members of the Press Fire Contingent will keep the ground. The motor cars should remain outside, having reversed position for return.

12 mid-day. Hoist American flag.

12.20 p.m. Open outside gates.

12.25 p.m. Arrival of Mr. and Mrs. ROOSEVELT, Mr. KERMIT ROOSEVELT and Miss ETHEL ROOSEVELT, the AMERICAN AMBASSADOR and Mrs. REID, the VICE-CHANCELLOR, &c.

They are received at the Entrance to the Press by the Secretary to the Delegates and the Controller of the Press, &c.

The party proceeds along the cloisters to the Learned Side, and ascends staircase to first floor.

12.30 p.m. Party will proceed through middle composing-room on the Learned Side.

[Works in progress: New English Dictionary—composition in progress from the original copy; correction of proofs, in slips and in pages; system of arrangement.—Composition of Music, Persian, Syriac, Hebrew, Burmese, Chinese: show books containing Chinese radicals, by means of which compositors who do not understand Chinese can do the work.—Above exhibits have been chosen as being on a single floor, and because of limited time.]

12.35 p.m. Party will descend back staircase leading from middle composing-room, and pass out into Quadrangle, cross in front of the private houses, and enter machine-room by one of the centre folding doors.

12.40 p.m. [Printing machines running. Party might be shown old platen machines; Huber machines (American); sheet of India paper Bible printed on one of these, containing 128 pages; Miehle machines (American). Party will leave the machine-room by end door, crossing at once into Gilling-room, and will be conducted thence to entrance of Press (table and chairs in archway.)]

12.45 p.m. Work stopped. Employees assemble quietly in Quadrangle and form semicircle. Women and girls enter Quadrangle by staircase next Electro Foundry. Firemen show positions.

12.50 p.m. Copy of Mr. ROOSEVELT's Romanes Lecture, specially bound at the Oxford Bindery, will be presented by the Vice-Chancellor; and copy of Keepsake, commemorating the visit, printed on silk in the traditional manner, will be presented to Mrs. ROOSEVELT by one of the youngest employees from the Girls' Department of the Bindery.

A small exhibit of similar silk Keepsakes, including one presented to the late Queen Victoria in 1832, will occupy Visitors while members of the party sign Visitors' Book (on table in readiness).

12.55 p.m. Front gates of the Press will be reopened, and party will enter motor cars and depart.

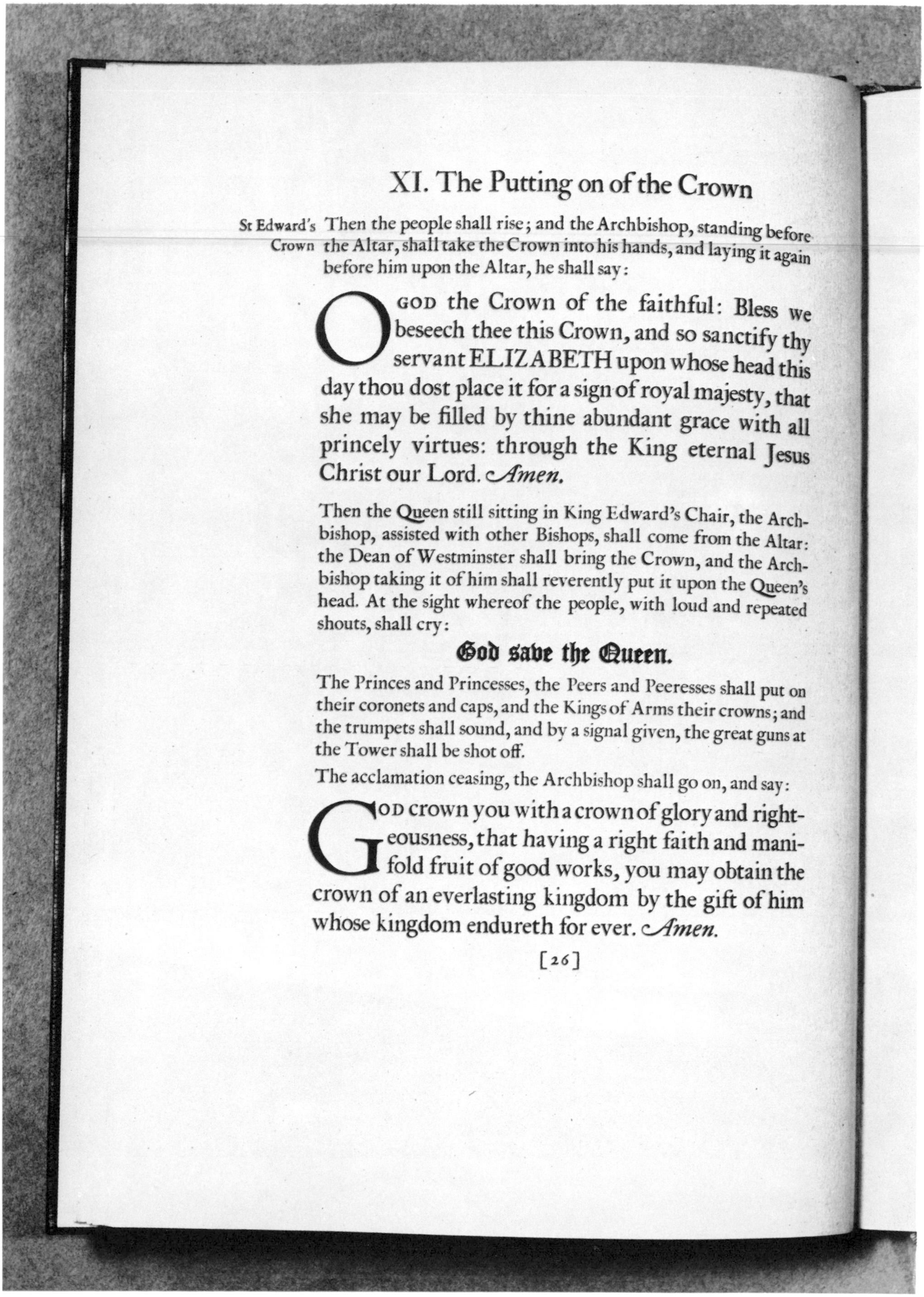

XI. The Putting on of the Crown

St Edward's Crown

Then the people shall rise; and the Archbishop, standing before the Altar, shall take the Crown into his hands, and laying it again before him upon the Altar, he shall say:

O GOD the Crown of the faithful: Bless we beseech thee this Crown, and so sanctify thy servant ELIZABETH upon whose head this day thou dost place it for a sign of royal majesty, that she may be filled by thine abundant grace with all princely virtues: through the King eternal Jesus Christ our Lord. *Amen.*

Then the Queen still sitting in King Edward's Chair, the Archbishop, assisted with other Bishops, shall come from the Altar: the Dean of Westminster shall bring the Crown, and the Archbishop taking it of him shall reverently put it upon the Queen's head. At the sight whereof the people, with loud and repeated shouts, shall cry:

God save the Queen.

The Princes and Princesses, the Peers and Peeresses shall put on their coronets and caps, and the Kings of Arms their crowns; and the trumpets shall sound, and by a signal given, the great guns at the Tower shall be shot off.

The acclamation ceasing, the Archbishop shall go on, and say:

GOD crown you with a crown of glory and righteousness, that having a right faith and manifold fruit of good works, you may obtain the crown of an everlasting kingdom by the gift of him whose kingdom endureth for ever. *Amen.*

[26]

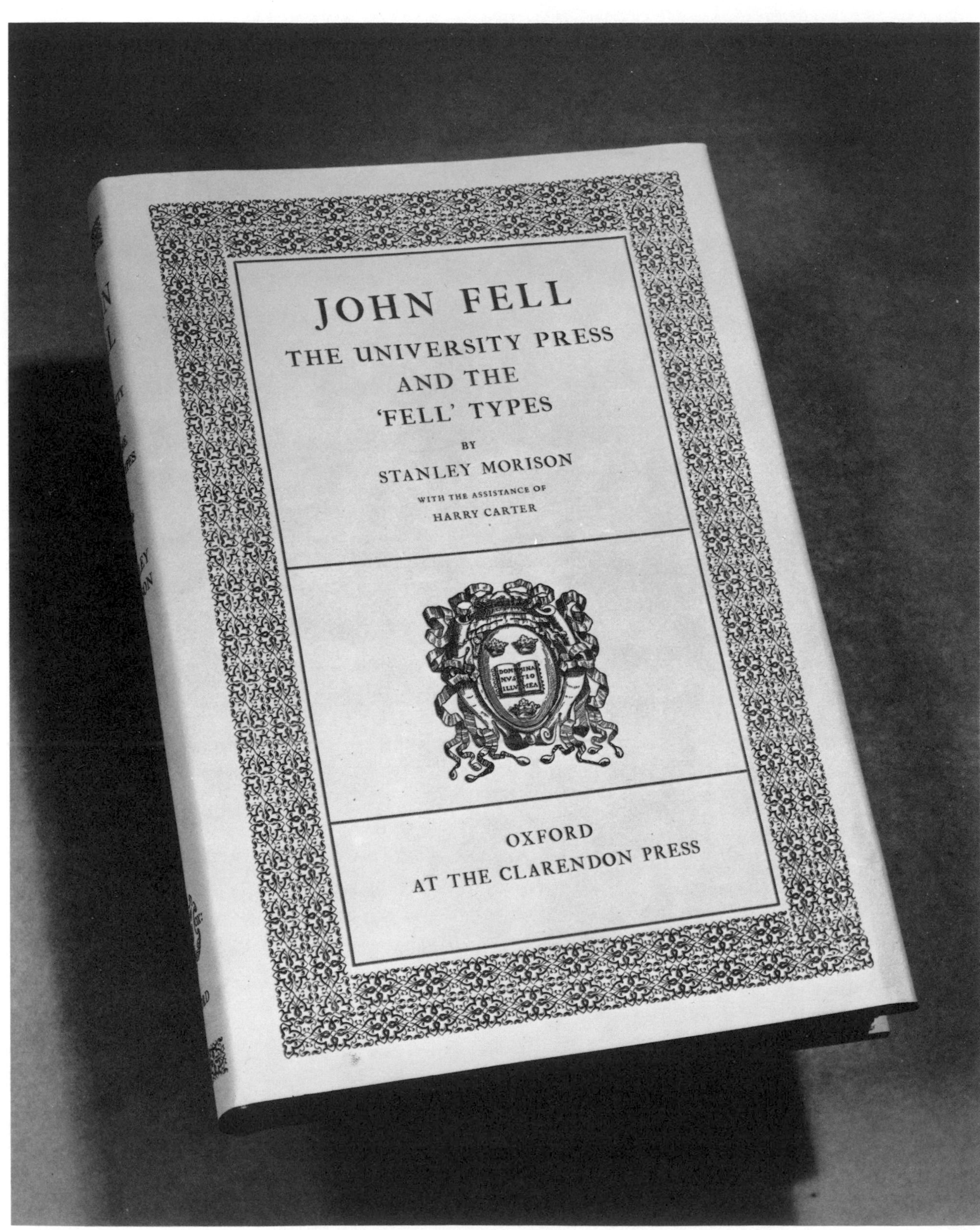
JOHN FELL
THE UNIVERSITY PRESS
AND THE
'FELL' TYPES
BY
STANLEY MORISON
WITH THE ASSISTANCE OF
HARRY CARTER
OXFORD
AT THE CLARENDON PRESS

too, he would never permit the strong-willed Warden of Wadham, Gilbert Ironside, to hold the office 'because a thwarter of him in severall public matters relating to the University'.[1] Ironside had to wait until the year after Fell's death to hold office.

From all that has been seen Fell was a consistent Royalist, a thorough Tory, an absolute Anglican, and a strict administrator, all in the Laudian sense; and never more so than in his dealings with the University; for, as Wood critically observes, Fell 'endeavoured to reduce the University to that condition as it stood in Laud's time'.[2] Such a man, with such a record, was clearly marked out for promotion in a period of reaction against nonconformity. Moreover, in the seventeenth century ecclesiastical preferment was generally regarded as the ultimate goal of Heads of Houses. Since 1565, when Thomas Sampson was deprived of the Deanery, only one Dean of Christ Church had not been rewarded with a bishopric, apart from Samuel Fell, whose career was interrupted by the Civil War, and John Owen the Independent. Fell, however, was not eager for such advancement because he felt he could not accept it without abandoning the two main passions of his life, his work at Christ Church and on the Press. He was so tenacious of both that the one, as has been seen, he described as 'the business of my life',[3] and of the other would say that he would sooner give up his bed than abandon it.[4] Since he would never relax his hold on the Press or give up the Deanery, his acceptance of a bishopric could only be possible on terms that would make him a pluralist. As Prideaux wrote:

Fell as Laud's disciple.

> Mr. Dean is soe eager and busy at the presse, and soe far engaged to prosecute the worke thereof, that, although he should be nominated to London, he will not as he hath declared accept of it, nor of the Bishoprick of Oxford, if Compton leave us, he beeing resolved as he sayth not [to] keep pluralitys.[5]

§ FELL AS THE CREATOR OF AN INSTITUTIONAL LEARNED PRESS WITHIN THE UNIVERSITY

The development of the Dean's interest in what he called the 'work of the Press' was gradual. Though Fell became Dean of Christ Church in 1660 and a Delegate of the Press in 1662, it was not until 1668 that he appears to exhibit strong personal interest in the 'work'. Samuel Clarke was still the Architypographus, and he was as active as the finances of the Press allowed. It was after Clarke's death in December 1669 that Fell entered whole-heartedly into the 'work'. Soon he had collected some powerful friends to aid him. The chief among these were Sir Leoline Jenkins, Principal of Jesus, Sir Joseph Williamson of Queen's, and Dr. Thomas Yate, Principal of Brasenose. Three of them were Delegates. The new company consisted of Jenkins, Williamson, Yate, and Fell. The latter was the driving force. Yate, who was possessed of means, was at one and the same time what we should call the director, the publicity agent, the financier who supported what capital Fell was not able to raise, and the business manager.[6] Thus Fell was freed to work at the great, immediate, and inescapable problem of furnishing the Theatre Press with type. 'It has always bin my opinion, that we must first secure to ourselves a good founder & a Stock of letters' he wrote.[7] He knew this from his experience of the Press since 1662 when he first became a Delegate and the printing for the University was conducted by the craft-printers, then Leonard Litchfield II, Anne Litchfield, and Henry Hall, who enjoyed semi-independence from the Delegacy provided their payments were not in arrear.

The Undertakers for Printing.

It was seven years before any appreciable change in the situation occurred. In May 1669 Fell had gained for the idea of the 'learned imprimerie' an adherent and an endowment of the greatest practical advantage, and immediately set men to work. On a day in July 1669 Fell read to a choice assembly, brought together within the Sheldonian

1 *Life*, iii, p. 224.
2 Ibid., i, pp. 348–9.
3 P. 35 above.
4 *Life*, iii, p. 198.
5 *Letters of Humphrey Prideaux to John Ellis*, Camden Soc., 2nd series, vol. 15, pp. 47–48: 8 Nov. 1675.
6 Johnson and Gibson, *Print and Privilege*, p. 60.
7 S.P. Dom., Car. II, 81, No. 27 (Nov. 1671).

£45/-
([illegible])